Praise for *The ELL Teacher's Toolbox 2.0*

"This collection of immediately usable strategies is a godsend for teachers of English language learners, which should be no surprise to fans of Ferlazzo and Sypnieski. This is a book you'll want to put on the desk of all the ELL teachers you know."
— *Dr. Shanna Peeples, National Teacher of the Year 2015*

"A grab-and-go book of strategies for teachers of English learners. With this book, all educators can be teachers of both content and language at the same time. *The ELL Teacher's Toolbox 2.0* turns principles into practices."
—*Tan Huynh, teacher, consultant, blogger at EmpoweringELLs.com*

"This book combines clear strategies by teachers for teachers in real classrooms. It includes a research base, points out connections to standards, and has tips on what to watch out for. A genuine all-in-one approach that's a winning formula for the classroom!"
—*Giselle Lundy-Ponce, American Federation of Teachers*

The ELL Teacher's Toolbox 2.0

The ELL Teacher's Toolbox 2.0

Hundreds of Practical Ideas to Support Your Students

LARRY FERLAZZO AND KATIE HULL SYPNIESKI

JB JOSSEY-BASS™
A Wiley Brand

Copyright © 2025 John Wiley & Sons, Inc. All rights, including for text and data mining, AI training, and similar technologies, are reserved.

Published by John Wiley & Sons, Inc., Hoboken, New Jersey.
Published simultaneously in Canada.

ISBNs: 9781394171675 (paperback), 9781394171682 (ePub), 9781394171699 (ePDF)

Except as expressly noted below, no part of this publication may be reproduced, stored in a retrieval system, or transmitted in any form or by any means, electronic, mechanical, photocopying, recording, scanning, or otherwise, except as permitted under Section 107 or 108 of the 1976 United States Copyright Act, without either the prior written permission of the Publisher, or authorization through payment of the appropriate per-copy fee to the Copyright Clearance Center, Inc., 222 Rosewood Drive, Danvers, MA 01923, (978) 750-8400, fax (978) 750-4470, or on the web at www.copyright.com. Requests to the Publisher for permission should be addressed to the Permissions Department, John Wiley & Sons, Inc., 111 River Street, Hoboken, NJ 07030, (201) 748-6011, fax (201) 748-6008, or online at http://www.wiley.com/go/permission.

Certain pages from this book (except those for which reprint permission must be obtained from the primary sources) are designed for educational/training purposes and may be reproduced. These pages are designated by the appearance of copyright notices at the foot of the page. This free permission is restricted to limited customization of these materials for your organization and the paper reproduction of the materials for educational/training events. It does not allow for systematic or large-scale reproduction, distribution (more than 100 copies per page, per year), transmission, electronic reproduction or inclusion in any publications offered for sale or used for commercial purposes—none of which may be done without prior written permission of the Publisher.

The manufacturer's authorized representative according to the EU General Product Safety Regulation is Wiley-VCH GmbH, Boschstr. 12, 69469 Weinheim, Germany, e-mail: Product_Safety@wiley.com

Trademarks: Wiley and the Wiley logo are trademarks or registered trademarks of John Wiley & Sons, Inc. and/or its affiliates in the United States and other countries and may not be used without written permission. All other trademarks are the property of their respective owners. John Wiley & Sons, Inc. is not associated with any product or vendor mentioned in this book.

Limit of Liability/Disclaimer of Warranty: While the publisher and author have used their best efforts in preparing this book, they make no representations or warranties with respect to the accuracy or completeness of the contents of this book and specifically disclaim any implied warranties of merchantability or fitness for a particular purpose. No warranty may be created or extended by sales representatives or written sales materials. The advice and strategies contained herein may not be suitable for your situation. You should consult with a professional where appropriate. Further, readers should be aware that websites listed in this work may have changed or disappeared between when this work was written and when it is read. Neither the publisher nor authors shall be liable for any loss of profit or any other commercial damages, including but not limited to special, incidental, consequential, or other damages.

For general information on our other products and services, please contact our Customer Care Department within the United States at (800) 762-2974, outside the United States at (317) 572-3993. For product technical support, you can find answers to frequently asked questions or reach us via live chat at https://support.wiley.com.

If you believe you've found a mistake in this book, please bring it to our attention by emailing our reader support team at wileysupport@wiley.com with the subject line "Possible Book Errata Submission."

Wiley also publishes its books in a variety of electronic formats. Some content that appears in print may not be available in electronic formats. For more information about Wiley products, visit our web site at www.wiley.com.

Library of Congress Control Number is Available:

Cover Design: Wiley
Cover Art: © Thomas Vogel/iStockphoto

SKY10095928_011025

Contents

About the Authors xxi
Acknowledgments xxiii

Introduction 1

I Reading and Writing 3

1. Independent Reading 5
Application 6
    Selecting Books 7
    Student-Teacher Check-Ins 8
    Writing and Talking About Books 8
    Publishing Student Successes 8
    Working with Students Not Literate in Their Home Language 9
Teaching Online 9
What Could Go Wrong? 10
Differentiation Recommendations for Independent Reading 10
Technology Connections 11

2. Text Engineering 15
Application 16
Teaching Online 17
What Could Go Wrong? 17
Technology Connections 17

3. Graphic Organizers 22
Application 23
- *Reading* 23
- *Writing* 24
Teaching Online 25
What Could Go Wrong? 26
Differentiation Recommendations 26
Technology Connections 26

4. Vocabulary 39
Application 40
- *Four Words Sheet* 40
- *Word Chart* 41
- *Teaching New Words During Reading* 42
- *Context Clues* 43
- *Academic Vocabulary* 43
- *Clines* 44
- *Word Webs* 45
- *Interactive Word Wall* 45
- *Cognates* 47
- *From Clues to Words* 47
Picture Dictionaries 48
Teaching Online 49
What Could Go Wrong? 49
Differentiation Recommendations for Vocabulary 50
Technology Connections 50

5. Activating Prior Knowledge 59
Application 60
- *KWL Charts* 60
- *Anticipation Guides* 61
- *Multimedia* 61
- *Quickwrites* 62
- *Vocabulary* 62
- *Preparatory Texts* 62
- *Home Language Materials* 63
- *Field Trips—Real or Virtual* 63
Teaching Online 63
What Could Go Wrong? 64
Differentiation Recommendations 64
Technology Connections 64

6. Sequencing 68
Application 69
Strip Stories 69
Sentence Scrambles 70
Comic Strips 71
Teaching Online 71
What Could Go Wrong? 72
Differentiating Recommendations for Sequencing Activities 72
Technology Connections 73

7. Clozes 80
Application 81
Teaching Online 82
What Could Go Wrong? 83
Differentiation Recommendations 83
Technology Connections 84

8. Language Experience Approach (LEA) 93
Application 94
"Classical" Version 94
"Gamified" Version 95
Teaching Online 96
What Could Go Wrong? 96
Differentiation Recommendations 97
Technology Connections 97

9. Jigsaw 99
Application 100
Beginners and Low-Intermediates 100
High-Intermediates and Advanced 102
Teaching Online 104
What Could Go Wrong? 104
Differentiation Recommendations 104
Technology Connections 105

10. Reading Comprehension 113
Application 115
Reading Strategies 116
Read Alouds and Think Alouds 117
Whole-Class Readings 118
Close Reading 122

    Teaching Online 126
    What Could Go Wrong? 126
    Differentiation Recommendations 127
    Technology Connections 127

11. Inductive Learning 133
    Application 134
        Picture Word Inductive Model (PWIM) 134
        Text, Phonics, and Picture Data Sets 136
        Concept Attainment 138
        Other Inductive Strategies 139
    Teaching Online 139
    What Could Go Wrong? 140
    Differentiation Recommendations 140
    Technology Connections 141

12. Retrieval Practice 150
    Application 151
        Quizzes and Tests 151
        Retrieval Practice Notebooks 152
    Teaching Online 153
    What Could Go Wrong? 153
    Differentiation Recommendations 154
    Technology Connections 154

13. Teaching Grammar 158
    Application 159
    Teaching Online 160
    What Could Go Wrong? 160
    Differentiation Recommendations 161
    Technology Connections 161

14. Writing Frames and Writing Structures 165
    Application 166
        Learning About the Importance of Writing in English Language Acquisition 167
        Writing Frames 168
        Writing Structures 169
    Teaching Online 170
    What Could Go Wrong? 171
    Differentiation Recommendations 172
    Technology Connections 172

15. Quoting, Summarizing, and Paraphrasing **183**
- Application 184
  - *Quoting* 184
  - *Summarizing* 185
  - *Paraphrasing* 186
- Teaching Online 188
- What Could Go Wrong? 188
- Differentiation Recommendations 188
- Technology Connection 189

16. Choice Boards/Learning Menus **193**
- Application 194
- Teaching Online 194
- What Could Go Wrong? 194
- Differentiation Recommendations 194
- Technology Connection 194

17. Using Photos or Other Images in Reading and Writing **199**
- Application 200
  - *Slideshow Annotation* 200
  - *Close-Read Photos and Other Images* 200
  - *Using Images to Teach "Claim" and "Evidence"* 201
  - *Unveiling Parts of an Image* 202
  - *Writing Captions and Cloze Captions* 202
  - *Compare and Contrast* 202
  - *Picture Story* 203
  - *Sensory Details* 204
  - *Artificial Intelligence Unit* 204
- Teaching Online 205
- What Could Go Wrong? 205
- Differentiation Recommendations 206
- Technology Connections 206

18. QSSSA **214**
- Application 218
  - *Question* 219
  - *Signal* 219
  - *Stem* 220
  - *Share* 220
  - *Assess* 220
- Teaching Online 221
- What Could Go Wrong? 221
- Differentiation Recommendations 222
- Technology Connections 222

19. Error Correction Strategies 228
Application 229
Concept Attainment and Concept Attainment Plus 229
Games 230
Encourage a Growth Mind-Set 230
Giving Individual Feedback 230
Self-Correction 231
Recasts 232
Teaching Online 233
What Could Go Wrong? 233
Differentiation Recommendations 233
Technology Connections 234

20. Revision 237
Application 238
Revising an Essay 238
Revising for Homework 240
Teaching Online 241
What Could Go Wrong? 241
Differentiation Recommendations 241
Technology Connections 242

21. Problem-Posing 244
Application 245
Teaching Online 248
What Could Go Wrong? 248
Differentiation Recommendations 248
Technology Connections 249

22. Project-Based Learning and Problem-Based Learning 251
Application 252
Examples of Project-Based Learning We've Done with ELLs 252
Examples of Problem-Based Learning We've Done with ELL Students 253
Project- and Problem-Based Project Process 253
Bonus Section: Object-Based Learning 255
Teaching Online 256
What Could Go Wrong? 256
Differentiation Recommendations 256
Technology Connections 257

23. Learning Games for Reading and Writing 263
Application 264
Nine Box Grid 264
Phonic Darts 265
Fill-in-the-Blank 265
Flyswatter Game (with or Without Flyswatters) 265
Name It 266
Round-and-Round She Goes 266
Writing Bingo 267
Sentence Scrambles 267
Academic Language Sentences 268
Pictionary 269
Team-Writing Sentences 269
Guess The Sentence (sometimes known as "Hangman") 269
Categories 269
What Doesn't Belong? 270
Connecting Four 270
Writing More 271
Summarize This! 271
ESL/ELL Wordle 272
Popular Board Game Adaptations 273
Teaching Online 273
What Could Go Wrong? 273
Differentiation Recommendations 274
Technology Connections 274

II Speaking and Listening   277

24. Dictation 279
Application 280
Paired Dictation 280
Dictogloss (and Variations) 280
Picture Dictation 282
Information Gap 282
Teaching Online 283
What Could Go Wrong? 283
Differentiation Recommendations 284
Technology Connections 284

25. Conversation Practice **285**
Application 286
- *Dialogues* 286
- *1-2-3* 288
- *Ask-Answer-Add* 289
- *Conversation Cheat Sheets* 290
- *Pronunciation Feedback* 290
- *Self-Assessment* 291

Teaching Online 291
What Could Go Wrong? 291
Differentiation Recommendations 291
Technology Connections 292

26. Total Physical Response (TPR) **296**
Application 296
- *TPR Extension Activities* 297

Teaching Online 299
What Could Go Wrong? 299
Differentiation Recommendations 299
Technology Connections 299

27. Music **302**
Application 303
- *Typical Sequence* 303
- *Topical Projects* 305
- *Personalized Song Lessons* 306
- *Chants* 307

Teaching Online 307
What Could Go Wrong? 308
Differentiation Recommendations 308
Technology Connections 308

28. Using Photos or Other Images in Speaking and Listening **315**
Application 316
- *Photo Collages* 316
- *Back and Forth* 316
- *If Animals or Inanimate Objects Could Talk* 316

Teaching Online 317
What Could Go Wrong? 317
Differentiation Recommendations 317
Technology Connections 317

CONTENTS xv

29. Video **320**
    Application 321
        Guidelines 321
        Typical Sequence 322
        Showing a Video Before or After Reading 324
        Back to the Screen 324
        Sequencing 325
        True or False 325
        Pause and Predict 325
        Students Creating Videos 326
    Teaching Online 327
    What Could Go Wrong? 328
    Differentiation Recommendations 328
    Technology Connections 328

30. Listening **333**
    Application 334
        The Why and the How: Listening Benefits and Metacognitive Listening 334
        Listening Language Frames 335
        More Listening Ideas 336
        Listening for Details/Correcting the Mistakes 338
    Teaching Online 338
    Differentiation Recommendations 338
    What Could Go Wrong? 338
    Technology Connections 339

31. Learning Games for Speaking and Listening **342**
    Application 343
        Nine Box Grid 343
        Answer—Question 343
        Letter Scavenger Hunt 344
        Sound Effects 344
        Guess the Word 345
        Telephone 345
        Running Dictation 345
        Four Truths and a Lie 345
        Video Game Walk-Throughs 347
    Teaching Online 347
    What Could Go Wrong? 347
    Differentiation Recommendations 347
    Technology Connections 348

III Additional Key Strategies — 351

32. Differentiation for ELLs in Content Classes with English-Proficient Students — 353
- Application — 354
  - *Dos and Don'ts* — 355
  - *Newcomer in Class* — 358
- Teaching Online — 361
- What Could Go Wrong? — 361
- Differentiation Recommendations — 362
- Technology Connections — 362

33. Supporting ELL Students with Interrupted Formal Education (SIFEs) — 365
- Application — 366
  - *Technology Support* — 366
  - *Phonics Instruction* — 367
  - *Home Language Instruction* — 367
  - *Encouragement, Patience, and Support* — 367
- What Could Go Wrong? — 369
- Teaching Online — 369
- Technology Connections — 369

34. Working with Long-Term ELLs — 371
- Application — 372
- Teaching Online — 373
- What Could Go Wrong? — 373
- Technology Connections — 374

35. Multilevel Classes — 375
- Application — 376
  - *Overall Strategies* — 376
  - *Content* — 376
  - *Process* — 377
  - *Product* — 377
  - *What Our Multilevel Summer School Class Looks Like* — 378
- Teaching Online — 379
- What Could Go Wrong? — 379
- Technology Connections — 380

36. Culturally Responsive Teaching **383**
Application 384
How Well Do I Know My Students? 384
Do My Words Reflect a Culturally Responsive Mind-Set When I Am Talking to Students and About Students? 385
How Are My Instructional Practices Culturally Responsive? 386
How Is the Curriculum I Am Using Culturally Responsive? 388
Teaching Online 389
What Could Go Wrong? 389
Technology Connections 390

37. Social Emotional Learning **391**
Application 392
Asset-Based Mindset 392
Sense of Belonging 395
Growth Mindset 396
Teaching Online 397
What Could Go Wrong? 398
Technology Connections 398

38. Motivation **402**
Application 403
Actions to Support Autonomy 404
Goal-Setting 404
Actions to Support Competence 405
Visualization 406
Temporal Comparisons 407
Shout-Out Whiteboard 407
Actions to Support Relatedness 408
Actions to Support Relevance 408
Teaching Online 409
What Could Go Wrong? 409
Technology Connections 409

39. Peer Teaching and Learning **417**
Application 418
Empathy Project 418
Peer Tutoring 419
Peer Mentoring 421
Sister Classes 421
Everyone Is a Teacher 422

Teaching Online 423
What Could Go Wrong? 423
Differentiation Recommendations 423
Technology Connections 423

40. Co-Teaching 437
Application 438
    Co-Teaching Don'ts and Dos 439
Teaching Online and Technology Connections 441

41. Working with Parents and Guardians 442
Application 444
    Communicating with Parents 444
    Supporting Parents 445
    Inviting Families to Participate in Classroom Learning 446
What Could Go Wrong? 446
Technology Connections 446

42. Translanguaging 449
Application 450
Teaching Online 451
What Could Go Wrong? 452
Technology Connections 452

43. Beginning the School Year 453
Application 454
    Greeting Students 454
    Student Names 454
    Course Expectations Activity 455
    Letter Exchange 455
    Partner Introductions 455
    Self-Portraits 457
    Language Maps 457
    My Summer Cloze Activity 458
Teaching Online 458
What Could Go Wrong? 458
Differentiation Recommendations 459
Technology Connections 459

44. Ending the School Year **465**
    Application 466
        Activities for the Last Few Months of School 466
        Activities for the Last Few Days of School 469
        Encouraging Summer Practice 472
    What Could Go Wrong? 472
    Differentiation Recommendations 472
    Technology Connections 473

45. Beginning and Ending of Class **482**
    Application 483
        Do-Now Activities 483
        Closure Activities 486
    Teaching Online 489
    What Could Go Wrong? 489
    Differentiation Recommendations 490
    Technology Connections 490

46. Zero-Prep Activities **492**
    Application 493
        Games 493
        Using Images 494
        Reading and Writing 495
        Dictation 495
    Teaching Online 496
    What Could Go Wrong? 496
    Differentiation Recommendations 496
    Technology Connections 497

47. Using Technology **498**
    Application 499
        Teaching Others 500
        Independent Study 500
        Homework 502
        Artificial Intelligence 502
        Learning to Type and Use the Keyboard 503
        Other Tech Equipment 503
    Teaching Online 504
    What Could Go Wrong? 504
    Differentiation Recommendations 505
    Technology Connections 505

48. Interactive Word Walls 513
- Application 515
- Teaching Online 517
- What Could Go Wrong? 517
- Technology Connections 517

49. Assessment 526
- Application 527
  - *Initial or Diagnostic Assessments* 527
  - *Formative Assessments* 528
- Teaching Online 531
- What Could Go Wrong? 532
- Technology Connections 532

50. Accelerated Learning 538
- Application 539
  - *Tutoring* 540
  - *Adding Instructional Time* 540
  - *Using Educational Technology* 540
  - *Scaffolds* 540
  - *Social Emotional Learning* 541
  - *Parent/Guardian Communication* 541
  - *Formative Assessments and Being Data-Informed* 541
  - *Student Engagement, Relevance, and Connection to Prior Knowledge* 542
  - *Simulations* 542
- Teaching Online 542
- What Could Go Wrong? 542
- Technology Connections 543

Appendix: English Language Arts Standards—Anchor Standards 548
- College and Career Readiness Anchor Standards for Reading 548
- College and Career Readiness Anchor Standards for Writing 550
- College and Career Readiness Anchor Standards for Speaking and Listening 551
- College and Career Readiness Anchor Standards for Language 552

Index 553

A variety of bonus material is available at www.wiley.com/go/ellteacherstoolbox2

About the Authors

Larry Ferlazzo teaches English and social studies to English language learners and English-proficient students at Luther Burbank High School in Sacramento, California. He has written, co-authored, or edited 13 books on education.

He has won numerous awards, including the Leadership for a Changing World Award from the Ford Foundation, and was the grand prize winner of the International Reading Association Award for Technology and Reading.

He writes a popular education blog at http://larryferlazzo.edublogs.org and writes a weekly teacher advice column for *Education Week*. His articles on education policy have appeared regularly in the *Washington Post*. In addition, his work has appeared in publications such as the *New York Times*, ASCD's *Educational Leadership*, *Social Policy*, and *Language Magazine*.

Ferlazzo was a community organizer for 19 years prior to becoming a public school teacher. He is married and has three children and five grandchildren.

Katie Hull Sypnieski has taught English language learners of all proficiency levels and English-proficient students in the Sacramento City Unified School District. She has served as a teaching consultant with the Area 3 Writing Project housed at University of California – Davis for the past 24 years.

She has co-authored three books on teaching ELLs and has co-edited three books on education. She has published articles and instructional videos for *Education Week*. In addition, she has co-authored articles for Edutopia, the *New York Times* Learning Network, and ASCD's *Educational Leadership*.

Sypnieski currently teaches English to English language learners and English-proficient students at Arthur A. Benjamin Health Professions High School in Sacramento, California. She is married and has three children.

Larry and Katie have co-authored two other books on teaching English language learners, *The ESL ELL Teacher's Survival Guide* and *Navigating the Common Core with English Language Learners*, both from Jossey-Bass/Wiley.

Acknowledgments

Larry Ferlazzo: I'd like to thank my family—Stacia, Rich, Shea, Ava, Nik, Katie, Karli, Federico, and especially my wife, Jan—for their support. In addition, I need to express appreciation to my co-author, Katie Hull Sypnieski, who has also been a colleague and friend for more than 20 years. I would like to thank my many colleagues at Luther Burbank High School, including Principal Jim Peterson, for their assistance over the years. Probably most important, I'd like to thank the many English language learner students who have made me a better teacher—and a better person.

Katie Hull Sypnieski: I would like to thank all the students I've had over the years for their determination, for their creative energy, and for helping me to grow as an educator and as a person. In addition, I am grateful for all of the support I have received from my colleagues, especially Larry Ferlazzo, my co-author, co-teacher, and friend. Finally, to all of my family members, especially my husband, David, and children, Drew, Ryan, and Rachel, I want to thank you for supporting me in this process—you are the best!

Larry and Katie: We must offer a big thank-you to Amy Fandrei and Pete Gaughan at Jossey-Bass for their patience and guidance in preparing this book, and to Jennifer Borgioli Binis at Schoolmarm Advisors for her assistance in developing our manuscript submission.

And, of course, we have to thank the four contributors to this second edition who authored chapters (you can see their complete biographies elsewhere in this book):

Valentina Gonzalez
Carol Salva
Carlota Holder
Stephen Fleenor

Introduction

We are back!

Bigger!

And even better!

The first edition of *The ELL Teacher's Toolbox* contained 45 chapters highlighting hundreds of strategies we had used in the classroom during our then-combined 35 years of experience in the classroom.

Now, we have well over 40 years combined classroom experience. And with that added experience, we have added 16 new chapters and have revised all 45 previous ones—some in minor ways, and others from top to bottom.

Most chapters now have a new differentiation chart, recommending ways to make each strategy accessible to students of all English proficiency levels.

We also discuss artificial intelligence in most chapters; however, keep in mind it's evolving so quickly that some of our comments may not be relevant by the time you read them.

But even as our ed tech recommendations become outdated, links to Larry's constantly updated blog will keep you up-to-date.

We have so much new content that a substantial amount, including 11 chapters, can now be found online and is freely available to everyone—no registration is required. In addition, most exhibits and figures from the book are there for downloading. To make space for more chapters in the hard-copy version, we also put references for all the chapters online. You can find all these resources and more at www.wiley.com/go/ellteacherstoolbox2. You can also access the page via the accompanying QR code.

The Bonus Strategies that you'll find online are:

Bonus Strategy 1: Literary Conversations
Bonus Strategy 2: Concept Attainment - +!
Bonus Strategy 3: Sentence Navigators and Sentence Builders
Bonus Strategy 4: Cooperative Writing
Bonus Strategy 5: Writer's Notebook
Bonus Strategy 6: Micro-Progressions
Bonus Strategy 7: Oral Presentations
Bonus Strategy 8: Debate
Bonus Strategy 9: Flashcards
Bonus Strategy 10: Learning Stations
Bonus Strategy 11: Textbooks

We also want to note that we are aware that the title of this book uses the term *English language learner*, which more and more is being recognized as a deficit-focused term, with replacement labels being ones like *emergent bilinguals* and *multilingual learners*.

There is no universal agreement yet on what term to use. We have decided to stick to the "ELL" description for this edition because it is still the most common term. However, as every strategy in this book tries to communicate, we certainly don't view our students through the lens of deficits.

As we said in the first edition, we want to make clear that we use the vast majority of these strategies with our English-proficient students, too. Good ELL teaching is better teaching for everybody!

We know you will apply these strategies in ways we haven't even thought of and, as always, look forward to hearing from you. Good luck to us all!

PART 1

Reading and Writing

STRATEGY 1
Independent Reading

What Is It?

Independent reading, also called *free voluntary reading, extensive reading, leisure or pleasure reading*, and *silent sustained reading*, is the instructional strategy of providing students with time in class on a regular basis to read books of their choice. Students are also encouraged to do the same at home. In addition, no formal responses or academic exercises are tied to this reading.

Why We Like It

We believe that one of the best ways for our ELL students to become more motivated to read and to increase their literacy skills is to give them time to read what they like! That being said, we *don't* just stand back and watch them read. We *do* teach reading strategies during classroom lessons and encourage students to apply them, conduct read alouds to generate interest, take our classes to the school library, organize and maintain our classroom library, conference with students during reading time, and encourage our students to read outside the classroom, among other things. All of these activities contribute to a learning community in which literacy is valued and reading interest is high.

In addition to independent reading having multiple language-learning benefits, we like it as a "warm-up" or "do-now" routine that students can easily begin before the bell even rings to officially start the class. It requires no initial teacher instruction after it becomes a routine, and it lets us focus, instead, on relationship-building activities like greeting each student by name, "checking in" with those we have reason to believe might be facing personal challenges, and helping those who aren't sure what book to read or online site to visit (see Strategy 45: Beginning and Ending of Class).

Supporting Research

Research shows there are many benefits of having students read self-selected books during the school day (Ferlazzo, 2011, February 26; Miller, 2015). These benefits include enhancing students' comprehension, vocabulary, general knowledge, and empathy, as well as increasing their self-confidence and motivation as readers. These benefits apply to English language learners who read in English and in their native languages (International Reading Association, 2014).

Encouraging students to read in their home language, as well as in English, can facilitate English language acquisition and build literacy skills in both languages (Ferlazzo, 2017, April 10). Extensive research has found that students increasing their first language (L1) abilities are able to transfer phonological and comprehension skills as well as background knowledge to second language (L2) acquisition (Genessee, n.d.). Research shows that providing choices is one way to support autonomy, a critical element in creating the conditions where student intrinsic motivation can flourish (see Strategy 38: Motivation).

Common Core Connections

According to the Common Core ELA Standards, "students must read widely and deeply from among a broad range of high-quality, increasingly challenging literary and informational texts" in order to progress toward career and college readiness (Common Core State Standards Initiative, n.d.b). The lead authors of the Common Core advocate for daily student independent reading of self-selected texts and specifically state that students should have access to materials that "aim to increase regular independent reading of texts that appeal to students' interests while developing their knowledge base and joy in reading" (Coleman & Pimentel, 2012, p. 4).

Application

Our students are allowed to choose whatever classroom-appropriate reading material they are currently interested in and are often given time to read each day (perhaps 10 minutes, and sometimes more, especially for students who might be more proficient in English). Our schools support ELLs with peer tutors (older students who receive class credit for working in our classrooms), and often ELLs will go into another room or outside and read their book to a tutor (see Strategy 39: Peer Teaching and Learning).

Our students' use of digital reading materials in the classroom has dramatically increased in the past few years. As part of our supporting student autonomy, in addition to providing hard-copy and online books, they may also choose to use that time to work on other independent practice sites that may provide oral or grammar practice, in addition to reading. We share these digital resources in the Technology Connections section.

For this time to be effective—in other words, for our ELL students to experience the various benefits of independent reading discussed in the research section—we scaffold the independent reading process in several ways.

SELECTING BOOKS

At the beginning of the year, we familiarize our students with the way our classroom libraries are organized—ours are leveled (beginner, intermediate, advanced) and categorized (fiction, nonfiction, bilingual). We organize our books in this way so that students don't have to waste time looking through many books that are obviously not accessible to them. For example, for a newcomer, having to thumb through 10 intermediate or advanced books before finding a readable one can easily lead to a feeling of frustration, not anticipation. Students, however, are free to choose a book from any section of the library, even if that means selecting a book at a higher reading level than we would select for them. That being said, we do our best to help students find books they are interested in that are also accessible to them.

We take Dr. Rudine Sims Bishop's (2015) perspective on diverse literature seriously and ensure that our students have access to texts that are "windows" and "sliding glass doors" where they can see other worlds and use their imagination, as well as "mirrors" where they can see themselves and their experiences reflected in what they read.

We also teach our students how to identify whether a book is too hard, too easy, or just right by reading the first couple of pages and noticing if most of the words seem unfamiliar (too hard right now), if they know the majority of the words (too easy), or if some of the words are familiar and some are new (just right). We also emphasize to students the importance of challenging themselves to improve (using a sports analogy works well—if you want to get better at basketball, you don't just work on the same shot every day) by sometimes practicing a little out of their comfort zones. We do allow students to use their phones or classroom dictionaries to look up words, but we also explain that having to look up every word usually indicates a book is too hard for now.

To ensure that all our students, including newcomers, have a hard-copy book option, we also have various bilingual and English-only (we can't ensure that we have a bilingual version for every student's home language) picture dictionaries, as well as bilingual books in various languages, available.

We do a similar series of introductions to the various online resources we use. Typically, we will introduce one site a day and require that all students use it for 20 minutes during class. That length of time typically provides them with enough of a sense of the site to know if they would like to revisit it—either during class or at home.

Speaking of online resources, we are writing this new edition near the beginning of what appears to be an artificial intelligence (AI) "revolution." We, like most educators, are experimenting with how and if to use it in the classroom, which is complicated by the fact that some AI tools are blocked by some districts.

One experiment we have been trying with ELLs is to provide "sentence frames" for students to get AI to write texts that they *want* to read. After all, you can't get much more high-interest than having students say what they want to read about!

Here are some sentence frames we have had students complete:

> *Write a story in English featuring (put your name here) as a soccer star that can be understood by a beginning English Language Learner.*
> *Tell me about (put any topic here) so a beginning English Language Learner can understand it.*

Unfortunately, we've found that some AI tools don't really recognize the language skills of a "beginning English Language Learner," so, instead, students have had to write "first-grader" or "second-grader." We assume that by the time you read this, AI abilities will have advanced considerably so that this problem no longer exists.

However, we believe that whatever AI exists at the time you are reading this book, the idea of ELLs using it to create their own accessible high-interest texts will still be a good one. See Technology Connections for up-to-date related resources.

STUDENT-TEACHER CHECK-INS

We use independent reading time to check in with individual students about their engagement, comprehension, and future reading interests. These are not formal assessments but are brief, natural conversations about reading ("Why did you choose this book? What is your favorite part so far? Which part is most confusing? How are you feeling about reading in English?"). We may also use the time to help students find new books, listen to students practice reading aloud, talk about new words they are learning, discuss which reading strategies they are using (see Strategy 10: Reading Comprehension), and glean information about their reading interests, strengths, and challenges.

WRITING AND TALKING ABOUT BOOKS

Sometimes we may ask students to respond to their daily reading in a quickwrite, in a drawing, or with a partner. Other times we ask students to respond to their reading in their writer's notebooks; see Bonus Strategy 5: Writer's Notebook (available at www.wiley.com/go/ellteacherstoolbox2) for a more detailed explanation of how we use them for reader response. We may also have students participate in one of the activities described in Bonus Strategy 1: Literary Conversations, such as creating a book trailer, conducting a book interview, or identifying and writing about a "golden line" (a passage they particularly liked).

PUBLISHING STUDENT SUCCESSES

We have our students keep track of the books they have read in English and in their home language, not as an accountability measure but as a celebration of their growth as readers. When they finish a book of any length, we give them a colored sticky note, and they write their name, the title of the book, and a four- to five-word rating, or blurb (e.g., "sad, but good ending" or "best graphic novel I've read!"). Students then stick their notes on the finished books wall (made of a large piece of colored paper).

We also have students keep a list of finished books in their writer's notebooks (see Bonus Strategy 5). We remind our students that it's not a race for who can finish the most books but that the most important goal is that all students are making their own progress. It's their option to include the online books they have read on the list.

Each quarter, we ask students to reflect on their independent reading (see Figure 1.1: End-of-Quarter Reading Reflection). At the end of the year, we celebrate all the reading our students have done with a visual project called *My Year of Reading*. Students use their sticky notes and lists of finished books in their notebooks to create a list of all the books they've read. Then they design a visual representation of their reading journey (a chart, a time line, a map, a bookshelf, etc.). See Figure 1.2: My Year of Reading Visual Project for the directions and Figure 1.3: My Year of Reading Student Example.

WORKING WITH STUDENTS NOT LITERATE IN THEIR HOME LANGUAGE

Independent reading can be especially challenging with English language learners who are preliterate or who have low literacy skills in their home language, particularly if they are older students. However, newer research (which we share with our students and their families) shows that learning to read creates deeper, stronger, and faster connections in the brain, even for those who are late to reading (Sparks, 2017). We frequently do lessons with all our students about how learning new things changes and strengthens the brain (Ferlazzo, 2011, November 26).

In our experience, one of the best ways to engage students facing these challenges and to build their literacy skills is to start through online reading activities in their home language and then move to English. The online sites we have found most useful are interactive and contain leveled texts, bilingual stories, visualizations, and audio support in which words are pronounced aloud in English and in the student's home language. Many of our students especially enjoy sites that incorporate music lyrics and videos. For teachers who have limited technology in the classroom, another option is to access printable books online at sites such as Learning A-Z or edHelper. See Technology Connections for a list of the sites we have found most useful. In addition, explore Strategy 33: Supporting Newcomer ELL & Students with Interrupted Formal Education (SIFES) for other ideas.

When we have a peer tutor available, we have had them use bilingual flashcards with students facing literacy challenges in their home language (see Bonus Strategy 9: Flashcards). Flashcards, along with students having a mini-whiteboard and marker, can be an effective interactive literacy activity. In addition, we've purchased relatively low-cost "talking" bilingual flashcards with audio card readers for students to use at home.

Teaching Online

Teaching online necessitates approaching independent reading differently. Typically, online classes may not meet daily and be of shorter duration. Because of the need to maximize "teaching time," that means independent reading needs to be truly "independent."

It requires having a robust selection of online sites (see Technology Connections), including local public library resources, where students can choose texts or practice activities and teachers can receive reports for accountability purposes. In addition, it's important to create an online version of a "finished books wall" where students can share their reviews (see Jamboard replacement suggestions in the Technology Connections section).

We've had long-term arrangements with various local "Friends of the Library" auxiliaries who organize fundraising book sales where they have donated books to our students for their home libraries. Creating similar arrangements could be particularly important for online students.

What Could Go Wrong?

Providing ELL students with access to high-interest books at their English proficiency levels can be challenging. Children's books, although often well written and available in multiple languages, are not always of high interest to adolescent learners. See Technology Connections for recommendations about where to purchase bilingual books appropriate for adolescent learners. We've also found that purchasing popular young adult fiction in English and in various home languages works especially well for our intermediate students. They can read the English version and use their home language copy as a reference—to check their understanding or to identify similarities and differences. There are also digital sites with "parallel texts" that, in effect, do the same thing. And, as we've said, many sites provide engaging features that support literacy development—glossaries, animations, audio tools, and so on (see Technology Connections for resources on digital reading).

Independent reading is a very important component of English language instruction; however, it is not a substitute for explicit reading instruction (see Strategy 10: Reading Comprehension). Ideally, it is a time when students can apply the reading skills and strategies they are learning in class to the texts they are reading independently. The teacher plays a big role in helping students reach this goal by consistently providing guidance and encouragement. It can quickly become an ineffective practice if students are not supported as they select books, read them, and interact with them. Teachers can fall into the trap of using student independent reading time to plan or catch up on paperwork. We certainly have done this and still do it now at times, but we try to resist the urge and we hope you do, too.

Differentiation Recommendations for Independent Reading

Newcomers (Preliterate or Low Literacy in Home Language): Offer online literacy activities in home language for independent practice, as well as online basic English literacy sites. Have peer tutors use basic flashcards and/or bilingual ones. Audio flashcard readers can also be purchased for independent use, as well as identifying online flashcard sites. See Bonus Strategy 9: Flashcards (available at www.wiley.com/go/ellteacherstoolbox2) for more ideas.	**Newcomers (Literate in Home Language):** Provide age-appropriate bilingual books and simple English ones. Offer access to online sites that have audio support for the text of English books, along with images.
Intermediate ELLs: Provide accessible English books, both hard-copy and online versions. Offer books with parallel texts, both online and on paper.	**Advanced ELLs:** Provide access to high-interest hard-copy and online books.

STRATEGY 1: INDEPENDENT READING

Technology Connections

There are numerous online sites that provide free, high-interest reading materials for all levels of ELLs. Links to these sites can be found here:

The Best Websites to Help Beginning Readers (http://larryferlazzo.edublogs.org/2008/01/22/the-best-websites-to-help-beginning-readers/).

The Best Websites for Beginning Older Readers (http://larryferlazzo.edublogs.org/2008/01/23/the-best-websites-for-beginning-older-readers/).

The Best Online Resources for Teachers of SLIFEs (http://larryferlazzo.edublogs.org/2008/12/06/the-best-online-resources-for-teachers-of-pre-literate-ells/).

The Best Websites for Intermediate Readers (http://larryferlazzo.edublogs.org/2008/01/26/the-best-websites-for-intermediate-readers/).

The Best Sources for Free and Accessible Printable Books (http://larryferlazzo.edublogs.org/2009/07/31/the-best-sources-for-free-accessible-printable-books/).

The Best Tools That Show "Parallel Text" – Same Sentences Translated into Different Languages Side-by-Side (https://larryferlazzo.edublogs.org/2019/12/31/the-best-tools-that-show-parallel-text-same-sentences-translated-into-different-languages-side-by-side/).

It's not always easy to find bilingual books in multiple languages, or ones that are appropriate and accessible to adolescent readers. We've found good selections at the places on this list: The Best Places Where You Can Order Bilingual Books (https://larryferlazzo.edublogs.org/2023/03/11/the-best-places-where-you-can-order-bilingual-books/).

Since our Hmong students came more than 20 years ago, the only students we have taught who have not been literate in their home language have been from Spanish-speaking countries. They've found the sites on this list helpful to begin literacy awareness: The Best Resources for Supporting Spanish-Speakers Not Literate in Their Home Language (https://larryferlazzo.edublogs.org/2023/03/14/the-best-resources-for-supporting-spanish-speakers-not-literate-in-their-home-language/).

We're sorry, but if you have preliterate or not literate students who speak other languages, you will need to create your own similar list for them. However, if that's the case, we'd love to hear from you and include a link to your list on Larry's blog so other teachers and students can benefit!

There are also many practice sites that include readings, oral practice, and interactive grammar activities (as well as accessible resources for other content classes). The ones our students seem to like best can be found here: The Best Sites Students Can Use for Independent Practice (https://larryferlazzo.edublogs.org/2022/07/19/the-best-sites-students-can-use-for-independent-practice/).

Though the Artificial Intelligence Revolution is likely to outpace the text in this book, you can stay updated on ideas for using it with your students here: A Collection of "Best" Lists About Using Artificial Intelligence in Education (https://larryferlazzo.edublogs.org/2023/01/01/a-collection-of-best-lists-about-using-artificial-intelligence-in-education/).

For additional information on the value of independent reading, explore the resources here: The Best Resources Documenting the Effectiveness of Free Voluntary Reading (https://larryferlazzo.edublogs.org/2011/02/26/the-best-resources-documenting-the-effectiveness-of-free-voluntary-reading/).

For different options of free virtual whiteboards, see The Best Alternatives to the Soon-to-Be-Deceased Google Jamboard (https://larryferlazzo.edublogs.org/2023/10/03/the-best-alternatives-to-the-soon-to-be-deceased-google-jamboard/) and/or The Best Online Virtual Corkboards (https://larryferlazzo.edublogs.org/2011/03/30/the-best-online-virtual-corkboards-or-bulletin-boards/).

Attribution

Portions of this section are adapted from our books, *The ESL/ELL Teacher's Survival Guide* (Ferlazzo & Sypnieski, 2012, p. 125–127) and *Navigating the Common Core with English Language Learners* (Ferlazzo & Sypnieski, 2016, p. 95–97).

All figures from this chapter, as well as 11 additional chapters, references, hyperlinked Technology Connections, and more online resources, can be found at www.wiley.com/go/ellteacherstoolbox2.

STRATEGY 1: INDEPENDENT READING 13

1. How many books did you read this quarter? List the titles (look at your sticky notes and your list in your writer's notebook). How do you feel about this number of books?
2. How do you feel about your progress in reading (what is getting easier, what is still challenging)?
3. What was your favorite book you read this quarter? Give at least three reasons why it was your favorite.
4. Are you reading mostly fiction books, nonfiction books, or a mix of both? Why do you think this is?
5. What strategies are you using to help you understand your book (summarizing, looking up new words, asking questions, etc.)?
6. What changes will you make as a reader next quarter (read more-challenging books, ask for book recommendations, read at home, etc.)?
7. What help do you need from your teacher or your classmates to become an even better reader (finding books, a quiet place to read in class, a partner to talk about my book with, starting a book club, etc.)?
8. Complete the following statement:
Reading is _____ because _____.

Figure 1.1 End-of-Quarter Reading Reflection

You have read many good books this year! You will demonstrate evidence of your reading and celebrate it by completing a final visual project. Follow this guide to complete your My Year of Reading Visual Project:

- Look back over your finished books list in your writer's notebook and your sticky notes from the finished books wall.
- Look at the titles you have read and think about how you might like to tie all of these books together.
- You may present your books on a poster in the form of a map, time line, game board, video game, advertisement, list, or any other creative way you want. You must include the title of each book.
- Complete a quick draft on a piece of scratch paper to show me your plan *before* I give you the final poster paper.
- On the poster paper, *sketch* your design with pencil before you use ink or color.
- You may use a combination of colored pens and colored pencils to complete your poster.

Figure 1.2 My Year of Reading Visual Project

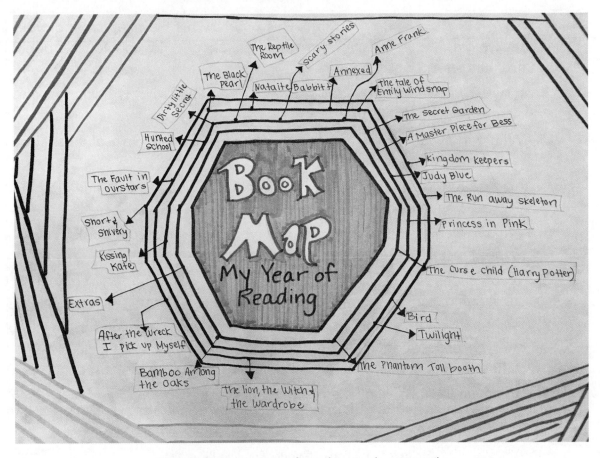

Figure 1.3 My Year of Reading Student Example

STRATEGY 2
Text Engineering

What Is It?

"Text engineering" is a concept and term, as far as we can tell, originally developed by Elsa Billings and Aída Walqui (2021). The idea is to "amplify" complex text by making it more accessible and not just "simplify" the words in it.

By "engineering the text," we're able to make design changes to the complex texts to further enhance their accessibility. This kind of accessibility can be supported by strategies like enlarging the text, including bold-faced subtitles, adding images, creating more white space around it where students can write notes, adding vocabulary definitions, etc.

This does not mean that providing ELLs with text that has been simplified does not have a role in instruction. "Simplified" text that has been rewritten to a lower Lexile level, perhaps through the use of artificial intelligence, can be an effective strategy to help students develop the prior knowledge they need to better access more complex texts that may or may not have been "engineered."

Why We Like It

As readers of this book already know, our ELL students are as smart as English-proficient students; they just don't know English well—yet. The quicker we can make grade-level content accessible to them, the better, and text engineering is a viable strategy for doing just that. We support "simplifying" texts to help students gain the prior knowledge necessary to make "engineered" complex texts accessible to them.

Supporting Research

We are not aware of extensive research on text engineering as a specific strategy. However, studies have clearly shown that teachers reviewing text prior to teaching it, identifying words and features that might be challenging to their ELL students, and then annotating the text in ways to make it more accessible is an effective method to develop the academic language skills of students (Neri et al., 2016). Explicitly highlighting key vocabulary words, as can be done in text engineering, is another specific practice supported by research (MDESSE, 2023). Studies have also found that teachers of ELLs sometimes "cushion" ELL students by providing them less complex text (Gersten et al., 2007). Text engineering can be one strategy to overcome that issue.

Common Core Connections

Engineering texts will help students achieve any or all of the Reading Standards!

Application

Educators Anne Lyneis and Maggie Roth (2020) share these key questions that educators should ask themselves before they begin to engineer a text:

- What makes this text complex?
- What vocabulary words will be important for students to know?
- What background knowledge will students need to understand the text and task?
- What scaffolding questions would help students access the text?
- How can I access students' prior knowledge?
- How can I divide the text into sections to make it easier to follow?

There are many ways to engineer text, depending on your answers to those questions. Here is a list of some of them:

- Divide text into small chunks of one or two short paragraphs each.
- Add subtitles as a heading for each "chunk" of text to alert the reader about main topics.
- Create white space where students can write notes.
- Include images with accessible captions providing useful information.
- Write "pre-questions" at the top of each chunked text to assist students to know what answers they should be looking for when reading it.
- Bring attention to key words or words that may be new to your students by putting them in boldface.
- Add images—with captions or without them.
- Include translations, cognates, and/or synonyms for key words.
- If the text is online, add voice narration to it.
- Add simple definitions for key words.
- Add a title.

STRATEGY 2: TEXT ENGINEERING

Engineering the text manually can be time-consuming. However, by the time you read this book, it is highly probable that artificial intelligence will have advanced to the point where if you upload to an AI chatbot a few examples of engineered text that you have created, along with a specific request, it should be able to create ones that you can use. It may need some human editing, but it should reduce your prep time considerably.

See Figure 2.1 for an example of engineered text.

Teaching Online

If anything, it's a bit easier to create engineered text online. Of course, if you're teaching online, there's also no guarantee that your students won't ignore you and just copy and paste the entire document into Google Translate! Be sure to talk with your students about the language acquisition value of initially trying to wrestle with the English text before using the translation option.

What Could Go Wrong?

Engineering texts can take a lot of a teacher's time. Don't spend hours and hours doing it! As we said earlier in the chapter, now that we are in the age of artificial intelligence, create two or three engineered texts manually, feed them to an AI chatbot, and ask it to create similarly designed ones for your desired topics. They won't be perfect, but editing them should take far less time than doing it from scratch. Be sure to confirm that all of the information they provide is accurate!

Technology Connections

For more information about, and examples of, text engineering, visit The Best Strategies for "Engineering" Text So That It's More Accessible to ELLs (https://larryferlazzo.edublogs.org/2022/02/16/the-best-strategies-for-engineering-text-so-that-its-more-accessible-to-ells/).

Attribution

Thanks to Anne Lyneis and Maggie Roth, and to Fishtank Learning, for letting us republish their questions (https://www.fishtanklearning.org/teacher-support/blog/remote-learning-english-learners/).

All figures from this chapter, as well as 11 additional chapters, references, hyperlinked Technology Connections, and more online resources, can be found at www.wiley.com/go/ellteacherstoolbox2.

The American Revolution[i]

[i] The images in this figure are from Wiki Commons. The text was generated by ChatGPT in response to the guiding questions. The resulting text was edited and reviewed for accuracy by the authors.

Figure 2.1 Engineered Text Example

Causes of the Revolution

Why did the American Revolution start?

The American **Revolution**, which took place from 1775 to 1783, was a **conflict** where 13 American colonies fought to gain independence from British rule. The colonists were **frustrated** with British policies, especially **taxation without representation,** and events like the Boston Tea Party in 1773 further **fueled** their desire for freedom. Tensions escalated, leading to the first battles at Lexington and Concord in 1775.

Revolution — a war to get a new government

Conflict — a fight

Frustrated — angry

Taxation without representation — forced to give money to the government without being able to vote (impuestos sin representación)

Fueled — increased

George Washington became the first President of the United States

Important People and Papers

Who were key people in the Revolution and what was an important paper they wrote?

Key figures such as Thomas Jefferson, Benjamin Franklin, and George Washington played **significant** roles in the revolution. Jefferson authored the Declaration of Independence, adopted on July 4, 1776, which **outlined** the colonies' reasons

Figure 2.1 (*Continued*)

for seeking independence and emphasized the right to life, liberty, and the **pursuit** of happiness. This **document** was crucial in rallying support for the revolutionary cause.

Significant — Important

Outlined — described

Pursuit — trying to get something

Document — important paper

Military Battles

What were key battles when armies fought each other?

The war saw many important **battles**, including Bunker Hill, Saratoga, and the decisive Siege of Yorktown. The Continental Army, led by George Washington, faced numerous challenges, including harsh winters and limited supplies. The turning point came with French assistance, providing **essential** military support and helping to **secure** key victories.

Battles — fights between armies

Essential — important

Secure — to get something

Figure 2.1 (*Continued*)

How the Revolution Ended

What did the end of the American Revolution mean to the United States and to the world?

The revolution **concluded** with the Treaty of Paris in 1783, where Britain recognized the United States as an independent **nation**. The American Revolution not only achieved independence for the colonies but also established a new nation based on democratic principles and individual rights. It **inspired** future democratic movements worldwide and **laid the foundation** for the growth and development of the United States.

Concluded — ended

Nation — country

Inspired — motivated, encouraged

Laid the foundation — the important beginning of something big (sentó las bases)

Figure 2.1 (*Continued*)

STRATEGY 3
Graphic Organizers

What Is It?

A graphic organizer is a visual display or template used to scaffold students' reading, writing, listening, and speaking activities. They support students in tackling demanding cognitive and linguistic tasks.

Although there are many different types of graphic organizers, some of the most common ones are story maps, KWL charts, Venn diagrams, concept maps, idea webs, cause-and-effect diagrams, and flow charts.

Why We Like It

The strategy of using graphic organizers is an essential part of our daily instruction. We use them often to promote active learning and engagement. They serve as critical scaffolds to move students toward more-complex tasks, such as writing academic essays or giving formal presentations. We've found that ELL students especially need the visual processing opportunities that graphic organizers provide, along with the academic language and structures contained in them. We try to give students practice with a variety of organizers and encourage them to reflect on which ones are more effective and why. We also provide time for students to create their own graphic organizers. We want students to be able to produce their own when we're not around to support their learning in future ELA classes and in other content areas. Most important, graphic organizers promote students' self-efficacy so they can take on increasingly more challenging academic tasks.

Supporting Research

Many studies support the use of graphic organizers in all subject areas to increase students' reading comprehension and vocabulary knowledge (Strangman et al., 2004, p. 6–7).

In addition, research has shown that they can be specifically beneficial to English language learners (Sam D & Rajan, 2013, p. 166–167).

STRATEGY 3: GRAPHIC ORGANIZERS

Studies also point to many positive effects of graphic organizers on student writing. When used in the prewriting process, they can have a major impact on students' ability to clarify and organize their thoughts before writing (Brown, 2011, p. 9).

Their use can also promote increased student motivation for writing (Tayib, 2015, p. 1).

Common Core Connections

Graphic organizers can be used to support a variety of learning tasks that can meet any of the Common Core Anchor Standards in all four domains! The graphic organizers shared in the Application section specifically support the Standards for narrative writing.

Application

In this section we will share how we scaffold a unit on story with our beginning English language learners (see our previous book, *Navigating the Common Core with English Language Learners*, 2016, for examples of how we scaffold a unit on argument with ELL students at all levels). We typically teach this unit in the final months of the school year, after first focusing on survival and core English skills.

READING

We start by providing our students with Figure 3.1: Narrative Word Chart to introduce our students to key words related to the genre. Word charts are critical tools used to support students in acquiring the vocabulary and academic language needed to access reading and writing tasks. Teachers and students can create different formats of word charts, which students can access in their binders or folders. Larger versions can be posted on the classroom wall.

We first read *The Story of Ferdinand* (Leaf, 1977). We read it aloud as students follow along in their own copies of the book and identify new words that they think are important to know. Then, after every third or fourth page we stop and ask students to write down three words that are new to them on Figure 3.2: Identifying Words While Reading. Students can work together and use an online dictionary to find the meanings. We remind them to try to restate the meaning using their own words and not just copy the definition.

Then, students get into small groups or pairs to complete a dictation activity for the pages we just read. They are given mini-whiteboards and markers, and they take turns reading a few sentences of the story to each other while the other writes the words down on the board (if necessary, students can "cheat" by looking at the book). The reader checks the accuracy of the writer. We then come back together as a class and repeat the process with the next few pages. Depending on student engagement, we may continue the process through the rest of the story or vary the process by simply reading a few pages without doing the vocabulary or dictation activities (see Strategy 24: Dictation).

In order to keep interest high with our teenage students (remember this example is a children's book), we encourage students to make connections between themselves and the text. For example, you may remember that Ferdinand has his favorite spot under the cork tree. At that point in the story, we pause and provide students with this sentence starter: "My favorite spot is ____ because ____." They create mini-posters on white copy paper and share them in small groups. Students responded to similar prompts throughout the story.

Next, we complete a story map together as a class—there are a zillion versions of story maps that can be found online. We make sure that the story map we select contains the genre-related words we are focusing on (see Figure 3.1: Narrative Word Chart) and is visually simple with enough space for students to write. We have found the most challenging part of the story map is helping our students understand *theme* and, to a lesser extent, *protagonist-antagonist*. To reinforce these concepts, we ask students to create a quick poster for three of their favorite movies or stories and to identify the theme and the protagonists and antagonists in each (we provide a teacher model as well).

We have students go back into the story and make a list of sensory words and details used in the text. We then work together to add additional related words to each column on Figure 3.2: Five Senses Chart. See Figure 3.3 for a student-completed example of this chart.

Next, we read the book *The Teacher from the Black Lagoon* (Thaler, 2000) using a similar process. We find this book is engaging and supports critical school vocabulary.

WRITING

After our reading, we revisit the narrative word chart to reinforce our understanding of the vocabulary and to make note of any new learnings. Students are then ready to apply their knowledge of these concepts to writing their own stories.

So, do we hand out the prompt and take a seat? No, we do not (though on some days it may be more tempting than others). We do hand out graphic organizers that support students as they progress through the writing process.

We often use backwards mapping or planning when developing a unit for our students. In other words, we think about what the culminating task will be (in this case, writing a story) and what instructional steps and scaffolding students will need to get there.

Here are some universal questions that we ask ourselves when creating or choosing graphic organizers to support students in navigating complex learning tasks. Following each question is an explanation of how we address it within the context of our unit on story.

1. What prior knowledge do students possess about the learning task? Is it necessary to build more background knowledge?

    In this instance, students have already built background knowledge by reading the two books and completing story maps and sensory detail charts.

2. What are the key elements students need to know in order to achieve the complex learning task?

    In this unit, students need to develop their own story with a setting, characters (including a protagonist and an antagonist), a plot containing conflict and a resolution, and a theme. They must also employ the narrative strategies of using imagery and dialogue. The graphic organizers we use (Figures 3.3–3.12) enable students to develop their ideas and language for each story element one at a time. This process increases motivation and decreases anxiety as students gradually build their writing skills and confidence. It also enables students to see how each organizer is connected and develops from the previous one. This steady advancement builds on research showing that one of the key factors in developing intrinsic motivation is seeing progress in one's work (also known as the progress principle, www.progressprinciple.com/).

3. What is the vocabulary level of students?

   A student's English proficiency level must be taken into consideration when developing a graphic organizer. For example, this unit is designed for beginners, so several of the graphic organizers (see Figures 3.5–3.8) contain a box for students to draw their ideas. After drawing, students can label the items they know and seek assistance from other students and the teacher to identify the English words that are new to them. Students can then use this bank of words to write sentences on the lines below their drawing.

4. What organizational structures or language techniques do students need to know in order to achieve the learning task?

   In the story unit, students need to sequence the events in their story and include a conflict and a resolution. Figure 3.10: Story Events provides a visual tool on which students can write the events of their story in order. Students also need to employ the narrative strategies of using imagery and dialogue. Figure 3.10: Story Events also asks students to incorporate sensory details from Figure 3.3: Five Senses Chart. Figure 3.11: Dialogue encourages students to create a dialogue between two characters and gives them an opportunity to practice structuring it with quotation marks. All of this practice boosts their confidence and serves to prepare them for the final task of writing a story.

Teaching Online

We have taught the story unit online, using the same books, the same process, and the same graphic organizers. Though it wasn't logistically possible for us to get hard copies of *The Story of Ferdinand* or *The Teacher from the Black Lagoon* to our students, it was easy enough to find YouTube videos of people showing and reading the books, which we would show on Zoom.

Then, either we took screenshots of the graphic organizers and inserted the images on an online whiteboard for students to complete or we replicated the graphic organizers on Google Drawings.

Students would share their work "speed-dating" in breakout rooms, and we would follow them up with class discussions.

Similar tech tools and teaching processes could be used for multiple topics.

What Could Go Wrong?

Providing students with graphic organizers without any instruction or modeling in how to use them can render them ineffective and result in student frustration. Graphic organizers that are overly complicated or have complex directions can have the same results. Have we ever passed out a graphic organizer without modeling it first? Of course! Have we used a mediocre graphic organizer because we didn't have time to make a better one? Yes! However, we try to minimize these situations and we hope you will, too.

   A note of further caution: Don't hand out a big packet of graphic organizers, no matter how cool you think they are. This will be a disaster and you may be greeted with expressions of disbelief. Having students complete them *one at a time* over several class periods will result in more-engaged students and better quality work. In addition, as students complete the graphic organizers, be sure to stop periodically so that they can share with partners what they have done. Teachers can also encourage students with higher English proficiency to help their classmates.

Differentiation Recommendations

Newcomers (Preliterate or Low Literacy in Home Language): Encourage students to use online translation tools to say and translate the graphic organizer text in their home language. They can use the same tools to say their responses and copy-and-paste or handwrite the home language and translated English versions into the graphic organizers. Students can also draw their responses.	**Newcomers (Literate in Home Language):** Add sentence starters to the graphic organizers as a scaffold. In addition, they can use translation tools to fill out graphic organizers, as well as also draw supporting images.
Intermediate ELLs: Use the assigned graphic organizers "as is."	**Advanced ELLs:** Invite students to use the teacher's recommended graphic organizers or to invent their own.

Technology Connections

We haven't found any huge benefits for our students in completing graphic organizers online—if we are teaching face-to-face—as opposed to with pencil and paper. That said, we sometimes have our students use online versions of graphic organizers for a change of pace. For a list of what we think are some of the better online mind-mapping and flow chart tools (all free and all accessible to English language learners) and sources for hard-copy graphic organizers, see The Best List of Mindmapping, Flow Chart Tools, & Graphic Organizers (https://larryferlazzo.edublogs.org/2009/02/09/not-the-best-but-a-list-of-mindmapping-flow-chart-tools-graphic-organizers/).

STRATEGY 3: GRAPHIC ORGANIZERS 27

For free virtual whiteboards, see The Best Alternatives to the Soon-to-Be-Deceased Google Jamboard (https://larryferlazzo.edublogs.org/2023/10/03/the-best-alternatives-to-the-soon-to-be-deceased-google-jamboard/) and/or The Best Online Virtual "Corkboards" (https://larryferlazzo.edublogs.org/2011/03/30/the-best-online-virtual-corkboards-or-bulletin-boards/).

Attribution

We were introduced to using *The Story of Ferdinand* (Leaf, 1977) in a genre-based short story unit by the WRITE Institute, though the series of lessons shared in this section are substantially different. For information on WRITE and their curriculum resources see https://writeinstitute.sdcoe.net/. Figure 3.5 was also inspired by a graphic organizer from the WRITE Institute.

All figures from this chapter, as well as 11 additional chapters, references, hyperlinked Technology Connections, and more online resources, can be found at www.wiley.com/go/ellteacherstoolbox2.

Word	Meaning in English	Meaning in Home Language	Picture
Protagonist			
Antagonist			
Characters			
Setting			
Conflict			
Events			
Dialogue			
Resolution			
Theme			

Figure 3.1 Narrative Word Chart

STRATEGY 3: GRAPHIC ORGANIZERS

Page Number, Word	Definition in English Using My Own Words	Definition in Home Language and/or Picture	My Own Sentence

Figure 3.2 Identifying Words While Reading

Name_____ **Five Senses Chart**	Sights
Sounds	Smells
Tastes	Touch

Figure 3.3 Five Senses Chart

Name_____ # Five Senses Chart	**Sights** • green grass • beautiful flowers • red cape • huge arena with many people • colorful flags
Sounds • quiet under the cork tree • a bumble bee buzzing • puffing and snorting • people yelling • people clapping • music playing	**Smells** • fresh flowers • grass • dust • food cooking • animals
Tastes • sweet grass • delicious food • salty • sweet	**Touch** • cool breeze • soft grass • painful sting • hot sun

Figure 3.4 Five Senses Chart Student Example

STRATEGY 3: GRAPHIC ORGANIZERS 31

Your Name _____

Setting

When does your story take place? _____

Where does your story take place? Draw it and use as many details as possible. What do the characters in your story see? What is the weather like? What objects, animals, are there? What colors do they see?

Describe the setting and include adjectives (colors, size, shape, temperature, smells, sounds, etc.). *Examples:* There is a blue sky. The school is big. The park is shaped like a square. The weather is very hot. It smells like bread. A dog is barking.

_____
_____
_____
_____
_____
_____

Figure 3.5 Setting

Your Name _____

Main Characters

What is the name of the protagonist? _____

Draw the protagonist:

Describe your protagonist: How old is he or she? What does he or she look like? How does he or she feel? What kind of clothes is she or he wearing? What is her or his hair color?

_____
_____
_____
_____
_____
_____
_____
_____
_____

What is the name of the antagonist? _____

Draw the antagonist:

Describe your protagonist: How old is he or she? What does he or she look like? How does he or she feel? What kind of clothes is she or he wearing? What is her or his hair color?

_____
_____
_____
_____
_____
_____
_____
_____
_____

Figure 3.6 Main Characters

STRATEGY 3: GRAPHIC ORGANIZERS 33

Your Name _____

Who are the other characters?

Name _____

Name _____

Name _____

Name _____

Figure 3.7 Supporting Characters

Your Name _____

Theme

What is the theme of your story? Circle one or create your own:

    Good beats evil.

    Love conquers all.

    Be true to yourself.

    Friendship is important.

    Beauty is on the inside.

    Being brave is better than being a coward.

    Racism is bad.

    It is important to be kind.

    We should try new things.

Other theme: _____

How will your story show that theme? Draw it:

[ ]

Describe the picture (for example, The strong man kills the monster. That shows that good is better than bad.):

_____
_____
_____

Figure 3.8 Theme

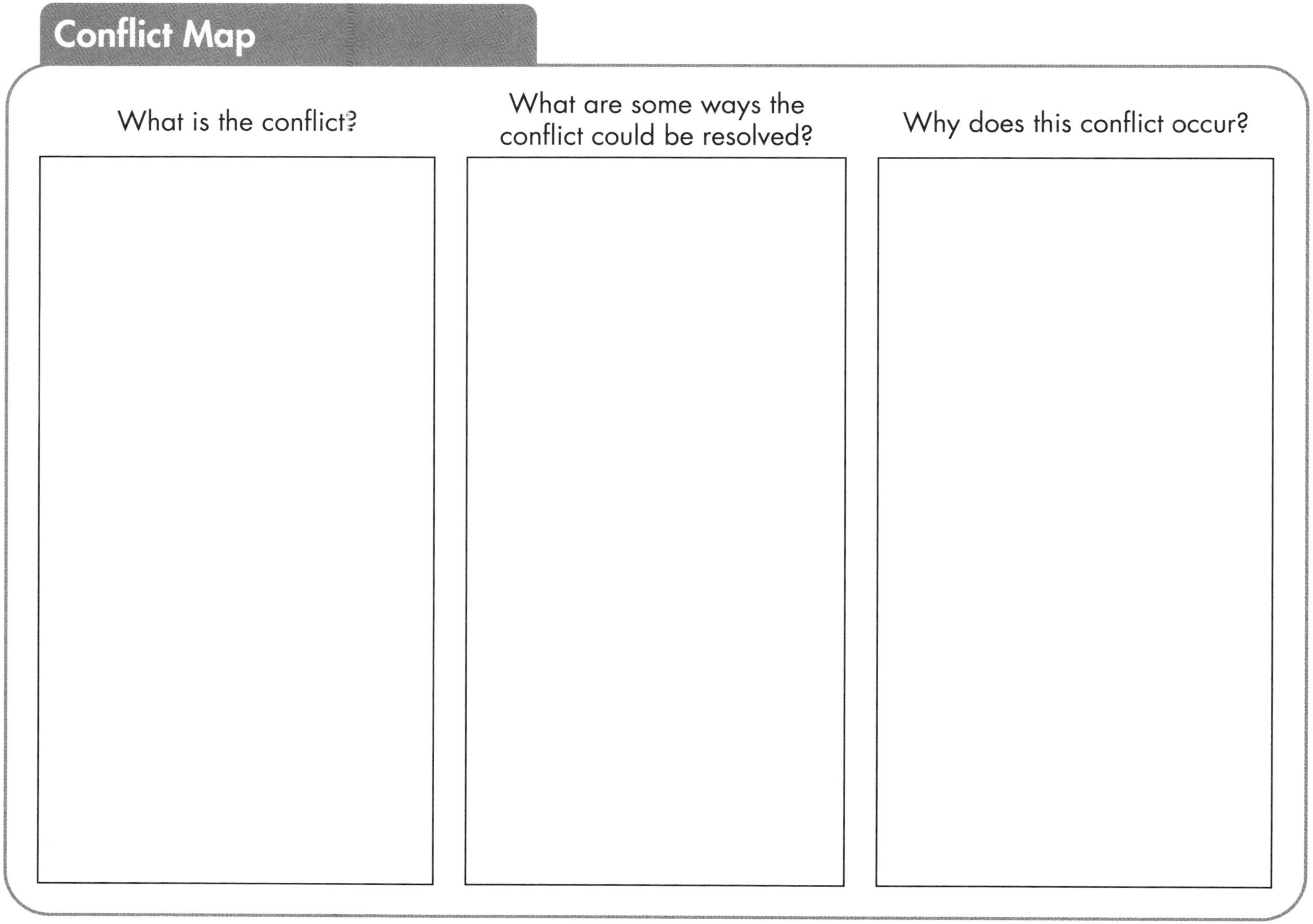

STRATEGY 3: GRAPHIC ORGANIZERS   35

Conflict Map

What is the conflict?

What are some ways the conflict could be resolved?

Why does this conflict occur?

Figure 3.9 Conflict Map   *Source:* Reproduced with the permission of NCTE/ReadWriteThink. This resource was provided by ReadWriteThink.org, a website developed by the National Council of Teachers of English.

Your Name _____

Story Events

Describe what happens. Please try to include words from the Five Senses sheet.

First:

Second:

Third:

Fourth:

Fifth:

Sixth:

Resolution:

Figure 3.10 Story Events

Your Name _____

Dialogue

What is a dialogue at least two of your characters can have and in which event (First? Second? Third?. . .)?

Be sure to use quotation marks!

This dialogue takes place in Event Number _____

Name of character:
_____

Name of character:
_____

Name of character:
_____

Name of character:
_____

Name of character:
_____

Name of character:
_____

Figure 3.11 Dialogue

Your Name _____

You may use a lined sheet of paper. Please write it in this order, using paragraphs:

1. Describe the setting.

2. Introduce the protagonist and antagonist.

3. Tell about the different events. Be sure to include a dialogue.

4. Write the resolution.

Figure 3.12 Write Your Story

STRATEGY 4

Vocabulary

What Is It?

Many of the other strategies we've discussed in this book are related to learning vocabulary—Strategy 1: Independent Reading, Strategy 9: Jigsaw, Strategy 11: Inductive Learning, Strategy 17: Using Photos or Other Images in Reading and Writing, and Strategy 23: Learning Games for Reading and Writing—just to name a few. We thought it would also be important to share examples of several other strategies we use, and provide a big-picture look at what generally works for English language learners in vocabulary instruction.

Respected education researcher Robert Marzano (2009) developed a widely used and research-backed six-step process for effective vocabulary instruction. We use it with minor modifications, and all the strategies listed under Application fit into at least one of the steps.

Here is that model with our personal tweaks:

1. First, the teacher pronounces the word—whether it's in the context of pre-teaching words needed for an upcoming text or unit, saying it while doing a read aloud, or introducing it as part of a cline or word web (see the Application section). We usually write it on the board or document camera, as well. Marzano doesn't explicitly point out the act of pronunciation in the six-step process. However, it's a crucial step for ELLs.

2. Next, the teacher describes the word using various examples—with an image or using different sentences.

3. Third, the student needs to actively process the word through writing his or her own definition (in English or in a home language) and drawing an image. Students can use an online dictionary for ideas, but they need to be reminded not to copy a definition word-for-word. Of course, this takes teacher modeling and student practice. We also encourage students to use the word in an original sentence.

These first three steps are completed right on the same day that the new vocabulary is introduced.

The following three activities are done within the next few days and beyond—reinforcing exercises (some of our favorites are students writing their own sentences using the words, categorization, clines, word webs and online exercises.), student discussions, and games.

It's clear that multiple exposures to new words in different contexts (Thornbury, 2013, describes this as the principal of re-contextualization and the principle of multiple encounters) are critical, though there is not universal agreement about the exact number of repetitions needed before the word is fully learned. Some researchers suggest 8 to 10 times in different contexts will do the trick (Rossiter et al., 2016).

Similar to Marzano, we're big fans of games for reinforcing new vocabulary, and there is no shortage of different options in Strategy 23: Learning Games for Reading and Writing.

Why We Like It

The strategies we list in the Application section are engaging to our students and can fit within the Marzano framework. Many of these strategies work in just about any instance or allotted amount of time. None of them require extensive teacher prep.

Supporting Research

Extensive research supports the importance of using multiple methods of vocabulary instruction rather than focusing on one or two (Ford-Connors & Paratore, 2015; National Reading Technical Assistance Center, 2010). These methods should include explicit instruction (prior to and during reading of the text), active student participation (such as writing their own sentences using the word and drawing images as part of their definitions), repeated exposure to words in different contexts (Rossiter et al., 2016), and wide reading (Feldman & Kinsella, 2005, p. 4). Marzano's (2009) six steps, which include many of these elements, have been shown to be widely effective.

Common Core Connections

There are four Standards under the heading "Vocabulary Acquisition and Use" in Language. Each of the applications we share meet one or more of these Standards.

Application

Here are nine specific instructional strategies that we use in vocabulary instruction.

FOUR WORDS SHEET

We ask that students identify four new words they learned that week during class or outside of class—and that they think are important—and complete Figure 4.1: Four Words Sheet. Every Friday, students share them with a partner using the question and sentence starters on Figure 4.2: Question and Sentence Starters List. This list roughly starts at easy and progresses to more difficult with the latter ones using academic language. Students choose which ones they want to use. After all students have shared with a partner, they each make a poster for one word to teach to the entire class and add it to the interactive word wall (see that section).

WORD CHART

A word chart is a simple graphic organizer used to pre-teach important vocabulary that students will encounter in an upcoming text or writing genre. The teacher identifies 10 or so key words and provides a copy of a word chart graphic organizer either with the words already printed or with blank spaces for students to write them. Figure 4.3 is the Narrative Word Chart we use in our story unit (see Strategy 3: Graphic Organizers).

The teacher pronounces two or three words at a time and then gives students several minutes to access any prior knowledge. See the Vocabulary section in Strategy 5: Activating Prior Knowledge for a description of the process we use to support students in rating their prior knowledge of words and Figure 5.2: Upstander Word Chart for an additional example of a word chart.

Depending on the unit of instruction, we also might first show students images or physical objects representing vocabulary words before directly teaching them the meanings. For example, when doing a unit with Beginners on Jobs and Careers, we first show an image of a type of job and then introduce the word for it. Recent research confirms vocabulary learning can be increased when teachers show an object (or picture of the object) to students prior to introducing the word (Ma & Komarova, 2019).

After assessing their prior knowledge, viewing any images, and writing what they already know about any of the words, we then ask students to look up the meanings online. Students write the definition in their home language and in English (with the admonition to put it in their own words and not copy it from a dictionary). In addition, we ask students to draw an image that represents the word. Research shows that drawing can significantly help learners recall word meanings (Wammes et al., 2016; Fernandes et al., 2018).

Students then share with a partner and make any needed revisions, and next the entire class reviews those words, with the teacher calling on individual students to share what they wrote and drew.

The process is repeated until all the words are reviewed. Afterward, we'll sometimes divide up the words and ask students to make a small poster for each word that we'll tape up on an interactive word wall (see that topic later in this section and in Strategy 48: Interactive Word Walls).

Just to change things up, we sometimes use a Frayer Model word chart. This well-known graphic organizer for vocabulary building was originally created by Dorothy Frayer and her colleagues at the University of Wisconsin (Frayer et al., 1969). It is visually represented with four squares and a circle for the vocabulary word or concept in the middle. Typically students are asked to explore the meaning of a word or concept using the four-square model by defining the word, describing its characteristics, providing a few examples of the word/concept, and offering a few non-examples.

For example, we have used a Frayer Model to teach the word "protagonist" by having students write its definition in the first box in English (*the main character, often the hero*) and in their home language. In the second box, students describe the essential characteristics of a protagonist (*brave, has empathy, experiences change, helps others*). Then, we ask students to list some examples of protagonists in books, stories, or movies they know (*Harry Potter, Ariel in The Little Mermaid*). Finally, students are asked to describe non-examples of a protagonist (*Voldemort, Ursula*). Of course, the examples and non-examples change from year to year depending on students' experiences and current movies! After completing a Frayer Model graphic organizer as a class, students can then work in pairs or individually to complete one for a different word or concept.

You can find a multitude of examples of Frayer Model graphic organizers by searching "Frayer Model" online.

TEACHING NEW WORDS DURING READING

The research cited previously finds that explicit instruction of new vocabulary before and during the reading of a text is an effective teaching and learning strategy. When we are reading a short text (e.g., a read aloud or think aloud; see Strategy 10: Reading Comprehension) we might see a word we suspect is new to many students and attempt to seamlessly teach it (e.g., "It was difficult [very hard, not easy] to do."). Many of these words end up on students' Four Words sheets.

When we are reading a short book together with a beginning or intermediate ELL class, such as *The Story of Ferdinand* (Leaf, 1977) or *The Teacher from the Black Lagoon* (Thaler, 2000), we'll show the pages on the document camera and read them aloud. We will quickly and explicitly teach key words that we think might be new to students and are crucial to understanding the story. We do not stop and teach *every* word. Then, we have students stop after we've read three or four pages and choose three words that are new to them. Next, they add these words to Figure 4.4: Identifying Words While Reading. They generally use an online dictionary and, as usual, we remind students to not copy what it says and, instead, use their own words. We next have students get into groups of two or three to share what they wrote and make any appropriate revisions. They then do a dictation activity with mini-whiteboards on the pages we just read together (see Strategy 24: Dictation) before we reconvene as a class and proceed to the next few pages.

Interestingly, no clear connection has yet been found in the research on vocabulary instruction suggesting that spending a lengthy period of time on teaching the meaning of a word (e.g., two to three minutes) is more effective than spending one or two minutes on it (Wright & Cervetti, 2016, p. 11). We are not surprised at this finding, based on Larry's experience of falling asleep during a professional development training session in which the trainer spent 30 minutes teaching the word *expedition*. The only exception to our time rule is when we teach academic language in a humorous and engaging manner that includes active student processing and physical movement.

CONTEXT CLUES

Explicit vocabulary instruction is a key part of our lessons, and research supports this practice as critical for English language learners (Gallagher et al., 2019). However, we also recognize that our students need support and practice in determining word meanings on their own as they are reading to build their comprehension and confidence as readers in English. Research backs our experience and has found that students can benefit from context instruction, but, interestingly, not from being taught a list of different types of context clues. Instead, learners gain more by doing actual practice in determining word meanings from context (Fukkink & de Glopper, 1998). In other words, it is a process of providing appropriate text that creates opportunities for students to more easily identify context clues, discuss what they find, and reflect on how they can apply these strategies in the future.

In addition, we also know that supporting students in the practice of context clues is ultimately more about improving reading comprehension than specific vocabulary learning. As literacy researcher Timothy Shanahan (2022) states, "the real purpose of using context is to comprehend the text, not to learn word meanings." However, we are discussing it here because many people think about context clues as a way to understand new vocabulary.

So what does this kind of practice with context clues look like in an ELL classroom?

We like the five-step approach developed by our friend and talented educator, Tan Huynh (2016). See Figure 4.5: 5 Steps to Teaching Context Clues, for a summary of the process he uses with ELLs. It involves the teacher first selecting a text for guided reading and identifying several words whose meanings can be determined from clues in the text. As the teacher reads the text aloud to students, they can pause at each pre-selected word and tell students that there are context clues for that word's meaning in the text. Students are then given time to reread that sentence and the sentences around it independently to search for clues which they can highlight or circle. Students can then be encouraged to share their clues in pairs or a small group and can work together to infer the meaning of the word. Finally, students can be asked to reflect in writing or through discussion on the process they used in determining word meanings through context clues.

ACADEMIC VOCABULARY

As you probably know, the authors of the Common Core Standards rely on research (Common Core State Standards Initiative, n.d.) dividing words into three categories called "tiers" (Beck et al., 2013). Tier One is composed of words used often in typical oral conversation. Tier Two includes general academic vocabulary often found in many different kinds of school texts (e.g., *vary, accumulated, request*), while Tier Three words are domain-specific and typically found in content textbooks (e.g., *photosynthesis, legislature*).

When it comes time to teach academic vocabulary, we mainly focus on Tier Two words because we feel we can get a bigger bang for the buck. These words will make more texts accessible to our students than Tier Three words. We generally teach academic vocabulary using two simple methods.

One way involves using vocabulary word lists (the Technology Connections section has suggestions of where to obtain them online for free) and teaching 8 to 12 Tier Two words from them each week. We give students a copy of one page of the word list to paste in their writer's notebook (see Online Strategy: Writer's Notebook). We pronounce a word, define it, and then write a humorous question and answer:

> Would you **compare** Mr. Ferlazzo to an egg?
>
> Yes, I would **compare** Mr. Ferlazzo to an egg because his bald head is smooth.

We write the question on the document camera, say it, have students repeat it, and then do the same with the answer. We do the same for two more words, and then students break into small groups of two or three to practice asking and answering the same questions. In addition, they write their own questions and responses using the same words and share them. Each time we do this process, they also practice some of the words, questions, and answers from previous lessons. This is always a high-interest activity, and students particularly look forward to developing sentences that make fun of Larry!

Another method we use when we want to change things up (especially second semester) or we have plenty of peer tutors involves displaying a slide with a question highlighting an academic word and sentence starter response. We model asking and answering the question; students copy it in their notebook and work on developing their own response. Students then go outside or to different parts of the classroom to practice in small groups led by a peer tutor or a student with higher English proficiency. Next, they present to another small group.

Figure 4.6: Academic Language Oral Practice is the first page of 107 question-and-answer sentence starters using academic vocabulary that we use throughout the year with our students. You can download the full list at our book's website, wiley.com/go/ellteacherstoolbox2. You can also create your own by asking an AI chatbot to make one.

A simple guide we keep in mind (and backed by research previously cited) when teaching academic vocabulary is that students need to SEE it, SAY it, WRITE it, and DRAW it! We also try to include body movements/gestures when teaching academic words because this practice can further boost learning (Wexler, 2022). For example, when teaching a word like "connect," we might make a gesture linking our fingers together.

CLINES

Clines are scales, or spectrums, of words that go from one extreme to the other (e.g., freezing, cold, room temperature, warm, hot, boiling). Two examples can be found in Figure 4.7: Clines.

We prefer to teach clines by first taping up words from the cline in different sections of the room. Then, we show a blank cline (just the line without the words) on the document camera and have students copy it down in their writer's notebook. Next, we ask students a series of questions, which they answer by going to the appropriately labeled part of the room (e.g., in the love-hate cline, we ask questions such as "How do you feel about Justin Bieber?" or "How do you feel about our school's cafeteria food?" Or, if you're feeling brave, you can ask "How do you feel about your teacher?"). We ask different questions quickly so students are moving relatively fast from one section of the room to another. Then, students return to their seats and we complete the cline on the document camera together.

As a follow-up, students could create their own unique clines tied to their interests (e.g., "I hate beets"; "I love salsa picante"). Time permitting, students can then orally share what they wrote with a partner.

There are many other word groupings suitable for clines. English teacher Jonny Ingham (n.d.) has several on his website: https://eflrecipes.com/2014/03/18/clines/. You can also search online "word groups for clines" or ask an AI chatbot for those word groups.

WORD WEBS

Word webs, semantic mapping, word maps are the names given to graphic organizers that in some way map connections between words. Teachers use them in all sizes and in varying degrees of complexity; search the web and you'll see what we mean. They typically have one word in the middle with lots of words connected to that central one as well as others branching off from each other.

In the picture word inductive model (PWIM) (see Strategy 11: Inductive Learning), we have students essentially do the same thing when they categorize words from the picture and add new ones. We just have them divide their papers into columns instead of creating a word web. We've never seen any advantage to having students write them as a map while using the PWIM. However, as in everything we do, we always remain open to learning how to do things in a better way.

We keep our word webs simple when we use them and generally they are in preparation for a writing assignment. We might use a version to help students identify words that fit under the five senses (see Strategy 3: Graphic Organizers). Or we'll identify an important word that is key to a text they are reading and that they will be writing about (e.g., the word *scared*) and have them identify synonyms in a word web. Additionally, word webs or maps can make connections between words more visible to students. That said, a word web or map can sometimes make connections between words more visible to some students. We want to provide our students with a variety of learning and organizational tools so they can choose what works best for them now and in the future.

There are several online tools that are ideal for ELLs to use when generating these kinds of word webs, which we discuss in the Technology Connections section.

INTERACTIVE WORD WALL

Many teachers are familiar with the idea of a word wall, though fewer might know the term *interactive word wall*. The traditional definitions for both, and their real-life uses, can vary widely. There's strong research supporting the idea that any version can assist vocabulary development by helping to create a print-rich classroom (Harmon et al., 2009; Southerland, 2011).

Because there is such a wide variance among them (just search *word wall* and *interactive word wall* online), we'll use this section to briefly explain what it means to us and how we apply it in our classrooms. See Chapter 48: Interactive Word Walls for a more extensive discussion of using word walls in the classroom.

Generally, the idea of an *interactive* word wall means that students interact with it in some way—it's not just a bunch of words stuck on the wall for decoration. Our interactive word walls typically have five elements (depending on the English levels of our students) and are often located in different parts of the classroom so they don't all just blend into each other. Some things they all have in common, however, are that the words are organized in some way, clearly written so they can be seen from most parts of the classroom, always being modified, and accompanied by an image (at least, most of the time).

The five elements of our interactive word wall are as follows:

- A labeled picture used with the weekly PWIM theme (see Strategy 11: Inductive Learning). This picture is almost always in the front of the classroom; these themes could be home, school, health, holidays, and so on; if we are in a classroom that has the appropriate physical layout we'll put retired labeled PWIM photos on the wall near the ceiling.
- A chart of irregular verb conjugations.
- A section devoted to total physical response (TPR) (see Strategy 26) words; easier words are regularly removed.
- A section devoted to important words related to the writing genre we are using at the time, such as the words in a narrative word chart (see Figure 4.3).
- A section devoted to new words identified by students as part of their Four Words assignment (see Figure 4.1).

Many of the words and pictures illustrating them—particularly for the writing genre and Four Words sheets—are created by students following these simple guidelines (with exemplars to demonstrate them):

- The words are written on a 4″× 11″ piece of construction paper.
- The letters need to be as large as possible, and they must contrast clearly with the background of the construction paper.
- Students can choose the color of the paper, and they must also devote at least some thought to considering if the color helps communicate the meaning of the word (e.g., blue for the word *ocean*).
- A simple and colorful picture representing the meaning of the word must be drawn on the last three or so inches of the paper.
- Or, teachers might give the option for students to select an online image to print out and glue onto the paper.

Trust us, having exemplars and these precise instructions are not overdoing it!

We don't want to have too many words on our walls. They can blend in and end up looking more like clutter instead of a scaffold. We retire words from the Four Words sheet every Friday; however, we retire them in a productive way—last week's words are turned around and shown through our window so the hundreds of students who walk past each day can see them. Knowing that their word posters will have an authentic audience also motivates students to do a particularly good job on them!

COGNATES

Cognates are words in different languages that have some similarity in spelling, meaning, and pronunciation. Although English does not have many cognates in most languages, it is estimated that more than 30% of English words have similar ones in Spanish (Colorado, 2007). These connections can provide a big benefit to our Spanish-speaking ELLs, and research has found emphasizing cognates can enhance vocabulary acquisition for ELLs even when the language of instruction is primarily in English (Post, 2021).

However, we don't necessarily teach remote lessons on cognates or the small number of false cognates (words that have similar spelling and pronunciation but don't share the same meaning). We feel that teaching cognates in isolation is equally as ineffective as teaching any vocabulary out of context. However, because we both speak Spanish, it is easy for us to identify and highlight cognates when we see them in the course of our teaching (however, usually our Spanish-speaking students beat us to it). For teachers who don't speak Spanish, it's a great opportunity to do a quick lesson on cognates and give a few examples (there are many lists online if you simply Google "list of cognates"). Then, invite and regularly remind students that you would love it if they would point out words that they believe are cognates in the texts the class is reading or that they are reading independently. Everyone can learn together!

FROM CLUES TO WORDS

This is a fun activity that we use occasionally in conjunction with the theme we're teaching with the PWIM. We first ask each student to think about words in their home language that are connected to the theme but they have not yet learned in English. We ask that each student write down four words in their home language. For example, if we are studying *home*, a student might write down the words *bathtub*, *tablecloth*, *attic*, and *basement* in their home language, because we probably have not already reviewed these less common words.

Next, students get into groups of two to four students who share the same home language. Students who don't have classmates who speak the same language often seem fine doing these next parts alone. The groups each decide on one word they want to learn, and they develop several clues that would help others who don't speak their language identify the word in English. Students can use drawing, drama, pantomime, and so on. They just cannot say the word in their home language. Each group performs their clues in front for all the other small groups. Every group has a mini-whiteboard. After each performance is finished, student groups can talk together to see if they know the English word (they can't use their smartphones!). Once they think they know the answer, they write it on their board. The teacher can provide the answer if no student knows the correct word.

This activity can also be used as a game with points being awarded to each group who writes the correct answer on their board within a minute. We haven't done so—students seem to have a lot of fun with this as it is. But it's certainly easy to make that modification.

Diglot stories, also known as diglot weave stories, can be another engaging activity to reinforce vocabulary. Diglot stories essentially "weave" together a student's home language (L1) and the target language they are learning (L2). Ideally, a diglot story is written in a student's L1 and the teacher strategically replaces certain vocabulary with L2 so that new language is introduced in a supported and engaging way. For example, a sentence from a diglot story for Spanish-speaking English language learners might look like "Había una vez un niño named Javier que vivía on a farm donde his family criaba pollos y ganado." Students can better understand the meaning of the new words because of the context provided in their home language.

We know it might be challenging to create diglot stories when a teacher isn't proficient in their students' home languages, but asking higher proficiency students to create simple versions for beginners can be an option. Also, we have had some success using an AI chatbot to create stories in Spanish on various themes (school, food, animals, etc.). Then, we replace several Spanish words with the English vocabulary we are currently studying. We hope by the time you read this, AI tools will be even more advanced and you will be able to ask an AI chatbot to create a diglot weave story on any theme in a variety of languages.

Picture Dictionaries

Picture dictionaries are a staple in English language learning classrooms. While interactive, online versions are popular and easily available, we still find value in using hard copies. We have bilingual picture dictionaries available in some languages and monolingual ones with pictures and just English words.

One of the ways we use them in the classroom is by having peer tutors (or higher proficiency students or the teacher) use the following simple sequence to teach new vocabulary:

1. Choose 10 words from a page in the picture dictionary. Teach students how to pronounce them by pointing to the image, saying the word, and asking the group to repeat it.

2. Quiz students verbally by pointing to an image and asking students to say what it is.

3. Teach students how to read and write the same 10 words. Peer tutors point to an image, say it, and write it on a whiteboard.

4. Then quiz students by pointing to an image, saying it, and asking them to write the words on their own mini-whiteboards.

5. Peer tutors can repeat this sequence with some or all of the words if they think their students need more practice.

6. Peer tutors can write a simple sentence on a whiteboard with one of the words, and ask their students to write a sentence using the same word. They can repeat that for each word.

Another picture dictionary activity that our students enjoy comes from educator Alycia Hamilton Owen. It involves asking students to do a scavenger hunt and look for specific categories of words (verbs, things that we see outside, proper nouns, etc.). Students enjoy when we gamify this activity by putting them in pairs and giving them a certain amount of time to find the words (with points awarded for the number of correct words in each category).

Students also enjoy playing games similar to "I Spy" where they sit next to a partner with a page of the dictionary open for both students to see. One student chooses an image (e.g., a soccer ball) and describes it to their partner (e.g., it is round, it is black and white) without saying the actual word. Their partner tries to guess the word based on the clues. Students can take turns describing multiple words and move on to a new page as time and interest allow.

Students can also be asked to create their own bilingual picture dictionaries individually, in small groups, or as a class. See the Technology Connections for a list of resources on using both hard-copy and online picture dictionaries.

Teaching Online

Most of these vocabulary strategies can be used online. Modeling the use of word charts and context clues will need to be done using a shared screen. Academic vocabulary can be practiced by students in breakout rooms and then shared with the whole class on Zoom. Students can contribute to shared online word walls using tools like Padlet or Google slides. Students can easily access vocabulary-building activities and interactive picture dictionaries online (see Technology Connections).

What Could Go Wrong?

Don't overdo it! Don't put a zillion words on the classroom walls, don't overwhelm students with too many words at one time, and don't re-create Larry's nightmare of spending a half-hour teaching one word.

Also, even though it's important for students to apply the new words they are learning, remember that it might be difficult for them to immediately use every one in an original sentence. During Larry's career as a community organizer, he learned community organizer Saul Alinsky's iron rule: "Never do for others what they can do for themselves. Never!" It would be a misinterpretation of that rule if you insist that ELLs immediately develop sentences using words they learned a few seconds earlier. Plan on providing lots of models and sentence frames for students who need that extra support.

Differentiation Recommendations for Vocabulary

Newcomers (Preliterate or Low Literacy in Home Language): Encourage students to draw or use images on word charts. Provide videos or use images when teaching new words. Use audio features of Google Translate or interactive online bilingual dictionaries that provide audio support.	**Newcomers (Literate in Home Language):** Encourage the use of home language and Google Translate during vocabulary instruction. Use texts and videos in a student's home language to build vocabulary knowledge. Students write simple sentences with vocabulary words.
Intermediate ELLs: Use all chapter strategies, with increasingly challenging academic vocabulary. Students write more complex sentences using vocabulary words.	**Advanced ELLs:** Use all chapter strategies, with increasingly challenging academic vocabulary. Students write more complex sentences and paragraphs incorporating vocabulary words.

Technology Connections

Technology offers a gold mine of ways to support vocabulary instruction:

- **Students creating 15-second videos:** We often have students easily create short narrated videos teaching new words with images and sentences. Some of their creations have even been featured on the *New York Times* website! See tons of examples, along with instructions, at The Best Resources for Learning to Use Video Apps Like Instagram (http://larryferlazzo.edublogs.org/2013/02/18/the-best-resources-for-learning-to-use-the-video-app-twine/).

- **Students monitoring their increasing vocabulary knowledge:** When students see obvious progress, it enhances intrinsic motivation and supports the development of a growth mind-set showing that success comes from effort (www.ascd.org/publications/educational-leadership/sept10/vol68/num01/Even-Geniuses-Work-Hard.aspx). One tool we use to make this happen is having students periodically take online vocabulary tests and note their scores. Invariably, they increase as the school year continues. We like one called Test Your Vocab (http://testyourvocab.com/), but there are many others that you can find by searching that same phrase: *test your vocabulary*.

- **There are many accessible and free online tools designed for vocabulary instruction:** These sites not only offer explicit instruction but also provide engaging and reinforcing games. Quizlet (https://quizlet.com/) is probably the most well-known one, and you can find others at A Collection of "Best . . ." Lists on Vocabulary Development (http://larryferlazzo.edublogs.org/2013/01/05/a-collection-of-best-lists-on-vocabulary-development/).

- **There are several online tools that easily and visually show synonyms and antonyms:** We use them when students are creating word maps. We have several listed on The Best Reference Websites for English Language Learners (http://larryferlazzo.edublogs.org/2008/11/13/the-best-reference-websites-for-english-language-learners-2008/).

- **There are many word lists we use for teaching academic vocabulary:** They can be found at The Best Websites for Developing Academic English Skills & Vocabulary (http://larryferlazzo.edublogs.org/2008/04/06/the-best-websites-for-developing-academic-english-skills-vocabulary/). This list also contains links to downloadable sentence frames using academic vocabulary.

- **There are lots of interactive picture dictionaries available online:** They can be found by searching "Interactive visual or picture dictionary" online. More ideas on using picture dictionaries can be found at The Best Strategies for Using Picture Dictionaries with ELLs at https://larryferlazzo.edublogs.org/2022/03/22/the-best-strategies-for-using-picture-dictionaries-with-ells/.

- **There is a wealth of research as well as numerous web tools focused on vocabulary learning:** An updated list can be found at The Best Sites Where ELLs Can Learn Vocabulary at https://larryferlazzo.edublogs.org/2009/07/15/the-best-sites-where-ells-can-learn-vocabulary/.

Attribution

Versions of some of these ideas appeared in our book *The ESL/ELL Teacher's Survival Guide* (Ferlazzo & Sypnieski, 2012, p. 132), and in our book *Navigating the Common Core with English Language Learners* (Ferlazzo & Sypnieski, 2016, p. 259).

Thanks to English teacher Jonny Ingham for his great ideas on using clines: https://eflrecipes.com/2014/03/18/clines/.

Our from clues to words activity was inspired by a somewhat similar idea that English teacher Judit Fehér (2015, p. 64) wrote about in *Creativity in the English Language Classroom* (www.teachingenglish.org.uk/sites/teacheng/files/F004_ELT_Creativity_FINAL_v2%20WEB.pdf).

Figure 4.4 was inspired by a graphic organizer from the WRITE Institute. For information on WRITE and their curriculum resources see https://writeinstitute.sdcoe.net/.

All figures from this chapter, as well as 11 additional chapters, references, hyperlinked Technology Connections, and more online resources, can be found at www.wiley.com/go/ellteacherstoolbox2.

Word and Definition in English

Definition in Primary Language

Picture

Sentence

Word and Definition in English

Definition in Primary Language

Picture

Sentence

Word and Definition in English

Definition in Primary Language

Picture

Sentence

Word and Definition in English

Definition in Primary Language

Picture

Sentence

Figure 4.1 Four Words Sheet *Source:* Reprinted from Ferlazzo & Sypnieski, Navigating the CommonCore with English Language Learners (2016, p. 75).

STRATEGY 4: VOCABULARY 53

Please take turns and ask your partner about their words using one or more of these questions.

Questions

1. Can you tell me a word you learned this week?
2. Please tell me a word you learned this week.
3. Please teach me a new word.
4. Please help me learn new words.
5. What is a word you learned this week?
6. Can you share a new word with me?
7. Can you teach me some new vocabulary?
8. Can you tell me about an interesting word you learned this week?
9. Please tell me a word you decided was important to learn this week.
10. Can you tell me about an interesting word you learned this week?
11. Can you share a new word with me that you think is useful?
12. Please tell me a word you decided was important to learn this week.
13. Can you review your new words with me?
14. What new words did you collect this week?
15. Let's examine your new words now. What is your first one? What is your second one? What is your third one? What is your fourth one?
16. Can you point out your new words to me and tell me what they mean?
17. What are your new words and what are their definitions?
18. Let's discuss new words. Can you please start with your list?

Answers

1. _____ is a new word I learned this week. It means _____ _____. I used it in this sentence: _____ _____.

2. I learned the word _____ this week. I read or heard it when _____ _____. It means _____. This is the sentence I used: _____.

3. _____ is a new word I learned this week. I read or heard it when _____. Its definition is _____. I used it in this sentence: _____ _____.

Figure 4.2 Question and Sentence Starters List

Word	Meaning in English	Meaning in Home Language	Picture
Protagonist			
Antagonist			
Characters			
Setting			
Conflict			
Events			
Dialogue			
Resolution			
Theme			

Figure 4.3 Narrative Word Chart

STRATEGY 4: VOCABULARY 55

Page Number Word	Definition in English Using My Own Words	Definition in Home Language and/or Picture	My Own Sentence

Figure 4.4 Identifying Words While Reading

5 Steps to Teaching Context Clues

Article # 15

1. Pre-select Words
Read the text prior to reading with students. Identify words that have context clues associated with it.

2. Notify students
As you read with your ELs, notify them of opportunities to use context clues to decipher the meaning of a word.

3. Search for clues
Have ELs independently re-read the text to search for clues.

4. Collaborative Discussion
Allow students to use the clues they found to infer the meaning of the vocab.

5. Metacognitive Reflection
Ask them to describe the steps of using context clues to construct the word's meaning.

EmpoweringELLs.com/blog

Figure 4.5 Five Steps to Teaching Context Clues

1. **What is a <u>list</u> of fun things you did during the summer?**
   During the summer, I _____, _____, and _____.

2. **Now that you have <u>finished</u> your first few days of school, how do you feel about your classes?**
   I feel _____ about my classes because _____.

3. **What is one <u>detail</u> you know about U.S. history?**
   One detail I know about U.S. history is _____.

4. **Can you <u>explain</u> to me something about the history of your home country?**
   One thing I can explain about the history of my home country _____ is _____.

5. **What is one thing you <u>must</u> do in this class if you want to get an A?**
   One thing I must do in this class if I want to get an A is _____ because _____.

For the rest of the oral language prompts, visit our book's website at www.wiley.com/go/ellteacherstoolbox2. You can also access it via this QR code.

Figure 4.6 109 Academic Language Oral Practice Prompts

58 THE ELL TEACHER'S TOOLBOX 2.0

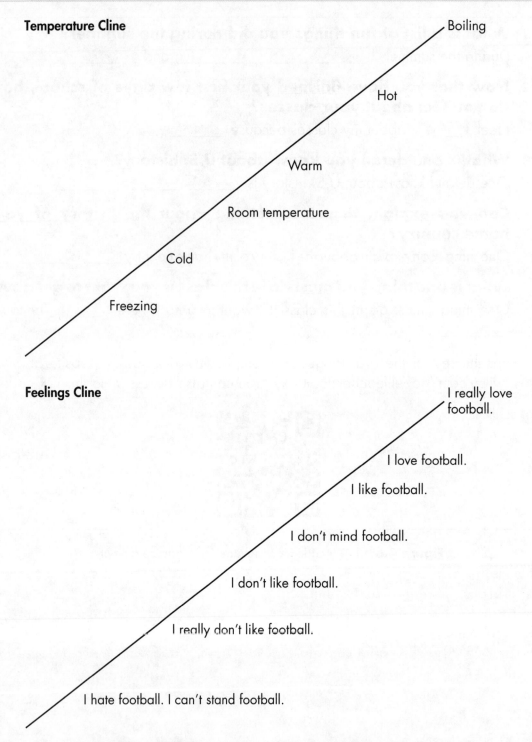

Figure 4.7 Clines *Source:* Reproduced with the permission of Jonny Ingham.

STRATEGY 5
Activating Prior Knowledge

What Is It?

Activating prior knowledge, also known as *activating schema,* is a well-known learning and teaching strategy of connecting students' prior or background knowledge to new concepts in order to promote deeper learning. In an ELL classroom, students possess varying levels of prior knowledge in English and academic content. Students also bring with them valuable funds of knowledge created through their cultural, family, and general life experiences outside of school (González et al., 2005; Lindahl, 2015). In order to help students maximize the language and content learning in a lesson, teachers must help students draw on their prior knowledge, including these funds of knowledge, and make connections to new learning.

We can't determine how to best help students build their understanding of a topic or concept until we find out what knowledge they already have about it. In other words, we need to identify what they know, what they don't know, and what they think they know.

Once we've determined what they know, we can then decide how much additional background building they need to understand new content. Building this background knowledge, however, does not mean pre-teaching all the information contained in a text or giving students the answers to upcoming questions on a topic. Instead, as educator Lauren Keppler (2016) says, it means giving students "experience with a foundational concept from which to build further knowledge" (para. 6).

In summary, activating prior knowledge means eliciting from students what they already know *and* building initial knowledge that they need in order to access upcoming content.

Why We Like It

We have found this strategy to be essential to our students' acquisition of English language skills and content knowledge. To go even further, this strategy lies at the heart of our teaching philosophy—our students *already* possess a wealth of knowledge and experiences that they can build on as they encounter new learning. It is up to us to facilitate this process by developing relationships with our students so that we learn what they already know and ensure that they feel comfortable sharing it.

Supporting Research

Research on the brain confirms it is easier to learn something new when we can attach it to something we already know (Carnegie Mellon University, 2015). Much research supports the idea that activating prior knowledge is a critical step in the learning process and a major factor in reading comprehension (Shanahan, 2013).

Additional research specifically with English language learners finds that activating and building prior knowledge plays a big role in improving their academic literacy (Short & Echevarria, 2004–2005).

Common Core Connections

Educators and researchers, along with the Common Core authors, recognize that activating prior knowledge is a necessary step in accessing complex texts, whether in the form of written words, images, charts, or other text types. However, you can have too much of a good thing. As the Common Core authors say, "Student background knowledge and experiences can illuminate the reading but should not replace attention to the text itself" (Coleman & Pimentel, 2005, p. 7).

The activities that follow serve to activate and build background knowledge as a support, not as a bypass, for students in meeting the Common Core Standards. We are confident that all of our suggestions here function as the kind of support encouraged by the Common Core.

Application

What follows is a variety of ways to activate students' prior knowledge and build further background knowledge in preparation for new learning. Activities for tapping prior knowledge are typically designed for use before reading activities, but we have used the ones listed here to also help students access writing, speaking, and listening tasks.

KWL CHARTS

Of course, the tried-and-true KWL chart is always an effective way of gauging student background knowledge about a topic or concept. Students write and share what they already know about the topic in the *K* (what I know) section. They then add questions in the *W* (what I want to know) section and write their learnings in the *L* section (what I learned) as they uncover new information through written and digital texts.

The K (what I know) section can provide teachers critical information on student background knowledge so we can plan our lessons accordingly. Students can also be encouraged to act as co-teachers when they have more knowledge on a topic and can share with those students who may have less. The W (what I want to know) section can be a resource for teachers to identify students' interests based on their questions in order to make lessons more relevant. A powerful extension can be added to this section (and an additional column) by asking students to consider why they want to know the answers to their questions. Finally, the L section (what I learned) provides both students and the teacher an opportunity to reflect on student learning.

Variations of KWL extend the chart to include columns for how students can find answers to their questions (online searches, personal interviews), what actions they might take after learning this new information (apply it, teach someone else, create something new), and what new questions they have based on what they've learned (Corbitt, 2016). Personally, we're old school when it comes to KWL and we like the original, simple version. More power to you if you want to expand your KWL horizons!

ANTICIPATION GUIDES

Anticipation guides ask students to think, write, and talk about their opinions on key themes or big ideas contained in upcoming texts and units of study. They are often organized as a list of statements that students have to agree or disagree with and explain why. This can be done in writing or speaking.

It can be helpful to have students revisit their anticipation guides at the end of a unit in order to reflect on changes in their thinking and in preparation for writing an essay. Figure 5.1: Anticipation Guide is an example of one we've used with our students during a mini-unit on sports drinks. Students are asked to read the statements and make a mark on a line indicating how strongly they agree or disagree with each statement. Then they explain their thinking and write down any reasons to support their opinion under each statement.

For a more kinesthetic version of an anticipation guide, students can respond to a series of agree or disagree statements by standing and physically placing themselves on a continuum (strongly agree on one side of the room, strongly disagree on the other, and other opinions at other places along the continuum). This is also called a *cline* (see Strategy 4: Vocabulary). We have also used the well-known four corners strategy by posting four statements in different parts of the classroom. We then ask students which statement they agree with most and tell them to go to that corner. Once there, students share with each other why they agree with that statement and then one student from each corner shares out to the whole class. This thinking and talking results in language building and developing curiosity about what is coming next.

MULTIMEDIA

The old saying "a picture is worth a thousand words" can really ring true in an ELL classroom! Many times before we start a new unit or text, we will show students a related video (with English subtitles), slideshow, or display a photograph on the document camera. Asking students to write or talk about it with a partner is a great way to instantly gauge prior knowledge, build background, and spark interest. A simple prompt could be "What did you notice?" or "What did you find interesting?" So many resources are now at one's fingertips—listening to music from an era being studied, viewing a newscast about a famous event, watching an interview with an author—and can be used to build background in an engaging way.

QUICKWRITES

Asking students to write to a quick prompt (e.g., "What do you think of when you hear the word *immigration*"?) related to a new topic of study (an immigration unit) is another way to activate and build student knowledge. Sharing these responses can be helpful in generating a class list of what is known and what questions students would like to find the answers to. Newcomers can respond to quickwrites in their home language or through drawing pictures of what they already know about the topic.

VOCABULARY

Writing about key vocabulary words prior to starting a unit can help both students and the teacher gauge student knowledge. We describe the use of word charts in Strategy 4: Vocabulary as a tool for pre-teaching key vocabulary in an upcoming unit. Sometimes we modify a word chart to include a section for prior knowledge about each word or concept. Figure 5.2: Upstander Word Chart is an example of one we used during a unit on upstanders. Prior to starting the unit, we ask students to write down any ideas or draw any related images for each word in the first column. As the unit progresses, students can update their word charts with any new learnings.

When introducing new vocabulary to students we often ask them to rate their knowledge of each word. You can find many examples of graphic organizers for this type of exercise online by searching "vocabulary knowledge rating sheet or chart." While we sometimes use a chart, most times we just use a word chart like the one in Figure 5.2, read each word aloud, and ask students to quickly rate their knowledge by noting a symbol next to each word on the chart. We display the following key:

+ = I know this word well and can explain it to a classmate.
✓ = I've heard or seen the word, but I don't know it well.
_ = I don't know this word at all.

PREPARATORY TEXTS

Providing simpler, preparatory texts in anticipation of a more complex reading task or concept can be very helpful in building ELLs' background knowledge and reading confidence. We often use the same text written in different lexile levels. There are many resources available online that make it easy to find or create these types of accessible texts (see Technology Connections). To be clear, we're not suggesting that teachers simplify the complex text they are planning to use for close reading. Instead, teachers can provide simplified texts addressing similar topics or themes in the complex text *as a way* to build background knowledge.

In Strategy 10: Reading Comprehension we also share strategies that students can employ *while* reading, which prepare them to access complex texts. Obviously we're not going to ask our newcomers to read a complex text, but that doesn't mean they aren't making their way toward this goal. They can employ the same pre-reading and reading strategies higher proficiency ELLs are using, but with simpler texts or texts in their home language.

HOME LANGUAGE MATERIALS

The preview, view, review instructional strategy is a common one in bilingual classrooms. Students are introduced to the lesson in their home language, taught the lesson in English, and review it in their home language. ELL teachers may not have the language capacity or the time, or may be facing the logistical challenge of multiple home languages in one class, but they can still provide students access to texts and videos in their home language as a means of building prior knowledge. For example, we often have students watch Spanish language BrainPop videos prior to watching the English versions and prior to our studying that topic. We have math teacher colleagues who do the same with Khan Academy videos.

If you are struggling to find materials in the home languages of your students, one option is to ask ChatGPT, Google's Gemini, or any other AI chatbot to create them. Of course, one challenge of using this option is that you won't be able to check the material for accuracy. See the Technology Connections section for more resources on providing fact-checked ELLs texts and videos in their home languages.

FIELD TRIPS—REAL OR VIRTUAL

Taking students on field trips in order to build background knowledge is an ideal strategy—nothing compares to real, hands-on learning. As education researcher Robert Marzano (2004) states, "The most straightforward way to enhance students' academic background knowledge is to provide academically enriching experiences" (p. 14). Marzano lists field trips as one of those "academically enriching experiences," and we wholeheartedly agree with him.

However, we know it isn't always possible to secure the funds or support to make these trips possible. Another option, though definitely not as effective as a real trip, is a virtual field trip. There are many online resources for finding and creating these types of virtual adventures for your students (see Technology Connections).

Teaching Online

All of the activities in this chapter can be used with students in online teaching. Students can complete digital copies of KWL charts and anticipation guides and be asked to share in breakout rooms or in the chat. Students can also view 360 pictures and videos through the use of a shared screen as well as go on virtual field trips the same way.

Teachers can ask students to share background knowledge on a topic in an interactive way by using an online whiteboard or Google slides.

What Could Go Wrong?

Just because you can build students' background knowledge on a topic doesn't mean you always should. Many teachers talk too much and get caught in the cycle of explaining every word, concept, or topic to their students. This nonstop yapping becomes background noise instead of background knowledge. Students can end up tuning out instead of tuning in.

It is also dangerous to assume that a student doesn't have prior knowledge of a concept or possesses incorrect understanding just because it *differs* from the teacher's prior knowledge. For example, asking students from different cultural backgrounds to write what they know about weddings or funerals may elicit very different responses from one written by the teacher.

Teachers should also be wary of assuming all students from a certain country or cultural background have the same prior knowledge or experiences. Nor should they put students in the role of ambassador and expect a student to be the sole resource on a whole culture, country, or ethnic background (Lundgren & Lundy-Ponce, n.d.). However, this doesn't mean that individual students, with preparation and their permission, can't be lifted up to share their unique cultural experiences at appropriate times.

Differentiation Recommendations

Newcomers (Preliterate or Low Literacy in Home Language): Encourage students to draw or use images to share their prior knowledge. Provide videos or use images to build background knowledge.	**Newcomers (Literate in Home Language):** Encourage the use of their home language and Google Translate when students are sharing prior knowledge. Use texts and videos in a student's home language to build background knowledge.
Intermediate ELLs: Use all chapter strategies, with increasingly complex text, vocabulary, and writing prompts.	**Advanced ELLs:** Use all chapter strategies with increasingly complex text, vocabulary, and writing prompts. In Anticipation Guide activities, ask students to support their opinions with reasons through either writing or speaking.

Technology Connections

For updated research and resources on activating and building background knowledge, see The Best Resources for Learning about the Importance of Prior Knowledge (& How to Activate It) (https://larryferlazzo.edublogs.org/2016/01/09/the-best-resources-for-learning-about-the-importance-of-prior-knowledge-how-to-activate-it/).

You can find resources for providing ELLs with texts or videos in their home language at The Best Multilingual & Bilingual Sites for Math, Social Studies, & Science (http://larryferlazzo.edublogs.org/2008/10/03/the-best-multilingual-bilingual-sites-for-math-social-studies-science/).

STRATEGY 5: ACTIVATING PRIOR KNOWLEDGE

For helpful information on virtual field trips and virtual reality experiences, see The Best Resources for Finding and Creating Virtual Field Trips (http://larryferlazzo.edublogs.org/2009/08/11/the-best-resources-for-finding-and-creating-virtual-field-trips/) and A Beginning List of the Best Resources on Virtual Reality in Education (http://larryferlazzo.edublogs.org/2017/02/27/a-beginning-list-of-the-best-resources-on-virtual-reality-in-education/).

Teachers can find lots of premade texts at different levels at The Best Places to Get the "Same" Text Written for Different "Levels" (http://larryferlazzo.edublogs.org/2014/11/16/the-best-places-to-get-the-same-text-written-for-different-levels/) or by using an artificial intelligence tool like ChatGPT. We have used the following prompt:

> You are a teacher of English language learners. Give 3 short texts on mummies in ancient Egypt. One text at the first grade level, one at a third grade level, and one at a sixth grade level.

We did find, however, that we still needed to make some adjustments to the texts. In addition, we have tried using language proficiency levels (beginning, intermediate, and advanced) instead of grade levels in the prompt, but they have not generated very effective results.

If you aren't getting good results from ChatGPT, you can always use one of the various AI teacher tools that include many features, including ones to differentiate text. You can find a list of these at Not Necessarily the "Best," But a List of AI Teacher Prep Sites (https://larryferlazzo.edublogs.org/2023/05/18/not-necessarily-the-best-but-a-list-of-ai-teacher-prep-sites/).

All figures from this chapter, as well as 11 additional chapters, references, hyperlinked Technology Connections, and more online resources, can be found at www.wiley.com/go/ellteacherstoolbox2.

Sports Drinks Versus Water

Read each statement. Think about *to what extent* (how much) you agree or disagree with the statement. Make a mark on the line to show your opinion. Then, write down any reasons for your opinion below the line.

1. Kids should only be allowed to drink water and low-fat milk.

_____

_____

Strongly   *Strongly*
Agree   *Disagree*

Why I think this:

2. Kids need to drink sports drinks when they are exercising or playing sports.

_____

_____

Strongly   *Strongly*
Agree   *Disagree*

Why I think this:

3. Schools should not sell sports drinks on campus.

_____

_____

Strongly   *Strongly*
Agree   *Disagree*

Why I think this:

Figure 5.1 Anticipation Guide

4. Sports drinks are better for you than soda.
_____
_____

Strongly   *Strongly*
Agree   *Disagree*

Why I think this:

Figure 5.1 (*Continued*)

WORD	WHAT I ALREADY KNOW ABOUT THIS WORD (related words, pictures, translation in home language)	WHAT I LEARNED ABOUT THIS WORD
bullying		
bystander		
upstander		
victim		
cyberbullying		

Figure 5.2 Upstander Word Chart

STRATEGY 6
Sequencing

What Is It?

Sequencing activities—cutting up text and having students put them back in the correct order—is a common language-learning task in the ELL classroom. But its value is not limited to English language learners: Benjamin Franklin famously developed his writing style by regularly cutting apart essays he liked and going back to them weeks or months later to challenge himself to put them back together again (Public Broadcasting System, n.d.).

There are several different types of sequencing activities. Strip stories are divided passages that, when reordered correctly, show an accurate story. Sentence scrambles (see Strategy 23: Learning Games for Reading and Writing) mix up words and punctuation in one sentence and challenge the learner to put them back in order. A third common sequencing task uses comic strips.

Why We Like It

We like this strategy for many reasons. One reason is these activities are clearly puzzles and, as we discuss in the Supporting Research section, can encourage participants to move into a state of *flow*, which is the highest form of intrinsic motivation. Second, strip stories in particular can let us hit two birds with one stone; it encourages the development of literacy skills *and* the content can be related to what we are studying at the time (U.S. history, school vocabulary, argument writing, etc.). Third, sentence scrambles are easy for teachers to create and can be a central part of lessons or easily fill up any extra time that might be left before the bell. And, fourth, students themselves can easily create all three—strip stories, sentence scrambles, and comic strips—for use by their classmates.

Just having students complete the activities can be beneficial to learning. However, why we *really* like this strategy is that we add an additional step most of the time that challenges students to develop higher-level thinking skills and metacognition. We do this by insisting—most of the time—they note *why* they put the items in that order. In other words, what were the clues they used that led them to the correct response?

Supporting Research

Teachers can frame sequencing activities as puzzles. Researcher Mihaly Csikszentmihalyi and others have found that looking at learning tasks and challenges as puzzles can promote the development of flow (Shernoff, 2013). Csikszentmihalyi (2008) suggests that an even better flow activity would be having students create their own puzzles that others can then solve (p. 129).

There is a substantial amount of research demonstrating the positive impact strip stories can have on English language acquisition (Kiftiah, n.d.). As far as we can tell, however, there have been no studies specifically done on sentence scrambles and reordering comic strips. However, because their process closely mirrors strip stories, we don't believe it's a stretch to say that research can also support these two versions of sequencing activities.

Research supports the benefits of students explaining their thinking to classmates or their teacher (Williams & Lombrozo, 2010) as well as explaining it to themselves (Ferlazzo, 2017, May 5).

Common Core Connections

Sequencing activities support the Reading Standards of understanding conventions and using context clues for understanding. Combining those two attributes with the fact that analyzing and interpreting text (found under the Language Standards) are the essence of sequencing activities, it's clear that sequencing lessons hit a Common Core home run.

Application

Here are specific how-to directions reflecting the steps we use to implement sequencing lessons in our classrooms.

STRIP STORIES

In some classes, strip stories are often a text that is cut into strips. The strips are then divided among students with instructions to discuss and determine the correct order.

We do it differently.

We like to give each student (sometimes they can work in pairs) a sheet with numbered passages out-of-order (the numbers are important because it makes it easier to review—as in "What number do you think is first?"). Next, we have students cut each one out and read them. Then, with a highlighter in hand they mark the clues they are using to determine the order for each strip. They then begin placing the strips on another piece of paper. Students will eventually glue the strips there, but only after we've checked to make sure they are correct. We will usually show students the first correct strip and model highlighting the clue word. After we see that most students have completed the second one, we'll have students check their answer with a classmate and ask for someone to share the number, and their clue, with the entire class. We then continue that process down the line.

Figure 6.1: First Day of School Strip Story is an example we use with ELL high beginners, and Figure 6.2 is the teacher answer key. Figure 6.3: Mexico Strip Story is an example we use with intermediate ELLs, and Figure 6.4 is the teacher answer key. You will notice that some answers are very obvious by the time or date, and others require a more careful reading of context clues to determine their position. As we mentioned previously, each strip is numbered to make it easier to have a classroom discussion about which ones go in what order (be sure to remind students not to order the strips based on their numbers!).

These strip stories can be simplified even further by reducing the number of words in each sentence *and* reducing the number of sentences in them. We've made them with as few as four simple sentences and then had ELL beginners create their own to share with classmates.

We've also found another advantage to having fewer sentences in a strip story. With fewer sentences, we "can get away with" not having students cut them up and, instead, just have them sequence the story by numbering the sentences and highlighting clues on the one sheet. We still believe cutting them out and pasting them on a sheet in the correct order is best because of the visual reinforcement it provides, but sometimes we just don't have the time. As the old adage goes, "We don't want the perfect to be the enemy of the good."

We taught a lesson on Dia de los Muertos (Day of the Dead) using this method by first showing a short accessible video on the holiday and then sharing the strip story; see Figure 6.5: Day of the Dead Strip Story (Figure 6.6 is the answer key). After students completed it, we asked them to create similar ones about a holiday in their country (for those from countries where the Day of the Dead was celebrated, we just asked them to choose another one) and share it with their classmates.

This activity can also be made *more* complicated with full paragraphs on each strip. We have also created versions that give a list of questions, and then the strip story is composed of the answers. For high-intermediates and advanced ELLs, it can be made more challenging by making more than one strip as part of the same answer. In other words, we divide an answer into two separate strips so that not only do students have to connect the correct answer to the question but also have to use context clues to determine the correct order of the sentences in the answer. We also talk in Strategy 25: Conversation Practice about how we use this sequencing strategy with dialogue.

In addition, we have our intermediate students create strip stories on topics of interest to them (newspaper stories on big soccer games are easy ones). They can copy and paste text off the web (with attribution, of course) after making sure there are clues, divide them into strips, and create an answer sheet and one that is out of order for their classmates to use. See Figure 6.5 for student instructions on how to create them (those are the steps we use to create strip stories, too!). The instructions contain several steps. Students should create their strip stories only after having completed a number of teacher-created ones. Then, as always, it would be important for teachers to model the instructional steps as well.

SENTENCE SCRAMBLES

As we've mentioned, sentence scrambles are just that—a sentence that has the words and punctuation scrambled and students have to put them in the correct order. These can be sentences that have been seen in previous text (e.g., ones written by the class using the Strategy 8: Language Experience Approach in or sentences in stories read by the class), sentences reinforcing a convention that we've recently taught, or a new fun sentence (e.g., "class love . this I").

They are great for games, which is why we talk about them in Strategy 23: Learning Games for Reading and Writing. They also are good formative assessment tools, and we often include them in periodic tests. And, as we explain in Strategy 23: Learning Games for Reading and Writing, it is also easy for students to create their own. When making sentence scrambles, though, we encourage students to copy sentences that are already written somewhere—a book, a text in their folder, and so on—and not create their own because of potential grammar or spelling errors. The tekhnologic blog (2015) has shared useful variations about how to use sentence scrambles.

They suggest writing the words of several sentences scrambled together on a whiteboard in front of the room with the words for each sentence in a different color. Then, students have to put the sentences together correctly. The same blog suggests making it into a listening and writing activity by dividing students into pairs, giving each partner different scrambles, and having them read the words for a sentence aloud so the other has to listen, write, and correctly reorder them. None of these modifications alters the primary focus of the activity, but they can serve to "mix it up" a bit so that students feel they aren't "doing the same old thing."

COMIC STRIPS

The use of comic strips almost explains itself. Identify comics with accessible language, cut them up, and have students put them back in order. Students can highlight clue words or be given a sentence starter to complete:

This box goes first because _____.
This box goes second because _____.
This box goes third because _____.
This box goes fourth because _____.

Students can even create their own comic strips for classmates to put in order. They don't have to be funny—they could be as simple as an event they experienced in the past or just their morning routine. In those cases, we would call them "picture stories" instead of "comic strips."

These kinds of student- or teacher-created "picture stories" make this activity particularly accessible for newcomers and/or for those not literate in their home language.

Teaching Online

It's easy to implement online versions of the first two activities described in this chapter. Obviously, one way to do strip stories is by just having students copy and paste sentences or paragraphs into the correct order. For sentence scrambles, it's fairly easy to create "drag-and-drop" activities in Google Docs or Slides—just search online for simple instructions.

It's even easier to create them in online learning game sites like Quizizz. Teachers can create them for students, or students can make them for their classmates to "play."

In addition, there are multiple sites where teachers can create and assign interactive worksheets that include these types of sequencing activities, along with others. See Technology Connections for the link.

It's fairly easy, though slightly teacher-labor intensive, to separate online comic strips "box by box" into digital images and then upload them to an online white board. Students can then reorder them correctly. Even better, students can create their own comic strips and mix up their sequence for classmates to put in the correct sequence. See the Technology Connections section for many different sites where students can create their own comic strips.

What Could Go Wrong?

When it comes to strip stories, the main problem is that it can take some students sooooooooooo looooong to cut up the strips. We try to deal with that issue by telling the class at the beginning that they only have a certain period of time to cut them (we don't threaten them with a consequence if they do not finish, but we will periodically announce the minutes as they count down). That usually does the trick.

Precutting the strips deals with that problem, but doing that can create other issues: It takes time to pass them out one at a time, it takes teacher time to cut them up, and they're harder to store for students who are absent that day.

And, as we mentioned earlier, an alternative to any cutting at all is having student's sequence a strip story with fewer sentences by numbering them on the paper.

A problem related to sentence scrambles is that ELLs will sometimes miss copying down a word or punctuation mark. So, we usually spot-check student-created scrambles before they are taught to their classmates.

Differentiating Recommendations for Sequencing Activities

Newcomers (Preliterate or Low Literacy in Home Language): Teachers provide simple and short "picture stories" that show an obvious sequence of events. Students narrate what they see in their home language to online translation tools and copy and paste or handwrite the home language and translated English versions under the images. They can create their own picture stories using the same language tools.	**Newcomers (Literate in Home Language):** Use strip stories with just a few lines and simple sentences, short scrambled sentences, and comic strips or picture stories with very accessible language. They can create their own comics, strip stories, and picture stories using simple English.
Intermediate ELLs: Use longer strip stories with more complex sentences, longer scrambled sentences, and more complex comic strips or picture stories using additional language. Also work in pairs when doing scramble sentences, with one reading the words aloud out of order to the other so they have to listen, write what they hear, and reorder them correctly. They can also create their own strip stories for classmates to sequence.	**Advanced ELLs:** Similar activities as those listed under Intermediate ELLs, but with increasingly complex sentences.

Technology Connections

If you don't want to create your own strip stories, you can find some freely available online at https://esolonline.tki.org.nz/ESOL-Online/Planning-for-my-students-needs/Resources-for-planning/ESOL-teaching-strategies/Oral-Language/Speaking-strategies/Strip-stories.

If you're making sentence scrambles for your students, it's easy for teachers to make a mistake and miss a word or punctuation mark (that's not an error limited to students). There are several free online tools that will automatically create them for you at The Best Sites for Creating Sentence Scrambles (http://larryferlazzo.edublogs.org/2010/03/29/the-best-sites-for-creating-sentence-scrambles/).

If, as a change of pace, you want students to create their own comic strips online, they can use one of the tools at The Best Ways to Make Comic Strips Online (http://larryferlazzo.edublogs.org/2008/06/04/the-best-ways-to-make-comic-strips-online/).

You can find links to many sites that allow you to create online interactive "worksheets" that could include the kinds of activities we discuss in this chapter at The Best Tools for Making Online Interactive Worksheets (https://larryferlazzo.edublogs.org/2021/06/16/the-best-tools-for-making-online-interactive-worksheets/).

A teacher time-saver, of course, for creating these kinds of sequencing activities is to use ChatGPT or other artificial intelligence tools. Though it may not understand what a "sequencing activity" or a "sentence scramble" is, it will understand a prompt like "Write five sentences about school that an early English language learner will understand" followed by "Mix up the words in each of those sentences." Always check for errors.

It is likely to understand what a strip story is and respond first to a prompt saying "Write a strip story about going to school with seven sentences that an early English language learner can understand" followed by "Put the strip story out of order."

Attribution

Versions of some of these ideas appeared in our book, *Navigating the Common Core with English Language Learners* (Ferlazzo & Sypnieski, 2016, p. 199).

The Strip Story instructions were modified from a document in Larry's book, *Helping Students Motivate Themselves* (Ferlazzo, 2011, p. 110).

As we mentioned, the teckhnologic blog shared some of sentence scramble modification described in the chapter (https://tekhnologic.wordpress.com/2015/03/12/word-jumble-practicing-sentence-structures/).

All figures from this chapter, as well as 11 additional chapters, references, hyperlinked Technology Connections, and more online resources, can be found at www.wiley.com/go/ellteacherstoolbox2.

1. Her second class was Math.
2. She liked her first day of class and was happy to tell her parents about it when she went home.
3. PE was her fourth class.
4. Consuelo was excited about her first day of school.
5. She liked that class because she liked to learn about the past.
6. Her brother drove her to the school in the morning.
7. Then she ate lunch with her new friends.
8. She liked that class because she liked to play.
9. She liked that class because she liked to draw.
10. Her fifth class was Science.
11. She first went to English class.
12. History was her third class.
13. She met her English teacher, Mr. Ferlazzo, who seemed very nice.
14. Her last class was Art.
15. She liked that class because she liked numbers.

Figure 6.1 First Day of School Strip Story (Student Handout)

STRATEGY 6: SEQUENCING

4. Consuelo was excited about her first day of school.

6. Her brother drove her to the school in the morning.

11. She first went to English class.

13. She met her English teacher, Mr. Ferlazzo, who seemed very nice.

1. Her second class was Math.

15. She liked that class because she liked numbers.

12. History was her third class.

5. She liked that class because she liked to learn about the past.

3. PE was her fourth class.

8. She liked that class because she liked to play.

7. Then she ate lunch with her new friends.

10. Her fifth class was Science.

14. Her last class was Art.

9. She liked that class because she liked to draw.

2. She liked her first day of class and was happy to tell her parents about it when she went home.

Figure 6.2 First Day of School Strip Story (Teacher Answer Key)

1. Mexico became an independent country in 1821.

2. In 1521, the Aztecs were overthrown by Hernán Cortés and other people who lived in Mexico but who did not like the Aztecs.

3. Spain enslaved people who lived there, and 24 million of them died by 1605.

4. The United States won, and took what is now California, Utah, Nevada, Arizona, and New Mexico from Mexico.

5. The Olmecs were the first society in the area we call Mexico and lived there over 3,000 years ago.

6. The Civil War lasted 10 years.

7. Even though it has these problems, many people still think Mexico can be "The Next Great Power" in the world.

8. From 1846 to 1848, Mexico fought a war with the United States.

9. In 1910, people revolted against a dictatorship in Mexico and began a civil war.

10. Spain then took over the Aztec Empire.

11. The Mayans were the most powerful people in Mexico between 250 and 900 AD.

12. Hernán Cortés came to Mexico from Spain in 1519.

13. In 1810, a priest named Miguel Hidalgo y Costilla called for the people of Mexico to revolt against Spain.

14. It has many factories, and many tourists, but faces many problems, including drugs.

15. Mexico now has a population of over 127 million people spread over 31 states.

Figure 6.3 Mexico Strip Story (Student Handout)

5. The Olmecs were the first society in the area we call Mexico and lived there over 3,000 years ago.

11. The Mayans were the most powerful people in Mexico between 250 and 900 AD.

12. Hernán Cortés came to Mexico from Spain in 1519.

2. In 1521, the Aztecs were overthrown by Hernán Cortés and other people who lived in Mexico but who did not like the Aztecs.

10. Spain then took over the Aztec Empire.

3. Spain enslaved people who lived there, and 24 million of them died by 1605.

13. In 1810, a priest named Miguel Hidalgo y Costilla called for the people of Mexico to revolt against Spain.

1. Mexico became an independent country in 1821.

8. From 1846 to 1848, Mexico fought a war with the United States.

4. The United States won, and took what is now California, Utah, Nevada, Arizona and New Mexico from Mexico.

9. In 1910, people revolted against a dictatorship in Mexico and began a civil war.

6. The Civil War lasted 10 years.

15. Mexico now has a population of over 127 million people spread over 31 states.

14. It has many factories, and many tourists, but faces many problems, including drugs.

7. Even though it has these problems, many people still think Mexico can be "The Next Great Power" in the world.

Figure 6.4 Mexico Strip Story (Teacher Answer Key) *Source:* www.history.com/topics/mexico/history-of-mexico and www.newsmax.com/Finance/GeorgeFriedman/mexico-power-economy-invest/2016/03/29/id/721358/.

1. Choose a passage that is in chronological order (a story, biography, or historical sequence). Make sure the passage is no longer than a page and a half and can easily be divided into at least eight sections.

2. Copy and paste the original passage onto a Google Doc or Word document and cite the author. Title this document *Strip Story Answer Key*. In this document, divide the passage into at least eight sections, making sure that there are clues in each one to help your classmates figure out the correct order.

3. Number each section, but start by making a section in the middle number 1. Then choose one on the top and make it number 2. Continue numbering them, but *not* in their correct order. Circle or underline the clue words on your answer sheet.

4. Now, individually copy and paste each section *out-of-order* onto another Google Doc or Word document. You will be printing this version for your classmates to complete. Be sure to leave space between each section because students will be cutting them out. Title this document *Strip Story for Students*.

5. Print out one copy of the Strip Story Answer Key and five copies of the Strip Story for Students.

Figure 6.5 Strip Story Instructions

1. Families remember the children who have died by making an altar. They put pictures of the children, candies, and toys on the altar.

2. Families make an altar for adults who have died. They put pictures of the adults on the altar. They also put their favorite things on the altar.

3. After they visit the graves, children paint their faces and wear costumes.

4. On November 1, families remember children who have died.

5. The Day of the Dead starts on October 31.

6. After they make an altar for adults who died, they visit the graves of people who died.

7. At the end of the Day of the Dead, everyone eats and tells stories about people who died.

8. On November 2, families remember adults who have died.

Figure 6.6 Day of the Dead Strip Story (Student Handout)

5. The Day of the Dead starts on October 31.

4. On November 1, families remember children who have died.

1. Families remember the children who have died by making an altar. They put pictures of the children, candies, and toys on the altar.

8. On November 2, families remember adults who have died.

2. Families make an altar for adults who have died. They put pictures of the adults on the altar. They also put their favorite things on the altar.

6. After they make an altar for adults who died, they visit the graves of people who died.

3. After they visit the graves, children paint their faces and wear costumes.

7. At the end of the Day of the Dead, everyone eats and tells stories about people who died.

Figure 6.7 Day of the Dead Strip Story (Teacher Answer Key)

STRATEGY 7
Clozes

What Is It?

Clozes, also known as *fill-in-the-blank sheets* and *gap-fills,* are relatively short texts that typically have words removed and replaced with blanks. This, at least, is the traditional definition of a cloze. There are, however, different variations that don't fit this exact description, which we will discuss in the Application section.

Why We Like It

Clozes can be excellent tools to help students enhance their vocabulary, use context clues, and develop metacognitive skills. Those last two benefits are primarily gained if students are challenged to explain the clues in the text that assisted them in choosing the correct answer. In addition, when teaching content (e.g., social studies or a unit on natural disasters in English class), the text can support that theme or unit. Clozes can also be used as an excuse for students to make multiple touches on the same text for increased comprehension (see Strategy 10: Reading Comprehension).

In addition, not only are clozes easy for teachers to create but students can also make them! They can then teach their clozes to classmates.

Supporting Research

Research has shown that the use of clozes with ELLs can result in a significant increase in vocabulary and, more important, an increased use of that new vocabulary in other contexts (Lee, 2008).

Clozes have also been shown to be an effective tool for helping students learn to monitor their reading comprehension and search for context clues to enhance understanding (Wright & Cervetti, 2016, p. 17).

Research shared in Strategy 6: Sequencing discusses how solving puzzles can increase intrinsic motivation leading to flow. We don't think it is a stretch to consider clozes as puzzles with the same resulting benefits.

Common Core Connections

Depending on how clozes are constructed and used, they can help meet all the points listed in the Language Standards, particularly the one on using context clues to aid comprehension. When clozes are used for double effect—in other words, students gain content knowledge from the text as well as practice grammar and learning vocabulary—they can also support some of the Reading Standards.

Application

There are several different types of clozes, but we follow a similar routine for most of them. First, we give each student a copy of the cloze and place one under the document camera. We ask students to put their pencils down and explain that we will read the cloze while they follow along. After we read it, we give students time to choose the correct words and also to identify the clues they use to help them make their choices. We ask that they circle, underline, or highlight the clue and connect them with a line to the word they chose. When giving students instructions, we always point out that clues might be found before *or* after the blanks. Of course, we'll model this the first (and probably a second and third) time we do clozes. We ask students to work on it alone and silently for a few minutes. After a certain period of time, we have students share their answers with a partner. Then, we'll review it as a class.

When there isn't a word bank (a list of the answers—in random order—at the top or bottom of the sheet) on the cloze for students to use, it's fine if they use a word that we didn't expect—as long as it makes sense. In fact, asking students to replace the "answer" word with synonyms can further extend student learning and provide an additional challenge. Sometimes, after we review a cloze, we'll also ask students to use the text for a follow-up activity—apply a reading strategy, pick a favorite line, or, perhaps, if the cloze is related to a topic we are studying, add information they learned to a KWL chart.

There are other ways to use clozes, and we will highlight them when discussing each figure. We should also point out that sometimes we use clozes as low-stakes formative assessments. In those cases, we do not create opportunities for students to share their answers with classmates.

Figure 7.1: Cloze with No Answers Shown—Jobs (Student Handout) is used with ELL beginners when we are studying jobs. There is not a word bank at the bottom of the page for students—they must only use context clues to complete the activity. The clues, however, are fairly obvious for students who have been studying English for a few months. A cloze like this is not appropriate for a newcomer. Figure 7.2 is the teacher answer key for this cloze.

Figure 7.3: Cloze with No Answers Shown—Art and Music (Student Handout) is another example of a cloze without a word bank. This one is slightly more difficult than Figure 7.2: Cloze with No Answers Shown—Jobs because some of the clues are found in sentences following the blank. In Figure 7.2, clues preceded each blank. In addition, the vocabulary is more challenging. We use it as part of a unit on art and music and have already pre-taught the vocabulary through words and pictures—sometimes we're even able to get our school's music teacher and one of his classes to invite us over for a lesson! Figure 7.4 is the teacher answer key for this cloze.

Figure 7.5 is a cloze on Helen Keller's life and contains a word bank below the text. We ask students to identify clue words even with a word bank. Figure 7.6 is the teacher answer key for this cloze.

Figure 7.7 is a cloze on Cesar Chavez and offers a different twist on clozes. Here, the emphasis is on teaching prepositions. In addition, the word bank is a series of two-word choices following each blank. Instead of highlighting or underlining the clues, we ask students to choose one of their answers and use a sentence frame to share the evidence they used to pick their answer. Figure 7.8 is the teacher answer key for this cloze.

Figure 7.9 offers a different type of challenge for students. This cloze passage about Vice President Kamala Harris has missing multi-word phrases instead of just single words. Students need to read the passage and choose which phrase from the "phrase bank" correctly completes the sentence. Figure 7.10 is the teacher answer key for this cloze.

Figure 7.11 is a fictional story about Juan and Maria. The blanks are short lines corresponding to the number of letters in the correct word, and the first letter is provided to students. The ending to this story tends to be enjoyed by adolescent readers. In addition to the usual clue-identification process, we'll often ask students to write their own ending. Figure 7.12 is the teacher answer key for this cloze.

Figure 7.13 is a particularly challenging type of cloze. We would only use it with higher-proficiency ELLs. In this cloze, which is about the history of the United States, we place the answer words at the end of sentences. However, we do not have any blanks—students have to identify where that answer word goes. They write the word where they think it goes in the space above the sentence with an arrow showing its correct location. You'll notice that the cloze is written double-spaced for that purpose. Instead of highlighting or underlining the clues, we ask students to pick two of their answers and use sentence frames to share the evidence they used to pick their answer. Figure 7.14 is the teacher answer key for this cloze.

As we discussed in *The ESL/ELL Teacher's Survival Guide* (Ferlazzo & Sypnieski, 2012, p. 137), clozes can also serve as models of writing that students will be expected to produce. The teacher can have students do a cloze that models their next writing assignment. Students can then mimic this style on their own. Figure 7.15: Persuading My Parents Cloze and Mimic Write is a cloze and writing frame modeling argument writing, and Figure 7.16: Persuading My Parents Student Sample is a paragraph produced by a student using that cloze as the model.

We give students Figure 7.17: Instructions for Making a Cloze when they are creating ones to teach their classmates. We use this assignment after they have had quite a bit of experience completing ones in class. It reflects a similar process we use to create our own clozes.

Teaching Online

The cloze strategy can easily be adapted online when teachers create clozes on class topics for students. The teacher can introduce the cloze process and model doing one the first time while sharing their screen on Zoom. Once students are familiar with the process, they can complete one on their own. Students could then share their answers and their thinking process behind their answer choices in breakout rooms or in the chat. Once students have had practice completing several cloze passages, they can be asked to create their own clozes to share with the teacher and/or classmates.

What Could Go Wrong?

We've learned from three common problems we've encountered using clozes. First, before we begin a cloze activity, we explain that there will be blanks in sentences and that students will need to decide which words belong in them. We then tell them that we will model two different ways of reading these sentences and they will vote on which version they think is most effective, in other words, which one helps them best figure out the correct word. We read the sentence the first time and say the sound "hmmmmm" when we reach the blank. The second time we read it, we say the word *blank* when we reach that space. Students generally pick the first option because in the second option saying the word *blank* can be confusing because it is a word! Once we start reading the cloze, we often get more than one student who wants to join us in saying "hmmmmm" in an exaggerated way, which distracts students from the text. We minimize this problem by addressing it before we start reading by saying, "Please remember that I am the only person who can say 'hmmmmm.' Raise your hand if you agree." We may not do this every time, but we always *remind* students of their prior agreement.

Second, when we ask students to create their own texts, some students or even entire classes do better if we pick six or seven texts ahead of time and let them choose from that selection. It is sometimes overwhelming and distracting to be given the entire Internet from which to choose, especially for middle school classes.

Finally, remember you can have too much of a good thing. Don't use the same kind of cloze all the time! We offer five different kinds (and we're sure there are more out there), so, please, mix it up!

Differentiation Recommendations

Newcomers (Preliterate or Low Literacy in Home Language): Use single-sentence clozes with a word bank, and students can access a tool like Read&Write for Google Chrome or Microsoft's Immersive Reader, which offer picture dictionary features. Also use Google Translate to provide audio support for text.	**Newcomers (Literate in Home Language):** Provide longer clozes with more complex text and a word bank, with or without the use of a tool like Read&Write.
Intermediate ELLs: Students can try different variations including clozes with word banks at the end of sentences, with phrase banks instead of just single words, with letter blanks, and without word banks.	**Advanced ELLs:** Teachers can provide increasingly complex cloze passages, and students can be asked to make their own and teach each other.

Technology Connections

Searching for "interactive online clozes" will yield many versions of clozes that students can complete online. However, many of these do not appear to have strategically placed blanks, and, instead, the gaps are either in arbitrary locations or are placed automatically after a certain number of words. We recommend always reviewing them prior to sharing them with students.

Ultimately, the best way to ensure that students are getting the most learning from doing online clozes is for teachers to create them. There are a variety of tools, including add-ons in Google Docs, that allow teachers and students to easily create different types of clozes. They can be found at The Best Tools for Creating Clozes (Gap-Fills) (http://larryferlazzo.edublogs.org/2012/04/30/the-best-tools-for-creating-clozes-gap-fills).

Teachers can save time by using an artificial intelligence tool, like ChatGPT, to create clozes on virtually any topic and at various levels of difficulty. These tools will generate a passage, select which words to remove, and create a word bank of answers. In our experience, the AI tools try to strategically remove words from the passage; however, we have found that its strategy is sometimes flawed and the word banks are not fully accurate. Nevertheless, making those corrections takes much less time than creating a cloze from scratch. And the good news that it will only get better as these tools develop!

This is an example of a prompt we have used to create a cloze:

> *Create a cloze passage about Rosa Parks for English Language Learners at the intermediate level with blank spaces for the missing words, along with a word bank containing the answers shuffled at the end.*

Attribution

Versions of some of these ideas appeared in our book, *The ESL/ELL Teacher's Survival Guide* (Ferlazzo & Sypnieski, 2012, p. 136–138).

All figures from this chapter, as well as 11 additional chapters, references, hyperlinked Technology Connections, and more online resources, can be found at www.wiley.com/go/ellteacherstoolbox2.

STRATEGY 7: CLOZES 85

People need to earn money to pay for food to eat and a place to live. People work at _____ to get money. Most adults work at jobs. The _____ you get to work at a job is called a wage or a salary.

If you work at the same kind of job for a long time then you have a career. Most people have more than one _____ during their lives.

People who graduate from high school make more money than people who do not _____ from high school. You can make even more _____ if you go to college.

It is important to work at a job to make money. It is also _____ to work at a job you like. Some people find a job they like to do. Some people do not like to work for somebody else. They start their own business.

Figure 7.1 Cloze with No Answers Shown—Jobs (Student Handout)

People need to earn money to pay for food to eat and a place to live. People work at **jobs** to get money. Most adults work at jobs. The **money** you get to work at a job is called a wage or a salary.

If you work at the same kind of job for a long time then you have a career. Most people have more than one **job** during their lives.

People who graduate from high school make more money than people who do not **graduate** from high school. You can make even more **money** if you go to college.

It is important to work at a job to make money. It is also **important** to work at a job you like. Some people find a job they like to do. Some people do not like to work for somebody else. They start their own business.

Figure 7.2 Cloze with No Answers Shown—Jobs (Teacher Answer Key)

Musicians play instruments. There are many different kinds of _____. You blow into flutes, horns, and tubas. You also blow _____ the trombone.

A violin has _____. A guitar also has _____. You hit drums to make music. You also _____ a xylophone to make sounds.

A large _____ of musicians playing instruments is called an orchestra. A smaller group of musicians is _____ a band.

Artists can draw, work with clay, and _____. Painters use different colors to paint a picture.

Figure 7.3 Cloze with No Answers Shown—Art and Music (Student Handout)

> Musicians play instruments. There are many different kinds of **instruments**. You blow into flutes, horns, and tubas. You also blow **into** the trombone.
>
> A violin has **strings**. A guitar also has **strings**. You hit drums to make music. You also **hit** a xylophone to make sounds.
>
> A large **group** of musicians playing instruments is called an orchestra. A smaller group of musicians is **called** a band.
>
> Artists can draw, work with clay, and **paint**. Painters use different colors to paint a picture.

Figure 7.4 Cloze with No Answers Shown—Art and Music (Teacher Answer Key)

> Helen Keller was born in Alabama in 1880. She lived on a farm. She got very sick when she was 18 months old. The _____ caused her to lose her sight and her hearing. *Blind* is another word for not being able to see. *Deaf* is _____ word for not being able to hear anything.
>
> Helen was angry that she could not see or _____ anything. She would _____ people and throw things. Helen's parents hired a teacher named Anne Sullivan to work with Helen. Sullivan would put things in one of Helen's _____. Then, Sullivan would spell out the letters of the word on Helen's other _____. So she would put a doll in one hand and then spell out *d-o-l-l* on Helen's other hand. Helen learned English this way.
>
> Helen learned to read using Braille, which are small bumps on pages. The _____ are letters and words.
>
> Helen also learned to talk. She wrote about her life and became very famous. Helen spent her life trying to help people.
>
> hands   hear   hand   bumps   sickness   another   hit

Figure 7.5 Cloze with Word Bank—Helen Keller (Student Handout)

Helen Keller was born in Alabama in 1880. She lived on a farm. She got very sick when she was 18 months old. The **sickness** caused her to lose her sight and her hearing. *Blind* is another word for not being able to see. *Deaf* is **another** word for not being able to hear anything.

Helen was angry that she could not see or **hear** anything. She would **hit** people and throw things.

Helen's parents hired a teacher named Anne Sullivan to work with Helen. Sullivan would put things in one of Helen's **hands**. Then, Sullivan would spell out the letters of the word on Helen's other **hand**. So she would put a doll in one hand and then spell out *d-o-l-l* on Helen's other hand. Helen learned English this way.

Helen learned to read using Braille, which are small bumps on pages. The **bumps** are letters and words.

Helen also learned to talk. She wrote about her life and became very famous. Helen spent her life trying to help people.

Figure 7.6 Cloze with Word Bank—Helen Keller (Teacher Answer Key)

Cesar Chavez was born in 1917. He worked in the fields as a farmworker when he was a child. He began a labor union _____ (for, to) farmworkers in 1962. The union wanted farmworkers to get more money and work in safer conditions. The union changed its name to the United Farm Workers. Many of the growers did not want to work _____ (of, with) the union.

Chavez and the union tried to get people not to buy grapes the growers grew. They did this _____ (to, two) pressure the growers to work with the union. Chavez also stopped eating for many days to show support for the farmworkers. This kind of action is called a *hunger strike*.

Many growers did agree to work with the union _____ (for, by) signing a contract saying they would pay the workers more and make it safer for them to work in the fields.

Chavez died in 1993. Many states celebrate his birthday on March 31st every year. The headquarters of the United Farm Workers was named a national monument, which is like a national park, in 2012.

Choose one of your answers and explain the clue you used to figure it out:

I chose _____ as the correct word because

_____.

Figure 7.7 Cloze with Word Bank at End of Sentences—Cesar Chavez (Student Handout)

Cesar Chavez was born in 1917. He worked in the fields as a farmworker when he was a child. He began a labor union **for** farmworkers in 1962. The union wanted farmworkers to get more money and work in safer conditions. The union changed its name to the United Farm Workers. Many of the growers did not want to work **with** the union.

Chavez and the union tried to get people not to buy grapes the growers grew. They did this **to** pressure the growers to work with the union. Chavez also stopped eating for many days to show support for the farmworkers. This kind of action is called a *hunger strike*.

Many growers did agree to work with the union **by** signing a contract saying they would pay the workers more and make it safer for them to work in the fields.

Chavez died in 1993. Many states celebrate his birthday on March 31st every year. The headquarters of the United Farm Workers was named a national monument, which is like a national park, in 2012.

Figure 7.8 Cloze with Word Bank at End of Sentences—Cesar Chavez (Teacher Answer Key)

Kamala D. Harris was born in Oakland, California, in 1964. Her father was born in Jamaica, and her mother was born in India, which makes her _____. While growing up, she was surrounded by a diverse community and went to both a black Baptist Church and a Hindu temple. She visited her grandparents in India _____. Kamala's mother was an activist and often took her daughter to _____. These experiences had a great impact on young Kamala, and she knew she wanted to spend her life fighting against injustice.

Kamala Harris has made history over and over again. In 2010, she was elected as the first African American and first woman to serve as California's Attorney General. Then in 2016, she was _____, becoming only the second African American woman to ever be elected to the U.S. Senate. Then in 2020, _____, the first African American woman, the first Indian-American, and the first person of Asian-American descent to be elected Vice President of the United States of America.

After winning the 2020 election with President Joe Biden, _____. She talked about being the first woman and woman of color to become U.S. Vice President and famously said, "But while I may be the first woman in this office, I won't be the last."

Figure 7.9 Cloze with Phrase Blanks—Kamala Harris (Student Handout)

STRATEGY 7: CLOZES

Phrase Bank (choose which phrase belongs in each sentence with a blank above):

elected as a Senator for California
Kamala gave a speech
the daughter of immigrants
civil rights marches and protests
Kamala Harris became the first woman
during the summers

Figure 7.9 (Continued)

Kamala D. Harris was born in Oakland, California, in 1964. Her father was born in Jamaica and her mother was born in India, which makes her **the daughter of immigrants.** While growing up, she was surrounded by a diverse community and went to both a black Baptist Church and a Hindu temple. She visited her grandparents in India **during the summers**. Kamala's mother was an activist and often took her daughter to **civil rights marches and protests**. These experiences had a great impact on young Kamala, and she knew she wanted to spend her life fighting against injustice.

Kamala Harris has made history over and over again. In 2010, she was elected as the first African American and first woman to serve as California's Attorney General. Then in 2016, she was **elected as a Senator for California**, becoming only the second African American woman to ever be elected to the U.S. Senate. Then in 2020, **Kamala Harris became the first woman**, the first African American woman, the first Indian-American, and the first person of Asian-American descent to be elected Vice President of the United States of America.

After winning the 2020 election with President Joe Biden, **Kamala gave a speech**. She talked about being the first woman and woman of color to become Vice President and famously said, "But while I may be the first woman in this office, I won't be the last."

Figure 7.10 Cloze with Phrase Blanks—Kamala Harris (Teacher Answer Key)

It was snowing very hard, and Juan and Maria were alone in the woods. "I'm scared," s_ _ _ Juan. "Don't worry," replied Maria, "I know how to get home." The wind was blowing v_ _ _ hard, and it was very cold. It was almost the end of the day, so it was getting d_ _ _. Juan had lost his cell phone, and Maria's battery had died. They had no way to call for help, and they had nothing they could use for light. Juan followed Maria as she w_ _ _ _ _ through the snow. Juan tripped and fell. He got very wet. Maria h_ _ _ _ _ him, and they began walking again. Finally, they saw lights from houses. They were very happy. T_ _ _ were almost out of the woods. But then a big monster came and ate both of them.

Figure 7.11 Cloze with Letter Blanks—Juan and Maria (Student Handout)

> It was snowing very hard, and Juan and Maria were alone in the woods. "I'm scared," s<u>ai</u>d Juan. "Don't worry," replied Maria, "I know how to get home." The wind was blowing v<u>er</u>y hard, and it was very cold. It was almost the end of the day, so it was getting d<u>ar</u>k. Juan had lost his cell phone, and Maria's battery had died. They had no way to call for help, and they had nothing they could use for light. Juan followed Maria as she w<u>al</u>ked through the snow. Juan tripped and fell. He got very wet. Maria h<u>el</u>ped him, and they began walking again. Finally, they saw lights from houses. They were very happy. Th<u>ey</u> were almost out of the woods. But then a big monster came and ate both of them.

Figure 7.12 Cloze with Letter Blanks—Juan and Maria (Teacher Answer Key)

> The United States first became a country in 1776. People who lived here fought a war with Great Britain to become independent. The people who lived here that war in 1783. (won)
>
> The United States was a lot smaller than it is now. There were only 13 states in the eastern part of the country.
>
> The country got a lot bigger by Native Americans, who lived here first, to move. (forcing)
>
> The United States bought land from France and Russia. The United States fought a war with Mexico and got more land.
>
> Many people came to the United States from other countries for a better life. (looking)
>
> A large number of people from Africa were to come to the United States to work as slaves. (forced)
>
> A war called The Civil War was fought between the northern part of the United States and the southern part of the United States. The South to keep slaves. (wanted)
>
> The North won, and the country slavery. (ended)
>
> Many white people treated Black people unjustly. This is still a problem today. Now, over 333 million people live in the United States.
>
> Choose two of your answers and explain the clues you used to figure it out:
>
> I put _____ between _____ and _____ because _____.
>
> I put _____ between _____ and _____ because _____.

Figure 7.13 Cloze with No Blanks—US History (Student Handout)

The United States first became a country in 1776. People who lived here fought a war with Great Britain to become independent. The people who lived here **won** that war in 1783. The United States was a lot smaller than it is now. There were only 13 states in the eastern part of the country. The country got a lot bigger by **forcing** Native Americans, who lived here first, to move. The United States bought land from France and Russia. The United States also fought a war with Mexico and got more land. Many people came to the United States from other countries **looking** for a better life. A large number of people from Africa were **forced** to come to the United States to work as slaves. A war called The Civil War was fought between the northern part of the United States and the southern part of the United States. The South **wanted** to keep slaves. The North won, and the country **ended** slavery. Many white people treated Black people unjustly. This is still a problem today. Now, over 333 million people live in the United States.

Figure 7.14 Cloze with No Blanks—US History (Teacher Answer Key)

Sometimes I need to persuade my parents to let me do things that I want to do. Last week, when I wanted to _____ up late and watch a movie, I had to convince my parents that it was a good idea. First, I had to think of a convincing _____ and support this reason with facts. For example, I told them that the reason I _____ be able to watch a movie is because I already completed my homework and set my cell phone. My parents disagreed with me and presented an _____ viewpoint. They argued that if I stayed up to watch a movie, then I would be too tired to _____ up on time and get ready for school in the morning. I reminded them that just last week I stayed up late finishing my homework and the next _____ when my cell phone went off at 6:00 a.m., I got up and got ready for _____ on time. This was a great counterargument because they were convinced and they agreed to let me watch my movie!

Sometimes I need to persuade _____ to let me do things that I want to do. Last week, when I wanted to _____, I had to convince _____ that it was a good idea. First, I had to think of a convincing reason and support this reason with facts. For example, I told them that the reason I should be able to _____ is because _____ disagreed with me and presented an opposing viewpoint. _____ argued that if I _____ _____, then I _____. I presented a counterargument when I said _____
_____
_____
_____.

Figure 7.15 Persuading My Parents Cloze and Mimic Write *Source:* Reprinted from L. Ferlazzo & K.H. Sypnieski, *ESL/ELL Teacher's Survival Guide* (2012, p. 138).

> <u>Persuade My Parents</u>
>
> One times I tried to persuade my parent to let me do things that I want to do. Last week, I wanted to wake up early to play basket in my brother school. I had to convince my parents that it was a good idea. One reason I used was it help me to get exercise and my body get stronger. Another reason was I already finished cleaning the house and I already did my homework.

Figure 7.16 Persuading My Parents (Student Sample)   *Source:* Reprinted from L. Ferlazzo & K.H. Sypnieski, *ESL/ELL Teacher's Survival Guide* (2012, p. 139).

---

1. Look for a passage online that seems interesting to you and is related to the topic we are studying in class. It should have at least 15 sentences, but not be longer than one page.
2. Copy and paste the original passage in a Google Doc and cite the author. Title this *Cloze Answer Key*.
3. Copy and paste it again in a Google Doc. Title this *Cloze*.
4. Read the passage carefully and select 10 words that you will replace with blanks. Do not have a blank in the first or last sentence of the passage and do not have more than one blank in the same sentence. Be sure that there are clue words for each blank. Highlight the clue words on your Cloze Answer Key.
5. Place the answer words on the bottom of the page. Be sure that they are not in the correct order.

Figure 7.17 Instructions for Making a Cloze

STRATEGY 8
Language Experience Approach (LEA)

What Is It?

The language experience approach (LEA) describes the process of the entire class doing an activity and then discussing and writing about it in a teacher-led process. The completed sentences can then be used in multiple follow-up activities to reinforce language learning.

Why We Like It

LEA can be a low-prep, high-energy lesson focused on student interests. It can be easily adapted to different subjects and, though it is most often used with ELL beginners, students at various degrees of English proficiency can benefit from its use.

Supporting Research

The LEA is one of the most widely used and effective instructional strategies in ELL classes. Substantial research has shown its positive impact on writing (Arvin, 1987), reading comprehension, and student motivation (Rahayu, 2013). It is often described as a best practice for ELL instruction (Howard Research, 2009, p. 30).

Common Core Connections

Using this strategy can assist students as they begin developing the skills to write informative, explanatory, and narrative text. In addition, it supports students in gaining an understanding of English conventions. Finally, it supports the Speaking and Listening Standard of "building on others' ideas" (Common Core State Standards Initiative, n.d.c).

Application

"CLASSICAL" VERSION

The LEA describes the process of the entire class doing an activity and then discussing and writing about it (however, a tutor working with a student one-on-one or in a smaller group could also use it). Here are the steps involved when we use it (portions of Steps 1 through 4 also appeared in *The ESL/ELL Teacher's Survival Guide,* Ferlazzo & Sypnieski, 2012, p. 55):

1. The class does a teacher-planned activity, such as one of the following:

   - Watching a short video clip
   - Taking a walk around the school
   - Making a simple musical instrument
   - Doing a simple science experiment
   - Creating a piece of art (we've used clay, painting, and origami)
   - Going on a field trip
   - Playing a board game
   - Creating a puppet or toy
   - Preparing a food
   - Playing Frisbee, soccer, or basketball outside
   - Performing a simple dance
   - Working in a school garden
   - Inventing and performing a short silent play (pantomime)
   - Just about anything else you can think of!

2. Immediately following the activity, students can be given a short time to write down notes about what they did (very early beginners can draw). Then, the teacher calls on students to share what the class did—usually, though not always—in chronological order ("What did we do first?"). The teacher then writes down what is said on a document camera, overhead projector, or easel paper. It is sometimes debated if the teacher should write down exactly what a student says if there are grammar or word errors or if the teacher should say it back to the student and write it correctly—without saying the student was wrong. We use the second strategy and feel that as long as students are not being corrected explicitly ("That's not the correct way to say it, Eva; this is"), it is better to model accurate grammar and word usage. Figure 8.1: Language Experience Approach Model shows an example of what we wrote after playing basketball outside for 15 minutes.

3. The class can chorally repeat each sentence after the teacher reads it aloud. Students can copy down the sentences and can add their own illustrations. Because the text comes out of their own experience, it is much more accessible because they already

STRATEGY 8: LANGUAGE EXPERIENCE APPROACH (LEA)   95

know its meaning. Instead of doing an activity, it is also possible to use common experiences already shared by all students in the class—for example, a folktale that might be known if all students come from the same home culture, a popular movie that everyone has seen, a major world event, or even what has happened in class that day.

4. The text can subsequently be used for different follow-up activities, including as a cloze (removing certain words and leaving blanks that students have to complete), a sentence scramble (taking individual sentences and mixing up the words for learners to sequence correctly), or mixing up all the sentences in the text and having students put them back in order. Students can also read the sentences out loud with partners and without looking at the text (ideally), take turns writing down what the other is reading. In addition, students could be assigned a sentence to illustrate and practice prior to reading it to the class while showing their drawing (time to practice would be essential—we never want to demand that beginning students speak without time to prepare).

Students can create categories for words in the sentences (verbs, nouns, words that begin with *r*, etc.) and add new words to the categories using their prior knowledge and a dictionary. Simple grammar lessons can be taught either during the original sentence writing (only if they can be done quickly—for example, that *went* is the past tense of *go*) or later.

Students with higher English proficiency can be asked to add more sentences on their own to the group-created ones or use the text as a model for writing another text about one of their personal experiences (e.g., playing soccer, cooking a meal, what happened in a different movie they saw, etc.).

ELL newcomers can be a little challenging. One way to support their language development and minimize potential learner frustration is by creating a "word bank" on the whiteboard prior to the activity. Depending on the activity, it could be one list of applicable words; lists divided into categories like "nouns," "verbs," and "adjectives"; or, to provide even more support, lists of words organized into "sentence navigators" or "sentence builders," which are puzzle-like structures where students choose words and put them in the correct order (see Bonus Strategy 3: Sentence Navigators and Sentence Builders). Newcomers who are literate in their home language could also write in that language and use Google Translate or another translation tool to share English versions of their sentences with the class. If they are not literate in their home language, they can speak the language to a translation tool and copy down and share both versions.

"GAMIFIED" VERSION

The "classical" LEA activity is excellent and is a tried-and-true lesson used by most ELL teachers.

We've also found that a "gamified" version of it can work equally well and provide a nice change of pace for the class.

In this activity, students are divided—or divide themselves—into pairs (in a mixed beginner/intermediate class, we think it works best to have one student of each level working together). Each group gets a mini-whiteboard, marker, and eraser. They are also given a number to write in the corner of their board.

The goal of the game is for the pairs to write sentences on their boards about a video clip they will watch. They get points based on the number, accuracy, and complexity of their sentences.

A student or peer tutor is assigned to be the "light turner-on-and-off person," and another is the score-keeper at the whiteboard in front of the classroom. The light is turned off, and a video is shown in the front (see Technology Connections for a list of engaging short ones) for a minute or so. Students are given a short period of time to write, and then the teacher yells "Stop," the light is turned on, and students hold up their boards.

The teacher walks (or runs) around calling out point totals for each group and looking for quick teaching opportunities ("Does women mean one or more?" "Right, more" "So should it be 'are' or 'is'?"). The light goes off again, and the process continues. The first time the game is played in class, students typically begin by writing one or two sentences and then figure out that they really can get more points based on the number of sentences or their complexity. Then groups begin to write three, four, or even five or six, or fewer with more words.

We allow students to "bet" earned points on the last clip, but tell them that to win the bet, they have to write sentences that are worth at least five points.

The atmosphere of these games can be electric, and the activity can also be exhausting for the teacher. It's definitely one for only occasional use!

Teaching Online

Though it's not possible for students to do something physically together when doing distance learning, with screen sharing, everyone can watch the same video or watch the teacher perform a simple science experiment.

Then, it's just a matter of the teacher sharing their screen while writing down the sentences students say about what they saw. One could say that the teacher could then just share the document without students copying down the final sentences on their own (and we are sure some students will ask for this!). However, that sort of passive learning is not likely to be very effective, so we recommend that students copy down the sentences on their own document, either by typing it or, even better, by doing it longhand (Ferlazzo, 2011, January).

What Could Go Wrong?

Writing down too many sentences or ones that are too complex can be frustrating to beginners, particularly students with little school experience or who are unfamiliar with the English alphabet. Keep the length of sentences short, the vocabulary simple, and the number of them low—not more than 6 to 10.

STRATEGY 8: LANGUAGE EXPERIENCE APPROACH (LEA)

Differentiation Recommendations

Newcomers (Preliterate or Low Literacy in Home Language): Use simple activities, like playing a soccer game or watching a short wordless video that can be described chronologically. Students can use online translation tools to say and translate what they did, as well as draw it. Keep sentences short.	**Newcomers (Literate in Home Language):** Students can also use online translation tools to say and translate what they did, as well as use teacher-created "word banks."
Intermediate ELLs: Use longer and more potentially complex activities, such as a wordless video that communicates a theme or message that needs to be identified. Have students write their own sentences about the activity.	**Advanced ELLs:** Students can be challenged to write more complex sentences about the group activity, and write sentences about a separate activity they did apart from class.

Technology Connections

Students can convert their sentences into an audio-narrated and illustrated slideshow online. See The Best Ways to Create Online Slideshows (http://larryferlazzo.edublogs.org/2008/05/06/the-best-ways-to-create-online-slideshows/).

Learn more about the Language Experience Approach by checking out The Best Resources for Learning How to Use the Language Experience Approach (https://larryferlazzo.edublogs.org/2021/07/09/the-best-resources-for-learning-how-to-use-the-language-experience-approach/).

Find videos to use for this activity at "Best" Lists of the Week: Teaching with Movies & Video Clips (https://larryferlazzo.edublogs.org/2018/06/13/best-lists-of-the-week-teaching-with-movies/).

Attribution

Portions of this section originally appeared in our book, *The ESL/ELL Teacher's Survival Guide* (Ferlazzo & Sypnieski, 2012, p. 54).

All figures from this chapter, as well as 11 additional chapters, references, hyperlinked Technology Connections, and more online resources, can be found at www.wiley.com/go/ellteacherstoolbox2.

First, we walked outside.

Second, we walked to the basketball court.

Third, we played basketball.

Fourth, Juan bounced the basketball.

Fifth, Julia threw the basketball.

Sixth, we drank water.

Seventh, we ran back to the classroom.

Figure 8.1 Language Experience Approach Model

STRATEGY 9

Jigsaw

What Is It?

The jigsaw strategy can be implemented with a number of different variations. Most, though, involve students becoming experts in a section of a text or an element of a broader topic (e.g., learning about different times of a famous person's life), which they then teach to other students who have become experts in different portions of the text. All students take turns teaching their classmates.

Why We Like It

There are so many reasons to like the jigsaw strategy! It generally produces high student engagement in all four domains—reading, writing, speaking, and listening; it is a great tool for differentiation (beginners can be given easier portions of the text); it can be used for any topic; and it can require minimal teacher preparation.

Supporting Research

Researchers share our enthusiasm for the jigsaw strategy. In fact, well-known education researcher John Hattie says that it is the *only* strategy that scores high in *all* sections of his newer four-quadrant model of learning: acquiring surface learning, consolidating surface learning, acquiring deep learning, and consolidating deep learning (Schwartz, 2017).

Other researchers have also found a number of academic benefits attributable to the jigsaw strategy for English proficient (National Association of Geoscience Teachers, n.d.) and ELL students (Sabbah, 2016).

Several studies have specifically found that the expectation to teach material has a positive impact on learning (Ferlazzo, 2012, April 22; Nestojko et al., 2014).

A jigsaw is also called an *information gap activity* (see Strategy 24: Dictation), a broader strategy used in many ELL classrooms. The idea behind an information gap activity is that one student is required to obtain information from a classmate in order to complete an activity. In other words, the student has to bridge the gap. It uses what researchers identify as a primary lever of motivation—the "curiosity gap" (Dean, n.d.a).

Common Core Connections

Apart from some of the Writing Standards, you can check off just about every other Standard with the jigsaw strategy—depending on the complexity of the text. Jigsaw can support students meeting the Writing Standards, too, if you have students use the process to kick off further writing about their topic.

Application

There are several different ways we use the jigsaw strategy in our classrooms, depending on the English proficiency level of our students, the time we have available for the lesson, and if we are teaching English or social studies.

BEGINNERS AND LOW-INTERMEDIATES

The teacher first prepares the materials. Figure 9.1: Driver's License Jigsaw is an example we have used with our beginners. It's simply a short article divided into five sections. We often create our own jigsaw materials or modify ones we've downloaded online (see Technology Connections for suggested resources).

After preparing the materials, the teacher needs to decide which vocabulary words are critical to pre-teach. In the case of Figure 9.1, we first taught these words or phrases: *driver's license, drive, car, one-half years old, prove, safely, live.*

After providing vocabulary instruction, the teacher divides the class into groups. For our lesson, we divided the class into five groups of three students each. We had cut the five sections in Figure 9.1 prior to the class and gave the number 1 section to Group 1, the number 2 section to Group 2, and so on. We were, however, strategic in determining which students would go into what group—here is where the differentiation ability of the jigsaw strategy shines. The students with the lowest English proficiency were in group 1 and the highest were in group 5. Middle-level students were in the other groups.

Students were then asked to practice reading their sentence(s) within their groups, working on their pronunciation and their understanding of the text. They first would seek the help of their group members and then ask the teacher. They were told they were going to teach classmates their text and that they would do it in a small group. Making it clear that they would be teaching in a small group was important to lower the stress level—we didn't want students to think they would have to read in front of the entire class. Students were able to refer to their written text when they taught it, but we also told them that the less they had to refer to it, the better.

While students were practicing reading their text aloud by taking turns in their small group, the teacher circulated and gave a letter to each student. Every group had one student who was a letter *A*, a letter *B*, and a letter *C*. If one group was a student short, the teacher would have filled in for him or her.

After students spent five to seven minutes practicing, they moved into their letter groups. Students then read their passages in the numbered order of the sections with group members softly applauding after each one read.

Last, after everyone had read their text, we asked them to put their sections away and gave them Figure 9.2: Driver's License Activity, a cloze–gap-fill using the entire text, along with three true-false statements and one question to answer. Students were asked to circle clues they used to determine the right answers to the cloze. For example, the answer for the first blank is *license* and the clue is the word *license* in the first sentence.

Students were asked to spend a few minutes completing the sheet silently. Then, after that time, we told them to share their answers with one or two other members of the group. We then reviewed the answers as a class.

To summarize, here are the seven steps to the jigsaw process that we follow (after we prepare the materials):

1. Teach the vocabulary needed for comprehension of the jigsawed text.
2. Divide the class into expert groups and distribute the appropriate texts.
3. Expert groups practice reading the text together.
4. Groups are then formed with one person from each expert group represented.
5. Experts teach their text to the new group.
6. Students complete a follow-up task (which could also be creating a poster summarizing the article, planning a role-play to perform, taking a simple test, playing an online game with review questions, etc.).
7. The teacher reviews the follow-up task with the entire class.

Figures 9.3: Nina's Break-In Part 1: Jigsaw and 9.4: Nina's Break-In Part 2: Questions About the Story come from Nancy Callan at ESL Jigsaws (www.esljigsaws.com/) and provide an idea of what a more-complex text and follow-up task might look like. Figure 9.5: Nina's Break-In: How to Use This Jigsaw contains a nice visualization of the jigsaw process that she uses in her classroom. We were inspired by her model and adapted it for our classroom situation.

We also sometimes use this kind of jigsaw to introduce new words before starting a new unit or theme. In that case, instead of distributing sections of text, we give students a portion of a word list (e.g., one group of four receives the same words; another receives the next few from the list). They then have to create draft posters with their words. These have to include the words, a definition (not just copying it down from the dictionary), a sentence using the word, and a picture. They then work with their expert groups (the students who have the same word or words) to revise their draft posters and practice their presentations. Next, they teach their word(s) to the new group. We then might distribute mini-whiteboards to all students for a follow-up formative assessment activity in which the teacher calls out words and students write down definitions or vice versa.

HIGH-INTERMEDIATES AND ADVANCED

Texts for students with a higher English proficiency could obviously be more complex. Here are examples of broader topics and the categories that could be used in jigsaws about them:

- Geography reports on countries: economy, culture, history, famous people, famous sites, politics, natural resources
- Biography reports on famous people: childhood, family as an adult, accomplishments, challenges, later years, and death
- Different wars: weapons, famous battles, leaders, causes, beginning and end
- Different sections of any lengthy article; there are many resources to obtain free articles that provide different versions depending on student English proficiency level, which is an easy way to differentiate jigsaws (see the Technology Connections section for online links)
- Different sports: how invented, famous players in the past, famous players in the present, key rules
- Articles published in different countries discussing the same current event (see the Technology Connections section for resources)
- Types of figurative language: metaphors, similes, personification
- Articles on different animals: habitat, diet, physical characteristics, behavior
- Some educators have used it with different types of math problems (Ferlazzo, 2018, April).

The jigsaw process we use with high-intermediate and advanced ELLs is a bit different, because they tend to have a higher level of well-placed confidence in their English literacy and oral ability. This increased English proficiency enables them to do more on their own and complete more-complex tasks.

As we do with beginners, we first identify the materials students will read (here, we generally use articles already written and not needing modification) and determine if any vocabulary needs to be pre-taught.

We determine group members—who is going to read what article. However, in this case, instead of immediately bringing group members together, we ask that students read it on their own and take preliminary notes for the presentation they will eventually make when they teach the article (see Figure 9.6: Student Jigsaw Instructions). First, they prepare their draft presentation on their own. Next, they meet with others who read the same article and share their initial plans. Third, students make revisions based on their expert group discussion. Finally, students get into mixed groups and teach their classmates.

We generally give guidelines about what students should include in their presentations. Figure 9.6 is one example for instructions we might provide students. Another example could be any variation of the versatile 3-2-1 structure. The instructions for a 3-2-1 poster could be "Write three words and why they're important, two phrases and why they're important, one sentence and why it's important, and draw a picture" (see the Technology Connections section for links to many other 3–2–1 ideas). We may sometimes provide a 3–2–1 graphic organizer. In addition, we remind students to paraphrase and not copy what the article says (see Strategy 15: Quoting, Summarizing, and Paraphrasing).

Next, students teach their article to the mixed groups (again, see Figure 9.6). *Sometimes*, we give all students a list of questions using academic language that they can use to ask presenters ("Can you clarify what you mean when you say _____?"). You can find many of these kinds of lists by searching online for "academic sentence starters for class discussions."

Our follow-up activity to this process is often a simple one (e.g., asking students to write down what was the most interesting thing they learned and *why* they found it most interesting). Sometimes, if we have the class time available, we'll have students take a simple test on the material that we have asked some artificial intelligence site to produce (though there may be class time available, we generally don't have teacher time to create it) or we may even ask each jigsaw group to create a short online game using Quizizz, Kahoot!, or another site with questions about their material that their classmates can play (with healthy, but yummy, snacks as prizes).

This process of a student first creating a draft on their own, meeting with others to share and discuss how to improve it, and then revising their original work based on those discussions promotes the concept of *collaborative* learning supported by the Common Core Standards (Ferlazzo & Sypnieski, 2016, p. 125). This contrasts with the cooperative learning that often appears in classrooms (including ours!) when student groups might be given directions to do a project together. There is also often a need for newcomers to work with a more-proficient ELL student in the jigsaw process and in other tasks in order to receive immediate peer support. In that case, cooperation can help newcomers develop the skills and self-efficacy to move toward more collaboration.

We should also note that collaboration also can mean two or more people working together to create new knowledge (Wisconsin Center for Education Research, n.d.) or something better than they could have created separately. We think this type of collaborative process is trickier to apply and demonstrate, though we do use it in Bonus Strategy 4: Cooperative Writing.

Again, though we believe that collaboration leads to better learning, it doesn't mean that a cooperative learning experience is "chopped liver." Because of time and logistics issues, for example, it's not unusual for us to do a cooperative jigsaw in History classes where small groups each read one page out of a textbook chapter and then make short group presentations. Figure 9.7: Student Textbook Jigsaw Instructions and Figure 9.8: Student Sentence Starters provide examples of how those activities are organized.

This process of a student first creating a draft on their own, then meeting with others to share and discuss how to improve it, and then revising their original work based on those discussions promotes the concept of *collaborative* learning supported by the Common Core Standards (Ferlazzo & Sypnieski, 2016, p. 125). This contrasts with the cooperative learning that often appears in classrooms (including ours!) when student groups might be given directions to do a project together. There is also often a need for newcomers to work with a more-proficient ELL student in the jigsaw process and in other tasks in order to receive immediate peer support. In that case, cooperation can help newcomers develop the skills and self-efficacy to move toward more collaboration.

We should also note that collaboration also can mean two or more people working together in order to create new knowledge (Wisconsin Center for Education Research, n.d.) or something better than they could have created separately. We think this type of collaborative process is trickier to apply and demonstrate, though we do use it in Bonus Strategy 4: Cooperative Writing.

Teaching Online

All aspects of the jigsaw instructional strategy can be used online. It's just a matter of providing digital reading materials (if students have to read an article), digital options for presenting their information (slideshows, "posters" like Google Slides, etc.), and the availability of "breakout rooms" in whatever videoconferencing tool you are using.

What Could Go Wrong?

Time, time, time! Do we follow the outlined jigsaw steps exactly all the time? Of course not! We've got a lot of ground to cover, there is only so much available time, and lots of unplanned events occur during the course of a school day. Sometimes we'll skip the follow-up activity, other times we'll shorten the time students can work on their own, or we'll not have people ask questions of the expert presenters. Flexibility is the rule—for this strategy and for all of them!

Students can get distracted, so jigsaw lessons are not a time for teachers to work on their computer and get caught up on grading. We need to be circulating around the room, listening, providing guidance, and offering support.

Lengthy step-by-step instructions can sometimes be more helpful to the teacher than for the students. However, it can work better and be less overwhelming to students if you place a sheet such as Figure 9.6: Student Jigsaw Instructions on the overhead or document camera, cover it up, and unveil each step as you progress through the activity.

Differentiation Recommendations

Newcomers (Preliterate or Low Literacy in Home Language): Use the Jigsaw model suggested for "Beginners and Low-Intermediates" (using very simple texts) and have digital copies of the texts that they can copy and paste into Google Translate or similar tool that will provide audio translation into their home language. Classmates or peer tutors who speak their home language can further assist in other parts of the activity.	**Newcomers (Literate in Home Language):** Use Jigsaw model suggested for "Beginners and Low-Intermediates" using simple texts.

> **Intermediate ELLs:** Depending on level of English proficiency, use either the Jigsaw model for "Beginners and Low-Intermediates" or the one for "High-Intermediates and Advanced," being sure to use texts at appropriate Lexile levels.
>
> **Advanced ELLs:** Use the Jigsaw model for "High-Intermediates and Advanced" with more complex texts. If class time allows, have students use academic question-starters for use in discussion. In addition, students can create online quiz games on materials for classmates to answer as the final activity in the process.

Technology Connections

It's easy for teachers to create their own jigsaw materials, though we generally either modify materials we download from edHelper.com (https://edhelper.com/) or Enchanted Learning (www.enchantedlearning.com/Home.html), which require a very low-cost subscription, or use ready-made materials we purchase from ESL Jigsaws (www.esljigsaws.com/). We've also used AI chatbots to create jigsaws after uploading examples.

In addition, you can find many different variations of how students can construct 3-2-1 posters when presenting as experts at The Best Ways to Use "3-2-1" as an Instructional Strategy(http://larryferlazzo.edublogs.org/2015/09/19/the-best-ways-to-use-3-2-1-as-an-instructional-strategy/).

Teachers can find articles from different countries covering the same topic at The Best Tools to Help Develop Global Media Literacy (http://larryferlazzo.edublogs.org/2009/03/12/the-best-tools-to-help-learn-global-media-literacy/) and articles about the same topic at different lexile levels at The Best Places to Get the "Same" Text Written for Different "Levels"(http://larryferlazzo.edublogs.org/2014/11/16/the-best-places-to-get-the-same-text-written-for-different-levels/).

Attribution

Professor Elliot Aronson originated the jigsaw strategy at the University of Texas and the University of California during the early 1970s (www.jigsaw.org/).

Nancy Callan at ESL Jigsaws (www.esljigsaws.com/) has developed many ideas and materials related to applying jigsaws in ELL classes.

All figures from this chapter, as well as 11 additional chapters, references, hyperlinked Technology Connections, and more online resources, can be found at www.wiley.com/go/ellteacherstoolbox2.

1. You need a license to drive a car.
2. You can get a driver's license in California when you are 16 years old.
3. If you are less than 17 ½ years old, you must take a driver's education class before you can get a license.
4. If you are over 17 ½ years old, you do not have to take a driver's education class.
5. You have to take a test where you write the answers down on paper. You also have to drive a car and show that you know how to drive safely. In addition, you must prove that you live in California. There are many ways to show that you live here.

Figure 9.1 Driver's License Jigsaw

Cloze

You need a license to drive a car. You can get a driver's _____ in California when you are 16 years old. If you are less than 17 ½ years old, you must take a driver's education class before you can get a license. If you are over 17 ½ years old, you do not have to take a driver's _____ class. You have to take a test where you write the answers down on paper. _____ also have to drive a car and show that you know how to drive safely. In addition, you must prove that you live in _____. There are many ways to show that you live here.

True or False (circle T or F):

1. You can get a driver's license in California when you are 15.   T   F
2. You can live in another state and get a California driver's license.   T   F
3. You have to take a test where you write the answers down on paper. T   F

Question

Do you want to get a driver's license? If your answer is yes, explain why. If your answer is no, explain why not.

I want to get a driver's license because _____
_____.

I do not want to get a driver's license because _____
_____.

Figure 9.2 Driver's License Activity

STRATEGY 9: JIGSAW

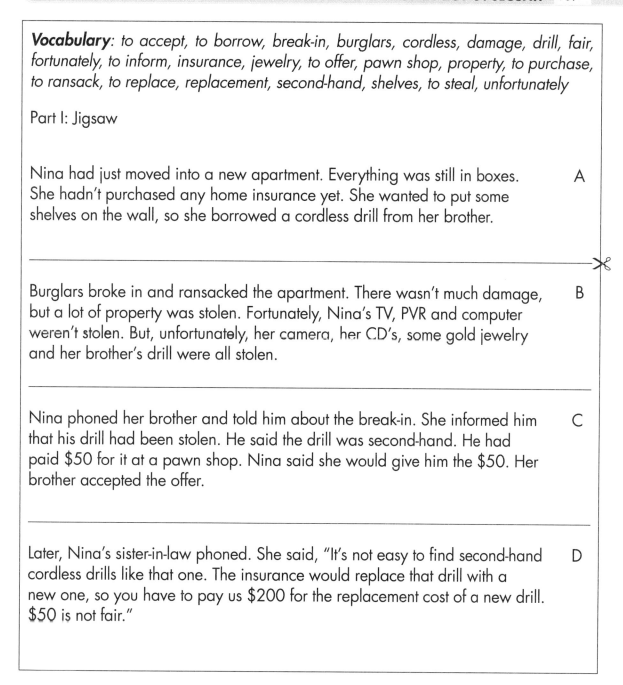

Vocabulary: *to accept, to borrow, break-in, burglars, cordless, damage, drill, fair, fortunately, to inform, insurance, jewelry, to offer, pawn shop, property, to purchase, to ransack, to replace, replacement, second-hand, shelves, to steal, unfortunately*

Part I: Jigsaw

Nina had just moved into a new apartment. Everything was still in boxes. She hadn't purchased any home insurance yet. She wanted to put some shelves on the wall, so she borrowed a cordless drill from her brother. A

Burglars broke in and ransacked the apartment. There wasn't much damage, but a lot of property was stolen. Fortunately, Nina's TV, PVR and computer weren't stolen. But, unfortunately, her camera, her CD's, some gold jewelry and her brother's drill were all stolen. B

Nina phoned her brother and told him about the break-in. She informed him that his drill had been stolen. He said the drill was second-hand. He had paid $50 for it at a pawn shop. Nina said she would give him the $50. Her brother accepted the offer. C

Later, Nina's sister-in-law phoned. She said, "It's not easy to find second-hand cordless drills like that one. The insurance would replace that drill with a new one, so you have to pay us $200 for the replacement cost of a new drill. $50 is not fair." D

Figure 9.3 Nina's Break-In Part 1: Jigsaw   *Source:* Reproduced with permission of Nancy Callan (http://esljigsaws.com/).

Please answer in full sentences together with your group.

1. Why didn't Nina have insurance?
   _____

2. Why did Nina borrow the drill?
   _____

3. How did the apartment look after the break-in?
   _____

4. What was stolen?
   _____

5. What wasn't stolen and why do you think those items were not stolen?
   _____
   _____

6. Where had Nina's brother bought the drill?
   _____

7. How much had the drill cost?
   _____

8. How much did Nina's sister-in-law want for the drill and why?
   _____

9. How much do you think Nina should pay for the drill? Why?
   _____
   _____

Figure 9.4 Nina's Break-In Part 2: Questions About the Story   *Source:* Reproduced with permission of Nancy Callan (http://esljigsaws.com/).

STRATEGY 9: JIGSAW 109

Nina's Break-In
Sample jigsaw courtesy of www.esljigsaws.com
1-888-ESL-BOOK

How to use this jigsaw:

Step One: (Teacher Preparation Stage): Photocopy 1/4 the number of copies of the jigsaw text and pictures as you have students. Cut each sheet of text and pictures into the 4 parts. Photocopy the follow-up task sheets (to be given out later).

Step Two: Preteach any new vocabulary, put students into groups, and give out an identical section of text to all members of a group. For a class of sixteen, your classroom should look like this:

A A   B B   C C   D D
A A   B B   C C   D D

Ask students to work together to memorize their section of text.
When students indicate that they're ready, take back the text passages.

Step Three: Regroup students into heterogeneous groups. Explain that they will be teaching the others their part of the story. At this point, for a class of sixteen, your classroom should look like this:

A B   A B   A B   A B
C D   C D   C D   C D

Go over comprehension checks before students begin telling their stories, such as: *Do you understand me? Should I repeat anything? What does that word mean?* etc.

Ask students to begin telling their part of the story, starting with person A. Circulate to assist with any problems and to check comprehension.

Step Four: Once students have finished telling all parts of the story, distribute the group exercises and stress that the group should work on them together. When all groups have finished, take them up with the whole class.

Figure 9.5 Nina's Break-In: How to Use This Jigsaw   *Source:* Reproduced with permission of Nancy Callan (http://esljigsaws.com/).

1. Write the number of your article at the top of the first page.
2. Read the article silently on your own.
3. Make notes:
   - The three most important points made in the article
   - A picture illustrating a main idea of the article
   - Do you agree with the author? Why or why not?
   - Prepare a thoughtful question to ask your audience about the topic of the article.
4. Meet with other classmates who are reading the same article (your teacher will assign the groups). In that meeting, share your notes and learn from others. You will also be given a letter.
5. Take your notes (and any changes you have made after hearing your classmates) and make a simple poster. You will have 10 minutes to create your poster.
6. Take your poster and meet with your letter group (the students who have the same letter as you). Take turns being the teacher and presenting your poster—starting with article number one and ending with the last article number.
7. After each teacher presents, all group members have 30 seconds to write down a question about the article. The teacher chooses one person to ask their question and then the teacher answers it.

Figure 9.6 Student Jigsaw Instructions

STRATEGY 9: JIGSAW 111

Your group is responsible for preparing a one- to two-minute presentation about your page in the book.

You must create a slide deck or poster and use index cards to help you present your slides/poster. Everyone must speak in the presentation.

Only put key words and draw a picture on the poster to help you in your presentation.

Your presentation must include:

- Three important words from the page and what they mean—in your own words.
- A one-sentence summary of the page—in your own words.
- Three other important facts from the page in your own words.
- A picture you draw (or find online) that helps people understand the chapter. Please explain how the image is connected to the page and chapter.

You must choose at least one of these additional options. You will receive extra credit if you do more than one:

- Use your laptop to look up more information about events or people talked about on your page and add them to your presentation and poster.
- Act out an event from the page.
- Connect something from the page to information we learned in a previous chapter or in a previous class activity.

Figure 9.7 Student Textbook Jigsaw Instructions

1. Three important words from the page and what they mean—in your own words.

   The word _____ **means** _____.

2. A one-sentence summary of the page.

   Our summary of the page is _____.

3. Three important facts from the page.

   One important fact from the page is _____.

   Another important fact from the page is _____.

   The third important fact from the page is _____.

4. A picture that helps people understand the chapter.

   This is a picture of _____. **It helps you understand the chapter because** _____.

You must choose at least one of these additional options. You will receive extra credit if you do more than one:

A. Use a laptop to look up more information about events or people talked about on your page and add them to your presentation and poster.

   We researched more information and we learned _____.

B. Act out an event from the page.

   We are going to act out _____ **from the page**.

C. Connect something from the page to another thing we learned in a previous chapter.

   The page said _____. **This is connected to what we learned about** _____ **because** _____.

Figure 9.8 Student Sentence Starters

STRATEGY 10
Reading Comprehension

What Is It?

The word *comprehension* comes from the Latin word *comprehendere*, meaning "to seize or take in the mind" (Comprehend, n.d.). Although the word *seize* may seem a bit dramatic when applied to reading, for many ELLs it feels like quite a victory when they have "seized" the meaning from a text in English!

There are several approaches we use in building the reading comprehension skills of ELLs so they can gain small victories every day. We discuss some of these ways as separate strategies, such as Strategy 3: Graphic Organizers, Strategy 4: Vocabulary, Strategy 5: Activating Prior Knowledge, and Strategy 11: Inductive Learning. In this section, we will describe other key methods that help our students increase their understanding of texts while developing skills and metacognitive tools they can apply in future reading situations. We refer to metacognition in several places in this book and like the definition we used in our last book:

> It is the self-awareness to know what our strengths and weaknesses are, and how and when to apply the former and compensate for the latter. Broadly explained, learners applying metacognitive strategies plan in advance for effective learning, monitor and make adjustments during the lesson/activity to maximize their learning, and reflect afterwards about which learning strategies worked and which did not for them. (Ferlazzo & Sypnieski, 2016, p. 31)

Why We Like It

We know, and research confirms, that students who are "actively engaged in their learning have better reading outcomes than do passive learners" (National Reading Technical Assistance Center, 2010, p. 12).

Therefore, the following strategies serve dual purposes—they help students become aware of the thinking processes that can build comprehension *and* keep them actively engaged as they are reading and learning.

Supporting Research

READING STRATEGIES

Many researchers have found that explicit instruction in reading strategies (such as monitoring for understanding, summarizing, asking and answering questions, etc.) can benefit comprehension (Education Endowment Foundation, n.d.; Filderman et al., 2022). Some also offer the reasonable caution that continuous reading strategy instruction taught day after day can "take a process that could bring joy, and turn it into work" (Willingham, 2012).

Most of the research on the effectiveness of teaching reading comprehension strategies has been focused on struggling readers who are considered English proficient, not ELLs, and particularly not ELLs at the middle or high school level (Snyder et al., 2016, p. 143). However, a study on ELL college students did indicate that higher reading abilities were related to the ELL's awareness and use of strategies while reading (Nordin et al., 2013, p. 476).

Our experience in the classroom corroborates what Stanford researcher Claude Goldenberg (2013) states: "It seems highly likely that we can help ELLs improve their comprehension by teaching comprehension skills directly, although if done in English, the impact will probably depend on English proficiency level" (p. 28).

We have indeed found that ELL students benefit from instruction in reading strategies, especially if they haven't been exposed to them in previous learning experiences. They also need additional time to practice how and when to apply them.

Taking all this into account, it's not entirely clear *how* reading comprehension strategy instruction directly affects reading outcomes for ELLs. However, limited research, common sense, and our own classroom experience strongly suggest that teaching comprehension strategies promotes engagement in the reading and language acquisition process.

READ ALOUDS AND THINK ALOUDS

Reading aloud is a foundational strategy linked to literacy development (Gold & Gibson, n.d.). Findings suggest that conducting teacher read alouds and think alouds can help students improve their reading comprehension, vocabulary, and listening skills while increasing their engagement in reading (Clark & Andreason, 2014, p. 174–175).

CLOSE READING

Research has linked the close reading of text by readers at all ability levels to increased reading proficiency. It has also been found to be an important part of college and career readiness (Boyles, 2012/2013). Reading a complex text that is challenging to understand can also help students to build stamina and persistence (Fisher & Frey, 2012) and can be one of the most successful interventions for improving reading comprehension, particularly among older students (Escamilla et al., 2022).

However, although close reading can assist students in building valuable skills, it should be viewed as just one tool in the toolbox. As teacher-researchers Douglas Fisher and Nancy Frey (2012) state, "Close reading must be accompanied by other essential instructional practices that are vital to reading development: interactive read-alouds and shared readings, teacher modeling and think-alouds" (p. 180).

Common Core Connections

The methods described in this section focus on building students' reading comprehension skills as they work toward meeting the Reading Standards. The section on Close Reading offers instructional moves to assist students in working with the types of complex texts called for in the Standards.

Application

Literacy teachers are familiar with the controversy surrounding reading instruction first characterized as a debate between phonics and whole language and that is now viewed as one between "the science of reading" and "balanced literacy." These debates are commonly referred to as the "Reading Wars."

Though we aren't going to spend time exploring that debate here (see Technology Connections for resources on this topic), we do feel it is important to note that researchers point out that a "one-size-fits-all" approach is not effective, especially for ELL students, and while phonics instruction has clear benefits for ELLs (as well as all students), it is not enough. Teachers of ELLs also need to be intentional about providing opportunities for students to develop vocabulary and oral language skills as they work to make meaning of text (August & Shanahan, 2010).

Effective reading instruction strategies for ELLs to a large extent reflect effective reading instruction for English-proficient students. The research does, however, point out a key distinction: ELLs require additional oral language support in order to become better readers (Claude, 2020). Many strategies for providing this kind of support can be found throughout this book, especially in the Speaking and Listening section. We highlight a few key practices here that we use to facilitate oral language development with our students:

- Providing time for students to do regular oral reading practice, including partner reading (see Bonus Strategy 1: Literary Conversations)
- Facilitating activities to build students' academic language and vocabulary (See Strategy 4: Vocabulary)
- Incorporating listening skills and practice into daily lessons (see Strategy 24: Dictation and Strategy 30: Listening)

- Creating opportunities for frequent, structured conversation practice (see Strategy 25: Conversation Practice)
- Offering a regular rotation of fun and engaging oral language activities like role-plays, games, songs, and storytelling (see Strategy 31: Learning Games for Speaking and Listening)

In addition, see the Technology Connections for more resources on oral language support.

In the following sections, we share how we directly support students in building their reading comprehension skills. For more on how we approach phonics instruction with ELLs, see Strategy 11: Inductive Learning.

READING STRATEGIES

As we stated previously, and as we have said in our first two books, we believe reading strategies are important scaffolds to support our students' comprehension of texts. We focus on several strategies recommended by the National Reading Panel Report of 2000 as most effective in assisting student reading comprehension. These include comprehension monitoring, cooperative learning, graphic and semantic organizers, story structure, question answering, question generation, summarization, and multiple-strategy use.

We also teach our students to use other common strategies, such as predicting, visualizing, making connections, evaluating, and inferring, in order to enhance their understanding of text. This is not a comprehensive list, however, and it is important to keep in mind what literacy expert Jennifer Serravallo (2010) says: "a strategy is never a single word or phrase—it's a series of actionable steps, a process to help readers tackle a skill that is not yet automatic for them." It is our goal to demonstrate these steps or processes for our students so they can practice them when faced with challenging text.

We introduce these strategies to our students with less English proficiency as well as to more advanced ELLs. Even though our beginning ELLs may not have the language to access higher level texts in English, we can give them access to strategies they can apply to understand more simple texts in English or texts in their native language.

Figure 10.1: Reading Strategies Word Chart is one way we help familiarize students with different reading strategies. For each word, students (with the teacher as a guide) draw what it means and then chorally read the sentence stems for using the strategy. We've also found it helpful to create hand gestures or body movements for each strategy. For example, when teachers are demonstrating the strategy of *making a connection* they can link their fingers together to create a connected chain or the teachers can close their eyes and point to their head to show *visualizing*. Students can then practice making the gestures with each other and even come up with their own versions. Research has confirmed many positive correlations between movement and increased learning (Ferlazzo, 2011, June 2).

As a follow-up to this activity, we use a reading strategies text data set (featured in our book *Navigating the Common Core with English Language Learners*, 2016) with our intermediate ELLs. See the Technology Connections section for the link to download this data set and see Strategy 11: Inductive Learning for more on text data sets.

Throughout the year, we model these reading strategies and provide students opportunities to practice them collaboratively and individually. Students often demonstrate their use of strategies in their independent reading through their reading response entries in their writer's notebooks (see Bonus Strategy 5: Writer's Notebook). We also periodically ask students to show us how they use reading strategies by writing one on a mini-whiteboard and sharing it with the class. In the upcoming sections, we describe how we model and encourage this strategy use through read alouds and think alouds, whole-class readings, and close reading.

Of course, the ultimate goal is for students to be able to identify which strategies are most effective in certain reading contexts and for these strategies to become automatic and transferrable as they read independently. Having this end goal in mind can help teachers to look for opportunities to ask their students to reflect on which strategies they are finding most helpful in which reading contexts.

READ ALOUDS AND THINK ALOUDS

We conduct read alouds with our students in order to spark their interest in reading; to model fluent, prosodic reading; and to increase their language development. Reading with prosody means reading aloud with proper intonation, expression, and rhythm. Research on the explicit teaching of prosody to students indicates it can improve fluency skills and reading comprehension (Calet et al., 2017, p. 7).

The read aloud process involves selecting a well-written, short piece of text (usually one to three paragraphs) related to our unit of study. We read it aloud to students and they follow along silently on their copy of the text. We may briefly supply a synonym or quick definition of an advanced word, but otherwise we do not stop to make any comments. Students can then respond to a variety of writing or speaking prompts that ask them to go back into the text and provide support for their answers (such as "What does the author mean by ?" or "Do you agree or disagree with and why?").

Sometimes we use read alouds to provide background knowledge or to pique student interest on an upcoming topic of study. Other times we give our students the chance to conduct their own read aloud with a partner or small group. They can choose their own texts, practice reading it aloud focusing on pronunciation and prosody, and create a writing or speaking prompt for their classmates.

Reading aloud, when structured carefully, can help less-proficient ELLs better understand what they are reading. We were introduced to an activity by educator Scott Thornbury (2017) called *Reading Aloud (Heads Up)*. In this method, students are given a sentence to read aloud. Then, instead of looking down at the page and reading it aloud, they must read it silently, look up, and then say the sentence aloud. Therefore, students must "hold the material in the mind in such a way that its meaning is processed, and then recall it meaningfully" (Thornbury, 2017). Students can say the sentence to another student, to a small group, or to the teacher, which naturally provides an authentic audience—a key to any meaningful language-learning activity.

Think alouds, sometimes known as *interactive read alouds,* serve as a great opportunity for teachers to demonstrate their use of reading strategies. We do think alouds with many different types of texts—fiction and nonfiction.

In this strategy, the teacher again reads a text aloud demonstrating prosody but also pauses every so often to share his or her thinking. We find it most effective for ELL students if we place the text on the document camera and demonstrate our use of reading strategies by writing annotations in the margins (we sometimes just share our comments orally with our most advanced ELLs). In other words, we may pause after reading the title and write down a question that comes to mind. Then we may read the first paragraph and pause to write a connection or summary statement in the margin.

Figure 10.2 is an example of a think aloud that Katie did with intermediate and advanced ELL students at the middle school level, but it could easily be used with older students. She worked with expert literacy teacher Dana Dusbiber to develop a unit examining the benefits of reading. The comments in italics have been inserted where the teacher broke from the text to share her thinking with students. The teacher also wrote her comments down on the copy of the think aloud under the document camera in order to make her thinking even more explicit to students.

Students can then practice making annotations on their own copies of the text, share them with a partner, and discuss them as a class. As with read alouds, students can develop their own think alouds by writing their thoughts in the margins, reading the text to a partner, and pausing to share their thoughts aloud.

Modeling our metacognitive processes of deciding which reading strategies to use and when to use them can assist students in employing these processes on their own (Boulware-Gooden et al., n.d.; Williams & Atkins, 2009, p. 39).

WHOLE-CLASS READINGS

We often use the following process when we are going to read a text (an article, a poem, a story) as a class. Although this is definitely not an exhaustive list of reading support activities, it does represent what we generally do. Prior to presenting a text to students, we often will "engineer" it to make it less intimidating and more accessible by adding headings, images, extra white space for appearance and for notes, etc. For more on our process of selecting and engineering texts to support student learning see Strategy 2: Text Engineering.

Before Reading

Vocabulary

Before reading a text with ELLs, we determine any key words or concepts that students will need to know in order to access the text. Sometimes we simply provide students with the words and their meanings. Other times we may give students a word chart (see Strategy 4: Vocabulary for an example of a word chart and further vocabulary strategies).

Activating and Building Prior Knowledge

We also consider ways to activate or build students' background knowledge in order to aid their comprehension and increase engagement. If the teacher knows the class is familiar with the topic of the text, they may simply provide students with the topic and ask them to share what they know with a partner and then with the class. If more explanation is needed, students could then do any or all of the following activities—start a KWL chart, do an anticipation guide, respond to a quickwrite, or watch a short video (see Strategy 5: Activating Prior Knowledge for more detailed explanations and examples of these activities). The teacher might also provide time for students to discuss or read about the topic of the text in their home language. Watching a video on the topic in their home language is another option. As we discuss in Strategy 5: Activating Prior Knowledge, teachers can also provide simpler, preparatory texts on a topic prior to reading a more complex one

Previewing Text Structure

We often ask students to scan the text we will be reading and look for what they notice about the text's structure. For example, we might ask, "Are there headings or any bold words? If so, what does that tell us?" "Does the text include quotations and what does that tell us?" This helps ELLs begin to notice the differences in text structures of different genres and to make predictions about the upcoming text.

Setting a Purpose

It is also helpful for ELL students to set a purpose for their reading, in other words, having a *why* for reading. Sometimes readers have multiple purposes—to learn new vocabulary and new information or to figure out an author's claim and find the evidence used to support it. Other times, a reader's purpose may simply be to read for enjoyment or to learn the steps of how to do something. In whole-class readings, we will often set the purpose so students know what to look for as we are reading (e.g., looking for describing words in the passage or identifying the author's claims and evidence).

During Reading

Reading the Text

We have found it most effective to read the text aloud to ELL students as they follow the words on their own copy of the text. This enables us to model pronunciation and prosody and frees students to focus on comprehension. As we described in Strategy 3: Graphic Organizers, sometimes we stop periodically and have students take turns dictating sentences from the text to a partner who writes it on a mini-whiteboard. This gives students the chance to practice reading the text aloud and builds their listening and speaking skills.

Providing our students with a variety of texts (whether they are written texts, digital texts, photographs, videos, infographics, etc.) and with a balance of highly accessible and more challenging texts are two key instructional goals we strive to meet. We also find it most effective to teach thematically—when all the texts in a unit are related to an engaging, meaningful theme. Thematic instruction is supported by research indicating its positive impact on student learning (Northwest Regional Educational Laboratory, 2012).

Figure 10.2: Think Aloud Example, which we discussed in the section Read Alouds and Think Alouds, is one of the texts used in a thematic unit for high-intermediates on the benefits of reading. Another text we used in this unit is Figure 10.3: Benefits of Reading Data Set. For this activity, we read the first few items of the data set aloud to students and then they took turns reading the rest with a partner. Then students reread each item and added an annotation (see next section). We then gave students the categories for the data set. They worked with a partner to determine which items fit into which category and either highlighted evidence in the text or wrote a sentence supporting their opinion. See Strategy 11: Inductive Learning for more information on inductive data sets.

Annotating the Text

As we read text with students, we often model using various reading strategies through annotation. For example, after reading a paragraph or two, we may pause and write a summary statement in the margin. We might underline a particularly descriptive sentence and draw a quick sketch in the margin of what we are visualizing as we read it. We encourage students to make their own annotations by marking up the text itself or, if this isn't an option, writing on sticky notes. We may model a specific strategy and then ask students to do it when they are new to the process. Once they've had practice with multiple strategies and when to use them, students can apply the ones that are most helpful. We also provide time for students to share their annotations with each other.

A note about highlighting: We model how to use highlighting as a tool for readers. It can help the reader focus on key ideas and stay engaged while reading. We also show students how effective highlighting can save them time when rereading in preparation for writing about the text. Instead of having to reread every word, students can quickly locate key ideas that are highlighted. We explicitly teach our students these dos and don'ts: *Do* highlight key words that express the main ideas. *Don't* highlight unnecessary words such as *and, but, it, the,* and so on or highlight all the words in a sentence. It takes modeling and practice, but we do notice improvement in our students' highlighting over time.

Some researchers have questioned the effectiveness of highlighting as a studying tool (Paul, 2013). Researcher Daniel Willingham (2016) has said that when teachers compare their classroom practice to research findings they should ask themselves, "How am I using this practice differently than it's been tested?" After examining these recent studies, we are confident in saying that our use of highlighting in the classroom is substantially different from how it has been used in the research. Test results have been the primary measure of effectiveness in those studies (Dunlosky et al., 2013). They have not measured the goals of improved writing quality and engagement, which, in our opinion, are more important than standardized test results.

Using Graphic Organizers

As we've described in our previous books and in this book, graphic organizers are a key scaffold for ELLs (see Strategy 3: Graphic Organizers). They are critical for supporting comprehension and sustaining student engagement in the reading process. Depending on the text and the goals of the lesson, we use a variety of graphic organizers that students complete during and after reading. For example, if we are reading an argument piece, we may provide students with a graphic organizer that contains boxes where students can write in the author's claims and evidence. Students can complete a story map when reading a story. It is helpful to use organizers that reflect the text's structure and for students to be actively involved in completing them (not just copying the teacher's model). Graphic organizers for a variety of text structures can easily be found online.

In addition, many of these graphic organizers contain sentence stems or frames with academic language. These activities can quickly be turned into oral academic language practice by asking students to share the ideas they've written in partners or small groups.

After Reading

Summarizing the Text

We often have students practice the important skill of summarizing what they've read. This can be done while students are reading by having them work in pairs or on their own to write summary statements for different sections of text. Students can then use these annotations to write a paragraph summary of the whole text after reading. In our second book, *Navigating the Common Core with English Language Learners* (2016, p. 122–124), we explain how we have students create a visual summary for a text they've read, which helps students and teachers monitor comprehension. Here are the quick steps for doing a visual summary activity:

1. Teacher divides the text into numbered sections and creates a simple chart containing the same number of boxes.
2. The teacher models rereading the first section of the text (referring to any highlighting or annotations as a support). Then the teacher draws an image (pictures or symbols) to represent the key ideas in that section. The teacher can also add key words, phrases, or a one-sentence summary of the ideas in that section.
3. Students then do the same process, either working with a partner or individually.
4. The teacher circulates offering assistance and selecting helpful student examples to display on the document camera.

Another application related to visually summarizing text comes from Katie's work with Dana Dusbiber. We previously referred to the think aloud (Figure 10.2) and the data set (Figure 10.3) they used with intermediate ELLs in a unit on the benefits of reading. After reading multiple texts on this topic and viewing several video clips, Katie and Dana provided students with Figure 10.4: "What People Say About. . ." Graphic Organizer to capture the key claims in each text. It can be completed following class readings of each text or it can be given to students after all the readings are finished. This type of tool helps students gather the key claims made in each text on one page in preparation for writing their own argument. Here is the writing prompt used in the Benefits of Reading Unit:

> According to the texts and videos we've studied in class, what are the benefits of reading books regularly? Do you agree with these claims and the evidence given to support them? To support your opinion, you may use examples from your own experiences, your observations of others, and anything you've read or watched (including the benefits of reading data set).

In Figure 10.4, each author or source studied during the unit is represented by an image (a stick figure, a book, a video screen) with an accompanying speech bubble. Teachers can first model how to put an author's main claim into their own words and then write it in the speech bubble. Students can work in pairs or small groups to write the main claims of the other authors or sources in the corresponding speech bubbles. Another option is to have students identify and copy a direct quotation representing the author's claim into the speech bubble. This graphic organizer helps to scaffold the process of including quotations from multiple sources, especially by providing space for the authors' names and the titles of the texts.

This organizer can be modified depending on the writing task. We've found it is very helpful for ELL students to see the different authors and their opinions all on one page—they can actually point to the claims with which they agree or disagree. Students can then use this organizer as a writing resource. For even more on summarizing, see Strategy 15: Quoting, Summarizing, and Paraphrasing.

Responding to the Text

Students can develop and demonstrate their comprehension by responding to a variety of speaking or writing prompts after reading. See Bonus Strategy 2: Literary Conversations for a list of creative response prompts and other helpful activities. See Strategy 25: Conversation Practice and Bonus Strategy 7: Oral Presentations for ways students can demonstrate reading comprehension while building their listening and speaking skills.

CLOSE READING

We've written extensively about how we do close reading with ELLs in *Navigating the Common Core with English Language Learners* (2016). In this section, we will summarize the process we use and introduce some new ideas we've come across since writing that book.

We use close reading once or twice during a unit to support our ELL students in accessing complex texts and applying reading comprehension strategies in more-sophisticated ways. Close reading differs from the other types of reading we do in class because we purposely choose increasingly complex texts. We also work on slowing down so that students have multiple touches with these texts. In other words, students read the text more than once and for different purposes—to comprehend the text on a basic level, to examine word choice and structure, to analyze the central ideas, and so on.

The other difference in close reading is that we tend to focus more on the Common Core–supported strategy of asking text-dependent questions when students are required to look for evidence in the text to support their answers. We are also more careful about building background knowledge before close reading. We try to make sure that any background provided is truly necessary for students to access the text. We don't want it to act as a substitute for what can be learned through close reading the text itself.

It is also important for the teacher to identify the purpose for close reading. In other words, asking, "What are the conceptual goals for students?" (e.g., identifying claims and evidence, finding figurative language and why it is being used) and "What are the language-learning goals?" (e.g., learning three new words based on the use of context clues). Then teachers can select a text that is appropriate for both goals. Another key consideration is text length. With ELLs we recommend that the text for close reading be anywhere between one paragraph and two pages, though we have had more success using texts on the shorter end of that range.

The close-reading sequence that follows appeared in our last book, *Navigating the Common Core with English Language Learners* (2016), and contains the process of close reading we usually do with students. This sequence is a summary containing a few examples of questions and answer frames. We have also added a final step we learned from literacy experts Douglas Fisher and Nancy Frey. See the Technology Connections section for a link to our *Navigating* book's website where you can download *all* the figures, including sentence frames, for free.

Step 1: Previewing the Text—What the Text Might Say

We teach our students to survey a text when seeing it for the first time and to ask themselves questions that can help them make some predictions. We provide students with questions and answer frames. For example:

1. What type of text is this (a story, an article, a poem, etc.)? How do I know this?
   ("I think this text is _____ because _____.")

2. What is the title of this text? What predictions can I make about the text based on the title?
   ("The title is _____. Based on this title, I predict and _____.")

3. Who is this text written for (who is the audience)? What makes me think this?
   ("I believe the text is written for _____ because _____.")

> The short headings in Steps 2, 3, and 4 come from literacy expert Timothy Shanahan (n.d.).

Step 2: Basic Comprehension and Decoding—What the Text Says

In this step, students read the text for the *first time* with the purpose of developing a basic understanding of it. The teacher can read aloud while students follow along on their copy of the text. At this time, the teacher can encourage students to underline a few unfamiliar words or jot down a couple of questions that come to mind. To assist students in understanding the text on a basic level, we provide literal-type questions along with sentence frames for student responses and encourage them to develop their own as well. After this first reading, students can work to answer a selection of teacher-provided questions along with any they generated on their own. Students should be encouraged to find evidence in the text to support their answers.

Here are two examples that work for fiction:

1. What is the setting of the text (setting means both place and time)?

    ("I think the text is set in _____ during _____. I think that because the author writes .")

2. Is there a conflict or problem in the text?

    ("I think a conflict or problem is _____ because the author writes _____.")

Here are two examples for nonfiction:

1. What is the text about?

    ("I think the text is about _____. The clues I see in the text are _____ and _____.")

2. What questions does the text make you wonder about?

    ("I wonder what/how/when/if/who because _____.")

Step 3: More In-Depth Meaning—Figure Out How the Text Works

Students read the text a *second time* in this step in order to dig a little deeper and focus more on the text's structure and language. This time, students can read with partners (taking turns every few sentences or every other paragraph) or read on their own. After reading, they again can choose from a selection of teacher-generated questions that push them to gain a greater understanding of the text. For example:

1. What is a context clue to the meaning of ?

    ("I think means because the author writes _____.")

2. Is there dialogue (people talking) in the text? If so, why do you think the author uses it?

    ("I think the author uses dialogue because they want to _____. For example, the author wrote _____.")

3. What did the author mean by ?

    ("I think when the author wrote he or she meant _____.")

Step 4: Picking It Apart—Analyze and Compare the Text

Students now read the text again on their own and choose one question to answer from a list of more analytical questions. For example:

1. Is the author pushing a particular position and, if so, what evidence does he or she give to support that position?

    ("I think the author believes _____. I think the evidence used to support this belief is _____. I think that evidence is valid/invalid because _____.")

2. Does this text remind you in some way of another text you have read? How?

    ("This text reminds me of because that text also _____.")

As part of this step, students can be given another text from the same author, in the same genre, or on the same topic. The text could be printed words, a close-captioned video, a comic strip, an infographic, and so forth. Students could repeat Steps 2, 3, and the beginning of Step 4 with the second text and then work to compare the two texts by answering a variation of the following question:

> Why do you think Text A contained certain information, text structures, or certain vocabulary while Text B did not?

Students could also use a graphic organizer, such as a Venn diagram, to compare the two texts.

Step 5: Taking Action—What the Text Inspires You to Do Now

We were introduced to the thinking behind this last step by Douglas Fisher and Nancy Frey (2016) in their *Edutopia* blog post "Questioning That Deepens Comprehension."

They explain that once students deeply understand a complex text, they can be inspired to act on the new information or insights they've gained. This action can take many forms and can look different for each student. Some ideas they suggest are writing about the text, presenting to the class, conducting further research on a topic, and participating in a debate, among others. We have offered our students these options along with several others:

- Writing a letter to the author of the text
- Creating a digital book summarizing the new information learned
- Forming a book club to read other texts by the author or a different author in the same genre
- Writing and illustrating a comic book based on the text
- Creating a video

Looking for opportunities for our students to take action can promote a sense of agency—a feeling that students are active participants in their lives and not just reactors to, or observers of, others, in other words, being the driver of a car and not just a passenger in it. This is particularly important to ELLs, many of whom have arrived in this country with little input into the decision to move.

> **Important note to teachers:** Remember, the close-reading process can and should be applied to other types of texts—photographs, charts, infographics, close-captioned videos, and so on. See Strategy 17: Using Photos or Other Images in Reading and Writing for ideas on helping students to do close reading with images. In Strategy 21: Problem-Posing we discuss a version of close reading we do with beginners that also leads to taking action, primarily in the community.

Teaching Online

Students can apply many of the strategies in this chapter in an online environment. Students can read, annotate, and highlight digital texts and teachers can monitor their progress using a variety of sites and applications (see Technology Connections for resources). Teachers can conduct read alouds, think alouds, and close reading activities using a shared screen, though there needs to be a focus on making them as interactive as possible (frequent prompts for students to respond to in a chat, break out room, or on a collaborative white board).

What Could Go Wrong?

Be strategic about the purpose and frequency of close reading with students. We like educator Laurie Elish-Piper's statement, "Close reading is like broccoli. It's good for you, but only in moderation" (Gallagher, 2015).

Doing a close reading of every text not only can overwhelm students but also can quickly squash their interest in reading. In addition, you can sometimes do a close read of a text *without* following every single step we list in the sequence, and we often do just that. As community organizers often say, "We live in the world as it is, not as we would like it to be." Time constraints and other real-life events force us to regularly modify our meticulously thought-out plans.

Asking students to think and read at higher levels, while keeping engagement high, is not an easy task for teachers. Research cautions that students may appear "busiest and most involved with material they already know" (Hendrick, 2015). We need to use strategies and texts that promote our students' curiosity and engagement in reading, but we also need to observe and assess their comprehension skills to ensure they are growing in reading and English proficiency.

Strategy 10: Reading Comprehension

Differentiation Recommendations

Newcomers (Preliterate or Low Literacy in Home Language): Use images and videos, preferably in a student's home language to build background knowledge to support reading comprehension. Encourage students to draw or use images to share their knowledge and in response to simple texts.	**Newcomers (Literate in Home Language):** Focus on just one or two reading strategies at a time. Encourage students to annotate texts using their home language. Also, use texts and videos in a student's home language to build background knowledge to support reading comprehension.
Intermediate ELLs: Use all chapter strategies, with increasingly complex text. Ask students to demonstrate their application of reading strategies through annotating the text.	**Advanced ELLs:** Do more frequent close reading activities using increasingly complex text. Have students create and conduct their own think alouds with classmates.

Technology Connections

For more resources on reading comprehension, see The Best Posts on Reading Strategies & Comprehension (https://larryferlazzo.edublogs.org/2015/03/19/the-best-posts-on-reading-strategies-comprehension-help-me-find-more/).

There are many resources on providing oral language support to ELLs, and they can be found at The Best Posts About Value of Oral Reading in Partners for ELLs & Others (https://larryferlazzo.edublogs.org/2020/04/13/the-value-of-oral-reading-in-partners-for-ells-others/).

Students can practice applying the reading strategies they are learning in class to online text. There are many sites where students can annotate and highlight while reading online. See a list of them at The Best Applications for Annotating Websites (http://larryferlazzo.edublogs.org/2008/12/18/best-applications-for-annotating-websites/).

For more information on the "Reading Wars," see The Best Resources for Learning About Balanced Literacy and the "Reading Wars" (https://larryferlazzo.edublogs.org/2014/07/09/the-best-resources-for-learning-about-balanced-literacy-the-reading-wars/).

For more on close reading with various types of texts, see The Best Resources on Close Reading, Paintings, Photos and Videos (http://larryferlazzo.edublogs.org/2015/08/05/the-best-resources-on-close-reading-paintings-photos-videos/) and The Best Resources on "Close Reading" (http://larryferlazzo.edublogs.org/2013/05/13/the-best-resources-on-close-reading-help-me-find-more/).

You can download Exhibit 5.3: Reading Strategies Data Set along with all the figures in The ESL/ELL Teacher's Survival Guide (Ferlazzo & Sypnieski, 2012) at that book's website (www.wiley.com/WileyCDA/WileyTitle/productCd-1118095677.html).

You can download Exhibit 3.3: Question and answer starter list for close reading at our Navigating the Common Core with English Language Learners (Ferlazzo & Sypnieski, 2016) website (www.wiley.com/WileyCDA/WileyTitle/productCd-1119023009.html).

If you'd like to access many of the resources we used to create the benefits of reading unit, see The Best Videos and Articles Where Athletes Explain How Reading and Writing Well Has Helped Their Career (http://larryferlazzo.edublogs.org/2013/07/13/the-best-videos-articles-where-athletes-explain-how-reading-writing-well-has-helped-their-career-help-me-find-more) and The Best Resources on the Study Finding That Reading Books Makes You Live Longer at (http://larryferlazzo.edublogs.org/2016/08/13/the-best-resources-on-the-study-finding-that-reading-books-makes-you-live-longer/).

For free virtual whiteboards, see The Best Alternatives to the Soon-to-Be-Deceased Google Jamboard (https://larryferlazzo.edublogs.org/2023/10/03/the-best-alternatives-to-the-soon-to-be-deceased-google-jamboard) and/or The Best Online Virtual "Corkboards" (https://larryferlazzo.edublogs.org/2011/03/30/the-best-online-virtual-corkboards-or-bulletin-boards).

Attribution

Versions of some of these ideas appeared in our book *Navigating the Common Core with English Language Learners* (Ferlazzo & Sypnieski, 2016, p. 100–107, 122–123, 128–130).

Our thanks to Douglas Fisher and Nancy Frey for their exceptional *Edutopia* blog post "Questioning That Deepens Comprehension" (www.edutopia.org/blog/questioning-that-deepens-comprehension-douglas-fisher-nancy-frey?utm_source=twitter&utm_medium=socialflow).

Our thanks to Sean Banville (n.d.) for his article "People Who Read Live Longer" (www.breakingnewsenglish.com/1608/160810-reading.html). His sites for English language learners offer a wealth of materials for students and teachers.

All figures from this chapter, as well as 11 additional chapters, references, hyperlinked Technology Connections, and more online resources, can be found at www.wiley.com/go/ellteacherstoolbox2.

Strategy	My Drawing or Translation	How It Works and How I Can Use It
Asking questions		I wonder _____. Why . . . ? Will . . . ? What does _____ mean?
Making predictions		I predict _____ because _____. Based on _____, I think that _____.
Visualizing		When I read _____, I picture _____. I visualize _____ because _____.
Summarizing		This story is about _____. The main idea is _____. From the text I learned _____ about _____.
Making connections		This reminds me of _____ because _____. _____ and _____ are similar because_____.
Evaluating		I agree (or disagree with) _____ because _____. In my opinion, _____.
Inferring		The text says _____ and I know _____, therefore I guess that _____. I infer _____ based on _____.

Figure 10.1 Reading Strategies Word Chart

People Who Read Live Longer [That's an interesting title—how does reading help you live longer?]

New research shows that people who read a lot live longer. The study was carried out by researchers from Yale University in the USA. The researchers said reading keeps the mind active, helps reduce stress, and makes us take better care of our health.

[This reminds me of the quote we read by President Obama about how reading helps him manage stress.] The researchers said that books help the brain more than newspapers and magazines, but any kind of reading will help us to live longer. *[I wonder why books are better?]* Even reading for half an hour a day could help us to live longer. In the study, researchers looked at the lifestyles of 3,500 men and women over a 12-year period. They looked at their reading habits, health, lifestyle and their education. All of the people were at least 50 years old at the start of the research.

The study is in the journal *Social Science and Medicine*. It found that people who read for up to 3.5 hours a week were 17 percent less likely to die during the study's 12-year research period than those who read no books. Those who read for more than 3.5 hours a week were 23 percent less likely to die. Researcher Becca Levy said: "Older individuals, regardless of gender, health, wealth or education, showed the survival advantage of reading books." *[So I think she's saying that no matter how old you are or how rich you are, reading will help you live longer.]* She suggested people swap watching TV for reading to live longer. *[Oh no! But I love "America's Got Talent"!]* She said: "Individuals over the age of 65 spend an average of 4.4 hours per day watching television. Efforts to redirect leisure time into reading books could prove to be beneficial."

Sources

http://www.dailymail.co.uk/health/article-3726386/Why-reading-help-live-longer-Immersing-good-story-mind-active-ease-stress.html

http://www.huffingtonpost.com/entry/those-who-read-books-live-longer-than-those-who-dont-study-finds_us_57a358c8e4b0104052a17cd2

https://www.rawstory.com/2016/08/a-new-study-has-found-that-avid-readers-appear-to-live-a-longer-life/

Figure 10.2 Think Aloud Example *Source:* This article is reprinted here with the permission of Sean Banville (www.breakingnewsenglish.com/1608/160810-reading.html)

(1) "Books showed me there were possibilities in life, that there were actually people like me living in a world I could not only aspire to, but attain. Reading gave me hope. For me, it was the open door."
—Oprah Winfrey

(2) "At an early age, I always felt there was something relaxing and enjoyable about reading . . . and I still feel that way today: Reading is the best way for me to clear my mind and slow down."
—Andrew Luck

(3) "If you are a reader, then you have the ability to educate yourself. When you have the ability to be a lifelong learner, there are no limits on what you can acquire in terms of knowledge and information. It represents the ultimate freedom of humankind."
—LeVar Burton

(4) "It is not enough to simply teach children to read; we have to give them something worth reading . . . something that will help them make sense of their own lives and encourage them to reach out toward people whose lives are quite different from their own."
—Katherine Paterson

(5) "Reading has given me an opportunity, just for those . . . 25 minutes before the game . . . to read and think about something else and get a sense of what else is going on besides the game of basketball. It's made me comfortable . . . It's just something that I decided to do at the beginning of the postseason, and it's worked for me."
—LeBron James

(6) "Reading gave me the ability to slow down, get perspective, and walk in somebody else's shoes."
—President Barack Obama

(7) "Reading in some small way makes me a more productive athlete, and being a pro athlete makes me enjoy the serenity that reading provides just a little bit more."
—Dan Grunfeld

Figure 10.3 Benefits of Reading Data Set

132 THE ELL TEACHER'S TOOLBOX 2.0

(8) "Whether reading books has made me a better president I can't say. But what I can say is that [reading books] has allowed me to sort of maintain my balance during the course of eight years."
—President Barack Obama

Categories

- Stress Management or Comfort
- The Power of Reading
- Empathy and Understanding Others
- Reading and Athletic Performance

Figure 10.3 (Continued)

Figure 10.4 "What People Say About..." Graphic Organizer

STRATEGY 11
Inductive Learning

What Is It?

When inductive methods are used in teaching and learning, students are presented with examples and are challenged to identify patterns in them. Inductive teaching uses a progression of going from the specific to the general. This instructional strategy contrasts with deductive teaching and learning in which the teacher presents the rule or concept and then reinforces it with examples. In other words, it applies a sequence of going from the general to the specific.

For example, an inductive phonics lesson on differentiating between the long and short *a* sound might start by showing a series of words, supported by images, using the patterns of *ai, a-e,* and *ay*. Students could be asked to categorize those words, identify additional ones that fit into those patterns, say the words to a partner, and develop rules for those patterns as they practice the language. A subsequent lesson would do the same with words using a short *a* sound.

A deductive lesson, however, might begin with a teacher listing the patterns where a long *a* is present, sharing a list of those words, and having students practice writing and saying them.

Why We Like It

We are proponents of the inductive method in many cases because it is more student-led than teacher-led. In addition, Duke psychology professor Dan Ariely (2016) often talks about the "IKEA effect"—we tend to value something more highly when we are involved in its creation as opposed to being presented with a finished product.

Supporting Research

Substantial research (Prince & Felder, 2007) finds that this kind of guided discovery or enhanced discovery teaching (Ferlazzo, 2016, October 2) not only enhances student autonomy and motivation but also results in greater learning of content, retention

(Stafford, 2011), and ability to transfer and apply knowledge to new situations (Ferlazzo, 2015, June 19). Students practicing the kind of "self-explanation" that is the focus of inductive learning have been repeatedly found to be more effective than "instructional explanations" by teachers (Birsa et al., 2018). The pattern-seeking that is supported by inductive learning has been found to be especially effective in acquiring first (University of Sydney, 2016) and new languages (Association for Psychological Science, 2013). Interestingly enough, this ability to recognize patterns is also being sought more and more by employers, as well (Wilson, 2015).

Common Core Connections

Inductive teaching specifically supports the Common Core State Standards. Induction is basically a strategy of noticing and seeking patterns. The Common Core explicitly promotes pattern-seeking—in word, sentence, and text structures; in oral discourse (Morrow et al., 2012); and in literature analysis (Common Core State Standards Initiative, n.d.e).

Application

Under the instructional strategy umbrella of inductive learning, we will explore several specific ways to implement this method in the English language learner classroom: the picture word inductive model, data sets, and concept attainment. We include additional ways under the "grab-bag" title of "Other Inductive Strategies." We will discuss concept attainment—plus (Bonus Strategy 2) as a separate instructional strategy because it requires a more lengthy explanation.

PICTURE WORD INDUCTIVE MODEL (PWIM)

As a Lesson

The PWIM (Calhoun, 1999) is a multistep language-development strategy that we use primarily with beginning English language learners. The steps and sequence can vary, but the following describes the general week-long process we use.

It begins with the teacher first choosing an image (including many different objects and people) based on the lesson theme (home, school, food, etc.). Figure 11.1: Man in the Kitchen is an example of an image we use in our unit on home. The photo is enlarged and laminated, and smaller paper copies are made for each student. Later, after students become familiar with the process, the class can be given the option to help choose the images.

> **Day 1:** All students come up to the large image and help label the objects by taking turns sharing the words they know. The teacher writes them, asking students to repeat each letter and then the word. The teacher adds new words that students do not know. The students return to their seats and copy down the words on their copy of the photo.
>
> Students work in pairs to categorize the words—either by word structure (words that start with the letter *r*) or by broader subjects (things, people, colors) and then add

new words that fit into those categories. Categories can either be student- or teacher-generated.

Day 2: After reviewing the words on the picture as a class, students are given a series of clozes or gap-fill sentences (see Figure 11.2: Kitchen Picture Cloze Sentences) describing the picture using some of the labeled words. Students complete the sentences, cut them out, and arrange the strips into categories on their desk (being sure to highlight the evidence they are using to support their being placed in a particular category). For example, in the case of Figure 11.2, two categories could be "things that are not living" and "things that are living." Next, students glue the cloze sentences on paper underneath the category title and leave space for additional sentences. They then begin to write new sentences (if they have a high-enough English proficiency level) describing the photo, which they add to their categories.

Day 3: Again, after reviewing the words on the picture, students complete writing new sentences and then turn the them (the cloze sentences and their own) into a paragraph for each category. By the end of the day, they have several parts of a simple essay completed.

Days 4 and 5: These activities depend on the English proficiency level of the students. Newcomers can write a list of potential titles for their essay and choose one to write at the top or complete paragraph frames for simple introduction and conclusion paragraphs. Others can learn to write simple topic sentences for paragraphs ("There are many things in the kitchen."). Higher-level English-proficient students can learn to write introductory paragraphs including hooks and thesis statements, along with conclusions.

Extensions: As students advance, many modifications can be made to the PWIM. In a multilevel class, different students, depending on their English proficiency level, can be asked to do different tasks:

- Instead of clozes, teachers can provide questions to students that they have to answer in sentences and then categorize their responses.
- Students can create clozes themselves that their classmates have to complete and categorize.
- Instead of providing cloze sentences, teachers can create paragraphs about the images with blanks needing to be filled in by students.
- Students can create and write stories about the people and the situation depicted in the image.
- Teachers can identify a somewhat similar image to one being used and have students create a Venn diagram comparing and contrasting one to the other.
- Students can develop thought bubbles for the people or animals in the picture or conversations between people in the image. Our students enjoy this activity.

- Assuming the image is hanging on a whiteboard (or projected on one), students draw what they imagine could be happening in other parts of the image if it were larger (Ferlazzo, 2016, September 23). Even though it gets pretty crowded up there, we sometimes assign groups of students to decide and draw what is happening in different "quadrants" beyond the existing image (Ferlazzo, 2016, September 23). Our students have had a lot of fun with this particular extension.

There are *many* ways to incorporate technology in the PWIM, and we primarily discuss them in the Technology Connections section. However, we did want to highlight one way in particular that we have used technology to make this model a very effective form of assessment.

As an Assessment

Our talented colleague Elisabeth Johnson showed us how to use the PWIM as an assessment tool.

In her ELL U.S. history class, after having used the PWIM for several months, she uploaded a variety of images representing topics they had covered. Then, each student had to create a presentation sharing several slides:

- First, the image labeled with words, like the images previously used in class
- Second, the words listed in three to five categories
- Third, 10 sentences correctly using the words to describe what they saw in the picture
- Fourth, the 10 sentences placed in three to five categories

This assessment strategy can be used in any subject area, and can also be easily made more challenging for students with higher English proficiency. For example, students could then be asked to turn the sentences into paragraphs, including topic sentences, and then convert them into an essay with introductory and concluding paragraphs.

TEXT, PHONICS, AND PICTURE DATA SETS

In the context of inductive learning, data sets are collections of texts, words, or pictures with a common theme. However, if you can't find a copy, searching online for "phonics sheets" will find many alternatives that can be taught in a similar way (creating or purchasing flashcards are another option).

Text Data Sets

Figures 11.3: International New Year's Traditions Data Set (for Intermediates), 11.4: John F. Kennedy Data Set (for Intermediates), and 11.5: Seasons of the Year Data Set (for Beginners) show three examples of text data sets. These data sets are composed of a series of one-sentence examples. Other data sets can be made lengthier and more complex depending on student English proficiency (such as the benefits of reading data set shared previously).

Here is a typical sequence we use while teaching a text data set:

Step 1: Teachers read each sentence or word aloud. For higher-level English-proficient students, texts can be more complex and not necessarily read aloud by the teacher. Instead, students can read them individually or in pairs. Teachers also can add a further step—having students apply a reading comprehension strategy such as summarizing, visualizing, or asking a question of each text item.

Step 2: Students categorize the sentences or words while highlighting evidence supporting their category placement. Teachers can supply the categories or ask students to develop their own. Students then cut and paste the sentences under the category names—this action can make it easier to do the next step. However, we sometimes skip this step due to time constraints and have students simply write the category name next to each sentence.

Step 3: Students add information to their categories either through prior knowledge or through further research (reading, video).

Step 4: Students can either turn those categories into paragraphs (and, ultimately, an entire essay) or be asked to create a poster summarizing the main points of each category and drawing a representative picture. In the latter case, students can subsequently present their posters in small groups.

After students become familiar with the process, we often have students create their own text data sets about topics of high interest (see Figure 11.6: Data Set Instructions for a student guide to create data sets). They then teach an inductive lesson to their classmates in small groups.

Text data sets can also be used to teach language skills and vocabulary, for example, one showing different examples of how punctuation can be used (question marks, exclamation points, quotation marks, etc.). Instead of using those sentences to create essays, students can make posters explaining the rules they have developed from the categorization activity. Or a data set describing events that take place during different parts of the day can be used to teach the concepts of morning, afternoon, and evening.

Phonics Data Sets

Phonics instruction is particularly important for students with interrupted formal education. We teach phonics inductively, and the easiest resource available for this activity is the book *Sounds Easy!* by Sharron Bassano (2002). A sample page from that book teaching the long *a* sound can be found in Figure 11.7. We follow the instructional directions found in the book, which include teachers showing an image on an overhead, saying the word that describes that image, and giving students a few seconds to write it down. Then, the teacher writes the correct word so students can see it and check their work.

We then have students extend this activity to include an inductive process similar to how we use a text data set. Students work in pairs to look for patterns among the words (e.g., *cake, gate, grape, rake*), categorize them (words that have the pattern "consonant-*a*-consonant-*e*"), and identify the appropriate rules (e.g., if the pattern is "consonant-*a*-consonant-*e*" then the word has a long *a* sound). They then consider other words they know or research new ones that follow the same rules. Next, they create posters listing their words and the appropriate rules to share with the class.

An additional extension activity we use is having students draw a picture using as many objects or actions as they can from the *Sounds Easy!* page or from their new ones. Then, they write sentences describing their picture or a story about it.

It is also important to follow up this kind of phonics instruction with phonemic-awareness activities, which we discuss in Strategy 33: Supporting Newcomer ELL & Students With Interrupted Formal Education(SIFEs) with Interrupted Formal Education (SIFEs). In addition, the first two games listed in Strategy 23: Learning Games for Reading and Writing are ones we often use as part of our phonics instruction, and we discuss how we play them there.

Picture Data Sets

Picture data sets can be used in similar ways to text and phonics data sets. They are most easily done online with thematically based categories that are created either by the teacher or student. For example, while studying signs, students can search online for signs fitting into these categories: labels or names, warnings, instruction, and information. There are many free online tools that enable users to create virtual corkboards, where students can easily copy and paste images of signs into categories (see Technology Connections). Students can also write the sign's message in their own words (e.g., "This sign says, do not drive fast."). Transportation is another easy theme for creating this kind of picture data set (e.g., public, cars, sea, air, people-powered, etc.). Students can even use their phones to take photos to add to their categories. Of course, similar projects can also be done by cutting out pictures from magazines and pasting them in categories on poster paper.

Follow-up activities include students presenting their picture data sets to a partner, a small group, or the entire class.

CONCEPT ATTAINMENT

The following explanation, except for the new figures, originally appeared in the *ELL/ESL Teacher's Survival Guide* (Ferlazzo & Sypnieski, 2012).

Concept attainment, originally developed by Jerome Bruner and his colleagues (Bruner, Goodnow, & Austin, 1956) is a form of inductive learning in which the teacher identifies "good" and "bad" examples of the intended learning objective (ideally, either taken from student work—with the names removed, of course—or teacher-created based on review of student writing).

First, the teacher develops sheets similar to the ones in Figures 11.8 and 11.9. Figure 11.8: Concept Attainment Example on Adjectives and Periods is designed to teach that adjectives come before nouns and that periods are placed at the end of sentences. Figure 11.9: Concept Attainment Example on *Has* and *Have* teaches when to use *has* and *have* correctly. The teacher would place the sheet on a document camera or overhead projector. At first, everything would be covered except for the *yes* and *no* titles. Then, the teacher would explain that they are going to give various examples, and students will identify why certain ones are under *yes* and others are under *no*.

After the first *yes* and *no* examples are shown, students are asked to think about them, and share with a partner why they think one is a *yes* and one is a *no*. After the teacher calls on people, if no one can identify the reason(s) (e.g., *have* is used with *they*), the teacher continues uncovering one example at a time. The think-pair-share process continues until students identify the correct reason. Then students are asked to correct the *no* examples and write their own *yes* ones. Last, students can be asked to generate their own *yes* examples and share them with a partner or the class. This inductive learning strategy can be used effectively to teach countless lessons, including ones on grammar, spelling, and composition (Ferlazzo & Sypnieski, *The ESL/ELL Teacher's Survival Guide,* 2012, p. 53).

OTHER INDUCTIVE STRATEGIES

Pre-Reading

Inductive strategies can also be used as a "pre-reading" strategy to introduce students to an upcoming unit. This idea, probably most appropriate for Intermediate and Advanced ELLs, is suggested by educators Matthew Perini, Harvey Silver, and Jay McTighe (2020). In this activity, students are first presented with a collection of 15 to 40 words (we would recommend the lower end of that number), including both words students would be familiar with and ones they would not, that are connected to an upcoming unit or text.

Then, after looking up the definitions of the words they don't know, they need to categorize all of them, while providing reasons for their sorting. Next, they make predictions about what the unit or text is going to be about or what they may be learning. Finally, during the unit or reading of the text, they keep track of, and share, the accuracy or inaccuracy of their predictions.

Scaffolding Writing

Inductive learning and teaching can provide helpful scaffolding for writing. After students become familiar with text data sets and have used them to develop essays, they can still use the inductive process to write essays on their own. We use Figure 11.10: Writing an Essay Flow Chart to guide students to apply this technique to writing. The figure uses the topic of cars as its subject, but it can apply to any topic.

Games

Only Connect was a popular British game show that, in effect, used an inductive teaching and learning process. In it, players had to create categories out of the given words. There are now many other online variations of the game, and it's also easy to play in class with mini-whiteboards. These are discussed in Strategy 23: Learning Games for Reading and Writing.

Teaching Online

All these inductive learning activities can be used in a distance learning situation through Google Docs, Microsoft 365 Online, or other shared online document tools. In remote teaching, online whiteboards, Google Docs, and Google Classroom (or whichever learning management system your district uses) are your, and your students', best friends.

What Could Go Wrong?

Of course, as with every instructional strategy, inductive learning can have a down side. In this case, inductive learning obviously can take a longer period of class time than a deductive lesson. Do we teach everything inductively? Of course not. When it comes to vocabulary, we might sometimes make a pedagogical decision to translate a word into a student's home language instead of spending an extra few minutes to find an image or act it out with gestures and objects. In other words, sometimes we decide that the time saved by teaching a concept explicitly and not inductively creates space for other better learning opportunities.

In addition, another problem of induction is that the conclusions reached through the process are based only on limited examples and do not take exceptions into account. Larry teaches this problem in his International Baccalaureate theory of knowledge classes using the famous example of many people believing all swans were white for many years until black swans were "discovered" in New Zealand. He also uses a more-recent example of playing basketball for years with his friend Don. Larry defends him well because Don almost always drives to the basket with his right hand. However, every now and then Larry is embarrassed on the court when Don chooses to go to his left.

Because there are so many exceptions to just about every rule in English, we "cover" ourselves by regularly telling our students that they will find exceptions to everything and that English is crazy. Most of the time, our students have already figured that out.

Differentiation Recommendations

Newcomers (Preliterate or Low Literacy in Home Language): Focus on teaching phonics inductively at first, primarily using images with words. If you have only one or two students in this situation and don't have a peer or volunteer tutor or student teacher, available to work with them, there are online phonics sites, some of which use artificial intelligence, where they can work independently. See Strategy 33: Supporting Newcomer ELL & Students with Interrupted Formal Education (SIFEs) and Strategy 47: Using Technology for more details. Teachers and students can also create picture data sets.	**Newcomers (Literate in Home Language):** Use the standard picture word inductive model, simple text data sets, and concept attainment for basic concepts.
Intermediate ELLs: Create a "higher bar" in the Picture Word Inductive Model, challenging students to write increasingly more complex sentences, paragraphs, and essays or stories about the images. If in a multilevel class, have students create picture word inductive and text data set lessons for students with a lower English proficiency (see Strategy 39: Peer Teaching & Learning).	**Advanced ELLs:** Once familiar with the Picture Word Inductive Model and with text data sets, students can create their own materials and use them to teach their classmates. They can be given topics, or the leeway to choose their own, and use the inductive strategy to research, organize, and write their own essays (see Figure 11.10: Writing an Essay Flow Chart).

Technology Connections

Of course, the picture word inductive model doesn't require laminating a large image. Though *we* still like doing it this way (call us old-fashioned) because it can be taped and displayed on the wall for students to always see, it's also easy to project the image on a whiteboard that can be annotated. Students can then be distributed hard copies of the image to annotate, or it can be shared to students online.

One technology-based extension activity that we have used with some success is that, after the entire class applies the PWIM to one image, we have asked students to find a similar image online and annotate it on their own.

With the advent of artificial intelligence, students—and teachers—can also create their own text-to-image images. Not only can that reduce or eliminate any concerns about copyright, but it can also increase students' sense of ownership of the activity.

AI can reduce the teacher time required to create text data sets. We have found that it's important to first "teach" AI what a text data set is and then give precise instructions for what we want it to produce. Even though its product typically requires a fair amount of editing, it still takes less time than creating one from scratch.

For example, here is the prompt we gave ChatGPT to create one text data set:

> *A text data set for a classroom lesson is a series of sentences on a particular topic that students can categorize. For example, if I want a text data set on the topic school, the data set would include twelve sentences about school that could be divided into the categories of classes, time periods and extracurricular activities. These sentences would be mixed up. Please create such a data set.*

You can see the result in Figure 11.11: ChatGPT-Created Text Data Set. It requires some editing to make it more relevant to our particular school, but it's a good start.

Technology also makes it as easy as pie for intermediate ELLs students to create their own text data sets (which they can then teach to their classmates) or to add to their already-created categories from teacher-created ones. All they have to do is use the copy-and-paste function for online text, along with including the URL address of their source. See Figure 11.6: Data Set Instructions, which is a student handout describing this process.

Though there are a variety of ways we have our students use AI to assist their language acquisition (see Strategy 47: Using Technology), we explicitly ask our students to not use it when they are creating their own data sets. During this activity, and during others, we often talk as a class about the fact that there will be many times when AI may make tasks easier for them, but at the same time not help them acquire English. We explain that we will use AI in a number of ways to assist in their language learning but would like them to wait to use it in other ways until they become more proficient in their English.

Picture data sets can be easily created by beginning ELLs by using any of many free and easy-to-use sites to create bulletin boards. See The Best Alternatives to the Soon-to-Be-Deceased Google Jamboard (https://larryferlazzo.edublogs.org/2023/10/03/the-best-alternatives-to-the-soon-to-be-deceased-google-jamboard/) and/or The Best Online Virtual

"Corkboards" (https://larryferlazzo.edublogs.org/2011/03/30/the-best-online-virtual-corkboards-or-bulletin-boards/).

Images can be found via Google or at other sites we recommend (http://larryferlazzo.edublogs.org/2016/08/14/the-all-time-best-sources-of-online-images/).

We would like to highlight one exceptional online inductive learning resource, The Smithsonian Learning Lab's Sorting Tool (https://learninglab.si.edu/news/create-interactive-sorting-activities). It allows teachers to create collections, or use existing ones, of Smithsonian objects for students to sort into categories. It's useful for all subject areas.

Additional information on inductive teaching and learning, including many other examples, can be found at The Best Resources About Inductive Learning and Teaching (http://larryferlazzo.edublogs.org/2015/01/16/the-best-resources-about-inductive-learning-teaching/).

Attribution

Portions of this section originally appeared in our book, *The ESL/ELL Teacher's Survival Guide* (Ferlazzo & Sypnieski, 2012, p. 41–43, 53, and 58).

Emily F. Calhoun (1999) is credited with developing the picture word inductive model in her book *Teaching Beginning Reading and Writing with the Picture Word Inductive Model*.

High school teacher and author Elisabeth Johnson introduced us to the idea of using the PWIM as an assessment strategy.

We learned about using inductive learning as a pre-reading activity from "3 Strategies for Deep Virtual Learning" by Matthew J. Perini, Jay McTighe, and Harvey F. Silver, which appear on the ASCD website (https://www.ascd.org/el/articles/3-strategies-for-deep-virtual-learning).

All figures from this chapter, as well as 11 additional chapters, references, hyperlinked Technology Connections, and more online resources, can be found at www.wiley.com/go/ellteacherstoolbox2.

STRATEGY 11: INDUCTIVE LEARNING 143

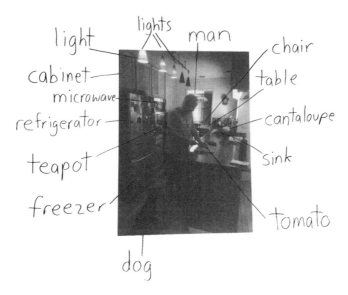

Figure 11.1 A Man in the Kitchen

1. The refrigerator is _____.

   closed   soft   tiny   open

2. The _____ is on the _____.

   tomato   man   stove   teapot

3. The _____ is above the stove.

   refrigerator   sink   microwave   dog

4. The _____ is behind the cantaloupe.

   man   dog   refrigerator   sink

5. The dog is looking at the _____.

   refrigerator   table   man   light

Figure 11.2 Kitchen Picture Cloze Sentences

6. There are _____ above the _____ and microwave.

freezer refrigerator dishes cabinets

7. The freezer is below the _____.

floor dog refrigerator chair

8. The _____ is cutting a tomato.

dog man chair teapot

Figure 11.2 (Continued)

Categories: Food, Names of New Year, Times of New Year, How New Year Is Celebrated

1. Many cultures celebrate New Year's Day on January 1st.
2. The Chinese New Year is also called the Lunar New Year.
3. There is always a big celebration in Times Square in New York City on New Year's Eve.
4. The Persian New Year is called Nauruz.
5. Khabse are cookies that are only made on Losar, the Tibetan New Year.
6. Rosh Hashanah is the name of the Jewish New Year.
7. Losar is the name of the Tibetan New Year.
8. Seven foods starting with the letter *s* are served on the Persian New Year.
9. Apples and honey are served on Rosh Hashanah.
10. The Vietnamese New Year is usually on the same day as the Chinese New Year.
11. The Islamic New Year is also known as the Hijri New Year.
12. In Vietnam the new year usually begins in February.
13. A shofar (ram's horn) is blown during Rosh Hashanah.

Figure 11.3 International New Year's Traditions Data Set (for Intermediates)

STRATEGY 11: INDUCTIVE LEARNING

Categories: Family, Accomplishments, and Challenges

1. John F. Kennedy was president of the United States from 1961 to 1963.
2. Kennedy was married to Jacqueline Kennedy and had three children. One died shortly after birth.
3. His ship was sunk in World War II and he almost died.
4. He was a United States senator from 1953 to 1961.
5. He was the first Catholic to become president. Some voters did not support him because of his faith.
6. He was assassinated by Lee Harvey Oswald on November 22, 1963.
7. Kennedy supported exploring space and promised that the United States would put a person on the moon.
8. He was the youngest person ever to be elected president.
9. He was the youngest president to die.
10. Kennedy wrote a book, *Profiles in Courage*, which won many awards.
11. He challenged the Soviet Union when that country put nuclear missiles in Cuba.
12. His father was the U.S. ambassador to England, and his two brothers became U.S. senators.

Figure 11.4 John F. Kennedy Data Set (for Intermediates)

Categories: Summer, Fall, Winter, and Spring

1. Students start going to school.
2. It's cold.
3. It rains or snows a lot.
4. It's very hot.
5. The leaves change color.
6. Christmas takes place during this season.
7. School ends when this season begins.
8. Cinco de Mayo takes place during this season.
9. Flowers bloom.
10. Most students don't go to school.

Figure 11.5 Seasons of the Year Data Set (for Beginners)

1. Choose a topic and pick at least four categories about that topic.
2. Create a document named *Data Set Answer Key* and type the names of your categories there.
3. Look for information on one category.
4. Choose at least three passages of no more than five sentences each that relate to that category.
5. Copy and paste those three passages on that document under the name of that category on the Data Set Answer Key.
6. Repeat this process with your other three categories.
7. Now, create a new document and title it *Data Set for Students*. Type the names of your four categories under the title.
8. Now copy and paste all 12 passages on to this document so they are mixed up. In other words, passages from the same category are not next to each other. Once they are mixed up, number each passage.

Figure 11.6 Data Set Instructions

STRATEGY 11: INDUCTIVE LEARNING *147*

Sounds Easy! _____

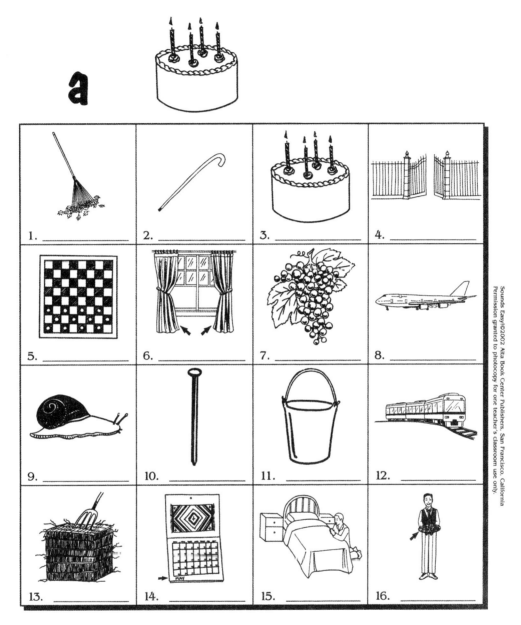

Figure 11.7 Page from *Sounds Easy! Phonics, Spelling, and Pronunciation Practice*
Source: Reproduced by permission of S. Bassano. Palm Springs, California USA. Copyright 2002 ALTA English Publishers.

Yes	No
He has a brown shirt.	
	She has a t-shirt pink.
She has a small dog.	
	The eagle has eyes big.
She has blue eyes.	
	He has hair black.

Figure 11.8 Concept Attainment Example on Adjectives and Periods

Yes	No
She has shoes.	
	She have a small house.
She has a black shirt.	
	He have two cars.
He has blue eyes.	
They have a big house.	
	They has a dog.
John and Ana have a dog.	
	Carlos, Ava, and Leo has a cat.

Figure 11.9 Concept Attainment Example on *Has* and *Have*

STRATEGY 11: INDUCTIVE LEARNING 149

Writing an Essay

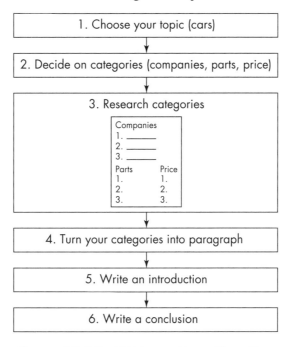

Figure 11.10 Writing an Essay Flow Chart

1. I have English class in the morning.
2. After lunch, we have a science experiment in the lab.
3. The math teacher assigns homework every day.
4. I enjoy playing soccer during recess.
5. In the afternoon, we have art class.
6. Our school offers a chess club for students interested in strategy games.
7. The history lesson is after the break.
8. We have a basketball practice in the gym after school.
9. During lunchtime, we can play board games in the cafeteria.
10. On Fridays, we have a music class where we learn to play instruments.
11. I participate in the school choir during music periods.
12. The school organizes a debate club for students interested in public speaking.

Figure 11.11 ChatGPT-Created Text Data Set

STRATEGY 12
Retrieval Practice

What Is It?

Retrieval practice is the . . . practice of remembering something that you've learned previously without any reminders or clues being immediately available to you. In other words, the information you're remembering is not in front of you on a piece of paper. Flashcards and quizzes are the most common examples of retrieval practice, but there are many other types, as well. Retrieval practice will then make that information more easily available to you in the future when you need it. It increases the likelihood that the knowledge you have acquired will be moved into long-term memory.

Why We Like It

We like this strategy because it can be used in many different forms, and it's not too difficult to help students understand its value, too. Many teachers, including us, use (and have used) versions of it (flashcards, quizzes, tests) without knowing the term "retrieval practice." Because of that prior knowledge, it's relatively easy to apply it in different ways once learning more about it.

Supporting Research

Hermann Ebbinghaus created a mathematical formula in 1885 that has since been replicated suggesting that we tend to forget *a lot* of what we learn 24 hours after first learning it. Retrieval Practice is one way to "beat" this curve by moving knowledge into long-term memory. There is so much research available finding its effectiveness as a learning strategy (i.e. Adesope et al., 2017; Agarwal et al., 2021) that there is little dispute about its overall effectiveness, though valuable research still can be done about particular ways to apply it. Studies have also found that making students aware of its benefits can enhance its effectiveness in the classroom (Simon et al., 2023). Specific research on ELLs has found that quizzing, flashcards, and "brain dumps" (all which are discussed in this chapter or elsewhere in this book) are specifically useful in vocabulary instruction (Strong, 2023). Finally, games where students have to recall knowledge they have learned have also been found to be an effective form of retrieval practice (Whitt & Haselgrove, 2023).

Common Core Connections

Though increased retention of knowledge can have a positive impact on all of the Common Core Standards, it can have a particular impact for ELLs in the four standards under the heading "Vocabulary Acquisition and Use."

Application

We'll cover a few ways we use retrieval practice with our ELL students. We'll discuss some in detail, including how we teach students about retrieval practice in the context of open-book tests and "brain dumps," along with "retrieval practice notebooks."

Flashcards are another key retrieval practice tool, and we devote an entire separate chapter to it (see Bonus Strategy 9: Flashcards available at www.wiley.com/go/ellteachers toolbox2). Learning games that require active recall also use retrieval practice strategies, and we have two other chapters on them (see Strategy 23: Learning Games for Reading and Writing and Strategy 31: Learning Games for Speaking and Listening).

We discuss "do-nows" in Strategy 45: Beginning and Ending of Class. It is easy to incorporate retrieval practice in that activity by including questions based on previous lessons. For example, in an ELL History Class, we sometimes include three questions: one based on a lesson from the day before, another from a week earlier, and a third from the previous month.

QUIZZES AND TESTS

Some educators suggest that retrieval practice is a *learning* strategy and not an *assessment* strategy, so that tests don't really count as retrieval practice. We're not convinced that there is a difference. Though research is not definitive on this topic, some believe that retrieval practice is most effective in a low-stakes environment. Since we consider most of our tests to be "low-stakes," the difference doesn't really matter in our classrooms.

In Larry's ELL History classes, open-book tests are the rule. However, he incorporates retrieval practice in some different ways.

First, he teaches his students about the concept through the use of two read alouds (Figure 12.1: Knowledge Read Aloud and Figure 12.2: Memory Read Aloud). They are designed to introduce students to the idea of retrieval practice and how they will be applied in class. Basically, students first try to answer the questions on the test with their book closed. After they have tried doing the test using that method, they can then check their answers by using the book—there is no grade penalty for doing so. It's an effort at encouraging students to practice self-regulated learning.

In addition, students in those classes are asked to add a page to their test called a "brain dump." This form of "free recall" (Agarwal, 2018) asks students to write down anything else they can remember about the topic (without looking at the book) that is being studied that was not on the test. Larry is regularly more impressed by what students write there than by their test answers.

In our ELL newcomers classes, we use retrieval practice in three important ways:

1. During the week, regularly having students quiz each other (or have a peer tutor quiz them) using mini-whiteboards on words or grammar we are learning.

2. Peer tutors, or absent them, we give a practice test midweek prior to Friday's "official" test. In addition to these practice tests being another form of retrieval practice, they have been found to reduce test anxiety (von der Embse & Witmer, 2014).

3. Spend one week each month reviewing words and grammar that were learned during the previous three weeks. We didn't take this time in the past in an effort to "cover" everything we felt needed to be covered. We learned the hard way that knowledge not reviewed is often knowledge not remembered.

RETRIEVAL PRACTICE NOTEBOOKS

We initially developed and used "retrieval practice notebooks" in a support class for long-term ELLs and then later used them regularly in our intermediate ELL class as a language practice activity and to also support our students in their other classes.

First, as in the History class example, we taught our students about retrieval practice through a read aloud (see Figure 12.3: Learning and Remembering Read Aloud). We modify it depending on the English language proficiency of the class.

We then give each student a composition notebook. In it, we ask them each day to write one sentence about what they think was the most important thing they learned in each of their classes during the previous day (they can also draw it). We will share some models, and periodically use concept attainment (see Strategy 11: Inductive Learning) using both "good" and "bad" examples from their notebooks to help them refine their writing. This is particularly important since they frequently have a challenge distinguishing between "what they did" and "what they learned." We then often, though not always, do "speed dating," where students share what they wrote with a few of their classmates and then ask a few to share examples out loud with the entire class.

We "mix it up" sometimes by asking students to review what they wrote during the previous week and pick the one thing they think is most important and why, or what is an example of something they learned that they can apply outside of school. Sometimes we'll ask them to focus on "what they did" by asking them to highlight what activity in each class they liked the most that week (which, if we have time, we'll share with that teacher).

It's also easy to alternate the use of composition notebooks with a digital one where students can write and also include images.

The entire process usually takes 10 minutes or less. If it's done the same way each day, it can get a bit boring for students. But that's why it's critical to regularly change it around; it's fine to keep the same basic format, but adding questions, changing how responses are shared, alternating between hard paper and digital notebooks are all ways to keep the activity fresh.

Finally, a not insignificant benefit to this activity is that the students' content teachers love it! And any way we encourage non-ELL teachers to appreciate ELL students more is definitely a net positive.

Teaching Online

All the strategies discussed in this chapter can be utilized online. However, helping students understand its learning value is even more critical in an online environment. Teachers won't be at their home ensuring that they are actually "remembering" and not looking up the answer, so students will need to "own" its importance themselves.

What Could Go Wrong?

Using retrieval practice activities like quizzes and do-nows to emphasize student recall of facts and information is a valid and important goal. However, it's also easy to fall into the trap of just using it for that purpose and not using it to also challenge students to apply higher-order thinking skills to retrieval practice.

Ways to incorporate higher-order thinking skills into retrieval practice could include:

- Categorizing (List all the words you can think of related to school or make a list of irregular verbs.)
- Knowledge transfer (What are two things you learned last week that you can apply outside of class, and how can you apply them?)
- Argument (List five adjectives and explain which one best describes this class, or What are three things we learned about the January 6th Insurrection and what is your opinion about it?)
- Summarizing (Which of these three statements most accurately portray the reasons given for the imprisonment of Japanese-Americans during World War II?)

For retrieval practice notebooks, the biggest mistake that can be made, and we have made it, is getting into the rut of doing it the same way every day. We included ideas in the narrative about how to mix it up, and we would strongly suggest you heed them.

Differentiation Recommendations

Newcomers (Preliterate or Low Literacy in Home Language): Retrieval practice can begin with simple activities, like having teachers or peer tutors say a word and then have students point to objects or images. Flashcard activities work well for all ELLs, especially with students in this "category." See Bonus Strategy 9: Flashcards (available at www.wiley.com/go/ellteacherstoolbox2) for specific ideas. Students can also benefit from drawing what they learned in retrieval practice notebooks. And games can be fun retrieval practice activities for *all* students.	**Newcomers (Literate in Home Language):** "Do-nows," quizzes, games, and retrieval practice notebooks (with Google Translate assistance) can be successfully used with students. "Brain dumps" ("List all the words you can think of related to food") can also work well.
Intermediate ELLs: More complex "do-nows," quizzes, and games can be used with this group, and teachers can have higher expectations for what is written and shared in the retrieval practice notebook.	**Advanced ELLs:** All the strategies listed in the chapter can be used, incorporating questions with greater complexity. In addition, students themselves can be asked to create the questions used in games, tests, do-nows and, in fact, online games themselves.

Technology Connections

To learn even more about retrieval practice and different ways to apply it in the classroom, visit The Best Resources for Learning About Retrieval Practice (https://larryferlazzo.edublogs.org/2017/10/22/the-best-resources-for-learning-about-retrieval-practice/).

Though, at least in our experience, it's likely that only the most self-motivated students will spend a significant amount of their own time using retrieval practice at home, we always do place links to Quizizz and Kahoot games, as well as to other sites, on our Google Classroom for students to use (assuming they have Internet service at their residence).

Of course, artificial intelligence offers another potentially engaging way for students to study on their own. Using a chatbot or, by the time you're reading this, some other more advanced tool will be able to quiz students on any topic of their choosing.

STRATEGY 12: RETRIEVAL PRACTICE

All figures from this chapter, as well as 11 additional chapters, references, hyperlinked Technology Connections, and more online resources, can be found at www.wiley.com/go/ellteacherstoolbox2 and the following QR code.

As we have been learning about the past, we have also been learning about how it is connected to today and in the future.

For example, when we talked about how the National Anthem was created, we also talked about the protests begun by Colin Kaepernick. We learned a little bit about the real story of the Mexican-American War and its impact on us today. When learning about Harriet Tubman, we learned about the controversy related to putting her image on the 20-dollar bill.

It is important to have knowledge, and to remember it, so we can think about how yesterday helps shape today and tomorrow. This knowledge will help us participate in making decisions about what happens in our country.

We are learning many things this year in U.S. History. In fact, you might be learning more in this class than in any other U.S. History class in this school since this is the first time you are studying it. Most other students who have been in this country longer than you have spent many years learning about our country's history.

And at the same time you are learning about history, you are learning a new language.

It's a lot to learn.

And a lot to remember.

Writing Prompt:

Please write a one- or two-sentence summary—in your own words—of this read aloud. Do you agree with what it says? Why or why not?

Figure 12.1 Knowledge Read Aloud

Our first read aloud talked about the importance of knowledge and memory. There are two main types of memory: short-term memory and long-term memory. In our short-term memory, we remember things for a short time before we forget them or until we transfer that knowledge to long-term memory.

We keep things in our long-term memory that we are going to remember for a longer time.

Scientists have found that one of the best ways to help move knowledge into our long-term memory is through "retrieval practice." It's basically forcing ourselves to remember things.

We are going to start doing this through two ways:

- First, some of the warm-ups will ask you to write down answers to questions about things we've learned before. You will not be graded on it. But we hope that it might encourage you to focus more on what we study in class so you will remember more. The more you remember, the more you will be able to be an active citizen in today's world and apply what you know to what's going on today. We all know that we have many challenges right now in our world.
- Second, when we do the unit tests, you will first try answering them without looking at the book. Then, after you have tried answering them without the book, you will have a chance to review and change your answers with the book. You will be graded only on your final answers.

When you take each test, though, we'll ask you to write down in your notebook how many questions you answered on the test correctly without looking at your book. The teachers won't look at what you wrote, but you will know how much each time you really learned and will remember. Like the warm-ups, we hope that this process will also encourage you to focus more on what we study in class so you will remember more.

Writing Prompt:

Please write a one- or two-sentence summary—in your own words—of this read aloud. Do you think the two changes are worth trying? Why or why not?

Figure 12.2 Memory Read Aloud

STRATEGY 12: RETRIEVAL PRACTICE 157

Scientists have discovered that without any reinforcement, information is quickly forgotten—"roughly 56 percent in one hour, 66 percent after a day, and 75 percent after six days" (Source: Tereda, 2017).

They have also found that the best kind of reinforcement is called "retrieval practice." This means you are pushed to remember what you learned in one place and in one situation in a different one. Retrieval practice could be tests and quizzes, flashcards, or students sharing the most important thing they learned at the end of class.

When you are pushed to "retrieve" that information, it then gets put into what is called long-term memory.

You may or may not think it's important to remember a lot of what you learn in your classes.

However, it is important for three reasons:

- Of course, there will be tests in your classes (called "summative") where you need to use the information you learned to answer questions or do projects way-past six days after you originally learned it.
- Much of what you learn this year will help you do well in future classes you will take here and in college. If you forget the writing skills you learn in ninth-grade English, you are going to have a lot of problems in tenth-grade English; not remembering what you learn in geography is going to make your world history class much harder next year.
- When we're young, even though we tend to think we know all the answers, we don't necessarily know what knowledge will help us in the future. That doesn't mean we need to try to remember everything we learn. It just means we need to be aware that some things we don't think are important may be important in the future. It may not be wise to just dismiss a great deal of information from classes as not very useful to us.

Reference: Tereda, Y. (2017, September 20.) Why Students Forget—and What You Can Do About It. *Edutopia*. Retrieved from www.edutopia.org/article/why-students-forget-and-what-you-can-do-about-it

Prompt:

What does this read aloud say about the importance of memory and retrieval practice. Do you agree with it? Please support your position with examples from the article, other texts you've read, and/or your observations and personal experiences.

Figure 12.3 Learning and Remember Read Aloud

STRATEGY 13

Teaching Grammar

What Is It?

Grammar is a key element of language, and students need to learn it to develop English language fluency. Unfortunately, much grammar instruction in our schools, and not only in our ELL classes, is the "drill-and-kill" variety. This chapter will offer some ideas for grammar instruction that might make it more engaging—and effective—for students and teachers alike.

Why We Like It

We like the strategies discussed in this chapter because they prioritize student engagement. You will not often find "drill-and-kill" and "engagement" in the same sentence! Don't get us wrong—we're not opposed to having students spend limited time completing short worksheets reinforcing important concepts. But they have to be on the "undercard" to the "main event."

Supporting Research

Researchers agree that understanding grammar is a critical part of acquiring English to communicate effectively (Zhang, 2009). Studies have found that teaching it interactively through small groups (Mu, 2010) using puzzles and games can be effective strategies for grammar instruction (Fauzi & Munawaroh, 2024). Finally, it's important to pursue opportunities to teach grammar in context (Mart, 2013)—in other words, teaching grammar skills when doing other aspects of the curriculum, like reading, writing, during read alouds, etc. (Williams-Pinnock, 2021).

Common Core Connections

The Anchor Standards for Language specifically call out the importance of understanding the conventions of grammar and usage in speaking and writing.

STRATEGY 13: TEACHING GRAMMAR

Application

Here's the process we typically use over a day or two when teaching grammar. (Do we use every step *every* time? No! But we do use all the steps more often than not.)

1. We teach the grammar concepts in the sequence laid out in the district "mandated" grammar book. Most textbooks, to a large extent, use similar sequences, and we don't have strong preferences about the order. The added advantage of using it is that it lets us say that we are using the district textbook, even though we may be ignoring other large parts of it.

    Though we are agnostic about the sequence, we are definitely not agnostic about the relatively minor role it has in our teaching.

    So, we'll begin with a short explicit lesson on a grammar topic (or two connected ones), followed by students, generally in small peer tutor-led groups, completing the textbook practice questions that reinforce the concept.

    After students have completed the textbook exercises, we have them write several original sentences using the targeted grammar concept. We find that it is important to have students actively apply and produce new grammar knowledge as quickly as possible.

2. Next, we give students a chart that might look something like Figure 13.1: Sentence Puzzle. We borrowed the name and modified the idea from language teacher Gianfranco Conti. The chart identifies different parts of a sentence (Figure 13.1 is a simple "Subject-Verb-Object," but others might be "Subject-Verb-Adjective" or "Subject-Verb-Adjective-Object" depending on what we are covering that day). We'll say five or six simple sentences (or give a list of the sentences for a peer tutor to say) that include the grammar topic and ask students to write the words in the appropriate sections of the chart. This activity reinforces the grammar topic *and* serves as listening practice (Conti, 2016b).

3. Then, students complete one or two pages of sentence navigators (Bonus Strategy 3: Sentence Navigators and Sentence Builders) that also apply the grammar topic and perhaps introduce or review other grammar topics or vocabulary. We also include "expanding sentences" in them, where there may be an additional word, two or three beyond the ones used in the sentence puzzles. Students may not fully understand why an article is used in one of the sentences or what an exclamation point is but, as Gianfranco Conti suggests, by incorporating future topics to be covered, it allows students to begin to develop prior knowledge that they will be able to connect to in future lessons. He calls this "planting the seed" (Conti, 2016a).

    We provide the correct sentences we want used in the navigators, and peer tutors create the entire worksheets during their "downtime" (for example, when students are doing independent practice on laptops). Since peer tutors are sometimes absent, we also generally have one or two extra tutors who fill in for them. When everyone is there, these extra tutors can be available to create materials. AI chatbots can also be used.

4. Next, comes expanded scrambled sentences (see Figure 13.2: Expanded Sentence Scramble & Answer Sheet, which we used when teaching about quotation marks when our students were writing a story). Less English-proficient students can just work on the first one in each category, while more proficient students can complete all of them. These are typically done in peer tutor-led groups.

   It's pretty easy for teachers to create these and is becoming even easier with artificial intelligence. Upload a couple of example sheets to a chatbot, explain the grammar topic you want to focus on, and tell it to replicate one in a similar form.

   You'll note that Figure 13.2 shows an easy way to differentiate instruction—the three sentences in each section get progressively more complex. Students less proficient in English can just be asked to "unscramble" the first sentence in each section, instead of doing all of them.

5. We "wrap up" the lesson with an online Quizizz or Kahoot game reinforcing the concept, which also functions as a formative assessment.

Follow-up:

- Based on what we see in formative assessments and in student writing, we'll also periodically do concept attainment exercises (see Strategy 11: Inductive Learning) to review certain grammar topics where additional support is needed.
- One of the main online sites for student independent practice is an online grammar tool called Quill. There are a number of other options, and these sites are a relatively engaging way to reinforce grammar concepts. They can also, as Dr. Conti suggests, "plant more seeds" for future grammar instruction.
- We are always looking for opportunities to highlight grammar concepts when practicing reading and writing during other times. In other words, we try to apply the evidence-supported idea of "teaching grammar in context" (Mart, 2013).

Teaching Online

All these grammar-teaching ideas can be used online, though, as in practically all the strategies discussed in this book, it would be important to emphasize to students that asking artificial intelligence for the answers without first trying themselves won't help them learn English.

What Could Go Wrong?

Don't rigidly stick to any kind of "formula" when teaching grammar. "Go with the flow," and use our suggested sequence when it seems to make sense and work, making adjustments whenever appropriate. Don't forget to teach grammar in context! It's easy for teachers to think once the grammar concept has been taught that we can put it out of our mind, but there's so much else to teach! Do whatever you need to do to remind yourself to include highlighting grammar elements when teaching other lessons.

Differentiation Recommendations

Newcomers (Preliterate or Low Literacy in Home Language): Initially reducing the number and simplifying the grammar exercises these new students have to do is an easy way to differentiate instruction. As noted in the narrative, having scrambled sentences progressing in complexity can help students learn at their language level and gain self-confidence. At the time we are writing this book, artificial intelligence–powered text-to-video tools have not reached a point of high quality. However, when they do, students (or teachers or peer tutors) may be able to type in sentences that would then be "acted out" on video. These might be able to enhance comprehension.	**Newcomers (Literate in Home Language):** These newcomer students should be able access the entire grammar teaching process as outlined in the chapter.
Intermediate ELLs: Not only should intermediates be able to access the entire outlined grammar-teaching process, but they should be able to create some of the teaching materials that can be used by their classmates, like the sentence navigators and expanded sentence scrambles.	**Advanced ELLs:** Again, these students will be able to benefit from the grammar teaching sequence and should be able to create more complex teaching materials that can be used by their classmates and newcomer/intermediate classes.

Technology Connections

Get more ideas about grammar instruction, including recommended practice websites for students, at The Best Sites for Grammar Practice (https://larryferlazzo.edublogs.org/2008/12/07/the-best-sites-for-grammar-practice).

Attribution

Thank you to Gianfranco Conti for some excellent grammar teaching ideas! *Gianfranco Conti, PhD*

All figures from this chapter, as well as 11 additional chapters, references, hyperlinked Technology Connections, and more online resources, can be found at www.wiley.com/go/ellteacherstoolbox2.

Example teacher-read sentence:

1. The boy throws the ball.

Subject	Verb	Object
1. *Boy* or *The boy*	throws	*ball* or *the ball*
2.		
3.		
4.		
5.		
6.		

Figure 13.1 Sentence Puzzle

Name:_____ Date:_____ Per.__

1. "hello. boy the said " ,
2. hello boy the said little " , . "
3. The hello little said little " , . " boy

_____
_____
_____

1. ! Ferlazzo Ricardo. said is "Mr. great"
2. ! Ferlazzo a Ricardo. teacher said is "Mr. great"
3. ! Ferlazzo really a Ricardo. said is "Mr. great" teacher

_____
_____
_____

Figure 13.2 Expanded Sentence Scramble & Answer Sheet

1. you?" are asked Alma . " how
2. you?" asked today Alma . " how are
3. you?" today doing Alma . " how asked are

_____
_____
_____

1. " Sara. stop" yelled !
2. " Sara. stop" it ! yelled
3. Sara stop" it now yelled ! .

_____
_____
_____

1. Yissel. "Give me," it to " asked
2. Yissel. please "Give me," to " asked it
3. Yissel. "Give me," to " now asked it please

_____
_____
_____

Figure 13.2 (Continued)

Answer Sheet

1. The boy said, "Hello." OR "Hello," said the boy.
2. The little boy said, "Hello."
3. The happy little boy said, "Hello." OR The little happy boy said, "Hello."

1. "Mr. Ferlazzo is great!" said Ricardo.
2. "Mr. Ferlazzo is a great teacher!" said Ricardo.
3. "Mr. Ferlazzo is a really great teacher!" said Ricardo.

1. "How are you?" asked Alma. OR Alma asked, "How are you?"
2. "How are you today?" asked Alma.
3. "How are you doing today?" asked Alma.

1. "Stop!" yelled Sara.
2. "Stop it!" yelled Sara.
3. "Stop it now!" yelled Sara.

1. "Give it to me," asked Yissel.
2. "Please give it to me," asked Yissel.
3. "Please give it to me now," asked Yissel.

Figure 13.2 (Continued)

STRATEGY 14
Writing Frames and Writing Structures

What Is It?

Writing frames are commonly described as templates that include sentence starters, connecting words, and an overall structure that provides extensive scaffolding to a student responding to a question or prompt (Warwick et al., 2010, p. 4). Writing structures is the term sometimes used to describe a "series of instructional prompts" designed to support students creating sentences themselves in responding to a question or prompt (Carthew & Scitt, 2015, p. 3).

These definitions are not necessarily formally recognized universally by educators or researchers. We tend to view writing frames and writing structures as a continuum. Both are steps along the way where students can use their experience to apply the writing strategies they have gained to writing situations in which no teacher scaffolds are available to them.

Individual sentence starters can perform similar functions in response to simple questions (you'll find an example in Strategy 4: Vocabulary and in other portions of this book) and are at the very beginning of the continuum. Here, though, we are concentrating on assisting ELLs to write lengthier pieces of writing.

Why We Like It

Writing frames and writing structures hold many benefits for English language learners:

- Providing models for how words and phrases look within a logical context
- Allowing teachers and students to focus on the key target language that is the emphasis of that current lesson
- Reducing student stress levels—as second-language learners ourselves (Spanish), we know it can be intimidating to be given a question or a task, along with a blank piece of paper

- Building on the Zeigarnik effect, which says we tend to want to finish something that we have started (Dean, n.d.b); sentence starters can have the effect of calling out to students that they want to be completed

Supporting Research

Writing frames and writing structures have been found to support greater writing fluency among English-proficient students (Carthew & Scitt, 2015; Warwick et al., 2010; Zeleo, 2021). In addition, they have also been shown to be effective when used with English language learners (George, 2011; Reyes, 2015).

Common Core Connections

No surprises here—writing frames and writing structures fit in with most of the Writing Standards. If you use ideas in the Technology Connections section, you can hit them all!

Application

As we mentioned when we first described this strategy, we view it as part of a continuum—beginning with simple single-sentence starters (also called stems); then moving on to writing frames that are basically fill-in-the-blank sentences; followed by writing structures in which scaffolding is provided but sentences are student-created; and, finally, to students using all their past experience and present skills to write without teacher-generated scaffolds.

And, as we've discussed in several chapters, we acknowledge to students that artificial intelligence is creating a world where they may very well not be required to do a lot of writing "from scratch" during their lives. Nevertheless, we explain, it will be important for them to do this kind of writing to help them acquire fluency in English, to make sure that AI is writing accurately, to improve on the quality of AI writing when they review it, and to be able to develop their own writing voice.

We introduce the importance of writing for the purpose of learning English through a simple lesson we describe in the next section. We should point out that we both do a different kind of lesson with our English-proficient students about the value of writing—for learning content, for processing emotions, for reflection. However, we feel our lesson plan for ELLs not only has to be more accessible language-wise, but we also recognize that ELLs can gain some of those same benefits from writing in their home language and not in English.

We certainly support the development of writing skills in our students' home languages (see Strategy 42: Translanguaging). But it is also our responsibility to help them develop writing skills in English. So, because of that responsibility, the content of our ELL lesson has a different focus.

We should also point out that most of the time we have students use writing frames and writing structures with pen/pencil and paper, for their first drafts at least. We do this both because it tends to be student preference and because it reduces the temptation to use artificial intelligence to do their writing for them (we also discuss the benefits and pitfalls of Google Translate in the "What Could Go Wrong" section of this chapter). However, we sometimes encourage students to use ChatGPT or Gemini for revision purposes, as we explain in Strategy 20: Revision.

LEARNING ABOUT THE IMPORTANCE OF WRITING IN ENGLISH LANGUAGE ACQUISITION

We begin our lesson by explaining what we said earlier—that though they will be using artificial intelligence a lot in their lives to help their writing, it's also important for them to learn to write in English on their own because learning to do so is critical to their success in learning English.

We also point out that this does not mean that we'll never suggest that they use artificial intelligence. In fact, we think AI can have an important role in helping them learn to read and speak English and to also improve their writing skills, particularly in revising and editing what they write from "scratch." We discuss these ways in Strategy 1: Independent Reading, Strategy 25: Conversation Practice, and Strategy 20: Revision.

Next, after we give all students mini-whiteboards, we ask them to think for a minute about why they think learning to write in English is important. We ask them to write their thoughts on their whiteboard and then have them share what they wrote with a partner. We tell them they can change what they wrote on their board if they want based on what their partner said.

We then ask everyone to lift their boards up and ask a few to say what they wrote. During this time, we write a list of their ideas on a sheet at the document camera.

We then add other reasons to the list—if they have not been shared. If we are teaching intermediate or advanced ELLs, we talk about them like this:

- Writing gives you more time to think about and remember vocabulary and grammar rules than when you're speaking, so it serves as a good practice tool. It will help you speak more easily and confidently because writing and speaking both require you to produce language.
- It's easier to see how you have progressed in your English by comparing what you wrote before with what you write today and what you will write in the future.
- Artificial intelligence tools make mistakes. You need to know how to write in English so you can fix those mistakes.
- You're not always going to have access to artificial intelligence, so there will likely be times when you will have to do some writing in English.

If we are doing this lesson with beginning ELLs, we simplify these four reasons:

- Writing gives you more time to think about English and lets you practice.
- It lets you see how much you get better over time.

- It helps you see and fix mistakes made by artificial intelligence.
- It helps you communicate when you don't have artificial intelligence around.

With intermediates or advanced ELLs, we then ask each student to create a poster using one of the following sentence starters:

A time when writing in English helped me improve my English was when..... OR

I think the most important reason for learning to write in English is.....because.....

We ask them to illustrate their posters, share them with classmates, and then tape some to the classroom walls to act as reminders for the future.

With beginning ELLs, we ask them to create a poster to decide which one of the reasons they think is most important for learning to write in English and then use this sentence starter:

I think the most important reason for learning to write in English is.....

We ask them to illustrate their posters, share them with classmates, and then tape some to the classroom walls.

WRITING FRAMES

Writing frames are extended fill-in-the-blank outlines and can be an important scaffold for English Language Learners.

Figure 14.1: George Washington Writing Frame is an example of a fill-in-the-blank writing frame. These writing frames differ from clozes because the blanks can require more than one word.

Figure 14.1 was given to beginning ELL students after we did a teacher read aloud and watched a simple animated video (with English subtitles) on George Washington. Students were asked to write a response to the question, "Why is it important to know about George Washington?" We were trying to teach the concept of topic sentences and supporting details. We read the writing frame aloud before students were given a few minutes to write on their own. They then shared what they wrote with a partner—orally and by showing them. Next, they were given a minute to make changes based on feedback from their partner. We then reviewed topic sentences and supporting details in a visual way by holding up our wooden stool and explaining that the top was like a topic sentence and the legs were the supporting details.

Figure 14.2: Mexico Writing Frame is an example of a more-complex writing frame for intermediate ELLs. After studying a text data set (see Strategy 11: Inductive Learning), students were given this writing frame, called an *ABC model* (*a*nswer the question; *b*ack it up with a quotation; make a *c*omment or *c*onnection).

STRATEGY 14: WRITING FRAMES AND WRITING STRUCTURES

After students completed it, we then used a pair-share process. While that sharing was going on, we were circulating around the room looking for student examples that we could show to the class (with student permission)—particularly ones that had a good paraphrase of the quotation they used. Paraphrasing well is not easy for ELLs, which is why we have a separate strategy on it (see Strategy 15: Quoting, Summarizing, and Paraphrasing).

After students shared with a partner, they had a chance to make revisions, and we then highlighted examples of finished student work on the document camera.

Figure 14.3: Writing About a Movie and Figure 14.4: Writing About a Book are writing frames that we offer to students to use at home for "extra credit" or for a practice writing assignment in class. As you can see, they are almost identical.

WRITING STRUCTURES

As we have previously explained, writing structures do not usually contain sentence starters or connectors. Instead, questions or additional prompts are provided by the teacher. For example:

- Figure 14.5: Mexico Writing Structure illustrates one way to turn the Mexico Writing Frame into a writing structure using the ABC format. It turns the sentence starters into questions.
- Figure 14.6: ABC Writing Structure is a writing structure from our colleague Jen Adkins that also uses the ABC format but contains less scaffolding.
- Figure 14.7: PEE Writing Structure is a writing structure from our colleague Antoine Germany and uses the PEE format: *point, evidence, explain*. Obviously this acronym, if used in younger learners, may elicit some giggling.
- Figure 14.8: RACE Writing Structure contains several graphics from teacher Meghan Everette illustrating the RACE writing structure (*restate, answer, cite the source, explain/examples*).
- Figure 14.9: AREE! Writing Structure is our final writing structure graphic. It's from our colleague Mary Osteen, who calls it AREE (she enjoys pronouncing it like a pirate *ARRRR!*). It stands for *assertion, reason, evidence, explanation*. What makes it even more effective is the grid puzzle she uses with students to teach its elements. That grid can be found in Figure 14.10: AREE! Writing Structure Teaching Grid.

Perhaps the most popular writing structures in many schools are the ones found in the well-known book, *They Say, I Say: The Moves That Matter in Academic Writing* (Graff & Birkenstein, 2015). We use those resources with our more-advanced ELLs. See a link in the Technology Connections section for online resources.

When applying any of these writing structures, we often use a follow-up process similar to what we do with writing frames—pair-share, circulate around the room to identify exemplars, then give students time to revise. In addition, we will often use examples of student writing to prepare concept attainment lessons highlighting specific conventions (see Strategy 11: Inductive Learning).

One more example worth sharing: Kernel essays, introduced to us by experienced educator Gretchen Bernabei, are a sister strategy to writing structures. They familiarize students with the text structures of various writing genres, including expository, argument, and narrative, and assist them in developing kernel ideas that can later be developed into longer writing pieces.

The kernel essay process involves students using a text structure (divided into sections or boxes with a prompt or question for each box) in order to write one-sentence responses for each prompt. This series of sentences is called a *kernel essay*. Students then read their kernel essays aloud to other students in order to see whether that structure works for their topic and whether it is worth developing into a longer piece of writing. For example, the teacher could show students this memory text structure:

Table A Memory

Where You Were	Moment It Started	Next Moment	Final Moment	What You Thought

Next, the teacher could give the following questions one at a time with students writing one-sentence answers for each:

1. Where were you and what were you doing?
2. What happened first?
3. What happened next?
4. What happened last?
5. What did you learn or realize?

For more explanation on this strategy, multiple examples of text structures, and its applications in content area writing, see a link to Gretchen's website in the Technology Connections section.

Teaching Online

All these writing frames and writing structures can be used while teaching remotely. The lesson on artificial intelligence and writing is a particularly important one to do in a distance learning format since everything is done online and the temptation to use an AI shortcut may always be there.

STRATEGY 14: WRITING FRAMES AND WRITING STRUCTURES

What Could Go Wrong?

A critique of writing frames and writing structures is that they can restrict students to formulaic writing methods. Because of that potential issue, it is important for teachers to constantly remind ourselves that the goal is to help students progress to the point where teacher-provided writing scaffolds are no longer needed. We want to move students forward on a continuum from the most heavily scaffolded to the least scaffolded through practice, peer-to-peer collaboration, and teacher feedback. After students become proficient with writing structures, we remind them that they are just guides—they should feel free to experiment and even create their own writing structures to share!

You also don't want to teach *all* the writing structures we've included in this strategy. You can have too much of a good thing—teaching all of them can turn into alphabet soup in our students' minds. Pick one and try it out. If it's not a good fit for you or your students, forget about it. If it works well, use it several more times. Then, consider trying out another one. Plan on regularly using two or three different structures over the course of a year so that students acquire different models they can use in future situations when teacher scaffolding is not available.

As we discussed previously, writing can be a scary endeavor for ELLs and often results in an overreliance on Google Translate. It's a tricky balance—the app can be a great asset for communicating with students (not to mention with their parents!) with whom you don't share a language—but it also can become a crutch that hinders written language acquisition. Students can easily get into the habit of writing sentences and even entire essays in their home language and then copying and pasting the Google Translate English version.

We deal with this issue by facing it head-on and asking students to use Google Translate for words only and not entire sentences when they are writing (however, they can use it to translate larger portions of text when reading). Students understand that using it will not help them write (especially if we show the class a Google Translate version of a passage—one not necessarily written by a student—and point out its deficiencies), but that doesn't always stop them! Fear of mistakes and the siren call of ease can be hard to resist for all of us. We assist with regular gentle, but firm, reminders.

The same holds true with students using artificial intelligence. Even though we do the AI lesson we described earlier in the year and even though the posters students have created stay on the wall as reminders and *even though* we regularly remind students that they won't be penalized for their writing mistakes and *even though* we assure them that they will be allowed to use AI to revise their writing and correct their mistakes, there still may be students who can't seem to stop themselves from using it early in the writing process.

To avoid having to spend time "monitoring" student use of AI, we find that the most simple way for us to know if they are using it, as well as Google Translate, inappropriately is by having students do a simple writing assessment every other month or so using pen/pencil and paper (see Strategy 49: Assessment) with laptops closed. Keeping those handy and accessible are easy reference tools for us to identify who might be using their genuine "voice" and who, instead, might be using what the computer is producing.

In addition, these writing assessments also serve as effective formative assessment tools for us and students alike to be able to track progress over time.

Differentiation Recommendations

Newcomers (Preliterate or Low Literacy in Home Language): Introduce basic sentence starters and sentence frames in home language, followed by simple sentence starters and sentence frames in English. Use Read&Write for Google Chrome or Microsoft's Immersive Reader, which offer picture dictionary features, and Google Translate to provide audio support for text.	**Newcomers (Literate in Home Language):** Introduce sentence starters, moving to sentence frames and then to paragraph writing frames, all in English. Then, gradually move to more lengthy writing frames and, next, to writing structures.
Intermediate ELLs: Begin by introducing sentence starters and sentence frames, and quickly move to paragraph writing frames, more lengthy writing frames, and increasingly more complex writing structures.	**Advanced ELLs:** Begin with academic language-oriented writing frames and then to increasingly more complex writing structures.

Technology Connections

The writing structures we've shared here are just the tip of the iceberg. You can find many more at The Best Scaffolded Writing Frames for Students (http://larryferlazzo.edublogs .org/2016/12/01/the-best-scaffolded-writing-frames-for-students/).

As we've mentioned elsewhere in the book, having an audience beyond just the teacher can be very motivating for students. There are many places where their work can be published, and a number are shared at The Best Places Where Students Can Write for an "Authentic Audience" (http://larryferlazzo.edublogs.org/2009/04/01/the-best-places-where-students-can-write-for-an-authentic-audience/).

Links to online "They Say, I Say" resources can be found at http://larryferlazzo.edub logs.org/2015/07/05/they-say-i-say-is-a-great-writing-resource/.

For more on the strategy of kernel essays see Gretchen Bernabei's website at http:// trailofbreadcrumbs.net/writing-strategies/kernel-essays/.

For additional strategies for dealing with artificial intelligence and Google Translate in the ELL classroom, visit The Best Posts About Using Artificial Intelligence with ELLs (https://larryferlazzo.edublogs.org/2023/06/04/the-best-posts-about-using-artificial-intelligence-with-ells/) and The Best Ideas for Using Google Translate in the ELL Classroom – Please Add Your Own! (https://larryferlazzo.edublogs.org/2022/07/09/the-best-ideas-for-using-google-translate-in-the-ell-classroom-please-add-your-own/).

STRATEGY 14: WRITING FRAMES AND WRITING STRUCTURES

Attribution

Thanks to our colleagues Antoine Germany, Jen Adkins, and Mary Osteen for letting us reproduce their writing structure graphics.

Thanks to Meghan Everette and to Scholastic for letting us reproduce the RACE materials.

Thanks to Gretchen Bernabei for letting us share about her kernel essay ideas.

All figures from this chapter, as well as 11 additional chapters, references, hyperlinked Technology Connections, and more online resources, can be found at www.wiley.com/go/ellteacherstoolbox2.

There are many reasons why it is important to know about George Washington. He was _____. He was also _____.

In addition, it is important to know about him because every February people in the United States celebrate _____ and we don't go to school.

Figure 14.1 George Washington Writing Frame

Name_____ Date_____

What is the most interesting thing you learned about Mexico from the data set?

Planning to Write

Use the ABC outline to answer the question:

Answer the Question

_____ is the most interesting thing about Mexico.

Back It Up with Evidence to Support Your Answer

The author says that _____.

OR

The author says, "_____."

This means _____.

Make a Comment and Connection

This is interesting because _____.

It reminds me of _____.

Putting It All Together

Put all your sentences together in one paragraph and write it below—be sure to indent!

Figure 14.2 Mexico Writing Frame

STRATEGY 14: WRITING FRAMES AND WRITING STRUCTURES 175

Student Name: _____ Date: _____

Title of Movie: _____

1. Who were the main characters in the movie?
   The main character was _____ **OR**
   The main characters were _____ *and*
   _____.

2. Who was your favorite character and why did you like him/her?
   My favorite character was _____
   because _____.

3. Where did the movie take place (you can list more than one place)?
   The movie took place in _____.

4. What was the problem in the movie and how did it get solved?
   The main problem in the movie was _____.
   It was solved by _____.

5. What happened in the movie?
   First, _____.
   Second, _____.
   Then, _____.
   Next, _____.
   Finally, _____.

6. Did you like the movie? Why or why not? *I liked/didn't like the movie because*
   _____
   _____.

Figure 14.3 Writing About a Movie

Student Name: Date:
Title of Book: Author:

1. Who were the main characters in the book?
    The main character was _____ **OR**
    The main characters were _____
    and _____.

2. Who was your favorite character and why did you like him/her?
    My favorite character was _____
    because _____.

3. Where did the book take place (you can list more than one place)?
    The book took place in _____.

4. What was the problem in the book and how did it get solved?
    The main problem in the book was _____.
    It was solved by _____.

5. What happened in the book?
    First, _____.
    Second, _____.
    Then, _____.
    Next, _____.
    Finally, _____.

6. Did you like the book? Why or why not? *I liked/didn't like the book because*
    _____
    _____.

Figure 14.4 Writing About a Book

STRATEGY 14: WRITING FRAMES AND WRITING STRUCTURES

Name _____

Date _____

What is the most interesting thing you learned about Mexico from the data set?

Planning to Write

Use the ABC outline to answer the questions:

A. What is the most interesting thing you learned about Mexico?

B. What is a quotation from the data set that backs up or supports your answer? What does the quotation mean in your own words?

C. Why is it interesting? What does it remind you of?

Putting It All Together

Please put all your sentences together in one paragraph:

Figure 14.5 Mexico Writing Structure

ABC Literature Response Format
A–Answer the prompt/Make a point

 Back it up with evidence from the text

C–Comment with further opinion or personal connection

"ICE" your B!!

I-Identify who said the quote
C-Copy the direct quote
E-Explain: (1) What the quote means: what the author is saying
(2) How the quote helps to prove your point

**REMINDER: Each of these steps MAY take multiple sentences.

Figure 14.6 ABC Writing Structure *Source:* Reproduced with permission of Jen Adkins

PEE

PEE Stands for POINT EVIDENCE EXPLAIN

P-make your point (what are you trying to get at?)

For example: Cell phones are better than landlines.

E-You need to support your point with some evidence.

For example: Cell phones are better than landlines. I think this because mobiles (on average) cost less and you can do a lot more with them.

E-You need to explain your evidence in more detail and how it relates/proves your point.

For example: Cell phones are better than landlines. I think this because mobiles (on average) cost less and you can do a lot more with them. This proves that mobiles are better than landlines and shows a couple of reasons why they are better. They are also a lot better because you are less restricted with cell phones and can freely move without being controlled by connection problems.

Make Your Point: _____.

Support Your Point with Evidence: I know this because _____
_____.

Evidence Details and How It Proves Your Point: This shows
_____. In addition, we know _____
_____.

Figure 14.7 PEE Writing Structure *Source:* Reprinted with permission of Antoine Germany.

RACE TO A GREAT ANSWER

RESTATE
ANSWER
CITE THE SOURCE
EXPLAIN / EXAMPLES

R	**R** stands for *restate the question*. We want students to practice flipping the question into part of their answer. This avoids students starting with *because-* or *yes* and sets them up to actually answer the question given. Often students who don't or can't restate the question are going to provide an incomplete or off-base answer.
A	**A** stands for *answer the question*. Here is where students give the simple or direct answer. **R** and **A** are usually contained in the same sentence.
C	**C** stands for *cite the source*. This is where students find the supporting evidence in the text for their answer.
E	**E** stands for *explain* or *examples*. Often, the evidence cited needs further explanation to tie back to the answer. Other times, just giving another example or extending the answer will suffice.

R	The lesson the reader should learn is
A	Never tell a lie.
C	In the story, the boy cries wolf three times. The first two times, the villagers come, but then they don't believe him when the wolf actually shows up.
E	The boy lied so he wasn't believable. That is why you shouldn't tell lies.

Figure 14.8 RACE Writing Structure *Source:* Reprinted by permission of Scholastic Inc. From blog by Meghan Everette https://www.scholastic.com/teachers/blog-posts/meghan-everette/responding-texthow-get-great-written-answers/ from Scholastic.com. Copyright by Scholastic Inc.

STRATEGY 14: WRITING FRAMES AND WRITING STRUCTURES

R	The animals that rely on the cactus life cycle to survive include
A	bats, birds, and insects.
C	In the text it says the bats eat the fruit of the cactus in the mature stage.
E	The birds use a mature cactus as a home. Both birds and bats use the seed stage for food. When the cactus dies, insects use the body for nutrients.

Figure 14.8 *(Continued)*

Argument = AREE!

Assertion: a claim or thesis

Reason: reasons why the claim is true

Evidence: proof, usually data or examples, quotations, statistics, etc.

Explanation: Explain/comment more about your evidence

Figure 14.9 AREE! Writing Structure *Source:* Reproduced with permission of Mary Osteen.

	Assertion	**Reasoning**	**Evidence**
1	The minimum driving age should be raised to 18.	Raising the driving age will save lives by reducing accidents.	16-year-old drivers have three times as many crashes as drivers aged 18 and 19.
2	Television is a bad influence.	Television shows too much violence.	
3	The United States should not have the death penalty.		Since 1973, 190 people have been released from death row because they were exonerated.
4		Eating junk food is bad for your health.	Junk foods are high in fat and sugar. Too much fat and sugar puts you at risk for diabetes and heart disease.
5		Allowing younger people to vote would increase their involvement in politics and society.	
6			Incidents of school violence have shown that students use their cellular phones to notify police and parents.
7	Schools should not use animal dissection in classes.		

Figure 14.10 AREE! Writing Structure Teaching Grid   *Source:* Reproduced with permission of Mary Osteen.

STRATEGY 15
Quoting, Summarizing, and Paraphrasing

What Is It?

We all know what quoting entails, and this is how we describe it to students: writing the exact words that someone else has said or written, putting these words within quotation marks, and attributing them to the original source.

Summarizing is saying or writing the main idea or ideas that someone else said or wrote and typically contains many fewer words than are found in the original text.

Paraphrasing is putting what someone said or wrote into your own words and is typically a similar length to the original passage.

Having students understand how to quote, summarize, and paraphrase are critical skills for academic writing success. This strategy in our book is more of a series of lessons done at different times to help students acquire those abilities. Once they are learned, quoting, summarizing, and paraphrasing become important strategies students can use to help them with their reading and writing. Teachers can use them as effective formative assessment tools.

Why We Like It

We like using this strategy, of course, because it's critical to student academic success, and we believe it has a positive impact on language acquisition. More important, though, we think that summarizing and paraphrasing especially provide a superior opportunity to highlight the *assets* English language learners (and all students) bring to class instead of the supposed *deficits* they carry. By helping students learn these concepts through seeing that they already paraphrase and summarize frequently, we reinforce the reality that ELLs are as intelligent as any other student in our schools. It's not a question of intelligence—instead, it's a challenge of language. It's a reminder that we can be more effective educators by remembering to look at our students through this lens of assets and not deficits.

Supporting Research

The National Reading Panel in 2000 identified summarization as an important skill for reading comprehension (Sedita, 2016; Shanahan, 2019) More recent studies have supported that finding and reinforced its importance for long-term learning (Khathayut & Karavi, 2011; Lawson & Mayer, 2021).

Research has found that paraphrasing skills have a positive impact on ELL student reading comprehension—they are able to better focus on the key ideas in the text. Subsequently, the quality of student writing improves because they are able to write better once they have clarity about what they want to communicate (Hans, n.d., p. 7). Similar results have been found when teaching summarization techniques (Khathayut & Karavi, 2011).

Common Core Connections

Reading a text, analyzing it for main ideas, and identifying context clues to assist with comprehension all fall under the Language and Reading Standards. The writing required in paraphrasing and summarizing also fits into a number of the Writing Standards.

Application

There are many different lessons out there about teaching quoting, summarizing, and paraphrasing to English language learners and English-proficient students. Many, if not most, teach all three at the same time in order to compare and contrast them. We think that this strategy can be overwhelming to students, and we take a different tack.

QUOTING

We generally begin by introducing the idea of quotations and quotation marks in the context of having students write dialogue—whether it is imagining a conversation between two people in a photo used in the picture word inductive model (see Strategy 11: Inductive Learning) or in a story they are writing (see Strategy 3: Graphic Organizers) or in a simple autobiographical incident essay. We also, through simple ABC paragraphs (see Strategy 14: Writing Frames and Writing Structures), familiarize students with how to use quotations when working with text written by others.

We explain that quotation marks are used to represent exactly what someone says. Further, we explain that if you copy what someone else says or writes without quotation marks, then it's like stealing.

It typically does not take very long for students to gain an understanding of this concept. We also explain that copying other people's words can get them into trouble at school.

Nevertheless, many ELLs continue to be scared of making mistakes and may still copy work without providing attribution or quotation marks. We continually reinforce its importance, and writing frames and writing structures (see Strategy 14) provide excellent and regular opportunities to do so.

STRATEGY 15: QUOTING, SUMMARIZING, AND PARAPHRASING

SUMMARIZING

We look for a good opportunity to teach summarizing after we have taught quoting—the following week, month, quarter. Generally, we do it after we have read a story as a class and are going to watch a short animated adaptation of it (e.g., *The Story of Ferdinand* [Leaf, 1977]). We periodically stop the video and ask for summaries. This process tends to work well because students have already acquired much of the vocabulary and experience needed to comprehend the story.

The teacher begins this lesson by writing the word *summarize* on the board or document camera. With words and gestures, the teacher explains that when we summarize, we take many words and turn them into a few words. The teacher tells students that they may not realize it, but that they summarize all the time—when a friend asks them what happened in the movie they just saw, when their parents ask them what happened in school that day, and when a classmate asks them in January what they did during winter break. They don't spend hours explaining every single thing that happened! No, they summarize with a few words. And the summary is in their own words—they don't quote someone else (this could be a good time to remind students what a quotation is). Again, teachers can use their hands to illustrate going from a lot to going to a little. The teacher explains that learning to summarize in English is a skill they can use to help them understand something they have read or watched.

After providing that mini-lesson, and before showing the video, a teacher can pass out a sheet such as Figure 15.1: Summarizing Examples (the humorous first example always generates student reaction!). The teacher reads the first example and the three options for a good summary. Then, the teacher explains why each option is either good or bad and circles the correct answer.

The teacher then reads the next example and the options and asks students to take a minute and silently circle the correct answer. The teacher then asks students to think about the reason why each one is either right or wrong and to explain the reasons to a partner. Afterwards, the teacher calls on students to share their responses and reasons. This same process is repeated with the last two examples.

Next, the teacher passes out mini-whiteboards to students and explains that they are going to watch a video of the story they recently read. The video will be paused every few minutes and then students will write down on their board a summary of what they watched. The teacher will model it the first time, and then the students will do it during the rest of the video.

Each time the teacher stops the video, students can write quietly and show their boards when complete (newcomers can draw their summaries). The teacher can give feedback. Remember—we're not looking for perfect grammar or spelling here! The primary point of the exercise is teaching and assessing if students understand and can apply the concept of summarizing.

A subsequent reinforcing activity we've sometimes done is to ask students to make posters of their favorite (classroom-appropriate) movie, including a summary of the plot. Depending on the English-proficiency level of the students, we might provide a simple writing frame or writing structure as a scaffold. Once students acquire this summarizing skill, of course, we ask them to regularly summarize portions of a text (see Strategy 10: Reading Comprehension).

The "Summarize This!" game in Strategy 23: Learning Games for Reading and Writing is a fun way for students to practice summarizing following these explicit lessons on the skill.

Note that our lessons for quotations and summarizing emphasize explicit instruction. Though we are big fans of assisted-discovery learning (e.g., inductive), we also think that explicit instruction is a key component of any classroom. Balance is the key!

PARAPHRASING

We believe that paraphrasing is difficult to teach and learn, and that is why we generally teach it last. Contrasting paraphrasing with what it is not—quoting and summarizing—can be one more way to help students understand the concept.

The teacher can begin by writing the word *paraphrasing* on the class whiteboard or document camera. The teacher explains that *paraphrasing* means putting what someone else said or wrote in your own words. The teacher tells students that they do something like paraphrasing all the time when they don't know the exact word for something. For example, if you don't know the word for this (the teacher points to a microwave), you might call it "the thing that cooks fast." That is a type of paraphrasing—you are putting something in your own words and showing that you understand it.

The teacher writes the word *quotation* and asks students to take a minute and remember what that word means. After a minute, the teacher asks students to share with a partner what they remember and then calls on one or two students to share with the entire class.

Then the teacher explains that paraphrasing means taking a quotation and putting it in your own words. Paraphrasing helps you make sure you understand the quotation, and it shows readers that you understand it, too. The teacher explains that students will use quotations and paraphrases when they write essays in school to support what they believe.

The teacher then says they are going to show good and bad examples of paraphrasing. Using the concept attainment strategy (see Strategy 11: Inductive Learning for instructions), the teacher will first put Figure 15.2: Concept Attainment Paraphrasing 1 on the document camera and use the inductive process to elicit from students why some examples are *yeses* and others are *nos*.

There are too many *yeses* and *nos* about paraphrasing to teach in one concept attainment sheet, so the teacher will use two of them. The reason the first example is under the *no* category is that it is just a quotation. The reason for the second example is that it does not cite the source.

The reasons for the *yes* examples, which can be elicited from students when reviewing either this figure or the next one, are as follows:

- It is a similar length to the quotation.
- Some words are changed (synonyms).
- Key words are often kept.

STRATEGY 15: QUOTING, SUMMARIZING, AND PARAPHRASING

- The order of words are changed.
- The source is cited.
- Complex words are simplified.
- The paraphrase is accurate.
- The student's opinion is not included within the paraphrase.

After having students, with teacher guidance, determine why the examples in the figure are *yes* and *no*, the teacher puts Figure 15.3: Concept Attainment Paraphrasing 2 on the document camera and uses the same process. The *no* reasons for Figure 15.3 are that the first example is a summary (the teacher might want to remind students about their previous lessons on summaries) and the second example is not an accurate paraphrase of the quote. If students don't identify all the reasons for the *yes* examples, the teacher can explicitly point them out.

The teacher should have student copies of both concept attainment sheets available to pass out *after* the process is complete. This will provide students with models as they complete the next activity, which is Figure 15.4: Paraphrase Sheet (note that some of the passages there are intentionally similar to ones found in the concept attainment sheets to function as an additional scaffold). The teacher will tell students that it's now their turn to write paraphrases of the quotations on the sheet. The teacher tells the students they will do one at time—after a few minutes, students will share with a partner, and then one or two examples will be shared with the entire class. Then students will proceed to the second quotation, where the process will be repeated. Finally, students complete the third quotation.

By that time, most—and, with luck, all—students will have a grasp of how to write paraphrases. They should be able to apply it to future writing and, as with summarizing, teachers can also ask them to do it periodically when annotating a text.

We are fully aware that our teaching suggestions for quoting, summarizing, and paraphrasing—and for other strategies in this book—might be viewed as somewhat simplified and not covering sophisticated nuances. We are making these choices intentionally and do not view it as dumbing down our teaching. We believe the strategies we use to teach our students support language acquisition, maximize higher-order thinking, meet Common Core Standards, and prepare them to be lifelong learners and have a long and successful academic career. As the authors of the Common Core Standards state:

> Teachers should recognize that it is possible to achieve the standards for reading and literature, writing & research, language development and speaking & listening without manifesting native-like control of conventions and vocabulary. (Council of Chief State Officers and the National Governors Association, n.d., p. 1)

Teaching Online

All these lessons can be done online with videoconferencing, shared screens, and breakout rooms. However, at the risk of sounding like a "broken record," it's critical to do some kind of lesson on ethical use of AI, similar to the one found in Strategy 14: Writing Frames and Writing Structures, because the temptation to use it as a shortcut may be especially strong in distance learning environments. The tricky part, of course, is that teachers can't actually see what students are doing, and some might be tempted to seek assistance from AI chatbots before trying to develop answers for themselves.

What Could Go Wrong?

In our experience, things generally go pretty well—including with beginning ELLs—when teaching quoting and summarizing. Paraphrasing, though, can be an entirely different kettle of fish. Intermediate ELLs often find it challenging, as do many of our English-proficient students. We suggest that it doesn't make sense to even try teaching paraphrasing until students reach the high-beginning stage at least. We'd also recommend having students continue to practice, including having them try the online exercises found in the Technology Connections section.

Differentiation Recommendations

Newcomers (Preliterate or Low Literacy in Home Language): Quotation marks are used in similar ways in many languages, though the punctuation may be slightly different. So, when teaching quoting, it might make sense to just use examples from student home languages to teach the concept. The same summarizing lesson in the chapter can be used with this population, but more simple examples than the one in Figure 15.1: Summarizing Examples should be given for student practice. An AI chatbot can create them if a teacher does not have time to do so. Teaching paraphrasing is probably best saved for a later time when the student's English proficiency is at a higher level.	**Newcomers (Literate in Home Language):** Students should be able to access the lessons and materials in the chapter.
Intermediate ELLs: Use lessons and materials in the chapter. If in a multilevel class, students could create practice examples for newcomer classmates.	**Advanced ELLs:** Begin with lessons and materials in the chapter, and then provide more complex examples and materials. For example, students could begin to summarize longer pieces of text and different kinds. To support them, multiple graphic organizers can be found online when searching "summarization graphic organizer for informational text," "summarization graphic organizer for argument text," etc.

STRATEGY 15: QUOTING, SUMMARIZING, AND PARAPHRASING

Technology Connection

Additional suggestions for teaching about plagiarism *and* online interactives for students to reinforce the skill of paraphrasing can be found at The Best Online Resources to Teach About Plagiarism (http://larryferlazzo.edublogs.org/2009/09/21/the-best-online-resources-to-teach-about-plagiarism/).

There are many free online games available to reinforce the important elements of quoting, summarizing, and paraphrasing at sites like Quizizz and Kahoot! Searching those terms will result in many relevant games, and teachers can also easily create their own. See links to these game sites at The Best Online Games Students Can Play in Private Virtual "Rooms" (https://larryferlazzo.edublogs.org/2009/02/10/the-best-online-games-students-can-play-in-private-virtual-rooms/).

Students can also test themselves at ChatGPT, Google's Bard, or other AI chatbots. For example, they can fill-in-the-blank using this kind of passage: Is (student types in their summary) a good summary for the following passage: (student types in the entire passage)?

In our experience, the chatbot typically gives an accurate response to this kind of paraphrasing or summarizing question. It would also be easy for the student to request the chatbot's feedback in their home language.

All figures from this chapter, as well as 11 additional chapters, references, hyperlinked Technology Connections, and more online resources, can be found at www.wiley.com/go/ellteacherstoolbox2.

1. All the students in school love Mr. Ferlazzo. They want to be in his class because they know they will learn a lot from him. He is very smart and kind. He is never absent, is never angry, and gives treats to his students every day. The students in his class are very lucky!

   Circle the summary:

   a. All the students in school love Mr. Ferlazzo.

   b. Students think Mr. Ferlazzo is a good teacher.

   c. "He is very smart and kind."

2. One bite from the black mamba snake can kill a person within 20 minutes. They don't just bite once—they will keep on biting you! They are very fast so you cannot run away from them.

   Circle the summary:

   a. Snakes are fun!

   b. "One bite from the black samba snake can kill a person."

   c. Black mamba snakes are very dangerous and can kill you.

3. Over 300 million people live in the United States. It is a big country. It has a strong military. There is a lot of money in the United States. Many people visit the United States.

   Circle the summary:

   a. It is a big country.

   b. The United States is a powerful country.

   c. I live in the United States.

4. It was a sunny day. The woman walked her little dog down the street. As they were walking, they saw a man walking with a big dog across the street. The big dog started barking at the woman and the little dog. The little dog started crying and tried to run away from the big dog.

   Circle the summary:

   a. The big dog didn't like the little dog, and the little dog was afraid of the big dog.

   b. The man didn't like the woman.

   c. "It was a sunny day."

Figure 15.1 Summarizing Examples

STRATEGY 15: QUOTING, SUMMARIZING, AND PARAPHRASING   *191*

"Failure is success if we learn from it."
—Malcolm Forbes

YES, This Is a Good Paraphrase

Malcolm Forbes said that we can still learn when things go badly.

Malcolm Forbes suggests that even if we fail, we can get something good out of it.

NO, This Is Not a Good Paraphrase

"Failure is success if we learn from it."

Even if we fail, we can get something good out of it.

Figure 15.2 Concept Attainment Paraphrasing 1

"Elephants' brains are bigger than the brains of any other land animal, and the cortex has as many neurons as a human brain. The ability of elephants to learn is impressive, and they are also self-aware—they can actually recognize themselves in mirrors!" (http://healthypets.mercola.com/sites/healthypets/archive/2015/08/22/10-most-intelligent-animals.aspx)

YES, This Is a Good Paraphrase

The Healthy Pets website says that elephants have big brains and have lots of connections inside them. The website also says the elephants know it's them when they look in a mirror and that they can learn a lot.

NO, This Is Not a Good Paraphrase

The Healthy Pets website says that elephants are smart.

Figure 15.3 Concept Attainment Paraphrasing 2

YES, This Is a Good Paraphrase	NO, This Is Not a Good Paraphrase
The Healthy Pets website says elephants have the ability to learn many things and that they have big brains and lots of connections inside them. The website also states that elephants know it's them when they look in a mirror.	The Healthy Pets website says that elephants are very big, ugly, and smell bad. They also look in the mirror a lot.

Figure 15.3 (Continued)

Name _____
Period _____

Paraphrase each of these quotations:

1. "Without education, you are not going anywhere in this world."—Malcolm X
   _____
   _____
   _____

2. "Dolphins are considered some of the smartest animals on Earth... Dolphins have been shown to recognize themselves in mirrors, to create language-like personalized whistles, solve problems and even follow recipes." http://bigthink.com/paul-ratner/what-are-the-smartest-animals-on-the-planet
   _____
   _____
   _____

3. "Mistakes are opportunities to learn. Students who are not afraid of making mistakes will do better in school."—Katie Hull Sypnieski
   _____
   _____
   _____

Figure 15.4 Paraphrase Sheet

STRATEGY 16
Choice Boards/Learning Menus

What Is It?

Choice boards (a variation are called learning menus) share a number of different assignments, and students need to choose some to complete. They are often divided into categories, and students select one from each section. They can be offered to students on paper, or online. If done online, they can often include links to additional resources.

Choice boards might be divided into categories like Listening, Speaking, Reading, and Writing. Students could be given three different choices of related activities in each category and be asked to complete one of them within a certain period of time.

In learning menus, the categories might be Appetizer, Main Dish, and Dessert, with less complex tasks under Appetizer and Dessert, and more challenging ones under Main Dish.

Why We Like It

Choice is a key element required for intrinsic motivation (see Strategy 38: Motivation), and offering choice boards/learning menus to students creates an easy opportunity to further that engagement goal. They can also serve as a nice outlet for creativity. We have often been surprised, for example, by the artistic talent of some of our students who choose an option requiring more of those kinds of skills.

Supporting Research

Researchers find that choice boards/learning menus support student autonomy and choice that is integral to creating the conditions students need for intrinsic motivation to flourish (Poulos, 2024). More research on the role of choice in the classroom can be found in Strategy 38: Motivation.

Common Core Connections

Choice boards/learning menus on their own do not necessarily support Common Core Standards. The key to making those connections is what teachers put on the boards/learning menus as assignments.

Application

There's not much to say about choice boards/learning menus apart from showing several examples, which we do in the figures.

Figure 16.1: Newcomers Quarterly Assessment is one we use with our students as a quarterly assessment and offers choices in writing, reading, speaking, and listening.

Figure 16.2: Homework Choice Board is from ELL teacher Miguel Miguez. He uses it in a variety of ways depending on his teaching context, including asking students to complete one task each week.

Figure 16.3: Online Choice Board shows an online choice board created by ELL teachers Michelle Makus Shory and Irina McGrath. The figure offers two different versions of the same content.

There are countless versions of choice boards and learning menus online. See the Technology Connections section for a link to many of them, or just search online.

Any artificial intelligence–powered chatbot will create one for you, too, which you can easily edit.

Teaching Online

Choice boards/learning menus can easily be done online and, in fact, can be made more accessible to ELLs through the use of multimedia and online translation tools.

What Could Go Wrong?

Even the "easiest" items on a choice board/learning menu should have an important language acquisition goal. Don't get seduced into putting any "fluffy" or "cute" assignments that may sound good but lack rigor.

Differentiation Recommendations

Newcomers (Preliterate or Low Literacy in Home Language): Creating a completely separate choice board for these students might be the easiest differentiation strategy. If it's created online, use of audio narration for the text and/or offering translation options will increase its accessibility.	**Newcomers (Literate in Home Language), Intermediate ELLs, and Advanced ELLs:** In a single-level or multilevel class, creating separate choice boards can work well. Providing an extra level of activities for "extra credit" can also provide needed challenges to your most motivated students.

Technology Connection

Find lots of examples of choice board/learning menus at The Best Posts and Articles About Providing Students with Choices (https://larryferlazzo.edublogs.org/2010/12/21/the-best-posts-articles-about-providing-students-with-choices/).

Attribution

Thanks to ELL teacher Miguel Miguez for letting us include his homework choice board (https://onthesamepageelt.wordpress.com/2018/10/24/developing-learner-autonomy-a-homework-choice-board/).

Thanks to Michelle Makus Shory and Irina McGrath for letting us share their online choice board (https://sites.google.com/view/ell20/scaffolding/scaffolding-makeovers/choice-board-makeover).

All figures from this chapter, as well as 11 additional chapters, references, hyperlinked Technology Connections, and more online resources, can be found at www.wiley.com/go/ellteacherstoolbox2.

Show how well you know English through writing, reading, speaking, and listening. No phones, no laptops, no Google Translate. You may ask your peer tutor for limited assistance.

For Writing (choose one):

- Write a dialogue with at least 12 lines. Each line must have at least four words, and more is better.
- Write a short story different from what you wrote about earlier (it must be the same length as that one).
- Write about a memory (autobiographical incident) different from what you wrote about earlier (it must be the same length as that one).
- Write a paragraph about your family (it must be at least seven sentences).
- Write a letter to a friend or family member saying what you appreciate about them (it must be at least seven sentences).
- Write a letter to Mr. Ferlazzo or to your penpal saying what your hopes for the future are and why (it must be at least seven sentences).

For Reading (choose one):

- Choose a book. You will go to Voice Typing on the Google Doc in Google Classroom under "Reading Exam." You will read for at least one minute into the Google Doc (reading for longer is great!). You can practice with your peer tutor for a few minutes before you do the exam. You can re-record it as many times as you would like.
- Choose a book. You can practice with your peer tutor for a few minutes. Then, your peer tutor will record your reading for at least one minute (reading longer is great) and send the recording to Mr. Ferlazzo. You can re-record it as many times as you would like.

For Speaking (choose one):

- Go to Voice Typing on the Google Doc in Google Classroom under "Speaking Exam." You will speak for as long as you can; try to talk for at least one minute (speaking for longer is great!). You can write up to 10 words on an index card to help you remember what you are going to say. Your peer tutor

Figure 16.1 Newcomers Quarterly Assessment

STRATEGY 16: CHOICE BOARDS/LEARNING MENUS

will count the words. You can practice with your peer tutor for a few minutes before you do the exam.

- Write a dialogue of at least 12 lines (you may work with another student). Practice the dialogue with a partner. When you are ready, go to Mr. Ferlazzo to perform it. You will receive extra credit if you are willing to perform it in front of the class.

For Listening (choose one):

- Go to Brainpop. Then go to Brainpop, Jr. Choose any video you want. Watch it two times. Then take the Easy Quiz. Be sure to click "Submit to Teacher." Then take the Hard Quiz. Then click "Submit to Teacher." You can watch more videos and take more quizzes for extra credit.
- Go to Google Classroom. Choose any of the interactive videos listed there. Answer the questions. You can watch more videos and answer more questions for extra credit.

Figure 16.1 (*Continued*)

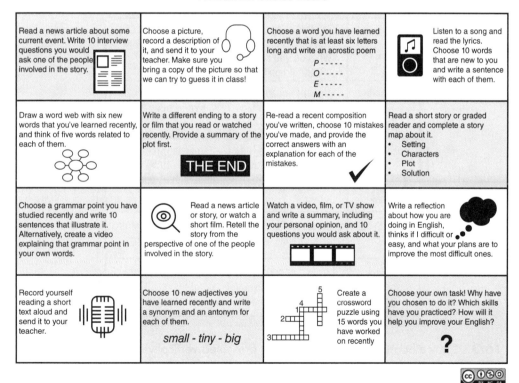

Figure 16.2 Homework Choice Board *Source:* Created by Miguel Miguez, OnTheSamePage, published with permission

198   THE ELL TEACHER'S TOOLBOX 2.0

Before

Pick three to create a tic-tac-toe.

Use the vocabulary list to create an image with all the words.	Read this article [url] answer the questions.	Play this Kahoot with our vocabulary words.
Use Listenwise [url] to listen to MLK's most famous speech.	View this short video [url]. What did you already know? What did you learn?	Create a post on our Padlet board. Use video to explain what you learned.
Why is it important to learn about MLK? Share on Flipgrid.	View this image [url]. Who is this? What do you know about him?	Create a post on our Padlet board. Write what you learned.

AFTER

Pick one from each row.

Background	View this image [url]. Who is this? What do you know about him?	View this short video [url]. What did you already know? What did you learn?
Vocabulary	Use the vocabulary list to create an image with all the words.	Play this Kahoot with our vocabulary words.
Read/Listen	Read this article [url] answer the questions.	Use Listenwise [url] to listen to MLK's most famous speech.
Write/Speak	Create written post on our Padlet board.	Create a video post on our Padlet board.
Reflect	Why is it important to learn about MLK? Share on Flipgrid.	What did you learn about yourself? Write your thoughts.

Figure 16.3   Choice Board Makeover (should be presented vertically)   *Source:* Created by Michelle Makus Shory and Irina McGrath. Used with permission.

STRATEGY 17

Using Photos or Other Images in Reading and Writing

What Is It?

Who doesn't use photos or other images while teaching English language learners? The visual support that they provide is a tremendous aid to comprehension and communication.

There are a million ways to use photos and other images in the classroom. For reading and writing instruction (we share other ideas in the Speaking and Listening part of our book), however, there are three primary ways *we* use them. One is while teaching inductively with the Picture Word Inductive Model (PWIM) and with phonics (see Strategy 11: Inductive Learning). Another is through cooperative drawing (see Bonus Strategy 4: Cooperative Writing). The third is a simple process we use when we teach our ELL social studies classes, which is described in the Application section.

In addition to those three primary uses, we will share a number of other simple ways we periodically use photos and other images in our classes to support reading and writing.

Why We Like It

When teaching ELLs (and anyone else, for that matter!), scaffolds such as photos and images only increase the odds of successful teaching and learning. They are a superior tool for differentiated instruction—newcomers can label objects, and advanced ELLs can answer more-complex questions and write a story about it. Plus, they're free and accessible, and teachers and students can easily make their own, to boot!

Supporting Research

Many researchers have identified benefits of using visuals with ELLs in multiple contexts (Petrie, 2003; Khafidhoh, 2019; Tan et al., 2020). Images can also serve as a catalyst (Petrie, 2003; Khafidhoh, 2019; Tan et al., 2020) for improved ELL student writing.

Common Core Connections

Common Core Standards highlight the importance of being able to close-read and analyze and evaluate diverse forms of visual media (Common Core State Standards Initiative, n.d.d). In fact, there is one Standard within the Reading Anchor Standards that focuses on this skill.

Application

As we previously stated, the applications we discussed in inductive learning and in cooperative writing are two of the main ways we use visual images in the classroom. Here are a few others.

SLIDESHOW ANNOTATION

After intermediate ELL students have spent time studying a unit (in geography, the unit might be Brazil; in world history, it might be World War II), we show a slideshow of related images. Students have all the materials we've used for that unit on their desks. When each new image is shown, students are asked to write a description of the image, along with connecting it to something they have previously learned (see Figure 17.1: Slideshow Notes). Every three slides we have partners share and then invite some comments to be shared with the entire class.

This activity reinforces what students have previously learned, creates opportunities for them to make multiple touches on different texts they have read as they search for connections, and lets them write and receive feedback on their commentary.

CLOSE-READ PHOTOS AND OTHER IMAGES

When students close-read images they can apply many of the same strategies used to analyze written text (see Strategy 10: Reading Comprehension). One lesson we do is project an image on the board and have students answer a series of reading strategy-related questions about it (interspersed with pair-share and classroom discussion activities).

Figure 17.2: Examining an Image is a photo analysis sheet that we have ELL beginners use to analyze an image, and Figure 17.3: Examining an Image (for Intermediates) is one we use with intermediates. In a mixed-level class, it's often possible to have students annotate different sheets at the same time while viewing the same photograph. When we are using Figure 17.3 in an ELL Social Studies class, we also sometimes add one or two additional assignments:

- Think about what we have already learned about the topic in the image and the time period. Please summarize what you know.
- Based on what you know about the topic and the time period, what do you predict may happen to the people and place in the picture in the future?

STRATEGY 17: USING PHOTOS OR OTHER IMAGES IN READING AND WRITING

We sometimes use a variation of pair-share during this activity. We label each row of students as A or B. The Bs move to the desk in front of them after each question is answered. They then share with the student next to them. This gets students up and moving and talking with multiple students about their work during the course of a class period.

Another option, depending on time constraints, is to just write one to three of the questions on the board from the analysis sheets and have students respond to them.

Additional or alternative questions could include these:

- How do you think the person who took the photograph or image felt at the time and why?
- Imagine a conversation between two or more of the people in the photo or image—what would they be saying to each other?
- What do you think each of the people in the photo or image is thinking and why?
- If the image included areas outside of the frame, what else would you see?
- Does this image remind you of anything connected to your life?
- Sometimes, we show an image and ask students to choose a question-starter from each level of Revised Bloom's Taxonomy and answer it (see Figure 17.4: Bloom's Questions for Images).
- English teacher Betsy Markman uses a much more simple activity along these lines, which we have also used on occasion as a warm-up. She shares an ongoing slideshow of images, and each slide has the title "What Happened?" and spaces for students to respond to three simple prompts: "Before," "During," and "After."

USING IMAGES TO TEACH "CLAIM" AND "EVIDENCE"

We were inspired by teachers Claudia Leon and Margaret Montemagno by what they wrote in the *New York Times* Learning Network about using images to teach ELLs about "claim" and "evidence" (Leon et al., 2018).

In our slight modification of their lesson, after we share model responses, we show students an image and then give them a sheet with the following instructions:

1. First, write words for what you see.
2. What do you think is happening in the picture? In other words, what is the story behind the picture? This is called a *claim*.
3. What do you see that makes you say that? This is called *evidence*. Give at least two pieces of evidence.
4. What do you think happened next? This is called a *claim*.
5. What do you know or what do you see that makes you say that? This is called *evidence*.
6. Write a question that you have about the picture:
7. Put all your answers together in one paragraph:

UNVEILING PARTS OF AN IMAGE

In one activity we've used the first step to show a screenshot of a small section of a painting or photo. Next, we ask students to write what they see and predict what they think will be in the full image. Then, we gradually show more and more of the image while periodically stopping to ask students the same question. If you don't want to take the time to make screenshots, just show a picture on a doc cam or overhead and cover it up with another piece of paper. Then, move the paper gradually to show larger portions of the image.

WRITING CAPTIONS AND CLOZE CAPTIONS

After introducing students to the concept of photo captions (we explain them as "titles for pictures" and show several examples), we sometimes will project a funny photo on the class whiteboard and ask students to write a caption for it (searching *collections of funny photos* online will yield tons of classroom-appropriate and -inappropriate pictures, so don't search while the computer projector is on!).

There are also news sites with photo galleries that allow you to *not* show the captions to photos. We have shown an image from one of them with captions off, had students write their own, and then compare them with what appears after we click captions on. Another version that works particularly well for ELL beginners is for the teacher to retype the captions as a cloze with three potential words as answers that students can choose for the blank (teachers can also modify the captions to make them more accessible). Then the teacher can project the image on the screen with the typed cloze below it. Students can have mini-whiteboards where they write what they think is the correct word and why. There are also specific sites for ELLs where they can post their own captions. See the Technology Connections section for these resources.

If you're feeling ambitious, and we only felt that way one year, you can cut out a bunch of photos from the newspaper and then clip their captions. Students then have to match the captions with the picture and write about the clues they used to connect them. It's a great activity, and the photos and captions can be reused (at least until they get too beat up). Or, even better, laminate them.

COMPARE AND CONTRAST

There are three ways we use the idea of compare and contrast with images.

1. This first one is great for ELL beginners. If you search *spot the difference picture* or *find the difference pictures* online, you will find many examples of two very similar pictures that have a few, hard-to-spot differences between them. We will divide students into pairs, project one of the images onto the class whiteboard, and provide sentence frames like these (or, if we are better prepared, print out sheets in advance with many of the same frames on it):

    The top picture has/doesn't have a _____ on the _____ (right, left).

    The bottom picture has/doesn't have a _____ on the _____ (right/left).

STRATEGY 17: USING PHOTOS OR OTHER IMAGES IN READING AND WRITING

After the teacher provides a model or example, we give students a certain period of time to identify as many differences as they can and write down the sentences describing them. Sometimes we make it a game or contest, and sometimes it's an activity minus the competitive aspect. Either way, students learn from it and have fun at the same time.

Because we're not very good at the game, we try to show pictures that come with an answer key!

With the advent of artificial intelligence, there are free tools that let you upload an image and it will produce several that just have minor differences. Students can create their own "Spot the Difference" images with these that they can share with their classmates. See the Technology Connections sections for details.

2. The second way we use a compare-and-contrast activity is through projecting two pictures and having students create a Venn diagram. With beginning ELLs, we'll often stop at a completed Venn diagram (of course, we model one first). With high beginners, we may have them complete a writing frame compare-and-contrast essay, while having intermediates use a writing structure to complete an essay (see Strategy 14: Writing Frames and Writing Structures).

3. There are several online tools that display engaging images from around the world (see the Technology Connections section for links to them). There are *many* ways to use these sites for English language acquisition. Teacher Miguel Míguez has created two infographics sharing different assignments he gives to his students, and has given us permission to share them here. Figure 17.5: Window Swap Assignments is one he uses with a website called Window Swap (https://www.window-swap.com/), where users share pictures of what they see outside of their home's windows, and Figure 17.6: Wonders of Street View is one he uses with a website of the same name (https://neal.fun/wonders-of-street-view). Many of these assignments can be used with images from other sites or with photos taken by students themselves.

PICTURE STORY

This is a simple lesson that requires little teacher preparation, and we've found that it's generated high student engagement and learning—so what's not to like?

The teacher displays any picture containing at least two people on the document camera or from the computer projector, ideally one that is connected in some way to the theme or unit the class is studying. Students are then divided into pairs and have to develop a simple story about the picture based on a series of teacher prompts:

What are their names?
How long have they known each other?
What are they talking about?
Where do they live?

What problems do they have?

What are they thinking?

What are they going to do later today?

What will they be doing 10 years from now?

If you are teaching argument writing, you could tell students that one of the people in the picture is trying to convince the other of something—what is it? Then have them imagine the elements of an argument taking place between the people in the picture. You could follow the same model for expository text by telling students one of them is giving the other instructions—to do what? Or it could just be more of a fun exercise to practice language conventions such as punctuation and spelling.

SENSORY DETAILS

After we teach about sensory details and the different words that can be used to portray them, we sometimes have students create a simple slideshow. They choose five pictures (to represent the five senses: sight, smell, taste, tough, and hearing) online or take their own pictures (or, with the advent of artificial intelligence, create them) that they feel offer opportunities for them to use the sensory detail words in writing about them.

Next, students write several sentences about each image, using words portraying that particular sense. They add them to their slideshow and then present them to classmates through a "speed-dating" procedure, sharing each image and just one or two of the sentences they wrote about them to a classmate before switching seats to present to another one. We use speed-dating a lot in our classes, and this kind of "active learning" has a lot of research backing-up its effectiveness (Galindo, n.d.).

ARTIFICIAL INTELLIGENCE UNIT

Students and teachers can use artificial intelligence text-to-image tools to create their own images for use in all the previous lessons. We have also applied these tools in a short AI unit that has generated positive student feedback. We have used Padlet's "I Can't Draw" feature for these lessons, but there are many other similar tools you could use instead. Here is a simple summary of what that unit looks like:

Day One: With teacher moderation controls turned on in Padlet and the comment feature turned off, students are invited to use AI on their devices to create four or five classroom appropriate images of their choice. Students then share the sentences they used to create the images, along with the images themselves, in small groups or in a "speed-dating" style to their classmates.

Day Two: Either with student examples from the previous day or with teacher models, students are asked to write more complex sentences with more detail and/or more than one sentence to create their images. Students then share them the same way they did a day earlier.

Day Three: Game Day! Students are divided into teams with mini-whiteboards, and the class is shown a teacher-created picture. Students have to guess what prompt the teacher used to create the image, and are given points based on how close they are to the actual prompt. Each student team then gets a chance to create an image for the rest of the class to guess, and they decide with the teacher how many points each team should receive.

Day Four: Students continue to create more complex sentences to create images, and their classmates leave comments on them using teacher-provided sentence starters like this:

- I like your picture because.....
- Your picture reminds me of . . . because.....
- One question I have about your picture is............?
- I can relate to this picture because........

Day Five & Day Six: The teacher models a simple story with sentences illustrated by text-to-image photos, and students create their own. They share them with their classmates through speed-dating.

Teaching Online

All of these activities can be done with various online tools, including Google Slides, Google Drawings, Google Classroom and/or other sites with similar features. Students can work in groups and share their creations in breakout rooms.

What Could Go Wrong?

Our regular refrain is not to overdo it! Don't have students annotate a slideshow that has 20 slides and don't feel like every question in the photo analysis forms has to be assigned during a lesson.

Why do we harp on not making this mistake, you might ask? An excerpt from Larry's book, *Helping Students Motivate Themselves* (2011, p. 93), provides an answer:

> Nobel Prize winner Daniel Kahneman tells about an experiment done in the 1990s when two groups of patients were given colonoscopies. One group "finished" when the procedure was completed. The other group stayed a while longer, believing the procedure was continuing when in fact it had ended, so the pain was gone or reduced dramatically. The second group described the procedure afterward as much less painful than the first group did, even though both groups had recorded similar levels of pain during the procedure except for the extra time provided the second group. Kahneman uses this example to explain that we have an "experiencing self" and a "remembering self."

The "remembering self" is composed of the one or two "peak" moments we have had in a situation combined with how it ends (this is known as the "Peak-End Rule"). It is the remembering self that tends to stick with us and the one we use to frame future decisions.

We want our students to leave our rooms having had peak moments and a good end. We want them to leave feeling like they want to learn more with us and enter our classroom the next day with the same frame of mind.

Are we able to succeed with every student every day of the year? Of course not. But it's not a bad thing to strive for, right?

Differentiation Recommendations

Newcomers (Preliterate or Low Literacy in Home Language): Use most, if not all, of the strategies in the chapter with the assistance of Google Translate or other similar tools that are voice activated. Encourage the use of simple text.	**Newcomers (Literate in Home Language):** Use all chapter strategies with relatively simple English text.
Intermediate ELLs: Use all chapter strategies and encourage increasingly complex text, especially when writing about "claims" and "evidence" because of its transfer to other academic subjects. Introduce Revised Bloom's Taxonomy sentence starters when appropriate.	**Advanced ELLs:** Use all chapter strategies with increasingly complex text. Students can create or identify images and create materials for use by their classmates. Encourage the use of Revised Bloom's Taxonomy sentence starters, especially the higher levels, when appropriate.

Technology Connections

There are many places on the web where the activities we listed in this strategy can be done by students online—whether as a change of pace or as a way to create content for a class blog so that others can view student work. In addition, we've collected, and continue to update, resources at the following links, including places to find engaging images to use in these lessons:

The Best Online Tools for Using Photos in Lessons (http://larryferlazzo.edublogs.org/2012/10/19/the-best-online-tools-for-using-photos-in-lessons/).

The Best Resources on Using "If This Animal or Image Could Talk" Lesson Idea in Class (http://larryferlazzo.edublogs.org/2015/08/01/the-best-resources-on-using-if-this-animal-or-image-could-talk-lesson-idea-in-class/).

The Best Resources on Close Reading Paintings, Photos and Videos (http://larryferlazzo.edublogs.org/2015/08/05/the-best-resources-on-close-reading-paintings-photos-videos/).

STRATEGY 17: USING PHOTOS OR OTHER IMAGES IN READING AND WRITING

Teachers and students can find more information on using "Spot the Difference" images in language instruction, including easy ways to create your own, at Using "Spot the Difference" Pictures with ELLs (https://larryferlazzo.edublogs.org/2017/09/19/using-spot-the-difference-pictures-with-ells/)

You can find many images from around the world to use with Miguel Miguez's infographics at The Best Tools for Taking Students "Around the World" (https://larryferlazzo.edublogs.org/2021/05/30/the-best-tools-for-taking-students-around-the-world/).

For more ideas on how to use Artificial Intelligence's text-to-image features in language acquisition classes, you can visit The Best Resources for Teaching and Learning with AI Art Generation Tools (https://larryferlazzo.edublogs.org/2023/01/01/the-best-resources-for-teaching-learning-with-ai-art-generation-tools/).

Attribution

Versions of some of these ideas appeared in our book, *Navigating the Common Core* (Ferlazzo & Sypnieski, 2016, p. 177).

We were inspired by teacher Colette M. Bennett's blog post on using photo fragments (https://usedbooksinclass.com/2013/10/03/close-reading-constables-the-hay-wain-and-turners-the-fighting-temeraire/).

Thanks to teacher Miguel Míguez for use of his infographics (https://onthesamepagelt.wordpress.com/2020/08/01/describing-windows-around-the-world/ and https://onthesamepagelt.wordpress.com/2023/01/29/wonders-of-street-view-some-activity-ideas/).

Teacher Betsy Markman shared her simple warm-up activity with photos.

All figures from this chapter, as well as 11 additional chapters, references, hyperlinked Technology Connections, and more online resources, can be found at www.wiley.com/go/ellteacherstoolbox2.

Student Name _____		
Date _____		
Slide Number and What It Is	**Describe What You See ("I see _____.")**	**Make a Connection to Something You Learned ("This makes me remember _____ because _____.")**

Figure 17.1 Slideshow Notes

STRATEGY 17: USING PHOTOS OR OTHER IMAGES IN READING AND WRITING 209

1. List the people, objects, and activities you see in the picture:

People	Objects	Activities

2. Write three sentences about the image:

3. Write a title for the image:

4. What might the people in the image be thinking or feeling? Why?

5. Write one question you have about the image:

Figure 17.2 Examining an Image   *Source:* The National Archives Education Stuff, Licensed under CC0 1.0 Universal license.

1. Describe the objects in the image.

2. Describe the people and/or animals in the image.

3. Describe the different activities you see happening in the image.

4. Describe the mood of the image. Is it happy, sad, or something else? What evidence do you see that supports your answer?

5. Write a title for the image and explain why you chose that title.

6. What might the people in the image be thinking or feeling? Why?

7. If you could see outside the frame of the image, what things or people would be there? What do you think would be happening? Why?

8. What year do you think the image was taken or made? What evidence do you see that supports your answer?

9. What questions do you have about the image?

Figure 17.3 Examining an Image (for Intermediates)

Remembering:

Describe what you see in the picture.
I see. . . .
Close your eyes. What parts of the picture do you remember the most?
The parts of the picture that I remember the most are. . . .
What places, events, or things does the picture remind you of?
The picture reminds me of . . . .

Understanding:

What year and what time of year do you think the picture was taken?
I think the picture was taken. . . .because. . . .
What do you think is happening in the picture?

Figure 17.4 Bloom's Questions for Images

I think. . . .
What do you think the picture is trying to show?
I think the picture is trying to show. . . .

Applying:
How could you change the picture to make it look more interesting?
I would. . . .to make it look more interesting.
What would you use this picture to teach about in a lesson?
I would use this picture to teach. . .
How could you use this picture in a lesson for another class?
I could use this picture in . . . . .class because. . . .

Analyzing:
Why do you think a person took this picture?
I think a person took this picture because. . .
Where and when do you think this picture was taken?
I think this picture was taken. . . .because. . . .
When you look at this picture, what do you think is the most important person and/or the most important object?
I think the most important person in the picture is. . . . . because. . .
I think the most important object in the picture is. . . .because. . . .

Evaluating:
Do you like the picture?
I like/don't like the picture because. . . .
If you were going to take a picture of the same subject—for fun or for a class—what, if anything, would you change?
I would change. . .because. . . . OR I would not change anything because. . .
How does the picture make you feel?
The picture makes me feel. . .because. . .

Creating:
What do you imagine is happening outside the four sides of the picture?
I imagine that. . . . .
What caption or title would you give the picture and why?
I would give it a caption or title of. . . .because. . . .
Please write a story with a beginning, middle, and end about the picture.

Figure 17.4 (*Continued*)

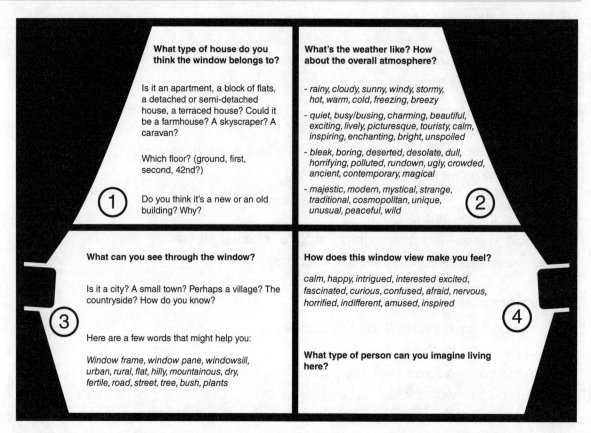

Figure 17.5 Window Swap Assignments Created by Miguel Míguez, https://onthesamepageelt.wordpress.com/2020/08/01/describing-windows-around-the-world/, Reprinted with permission

STRATEGY 17: USING PHOTOS OR OTHER IMAGES IN READING AND WRITING 213

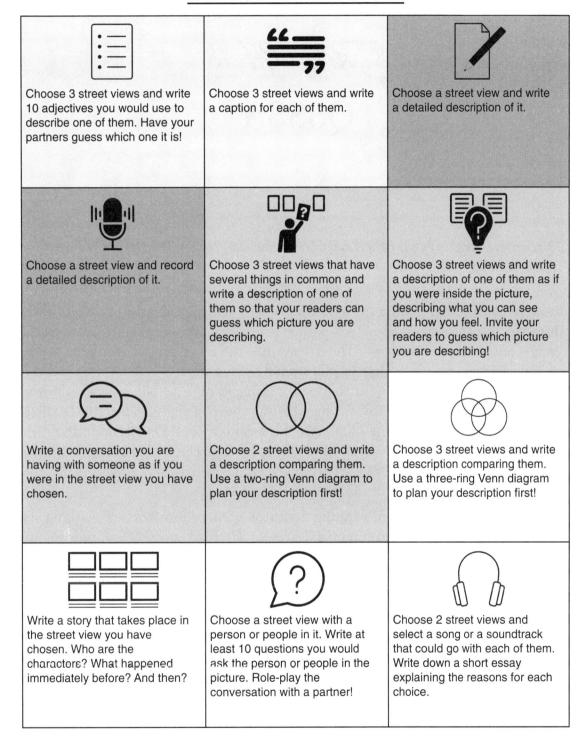

Figure 17.6 Wonders Of Street View Created by Miguel Míguez, https://onthesamepageelt.wordpress.com/2023/01/29/wonders-of-street-view-some-activity-ideas/ , Reprinted with permission

STRATEGY 18
QSSSA

This chapter is written by our friends and talented educators Dr. Stephen Fleenor and Dr. Carol Salva.

Dr. Stephen Fleenor is a scientist-turned-educator who is inspired by the principles of sheltered instruction and growth mind-set, particularly in the advancement of academic language in content-area classrooms. He is currently the chief digital officer at Seidlitz Education and previously served as an educational consultant at Seidlitz. Prior to working with Seidlitz, Dr. Fleenor was an instructional coach and high school science teacher at a Title I school in San Antonio, Texas, where he was awarded the Edgewood ISD District Teacher of the Year Award and the KENS5 ExCEL Award in 2017. Dr. Fleenor is the author of *Teaching Science to English Learners* with Tina Beene and *The Visual Non-Glossary*. He holds a PhD in Developmental Biology from Oxford University and a Masters in School Leadership from the University of the Incarnate Word.

Dr. Carol Salva is an award-winning educator with proven success working with unschooled/under-schooled multilingual learners classified as SLIFE (Students with Limited or Interrupted Formal Education) or ELD (English Language Development) students. She is a key Seidlitz Education consultant for training, coaching, modeling, and supporting program leaders. Dr. Carol Salva is a coauthor of *Boosting Achievement: Reaching Students with Interrupted or Minimal Education* and a coauthor of *DIY PD: A Guide to Self-Directed Learning for Educators of Multilingual Learners*. She has taught elementary, middle, and high school. Dr. Salva holds a doctorate in education in the area of ethical leadership from the University of St. Thomas in Houston, Texas. She also has her master's degree in education administration.

What Is It?

QSSSA is a popular routine educators of English Language Learners use to facilitate structured, equitable, and meaningful student-to-student dialogue. This acronym stands for Question, Signal, Stem, Share, Assess. According to Seidlitz and Perryman (2021, p. 73), student conversations structured through QSSSA empower students to equitably use specific language about a clearly defined topic.

Structuring dialogue with the QSSSA routine allows students a chance to share ideas and points of view with each other. This happens when a small group of students is guided by sentence stems or sentence frames to briefly discuss a topic. The teacher sets up and monitors the conversations and then assesses the entire class to ensure the students are achieving the lesson objectives.

THE QSSSA ROUTINE

Question: Ask a question based on a key concept.

Signal: Ask students for a signal to indicate readiness.

Stem: Provide the target language for students to use (or to direct thinking).

Share: Allow students to share in pairs or small groups.

Assess: Evaluate whole-group student understanding.

This structure begins with the teacher asking a **question.** The teacher offers "wait time" by asking students to provide a **signal** (such as a thumb up or hand in the air) when they are ready with an answer. The teacher then provides a sentence **stem** for the students to use with a partner for **sharing** responses. The stem directs thinking and offers clarity but could also include target academic language such as *"To calculate the median, I would...."* The teacher then **assesses** students by randomly calling on a few learners, rotating between different groups, or asking them to write something such as an exit ticket or a two-minute quick write.

Each part of the routine offers positive outcomes for the learner and the educator. Consider some of the language and learning considerations for each part of the routine:

QUESTION: The question is the thinking prompt that drives the students' conversation. For the educator, the question is based on a key concept that is explicitly linked to the lesson objectives, thus serving as an essential part of the lesson plan.

SIGNAL: By allowing students to show a signal to indicate when they are each individually ready to share, the signal provides students exactly as much time as they need to craft a response and/or think deeply about the concept. This think time leads to more meaningful and equitable student conversations. For the educator, the signal provides a gauge for how much think time to provide, as well as an indication of how prepared students are to answer the question.

STEM: The sentence stem offers an opportunity for students to practice targeted academic language. It offers a model of an academic register that is important for elevating the dialogue of the class. Some learners are just repeating it (important for oral language practice) but others benefit from the clarity that the stem provides. Research shows that "Teacher Clarity" has a strong positive impact on student learning (Hattie, 2008, p. 47). Identifying one or more sentence stems in advance is helpful for educators to intentionally plan out the language goals of the lesson.

SHARE: This is a low-stress opportunity to talk. It provides a source of confidence for learners as well as builds on their response by exposing them to diverse viewpoints. For the educator, the share is an opportunity to monitor students' dialogue and gauge class-wide understanding.

ASSESS: Assessment mostly happens through randomization (through popsicle sticks, seat numbers, or web apps such as Class Dojo or Wheel of Names). The random call in this routine is not a "gotcha" for students who are not prepared to answer. In fact, the random call is designed to offer students a win in class. Using randomization to call on students sends the message that anyone in the class should be able to answer the question when collaborating with peers. Teachers can clear up misconceptions at this point, praise where groups are thinking correctly, and make sure everyone is being held accountable for the conversation that was just had. Students are much more likely to engage in the student-to-student talk when held accountable for that conversation. The random call allows teachers to call on students with equity, to get a formative assessment on what groups are thinking, and also to send that strong message that everyone's voice is important.

In addition to randomly calling on students, assessment can also happen by asking all students to write down their responses or asking one student from every group to share using a random indicator (for example, asking the student closest to the door in each group to share). All three of these modes of assessment are equitable and give the teacher valuable information about the class's understanding. Asking for volunteers is *not* equitable because it gives preference to more confident or gregarious students. However, following up a random call with an invitation for volunteered responses communicates to the class in an equitable way that all perspectives are valued.

Why We Like It

This strategy is widely used and extremely popular among content teachers at every grade level, as well as being used effectively in ELL classes. Educators understand that peer-to-peer interaction is important. But that can often go wrong when we simply ask students to talk with each other. Indeed, teachers often share with us cringe-worthy stories of telling their students to turn and talk, only to find many students silently looking at the floor and many more talking about anything other than academic content. However, when we are explicit about how students are to engage in discussion and when they can trust a routine that offers support, we are reducing a lot of the problems that arise when we ask them to work with a partner or in groups. During structured conversations, we often see enhanced understanding of topics, less off-task behavior, and fewer classroom management problems. QSSSA offers that structure seamlessly.

A quick Internet image search for "QSSSA" will reveal more than a decade of examples for how teachers are using this technique at every grade level. Educators love it because it offers so much bang for your buck! Students have wait time to process what is being asked, they are practicing academic language (syntax, vocabulary, pronunciation, etc.) in a low-stress way, and the cognitive load is on the students when they are collaborating

(Salva & Matis, 2017). Additionally, routinely using QSSSA transforms classroom culture to be more language-rich, equitable, and inclusive.

A TOOL FOR ACADEMIC LANGUAGE DEVELOPMENT

QSSSA provides tiers of linguistic support. The first tier is the sentence stem, which provides the structure to craft a response using academic language. This is especially true if sentence stems are differentiated for various levels of English proficiency (see the "Application" section). The second tier is peer-to-peer support. When students share with each other, they build their listening and speaking skills, as well as receive multiple exposures to academic concepts and vocabulary. We encourage the use of open-ended questions when possible to allow students to hear multiple perspectives about a topic. Lastly, the whole-group interaction during the Assess portion of a QSSSA provides even more exposure to academic language, as well as gives the teacher an opportunity to authoritatively model proper academic language. For example, in a QSSSA about the social studies concept of *entrepreneurship*, several students might share during the assess:

- Entrepreneurship is important because it gives jobs.
- Entrepreneurship is important because it is the free market.
- Entrepreneurship is important because it makes business.

Note that students have already begun structuring academic language in their answers by using the sentence stem "*Entrepreneurship is important because. . . .*" The teacher can then offer responses that value students' contributions while modeling correct academic language:

- *Yes, you're right, entrepreneurship does create jobs and new employment opportunities.*
- *I like how you're connecting entrepreneurship to the free market, because when entrepreneurs build businesses, the free market grows.*
- *Entrepreneurs do start businesses, so businesses are more diverse. Great answer!*

Routine use of QSSSA is an enormously effective way to grow academic language in a classroom for all students.

A TOOL FOR EQUITY

QSSSA makes learning equitable in two ways. First, its use of randomization when assessing ensures that all students—not just the most confident or most likely to raise their hands—are given an equal chance to participate. Importantly, however, QSSSA is much more than just randomization. This is because QSSSA gives students everything they need to be successful once that name is called: think time, language structure (through sentence stems), low-stakes practice with peers, and open-ended questioning that allows for multiple approaches to learning. Once the "QSSS" of QSSSA has been provided, teachers can be confident that all students will be prepared to be called on.

QSSSA also makes small-group conversations equitable. Whereas simply asking students to turn and talk results in the more talkative and/or confident students dominating a conversation, QSSSA equitably prepares all students for the conversation by giving language support and ample think time. Additionally, structuring the conversation by instructing students who will speak first using a random indicator (the person with the longest hair, or the person closest to the window, for example) ensures that different students start off the conversation every time.

Supporting Research

We see language learners advancing with their English fastest when we offer both comprehensible input (Krashen & Terrell, 1983) and low-stress opportunities for output (Swain, 2005). The QSSSA routine allows learners to negotiate meaning and also have a low-stress opportunity to practice targeted language. The QSSSA routine can provide an opportunity for maximum classroom engagement. This is critical as student-to-student communication using academic language results in much higher achievement for the average student (Zwiers, 2023).

The *7 Steps to a Language-Rich, Interactive Classroom* is a second-language acquisition model that uses QSSSA prominently as a strategy to engage students in structured academic conversations. Recent research has shown that middle school students receiving the *7 Steps* as part of their instructional model were significantly more successful on state standardized math, reading, and writing assessments (Seidlitz & Perryman, 2021).

Common Core Connections

This routine meets a number of Language Standards. Facilitating QSSSA also meets the Speaking and Listening standard of helping students "prepare for and participate effectively in a range of conversations." Because QSSSA can be used as a learning tool for any content, QSSSA also aligns to all of the Common Core content standards.

Application

The QSSSA routine can be facilitated at any point of the lesson: as part of a warm-up to activate background knowledge, before or after a student writes to reflect on learning such as with an exit-slip, as a two-minute quick write or a one-minute quick jot, during or after a direct teach to check for understanding, or in combination with a hands-on experience such as a manipulative or a laboratory activity.

When a student-to-student dialogue takes place, the teacher is offered a formative assessment that should drive instruction. As conversations are taking place, the teacher may ask themself: Are students getting it? Where are misconceptions? Who might need to be in a small group tomorrow? The students are also benefiting from the QSSSA routine. They are getting wait time, oral language practice, and an opportunity to negotiate meaning with peers. But they also get an opportunity to build on their ideas. Research tells us that there is a significant effect on learning when we offer students effective ways to reflect and evaluate their learning (Hattie, 2008). We thus recommend deliberately planning one or more QSSSAs in each lesson, both as a formative assessment opportunity for the teacher and as a valuable learning opportunity for students.

When executing a QSSSA during the lesson, here are several tips to make the QSSSA more effective.

QUESTION

According to Seidlitz et al. (2024, p. 14), effective questions for QSSSAs should be:

- Accessible to everyone in the classroom
- Thought-provoking
- Opportunities to model respectful discussion practices

This is best achieved by posing *open-ended* questions, or questions that do not have one single correct answer. Typically, open-ended questions begin with *why* or *how*, whereas closed-ended questions begin with *what*. For example, whereas "What is the theme of this passage?" is a closed-ended question with one correct answer, the question "How is the theme 'betrayal' depicted in this passage?" can have several different answers. This is particularly important when the teacher seeks to validate students' responses (see the "Assess" section).

Open-ended questions are not easily generated in the moment and often require some planning. The book *QSSSA* features a planning tool to help teachers convert closed-ended questions into open-ended questions (Seidlitz et al., 2024, p. 19-23).

SIGNAL

A simple and powerful approach to ensure all students participate in the QSSSA is to "reverse" the signal. In this approach, students are all asked in unison to give a signal and then undo the signal when they are ready. For example, instead of instructing students to "raise your hand when you are ready to share," instruct students by saying this:

Can everyone raise their hands? Great, keep your hand up. Think about this question. Teacher asks the question. When you are ready to answer this question, show me by lowering your hand.

This is especially effective when students are provided additional visual support, such as:

- A structured visual (see Figure 18.1: Example of a Structured Visual)
- An anchor chart
- A page of the textbook or the notes
- A graphic organizer

This can cause students to think deeply about the question and prepare themselves for a rich peer-to-peer conversation. Figure 18.2: Example Signals shows some example signals.

STEM

For classrooms with diverse levels of English language proficiency, it can be helpful to provide multiple sentence stems for students to choose from. Beginning-level English learners benefit from a closed-ended, fill-in-the-blank sentence frame (even if the question is open-ended), especially when paired with a word bank or labeled visual. Advanced-level English learners and fluent English speakers might benefit from more open-ended sentence stems. For example, for the question "How does compaction occur?" the teacher could provide three sentence stems:

- *Compaction occurs before_____.*
- *Compaction occurs when...*
- *During the process of compaction, ...*

All three sentence stems can be displayed, and students can be instructed to pick any one. In our experience, students choose the most appropriate sentence stem for themselves the vast majority of the time.

SHARE

Student conversations during the Share portion of QSSSA can be made much more equitable by specifying who will speak first in the conversation. This can be through a random indicator that is different every time so that a different student shares each time. In addition to ensuring all students are given the opportunity to lead the discussion, specifying who speaks first creates a layer of peer-to-peer accountability that engages students in discussions even more. Figure 18.3: Example "Who First" Indicators provides some example indicators for who shares first.

ASSESS

At first appearance, the Assess portion of the QSSSA might seem the most intimidating for students. However, when done properly, it actually can be one of the biggest tools for building confidence in students! Here are two strategies for building confidence during the Assess stage:

- Encourage students to share their response, or their partner's. This feels like a source of support for students if they are not confident in their answer, and it encourages them to actively listen to their partner during the Share!
- Look for ways to give students positive feedback for their responses. Even if a student provides a totally incorrect response, they can be praised for using a

vocabulary word or going in a specific direction with their thinking. This is especially easy if the QSSSA was structured with an open-ended question. For example, imagine an algebra problem that requires students to multiply both sides by 2. If a student (incorrectly) answers, "I found the value of x by dividing both sides by 2," the teacher can respond, "That's great that you're applying the operation to both sides, Samuel! Did anyone else do this? Did anyone *multiply* by 2 on both sides? Why did you do that, Cynthia?"

Both of these strategies help us shift the narrative away from questions as quizzing toward questions as invitations to contribute to the class conversation.

For more examples, see Figure 18.4: Elementary QSSSA Examples, Figure 18.5: Secondary QSSSA Examples, and Figure 18.6: QSSSA Script.

Teaching Online

QSSSA can be facilitated in a synchronous or asynchronous learning environment.

The key to a *synchronous* conversation structured through QSSSA is to use breakout rooms, which are available on all major web meeting platforms. Students can **share** during the breakout room and then unmute whole-group in the meeting during the **assess**.

The key to an *asynchronous* conversation structured through QSSSA is to use video platforms such as Padlet. Students can be instructed to view and respond to other students' videos, and teachers can **assess** by also viewing and responding to students' videos.

What Could Go Wrong?

A common misconception is that the QSSSA routine should be used every time we ask students to think about their learning. The routine offers many benefits, but trying to facilitate a structured conversation every few minutes in class might not be practical or necessary. Instead, a teacher might consider the best placement in the lesson based on the purpose of having students in dialogue with each other. The routine can be used to activate background knowledge, to internalize content, or to reflect and evaluate what they have learned. A good gauge about when to use QSSSA is to evaluate the depth and participation of conversations: if students are speaking with academic language, in depth, and equitably, then conversations can be set up with less structure (such as simply saying "Talk about this with your group"). If participation falls, however, the immediate and effective correction is to employ QSSSA structures.

Students may also struggle to participate if they are unfamiliar with a question, or totally lack the background knowledge to answer a question. This can be helped by cuing students to a reading passage, notes, or a structured visual or anchor chart (see the "Application" section). Alternatively, before showing students a video, before having them read something, or even before direct instruction, the teacher can guide students to pay close attention to something specifically, letting them know that this will be what they will be having a conversation about.

Lastly, educators may find it challenging to facilitate the structure when students are not used to participating in class. Practicing without content (questions that anyone can answer) may be helpful for students to get comfortable with the routine. Students may also be reluctant if they do not understand the reason we want them speaking to each other. Sharing the research and relevance of speaking in class can go a long way in supporting a learner's desire to participate. Implementing QSSSA goes part-and-parcel with building a culture of student conversations, and this can be communicated to students.

Differentiation Recommendations

Newcomers (Preliterate or Low Literacy in Home Language): Use simple models with visuals to support comprehension. Echo read the sentence starter with the class and have it displayed (language practice). Tap each word of the sentence stem (to support directionality, high-frequency word recognition, reinforce phonetics, and more). The classroom environmental print should have visuals with vocabulary. Students can use translated word banks with a few keywords that can be "plugged in" fairly easily. Set them up with a literate "buddy" in class for support. Focus on creating opportunities for quick-and-easy success. Be open to hearing student responses that are a combination of their home languages and English.	**Newcomers (Literate in Home Language):** Everything listed in the "Low Literacy box" is important for literate newcomers as well, but expect quicker progress. Ask students to look for commonalities in the alphabet, cognates, etc. Allow use of technology to negotiate meaning but encourage students to look up only keywords and phrases. Counsel students to understand that the "share" part of the QSSSA is the best place to negotiate meaning and clear up misconceptions.
Intermediate ELLs: The previous scaffolds support these students' progression with proficiency as they gain the ability to use more complex sentences in English. They will have more comprehension but still need oracy and English literacy practice to build the ability to authentically extend their ideas in English. These students can be effectively paired with beginners (to support the beginners' comprehension) or more proficient English speakers (to offer opportunities for more complex English language exposure).	**Advanced ELLs:** Echo reading the sentence starter offers all students the reminder to use grade-level vocabulary and sentence structures during the share. As noted above, this quick daily practice would result in much more academic language being used by these students in speaking and in writing. These students can also act as "peer tutors" to assist less English-proficient students in a multilevel class.

Technology Connections

Technology can be particularly well employed during the Assess portion of QSSSA. Mentimeter and Nearpod are both web apps that offer the ability for students to submit written responses to a class page, which the teacher can project and everyone can see. Additionally, the web apps Wheel of Names and Class Dojo offer a fun, interactive way to randomly call on students.

STRATEGY 18: QSSSA 223

Molly Lange Shackelford of Louisville, Kentucky, created her QSSSA template slide deck with several QSSSAs ready to go as a starter for us (Figure 18.6). She shares it with the teachers she supports and offers it out to the world so we can all just click through the slides to help students get familiar with the routine. See more at https://bit.ly/ShackelfordQSSSA.

Dr. Fleenor developed the following template to display all of the QSSSA structures on a single slide. The template also offers two examples using a word bank, visual, and differentiated sentence stems. You can make a copy of the template at http://bit.ly/QSSSAtemplateS.

The QSSSA script was developed by Michelle Gill (@MrsGill_) in Alberta, Canada. Michelle wanted her teachers to have a simple way to implement the routine (reading a script). She also created a "Why" column to offer some of the relevance of each step. You can download that script at bit.ly/QSSSAscript.

All figures from this chapter, as well as 11 additional chapters, references, hyperlinked Technology Connections, and more online resources, can be found at www.wiley.com/go/ellteacherstoolbox2.

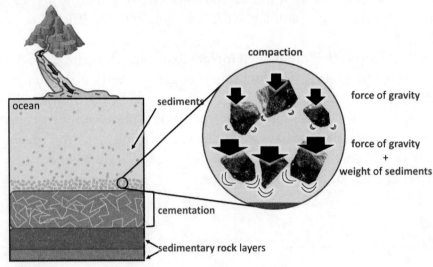

[CC BY-SA 4.0] Stephen Fleenor/Seidlitz Education For image attribution, see www.thevisualnonglossary.com/att.html#S5019

Figure 18.1 Example of a Structured Visual Reprinted with permission from The Visual Non-Glossary (http://www.thevisualnonglossary.com)

Example Signals
Raise your hand, and lower when ready
Put your fist on your chin, and lower when ready
Stand up, and sit down when ready
Raise a pen, and lower the pen when ready
Place a hand flat on the desk, then take it off when ready

Figure 18.2 Example Signals

Example "Who Goes First" Indicators
Student closest to the door
Student closest to the window
Student with the brightest shirt
Student with the darkest shirt

Figure 18.3 Example "Who First" Indicators

STRATEGY 18: QSSSA

	Question	Signal	Stem	Share	Assess
Math	What is the sum of three and four?	Raise hand when ready to respond	The sum of three and four is. . .	Turn to Your Partner, Random Calling on Students	Have students solve problems 1–5 in workbook.
Social Studies	What is one change that resulted from the Industrial Revolution?	Thinker's Chin	One change that resulted from the Industrial Revolution is. . .	Numbered Heads Together	Have students share with their table group and then illustrate in their journal the change they selected.
Science	What is a characteristic of an insect?	Stand when ready	One characteristic of an insect is. . .	Think, Pair, Share	Have students label or illustrate some characteristics of insects.
Language Arts	What is the main idea?	Put your pen down when finished writing a response	The main idea is. . .	Inside/Outside Circle	Randomize and rotate responses within whole group.

Figure 18.4 Elementary QSSSA Examples From QSSSA (p. 8–9), by Seidlitz et al., 2024, Seidlitz Education. Reprinted with permission.

	Question	Signal	Stem	Share	Assess
Math	What are some important things to remember when deriving the equation of a parabola?	Raise your hand when you can complete this sentence	One important thing to remember when deriving the equation of a parabola is. . .	Share in groups of three	Randomly call on students.
Social Studies	Do you support Sam Houston's position on secession?	Place your hand on your chin when you can complete this sentence	I support/oppose Sam Houston's position because. . .	Numbered Heads Together	Randomly select groups to respond.
Science	What are some unusual characteristics of annelids?	Stand up when you can complete this sentence	The most unusual characteristic of annelids is. . .	Share in groups of two	Randomly call on students.
Language Arts	Do you think Esperanza's family made a wise decision?	Put your pen down when you can complete this sentence	I think Esperanza's family made/did not make a wise decision because. . .	Share answers with several partners	Have students write their perspectives in journals.

Figure 18.5 Secondary QSSSA Examples From QSSSA (p. 8–9), by Seidlitz et al., 2024, Seidlitz Education. Reprinted with permission.

QSSSA Script	Why?
Class, without calling out answers think about this question: **QUESTION**	Linked to objectives and lesson goals, to activate prior knowledge for ELLs.
When you think you have an answer in mind let me know by: **SIGNAL**	Build in wait time for ELLs to process.
When you discuss your answers, I want you to respond in this format.... (*When you talk with your partner, I want you to sound like this. . .*) (*I'm listening for ". . ."*) **STEM**	Provides opportunity for students to practice targeted academic language.
Turn to your partner and discuss. . . (*Please find someone who. . . and use a complete sentence to discuss.*) (*please compare ideas with your partner.*) **SHARE**	Low-stress opportunity to talk. Chance to compare the responses of others, and 100% of the class practices targeted language.
Everyone please write your response. **ASSESS**	Scaffolds for ELLs, ensures students are prepared to respond.

Figure 18.6 QSSSA Script (see the Technology Connections for an online version) Adapted from script by Michelle Gill. Used with permission. QSSSA is adapted from *7 Steps to a Language Rich, Interactive Classroom* by John Seidlitz and Bill Perryman.

STRATEGY 19

Error Correction Strategies

What Is It?

This strategy is really a series of different steps we take to deal with the very tricky issue of error correction. When it comes to reading and writing (as well as speaking), our ELLs make plenty of them.

The question is: How can we best assist our students to learn from their mistakes and at the same time not have our corrections be de-motivators?

Don't believe anyone who tells you they *know* the best way to handle this critical component of language instruction. This is one of those areas in which there is definitely no best answer. However, we can share with you what seems to work for us and our students and what research guides us in our practices.

Why We Like It

As we discuss in the next section, research is mixed on the best ways to provide student error correction. Given that murkiness, and given the uniformly strong evidence in favor of the effectiveness of the inductive process and games (see Strategy 11: Inductive Learning and Strategy 23: Learning Games for Reading and Writing), we emphasize error correction through these two methods in our classroom practice. In addition, we also apply *one* method of feedback that has been found to be somewhat effective for student writing—pointing to an incorrect word as a prompt for student self-correction. Finally, research suggests that encouraging a growth mind-set among students—the idea that mistakes are just opportunities to learn and not obstacles to be avoided—can have a positive impact on overall academic performance (Ferlazzo, 2012, October 13).

Supporting Research

Though there does appear to be consensus on which three types of correction for oral errors might make sense to apply—immediate correction, correction after students have completed everything they want to say, and postponed correction at some later time—there is no agreement on if any of the three are actually effective (Zhou, 2020).

There does appear to be much more evidence demonstrating the ineffectiveness of the typical ways teachers provide feedback on written work, such as marking a student's paper (Conti, 2015, May 7; 2017; Sparks, 2023).

One practice that seems to have some evidence of success in feedback on writing, however, is pointing to an incorrect word as a prompt for student self-correction (Conti, 2015, May 20).

All of the error correction strategies we share here fit into the category of what some researchers characterize as "agentic feedback" (Mutoni Griffiths, 2023). The idea is that teachers just don't tell students what they've done wrong. Instead, we provide guidance and challenge students to figure out the specifics or, in the case of "self-correction," create the conditions where students can "preempt" making an error. In other words, students gain more agency in the process.

There is an important caveat that we teachers need to keep in mind when considering the results of all these studies. And that caveat was expressed clearly by education researcher Dylan Wiliam, who said, "In education, everything works somewhere and nothing works everywhere" (Wiliam, 2022). His point is especially relevant to error correction because, though a substantial number of studies have found the conclusions that we have shared, others have also found different ones for various ethnic and cultural groups (Schenck, 2021).

The lesson for all of us educators is that when applying these error correction strategies, and any of the strategies shared in this book, we need to do so in the context of knowing them, their assets, their dreams, and their challenges. As our experience has shown us, and as research has demonstrated, people tend to listen to critical feedback only when they feel valued (Berinto, 2018).

Common Core Connections

Really, what Common Core Standard does not apply to students learning from their mistakes and developing the resilience to recover from them?

Application

These are the four primary error-correction strategies we use in our classrooms. We will also describe a fifth strategy—recasts—which we only use in two very specific circumstances.

CONCEPT ATTAINMENT AND CONCEPT ATTAINMENT PLUS

In Strategy 11: Inductive Learning and in Bonus Strategy 2: Concept Attainment—Plus, we explain in detail how we take student writing mistakes and create the conditions for them to identify what is wrong and correct it.

GAMES

Here are our versions of two games incorporating student mistakes:

Buy a Mistake

This is our version of a popular game among ELL teachers called *Grammar Auction*. We type up a list of sentences containing written student mistakes (either actual student-written sentences or ones we create) and put an amount next to each one (e.g., $10 if we think it's a particularly tricky one, $5 if we think it's medium hard, and $1 if we think they'll pick up on it right away). We divide students into teams, with each group having a mini-whiteboard. We'll show one sentence and give students a minute to write the correct version on their board. If it's right, they get the dollar amount. If it's wrong, in our version they don't lose anything. The team with the most money at the end of the game wins.

Correct a Sentence

Here, we again type up a list of sentences containing student mistakes. In this game, though, after we divide students into teams, we give each team a sheet containing all the sentences, and they have to race through to correct them all in a certain period of time. At the end of that time (depending on the number of sentences—it could be 5 to 15 minutes), the team who has accurately corrected the greatest number of sentences is the winner. The first team to finish all of them correctly receives bonus points.

ENCOURAGE A GROWTH MIND-SET

In our book *Navigating the Common Core with ELLs,* we share a lesson plan designed to help students not be hesitant to take risks and make mistakes (Ferlazzo & Sypnieski, 2016, p. 82). Its essence is first to have students make a list of the times they spoke or wrote English incorrectly over the previous few months and what they learned from each experience. Afterwards, we all reflect on the long list of things students would not have learned if they had not been willing to take risks using their new language. This lesson plan can be downloaded for free at our book's website. See the Technology Connections section for the link.

GIVING INDIVIDUAL FEEDBACK

Of course, providing individual feedback can be a key error correction tool. How we use this tool is guided by a number of considerations:

- What type of relationship do we have with this student? Are they new to the class and to this country? Have they been with us for several months, and what do we know about them? The better relationship we have, the more candid the error feedback can be. In addition to the quality of the relationship, some researchers have found that

STRATEGY 19: ERROR CORRECTION STRATEGIES   *231*

"novice" language learners tend to do better with more positive feedback, while those who are more experienced tend to prefer more critical comments (Grant, 2013).

- Is it an error or a mistake? In linguistic terms, a *mistake* is doing something wrong that you have already been taught or should have known. An *error* is doing something incorrectly that you haven't yet been taught (Error, n.d.). Individual feedback on mistakes might be worth doing carefully. Generally, we hold off on doing feedback on errors and, instead, use them for class mini-lessons. This distinction between students doing something incorrectly that they have already been taught and their doing something incorrectly without having any prior knowledge of the concept *is* an important instructional consideration. Whether you call it a mistake or an error *is not* very important because the vast majority of people in the world, including us, do not care.

- When there are written mistakes, we point to it—whether it be a word or a punctuation issue. Students are typically then able to correct it then and there. Or, in the case of playing the Running Dictation game we discuss in Strategy 24: Dictation, after students *believe* they have accurately copied down each sentence, we'll just point to the sentence or sentences that contain errors. This kind of error correction turns students into "detectives" who have to do a deeper analysis of their work (Wiliam, 2016).

- We give very minimal feedback on oral mistakes—unless we are asked—as long as they do not seem to affect the primary message that the students want to communicate. We want to encourage them to talk and are thrilled when they are willing to do just that!

- If we have a solid relationship with a student, and if the student appears to be highly motivated, we will have a conversation explaining how we handle providing feedback on incorrectly used language. We then ask if that is what the student would like us to do, or if they would prefer more intensive individual correction. Invariably, these students choose the latter and appear to benefit from it.

SELF-CORRECTION

It may not be entirely accurate to describe "self-correction" as a form of "error correction" since the teacher is not there making the correction in "real time." Instead, the teacher is creating the conditions where students preempt themselves from making the error or mistake in the first place.

The way we put this strategy into practice is through use of an editing checklist, which researchers have found effective with ELLs (Cahyono & Amrina, 2016) and/or an "improvement rubric" that students can use to guide their writing.

Many different examples of editing checklists can be found online by searching "editing checklist." These checklists may include questions like "Have I put a period at the end of each sentence?" It is also possible to ask an artificial intelligence tool like ChatGPT to create a similar type of checklist, though we have found it requires a *very* detailed prompt to get a useful result.

A simple editing checklist can be used by students to help guide and double-check their work. As we're sure every teacher who has applied this kind of self-correction technique has found, however, providing this kind of scaffold to students and asking them to use it is no guarantee that they actually will! Nevertheless, some students will at least try to use it, and, in an ideal world, its guidelines may begin to be internalized by them, and they may develop a greater capacity for self-assessment.

Rubrics, as most teachers know, are a different approach to feedback that rely on attributes of quality that can be used by students and teachers alike to help guide student work and assess it. We prefer to use "improvement rubrics" (Ferlazzo, 2012, October 31). These kinds of rubrics, unlike most, do not utilize deficit language and emphasize what students have done instead of what they have not done. We use numbers to keep it simple for students and to avoid a text-heavy rubric. See Figure 19.1: Improvement Rubric for an example used by intermediate ELL students to compare an essay they wrote at the beginning of the year with one that they wrote several months later.

These editing checklists and rubrics can also be used by students in a peer assessment format, with students checking each other's work.

RECASTS

Recasts are a subtle form of error correction where the teacher/tutor reformulates a mistake or error back to the learner in the correct form. For example, the learner might say, "I go to San Francisco yesterday" and the teacher/tutor might respond, "Oh, you went to San Francisco yesterday." If the recast is made verbally, the teacher/tutor might put an emphasis on the word "went" when they say it.

Recasts are one of the most popular forms of error correction. Unfortunately, because of their subtlety, they are also one of the least effective forms because students don't necessarily notice them (Lyster & Ranta, 1997).

We only use recasts in two circumstances. One is during Strategy 8: Language Experience Approach when students are sharing sentences they wrote about the shared activity, and teachers are writing them down on the document camera or whiteboard. In those cases, we recommend that teachers use recasts to write correct versions of student sentences. We feel that, since we subsequently use the sentences for multiple other activities like sentence scrambles and oral reading, those extra exposures reinforce the correct language. In other words, they are not "one-and-dones."

The other occasion when we use recasts is when a "sister class" is responding to students' dialogue journal. This activity is discussed further in Bonus Strategy 5: Writer's Notebook available at www.wiley.com/go/ellteacherstoolbox2. There, ELL students write to penpals in another class, and those students use recasts in their responses. In this activity, we feel the primary learning benefit for our students is writing to an "authentic audience" (someone other than the teacher) and learning correct grammar is "gravy." In reality, the recasts themselves are the primary learning benefit for the *responding* English-proficient students, who need to reflect on their grammar knowledge and use their metacognitive skills to write their answers. This kind of learning helps the sister class teacher see the self-interest in participating in the pen-pal activity.

Though the actions we have listed here are the primary ways we offer feedback, we need to end by highlighting that we also often just point out mistakes and errors in class and correct them. As long as we have helped develop a classroom culture of risk-taking and support, those kinds of corrections are generally well received.

Dylan Wiliam, the education researcher who we quoted earlier in the chapter, provides a useful guideline for student feedback that we view more as aspirational than truly reflective of our classroom practice. He recommends that 25 percent of classroom feedback be teacher-to-individual-student; 25 percent teacher-to-the-entire-class; 25 percent be peer-to-student; and 25 percent be student self-assessment (Wiliam, 2023).

We think that is a helpful proportion to keep in mind but, as with everything in this book, we think these recommendations are best viewed more as a compass, and not as a fixed road map.

Teaching Online

As most of us discovered during pandemic-related distance learning, it is not easy to develop relationships in a remote teaching environment. This difficulty offers challenges for error correction; it's hard, but not impossible, in that situation to develop a sense of trust and rapport with students, particularly when students might not even turn on their cameras for us to see them!

What Could Go Wrong?

Each one of our students is an individual, and it is easy to miscalculate the fine line between what is the appropriate amount of correction and what amount will result in de-motivation. Many of our students come from highly vulnerable personal situations, which affects their learning outlook. Be aware and be flexible!

Differentiation Recommendations

Newcomers (Preliterate or Low Literacy in Home Language): Emphasize positive feedback. Support development of a growth mind-set, provide individual comments, and incorporate concept attainment and games.	**Newcomers (Literate in Home Language):** Emphasize positive feedback, adding in more critical comments as they develop increased English proficiency. Support development of a growth mind-set, provide individual comments, and incorporate concept attainment and games. Teacher creates basic editing checklists and rubrics for self-correction and peer assessment.
Intermediate ELLs: Provide positive feedback but can add increased critical commentary, especially following an explicit individual or class discussion about its value. Support development of a growth mind-set, provide individual comments, and incorporate concept attainment and games. Teacher creates more complex editing checklists and rubrics for self-correction and peer assessment.	**Advanced ELLs:** Provide positive feedback, and provide even *more* critical commentary—again, following an explicit individual or class discussion about its value. Support development of a growth mind-set, provide individual comments, and incorporate concept attainment and games. Invite students to co-create editing checklists and rubrics for self-correction and peer assessment.

Technology Connections

Practicing comprehension, writing, and pronunciation at online sites that provide immediate feedback and that generally use artificial intelligence in an adaptive learning context (each subsequent question is dependent on the learner's responses; it might be more challenging, easier, reinforce the previous concept, or introduce another one) is another way to reinforce language acquisition and practice weak areas. There, the only one who knows when you make a mistake is the computer. Though research is not conclusive, it appears that this kind of feedback *might* even be a more effective form of error correction than other ways (Li, 2010). You can find lists of these sites here:

- The Best Sites for Grammar Practice (http://larryferlazzo.edublogs.org/2008/12/07/the-best-sites-for-grammar-practice).
- The Best Sites for Online Pronunciation Feedback – Do You Know Others? (https://larryferlazzo.edublogs.org/2020/02/08/the-best-sites-for-online-pronunciation-feedback-do-you-know-more).
- The Best Free Online Tools Using Adaptive Learning (https://larryferlazzo.edublogs.org/2023/01/01/the-best-free-online-tools-using-adaptive-learning).

We have also had our students use artificial intelligence in other ways to help promote English acquisition and create supportive opportunities for error correction. We learned one idea we use from Spanish teacher Agnieszka Figlewicz. We ask students as homework to put various small portions of their writing—one-to-four sentences at a time—into ChatGPT, Gemini, or Poe or any other AI chatbot and precede it with instructions like this:

> *If this sentence is written correctly, tell me so. If it is not, rewrite the sentence correctly and explain any errors very simply in Spanish [or whatever is the student's home language]:*

Students then copy and paste, screenshot, or paste a link to it in a document they share with us.

There are also AI sites specifically designed for language learners that provide additional scaffolds for this exact kind of language feedback. See a Collection of "Best" Lists About Using Artificial Intelligence in Education (https://larryferlazzo.edublogs.org/2023/01/01/a-collection-of-best-lists-about-using-artificial-intelligence-in-education) to find the most up-to-date and most useful AI sites.

Risk-taking is essential in learning a new language. Encouraging students not to shy away from taking them is important, and you can get many ideas on how to do that in the classroom from these sources.

- The Best Ways to Use Mistakes When Teaching Writing (http://larryferlazzo.edublogs.org/2013/11/07/the-best-ways-to-use-mistakes-when-teaching-writing)

STRATEGY 19: ERROR CORRECTION STRATEGIES

- The Best Posts, Articles & Videos About Learning from Mistakes and Failures (http://larryferlazzo.edublogs.org/2011/07/28/the-best-posts-articles-videos-about-learning-from-mistakes-failures)
- The Best Resources on Helping Our Students Develop a Growth Mindset (http://larryferlazzo.edublogs.org/2012/10/13/the-best-resources-on-helping-our-students-develop-a-growth-mindset)
- You can download our growth mind-set–related resilience lesson plan at our *Navigating the Common Core with English Language Learners* website (www.wiley.com/WileyCDA/WileyTitle/productCd-1119023009.html).

You can find additional ideas about error correction at:

- The Best Resources on ESL/EFL/ELL Error Correction (https://larryferlazzo.edublogs.org/2011/09/04/the-best-resources-on-esleflell-error-correction)
- The Best Resources for Learning How to Best Give Feedback to Students (https://larryferlazzo.edublogs.org/2010/11/10/the-best-resources-for-learning-how-to-best-give-feedback-to-students)

Attribution

Versions of some of these ideas appeared in our book, *Navigating the Common Core with English Language Learners* (Ferlazzo & Sypnieski, 2016, p. 82, 254).

Spanish teacher Agnieszka Figlewicz shared her idea with us for having students use artificial intelligence for homework.

All figures from this chapter, as well as 11 additional chapters, references, hyperlinked Technology Connections, and more online resources, can be found at www.wiley.com/go/ellteacherstoolbox2.

ESSAY 1:	ESSAY 2:
I opened my essay with an attention grabber (a hook). 1 2 3 4	I opened my essay with an attention grabber (a hook). 1 2 3 4
I used a thesis statement saying the main idea of the essay. 1 2 3 4	I used a thesis statement saying the main idea of the essay. 1 2 3 4
I organized my essay into paragraphs. 1 2 3 4	I organized my essay into paragraphs. 1 2 3 4
I used topic sentences in all my paragraphs. 1 2 3 4	I used topic sentences in all my paragraphs. 1 2 3 4
I used the correct verb tenses (past or present). 1 2 3 4	I used the correct verb tenses (past or present). 1 2 3 4
Punctuation was correct throughout the essay, including in dialogues. 1 2 3 4	Punctuation was correct throughout the essay, including in dialogues. 1 2 3 4
I wrote a conclusion in which I summarized my main points and left the reader with something to think about. 1 2 3 4	I wrote a conclusion in which I summarized my main points and left the reader with something to think about. 1 2 3 4

Figure 19.1 Improvement Rubric   Originally published in Helping Students Motivate Themselves by Larry Ferlazzo, Routledge, 2011. Reprinted with permission of the publisher.

STRATEGY 20

Revision

What Is It?

In the United States, the word *revision* is generally used to describe the act of reviewing a piece of writing and making improvements to it. In the United Kingdom and Commonwealth countries, it's more often used to describe the act of studying and preparing for exams (American English. . ., n.d.). We are using the former definition as we talk about the strategy, which is a series of steps we use to help ELL students improve their writing.

Why We Like It

We like doing revision for two reasons—it seems to help our ELLs improve their writing and they also usually don't object to it! We find much more resistance to revision in our classes with English-proficient students. A perfect example of this perspective is shown in a video we wrote about in our last book (*Navigating the Common Core with English Language Learners*, 2016, p. 171). In the video:

> President Obama is being interviewed by a middle school student (https://www.youtube.com/watch?v=e7C8vEDhhVQ). As the president is explaining the importance of students revising their writing, the student interviewer cuts him off saying, "Yeah, I think you've pretty much covered everything about that question." We think that reaction "pretty much" sums up how many of our [English-proficient] students feel about the revision process—they'd rather just move on!

Our experience with ELLs seems to be shared by many other educators—ELL students are generally open to revising more often (Kietlinska, n.d., p. 70). This *might* be attributable to the fact that researchers have found many ELLs believe that their learning is based more on effort than natural-born intelligence (Byers-Heinlein & Garcia, 2015). In other words, it appears that ELLs might be more prone to having a growth mind-set and to see mistakes as opportunities to learn (Decades of Scientific Research. . ., n.d.).

This doesn't mean that ELLs are not afraid of making mistakes or never get frustrated. However, every day they are likely to be in a situation in which they see an immediate gain in understanding and communicating based on their efforts. This success can be experienced in being better able to understand ordering in a restaurant, watching an English-language TV show, comprehending a text, communicating in writing, or socializing more easily with English-speaking friends.

We should point out that artificial intelligence now brings an entirely different aspect to the idea of revision. We have sometimes incorporated its use as a new step in the standard revision process we have applied for years in our classrooms, in addition to encouraging students to use it in a simple new revision process we like to have students do as homework.

Supporting Research

There does not seem to be clarity among researchers about the best ways to assist ELLs in revising their writing, but they all seem to agree that one of the best things teachers can do is to give ELLs more time—more time to write, more time to think, more time to revise (Kietlinska, n.d., p. 70). This need is one of the major reasons why many researchers recommend including an opportunity for peer review and feedback (Decades of Scientific Research, n.d., p. 8; Kietlinska, n.d., p. 80)—this process provides more time, as well as social support. Individual tutoring is generally considered the most-effective way to provide feedback for revision (Kietlinska, n.d., p. 85), and we discuss some ways to do that in Strategy 37: Social Emotional Learning. Finally, researchers typically suggest that the feedback process should focus on the content first and grammar later (Kietlinska, n.d., p. 75).

Common Core Connections

Revision of student writing can assist in meeting several of the Standards, including one Writing Standard that is specifically *about* revision: "Develop and strengthen writing as needed by planning, revising, editing, rewriting, or trying a new approach." Remember, however, as we mentioned previously, that the Common Core authors have made it very clear that ELLs can meet the Standards without exhibiting "native-like" skills in all areas. We don't need to be the grammar police!

Application

REVISING AN ESSAY

We typically use the following multistep process in assisting our students with revision (you can read about revision strategies we use more occasionally in our book, *Navigating the Common Core with English Language Learners*, 2016, p. 173). Please note that we used the word *typically* and not *always*. Sometimes, because of time constraints, we'll work on revising just a portion of an essay and not the entire piece:

1. After pre-planning their essay with a graphic organizer (see Strategy 3: Graphic Organizers), students write out their first draft with pen on paper. As we have discussed in previous chapters, we ask students to use Google Translate only "for words,

not for sentences." More often than not, our request is heeded, but not always. We encourage students to read their essay out loud, though quietly, in the classroom or outside, because research suggests that writers are more likely to catch errors through using that practice (Nebel, n.d.).

2. We review a hard copy of their essay with each student, primarily focusing on key issues such as these: Is it basically communicating what they want it to say? Is the content corresponding with the essay's purpose? Does it have an introduction, topic sentences, and so on? We generally don't cover grammar issues at this time, though we *might* point out one or two of them. See Strategy 19: Error Correction Strategies for more specific advice about giving critical feedback to students.

3. Students will then type out their essay on laptops. In addition to incorporating our feedback, students can use the grammar and spelling corrections provided by Google Docs or Microsoft Word.

4. Sometimes we have students copy and paste the following prompt, followed by their essay into ChaptGPT or any other AI chatbot that is available. Of course, the prompt can be changed to ask for even more specific feedback, on claims, evidence, etc. But we've found this simple version has worked well:

   You are a teacher of beginning English language learners. You want to make as few corrections as possible to the following essay. You don't want to hurt their feelings, but you want them to learn a few key things about writing in English. Rewrite the essay with as few changes as possible. Then, afterwards, explain in Spanish (or a different home language) why you made those changes.

5. In an ideal world, we have the time then to meet individually with each student to check with them to see if they agree or disagree with the chatbot's changes, and usually offer one-or-two additional suggested changes.

   Because of time issues, we often will then skip to step 9 when students turn their essays into slideshows and then share via speed-dating. However, we occasionally, instead, move on to the peer review process.

6. Students will work with a partner using a peer reviewing process. We print out two copies of each essay—one is for the peer reviewer. Each student also gets one copy of Figure 20.1: Peer Review Sheet.

   The first student who gets their essay reviewed reads the essay aloud, and the reviewer follows along on their copy. During this time, the writer and the reviewer make notes about mistakes and improvements, primarily targeting grammar and sentence construction issues. After the writer is done reading, the writer and the reviewer discuss the points they both noted. Then, the reviewer goes through the peer review sheet one section at a time taking a minute or so to silently read that section of the essay and noting suggestions on the sheet. After they are done with each section, the reviewer shares comments with the writer, who makes notes on their copy of the essay. This process is repeated until the entire sheet is completed, and then the roles are reversed.

Note that teachers will probably want to modify the peer review sheet to reflect the essay their students are writing.

7. We'll then quickly review this marked-up version of the essay with the student and, depending on the student's English proficiency and overall confidence level, may give specific feedback on one or two grammar issues by pointing at the mistake and having students identify the correction. More importantly, we'll note to ourselves what specific skills we need to cover in future lessons.

8. Students will next return to the electronic version of the essay they saved. Then they will make the revisions identified in the peer review process and in the follow-up conversation we had with them.

9. Students will print out two copies of their essay—one for us to keep in a file where we can track student progress and one they can glue into their writer's notebook (see Bonus Strategy 5: Writer's Notebook, available at www.wiley.com/go/ellteacher stoolbox2).

10. Sometimes we'll give students another opportunity to review and revise their essay by having them turn it into a narrated book or slideshow presentation, which they will post on our class blog. We then show it to the entire class. Students love it! Not only does this extra step provide more time for ELLs to revise (remember in the research section that's what everyone agrees they need), but also it is an excellent opportunity for pronunciation practice. You can see a link to the free tools we use in the Technology Connections section.

Then, it's time to move on to the next essay or project!

REVISING FOR HOMEWORK

We shared this next activity in the previous chapter, Strategy 19: Error Correction Strategies, and feel that reprinting it here again is valuable for readers.

We learned this idea from Spanish teacher Agnieszka Figlewicz and have put it to good use, primarily as homework but also sometimes in class.

We just ask students to paste this prompt into ChatGPT or another AI chatbot:

If this sentence is written correctly, tell me so. If it is not, rewrite the sentence correctly and explain any errors very simply in Spanish [or whatever is the student's home language]:

We then ask students to try writing the most complex sentences they think of and then learn from the chatbot. We have them repeat this activity with several sentences. If there is time, students share what they learned with a partner, and they copy and paste the conversation into a document they share with us, or paste a link to it.

We emphasize that, in this activity, they should stretch themselves, and that making errors is perfectly fine. Often, we'll ask students to share what they thought was the important thing they learned about English from that particular activity.

Teaching Online

All aspects of these revision applications can be done online and in breakout rooms, though the peer revision process is obviously a bit trickier. However, it can be done through the use of shared screens.

We recognize that student use and misuse of AI for writing can be more tempting when all instruction is through distance learning. All we can do is instruct students on ethical AI use (see Strategy 14: Writing Frames and Writing Structures), continually bring up reminders, and have candid and caring conversations if we believe the problem arises.

What Could Go Wrong?

Don't feel like you have to follow our nine-step process every time you have students write an essay! You won't have time, and even your ELLs, though they are likely to be less resistant to revision than other students, may get burnt out. We're generally able to use this entire process once every quarter.

We talk more extensively about how we frame the ethical use of Artificial Intelligence, including chatbots and Google Translate, in Strategy 14: Writing Frames and Writing Structures. Nevertheless, that kind of preparation and regular reminders do not guarantee that students will always follow them. In that chapter and in others, we also recommend regular handwritten formative assessments for a variety of purposes, including to help us become aware if AI use is a problem.

Differentiation Recommendations

Newcomers (Preliterate or Low Literacy in Home Language): Focuses on sentence-level writing and revision, gradually increasing to slightly more lengthy writing. Students can access a tool like Read&Write for Google Chrome or Microsoft's Immersive Reader, which offer picture dictionary features. Also use Google Translate to provide audio support for text. Teacher leads with praise.	**Newcomers (Literate in Home Language):** Teacher leads with praise and focuses on no more than one or two suggestions for improvement. Use an AI chatbot prompt like the model in this chapter requesting simple feedback.
Intermediate ELLs: Teacher leads with praise and then offers more critical feedback. Instead of focusing on one or two suggestions, perhaps increase it to three. Use an AI chatbot prompt like the model in this chapter, perhaps editing it to request slightly more critical feedback and additional details.	**Advanced ELLs:** The teacher leads with praise and then offers increasingly critical feedback. Use a prompt with an AI chatbot to request more critical feedback and additional details (vocabulary choices, suggestions for more complex sentences).

Technology Connections

Not all our ELL students are thrilled with revision. Good, student-friendly videos and images that show its importance can be found at The Best Resources for Getting Student Writers to "Buy-into" Revision (http://larryferlazzo.edublogs.org/2015/07/23/the-best-resources-on-getting-student-writers-to-buy-into-revision-help-me-find-more/).

Students can use many tools to turn their essays into narrated books. You can see the links to the online tools we use at The Best Ways to Create Online Slideshows (https://larryferlazzo.edublogs.org/2008/05/06/the-best-ways-to-create-online-slideshows/).

All figures from this chapter, as well as 11 additional chapters, references, hyperlinked Technology Connections, and more online resources, can be found at www.wiley.com/go/ellteacherstoolbox2.

STRATEGY 20: REVISION 243

This sheet should be stapled on top of your essay

Name of Writer _____

Name of Reviewer _____

First, have the writer read their essay to you while you are looking at it. Mark down any grammar issues you find. After your partner is done reading, share your comments.

Essay Check List

1. Does it have a title related to the topic?

First Paragraph

1. Does it have a good hook?
2. Does it have a thesis statement communicating the main idea of the essay?
3. Does it have a sentence listing major topics the essay will cover?

Body Paragraphs

1. Does it have a topic sentence?
2. Does it have good supporting details?

Conclusion

1. Does it summarize the content that was covered in the essay?
2. Does it say why the essay topic is important?

Figure 20.1 Peer Review Sheet *Source:* Modified from Exhibit 4.2 in *Navigating the Common Core with English Language Learners* (Ferlazzo & Sypnieski, 2016, p. 175).

STRATEGY 21
Problem-Posing

What Is It?

Problem-posing is an element of the critical pedagogy concept developed by Brazilian educator Paulo Freire. The idea is to draw from students the issues and concerns they have about their lives and help them identify actions they can take to effectively respond to them. The Peace Corps, drawing on the work of Nina Wallerstein (Crawford-Lange, 1983), developed a multistep instructional strategy to also use this process as a language-learning opportunity (Schleppegrell & Bowman, 1995, p. 298).

Why We Like It

As we've said elsewhere and repeatedly in this book, looking at our students through the lens of assets, and not deficits, is a central element of our teaching beliefs. Problem-posing is a classic example of how students can use their own life experiences to learn and grow in an academic environment. In addition, it can assist them to use what they learn in our classrooms to improve their lives outside of school.

Last, it's a versatile strategy that can be used in just about any thematic unit. Unfortunately, all of us have problems and challenges!

Supporting Research

There appears to be limited research available specifically on this kind of problem-posing instructional strategy with its roots in Freirian critical pedagogy. However, this strategy has many similarities to culturally responsive pedagogy, and research finds that it can have a positive impact on student achievement (Liebtag, n.d.). Also see Strategy 36: Culturally Responsive Teaching.

Common Core Connections

The writing involved in this strategy connects to the Language Standards of acquiring and applying language conventions, as well as to the Standard of argument writing. In addition, depending on how much time the teacher wants to devote to the lesson, it can also support student Speaking and Listening Standards. Finally, the process of problem-posing is really a form of close-reading an image or dialogue (see Strategy 10: Reading Comprehension and Strategy 17: Using Photos or Other Images in Reading and Writing for more on close reading). This makes the strategy very relevant to several of the Reading Standards.

Application

There are eight (and sometimes nine) primary steps to our modified version of this instructional strategy:

1. Select a picture or short video clip portraying a national or international problem directly affecting students or a common challenge students and their families face (a photo of a long line of people wanting to apply for a job, a movie scene in which someone is a victim of crime, a photo of a child being bullied on a playground, an image of damage caused by a hate crime). Another option for high ELL beginners or intermediates is to have the teacher write a dialogue demonstrating the problem.

   Of course, a prerequisite of being able to use this strategy is having a *relationship* with your students and knowing their hopes, dreams, and concerns. Does this mean you have to spend hours asking them questions? Of course not. However, it does mean you can do the following:

   - Have all students do a simple introductory poster and small-group presentation sharing their likes, worries, dreams for the future, favorite songs, and so on.
   - Follow up that assignment with brief individual conversations about what they said. Just take a minute or two when they're working on computers or quietly reading a book.
   - Make arrangements with the classroom teacher they have during your prep period to pull each student out to have what our principal Jim Peterson calls a *walk-and-talk*. This is just a 15-minute walking conversation when you can check in with your student and learn more about them.
   - Visit the home of your student. Our local teachers union was one of the founders of the national Parent-Teacher Home Visit Project. See the Technology Connections section for more details.

2. Show the image or video clip, or a student and the teacher can act out the dialogue.

   Make sure you turn on the video's English captions—if available.

   If you are using a dialogue, be sure to arrange a brief practice time with the student or students.

3. Next, ask students to share what they believe is happening. What is the problem they think is being portrayed?

   Ask students to first describe what they see with simple prompting questions such as "Who is in the picture or video?" "Where are they?" "What is happening?" "What else do you see?" "How do you think the person is feeling?" Give students a minute to think about their responses before calling on them.

   Write student answers to the questions on the board or document camera and recast any errors. *Recasting* means writing and saying in correct English if something is said incorrectly (Student: "Boy in picture." Teacher: "There is a boy in the picture."). Students can copy what you write in the first question in Figure 21.1: Problem-Posing Graphic Organizer.

   Then, ask students what they think is the problem in the picture. Depending on the English proficiency level of the students, the teacher might have to teach what the word *problem* means (e.g., "It means something bad" and play-act being thirsty: "No water is a problem."). Write the response on the board or document camera and have students copy it down. Students could say more than one type of problem. If that's the case, as long as they make sense, write them down and have students copy the words in the second section of the graphic organizer.

4. This is followed by asking students if they, members of their family, or friends have ever experienced a similar problem now or in the past.

   The teacher can probably begin by saying that have either experienced it or have known former students or others who have experienced it and share that example. The teacher can write a simple sentence about it on the board or document camera. Students should not copy the sentence, but it can serve as a model.

   The teacher then asks students to share if they, their family, or friends are experiencing this problem now or have experienced it in the past. If some students say yes, the teacher can ask simple questions ("Are you having the problem?" "Is your family having this problem?" "When did you have this problem?" "Where are you having the problem?" "How does it make you feel?") and compose simple sentences on the board or document camera for students to copy in the second section in the graphic organizer. As always, after asking a question the teacher should ask students to think about it for 30 seconds or a minute prior to calling on someone to share. We also make a point of saying that it's okay if students just don't feel comfortable answering the question.

   If they have no experience with the problem, they can just circle that answer on the graphic organizer.

5. Ask students what they think caused the problem.

   The teacher first might have to define the world *cause* through doing some physical examples (e.g., putting a book on the floor and pretending to trip over it and asking, "Why did I stumble?" or telling students they are hungry and asking them why they think that is the case).

The teacher can then ask students what they think caused the problem and write down what they say on the board or document camera. Students can copy down all or some of the causes listed. They don't have to copy down any causes with which they don't agree.

6. Next, students can share potential solutions to the problem, including any ones they might have already tried.

   The teacher may need to teach the meaning of the word *solution* (he or she can refer back to the play-acting about needing water as being a problem. Then, go around play-acting asking students for water to see who will give it. Not only will it teach the world *solution* but also it will be fun to see who refuses to help!).

   If the process has been going on for a while, we sometimes will end it for the day at this point and ask students to think about potential solutions for homework. Other times, we will continue on to finish this multistep process on the same day.

   After giving students a minute to think about it, and then to share with a partner, the teacher asks students what they think are solutions to the problem that they have either tried in the past or think would work in the future. The teacher writes them down on the board or document camera and asks students to copy them on the graphic organizer.

7. Then, students are asked to choose which solution they think would be the best one.

   Students write their answer on the graphic organizer. Ideally, they can also explain in English why they think one is the best solution. However, that is not always possible for ELL beginners. In those situations, students can answer in their home language.

8. Finally, students are asked what they could do to help solve the problem.

   The graphic organizer provides a space for students to write down what they could do individually and what they could do with others.

   Students can make a simple illustrated poster or slideshow with their responses to each of the steps and practice reading them in small groups. We've also recorded their presentations and posted them online—with permission from them and their family (see the Technology Connections section).

9. In some cases, the final step is to have students decide if they want to take action to try to solve the problem. We use this multistep process several times during the school year, but it's not feasible to move to the action stage every time due to time constraints. However, when student energy is obvious, it makes sense to move forward.

   Actions can be simple or more complicated. In our classes over the years, actions have ranged from students making posters about the importance of picking up trash on school grounds to organizing a neighborhood-wide jobs fair with 20 job-training providers and 300 people in attendance. Other student actions have included organizing neighborhood campaigns to complete US Census forms, organizing a forum on the rights of immigrants, and writing letters to public officials about government immigration policy.

Teaching Online

Most of the steps in the problem-posing sequence can be done by sharing screens and partners discussing what they saw or wrote to everyone in the video conference or in breakout rooms. However, taking steps to try to solve the problem can be more challenging if everyone is online. Organizing support on social media and meeting with officials via video conferencing are possible strategies for getting around this issue.

What Could Go Wrong?

Don't feel like you have to complete this lesson in one day! The originator of the expression "Always leave them wanting more" is in dispute, but the advice is not! This strategy easily lends itself to being taught in chunks on different days.

Be politically savvy when it comes to the class deciding on student action steps. Don't put you or your students in the middle of a firestorm with administrators and parents. Don't encourage students to take actions that could make them or you politically vulnerable. Don't get involved in partisan politics.

Do encourage students to take fact-based actions such as the ones we described in Step 9 and, before anything is done, make sure you have support from your school administrators. This may be the first time any of your students have taken a step toward participating in public life, a step that may very well have put their lives in danger in their home countries. This makes it doubly important that teachers make sure that any action has the support of the school and parents.

Differentiation Recommendations

Newcomers (Preliterate or Low Literacy in Home Language): Should be able to participate in the entire problem-posing process, though are likely to need Google Translate audio support or support from another student who speaks their home language (or from the teacher, if they speak it). Will need translation support if organizing public events responding to identified problems.	**Newcomers (Literate in Home Language):** Should be able to participate in the entire process with minimal home language support. May need translation support if organizing public events responding to identified problems.
Intermediate ELLs: Participate in the entire problem-posing process, with expectations that they use more complex English sentences verbally and in writing when discussing problems, their causes, and possible solutions. Minimal translation support should be needed if organizing public events responding to identified problems.	**Advanced ELLs:** Participate in the entire problem-posing process, with even greater expectations of text and speaking complexity. Should be able to speak at public events responding to identified problems with no translation support.

Technology Connections

To learn more about making home visits to help build relationships with students and their families, visit The Best Resources for Learning About Teacher Home Visits (http://engagingparentsinschool.edublogs.org/2011/10/10/the-best-resources-for-learning-about-teacher-home-visits/).

We have recorded students presenting their problem-posing posters and posted it online. There are many tools for this kind of recording. Find them at The Best Ways to Create Online Slideshows (https://larryferlazzo.edublogs.org/2008/05/06/the-best-ways-to-create-online-slideshows/).

We mentioned various action projects our students took, including informing their neighborhood about the advantages of completing Census forms. You can read more about it, and see their posters, at Combining an "Assets" Perspective with an Authentic Audience (http://larryferlazzo.edublogs.org/2016/09/21/a-look-back-combining-an-assets-perspective-with-an-authentic-audience/).

Attribution

Versions of some of these ideas appeared in our book, *The ESL/ELL Teacher's Survival Guide* (Ferlazzo & Sypnieski, 2012, p. 45) and in our book, *Navigating the Common Core with English Language Learners* (Ferlazzo & Sypnieski, 2016, p. 201).

All figures from this chapter, as well as 11 additional chapters, references, hyperlinked Technology Connections, and more online resources, can be found at www.wiley.com/go/ellteacherstoolbox2.

Name _____

1. What do you see in the picture/video/dialogue?
   _____
   _____
   _____

2. What is the problem?
   The problem is _____.

3. Do you, your family, or your friends have this problem now, or have you had it in the past?
   Yes, I/we/they have this problem now when _____
   _____.
   Yes, I/we/they had this problem in the past when _____
   _____.
   OR
   No, I/we/they do not have this problem now and have not had it in the past.

4. What do you think is the cause of that problem?
   I think _____
   is/are the cause/causes of the problem.

5. What are solutions to that problem?
   One solution is _____.
   Another solution is _____.

6. What is the best solution to that problem?
   The best solution to that problem is _____
   because _____
   _____.

7. What is one thing you can do to help solve the problem?
   One thing I can do alone to help solve the problem is ___
   _____. One thing I can do with others is to ___
   _____.

Figure 21.1 Problem-Posing Graphic Organizer

STRATEGY 22
Project-Based Learning and Problem-Based Learning

What Is It?

There are more similarities than differences between project-based learning and problem-based learning (and we should point out that teachers have been doing these types of activities before the terms were invented).

Project-based learning is generally defined as students in small groups working on tasks that lead to a concrete project of some kind (a poster, slideshow, report), accompanied by a public presentation.

A *problem-based learning* activity can also lead to a product and/or presentation, but the focus is a real-word problem students must solve.

Either of these two activities can take anywhere between a few days and a few weeks.

Why We Like It

Both project-based learning and problem-based learning offer an engaging framework for countless language acquisition and leadership development activities.

Though we do both (and probably do more project-based learning activities because they tend to be simpler and take less time), we lean toward liking problem-based learning more since we feel that helping our students develop into "active" citizens in a democratic society is a priority for us. Problem-based learning is an excellent tool for students to practice that critical skill.

Supporting Research

Researchers have found that problem-based learning can result in increased achievement for ELLs in writing, reading, and communicative skills (Othman & Shah, 2013). Similar results have been found for ELLs through project-based learning (Essien, 2015). There is extensive research documenting the effectiveness of both kinds of activities with a broad range of students (i.e., De Vivo, 2022; REL, 2017; Nietzel, 2019; Ostby, 2022).

Common Core Connections

Like Strategy 37: Social Emotional Learning, it's a bit challenging to write a short section connecting the standards to project-based learning and problem-based learning. There are *many* ways both PBLs can be used to achieve the Common Core Standards. In fact, it connects to so many of them so well that their rise in popularity to a certain extent may be traced to the establishment of the Common Core Standards (Ellison & Freedberg, 2015). But *which* Common Core Standards they connect to can vary depending on exactly how you do it and which topics you choose.

So, as in Strategy 37: Social Emotional Learning, we've created a separate resource list filled with our choices of articles and reports detailing which PBL projects connect to what standards.

Check out The Best Resources to Help Connect Project & Problem Based Learning to Standards (https://larryferlazzo.edublogs.org/2024/06/29/the-best-resources-to-help-connect-project-problem-based-learning-to-standards/).

Application

We'll begin this section with short examples of both project-based learning and problem-based learning projects we've done in our ELL classes.

Then, we'll lay out the typical process we use in both types of activities.

Finally, we'll end with a short section on a related activity called "Object-Based Learning."

EXAMPLES OF PROJECT-BASED LEARNING WE'VE DONE WITH ELLs

Here are some examples of project-based learning efforts our ELL classes have done:

- To evaluate which building methods would be cooler in Sacramento's blazing climate, Hmong refugee students built several model homes using "Western" design and several using traditional Hmong methods using bamboo. They put thermometers in each one to measure results. We believe you can accurately guess which method was more successful!

- Small groups first identified their priorities for the kind of neighborhood they would like to live in. Using those priorities as part of a checklist, we then went on two field trips: first, walking around our school community and, then, going to the highest-income ZIP code in Sacramento (where, one year, someone called the police on us!). After comparing which neighborhood had the highest number of positive attributes on the lists, along with analysis of community data for each neighborhood, students then developed argument essays and presentations promoting which neighborhood they thought was the best one. During the many years we've done this project, students identify their school community as the one they like the best more than 90% of the time!

- As part of a series of lessons on the density of water and buoyancy, students researched online different kinds of boats. They then worked in teams to create models out of different natural or biodegradable materials to see which ones would carry the heaviest load without sinking, trying it out at first in aquariums in the classroom. Next, students tested their creations on an actual river near the school.

- At the end of the school year, students could choose any school appropriate topic they wanted to teach the class. However, they had to teach it using the key instructional strategies that had primarily been used during the year: inductive teaching, clozes, read alouds, etc. Though there wasn't time to use all their instructional materials, they had to teach at least one 20-minute lesson.

- Students worked in small groups to first identify what they could agree on for the characteristics of a "good" career. They then researched different occupations, worked with us to invite some people (including former ELL students) who were working in those jobs to speak with them, and made class presentations about which job or jobs they felt were right for them.

- Students worked in small groups and developed presentations on important elements of their respective home cultures (see Figure 22.1: Home Culture Project).

EXAMPLES OF PROBLEM-BASED LEARNING WE'VE DONE WITH ELL STUDENTS

Here are some examples of problem-based learning projects our students have tackled:

- After learning that our school's community might be shortchanged in government support because of low U.S. Census participation, students developed multilingual brochures encouraging Census participation and distributed them in the neighborhood.

- After conducting a series of individual conversations both inside and outside of school to identify community problems, students organized a school "fair" where multiple job training agencies had information booths.

- Muslim students were concerned about the lack of halal food. They met with cafeteria workers, researched school district food budgets, and successfully negotiated to have halal options available during each lunch.

PROJECT- AND PROBLEM-BASED PROJECT PROCESS

We want to emphasize that we do not consider ourselves to be experts in either project- or problem-based learning, and the processes we follow may not be in exact line with how experts do them.

However, these processes have worked for us and for our students. Does every project follow these exact steps to the letter? Of course not! As we've mentioned, our chapters are compasses, not roadmaps.

Step 1: Identify the focus of the project (sometimes referred to as an "essential" or "driving" question) or, in problem-based learning, identify the primary problem.

The driving questions for the project-based learning activities described in the previous section of this chapter were:

- Are "Western" or Indigenous building methods better in the face of our changing climate?
- What boat materials and designs work best, and what does it mean to "work best"?
- What are the elements of a good neighborhood?
- What is involved in teaching an effective lesson?
- What are the key factors that make a career a good one for me?
- What makes up a society's culture?

In problem-based learning, the problems are generally identified through students initiating individual conversations asking their peers and family members (we might ask that students ask six students, two school staff, two family members, and two non-family members in the community) to learn what they think are the biggest problems facing students in school and the biggest issues facing them and their families outside of school. A simple form with questions, along with a requirement to actually talk individually with people (not an impersonal survey—in Larry's community organizing career, he found that often people will write down in surveys what they think they should say instead of what they really feel), along with in-class practice and role-plays will generate lots of potential problems to work on, in addition to a tremendous amount of language practice. Sometimes, however, a more immediate issue may arise, like not having halal food in the school cafeteria. In those cases, entire classes might quickly coalesce around a single issue.

Step 2: Research what we know and don't know about the focus of the project or the problem, and develop a plan to learn what we need to know.

For this step, ELL teachers may need to provide an organized structure students can use for research.

Figure 22.1 is an example of one used for the home country's culture project-based learning project.

In problem-based learning, students might identify three or four of the most mentioned concerns in their conversations, perhaps housing, crime, jobs, and immigration legal advice. Then, the teacher would provide a research outline that could look like Figure 22.2: Community Problem Research Form: What Do We Know About the Problem Now?

At this point, in our experience, at least, teachers need to provide a large amount of assistance to students to help them figure out what are the most important pieces of information they don't know.

STRATEGY 22: PROJECT-BASED AND PROBLEM-BASED LEARNING

Step 3: *Implement the plan to find out needed information.*

In this step, students generally need a fair amount of scaffolding and a list of resources (or, as we did in the science project-based learning activities, a series of experiments) that teachers can provide in both project- and problem-based projects. Doing these kinds of activities does not mean they are free of explicit instruction!

Step 4: *Draw conclusions and act on it*, either through a presentation or report, which is typically the case in project-based learning; or through taking action to solve the problem, which is typically what happens in problem-based learning. We generally also ask that students do a reflective assignment explaining what they learned through the project-based learning process.

In problem-based learning, to help students narrow down the best solution, we guide them through the criteria community organizers use to narrow down a "problem" (something that is big) to an "issue," something that is specific and winnable in a short period of time. For example, unemployment was a big *problem* identified by our students. We were able to narrow it down to an issue by deciding to organize a fair for job training agencies at the school.

BONUS SECTION: OBJECT-BASED LEARNING

Though project-based learning and problem-based learning get most of the attention, there's also another variation of the inquiry method that we like that is called object-based learning.

There has been a fair amount of writing about it, and we point at resources to learn more about it in the Technology Connections section.

Larry has been particularly interested in it because he also teaches International Baccalaureate Theory of Knowledge classes (which always include many ELLs), and one of the main assessment tools asks students to answer prompts using objects.

We've used simple versions in our ELL classes, including the following:

- What is an object that is important to you? Display a picture of it and describe it, including what your history is with it, why it is important to you, and what you think it communicates to other people about you.

- What is an object that represents a challenge you face in school? How does it represent that challenge, and how do you think you can overcome that challenge?

- What are three objects that represent the biggest differences between your home country and the United States? Please be specific about what's different.

We also provide writing frames for students to use when responding to these prompts. See Figure 22.3: Object Writing Frame for an example.

Of course, it is important that educators teach the word "object" and provide examples when doing this activity.

Teaching Online

Everything in this chapter can be done in an online environment. The real question is if students will do it without taking any artificial intelligence shortcuts. Once again, it gets back to teachers having regular conversations with students about the appropriate and inappropriate ways to use AI and to developing solid relationships of trust.

What Could Go Wrong?

ELL students will need explicit vocabulary instruction and more scaffolds than an English-proficient class will need—obviously not because they are less intelligent but because they just don't have mastery of the English language yet. Especially the first time around on either project-based learning or problem-based learning, do not hesitate to provide as much direct instruction as necessary! Everyone, including our students, learns more from their successes than their failures (Ferlazzo, November 2019), so there is no shame in going overboard on providing scaffolds initially. There will be plenty of time to gradually remove them the next time around.

Differentiation Recommendations

Newcomers (Preliterate or Low Literacy in Home Language): It will be a challenge to engage these students in either PBL activity because the language involved can be fairly complex. It should be somewhat easier for project-based learning, since most of those activities are within the control of the teacher and they can have time to prepare with translated materials. Problem-based learning can be a bit of a wildcard since we really don't know what issues will come up. However, these students can participate in the initial activity of talking with people to learn what concerns they have. The conversations can be done in the student's home language with them making voice notes, or one of the growing number of simultaneous translation tools can be used. Object-based learning, on the other hand, should be very accessible to these students through the use of Google Translate or other similar tools.	**Newcomers (Literate in Home Language):** All of the project-based and problem-based activities discussed in the chapter were done by newcomer classes. Though not all the scaffolds that were used were listed in the chapter, they included pre-teaching vocabulary, graphic organizers, writing frames, sentence starters, and many more.
Intermediate ELLs: These students should be able to do all the activities discussed in the chapter, with fewer scaffolds and with more complex topics.	**Advanced ELLs:** These students can do all these activities with even fewer scaffolds and even more complex topics.

STRATEGY 22: PROJECT-BASED AND PROBLEM-BASED LEARNING

Technology Connections

For more ideas, visit The Best Resources for Learning How to Use Project-Based Learning & Problem-Based Learning in Your Classroom (https://larryferlazzo.edublogs.org/2022/07/19/the-best-resources-for-learning-how-use-project-based-learning-problem-based-learning-in-your-classroom/).

Learn more about object-based learning at Using "Object Based Learning" in the Classroom (https://larryferlazzo.edublogs.org/2022/08/11/using-object-based-learning-in-the-classroom/).

All figures from this chapter, as well as 11 additional chapters, references, hyperlinked Technology Connections, and more online resources, can be found at www.wiley.com/go/ellteacherstoolbox2.

You will be researching the culture of your family's original country or, in some cases, where there isn't really a home "country," you will research about your ethnic culture. You will be making a two-to-three-minute presentation in front of the class. You will be creating a Google Slide presentation of at least nine slides, including a title slide and a final slide where you will list your sources. Each element of a culture will have at least one slide. You will write notes on index cards. Use the slides for titles, a few key words, and an image that will support your presentation. Don't write everything you are going to say on the slides; write them on your index cards.

You will have two full periods to do online research (you can also ask your parents and grandparents for information), and then two days to create your slides and practice. You will present on the fifth day.

Figure 22.1 Home Culture Project (a much-expanded version of a similar figure found in Bonus Chapter 7: Oral Presentations, available at www.wiley.com/go/ellteacherstoolbox2)

When researchers write and talk about a culture, they usually say it has the following elements:

Language:

- Spoken & Written
- Gestures (classroom appropriate)

Social Organization:

- Who are the most important people in a community and why?
- What are the most important groups in a community and why?

Traditions (holidays, birth and death rituals, gender roles, role of the family, etc.)

Food

Arts (paintings, music, dance, etc. Please make sure it is classroom appropriate)

Religion

Form of Government

Culture Project Outline

You can add to this outline. You also do not have to follow this outline exactly. Use it to take notes. You will be writing down what you are saying on index cards.

You will begin your presentation saying your name and the name of your home culture. Your first slide should show a map of the area of the world where your family originally came from.

LANGUAGE:

The primary language spoken in my home culture is _____.

Other languages spoken in my home culture include _____ and _____.

The slide shows you a sentence written in my home culture's language and what it means in English.

One gesture that is popular in my home culture is _____.
It means _____.

Figure 22.1 (Continued)

SOCIAL ORGANIZATION:

In our home culture, one important person is _____.

This person is important because _____.

Another important person is _____.

This person is important because _____.

An important group or organization is _____.

It's important because _____.

Another important group or organization is _____.

It's important because _____.

TRADITION

There are many traditions in my home culture.

One is _____. (Explain what it is, when it happens, why it happens).

Another is _____. (Explain what it is, when it happens, why it happens).

Another is _____. (Explain what it is, when it happens, why it happens).

FOOD:

One traditional food in our culture is _____. It is made of _____ (show an image of it on your slide).

Another traditional food is _____. It is made of _____ (show an image of it on your slide).

Another traditional food is _____. It is made of _____ (show an image of it on your slide).

Figure 22.1 (*Continued*)

ARTS:

The arts are important in my home culture.

One example is music (play a 30-second portion of some music from your home culture).

Another is _____ (show an image of something drawn or painted).

Another is _____ (explain a traditional dance).

RELIGION:

People in my home culture have different religions, but the primary one is _____. This religion believes _____.

Other religions that are important in my home country include _____ and_____.

FORM OF GOVERNMENT:

The country where my family is from has a _____ kind of government. The head of the government now is _____.

ANYTHING ELSE YOU WOULD LIKE TO SHARE ABOUT YOUR HOME CULTURE:

Figure 22.1 (Continued)

STRATEGY 22: PROJECT-BASED AND PROBLEM-BASED LEARNING 261

What do we know about the problem now?

Names of Research Group Members _____

1. What is the problem you are researching?
   _____

2. How many people mentioned it in conversations?
   _____

3. How does the problem affect them? _____
   _____
   _____
   _____

4. Look at the conversation report forms and make a list of the students who spoke with people who listed this concern. Find out how strongly they think the person they spoke to feels about this problem (1 means not so much, 2 means somewhat, 3 means they feel it's very important). Put an average number for all of them here: _____
   _____

5. Does the problem affect anyone in your group? If so, who are they, and how does it affect them? _____
   _____
   _____

6. What are some ideas members of your group have for solving the problem?
   _____
   _____
   _____

Figure 22.2 Community Problem Research Form: What Do We Know About the Problem Now?

> Image of your object inserted here
>
> _____ is an object that is important to me. As you can see in the picture, it is _____, _____, and _____. I got it _____ (date). It is important to me because _____. I think what this object tells other people about me is that I _____ _____.

Figure 22.3 Object Writing Frame

STRATEGY 23

Learning Games for Reading and Writing

What Is It?

This strategy lists our favorite non-online games to reinforce reading and writing with English language learners. The Technology Connections section shares links to many ones that are online.

Why We Like It

There are countless games that teachers have used while teaching English language learners. Many, however, don't meet our criteria:

- They require very minimal teacher preparation time.
- The financial cost is nothing or next to nothing.
- Students enjoy them, but there is an emphasis on learning as much as there is on playing.
- After teacher modeling, students can lead the game or create game materials as a way of doubling language-learning opportunities.
- All students participate (or, at least, are *supposed* to participate) all the time—there are no opportunities to be eliminated from the game.

These games, similar to all the strategies in the book, are ones we periodically use in the classroom to support reading and writing. Strategy 31: Learning Games for Speaking and Listening, specifically reinforce those skills (our decisions on which section to put each game were sometimes arbitrary because most of them support all four domains).

And did we mention teacher prep time? ☺ We don't know about you, but with everything else on our plate, we don't need to find another 15 minutes to an hour to prepare materials for a game!

Supporting Research

Plenty of research shows that strategic use of games promotes language learning in several ways, including by increasing motivation and creating opportunities for low-anxiety communication in the target language (Martin, 2016; Mubaslat, 2011/2012). Education researcher Robert Marzano's examination of multiple studies has also found that games can have a relatively strong positive impact on student achievement (Marzano, 2010).

Research specifically targeting technology-based games (see the Technology Connections section) has also found that they can promote academic achievement (Shapiro, 2014). Studies conducted with language learners have found similar results (Ashraf et al., 2014; Yip & Kwan, 2006).

Common Core Connections

Specific Common Core connections would depend, of course, on the game and the target language it is reinforcing at the time. Most, if not all, of the games almost certainly support the Language Standards, including acquiring vocabulary, learning conventions, and demonstrating "knowledge of word relationships."

Application

Here are our favorite reading and writing games.

NINE BOX GRID

We use this simple game, which we learned and modified from English teacher Katie Toppel (2017) *a lot*. As you can see from Figure 23.1: Nine Box Grid with Health Care Words Example and Figure 23.2: Nine Box Grid Template, it's just a matter of putting nine words (or, when we teach phonics, letters) on a numbered three-by-three grid (for a total of nine boxes or spaces) on the class whiteboard.

Then, we give students mini-whiteboards (sometimes they play with a partner and sometimes individually), markers, and erasers or cloths (if you haven't invested in a class set of mini-whiteboards, we'd strongly advise you do so—either buying them from a store or making your own—search *make mini-whiteboards* online for instructions).

Next, we take out two huge foam dice we bought online for a few dollars. One student rolls the dice and then everyone gets one minute to write a sentence on their board using the chosen word or writing a word using the letter. If they roll an 11 or 12, they must use their choice of two words or letters on the grid. Students are told to hold up their boards at the end of a minute and the teacher gives some quick feedback.

Then, another student rolls the dice and the game continues. Unlike some of our other games, we don't keep score in this one and students enjoy it just the same.

After a few turns, we'll ask the rollers of the dice to change a word or letter on the grid. This move promotes more student engagement and ownership (though it can get a bit loud each time the dice roller is lobbied by the rest of the class when the student is at the board!).

We talk more about how we use Katie Toppel's game to promote speaking in Strategy 31: Learning Games for Speaking and Listening.

PHONIC DARTS

Years ago we were able to purchase a game called *Phonicball*. It's a series of Velcro dart boards with letters (one with consonants, another with vowels, and a third with phonic blends) instead of numbers. We have one student throw a Velcro ball at the board, and then, depending on the English proficiency level of the students, the student can have a certain amount of time to write as many words down on the whiteboard that start with that letter or, in the case of vowels, use the vowel that is selected. After students get their points for the words they wrote, they can practice saying the words in small groups.

Unfortunately, the company that made those Velcro boards went out of business years ago. But there are plenty of pictures of their products available if you search the web, and you can create your own versions. Searching for *Velcro ball dartboard* will lead you to instructions to make your own. Alternatives include drawing one on a poster board or projecting an image of it on the board, and having students throw a beanbag. Laying the poster on the floor and tossing a beanbag on it might, however, reduce the number of arguments you have about which letter the beanbag lands on.

FILL-IN-THE-BLANK

This simple game also requires mini-whiteboards—one per group. We usually have students divide into pairs and give each partner group a number. We then put the number on the board and give them points when they make a correct answer.

In this game, the teacher writes and reads or just says a cloze or gap-fill sentence ("Mr. Ferlazzo is a _____"; "I am going to _____ over the weekend.").

Students must fill in the blank and write a complete sentence on their board. They will get one point for every word they add if the sentence is correct—this feature encourages students to avoid the easiest answers. We also want to encourage some risk-taking, so students are not penalized if they add more than one new word and one is incorrect. However, if there is more than one error in their more-complex sentence, they do not get any points—no matter how many other words they use. In this game, as in all of the games, the teacher is the ultimate decider!

However, even though the teacher is the final judge, students can also take turns being the leader and giving the class their own clozes.

FLYSWATTER GAME (WITH OR WITHOUT FLYSWATTERS)

In this game, students will be running up to the class whiteboard and swatting words. You can buy several flyswatters for a few dollars, or you can just have students use a rolled-up a piece of paper, instead.

First, ask three or four students to go up to the classroom whiteboard. Then ask them to write—in large letters and scattered all over the board (it's even better if you have boards on two classroom walls so the words can be very spread out)—20 or so words recently studied by the class. Ideally, there is a vocabulary list they can quickly divide up among themselves.

Divide the class, or have them divide themselves, into three to six teams (the more the better), with each team having a number. Each team sends one member to the front with their back to the board (they can stand diagonally if the words are on two boards).

The teacher will either call out the word itself (the easiest version), a cloze or gap-fill sentence using one of the words, an antonym or a synonym (making it clear if it's one or the other), or make a related gesture. As soon as the word or clue is given, the students with the flyswatter can turn around and start swatting. The first person who swats the correct answer gets a point for their group and the second person gets one-half point. Group members cannot leave their seats, but they can help by shouting out directions or suggestions (if your classroom has thick walls). Each group rotates the person doing the swatting.

In this game, and in most of our games where students earn points, we let groups decide on how many they will bet on the last question in order to generate more suspense and enthusiasm, though it's not like there's a shortage of the latter by that time. Students can take turns leading the game, too.

You can do a less-noisy and more-sane version of this game by dividing the class into groups of four. Then have the four in each group write the same list of vocabulary words on index cards or small sheets of paper. Next, have them combine their desks so they are all facing each other and spread out the words between them. When the teacher calls out the word or clue, the first person in each group who slaps the correct word with their hand gets a point. You'll have multiple groups of four (expanding it to six is an option with desks at each end) playing and keeping score on their own. When we play this version, before the game begins we ask each group to choose a scorekeeper they trust.

NAME IT

This game has a few similarities to the flyswatter game. As in that game, the teacher will either call out a word itself (the easiest version), a cloze or gap-fill sentence using one of the words ("I will drive my ____ to work"), an antonym or a synonym (making it clear if it's one or the other), or make a related gesture. However, in this game students are divided into pairs with one mini-whiteboard per group and are given 60 seconds (as in all of these games, the time limit can be adjusted based on the English proficiency level of the students) to write down the words—they are not written on the classroom whiteboard. Remember, though, that teacher clues could result in more than one answer making sense, so flexibility about the correct response is required.

An easy modification of this game could be the teacher just saying sentences and having students write them correctly on their boards.

ROUND-AND-ROUND SHE GOES

This game incorporates one of the most versatile free sites on the web, ClassTools (www.classtools.net/), which has a huge number of easily usable online tools (search online for "online picker wheel" to find similar free tools). Round-and-Round She Goes uses the

STRATEGY 23: LEARNING GAMES FOR READING AND WRITING

Random Name Picker (n.d.) feature. It is basically a roulette wheel that lets you write anything you want in the different sections and then spin it with a click of your mouse. You can save your wheel for repeated use or make up new ones with different wording.

In the game, a teacher or student clicks the wheel for a spin and then student teams of two or three (again with one mini-whiteboard per group) have a time period to perform the task that is picked. The wheel could include vocabulary words that students have to use correctly in a sentence, irregular verbs that they have to write in the correct past tense, three words starting a sentence that they have to complete, a story topic that they have to write about—the possibilities are endless!

WRITING BINGO

This game is designed for high-beginner or intermediate ELLs. First, students write briefly about a topic of their own choosing. Then, they share their title and other students predict what words they think might be used in the short writing piece. They earn a point for every accurate prediction.

To start, the teacher writes a model short story or essay about a simple topic (favorite sport, favorite teacher, favorite food, least-favorite food, etc.). Ideally, it would be related to a theme the class has recently studied.

The teacher announces the topic of their essay and explains that they are going to read it to the class. Prior to reading it, though, students will be given a few minutes to write down words they believe will be used in the story. They will receive a point for every correct prediction.

After students have written down their predictions, they are told to put away their pens or pencils and are given a colored pencil (this reduces the chances of students cheating by writing down new words as they hear them). Every time they hear one of their words, they should cross it off the list. After the teacher reads their essay, students count their points and a winner is declared. Obviously, the teacher should double-check the winner's sheet.

Next, students are given 5 or 10 minutes to write a story or essay on a topic of their choice. The teacher can list ideas on the board to help students who have trouble thinking of a subject on their own. Students can be divided into groups of four (including a group leader) and the same process can take place with each group declaring a winner.

We were inspired to use this game by English teacher Sandy Millin (2013). We modified her original idea, so you might want to read how she uses the game.

SENTENCE SCRAMBLES

Sentence scrambles are words and punctuation in one sentence that are scrambled out of order. Students then have to put them in the correct sequence.

A lot of preparation is required for this game, and it is mostly student work. Students are given paper clips and many index cards or sheets of paper that they can cut into the size of index cards. They are asked to choose 10 or 15 sentences from their textbook or from the books they are reading. They write each word and punctuation mark in the sentence on a separate card. They must be copied down exactly, and even a period has to have its own card. If a sentence has five words and a period, then the student would need to prepare six cards.

Students are not creating original sentences (the needed checking for errors would not make this feasible). After they have completed one sentence, they mix up the order and clip them together. It's important to note that they do not mix sentences together—only the words from the same sentence. Trust us, teacher modeling of these instructions is critical to ensure that students clearly understand the required steps. In addition, we suggest that the first two sentence scrambles created by each student be checked by the teacher to ensure that these directions are followed—it's obviously easy for an ELL to copy a sentence incorrectly.

After all the sentence scrambles are done, one or two students are asked to shuffle them to ensure that the 10 or 15 scrambles done by each student are not together. They are shuffling the completed scrambles, not mixing up the words within a sentence. In other words, not all the sentence scrambles created by Juan are grouped together—they are mixed in with the scrambles from all the other students. Once mixed, the scrambles are all put into a box.

The next day, students are divided into teams of four or five students each and asked to put their desks together. The teacher gives each group 30 (this number may vary based on the English proficiency of the class) of the sentence scrambles, and the first group that completes them all correctly is the winner (it's always nice to have a prize for second place, too). As students place the words in what they believe is the correct order, the teacher can circulate and tell them if they are right or not. After they are checked by the teacher, the group paper clips them together and puts them on a tray or on another desk. Obviously, the teacher needs to be working quickly, too. If you have a large class, you probably want to make the groups larger and increase the number of sentence scrambles so you have to move around less often. But we've found that we can handle four or five groups at one time if we are fast on our feet. In the best of all worlds, there might be a student teacher, peer tutors, or English-proficient students from other classes who can be "drafted" to help evaluate the scrambles.

The sentence scrambles can be kept for future games or for practice as part of another lesson.

ACADEMIC LANGUAGE SENTENCES

We explicitly teach academic language, and we use this game to reinforce those words. However, this same game can also be used to review vocabulary words learned in a specific unit.

Students are in groups of two or three and have one mini-whiteboard per group. All students have access to their materials that list the academic language they have learned or their unit vocabulary.

Each group is given 90 seconds to write one sentence correctly using as many of the targeted vocabulary words as possible. Their group will gain one point for every word used correctly. At the end of that time, one person from each group stands up and reads the sentence (this step is optional). The teacher determines how many points the group should be given. Sentences cannot be reused exactly, but students can model sentences they write after ones that others have said. (Teachers don't have to worry about remembering all the sentences—students are the first to accuse others of copying their sentences!) To reduce copying, we usually keep this game short—only four rounds or so—and we tell students they can write two sentences during that last round to gain as many points as possible.

PICTIONARY

Everybody reading this book probably is already familiar with Pictionary. The teacher or a student draws an object, living being, or action on the front board or document camera, and then students (again with whiteboards) are given a minute to write down what they think is being drawn. We want to encourage full-class participation, so in our version people don't shout out their answers and students don't get points for being first. Everyone who has the correct answer written down 30 seconds after the drawing is completed receives a point and can bet it all prior to the last drawing.

TEAM-WRITING SENTENCES

In this game, students are divided into groups of four or five each with one whiteboard per group. One representative from each group stands in front of the classroom with the mini-whiteboard, and the rest of their group is seated in front of them.

The teacher, or a student, says a sentence, and the students standing in front have to write it out correctly. Though members of their group cannot get out of their seats, they can shout encouragement and suggestions. The first person who writes out the sentence correctly, including capital letters and punctuation, gets a point for their team.

All group members rotate to have a turn standing in front with the whiteboards.

GUESS THE SENTENCE (SOMETIMES KNOWN AS "HANGMAN")

We play this game without the problematic illustration of the hanged man and challenge students to determine not one word but all the words in a sentence. First, the teacher thinks of a sentence and draws short lines on the class whiteboard representing each letter of each word in the sentence (we use a different color marker for each word and leave a space between them).

Next, students are divided into small groups with one mini-whiteboard. Each group takes turns guessing letters (with luck, after some kind of analysis). If the letters are included in the words, the teacher writes them in their appropriate spot. If not, they are written at the bottom of the board.

The first group to write the entire sentence correctly is the winner. Any group can write what they think is the correct sentence and yell it out at any time. However, if they guess incorrectly, they cannot guess again until it is their turn to suggest a letter.

CATEGORIES

We use this game primarily for vocabulary review. Students are divided into pairs and, as usual, each group is given one mini-whiteboard. The teacher calls out names of categories (home, animals, things that move, things made of metal, things that people do for fun, etc.). Students are given one minute to write down as many (classroom-appropriate) items as they can on their whiteboard. They get a point for each one that is correct. This game can also create opportunities for speaking practice when there is a dispute about an answer—students had to convince us once that *fighting* qualified under "things that people do for fun."

The category could also be "words that start with the letter *b*." And, if you are teaching a more-advanced ELL class, you can even make it more challenging by combining two categories (e.g., "words that start with *t* and are in a home").

You can do this occasionally in reverse and throw in a question in which *you* give the words and *they* have to write the name of the category.

Another "twist" to this game can be to ask each group to choose a "spy" who can get one minute to walk around to other groups—without writing any notes or taking any photos—to find words to "steal" for their group.

WHAT DOESN'T BELONG?

As usual, students are divided into small teams with each group having a small whiteboard. In this game, the teacher writes down three or four words. The teacher shows and says the words to the class. One of the words in the group does not belong to the same category as the others (e.g., dog, cat, lion). Sentences could also be used (e.g., "I like you"; "I love this picture"; "I'm hungry"). Students have 30 seconds or a minute to write down the word that doesn't belong *and* write an explanation for their choice. Teams get one-half point if they choose the correct word and one-half point if they give the correct explanation. Also, as usual, students can bet a large amount prior to the last question.

After students become familiar with the game, they could create several posters. Each poster could be divided into three or four sections with one word or one sentence that doesn't belong. In addition to text, students could illustrate each word or sentence. Teachers can use them along with their own examples for the game. You can keep the best for future years, too.

CONNECTING FOUR

Only Connect was a popular British television game show where contestants were shown a number of words and had to find connections between different sets of four of them.

This categorization and connection concept is an example of inductive learning and can be a good game to play in the ELL classroom.

One way to play would be to have the teacher spend time creating a four-by-four grid of 16 words, ensuring that they could be divided into categories of four words each (like animals, games, sports, and school).

Or, you could just find one of the *many* free online versions of the game and "steal" from them. Write the words on the board or display them; have small groups of students with mini-whiteboards have a minute (or two) to write down their choices for the words and their categories; and then give groups a point for each collection they wrote down correctly. Next, move on to another set of 16 words and continue the process.

You can find these online versions of *Only Connect* by searching the Web for "Only Connect online." Several sites also allow players to create their own online versions, which either the teacher or the students can use.

STRATEGY 23: LEARNING GAMES FOR READING AND WRITING

Then, of course, there's always ChatGPT or another AI chatbot. Give it this prompt:

Please create an Only Connect grid of 16 words using the category games, school, food, and animals. Please mix up the words. Also give me the answer key.

You may have to do some minor editing, but the chatbot should be able to do most of the work.

WRITING MORE

In this game, we show a minute of a short, accessible, and funny video (see the Technology Connections section for links to them), and then students—working in pairs and sharing a mini-whiteboard— get one minute to write sentences about what they saw. The goal is to write as many sentences or, even better, fewer simple sentences and more complex ones.

After one minute of watching the video (students can also begin writing while the video is playing), we turn on the timer. Then, at the minute mark, we yell "Stop!" and ask students to hold up their whiteboards (later in the game most groups might ask for a second board so they could write more). We run to one group, spend 20 seconds looking over their board, quickly identify a teaching opportunity ("Does women mean one or more?" "Right, more"; "So should it be 'are' or 'is'?"), and give them a point total. Students typically start off writing one or two simple sentences and then figure out as the game goes on that they really can get more points based on the number of sentences or their complexity. Then groups begin to get three, four, or even five or six (those high numbers are often greeted by oohs and aahs from the rest of the class). We yell out the group number and their point totals, which the scorekeeper (who is either a student sitting out this game, a peer tutor, or a student teacher) posts.

Then we repeat the whole process again.

It's not an exaggeration to say the atmosphere when playing this game is often electrifying with student engagement at a very high level.

In the final round, groups can bet some or all of their points. But to win the bet, they have to earn at least five points with what they write on their whiteboard.

SUMMARIZE THIS!

This game works best after explicitly teaching summarization skills (see Strategy 15: Quoting, Summarizing, and Paraphrasing). Then, this game can be played, as we usually do, by having students read pages in a textbook in pairs and summarizing a page at a time, or in a similar way to "Writing More" with watching videos and having students summarize what they have just watched.

In Larry's ELL world history class, he explains that students will have 10 minutes to read a particular page in their textbook and write a summary on a whiteboard. He then goes around the room and gives students a point total for the quality of what they wrote. As he goes to each group, he holds their board so everyone can see and reads their summary out loud. He gives each group one, two, or three points, and quickly explains the reasons why (maybe they copied a sentence from the page, or they did or didn't include the real main idea of the page, etc.). A peer tutor writes the point total next to each group member on the front board.

IMPORTANT NOTE: Obviously, there needs to be a culture of trust, support, and respect in a class to be able to play this game, and the teacher needs to provide critical feedback in a kind and encouraging way.

This is done for three or four pages and the points are on the board (students can "bet" on the final page). The quality of everyone's summaries by the final page is very good!

This game can be played in a similar way by showing short segments of fun and accessible videos and having students write summaries of them.

ESL/ELL WORDLE

Here's how we adapt the popular word game for our ELL students:

1. First, we decide on the categories, which are based on the units we have been studying. So, for example, we might choose school, food, and home.
2. Next, we ask either ChatGPT or another chatbot for five-letter words that relate to each category, or we just search online for them.
3. Then, we draw a five-by-size box grid on the front whiteboard or display one at the front using a projector.
4. Students are then divided into small groups with mini-whiteboards and given a team number.
5. We explain the rules:
    1. The class will vote on which of three categories the word will come from.
    2. The first group will guess a word and have it written on the board.
    3. If I outline the letter in blue, that means that letter is in the word, but it is in the wrong place.
    4. If I outline the letter in red, that means that the letter is not in the word.
    5. If I outline the letter in green, that means that the letter is in the word and is in the correct place.
    6. If the guessed word is correct, that team will win a point.
    7. If the guessed word is incorrect, all teams will have 30 seconds to write the word they think is correct on their board. Teams will be told to raise their boards, and any team with the correct word will win a point. If no team has guessed the correct word, they will just be told it's incorrect and not which letters were in the correct word.
    8. If no team has guessed the correct word, the next team will guess the word and have it written on the board.

9. The process is repeated until there is a winner or until the board is filled.
6. If the class wants to continue playing the game, they can vote again if they want to keep the same category or switch.

POPULAR BOARD GAME ADAPTATIONS

So many popular board games can be used for language learning! Headbands, Guess Who, and Boggle are just a few of them. See Technology Connections for links to instructions for adapting them to the classroom, or just search the Internet for "adapting popular board games for ESL students."

Teaching Online

Obviously, the games requiring moving around the classroom, like "Flyswatter," don't translate well to online learning. However, most of the rest work fine in a virtual environment.

Students can work in groups in breakout rooms. When "time is up," they come back to the main room, wait for the teacher to say "Write Your Answer!" and then one person from each group clicks "submit" to the chatbox.

That being said, however, during our distance learning experience we pretty much stuck with the online games listed in the Technology Connections section, including the online Pictionary versions that were not blocked by our district's content filters.

What Could Go Wrong?

No surprise here—the primary potential problem is student cheating and the tensions created by it. We deal with that issue by beginning each game with a short explanation of the rules. Then, we ask everyone who agrees with following these rules to raise their hands. We've found that spending a minute doing this exercise reduces, though may not eliminate, the problem. If it still happens, we remind the student of the agreement they made. In a worst-case scenario, a repeat offender is told they cannot continue to play and a one-on-one conversation takes place after class.

The next big problem can be high noise levels for some of the games. Again, we cover this issue when we discuss the rules prior to the game, but generally still have to repeatedly remind students. Luckily, our classroom neighbors are patient and we periodically send them candy bars.

Prizes are another issue to consider. Many times the bell rings signaling the end of class and the end of the game, and no one really cares about a prize. Even when the games end in the middle of class time, it's clear that the games generate intrinsic motivation and students are not in it for the reward. Nevertheless, we always have on hand small and inexpensive packages of dried fruit or trail mix we purchase at warehouse stores or a couple of graham crackers. These are usually sufficient for the winners. Another option is to use Katie's one-liner: "You all have extra credit in my heart!"—though we cannot guarantee positive student reactions to that comment.

Differentiation Recommendations

Newcomers (Preliterate or Low Literacy in Home Language): When playing the games in this chapter, they should have a partner who is open to, and has explicit instructions about, not just to give the answers but to also *teach* their partners. That explicit instruction should be accompanied by a teacher model. In addition, students should be encouraged to play many of the most accessible online games at home on their own, including sites like Duolingo and LingoHut, two sites that are likely to be around for a long time.	**Newcomers (Literate in Home Language):** All of the games except, perhaps, for "Summarize This" would be accessible to them. Online games should be "vetted" by teachers for accessibility.
Intermediate ELLs: Most of the games in the chapter are appropriate for students with this proficiency level. If in a mixed-level class, it's often best to pair a newcomer with an intermediate when playing them. The teacher then would give explicit instructions to intermediates about how it's their responsibility not just to give the answers but to also *teach* their partners. That explicit instruction should be accompanied by a teacher model.	**Advanced ELLs:** "Summarize This" is particularly good for this group. Many more advanced games can be found online, and they can also create their own for classmates to play.

Technology Connections

There are many, and we mean *many*, online games geared toward English language learners.

To narrow them down a bit, check out The Best Online Games Students Can Play in Private Virtual "Rooms" (https://larryferlazzo.edublogs.org/2009/02/10/the-best-online-games-students-can-play-in-private-virtual-rooms/), which contains links to games like Quizizz, Kahoot!, and others. Students compete against each other on these sites using their own electronic devices. After a teacher chooses a game, students sign on with a code and can see their standings or how their teams are doing in the competition as they play. At the time of this book's publication, Quizizz is our favorite. However, they are all adding new features frequently and new similar gaming apps are coming online all the time, so we encourage you to explore them all to figure out which works best for you and your students.

Students can also create online learning games for their classmates to play. The Best Websites for Creating Online Learning Games (http://larryferlazzo.edublogs.org/2008/04/21/the-best-websites-for-creating-online-learning-games/) has a lengthy list of sites where they can easily make them. Teachers can also do the same, but with so many premade games out there on countless subjects, is that really how you want to spend your time?

Many of these online gaming sites now incorporate artificial intelligence into the creation of their games, so it's easier than ever to make a game that is more specific to your needs.

Students who are particularly motivated can ask ChatGPT or any other chatbot: *What are games someone who is learning can play with you to help them learn English?*

STRATEGY 23: LEARNING GAMES FOR READING AND WRITING

In response, they will receive a long list of potentially engaging options.

For an almost limitless supply of short and fun videos to use with some of the games listed in this chapter, visit "Best" Lists of the Week: Teaching with Movies & Video Clips (https://larryferlazzo.edublogs.org/2018/06/13/best-lists-of-the-week-teaching-with-movies/).

One final note:

The non-tech classroom games we listed here and the ones in the "Speaking and Listening" section of this book are just a drop in the bucket of the games teachers have developed for the ELL classroom. If you are interested in more, including links to ways for adapting popular board games for learning, you might want to explore The Best Ideas for Using Games in the ESL/EFL/ELL Classroom (http://larryferlazzo.edublogs.org/2013/10/27/the-best-ideas-for-using-games-in-the-esleflell-classroom/).

And if you want to really find out about more online learning games, explore to your heart's content at A Collection of "The Best . . ." Lists on Learning Games (http://larryferlazzo.edublogs.org/2010/08/28/a-collection-of-the-best-lists-on-games/).

Attribution

Portions of this section originally appeared in our book, *The ESL/ELL Teacher's Survival Guide* (Ferlazzo & Sypnieski, 2012, p. 239).

Thanks to Katie Toppel for the nine box grid (https://twitter.com/Toppel_ELD/status/852598723779493892).

Thanks to Carissa Peck (2012) for suggestions to modify the Flyswatter game (http://eslcarissa.blogspot.com/2012/09/flyswatter.html).

Thanks to Cristina Cabal (2016) for ideas on the Round-and-Round-She-Goes game (www.cristinacabal.com/?p=5269).

Thanks to Sandy Millin for inspiring us with her idea of writing bingo (https://sandymillin.wordpress.com/2013/10/15/writing-bingo/).

All figures from this chapter, as well as 11 additional chapters, references, hyperlinked Technology Connections, and more online resources, can be found at www.wiley.com/go/ellteacherstoolbox2.

2. sick	3. doctor	4. nurse
5. hospital	6. cough	7. appointment
8. medicine	9. broken	10. help

Figure 23.1 Nine Box Grid with Health Care Words Example *Source*: Reproduced with permission of Katie Toppel.

2.	3.	4.
5.	6.	7.
8.	9.	10.

Figure 23.2 Nine Box Grid Template *Source*: Reproduced with permission of Katie Toppel.

PART II

Speaking and Listening

STRATEGY 24

Dictation

What Is It?

There are many different types of dictation activities in an ELL classroom (see the Application section). They all share the common qualities of a teacher or student (or, in the case of tools shared in the Technology section, a recorded voice on the computer) saying or reading something while a listener is writing it down. This action is followed by a check for accuracy.

Why We Like It

Dictation is a very versatile strategy—it can be used for demonstrating comprehension, practicing listening and spelling, and assisting in pronunciation. Teachers can also use the text strategically to reinforce or clarify grammar issues facing students. It's also the kind of activity that can be easily adjusted to the amount of time available—you can use it for 20 minutes or during the final few minutes of class if you finish your primary lesson early.

Supporting Research

Studies have found that dictation activities can assist with grammar instruction (Kidd, 1992, p. 50; Tedick, 2001), listening comprehension (Kiany & Shiramiry, 2002, p. 61), spelling and punctuation (Alkire, 2002), vocabulary instruction (Yu et al., 2022), and student engagement (Kit, 2004).

Common Core Connections

Surprisingly enough, dictation activities do not appear to meet any of the Anchor Standards under Speaking and Listening. However, they do fall under a number of the Language Standards, including learning the "conventions of capitalization, punctuation and spelling when writing" and to "comprehend more fully when . . . listening." Don't ask *us* why that last one is not under the Speaking and Listening Standards!

Application

Here are several dictation methods we apply in our classes listed in order of ones we use most frequently to ones that we use less often.

PAIRED DICTATION

We've previously mentioned this method in several reading and writing strategies. It's a simple and effective one that we typically use after reading a few pages of a short and accessible text. We show the text on the document camera and make sure all students have copies (see the Technology Connections section about where to obtain free copies of accessible texts).

We then divide students into groups of two or three and give them mini-whiteboards, markers, and erasers. Each student takes a turn reading a sentence from the text while the other one or two are writing down what they hear. Ideally, the students doing the writing don't need to look at their copies of the text, but they can if necessary. The reader then checks for accuracy and gives corrective feedback in a supportive way.

This kind of supportive feedback needs to be modeled (e.g., "Oops! You forgot to capitalize the letter *T*.") in order to avoid inappropriate corrections (e.g., "You're dumb! You forgot a capital letter!").

A variation of this activity (especially for more-advanced ELL students) is for the reader to leave a blank in the sentence that is being dictated. This functions as a challenge for the listeners to remember or use their language knowledge to determine what word belongs in that space without having to resort to looking at the text. As in all clozes (see Strategy 7: Clozes), students can say or write a word that makes sense in the context even if it differs from the exact one found in the original text.

DICTOGLOSS (AND VARIATIONS)

Dictogloss is the word often used to describe this next dictation activity and it, too, has multiple variations. One option is to first select a short passage—perhaps a paragraph—from a familiar text (from the textbook, a story we've just read, etc.). We ask students to draw a line across their paper roughly one-third of the way down and then to draw one two-thirds down.

Next, we ask students to put their pencils down and carefully listen as we read the text at a regular pace. Prior to beginning to read, we tell students they are going to have to reconstruct what we say after hearing it a few times. Students do not write anything down after our first reading.

Next, we tell students we are going to read it again a little slower and they can write notes on the top third of their paper *after* we are done—we explain we want them to focus only on listening. After we finish reading a second time and students have had five minutes to silently write down notes, we give them a few minutes to compare with a partner and both can improve their notes.

Then, we ask them to put down their pencils and we read it again at the same pace as our second reading. Once we're done, students can either write additional notes in the second section of their paper or edit what they previously wrote down. They then can review their notes with a new partner and work toward writing a final text reconstruction on the bottom third of their page.

We also explain that their final version doesn't have to be a perfect copy of what we said, but the meaning should be the same, the grammar should be correct, and it should be as close as possible to what we read.

We then show the original passage on the overhead and ask students to reflect on how well they did. We have already done our own assessments while circulating during the activity and looking at student work in progress. We do not grade this exercise, as long as it appears that students are trying their best.

With beginning ELLs, ways to make dictogloss more accessible can be by doing the following:

- Providing them with a cloze of the text so they could view the words while they are being read. This way, they have to pay particular attention to fewer words.

- Asking students to number their paper leaving two blank lines for each dictated sentence. Then, instead of dictating an entire paragraph, just go through the same process of note-taking, pair-share, and reconstruction one sentence at a time.

- Writing a very simple text for students using vocabulary that they know, previewing any new words, and also providing photo support during the dictation activity.

Another dictogloss option is to either write or duplicate a short text that contains conventions or grammar issues that you have identified as particularly challenging for students. Hearing and writing down challenging grammar patterns can assist students in internalizing and acquiring them (Kidd, 1992, p. 51). For example, we've used this strategy to reinforce subject-verb agreement. We follow up the text reconstruction process with a class discussion of the targeted grammar concept.

An additional twist that we've used occasionally with intermediate ELLs is to pick a few words from the text we are using and replace them with a "mmmmmm" sound when we are reading it—basically turning it into an oral cloze. Then, when they have to reconstruct the text, they also have to determine which words they think belong in the blanks. When we use this version, we've typically deleted only the same types of words (only articles, only verbs, etc.), but don't feel obligated to use the same method. The key is that you have *some* kind of strategy for the deletions.

A final variation we've sometimes used is called "delayed dictation." In this instructional strategy, we first explain to students that we are going to read some sentences and, after we are done reading each one, we are going to ask them to wait 10 seconds (we'll tell them when time is up) before they write it down. These are sentences that they already have had exposure to—no surprises! Though some suggest that this modification can enhance retention in long-term memory (Smith, 2019), our primary reason for using it is because it's just a change from our usual form of dictation.

PICTURE DICTATION

In a picture dictation lesson, a teacher can draw an image—generally, though not always, reflective of the theme the class is studying. Then, without showing students the image, the teacher dictates what it looks like while students attempt to draw it based on the verbal description ("There is a big tree to the right of the house"; "The sun is in the sky on the left"; etc.). Inviting anyone to the document camera who is willing to share their masterpiece is always a fun way to end the activity. Larry, who has no artistic ability whatsoever, generally compares each drawing with one of his and asks for a class vote on which they think is the better image. He has not yet won—and it's been 22 years!

After the teacher leads this lesson once, future versions can have students drawing their own pictures and taking turns dictating their description in English to a partner. After checking for accuracy, the roles are reversed.

INFORMATION GAP

Information gap activities are often used in language-learning classrooms. Their basic definition is that students have to complete a task together, but neither student has all the information necessary to do it. They must communicate with each other to fill that gap. These activities often, though not always, fall under the umbrella of dictation.

To be truthful, despite their popularity, we haven't used the more-traditional text-based types of information gap lessons in our classrooms very often. Neither students nor we have been particularly engaged by them. Nevertheless, you'll find a link to a huge collection of them in the Technology Connections section if they work for you and you want printable copies or if you just want to give them a try.

However, there is one activity that falls under the information gap umbrella that we regularly use and that we'd like to share here.

Running Dictation

Running dictation, also known as messenger-and-scribe, is a staple of many ELL classrooms. We tape four to six sentences in different sections of the room and divide the class into pairs. One of them (the messenger) has the job of running to the different texts, reading them, and running back to their partner. Then, the messenger student has to tell the writer (scribe), who writes it down. Partners can alternate roles, if desired.

Newcomers can be part of a three-person group including two students with a higher English-proficiency level. We often play it as a game, with the first three pairs to write down all the sentences perfectly, including punctuation and capitalization, being declared the winners.

Students love the game, but it can get quite rowdy. We caution students about our neighboring classrooms and the need to keep the noise in check. In addition, our students cheat at this activity more than any other, so we make it very clear that photos of text cannot be taken by cell phones, no one can tear the text off the wall and bring it to their partner, students can't stand by the text and read it loudly to their partner across the room, and the messenger cannot grab the pen from the scribe and write the text—it must be verbally communicated. If you don't think your students will do any of these things, then we also have a bridge that we'd like to sell to you!

To mix things up, we sometimes put small pictures instead of text on the walls. Students then have to run back and forth and describe the image to their partner. Next, the scribe can either draw it or write down the description that the messenger is saying to them (we announce ahead of time if the scribe will be drawing or writing sentences). We then call a halt to the activity (usually after 10 minutes or so) and share the original images and the scribes' version of them on the document camera (often to great laughter). Students vote on who drew the most-accurate images (they cannot vote for themselves).

Teaching Online

Most, though not all, of these dictation variations transfer reasonably well to an online environment.

You might think that it wouldn't be possible to use running dictation in distance learning, but we did, and it was very successful. Here's how we did it.

After explaining the game, we paired up students into different breakout rooms. We then displayed three sentences. For example:

- *I am working very hard to learn English.*
- *If I don't study English at home, I will pay Mr. Ferlazzo one thousand dollars.*
- *Learning English is hard, but it will help me get the job I want in the future.*

One student (the *messenger*) went back and forth between the main room and the breakout rooms, and the *scribe* shared their screen there as the messenger told them the sentences.

Prior to playing the game, we made all students make "pinky promises" to not write the sentences down and not take pictures of them.

During the game, we took quick trips to the breakout rooms to see how it was going, and, one time, we did catch a group cheating. The messenger had respected the rule of not writing the sentences down and not taking pictures of them. But two of them had decided it was not against the rules for the messenger to come back to the breakout room and write down the sentences based on memory in the chat. We made sure to explicitly "forbid" that exercise in future games.

What Could Go Wrong?

Don't pick a text for dictation that's too long or that has too many new words for your students. Other than those points, along with our cautions about noise and student cheating during running dictation, it's hard to mess up dictation activities.

Be thoughtful about student partners prior to organizing a running dictation activity. Don't create opportunities for frustration by pairing up two less-proficient ELLs. Instead, consider grouping higher-level students with others newer to the language.

Differentiation Recommendations

Newcomers (Preliterate or Low Literacy in Home Language): Begin with paired dictation using very simple phrases that have been previously taught. When using running dictation, place them in a three-person group where one can be a partner and coach (with their consent, of course) or paired with a peer tutor or student teacher. Have a "coach" when doing picture dictation, as well. A displayed word bank could be helpful for more complex texts.	**Newcomers (Literate in Home Language):** All chapter dictation activities should be accessible, ensure that texts used are familiar to them, and words needed to describe pictures have been previously taught. A displayed word bank could be helpful for more complex texts.
Intermediate ELLs: Most of the activities can be used as described in the text, but with increasingly complex text. Picture dictation might be "too easy," though it could be used on occasion as a fun activity.	**Advanced ELLs:** Most of the activities can be used as described in the text, but with increasingly complex text. After practicing, students could take turns leading the class or small groups in dictogloss lessons.

Technology Connections

There are several excellent free online sites that provide dictations at different levels of English proficiency—ranging from simple one-word versions to complex paragraphs. Once users type what they believe they heard onto the site, their accuracy is automatically graded by its software. We have our students use them when we have access to technology at school, and they're great for home use, too. You can find them at The Best Sites for ELLs to Practice Online Dictation (http://larryferlazzo.edublogs.org/2017/07/15/the-best-sites-for-ells-to-practice-online-dictation/).

We briefly discussed traditional information gap activities in the language-learning classroom. You can find many different examples, including scores of free printable versions, at The Best Online Resources for "Information Gap" Activities (http://larryferlazzo.edublogs.org/2011/09/06/the-best-online-resources-for-information-gap-activities/).

You can obtain free copies of accessible texts for dictation and for other purposes at The Best Sources for Free & Accessible Printable Books (http://larryferlazzo.edublogs.org/2009/07/31/the-best-sources-for-free-accessible-printable-books/) and at The Best Places to Get the "Same" Text Written for "Different" Levels (http://larryferlazzo.edublogs.org/2014/11/16/the-best-places-to-get-the-same-text-written-for-different-levels/).

If you would like to learn more about using dictation in the ELL classroom, you can visit The Best Resources for Learning How to Use the Dictogloss Strategy with English Language Learners (https://larryferlazzo.edublogs.org/2011/04/21/the-best-resources-for-learning-how-to-use-the-dictogloss-strategy-with-english-language-learners/).

Attribution

Versions of some of these ideas appeared in our book, *The ESL/ELL Teacher's Survival Guide* (Ferlazzo & Sypnieski, 2012, p. 51) and in our book, *Navigating the Common Core with English Language Learners* (Ferlazzo & Sypnieski, 2016, p. 241).

STRATEGY 25

Conversation Practice

What Is It?

This strategy is really a series of activities that we use to help our students develop competence and confidence in oral communication.

Why We Like It

We want our students to be able to *communicate* with others in English. In order to make that happen, they will need to overcome anxiety, know the necessary language, and have a desire to apply it. We think the activities we use in our classroom and list here effectively assist students to achieve that trifecta.

Supporting Research

Communicative opportunities, such as dialogues, have been found to be one effective way to promote speaking skills (Dewi, 2011). Anxiety, self-confidence, and motivation are three factors often identified by researchers as issues holding back ELLs from speaking English (Tuan & Mai, 2015, p. 8). Studies have found that speaking anxiety for ELLs can be reduced by providing planning time prior to a conversational activity (Bashir, 2014, p. 220), which we do with many of the speaking activities discussed in the Application section. This planning time also can help increase confidence in learners that they can perform the task.

This sense of confidence and competence (feeling like you have the skills to perform the task) is one of four key elements researchers have found to be critical for developing intrinsic motivation. Autonomy (having some level of control over the work you have to do), relatedness (working with people you like and respect), and relevance (the work will help you achieve your goals or is something of interest) (Ferlazzo, 2015, September 14) are the other three critical factors. All the activities listed under the Application section and, in fact, in most of the Application sections in this book, are designed to build on these four pillars of motivation. Finally, some studies suggest that "simulations" are a particularly effective strategy for "accelerating learning" (Ferlazzo, 2023, February 14). The dialogues that we use in the classroom, and which we discuss in this chapter, certainly fulfill the definition of a simulation.

Common Core Connections

The first Standard under Speaking and Listening says, "Prepare for and participate effectively in a range of conversations..." If we were more wordy, that sentence could effectively serve as the name for this strategy instead of *conversation practice*. The last Standard in that section begins, "Adapt speech to a variety of contexts and communicative tasks..." That phrase also aptly describes all the activities we describe here.

Application

These are the activities we use the most in our classroom to promote conversational skills.

DIALOGUES

We use dialogues in multiple ways. One way is for the teacher to create short, simple, and funny dialogues related to the theme that is being studied. This means most dialogues in textbooks are out because they tend to be pretty boring. Figure 25.1: Holiday Dialogue is an example of one we use with high beginners—it's short, provides space for student choice, and injects a little humor into it all. The teacher first models it and then strategically creates student pairs (in other words, depending on the class situation, they may want to have partners with the same or different home languages and/or English proficiency levels). They practice for a while and then perform.

Another activity we do is to have the class select videos of their choice from Brainpop, Jr. (n.d.), show it to the entire class (with closed captions), and then have students complete the easy quiz feature in pairs with mini-whiteboards. Next, we have students work in pairs and use a simple word-play activity offered by the site. It lists several key words from the video and provides a form where students write a super-short skit about one of the words they just learned and act it out (you have to pay for Brainpop, but the cost is minimal if you buy the feature that allows only three log-ins at any one time). We ask students to use at least two words and offer extra credit if they include all four of them. Again, students practice and then perform them.

Of course, you don't need a Brainpop movie to do this activity. You can show any short video and identify the words on your own for students to use in a dialogue. In fact, sometimes we don't even preface this task with a video. For example, if we've been studying the theme of feelings, we'll just ask students to create a simple dialogue of, let's say, 10 lines using at least four words from the theme we've been studying.

In Strategy 6: Sequencing, we discussed ways to scramble sentences and then have students put them back in order. This kind of activity can work well with dialogues, too. Teachers can create dialogues and give a scramble such as the one we use in Figure 25.2

STRATEGY 25: CONVERSATION PRACTICE

(Figure 25.3 is the teacher answer key). After students cut and glue them in the correct order (being sure to highlight or underline the clues they used to figure it out), they can practice and perform the dialogue. Students can also create their own dialogue scrambles to challenge their classmates.

Critical Thinking Dialogues

The ability to develop an argument is an important skill to foster among students. Writing an essay is one way to develop that skill. However, we've found that a prelude to that—or something that can stand on its own—can be promoting student talk through what we call critical thinking dialogues that are helpful to ELLs and others. These can be particularly helpful in content classes.

After we've studied a topic (for example, the Mexican American War in a history class) or after we have discussed a current event or problem (for example, "Should the school cafeteria serve more food that is Halal?"), we'll introduce a dialogue where students have to take a position on a question and explain their reasons. We also try to inject a bit of humor in them (though levity might be inappropriate for some topics), and students practice in small groups and then perform them for the entire class or for another small group.

See Figure 25.4: Mexican American War Critical Thinking Dialogue for an example.

Artificial Intelligence Dialogues

Artificial intelligence chatbots like ChatGPT, as well as a number of other online AI-powered sites specifically targeting second language practice, offer another way for students to practice dialogues. This kind of low-anxiety setting has been found by researchers to support English language acquisition (Bibauw et al., 2022).

We encourage students to use them for homework, though, at times, we've had students use this exercise in class just to "mix things up." We definitely do it in class the first time so students become familiar with the process.

We ask students to use this kind of prompt as a model. The teacher puts the prompt in Google Classroom or whatever learning management system the school uses, and the student copies and pastes it into the chatbot. It obviously will change depending on the theme that is being studied at the moment, the home language of the student, and the language ability of the chatbot that is being used (of course, it also depends on if AI is blocked for students by your district's Internet content filter). In this case, the class is studying school vocabulary:

> *You will pretend to be a teacher at school. I will pretend to be your student. We will pretend to have a conversation. I will say something first, then you will respond. You are a teacher. I am a student. Let's have a conversation. I will say one sentence. Then you will say one sentence. You are not to invent an entire conversation. You will only respond to what I say. I am a Beginning English Language Learner, so please keep*

your answers short. After I tell you the conversation is over, please retype the entire dialogue and explain in Spanish any errors that I made. I will begin now. "Teacher, can I can go to the bathroom?"

Then, after several lines of conversation, they would paste this next prompt into ChatGPT:

The conversation is over, please retype the entire dialogue in English and explain in Spanish any errors that I made.

Puppet Dialogue

Sometimes, especially for beginners, speaking anxiety decreases if they can pretend it's not actually them engaging in the dialogue. Puppets can work as a good substitute. Also, having students imagine a conversation (supported by imagery) between animals or inanimate objects such as fruits and vegetables can create fun *and* confidence. Links to resources for these kinds of substitutions can be found in the Technology Connections section.

1-2-3

We described this activity in *The ESL/ELL Teacher's Survival Guide* (Ferlazzo & Sypnieski, 2022) and still use it regularly. This is a modification of an exercise developed by Paul Nation (2007) called the *4-3-2 fluency activity*. In his original activity plan, students line up (standing or sitting) facing each other. Each one must be prepared to speak on something that they are already quite familiar with. First, they speak to their partner for four minutes about the topic.

Then, they move down the line and say the same thing for three minutes to a new partner. Next, they move again and speak for two minutes. Then, the students on the other side do the same thing.

We developed a modification of this activity that "turned it on its head" and could be called 1-2-3 or, for beginners, even 30 seconds—one minute—90 seconds. The times could even be shortened more. In it, students are told to pick any topic they know a lot about, and they will be asked to talk about it to a partner for one minute (or 30 seconds, depending on the English level of the students) and then for two minutes and then for three. But they need to do some preparation prior to the speaking activity.

First, they should write down notes about what they might want to say. Next, students practice speaking by recording all or part of what they want to say on their cell phone or laptop (they could also practice with peer tutors if they are available). Afterward, students are told they have two minutes to review their notes before they have to be put away. Next the teacher models questions that students who are listening can ask the speaker if they appear to be stuck. It is also useful to model characteristics of being a good listener (such as maintaining eye contact and not talking to other students). Then students begin the speaking and switching process described earlier.

ASK-ANSWER-ADD

Neil T. Millington from Dreamreader, an excellent online site with free ELL lesson plans, and Todd Beuckens from Ello, a site filled with interactive listening activities, shared an activity they call *ask-answer-add* (Millington, n.d.). We've used it successfully with high-beginning ELLs and intermediates and share parts of their instructions with permission.

First, students are lined up facing one another. If the classroom is not big enough to accommodate two long lines (like ours), students can be seated across from each other in a snake-like series of rows. We often use this kind of set-up to facilitate speed-dating for students to share their work. One row is designated *A* and the other is *B*.

We put a series of questions on the board related to the theme we are studying. For example, if we are studying food, the questions might be as follows:

- What is your favorite food?
- What is a popular meal in your home country?
- What is your favorite dessert?
- What did you eat for breakfast this morning?
- What did you eat for lunch yesterday?
- What did you eat for dinner last night?
- What did you eat the last time you went to a restaurant?

We then announce to the class that everyone in row A is going to ask the student across from them in row B the first question. Everyone in row B is given a minute to plan their answer.

After a minute, it might go something like this:

Ask—A: "What is your favorite food?"
Answer—B: "My favorite food are pupusas" or "I love papaya salad."

Then, it's time for Student B, the one who answered, to *add* something more. The teacher can provide a model or example, along with 30 seconds for Student B to plan their add. The conversation could now look something like this:

Ask—A: "What is your favorite food?"
Answer—B: "My favorite food are pupusas." **Add**—"My mother makes them on holidays."

Then it's time for Student B to ask the next question on the board to Student A and repeat the same process. After they've done ask, answer, add, then everyone in row A can move down one person and start with the third question on the list.

Hold on, though! That's the process we use for mid-beginner students. For high-beginners and intermediates, we make it more challenging. After the first ask, answer, add we *don't* switch partners.

Instead, we give 30 seconds to Student A so they can formulate another question based on Student B's response and repeat the sequence one more time before we start all over again with a new partner.

As students become more confident and skilled, ask-answer-add can continue with the same partners repeating the sequence for several minutes.

CONVERSATION CHEAT SHEETS

In *The ESL/ELL Teacher's Survival Guide* (Ferlazzo & Sypnieski, 2012), we included a multi-page conversation cheat sheet containing over 60 simple question or answer frames beginning students can practice ("What time is it? It is _____."; "How are you? I am _____."). You can download them for free at that book's website. You can find the URL address in the Technology Connections section.

We also developed a *much* longer collection of conversation prompts and sentence starter responses. Figure 25.4: Conversation Starters is the first page of the list, and its entire 20 pages can be downloaded on our book's website in the same place the online chapters can be accessed. AI chatbots can create similar sheets tailored to your teaching priorities.

We post one question and sentence starter response at the beginning of each class, have students write them down in their notebook, and then students go outside to share their questions and answers in small groups (either with peer tutors or with their own small group leaders). Then, two groups pair up to share them again. If there is any extra time, they review previous prompts.

We also keep copies of all the prompts for students who arrive later in the school year. As ELL teachers know, we typically welcome new students every month of the year!

PRONUNCIATION FEEDBACK

Research has found that individuals generally believe their pronunciation is the best—we're not able to be accurate judges. The research emphasizes the importance of receiving more objective feedback (Ludwig-Maximilians-Universität München, 2020).

For that reason, we strongly encourage our students to use some of the many free AI-powered tools that can provide that kind of feedback in a low-stress environment. After all, in those situations, the only "judge" of their pronunciation skills will be computer code!

Students can use a chatbot like ChatGPT in a similar way that we described earlier in the chapter, but in this case give it instructions verbally and request pronunciation feedback or choose from the list of other sites found in the Technology Connections section. Here is a prompt that a student could paste or say to a chatbot:

> *You are an English teacher. I am a beginning English language learner. Please give me three simple sentences to read. After I read them, please give me feedback on if I am pronouncing the words correctly or not. Please give me this feedback on my pronunciation in Spanish.*

STRATEGY 25: CONVERSATION PRACTICE

SELF-ASSESSMENT

We discussed the progress principle in Strategy 3: Graphic Organizers. As we explained, researchers have found a key factor in building intrinsic motivation is people seeing themselves making progress.

An easy way to help students see the progress they are making in speaking is through having them record themselves speaking various dialogues over the course of the year and saving it to Google Classroom or whatever other Learning Management System is used by the school. We've found that it's very energizing for students to listen to prior recordings as the year goes on—their speaking improvement is very obvious to them. Links to recording tools can be found in the Technology section. Students love it, especially seeing their grades go up! Students, of course, can also just use their cell phone or laptop.

Teaching Online

All of these activities can work in an online teaching environment, though some may take a bit of creativity when organizing and using breakout rooms, especially when using the 1-2-3 lesson.

What Could Go Wrong?

Make sure you give students time to prepare! Our students don't need to be set up for failure by us. We're not talking about a huge amount of prep time. Often, 30 seconds is sufficient.

In addition, as we've often said in other strategies throughout this book—don't let any of these activities go on too long! There's no shortage of ways for students to learn English. Know when it's time to move on.

Differentiation Recommendations

Newcomers (Preliterate or Low Literacy in Home Language): KEEP IT SIMPLE! Just have them start off with simple question/answer dialogues that they can use with Google Translate ("How are you?" "I am fine?"). Encourage them to practice at home with audio artificial intelligence–powered chatbots, as described in the chapter. Ideally, during class, have a peer tutor work with them on these simple conversations while the rest of the class is doing more complex ones.	**Newcomers (Literate in Home Language):** Can use all the activities described in the chapter.
Intermediate ELLs: Can use all the activities described in the chapter. Students can also create their own dialogues, and expand their responses when using Figure 25.5: Conversation Starters.	**Advanced ELLs:** Can use all the activities described in the chapter. Students can also create their own dialogues and expand their responses when using Figure 25.5: Conversation Starters. The time limits in the "1-2-3" activity can be lengthened.

Technology Connections

For a list of artificial intelligence–powered sites that offer automatic pronunciation feedback, visit The Best Sites for Online Pronunciation Feedback – Do You Know Others? (https://larryferlazzo.edublogs.org/2020/02/08/the-best-sites-for-online-pronunciation-feedback-do-you-know-more/).

There are plenty of practice and recording sites for ELLs, and you can find links to the best of them at The Best Sites to Practice Speaking English (http://larryferlazzo.edublogs.org/2008/03/17/the-best-sites-to-practice-speaking-english/). You'll also find links to great apps where students can take photos of illustrated dialogues they have created (e.g., talking heads). They can then provide audio narration and post them on a class blog.

Other useful online sites for speaking practice can be found at The Best Sites for Developing English Conversational Skills (http://larryferlazzo.edublogs.org/2008/04/05/the-best-sites-for-developing-english-conversational-skills/) and The Best Websites for Learning English Pronunciation (http://larryferlazzo.edublogs.org/2008/03/31/the-best-websites-for-learning-english-pronunciation/).

For puppet ideas, check out The Best Resources for Using Puppets in Class (http://larryferlazzo.edublogs.org/2009/10/07/the-best-resources-for-using-puppets-in-class/).

You can download our conversation cheat sheets at The ESL/ELL Teacher's Survival Guide website (www.wiley.com/WileyCDA/WileyTitle/productCd-1118095677.html). It's Exhibit 4.3.

Attribution

Versions of some of these ideas appeared in our book, *The ESL/ELL Teacher's Survival Guide* (Ferlazzo & Sypnieski, 2022).

Thanks to Neil T. Millington from Dreamreader (http://dreamreader.net/), an excellent online site with free ELL lesson plans and Todd Beuckens from Elllo (www.elllo.org/), a site filled with interactive listening activities, for the ask-answer-add activity.

All figures from this chapter, as well as 11 additional chapters, references, hyperlinked Technology Connections, and more online resources, can be found at www.wiley.com/go/ellteacherstoolbox2.

STRATEGY 25: CONVERSATION PRACTICE 293

A	What is your favorite holiday?
B	My favorite holiday is _____.
A	What does your family do on _____?
B	We _____.
A	You should bring food from that day to Mr. Ferlazzo. He is a good person.
B	Yes/No I will/will not. I like him/I don't like him.

Figure 25.1 Holiday Dialogue

A	Okay, I will throw up now instead! Bleeeeaaaahhh!
A	But they tasted so good! And I was so hungry!
A	I have a stomachache!
B	Okay, I will take you to the doctor. Please don't throw up in my car!
B	But you don't feel so good, do you? You deserve to feel bad.
A	I feel better now. You don't have to take me to the doctor.
B	You should not have eaten 10 bags of Hot Cheetos!
B	Eeeewww, that's disgusting!
A	Please don't be angry. Help me. I need a ride to the doctor.

Figure 25.2 Dialogue Scramble

A	I have a stomachache!
B	You should not have eaten 10 bags of Hot Cheetos!
A	But they tasted so good! And I was so hungry!
B	But you don't feel so good, do you? You deserve to feel bad.
A	Please don't be angry. Help me. I need a ride to the doctor.
B	Okay, I will take you to the doctor. Please don't throw up in my car!
A	Okay, I will throw up now instead! Bleeeeaaaahhh!
B	Eeeewww, that's disgusting!
A	I feel better now. You don't have to take me to the doctor.

Figure 25.3 Dialogue Scramble (Teacher Answer Key)

Student One:	Did you know that the United States stole much of the western part of the country from Mexico?
Student Two:	Yes, it was not fair. Even a U.S. President who fought in the war, President Grant, called it "unjust."
Student One:	Mexico lost over half of its land!
Student Two:	It was so unfair!
Student One:	Do you think the United States should apologize to Mexico for what it did?
Student Two:	(Yes/No) because _____. What do you think, _____?
Student Three:	(Yes/No) because _____. What do you think, _____?
Student One:	(Yes/No) because _____.
Student Two:	I wonder what Mr. Ferlazzo thinks?
Student One and Student Three:	Nobody cares what he thinks!

Figure 25.4 Mexican American War Critical Thinking Dialogue

1. What has been the best thing that has happened in school?
   - The best thing that has happened in school during the first 10 days was _____.
   - The best thing that has happened in school during the first 10 days was _____ because _____.

2. How are you feeling today?
   - I am feeling (happy; hungry; lonely; sad; sleepy; tired)
   - I am feeling _____ because _____.

3. What kind of job do you want to do in the future?
   - I want to be a _____.
   - I want to be a _____ because _____.

4. Can you show me one of your favorite pictures on your phone?
   - This is one of my favorite pictures on my phone.
   - This is one of my favorite pictures on my phone because _____.

5. Who is your favorite singer or band?
   - My favorite singer is _____.
   - My favorite singer is _____ because _____.

For the rest of the conversation starters, visit our book's website at www.wiley.com/go/ellteacherstoolbox2. **You can also access it via this QR code.**

Figure 25.5 Conversation Starters (note there is a longer version of this Figure for the website in the website bonus folder)

STRATEGY 26
Total Physical Response (TPR)

What Is It?

Total physical response (TPR) is a popular activity in language-learning classrooms where students learn vocabulary by physically acting out actions typically performed and commanded by the teacher. It is primarily done with beginners and usually for a period no longer than 10 to 15 minutes during a day. TPR was originally developed by professor James J. Asher.

Why We Like It

TPR is a great way to get students moving, help ELLs gain confidence by learning new vocabulary easily, and get students to review previously learned words in a fun way.

Supporting Research

TPR has been found to be effective in teaching vocabulary (Howard Research, 2009, p. 34) and increasing student engagement with ELLs (Qiu, 2016). There is substantial research on the advantages of using movement when learning anything, including a new language (Ferlazzo, 2011, June 2).

Common Core Connections

TPR helps meet several Standards, including in Language where we are assisting students "to comprehend more fully when reading or listening" and in Speaking and Listening, where they must "adapt speech to a variety of contexts and communicative tasks."

Application

The following describes the TPR process we use with our beginning ELLs. First, we decide on five or six new words we want to teach that day. The Technology Connections section has links to sites that provide extensive lists of words that easily lend themselves to being taught through TPR, and they generally begin with the basics—*stand, sit, walk, point,* and so on.

Next, we ask two students to come up to the front and stand on either side of us. We then model the command (e.g., "sit") two times, and then we ask the two students in the front to do it afterwards. We think that students find it more helpful and interesting to have classmates modeling instead of always just the teacher. Our welcoming classroom environment and our own regular practice of making fun of ourselves seems to minimize student resistance toward coming to the front.

Then, the two students return to their seats, we write the word on the class whiteboard, and then ask the entire class to do the action—we don't physically model it this time.

After we repeat this sequence for that day's new words, we move on to the next step in the process. This time, without student or teacher modeling, we begin combining those new commands with previously learned ones (e.g., "Walk to your right and point to a student.") and students act them out. We also create funny combinations (e.g., "Hop on one leg and put your finger in your ear.").

Sometimes, we even try to trick students by saying a command and doing a different action to emphasize the importance of listening. As we mentioned, the positive atmosphere of TPR and our classroom tends to ensure that students find it funny and not embarrassing when they make a mistake.

We use TPR as a constant formative assessment activity and keep our eyes out for words that seem to be more difficult for our students. We reinforce those words with more practice and more modeling by us. This entire TPR process is less a map and more of a compass, so be flexible!

In addition, students can take turns teaching the class, and, best of all (in students' eyes, at least), periodically students can command the teacher to do whatever they want!

After 10 or 15 minutes of these activities, students add the new words on the board to their writer's notebook (see Bonus Strategy 18: Writer's Notebook available at www.wiley.com/go/ellteacherstoolbox2) and we move on to a different activity.

TPR EXTENSION ACTIVITIES

Using Mini-Whiteboards

To provide a "change of pace," we sometimes distribute mini-whiteboards and use them in one of two ways:

- We and, when the class is familiar with the activity, students act out the word and give everyone 15 seconds to write down on the board what we did.
- Students are divided into pairs. They take turns with one person acting out the word and the other writing it on the board and saying it.

Practical Stories

After students begin developing a higher English proficiency, we begin to move TPR sessions more into story-like sequences. For example, we model our morning routine ("go into the bathroom"; "wash your face"; "put toothpaste on your toothbrush"; "rinse your mouth"; "spit the water out," etc.) and have students act it out. Then, individual students could plan out their individual routine and teach their version using TPR.

Other routines we've used include these:

- Making breakfast
- Getting ready for bed
- Getting into a car
- Washing dishes
- Riding a bike to school and locking it up
- Taking care of a pet
- Making lunch
- Preparing dinner
- Cleaning the kitchen
- Changing diapers

We usually, though not exclusively, use these routines in parallel to the themes we are emphasizing during other parts of the class (e.g., home, school, food, etc.). In addition, we invite students to make their own suggestions (that's where the "changing diapers" sequence came from).

"Fun" Stories

After teaching a few specific words, we also sometimes turn the TPR "commands" into a fun short story, like this:

> *Stand up and look to the left.*
> *Pretend you see a ghost.*
> *Yell!*
> *Run around!*
> *Scare the ghost!*

Once students become familiar with the idea, we sometimes have small groups use Exhibit 26.1: TPR Story Planning Sheet to create and then teach their own five-sentence stories using words we've taught in previous days and weeks. Or, a group of students with a higher English proficiency level might just create a story and then teach it to the entire class.

Teaching Online

Using TPR in an online class can be challenging, with one of the main issues being that students may be reluctant to turn on their cameras so the teacher can't see if students are following along with the lesson.

If you can get over that hurdle, it shouldn't be too difficult to teach many of the typical words used in TPR lessons. And students can use some of the variations discussed in the chapter while working in breakout rooms.

What Could Go Wrong?

Don't try to teach too many new words at one time, and don't let TPR go longer than 15 minutes (we've actually found 10 minutes works best most of the time).

Differentiation Recommendations

Newcomers (Preliterate or Low Literacy in Home Language): Start with the basic words and the basic "moves" of TPR. Encourage them to draw images next to the words they copy down in their notebooks.	**Newcomers (Literate in Home Language):** Use basic TPR and then move to whiteboards and to acting out more complex "practical" stories and "fun" stories.
Intermediate ELLs: Skip the basics and immediately use multistep "practical" stories acting out different scenarios and do "fun" stories for a change of pace.	**Advanced ELLs:** The teacher can develop multistep "practical" stories acting out different scenarios and more complex "fun" stories. If in a multilevel class, advanced ELLs can develop simpler versions to teach to less English-proficient students.

Technology Connections

You can access downloadable word lists and short videos of the TPR strategy in action at The Best Resources for Learning About Total Physical Response (TPR) (http://larryferlazzo.edublogs.org/2016/09/10/the-best-resources-for-learning-about-total-physical-response-tpr/).

300 THE ELL TEACHER'S TOOLBOX 2.0

Attribution

Versions of some of these ideas appeared in our book, *The ESL/ELL Teacher's Survival Guide* (Ferlazzo & Sypnieski, 2022, p. 61).

All figures from this chapter, as well as 11 additional chapters, references, hyperlinked Technology Connections, and more online resources, can be found at www.wiley.com/go/ellteacherstoolbox2.

STRATEGY 26: TOTAL PHYSICAL RESPONSE (TPR) *301*

What is the problem? _____
How does the story end? _____
What are three verbs you can use in the story?

1. _____
2. _____
3. _____

What are the five lines of the story?

1. _____
2. _____
3. _____
4. _____
5. _____

Now that you have the five lines in the story, are there any other words you need to pre-teach? If, so, what are they? _____
Who will teach each line of the story?

1. _____
2. _____
3. _____
4. _____
5. _____

Practice!

MODEL:
Stand up and look to the right.
Pretend you see a monster.
Yell!
Cry!
Kill the monster

Figure 26.1 TPR Story Planning Sheet *Source:* Reprinted from *The ESL/ELL Teacher's Survival Guide,* © 2022 Jossey-Bass. Reprinted with permission.

STRATEGY 27

Music

What Is It?

Music can assist ELLs to develop their reading, writing, listening, and speaking skills. Though we'll list all the ways we use it in our classroom, we will specifically describe activities that maximize listening and speaking.

Why We Like It

Most students like music, and it's always an opportunity if we can leverage something they already like to help them learn English! In addition, anything we can do to get our ELLs speaking is a plus—and choral singing or chanting counts!

Supporting Research

As we shared in *The ESL/ELL Teacher's Survival Guide* (Ferlazzo & Sypnieski, 2022, p. 89):

> Extensive research has shown that using songs is an effective language-development strategy with English Language Learners (Schoepp, 2001). They are often accessible because popular songs tend to use the vocabulary of an eleven-year-old, the rhythm and beat helps students speak in phrases or sentences instead of words, and the word repetition assists retention (Li & Brand, 2009, p. 74). Neuroscience has also found that music can increase dopamine release in the brain and generates positive emotions. This kind of emotional learning reinforces long-term memory (Jensen, 2001).

More recent research has reinforced these same findings (Talada, 2015; Bokiev et al., 2018; Johansson, 2021). In addition to this research specifically on songs, there have also been studies showing that jazz chants, a rhythmic activity originated by Carolyn Graham, have positive effects on student engagement (Kung, 2013, p. 16) and English prosody (Felix, 2013, p. 15).

Common Core Connections

Our focus here is on the speaking and listening aspects of using music in the ELL classroom, so these activities certainly help students "prepare for and participate effectively in a range of conversations" (Common Core State Standards Initiative, n.d.c) and "adapt speech to a variety of contexts and communicative tasks, demonstrating command of formal English when indicated or appropriate" (Common Core State Standards Initiative, n.d.c). In addition, these lessons enhance listening comprehension. The other music-related ideas we mention also meet several other Language, Writing, and Reading Standards.

Application

TYPICAL SEQUENCE

This is a typical process we use with songs, though we don't use *all* steps *all* of the time.

Choosing the Song

We generally play songs that fit into the theme (home, school, feelings, etc.) or writing genre (narrative, argument, problem-solution) we're teaching at the time. However, we also choose songs for other reasons, including if we feel the song's messages might resonate with our students. Larry loves the musical *Hamilton*[1] and has used songs from the show with ELLs. We talk about those lessons later in this section. The *Hamilton* songs illustrate another important criterion that we use when choosing music for our classes—they must have simple choruses that don't require being sung too quickly. Our students may not be able to sing most of the words to a song, but focusing on the chorus reduces the difficulty, maximizes the fun, and creates lots of opportunities for repetition.

We also look for songs that can incorporate movement. There are old favorites, such as "Heads, Shoulders, Knees, and Toes," but also more mature songs, such as Bob Marley's "Get Up, Stand Up," in which it's easy to improvise our own moves. Substantial research documents that gestures and movement can support language acquisition (Ferlazzo, 2011, June 2).

So, our baseball-inspired equations for songs that we use in our classroom are as follows:

Relevance + Accessible chorus + Movement = Home run

Relevance + Accessible chorus = Triple

Note: We just haven't found that many popular songs that seem accessible to Beginning ELLs. Though we're always on the lookout for more, we primarily use "Hello, Goodbye," "You Are So Beautiful," "The Lion Sleeps Tonight," and "Three Little Birds."

---

[1] *Hamilton: An American Musical* (written and created by Lin-Manuel Miranda, who, incidentally, is a former seventh-grade English teacher) has been a huge hit in the United States. Its songs celebrate history and immigrants through the story of founding father Alexander Hamilton and is popular among the young and old alike.

Pre-Listening

We preview a song in similar ways we might preview a book. We might tell students the title of the song and ask them to predict what it might be about. Or, before we teach "I Just Called To Say I Love You," we might ask students what they think love is and to share with classmates whom they love and who loves them (if they feel comfortable doing so).

Free Listening

We then play the music and ask students to just listen to it—they don't see the lyrics and have no assignment except for listening to the song.

Sometimes, we'll play the song twice and, prior to the second time, ask students to make notes of the words they recognize. Afterwards, we'll ask them to draw simple pictures of the words they know—without labeling them. After they've drawn a few images, students can share them in small groups to see if other students can identify the words represented by the picture. This process is called *song pictures,* and we learned it from English teacher Nico Lorenzutti (2014).

Listening and Reading

We'll then distribute the lyrics to the song and encourage students to read along (particularly the chorus). Ideally, we show a lyrics video of the song at the same time. These are videos that scroll the lyrics as the song is being played. Just search *lyrics video* plus the name of the song and it is very likely you'll find one online. If a video is not available, the students just read lyrics that we have distributed to the class.

Saying and Singing

After listening to the song two or three times, we tell students that it's time to lip-sync—again, not necessarily all the words (though that would be great). We ask them to lip-sync the chorus, at least. This exercise helps them become comfortable with the words and rhythm of the song without having to take the risk of actually saying the words.

Some classes are filled with students who relish singing, some are filled with students who are all scared at the thought of singing, and some are half and half. We teachers play with the hand we're dealt, and if you're not confident that your students will sing you've got nothing to worry about—tell your students that, next, we are all going to say the words and not sing them. When it's time for the chorus, just lead the class in saying the words. It accomplishes the same goal of having students speak and, if they say it enough times, you might be surprised how easily some will slip into singing. Play the song two or three more times as students are saying or singing the words.

The teacher has to be up in the front lip-syncing and saying or singing in an exaggerated manner along with students. If we aren't willing to model taking that kind of risk, why should we expect students to do so?

Comprehension Activities

Following those pre-listening, listening, and singing activities, we might have students complete a cloze exercise as a follow-up exercise (probably on a different day). It's easy to print out lyrics, white out the words you want students to replace, and then make copies (sometimes we have a word bank at the bottom and sometimes we don't). We typically have students complete these clozes while we are repeatedly playing the song.

We might also do a sequencing activity in which we have copied and pasted the lyrics out of order. Students then have to cut them out and put them in the correct order while listening to the song a few times.

Extension Activities

There are multiple options for extension activities:

- Ask students to substitute words, write their own chorus, and sing it for the class. For example, if we've just learned "Hello, Goodbye," then students can change the words to *big* and *small*.
- Have students sing a chorus or an entire song together, record it on their phones and the teacher's phone, and post it on Google Classroom, or whatever Learning Management System your school uses. Oftentimes, students love to hear themselves sing (even if they say they don't).
- English teacher Nati Gonzalez Brandi gave us the idea of "drawing a song" (ELT Brewery, 2016). After students learn a song, she has them draw a representation of it with some words and some pictures, which they then present to the class. You can see links to examples in the Technology Connections section.
- There are several free online sites that, while playing a song, show the lyrics in a cloze format requiring listeners to fill in the blanks as they are listening. This can be made into a whole-class activity by giving everyone whiteboards and projecting the website on the front whiteboard.

TOPICAL PROJECTS

Trending popular music and music videos often offer opportunities for creative language-learning lessons. Here are two examples we've done with our ELL classes. You may or may not want to use these activities with your students. We offer them here more as inspirational examples so teachers can be on the lookout for upcoming popular music trends and be thinking if and how they might be used in the classroom.

Hamilton

As mentioned previously, Larry is a big fan of this Broadway musical. "My Shot" is one of his favorite songs from the show, though, similar to most of the songs, it's sung too rapidly for many English language learners. It does, however, have an accessible chorus. It emphasizes Hamilton's grit and ambition through repeating the line, "I am not throwing away my shot." After explaining what it means, having the class listen to the song, and then singing the chorus several times, Larry gave his students this sentence frame to respond to the question "How can you apply this idea to your own life?":

"I'm not throwing away my shot because _____." Things I will do to not throw away my shot are _____, _____, and _____.

Larry did something similar with another *Hamilton* song, including "I wrote my way out" in the chorus.

In both instances, he took advantage of a very fast-moving and popular song that had accessible lyrics to help ELLs find nuances of the language and support social emotional learning skills at the same time.

Again, the point of these examples is not to encourage you to use these *Hamilton* songs in your class (though you're welcome to do so). Rather, we offer them here as encouragement to get your creative juices flowing as you become aware of each year's popular hits.

PERSONALIZED SONG LESSONS

Personalized learning is a buzzword in education circles these days and often refers to using technology to fit lessons that are more personalized to a student's interests, strengths, and challenges. We're not using much tech in these two examples of personalized song lessons, but in each case we are building on each student's unique musical interest to leverage motivation for language learning.

My Favorite Song

Alma Avalos, a talented educator who worked with us in our classrooms, developed this two-part high-interest lesson. In Part 1, choose any song that you are confident will engage your students and meets the Relevance + Accessible Chorus + Movement equation we shared previously in this strategy. Then go through some of the Pre-Listening through Comprehension activities listed previously. Next, have students complete Figure 27.1: Song Lyric Analysis Sheet. Last, ask students to use an online tool that lets them easily write and illustrate their favorite lyrics to present to the class (doing it by hand is fine if tech is not available). See the Technology Connections section for resources.

After having completed Part 1, students then use their work as a model for Part 2. Each student chooses their own favorite song—whether it is in the home language or in English—and completes a similar form (see Figure 27.2), creates a visual representation of his or her favorite lyrics, and then presents them to the class, as well as playing the song.

It's easy to modify the number of lyrics and questions on the forms. Our students have always loved this exercise, and there has been very little resistance—if any—to making full-class presentations.

Personal Theme Song

We use this activity after students have learned the concept of theme in our narrative (story) writing unit (see Figure 3.8 in Strategy 3: Graphic Organizers). We ask students to think about a theme for their lives and often rewrite the list of themes we discussed when we first taught the concept, while clarifying that their personal theme doesn't have to be from the list. If students are high-beginner or intermediate ELLs, we sometimes have students take online quizzes designed to help people choose their theme song (just search online for *quiz to pick personal theme song* and you'll find many options), though we also point out that they don't have to agree with the results. We then give students a copy of Figure 27.2: My Favorite Song with minor changes—we replace the word *favorite* that appears two times with the word *theme*. Students then follow a process similar to Part 2 in the My Favorite Song exercise, including making a class presentation. We borrowed this idea from English teacher Shelly Terrell (2012).

CHANTS

The idea of using jazz chants, which are short, rhythmic lines that support vocabulary and grammar development to help in language acquisition, was developed by Carolyn Graham. Graham encourages teachers to create their own chants using a pattern of three syllables, two syllables, and one syllable, though we and many other teachers do not feel bound by that pattern. Figure 27.3: Information Chants is an example of one we use with our students to help learn the months and days of the week. After practicing saying the words in a non-chant way, we all then tap on a desk and chant in a unified beat. We sometimes have students record their chanting and post it on our Google Classroom.

A link to many more resources on chants can be found in the Technology Connections section.

Teaching Online

Practically all of these activities can be taught online. However, based on our experience, it's extraordinarily challenging to ensure that the majority of students are engaged in them. Getting students to sing in the classroom is difficult enough—getting them to sing when many might have their cameras turned off and other family members nearby might be "Mission Impossible."

There are obviously a number of activities that don't require singing. Regular reminders to students about keeping their eyes on the goal of learning English will be required to safeguard against students taking shortcuts, like easily checking the answers to clozes on another screen instead of using their own thinking skills. Learning English is hard, and even the most serious student might be tempted to take the easier road on occasion.

What Could Go Wrong?

As we already mentioned, sometimes students don't want to sing. If that's the case, don't worry about it—just have them say the words. Forcing students to sing will not lead to a positive classroom environment for learning.

Some students can get into loud pounding instead of light tapping when doing chants. As in all things, model desired behavior prior to doing the activity. This usually preempts disruptions.

Differentiation Recommendations

Newcomers (Preliterate or Low Literacy in Home Language): Use the songs listed that are accessible to beginners. Encourage them to primarily focus on the chorus that is repeated and to write down images above the words (they can use Read&Write for Google Chrome or Microsoft's Immersive Reader, which offer picture dictionary features as long as lyrics are in an online document) and Google Translate to provide additional assistance. Simple chants can also be accessible.	**Newcomers (Literate in Home Language):** All activities in the chapter are accessible to newcomers, though some might need additional scaffolding.
Intermediate ELLs: All activities in this chapter are accessible to intermediates. In a multilevel class, perhaps provide different types of clozes using lyrics—one version for newcomers (with a word bank, for example) and the other for intermediates (no word bank).	**Advanced ELLs:** Use songs containing more complex language. Provide clozes with fewer "clues." Have students create clozes for their classmates to complete. See Strategy 7: Clozes for student instructions on creating their own clozes.

Technology Connections

If you are looking for ideas of songs to use in the ELL classroom, you won't have to look further than The Best Music Websites for Learning English (http://larryferlazzo.edublogs.org/2008/01/30/the-best-music-websites-for-learning-english/). That list also contains links to free sites that show music videos and accompany them with clozes that students complete online. Unfortunately, many of the videos are blocked by school district content filters, but the site can still be used by students at home, and teachers can get specific clips unblocked and use them as an all-class activity.

There are also *many* lesson plans targeting specific songs that can be found on that "Best" list, and by just searching "(name of song) ESL lesson." In this chapter, we have focused on instructional strategies that can be applied to just about any song.

Karaoke sites can also provide fun singing opportunities; explore The Best Online Karaoke Sites for English Language Learners (http://larryferlazzo.edublogs.org/2008/10/15/the-best-online-karaoke-sites-for-english-language-learners/).

For student examples of the My Favorite Song activity, visit Here's a Successful Music Lesson We Did with Beginning ELLs (http://larryferlazzo.edublogs.org/2015/05/10/heres-a-successful-music-lesson-we-did-with-beginning-ells-hand-outs-student-examples-included/). And for online tools to use with that lesson, go to The Best Tools for Creating Visually Attractive Quotations for Online Display (http://larryferlazzo.edublogs.org/2013/02/23/the-best-tools-for-creating-visually-attractive-quotations-for-online-display/).

In Strategy 5: Clozes, we discussed how ChatGPT and other AI-powered chatbots can create accessible clozes. Teachers can use those same instructions to create clozes from song lyrics. AI tools can also automatically create comprehension questions for them. See The "Best" Tools for Automatically Turning Texts & Videos into Interactive Language Learning Tools (https://larryferlazzo.edublogs.org/2022/08/03/the-best-tools-for-automatically-turning-texts-videos-into-interactive-language-learning-tools/) for a list of sites that offer that feature.

There are now also many artificial intelligence–powered text-to-music sites that can bring the idea of "personalized songs" to a whole different level. The ones that provide the text lyrics along with the songs are the ones most helpful to ELLs. We've had students use them to create songs, for example, that include the "10 food-related vocabulary words" that we taught that week. Students then can listen to it while they are walking or biking to school. We've also used them to help reinforce grammar concepts like when to use "has" and "have" and have the whole class sing it. See a list of the sites we use at The Best Online Sites for Creating Music (https://larryferlazzo.edublogs.org/2008/10/01/the-best-online-sites-for-creating-music/).

Finally, you can watch lots of chant examples at The Best Sites (& Videos) for Learning About Jazz Chants (http://larryferlazzo.edublogs.org/2011/07/28/the-best-sites-videos-for-learning-about-jazz-chants/).

Attribution

Versions of some of these ideas appeared in our book, *The ESL/ELL Teacher's Survival Guide* (Ferlazzo & Sypnieski, 2012, p. 62–63).

Thanks to Nati Gonzalez Brandi for her drawing a song idea (https://myeltbrewery.wordpress.com/2016/10/17/beyond-gap-fills-using-songs-to-learn-a-language-why-how-and-which/).

Thanks to English teacher Nico Lorenzutti for the song pictures activity (https://americanenglish.state.gov/files/ae/resource_files/52_1_4_lorenzutti.pdf).

Thanks to Shelly Terrell for the personal theme song lesson (http://blog.esllibrary.com/2012/03/05/20-tips-language-through-song-lyrics/).

All figures from this chapter, as well as 11 additional chapters, references, hyperlinked Technology Connections, and more online resources, can be found at www.wiley.com/go/ellteacherstoolbox2.

Directions: Choose lyrics that you liked from the song and copy them onto this paper. You must choose five different lines or more. Please write neatly.

Name of Song:_____

My favorite lyrics:_____
_____
_____

When done copying the lyrics, *translate* them in your home language. (Use Google translate if you need help.)

1. Lyric:

   My translation:

2. Lyric:

   My translation:

3. Lyric:

   My translation:

4. Lyric:

   My translation:

5. Lyric:

   My translation:

Figure 27.1 Song Lyric Analysis Sheet

STRATEGY 27: MUSIC 311

Answer the following questions about two of your favorite lyrics:

A. Why did you choose these lyrics?

I chose lyric number _____ because
_____.

I chose lyric number _____ because
_____.

B. What are some new words you learned in these lyrics? What does each word mean in English?

_____ means _____.
_____ means _____.
_____ means _____.

C. How do these lyrics make you feel and why?

Lyric number _____ makes me feel _____ because
_____.

Lyric number _____ makes me feel _____ because
_____.

Figure 27.1 (Continued)

---

1. What is the name of your favorite song?

The name of my favorite song is _____.

2. Who is the artist?

The recording artist is _____.

3. What is the genre of the song?

_____ is the genre of the song.

4. Why did you choose this song?

I chose this song because _____.

Choose five lyrics or more from your favorite song.

Please copy them below. (If your lyrics are in your home language, please also write the English translated version. If the lyrics are in English, then also write them in your language.)

Figure 27.2 My Favorite Song

1. Lyric:

   My translation:

2. Lyric:

   My translation:

3. Lyric:

   My translation:

4. Lyric:

   My translation:

5. Lyric:

   My translation:

Answer the following questions about two of your favorite lyrics:

A. Why did you choose these lyrics?

   I chose lyric number _____ because _____.

   I chose lyric number _____ because _____.

B. What are some new words you learned in these lyrics? What does each word mean in English?

   _____ means _____.
   _____ means _____.
   _____ means _____.

C. How do these lyrics make you feel and why?

   Lyric number _____ makes me feel _____ because _____.

   Lyric number _____ makes me feel _____ because _____.

Figure 27.2 (Continued)

STRATEGY 27: MUSIC 313

January is the Winter.
February is the Winter.
March is the Spring.
March is the Spring.

April is the Spring.
May is the Spring.
June is the Summer.
June is the Summer.

July is the Summer.
August is the Summer.
September is the Fall.
September is the Fall.

October is the Fall.
November is the Winter.
December is the Winter.
December is the Winter.

Monday starts the week.
Monday starts the week.
Then comes Tuesday.
Then comes Tuesday.

Figure 27.3 Information Chants

Wednesday comes next.
Wednesday comes next.
Then comes Thursday.
Then comes Thursday.

School ends Friday.
School ends Friday.
Next comes the weekend.
Next comes the weekend.

The weekend starts with Saturday.
The weekend starts with Saturday.
The weekend ends with Sunday.
The weekend ends with Sunday.

Figure 27.3 (*Continued*)

STRATEGY 28
Using Photos or Other Images in Speaking and Listening

What Is It?

Photos and other images can be used to promote reading and writing, as we shared in Strategy 17: Using Photos or Other Images in Reading and Writing. Though many of the ideas we shared in that strategy have speaking and listening components, the three activities we share in this section use images primarily to promote speaking and listening.

Why We Like It

We've found that these applications have been successful in encouraging students to listen with intention and to speak. It is not often an easy job to get our teen ELLs to do either, and we kissed a lot of frogs before we found these effective activities.

Supporting Research

Previously cited studies in Strategy 17: Using Photos or Other Images in Reading and Writing clearly support the use of visuals in ELL classes. In addition, there is specific research that suggests using images can enhance student motivation to engage in speaking activities (Trang, n.d., p. 4).

Common Core Connections

All the activities listed here support the Language Standards of developing the ability to apply English conventions and to become a skilled listener. The Speaking and Listening Standard saying that students must "prepare for and participate effectively in a range of conversations and collaborations with diverse partners, building on others' ideas and expressing their own clearly and persuasively" is also a slam dunk!

Application

In Strategy 17, we discussed numerous ways to use photos or other images in reading and writing activities. Many of those lessons can be easily extended to the speaking and listening domains. Here are some photo activities that lend themselves particularly to speaking and listening.

PHOTO COLLAGES

Photo collages are great tools to use in class for listening and speaking practice. News organizations, especially the *New York Times,* publish online photo collages in grid form about specific topics (summertime, pigeons, dog show winners, etc.). We project them on our whiteboard before class and write a visible number on each image in the grid. We give students mini-whiteboards and explain, "I'm going to describe one of the images and ask you which number I'm talking about." For example, a teacher describing the pigeon images could, after teaching any specialized vocabulary needed, say, "Two eyes are showing and its beak is pressed down to its chest." Once students understand how the strategy works, we sometimes change the collage and pair students up to continue on their own.

There are plenty of online tools that let you easily create your own collages from photos on the web or pictures you take. Not only can teachers make ones to project for the class but also students can make collages for use in this activity. See the Technology Connections section for links to ready-made collages and do-it-yourself tools.

BACK AND FORTH

We build on the idea of using photo collages by reproducing pages from the book *Back & Forth: Photocopiable Cooperative Pair Activities for Language Development* (Rodgers et al., 1985). An example of one of its pages can be found in Figure 28.1. They are basically a series of image strips that are very similar to one another. After quickly teaching any needed vocabulary, we divide the class into partners. Then, we have one student describe the image they have in mind ("The man and dog are walking to the right.") and the other has to point to the correct one. After students become familiar with the exercise, we sometimes have them create their own similar picture strips.

IF ANIMALS OR INANIMATE OBJECTS COULD TALK

As we discuss in Strategy 25: Conversation Practice, sometimes ELLs, particularly beginners, have less anxiety about speaking if they do it through other objects—such as puppets. In those cases, it can feel like the object is doing the talking (as well as making any mistakes) and not the student.

The same idea is at work with this activity. We often show funny images of animals, and students then have to write and say what they believe the animal is thinking at the moment the photo was taken. It can be a short and fun exercise for students. You can find links to lots of examples, as well as to many usable images, in the Technology Connections section.

STRATEGY 28: USING PHOTOS OR OTHER IMAGES IN SPEAKING

Teaching Online

Nothing complicated here—all of these instructional strategies can be used online with screen sharing and breakout rooms.

What Could Go Wrong?

Be sure to give students time to prep! Don't put a collage up on the board and give students five seconds to answer your questions. Don't give students just a few seconds to write down what they think the funny-looking duck is thinking! Provide sentence starters to newcomers or give them a list of answers to choose from.

Differentiation Recommendations

Newcomers (Preliterate or Low Literacy in Home Language): Use most, if not all, of the strategies in the chapter with the assistance of Google Translate or other similar tools that are voice activated. Provide sentence starters. The Back & Forth activity may be too challenging until they gain higher English proficiency.	**Newcomers (Literate in Home Language):** Use all strategies as described in the chapter. Provide sentence starters.
Intermediate ELLs: Use more complex Back & Forth images, and expect them to create more complex ones, as well.	**Advanced ELLs:** Write longer dialogues and extended stories for the "If Animals or Inanimate Objects Could Talk" activity.

Technology Connections

Find links to photo collages made by news organizations and online tools to create your own at The Best Ideas for Using Photos in Lessons (http://larryferlazzo.edublogs.org/2010/06/27/the-best-ways-to-use-photos-in-lessons/).

Find links to fun examples of animals "thinking" and images your students can use at The Best Resources for Using "If This Animal or Image Could Talk" Lesson Idea in Class (http://larryferlazzo.edublogs.org/2015/08/01/the-best-resources-on-using-if-this-animal-or-image-could-talk-lesson-idea-in-class/).

Instead of potentially feeling overwhelmed by looking for photos on a certain theme using a search engine, consider going to ELTPics and their free categorized photo sets (www.flickr.com/photos/eltpics/albums) and take advantage of the work that other ELL teachers have done (you can also contribute your own photos there).

Attribution

Thanks to Alta Book Center Publishers for letting us reprint a page from *Back and Forth* (https://altaenglishpublishers.com/product/back-forth-photocopiable-cooperative-pair-activities-for-language-development/).

All figures from this chapter, as well as 11 additional chapters, references, hyperlinked Technology Connections, and more online resources, can be found at www.wiley.com/go/ellteacherstoolbox2.

STRATEGY 28: USING PHOTOS OR OTHER IMAGES IN SPEAKING 319

BACK & FORTH: PAIR ACTIVITIES
Exercise 2.6
PARTNER

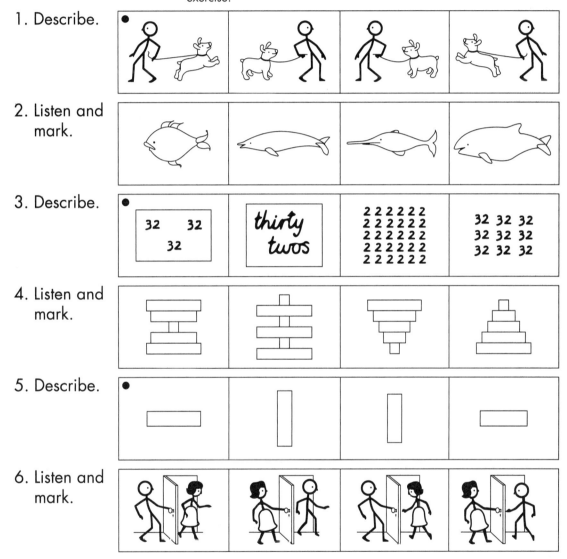

Figure 28.1 Back-and-Forth Page   *Source:* Reproduced by permission. Palm Springs, California USA. Copyright 2014 ALTA English Publishers.

STRATEGY 29

Video

What Is It?

Using video in the ELL classroom is a great way to boost language skills and motivation. Videos can play a range of roles in learning—students can watch them to build listening skills and comprehension or practice speaking by creating their own.

In Strategy 21: Problem-Posing, we discuss the use of video as a way to help students develop critical thinking and writing skills. We also explain the use of a video activity to build students' summarizing skills in Strategy 15: Quoting, Summarizing, and Paraphrasing. And, we describe students using videos to create dialogues and practice pronunciation in Strategy 25: Conversation Practice.

Here, we will share some ways to use video as an instructional strategy to specifically increase students' speaking and listening abilities.

Why We Like It

Who doesn't enjoy watching engaging videos? It's something many of us do on a regular basis, and many students do it daily and sometimes hourly! We can build on this interest by bringing some of the videos they are already watching at home or sharing with their friends into the classroom, as well as introducing new ones to them. Videos are excellent tools for language study because students can *listen* to English being spoken; *see* facial expressions, gestures, and body language among other visual cues; and *read* the English subtitles all at the same time. In addition, they can be re-watched as many times as needed. Students are also highly motivated to create their own videos (something many of them already do) and share them with authentic audiences online.

Supporting Research

Research shows the use of video in ELL instruction can benefit learners' comprehension, language skills, and motivation (Almurashi, 2016; Morat, Shaari, & Abidin, 2016). Specifically having students watch videos with same-language subtitles (e.g., watching a video in English with English subtitles) can result in better word recognition and comprehension skills (Brady-Myerov, 2015).

Common Core Connections

Using videos for listening and speaking practice can support many of the Speaking and Listening Standards. One of them is being able to "integrate and evaluate information presented in diverse media and formats, including visually, quantitatively, and orally."

Application

This section contains general guidelines for using videos, a typical sequence we follow when showing clips, and several additional ways we use them in class (note that in Strategy 14: Writing Frames and Writing Structures, we include a figure that can be used by students to write about movies and videos they watch at home).

GUIDELINES

We keep the following considerations in mind when we use videos to build speaking and listening skills (and for any other reason):

- **Video length:** Short clips (usually one to five minutes) work best at keeping students engaged while offering enough context and language for study. Another option is to use a longer video divided into shorter chunks with activities and discussion. Research on video length and student engagement reveals the optimal length to be six minutes or less, and we prefer the less (Guo et al., 2014).

- **Purpose:** Video clips that directly relate to the topic of study are helpful in deepening understanding while building language skills. Selecting relevant and engaging video clips can increase student participation and language-learning opportunities.

- **Accessible vocabulary:** Students don't need to know all the words in a video in order for it to be effective. However, between the visual support and the subtitles contained in the video, students should be able to get the gist—the overall meaning or main idea. It can be helpful to keep the idea of *comprehensible input* in mind when selecting a video (or a text) to use with ELLs.

    Linguist Stephen Krashen, along with many other researchers, proposes that learners can make more progress and acquire a language more naturally when some of the language input they are receiving is slightly above their current English proficiency level (Krashen & Terrell, 1983; Wong & Van Patten, 2003, p. 418). In other words, they can use their present English skills to acquire new vocabulary and language structures. In terms of video, this means that students can understand the gist of the video without initially knowing all the words. The speed of the words being spoken in a video and accent also enter into this accessibility equation.

- **Video and audio quality:** When viewing videos, ELLs are navigating new content in a new language. We don't want to make this process even more difficult by using video clips that have poor visual or audio quality. This can be distracting and frustrating for everyone!

- **Subtitles:** As we discuss in the Supporting Research section, turning on the closed captioning feature can boost students' literacy skills. Of course, there may be times when we want students to do a specific activity without using the subtitles (e.g., watching a brief conversation with the sound off and having students write what they think the people might be saying), but, most of the time, we find it helpful to turn on this feature.

- **Active, not passive viewing:** We've all experienced turning our students and ourselves into zombies when a video clip goes too long! To avoid this, we break longer videos into shorter clips and provide opportunities for students to be active while viewing—by asking them oral or written questions, having them take notes, or working with a partner to discuss the video, and so on.

  New research has pointed specifically to the effectiveness of giving students questions *before* viewing a video in order to enhance learning and focus. Researchers found that students who were provided these pre-questions were better able to learn and recall not only the answers to those questions but also material from other parts of the video (Carpenter & Toftness, 2017; Willingham, 2017).

- **Access to video:** School district content filters may block certain videos, especially ones from YouTube, even though they are educationally appropriate. Don't wait until your lesson starts to check if the video is accessible. If it's not, you can always download it at home.

TYPICAL SEQUENCE

We use the following general process when incorporating videos into lessons with ELLs. It is similar to the one we describe in Strategy 27: Music. Again, we may not follow *all* the steps *all* of the time. In fact, when we show a video as part of the Language Experience Approach (see Strategy 8), we just show the video and then have students write sentences about what they saw.

Note that there is another discussion to be had about when to show a video if it is part of a lesson that includes students reading about the same topic. We have not found any clear research-based conclusion about if a video should be shown before or after a reading in terms of which one enhances English acquisition and comprehension. We talk further about the questions related to the timing of when to show a video after we explain our process of actually showing it.

Choosing the Video

As we stated, we choose videos that are short (typically one to five minutes), or if they are longer, we break them into shorter clips. We also select video clips that are related to a topic of study and are engaging and accessible to our students. Then, we make sure the video is unblocked by our school district. Finally, we turn on the subtitles.

It can be challenging to find movies and videos that are accessible to Newcomers. The Technology Connections section includes links to lists of many that can be used in lessons, including many animated voiceless videos that work well with students with any English proficiency level.

Before Watching

Before showing a video, we often tell students the title and its type (an advertisement, a movie clip, etc.) and ask them to make one or two predictions to share with a partner. Sometimes these predictions can turn into pre-questions for students to investigate while viewing the video. Other times we create a few pre-questions and write them on the board for students to reference while they are watching the video (e.g., "What is the penguin trying to do? Was the penguin successful? Why or why not?").

While Watching

When using a video clip, we often show it to students one time without stopping and assign no task other than to watch it. Then, we show it again with a task in mind—giving students a couple of pre-questions and having them share the answers or pausing a few times to have students make predictions, ask questions, or summarize what is happening.

After Watching

After watching a video clip, we often ask students to revisit their initial predictions and revise them. We also check for understanding by providing students with a few questions to answer. Sharing these responses in small groups can provide speaking and listening practice. Some examples of questions we give to students can be found in Figure 29.1: Video Thinking Sheet. This sheet can be used with almost any video and contains questions and answer stems for students to complete before and after watching a clip.

Another option is for each student to come up with a few questions based on the video and invite a partner to answer them. We have also had students use their answers to create a mini-poster about the video, which contains the video title, two to three sentences about it based on their question responses (e.g., their favorite part or two things they learned), and an illustration representing a key idea in the video. Students can then informally present their mini-posters in small groups or to the class.

Along with the typical sequence we just described, here are five video activities that we use to specifically help students develop their speaking and listening skills.

SHOWING A VIDEO BEFORE OR AFTER READING

As we mentioned earlier, we can find no clear research-based conclusion about if ELLs should read about a topic before or after watching a video about it. Here, however, is what our experience suggests:

It seems to us like it's one of those education questions that might have an answer beginning, "*It depends.* ...":

It depends on the students' English proficiency level. We would bet dollars to donuts that most newcomers would strongly prefer watching a video first because they would likely gain more background knowledge from the audio, closed captions, and images that would increase their odds of good reading comprehension. This has been our experience when teaching newcomers.

It depends on what scaffolds are used with ELLs to support their reading comprehension. If teachers apply a number of the instructional strategies in Strategy 4: Vocabulary, then they might be more likely to feel confident in comprehending the text without gaining prior knowledge from watching the video. This has been our experience when teaching intermediate and advanced ELLs.

Every class is different, though. We recommend trying it out both ways and then asking which one your students prefer. If most like it one way, then go along with that process. If it's divided, just take turns doing it the two different ways.

BACK TO THE SCREEN

Back to the screen, also called *back-to-back* by some educators, is a popular video activity in our classroom. We were introduced to it by Laurel Pollard and Natalie Hess in their book *Zero Prep: Ready-to-Go Activities for the Language Classroom*.

In this activity, the teacher chooses a short clip (movie clips with a lot of action work best) and divides the class into pairs. One group turns their desks so they face the screen and the other students have their backs to it. The teacher starts to show the clip with the sound off and the person who can see the screen describes in English what is happening to their partner. The teacher then pauses the video, students switch places, and the teacher hits play and the roles are reversed. Depending on the length of the clip, this switch can happen three or four times (we usually change every two minutes or so). The pairs then work together to write a chronological sequence of the events in the clip. They can share with another group and then with the class. The activity concludes with the class watching the whole clip with the sound turned on (if extra support is needed, the whole clip can be shown to the class *prior* to creating the chronological sequence).

We described this activity in our first book *The ESL/ELL Teacher's Survival Guide* (Ferlazzo & Sypnieski, 2022, p. 94) but have since improved it in a few ways. We've found it helpful to scaffold the activity for beginners by writing key words from the clip on the board. If any are new words, we quickly provide the definition or ask students to translate them into their home language. Students can then access these words when they are talking to their partners and writing their chronologies. If we have newcomers in class, we often have them pair up with a more-proficient student so they can watch the clip and listen to what their partner is saying to the other partner. We've also paired up newcomers who speak the same home language to do the activity in that language.

Then, they can write the chronology in their home language and work to translate it, or parts of it, with assistance from the teacher, a student with higher English proficiency, or Google Translate.

SEQUENCING

In this activity, students are given sentence strips containing different events in the video clip and they have to put them in order after watching it. As we explained in Strategy 6: Sequencing, we print out the strips on one sheet in mixed-up order (AI chatbots can help). Then, students can cut them out before doing the sequencing activity. Once students put the strips in an order, they can compare with a partner, and then the class can come to agreement about the correct sequence. Here's where the speaking practice comes in—students can get into pairs and re-watch the video clip with the volume off while taking turns narrating the events as they happen. Newcomers can participate in a similar activity using flashcards with just a word or short phrase on them. They can also work to put the flashcards in the correct sequence and then practice narrating the video by saying the words aloud in order.

As an extension, the teacher can show another video, but this time the students can create the sentence strips (or flashcards) describing the main events in the clip. Then students can practice narrating the video using their sentence strips. This can be done in small groups or as a class, and students can note the similarities and differences between their narrations.

TRUE OR FALSE

This is a quick and easy activity to keep students active during a video and to encourage speaking and listening practice. The teacher shows part of a video clip and pauses to ask students a true or false question based on what they just watched. Students can respond by writing their response on a piece of paper or on a mini-whiteboard. To increase the challenge students can be asked to also write a reason why they think a statement is false. Then they can share their response with a partner and the teacher can select a few pairs to share with the class. The teacher can continue the video and repeat the process a couple more times.

PAUSE AND PREDICT

The pause and predict activity is exactly that—the teacher pauses a video so students can predict what is coming next. Students can write their predictions down or simply share them aloud with a partner. They can be encouraged to share the thinking behind their predictions with the simple sentence frame, "I predict because." Students can revisit their predictions after viewing the whole video clip and share (by writing or speaking) how and why they were correct or not.

Figure 29.2: Pause and Predict Sheet is a simple form we've used to scaffold this activity for intermediate students. The sentence frames contained in this figure could also just be written on the board for student use. The teacher can divide a video clip into four sections. After showing the first section, the teacher can pause the video and ask students to make a prediction about what is coming next and why they think that is the case. Each student can write their prediction in sentence frame number 1 on the pause and predict sheet. The teacher can have students share these or just move on and have them share at the end. Then the teacher shows the second section of the clip and students write new predictions in sentence frame number 2. The teacher can use the same process after showing section 3 and then show the last section to students. Then, students can watch the whole video again without any stops. They can revisit the predictions they made by completing the bottom half of the pause and predict sheet and share their new learnings in pairs or small groups.

STUDENTS CREATING VIDEOS

How-To Videos

Showing students how-to videos, also called *tutorials,* is another way to build speaking and listening skills. We start by showing students several simple how-to videos that only have five or six steps. Before watching, we encourage students to pay attention to the different steps. After watching the video, we give students time (either in pairs or individually) to write down the steps in order. We then play the video again and students can make any necessary changes. This activity can reinforce ordinal numbers by asking students to use them when writing the steps (e.g., first, second, third, etc.). Students can study the steps and then practice saying them in order with a partner.

We have also had our students make their own how-to videos by thinking of something they know how to do and writing down the steps using ordinal numbers. Then, they practice saying each step while also demonstrating it. Demonstrations could include fun pantomimes and pictures as stand-ins for real objects, animals, or people. We use our phones to record the students' demonstrations, show them to the class, and, with permission, post them on our class blog. Some examples from past years include how to tie a tie, how to make papaya salad, and how to brush a cat. See the Technology Connections section for more resources on creating online tutorials.

Thematic Report Videos

Thematic reports are simple writing frames that we have students complete near the beginning of different thematic units we cover in class. For example, when we are studying the topic of community and neighborhoods, students briefly write and draw about their neighborhood; when we are studying food, students briefly write and draw about their favorite meal. Many of these student hand-outs can be found in our book, *The ESL/ELL Teacher's Survival Guide*, second edition, and can be downloaded for free at that book's website.

An example of one can be found at Figure 29.3: Thematic Report: My Favorite Story. We use this one when we begin our unit on reading and writing stories.

After students complete these forms and practice reading and showing them to classmates in a "speed-dating" style, we have either a student in the class or a peer tutor go around and invite students outside one by one to take a picture of the sheet and then record them saying what they wrote. Though there are many free apps that allow you to easily create these videos, Adobe Express and Microsoft Flip are probably the two most popular ones and are likely to be around for a long time.

We have the student doing the recording take our phone during the "warm-up" time and record four or five students each day until they get through everyone.

Showing the videos to the entire class a few at a time in the final minutes of class, with the ending of each video greeted with loud applause, is a positive way to end the day on a good note.

Artificial Intelligence Videos

We discussed a teaching sequence in Strategy 17: Using Photos or Other Images in Reading and Writing of how we use AI-powered text-to-image tools to teach writing.

We have used a similar sequence—in a limited way—with students using text-to-video tools.

We say "in a limited way" because, at the time we are writing this book, the technical abilities of text-to-video tools are far behind those of text-to-image ones.

However, these tools will be catching up soon and are likely to have reached a point when you are reading this passage that you could use the complete sequence from that chapter for videos.

See the Technology Connections section for resources where you will be able to find these up-to-date tools.

Vocabulary Videos

See Strategy 4: Vocabulary for details on how students can create short animated videos on new vocabulary words.

Teaching Online

All of these activities can be done online; though we know we may sound like a "broken record," it will be important to have early discussions with students about the ethical uses of Artificial Intelligence so that they don't use AI tools to short-change their learning.

Videos can be shown through screen sharing, and students can do the various assignments on a shared Google Slide with each student assigned a specific slide. Of course, if you use this strategy, you will also need to talk with the class about not copying or deleting another student's work, or changing the entire presentation style of the slideshow. We've found that starting that discussion by emphasizing the importance of a class culture of mutual respect, and then ending it by explaining how you can identify "who does what" on the slide by looking at its history, usually does the trick.

What Could Go Wrong?

Having access to millions of free videos online can be a double-edged sword. It is wonderful to be able to search for videos containing specific features or on certain topics, but the results can be overwhelming. See the Technology Connections section for links to many videos that are specifically effective with ELLs.

Differentiation Recommendations

Newcomers (Preliterate or Low Literacy in Home Language): These students will do well with watching voiceless videos and using Google Translate to assist them in first saying, and then writing, what they saw. They will need extra assistance from another student who speaks their language, a bilingual aide, or a peer tutor to fully participate in the other video activities described in the chapter, at least until they develop a higher English proficiency.	**Newcomers (Literate in Home Language):** All the activities described in the chapter would be accessible to them.
Intermediate ELLs: Doing all the activities described in the chapter, but showing videos using more complex language and challenging them to create longer and more complex videos in English.	**Advanced ELLs:** Again, doing all the activities described in the chapter, but showing videos with even more complex language and challenging them to create even longer and even more complex videos in English. Expect that they can produce more complex language when completing video comprehension and prediction questions.

Technology Connections

For links to numerous movie and video clips and ideas for using them with ELLs, see these sites:

- The Best Popular Movies/TV Shows for ESL/EFL (& How to Use Them) (http://larryferlazzo.edublogs.org/2008/04/26/the-best-popular-moviestv-shows-for-eslefl/)
- "Best" Lists of the Week: Teaching with Movies & Video Clips (https://larryferlazzo.edublogs.org/2018/06/13/best-lists-of-the-week-teaching-with-movies/)
- The Best Movies to Show ELL Newcomers – Contribute Your Own Suggestions (https://larryferlazzo.edublogs.org/2022/07/09/the-best-movies-to-show-ell-newcomers-contribute-your-own-suggestions/)

For multiple examples of how-to instructional videos, see The Best Online Instructional Video Sites (http://larryferlazzo.edublogs.org/2008/07/24/the-best-online-instructional-video-sites/).

For an up-to-date list of artificial intelligence tools useful to educators, including ones for using in text-to-video projects, see The Best New – & Free – Artificial Intelligence Tools That Could Be Used in the Classroom (https://larryferlazzo.edublogs.org/2023/01/25/the-best-new-free-artificial-intelligence-tools-that-could-be-used-in-the-classroom/).

For ideas on how to use Instagram to make student-created videos (particularly short ones on vocabulary words), see The Best Resources for Learning to Use Instagram (http://larryferlazzo.edublogs.org/2013/02/18/the-best-resources-for-learning-to-use-the-video-app-twine/).

Attribution

Versions of some of these ideas appeared in our book, *The ESL/ELL Teacher's Survival Guide* (Ferlazzo & Sypnieski, 2012, p. 67).

Thank you to Laurel Pollard, Natalie Hess, and Jan Herron for their great activity back to the screen, which is just one of many excellent lesson ideas in their book *Zero Prep: Ready-to-Go Activities for the Language Classroom* (https://altaenglishpublishers.com/product/zero-prep-activities-for-all-levels-activities-for-the-language-classroom/).

All figures from this chapter, as well as 11 additional chapters, references, hyperlinked Technology Connections, and more online resources, can be found at www.wiley.com/go/ellteacherstoolbox2.

Before watching:

What is the title of the video?

Based on the title, what do you predict it might be about?

Write three words that you think you might hear in this video.

After watching:

Were your predictions correct? Why or why not? Did you hear any of the words?

Write two important things you noticed in the video:

Write a question you have about the video:

Write the part of the video that you liked most:

Write how this video made you feel:

If you had to use only five words to describe this video, what would they be?

If you could give this video a new title, what would it be and why?

Figure 29.1 Video Thinking Sheet

Making Predictions

1. I predict _____
   because _____.
2. I predict _____
   because _____.
3. I predict _____
   because _____.

Revising My Predictions

1. My first prediction was _____ (right/wrong) because _____
   _____.
2. My second prediction was _____ (right/wrong) because _____
   _____.
3. My third prediction was _____ (right/wrong) because _____
   _____.

Figure 29.2 Pause and Predict Sheet

Name _____ Date _____

My favorite story is about _____. The hero of the story is _____. The other people or animals in the story include _____ and _____.
It takes place in _____. I like the story because _____.

Draw something that happens in the story here and then write what happened below it:

This is a picture of when _____.

Figure 29.3 Thematic Report: My Favorite Story

STRATEGY 30

Listening

What Is It?

Active listening, inside and outside the classroom, means to actively focus on understanding what you are *listening* to as opposed to *hearing* language being used around you. It's similar to the difference between listening to instructions and hearing music playing in the background. Common activities in ELL classrooms involve students listening to something (a text, a dialogue, a song, a video clip, etc.) and completing a task that requires them to listen for certain language or content. Although this is certainly a helpful practice, we also want our students to know *why* listening skills are important and *how* they can improve these skills. The activities in this section support those goals.

Why We Like It

Listening can often be a hidden skill that gets less attention in the classroom. We try to make it more visible to students because it is so critical to the development of skills in every domain! Good listening skills can obviously increase language learning and content knowledge. Active listening also has many benefits in life in general, especially in the workplace and in our personal relationships. We like to make our students aware of these benefits because it helps create further motivation to practice these skills.

Students often need this extra support because listening to authentic speech in a new language can be a frustrating and overwhelming task. Helping them see the immediate and long-term impacts of active listening can help them stay motivated to apply this skill in and out of the classroom.

Supporting Research

Research has found a significant positive relationship between ELLs' metacognitive awareness and listening performance and thus supports a process-oriented approach to listening instruction (Goh, 2014; Vandergrift & Goh, 2011; Plonsky & Dalman, 2011). A process approach assists students in learning listening strategies and becoming aware of which ones work best, and least best, for them.

Common Core Connections

As in Strategy 24: Dictation, specific listening activities hit more of the Language Standards than the Speaking and Listening ones. They specifically meet the Language Standard that requires students to "apply knowledge of language to understand how language functions in different contexts . . . and to comprehend more fully when reading or listening."

Application

This book includes many ideas that support students in building their listening skills. Strategy 24: Dictation, Strategy 27: Music, Strategy 29: Video, and Strategy 31: Learning Games for Speaking and Listening all contain specific listening activities and resources. These types of lessons help students develop their listening comprehension skills in English as they progress in other domains. Another key element of listening instruction, however, involves making students aware of the value of these skills and how to improve them.

THE WHY AND THE HOW: LISTENING BENEFITS AND METACOGNITIVE LISTENING

We help students become more aware of the benefits of listening in their lives. We explore this idea by asking students to think and write about how *active listening* (fully concentrating in order to understand, remember, and respond to what is being said) can benefit them right now. Students usually come up with answers such as being able to help their families, to learn English more quickly, and to have better relationships with friends. We also have students think about how active listening might be important in their future. We share research that shows that listening is seen as one of the most important traits in leaders and among colleagues in the workplace (Nowogrodski, 2015; Rodriguez, 2012).

After students consider the value of listening skills in their lives, they are often more motivated to learn, use, and evaluate different listening strategies. Research supports this type of strategy instruction—ELLs can make more progress if they are aware of how listening processes work and apply them in their own listening (Vandergrift, n.d.). Helping students understand metacognition (being aware of how and when to use different learning processes) can improve their listening skills in English and in their home language.

We described one way of doing this in our book *Navigating the Common Core with English Language Learners* (Ferlazzo & Sypnieski, 2016, p. 237). We give students Figure 30.1: Listening Practice Sheet before starting a listening practice activity using any of a variety of texts—a video, podcast, news report, dialogue, TED Talk, and so on. We write the title and type of text on the board (e.g., a radio news report titled "Earthquake in Turkey and Syria"). Then we ask students to write anything they know about the topic and the type of text in the first section of Figure 30.1. Students share with a partner and work together to generate more ideas. Students then write a few predictions based on this knowledge. We model how to make predictions about the content (e.g., "I predict the news report will give information about how big the earthquake was and if it caused any damage.") and how the content will be delivered (e.g., "I predict the news report will contain audio interviews with people who lost their homes and will describe the damage to the area."). Students write their predictions in the first section labeled "Before Listening" in Figure 30.1 and share them with each other, adding any new ideas from their partner.

Students then move to the second section of the listening practice sheet and are asked to list strategies they think might be helpful in understanding this particular text. We guide students to remember the different strategies they use while reading and explain that they can apply many of those when listening to texts—including activating prior knowledge, making predictions, visualizing, asking questions, summarizing, using context clues to determine word meanings, and so on. We list these strategies on the board or document camera and ask students to consider which strategies might be helpful, or not, based on the type of listening text (e.g., activating prior knowledge can help us prior to listening to a news report) and their prior listening practice experiences (e.g., summarizing helped me last time I listened to a news report).

During the listening task, it is important for the teacher to pause and replay the listening text several times so students can use these strategies. The teacher should model this process the first time students are doing the activity. Students can also use their own laptop or device with headphones so they can pause on their own and re-listen when needed. See the Technology Connections section for links to sources of good, free audio recordings accessible to ELLs.

Once they've finished the listening task, we ask students to reflect on which strategies were most helpful to their understanding and what was difficult, so they can set goals for improvement. Students write these reflections in the third section of Figure 30.1 and then share them in a class discussion.

We want to restate that the point of this listening exercise is *not to give a comprehension quiz on content*. Rather, its purpose is to challenge students to see for themselves (with our assistance) what strategies they can use to become better listeners in English and in their home language.

Helping students practice these types of listening strategies and metacognition (thinking about which strategies to use, when to use them, and why they help) is easier to do in a classroom environment where students or the teacher can pause the task at any time. It is much more difficult to employ these processes to listening situations out in the world—students can't hit pause when someone strikes up a conversation or when the pharmacist is explaining a medication to them. However, we can help make these processes more automatic by providing this type of practice in the classroom and encouraging them to try it on their own. We can also give them the language to improve their understanding in these situations. The next section contains ideas on how to provide this kind of support.

LISTENING LANGUAGE FRAMES

Teaching students the words and language structures they can use to improve their understanding provides an opportunity for growth in listening, communication, and confidence. Students need to know what to do when they don't understand something and when they think they do understand it but want to confirm that it is correct. When someone says something an ELL doesn't understand, they need to know different ways that they can ask for clarification in English. (e.g., Teacher: "Everyone take out your outline." Student: "Excuse me, what does *outline* mean?"). ELLs also need to be able to paraphrase what they've heard as a comprehension check when they are not 100% sure of their understanding (Teacher: "Everyone take out your outline." Student: "Just to be clear, the *outline* is the paper with the boxes, right?"). We use Figure 30.2: Listening Frames to have students practice these skills.

We provide copies to each student and have a large version posted on the wall. Students can then practice using these questions as they participate in small-group discussions. The teacher can also provide dialogues containing these language frames that students can practice and then perform (see Figure 30.3: Sample Dialogue).

Students can be asked to underline the phrases in the dialogue that demonstrate active listening. Students could also write their own dialogues for other listening situations (e.g., talking with a teacher, making a phone call to get information, talking to a neighbor about a problem, or anything else relevant to their experiences).

MORE LISTENING IDEAS

All of our books include a variety of ways to specifically support students' listening skills. Here are a few more ideas we've either come across or made better since our last two books were published.

Back-to-Back

Back-to-back is a listening activity frequently used for team-building and to improve communication skills. In our classroom, we use it as a modified dictation activity with a challenging twist. Because students are seated back-to-back, they have to listen carefully to their partner without the visual support of lip reading, facial expressions, body language, or gestures.

Students can do various tasks while seated back-to-back. One option is to give Partner 1 a mini-whiteboard and Partner 2 a picture. Partner 2 must describe the picture as Partner 1 listens and draws. This option always elicits laughter when the real picture is compared to the student-drawn one! Another way to do back-to-back is to give Partner 1 the name of an animal written on a piece of paper. They must describe the animal and give clues without saying the animal's name. Partner 2 listens and tries to guess the animal. The same process could be used with one partner describing a place or a famous person for the other partner to guess. Students can also take turns dictating from a text they've recently read while the other person writes what they are hearing on a mini-whiteboard.

Back-to-back provides another opportunity for students to use the listening language frames in Figure 30.2 because they frequently need to ask for clarification during this activity.

Different or Same?

This is a listening activity that encourages students to listen closely to each other and to interact in a meaningful way. We were introduced to it by teacher trainer and writer Adrian Tennant (n.d.) in his blogpost "Listening Matters: Active Listening."

The teacher writes a student- or teacher-generated topic on the board (e.g., "What I did over the weekend"; "What I like about our school"; "What I don't like about learning English"). Students take a few minutes to write or make notes about the topic. Then the teacher puts students into pairs and tells them they will have three minutes to have a conversation about the topic, and—here's where the *conversation* and *active listening* parts happen—they must identify two things that are the same and two things that are different as they discuss the topic. Once time is up, the teacher can call on pairs to share any similarities or differences they found.

Choose Your Own Adventure

These stories, also called *action mazes,* are always a hit with students. Students are periodically given choices of what they want characters to do, and then they participate in the construction of the story itself. There are numerous choose your own adventure stories on the web that are accessible to ELLs (see the Technology Connections section for a list of links to the best ones). Our students enjoy reading these stories online and writing their own in small groups or using online sites to create them (also listed in Technology Connections). However, we also do a low-tech version of choose your own adventure that specifically targets listening practice.

We first tell students they need to listen carefully without taking any notes because they will be reconstructing the story with a partner when we are done reading it. We sometimes choose an online story (from one of the recommended sites we list) and read it from our tablet or laptop.

Other times, if we are feeling ambitious, we create the story on our own or on the fly. When it comes time for students to make a choice (e.g., which door a character should go through), they vote by show of hands, and the winning choice is announced and made. The same process is continued until the best ending to the story is chosen.

Then it is time for students to get into pairs or groups of three and retell the story. Students write down everything they remember and then meet with another pair or group to compare notes and make any changes. We end the activity by asking for volunteers to read their reconstructions of the story to the class.

Of course, if teachers are pressed for time or if their brains are dulled by too much work (as ours often are), they can always insert ideas into an AI chatbot to create a personalized choose your own adventure story to read to the class.

LISTENING FOR DETAILS/CORRECTING THE MISTAKES

This activity challenges students to carefully listen to a text and make "corrections" to a written transcript which contains missing or incorrect details. We like to use a simple narrative or short informational text on a topic being studied in class. We provide students with a transcript of the text which we have modified to include incorrect details (e.g., different dates, places, names, sequences) or missing details. We then read the text slowly to the class, and students make any corrections (adding, deleting, or changing words) to their copy of the transcript. We often reread sentences based on student needs. Students can then compare their "corrections" with a partner or in small groups.

Another related activity could be the teacher identifying a listening text (for example, a podcast transcript) and then feeding it into an AI chatbot with instructions to turn it into a close passage.

Teaching Online

All of these listening activities can be used in an online setting with teacher modeling on a shared screen and students collaborating in breakout rooms. Students can be asked to identify the listening strategies they are finding most useful in an online learning setting and which ones they might want to practice.

Differentiation Recommendations

Newcomers (Preliterate or Low Literacy in Home Language): Use the activities described in the chapter but with very short and simple listening text types (narrated stories, videos, radio news reports, songs, etc.) in English using topics being studied in class. Students can demonstrate comprehension by drawing what they hear and/or using Google translate to summarize in their home language. Students can also practice the metacognitive listening activity by listening to texts in their home language, if available.	**Newcomers (Literate in Home Language):** Use the activities described in the chapter with accessible text types. Students can practice the metacognitive listening activity by listening to texts in their home language, if available.
Intermediate ELLs: Gradually increase the complexity of listening text types and spend more time having students practice metacognitive listening skills with them.	**Advanced ELLs:** Challenge students to listen to texts with multiple speakers or speaking at a faster rate. Include metacognitive listening activities more frequently.

What Could Go Wrong?

It is safe to say that many teachers, not just those of ELLs, underestimate the importance of explicit instruction in listening skills. For ELL students, listening in English can be one of the most-challenging skills to practice and is often one area in which they lack confidence. Teachers can help students boost their confidence over time by providing fun, meaningful listening practice. Don't do it once and check it off your list!

Technology Connections

For more ideas on helping ELLs improve their listening skills and for tons of links to accessible listening sites, see The Best Ideas to Help Students Become Better Listeners (http://larryferlazzo.edublogs.org/2012/07/23/the-best-ideas-to-help-students-become-better-listeners-contribute-more/) and The Best Listening Sites for English Language Learners(http://larryferlazzo.edublogs.org/2008/05/28/the-best-listening-sites-for-english-language-learners/).

For more resources on choose your own adventure stories, including places students can read them and write them online, see The Best Places to Read & Write "Choose Your Own Adventure Stories" (http://larryferlazzo.edublogs.org/2009/05/02/the-best-places-to-read-write-choose-your-own-adventure-stories/).

For further information on metacognition, see The Best Posts on Metacognition (http://larryferlazzo.edublogs.org/2012/05/13/my-best-posts-on-metacognition/).

Attribution

Portions of this section are adapted from our book *Navigating the Common Core with English Language Learners* (Ferlazzo & Sypnieski, 2016, p. 235–238).

Thank you to Adrian Tennant for the great ideas in his blogpost "Listening Matters: Active Listening" (www.onestopenglish.com/skills/listening/teaching-tips/listening-matters/listening-matters-active-listening/554465.article).

All figures from this chapter, as well as 11 additional chapters, references, hyperlinked Technology Connections, and more online resources, can be found at www.wiley.com/go/ellteacherstoolbox2.

Title of listening text:_____

Type of text: _____

1. Before listening: "What do I already know? What predictions can I make?"

2. While listening: "What strategies can I use to help me understand what I'm listening to?"

3. After listening: "Which strategies helped me the most? What will I do next time?"

Figure 30.1 Listening Practice Sheet   *Source: Navigating the Common Core with English Language Learners: Practical Strategies to Develop Higher-Order Thinking Skills* (Ferlazzo & Sypnieski, 2016, p. 237).

Asking for Clarification

Could you repeat that, please?

What do you mean by _____?

Could you explain that more?

What does the word _____ mean?

Can you give me an example of _____?

I'm confused when you say_____. Can you explain it to me?

Checking for Understanding

So, what you're saying is . . .

You said _____. Does that mean _____?

If I understand you correctly, . . .

You mean _____, yes?

So, an example of _____ is _____, right?

Just to be clear, you mean _____, right?

Figure 30.2 Listening Frames

Doctor:	How are you feeling?
Patient:	Not good in my throat.
Doctor:	Tell me about your symptoms and when they started.
Patient:	Could you repeat that, please?
Doctor:	Yes, I asked what are your symptoms and how long you've been experiencing them?
Patient:	What does the word *symptoms* mean?
Doctor:	Oh, that means where does your throat hurt and is anything else wrong?
Patient:	My throat hurts right here and my head feels bad since Saturday.
Doctor:	Well, you don't have a fever so I think you just have a cold. Drink a lot of fluids, take some aspirin, and get some rest.
Patient:	What are *fluids*? Can you give me an example?
Doctor:	Fluids are liquids like water or juice.
Patient:	Oh okay. So Gatorade is a fluid, right?
Doctor:	Yes, you can drink some Gatorade along with your medicine.
Patient:	So I need to take some aspirin, go home to rest, and drink some fluids, yes?
Doctor:	You got it! Hope you feel better soon!
Patient:	Thank you so much.

Figure 30.3 Sample Dialogue

STRATEGY 31

Learning Games for Speaking and Listening

What Is It?

This strategy lists our nine favorite games to reinforce speaking and listening with English language learners.

Why We Like It

We like these games for the same reasons we like the ones listed in Strategy 23: Learning Games for Reading and Writing. Students enjoy them and learn from participating in the activity. Plus, they all require minimal teacher prep time!

Supporting Research

Again, the same research we cite for the reading and writing games holds true for these speaking and listening ones. This book is long enough, so we don't think it's necessary to reprint those citations here. However, there is one piece of additional research we'd like to share: Many of us who try to learn a new language feel very anxious when prompted to speak in that language. Researchers have found the same issue with ELLs (Bashir, 2014, p. 217; Boonkit, 2010, p. 1305; Savaşçı, 2014, p. 5). Games can provide a low-risk and positive atmosphere that can lower student anxiety.

Literacy researcher Stephen Krashen has identified anxiety as one of the elements of the "affective filter" that influences language acquisition. The higher the affective filter, which also includes motivation challenges and low self-confidence, the more difficult it is to learn a new language. The lower the affective filter, the easier it is to learn a new language (Du, 2009). Games are just one tool that teachers can use to lower the affective filter for our students. Other ways include creating a supportive and welcoming classroom environment, developing positive teacher-student and student-student relationships, and making lessons relevant and engaging to students.

STRATEGY 31: LEARNING GAMES FOR SPEAKING AND LISTENING

Common Core Connections

These activities will assist students to meet several Language Standards. They include using conventions and grammar in speaking and enhancing comprehension when listening.

Application

Many of the games in the Reading and Writing section have obvious connections to speaking and listening as well. The following seven games are particularly effective in building speaking and listening skills with ELLs.

NINE BOX GRID

You might remember Katie Toppel's Nine Box Grid game that we shared in Strategy 23: Learning Games for Reading and Writing. In that version, we drew a grid on the class whiteboard. In this case, students are assigned a partner, each group gets its own pair of dice, and each student gets a sheet like the one in Figure 31.1. Students take turns rolling the dice and have to use the word that they roll in a sentence. If they roll an 11 or 12, they must use their choice of two words on the grid. The other students provide feedback using the sentence starters in the image. If students are not sure if the word was used correctly, they call the teacher over to judge. On occasion, we give students a grid sheet where we've typed the words. Most of the time, however, we have students create their own template using their choice of nine words from the theme or picture word inductive model (see Strategy 11: Inductive Learning) we've been studying that week.

As in the reading and writing version, this activity has game-like qualities but we don't keep score.

ANSWER—QUESTION

In this game, students are asked to make a list of six things (it could be less or more). We got the idea for this game (which we slightly modified) from English teacher Larissa Albano (2017), and the example she uses is to have students make a list of six things they did the previous day. Students then get into groups of three with two mini-whiteboards. One student says the first answer, and then the other two are given 30 seconds to come up with a corresponding question. They have to write it down on their board without the other seeing it. When time is up, they hold up their board and say what they wrote. If the student who shared the answer approves of the question, then the questioner gets a point (as always, the teacher can be consulted as needed).

Here's Larissa's example:

The answer is "I ate fish and chips."
Question by Maria: "What did you eat for lunch yesterday?"
Question by Francesco: "What did you eat for dinner yesterday?"

Here are other topics we've used for this game, including an example of an answer and a corresponding question:

- Six actions you want to take in the future ("be a doctor"—"What kind of job do you want?")
- Six favorite things or people ("soccer"—"What is your favorite sport?")
- Six things in your house ("television"—"What is in your living room?")
- Six things you don't like ("beets"—"What kind of food don't you like?")
- Six physical problems ("my head hurts"—"Do you have a headache?" or "How does your head feel?")
- Six feelings (student acts out a feeling—"Are you angry?" or "What are you angry about?")

LETTER SCAVENGER HUNT

There are many variations of this game (search *letter sounds scavenger hunt* or *letter scavenger hunt* online). In the version we play, students are divided into groups of three with one mini-whiteboard for each group. The teacher then calls out a letter or says a letter sound (e.g., "buh" for *b*). Each group then has about a minute to find one object in the classroom that begins with that letter or sound and bring it back to their group. Then, the group has to write down the name of that object *and* come up with another word that also begins with the same letter or sound. At the end of that time limit, the teacher calls on one of the students in the group to stand and say the name of the object the teacher found and the word the teacher wrote (this is to make sure they all know how to say it because they don't know who the teacher is going to choose to speak). Each group gets a point for every word they say correctly and can bet all their points on the last round.

We read about a neat twist on this game at FluentU (Genesisd, n.d.). Instead of saying the letter or letter sound, we sometimes say a word and tell students they have to find an object that begins with the same letter or letter sound (or even one that *ends* with the same letter or letter sound). This change makes it slightly more challenging for students.

SOUND EFFECTS

Students are divided into pairs and each group receives one mini-whiteboard. The teacher goes to an online sound effects site and plays a sound. Students have 20 seconds to describe the sound that is being played. Generally, we also share a list of the different kinds of sounds that function as a scaffold.

We usually play this game during a thematic unit and have found it works best when learning about animals, home, and transportation. We share links to sound-effect sites and other ways to use sound in the Technology Connections section, including for creative story prompts.

GUESS THE WORD

This is probably one of the oldest games used in language classes and the model has been exploited in more than one commercial game. We divide the class into pairs and give each group a whiteboard. First, each pair has to choose a word and then develop a series of clues in words or phrases that would help the class guess their word (shape, color, what you do with it, where it can be found, noun or verb, living or thing, etc.). The clues cannot use the word itself or any other forms of the word. Students then share all their clues and the class is given 30 seconds to write a guess on their board. Correct answers are worth one point.

Cambridge University Press developed an excellent website on which English students from around the world could record themselves presenting their clues. Though they've ended that part of the program, they still have some of the best video examples up on their site. Those videos can still be used in classes. Even though the site is not accepting new student-created ones, if you feel ambitious you can always connect up with a "sister class" elsewhere to each make videos for the other! Nothing beats an "authentic audience" (someone other than the teacher) for student motivation! See the Guess What site in the Technology Connections section for more information, as well as links to many sites that facilitate sister class connections.

TELEPHONE

Telephone is a tried-and-true game that has been used for years in language-learning classrooms. We use it by first dividing the class into halves or thirds. We then ask the students seated at the front of each group to come up so that we can whisper a sentence in their ear. They each then go back and whisper it in the next student's ear and so on. The winner is the group that has whispered the message to everyone and the last person comes up to the teacher and correctly repeats the original sentence. This seldom occurs the first time around. Then the teacher re-whispers the sentence to the student in front and they do it all over again.

There are online games that let students do versions of this telephone game, and teachers can create private virtual rooms so they are playing only with classmates. See the Technology Connections section for information.

RUNNING DICTATION

We described running dictation in Strategy 24: Dictation and felt we needed to mention it again here because it is one of our (and our students') favorite games!

FOUR TRUTHS AND A LIE

Most teachers have some familiarity with the game "Two Truths and a Lie." Here is how we modify it for our intermediate ELL classes (it tends to be too challenging for newcomer students, though not impossible):

First, the teacher models it. For example, Larry might write these things about himself:

1. I have five children.
2. I lived in New York City at one time.

3. I like dogs.
4. I play basketball every week.
5. I don't like green beans.

He would then give examples of questions someone could ask to help determine which one is a lie, and which ones are true, like:

1. What are the names of your children?
2. What years did you live in New York City?
3. Why do you like dogs? Have you ever had a dog? What were their names?
4. What position do you play in basketball?
5. Why don't you like green beans?

Of course, he points out, they could ask him those questions, and he could also lie in his answers!

Larry would then have all students write their own "four truths and a lie" (typically on a shared Google Slides presentation, with each student getting their own slide). He asks students to really try hard to write down things that even their friends might not know about them.

Students then divide into small groups with each having a mini-whiteboard, marker, and eraser. Each also gets one or two sheets of paper.

Larry calls up one student to sit in the front and projects that student's "Four Truths and a Lie" on the front screen.

Each group is given one minute to write as many questions about them that they can think of on their board or sheet (they can use either). They need to choose one person to ask one of the questions.

The teacher calls on the first group to ask their question and receive their answer. The next group is given 10 seconds to decide which of their questions they are going to ask, since the preceding group might have asked one of theirs. After five groups have asked their questions and received their responses, each group has to write on their board which one they think is a lie. The teacher asks them to hold their board up, and groups that guessed the "true lie" receive a point.

The game continues, though a different person from each group has to actually say the question each time.

It's always best to end a game with students wanting more, so we typically end it after we've examined the "truths and lies" from no more than five people, and sometimes less. It's a game we play consistently, though, throughout the year, until we get through everyone's "truths and lies."

One important note is that we begin by first taking volunteers to start off being in front of the class, and we often will encourage a few privately. Of course, we also give every student the option to not participate until they feel comfortable being in front of the class and it's okay if that is never.

STRATEGY 31: LEARNING GAMES FOR SPEAKING AND LISTENING

VIDEO GAME WALK-THROUGHS

For years, we've printed out "walk-throughs" (directions about how to win the game) for online escape room and adventure games.

Then, students "pair up" and take turns with one reading the walk-through aloud and the other playing the game. There are usually simple prizes for the first several pairs to reach its end.

They are super-energizing, and students are highly motivated to learn the English they need to win the game!

Unfortunately, the end of Adobe Flash software meant that many of those games went offline, and then people stopped making text walk-throughs for the games and, instead, recorded them.

Larry began asking peer tutors to watch the walk-through videos and convert them to text when they had time. There aren't as many of these kinds of video games around as there once were, and many are blocked by district Internet content filters.

You can find a link to resources for these kinds of online games, and Larry will add walk-throughs to any games if and when his peer tutors find the time to create them!

Teaching Online

All of these games can be played online with shared screens and breakout rooms, along with other various modifications. For example, The Nine Box Grid games would need to be played with an "online dice roller" (just search the term and you'll find multiple versions).

What Could Go Wrong?

The same concerns we share in Strategy 23: Learning Games for Reading and Writing hold true for the ones here—student cheating, noise levels, and prizes. These concerns can all be managed, however—just check out the "What Could Go Wrong" section in Strategy 23 for our suggestions on how to do it.

Differentiation Recommendations

Newcomers (Preliterate or Low Literacy in Home Language): Most games are played in small groups, so make arrangements to have students in this group have a "buddy" with a higher English proficiency. If the "buddy" does not speak the student's home language, they can use Google Translate.	**Newcomers (Literate in Home Language):** All the games described in the chapter should be accessible to these students except, perhaps, for Four Truths and One Lie.
Intermediate ELLs: Can play the games described in the chapter, including Four Truths and One Lie using more complex language, though one or two (like the Sound Effects Game) may be too easy.	**Advanced ELLs:** Can play the games described in the chapter using more complex language. Can be asked to *create* video game walk-throughs.

Technology Connections

Students can find many online sites, including speaking and listening games, at The Best Sites to Practice Speaking English (http://larryferlazzo.edublogs.org/2008/03/17/the-best-sites-to-practice-speaking-english/).

Sites for sound effects and ideas on how to use them in class can be found at The Best Resources & Ideas for Using Sound Effects in ELL Lessons (http://larryferlazzo.edublogs.org/2017/07/20/the-best-resources-ideas-for-using-sound-effects-in-ell-lessons/).

Learn how your students can create guess-a-word videos and access others at "Guess What" Is a Great "New" Game—Plus ELLs Can Create a Video for an Authentic Audience (http://larryferlazzo.edublogs.org/2016/07/12/guess-what-is-a-great-new-game-plus-ells-can-create-a-video-for-an-authentic-audience/).

Online versions of the telephone game seem to come and go. Drawception (n.d.) (https://drawception.com/) is one that combines the concept with a drawing feature. As new ones come online, we'll be posting them at The Best Online Games Students Can Play in Private Virtual "Rooms" (http://larryferlazzo.edublogs.org/2009/02/10/the-best-online-games-students-can-play-in-private-virtual-rooms/).

Attribution

Versions of some of these ideas appeared in our book, *The ESL/ELL Teacher's Survival Guide* (Ferlazzo & Sypnieski, 2012, p. 242).

Thanks again to Katie Toppel for the nine box grid game idea.

Thanks to Larissa Albano for her great game, which we call *Answer—Question* (http://larissaslanguages.blogspot.com.es/2017/04/the-dice-game-fun-low-prep-speaking-game.html).

Thanks to Genesis Davies at FluentU (www.fluentu.com/blog/educator-english/esl-listening-games/) for the scavenger hunt idea.

Find "sister classes" to share these student video creations at The Best Ways to Find Other Classes for Joint Online Projects (https://larryferlazzo.edublogs.org/2009/05/30/the-best-ways-to-find-other-classes-for-joint-online-projects/).

Learn more about walk-throughs and online video games at Using Online "Point-and-Click Escape the Room" Games with ELLs (https://larryferlazzo.edublogs.org/2023/10/01/using-online-point-and-click-escape-the-room-games-with-ells/).

STRATEGY 31: LEARNING GAMES FOR SPEAKING AND LISTENING   349

All figures from this chapter, as well as 11 additional chapters, references, hyperlinked Technology Connections, and more online resources, can be found at www.wiley.com/go/ellteacherstoolbox2.

prey 10	message 2	attack 3
predator 4	recognize 5	shelter 6
feature 7	attract 8	repel 9

Partner responses:

Nice job using the word _____ in a sentence.

I don't think you used the word _____ correctly. Try again.

Figure 31.1 Nine Box Grid *Source:* Reproduced with permission of Katie Toppel.

PART III

Additional Key Strategies

STRATEGY 32

Differentiation for ELLs in Content Classes with English-Proficient Students

What Is It?

Many schools are not able to have classes exclusively for ELL students. In those cases, ELLs are in mainstream classes—with or without an ELL co-teacher (see Strategy 40: Co-Teaching). We think most, if not all, of the strategies in this book are useful in mainstream classes and, in fact, use them in *all* of the classes we teach. Good teaching for ELLs is good teaching for all students. In fact, Larry co-authored an article with Ted Appel, our former principal, talking about how our school wanted to get as many ELLs as possible to enroll because their presence challenged our teachers to improve their craft. As they wrote:

> All of our teachers have had to learn how to effectively teach English Language Learners simply because all of our classes have significant numbers of ELLs in them. Graphic organizers, visual supports, cooperative learning, modeling, and accessing prior knowledge are just a few of the instructional strategies that are used school-wide.
>
> Of course, all of these teaching methods are effective with any type of struggling student, whether they are struggling because of language or because of some other challenge.
>
> Our large number of English Language Learners pushed our school and faculty to invest in professional development so that our teachers would learn and refine these skills. Time and resources have been made for extensive in-service training and peer-to-peer support, including observations and weekly "study teams" where groups of teachers meet to enhance their professional practice. (Appel & Ferlazzo)

In fact, recent studies reinforce these beliefs; researchers found that the presence of ELLs in classes have a positive impact on the academic achievement of English-proficient students (Figlio, et al., 2021). The researchers don't seem quite sure what to attribute this to (they suggest that one reason might be the presence of less-disruptive classroom behavior), but it seems pretty clear to us it's because, as we've said, making content more accessible helps everybody (the study doesn't even appear to consider that possibility!).

In our previous books, we have separate chapters devoted to specific strategies English, math, art, social studies, and science teachers can use to make their content more accessible to ELLs. The strategy here is designed to provide a few general suggestions to content teachers who have one or more ELLs placed in their classes.

Why We Like It

It's a safe bet to say that most English language learner students are *not* in classes exclusively for them most of the time. Given that fact, it's important for those of us who are primarily ELL teachers to be able to offer practical advice to mainstream content teachers. As a graphic we saw in Carol Salva and Anna Matis's book, *Boosting Achievement*, explains, content teachers tend to be trained to use language to teach concepts, whereas ELL teachers use concepts to teach language (p. 58). By combining our expertise, everybody wins!

Supporting Research

The recommendations we share in the Application section are consistent with extensive research done on differentiation for ELLs in content classes (Baecher, 2011; Dahlman, Hoffman, & Brauhn, n.d.; Ford, n.d.; Ullom, 2022).

Common Core Connections

The suggestions in this strategy can be used by all content teachers to help their students—ELLs and non-ELLs alike—achieve the Standards they are teaching in each lesson.

Application

We've divided this section into two parts. In the first dos and don'ts list, we've modified and revised a section from *The ESL/ELL Teacher's Survival Guide* (Ferlazzo & Sypnieski, 2012, p. 12, 210) to provide a quick summary of the key points we think content teachers should keep in mind when they have ELLs of various levels in their classes.

In the second part, we discuss how mainstream content teachers can handle an unfortunately all-too-common experience—a newcomer with zero or next-to-zero English proficiency being placed in their class.

DOS AND DON'TS

Here are a few basic best practices that might help teachers respond to the needs of these students. We also feel it is important to include a few worst practices in the hope that they will not be repeated!

Use Proactive Strategies to Activate and Build Prior Knowledge

Do use the many ways to activate and build prior knowledge we discuss in Strategy 5: Activating Prior Knowledge. These include accessing huge amounts of online resources for many content areas that are available in students' home languages as well as sites that offer multiple versions of the same text provided at different lexile levels. See the Technology Connections section in Strategy 5 and here for links to them.

Don't erroneously think that all you have to do to teach ELLs is to speak louder. We understand that all of us are very busy carrying our regular teacher load. However, remember that good ELL teaching is good teaching for everybody. All your students will benefit from your increased attention to the scaffolding required by ELL students.

Recognize the Many Assets ELL Students Bring to the Table

Do remember all the assets that ELL students bring to the table—they are as intelligent as any other student in your class. ELLs just have a temporary challenge of learning a new language. In addition, they have demonstrated grit and perseverance in their lives, important qualities for success. Look for opportunities when they can model those characteristics to the class as well as times their international experiences can contribute to classroom topics.

Don't look at ELLs through a lens of deficits. For example, if they come from a country where certain numbers and some mathematical equations are written differently, view it as an opportunity for them to teach your class something new about the world. Don't just view it as a mistake that needs to be corrected.

Modeling

Do model for students what they are expected to do or produce. This is especially important for new skills or activities. This can be done by explaining and demonstrating the learning actions, sharing your thinking processes aloud, and showing good teacher and student work samples. Modeling promotes learning and motivation as well as increasing student self-confidence—they will have a stronger belief that they can accomplish the learning task if they follow steps that were demonstrated.

Don't just tell students what to do and expect them to do it.

Rate of Speech and Wait Time

Do speak slowly and clearly and provide students with enough time to formulate their responses, whether in speaking or in writing. Remember, they are thinking and producing in two or more languages! After asking a question, wait for a few seconds before calling on someone to respond. This wait time provides all students with an opportunity to think and process and especially gives ELLs a needed period to formulate a response.

Don't speak too fast, and if a student tells you he or she didn't understand what you said, never, ever repeat the same thing in a louder voice!

Use of Nonlinguistic Cues

Do use visuals (such as pictures), sketches, gestures (Pilegard & Fiorella, 2021), intonation, and other nonverbal cues to make language and content more accessible to students. Teaching with visual representations of concepts can be hugely helpful to ELLs. Use word charts such as the ones recommended in Strategy 4: Vocabulary.

Don't stand in front of the class and lecture or rely on a textbook as your only visual aid.

Giving Instructions

Do give verbal *and* written instructions—this practice can help all learners, especially ELLs. In addition, it is far easier for a teacher to point to the board in response to the inevitable repeated question, "What are we supposed to do?"

Don't act surprised if students are lost when you haven't clearly written and explained step-by-step directions.

Check for Understanding

Do regularly check that students are understanding the lesson. After an explanation or lesson, a teacher could say, "Please put thumbs up, thumbs down, or sideways to let me know if this is clear, *and it's perfectly fine if you don't understand or are unsure—I just need to know*." This last phrase is essential if you want students to respond honestly.

Teachers can also have students write answers to specific comprehension questions on a sticky note that they place on their desks or on mini-whiteboards. The teacher can then quickly circulate to check responses.

When teachers regularly check for understanding in the classroom, students become increasingly aware of monitoring their own understanding, which serves as a model of good study skills. It also helps ensure that students are learning, thinking, understanding, comprehending, and processing at high levels.

Don't simply ask, "Are there any questions?" This is not an effective way to gauge what all your students are thinking. Waiting until the end of class for students to do a written reflection is not going to provide timely feedback. Also, don't assume that students are

STRATEGY 32: DIFFERENTIATION FOR ELLs IN CONTENT CLASSES 357

understanding because they are smiling and nodding their heads—sometimes they are just being polite!

Encourage Development of Home Language

Do encourage students to use their home language (L1) to support learning in your classroom. Research has found that learning to read in a home language can transfer to increased English acquisition (Ferlazzo, 2017, April 10). These transfers may include phonological awareness, comprehension skills, and background knowledge.

Identify the home languages of your ELL students, make sure you have the appropriate bilingual dictionaries in your classroom, and allow students to access their smartphones to use for translation. Google Translate also lets students takes pictures of, and then translate, writing on the board and textbook pages.

Although the research on transfer of L1 skills to L2 cannot be denied, it doesn't mean that we should not encourage the use of English in class and out of the classroom.

Don't ban students from using their home language in the classroom. Forbidding students from using their primary languages does not promote a positive learning environment where students feel safe to take risks and make mistakes. This practice can be harmful to the relationships between teachers and students, especially if teachers act more like language police than language coaches.

Provide Graphic Organizers and Sentence-Starters

Do use the strategies and resources we provide in Strategy 3: Graphic Organizers, Strategy 4: Vocabulary, and Strategy 14: Writing Frames and Writing Structures. Graphic organizers can help all students, and particularly ELLs, organize what they are learning and help them make connections between new and prior knowledge. Sentence starters can help ELLs communicate what they already know.

Don't think your secondary students should have already outgrown these kinds of scaffolds and don't think of them as a form of cheating. Scaffolds can be temporary and even Michelangelo needed them in order to paint the Sistine Chapel. View scaffolds as a helpful hand up and not an unjustified handout.

Note-Taking Strategies

Do explicitly teach note-taking strategies. For ELLs in content classes, academic listening is a critical skill that places the heaviest processing demands on students. Providing note-taking scaffolds is a key accommodation teachers can use with their ELLs to help students process new vocabulary. A note-taking scaffold can look similar to a cloze passage and include the most important content with blanks for students to fill in as they listen throughout the lesson. For example, a social studies scaffold sheet might have several lines similar to "was the primary cause of the Civil War." As students gain more experience with academic listening and note-taking, teachers can gradually remove the scaffold or adjust it to include only a few key words.

Don't assume that students, including ELLs, know how to take notes during a lesson, when you are talking, or when they are watching a video. And don't assume that they see value in doing so.

Cooperative and Collaborative Learning Opportunities

Do create opportunities for cooperative and collaborative learning. Many of your English-proficient students may be more than willing to provide additional support to ELL students. ELLs may also be more open to asking for help from their classmates. If you have a small group of intermediate ELLs, often grouping them together (or sitting them near each other) may provide opportunities for mutual support. Ideally, they could also work with others who have expressed an interest in helping them.

Don't lecture. It's not good for ELLs or for your other students. See the Technology Connections section for links to research documenting its ineffectiveness.

Videos Showing These Strategies in Action

Do take a few minutes and look at a collection of short videos we've put together that demonstrate these instructional strategies and modifications in action. You can find the link in the Technology Connections section.

Don't assume you know all the ways to implement these strategies by reading about them in this book and in others.

NEWCOMER IN CLASS

Although we don't have any hard data on this, we hear enough anecdotes to suspect that this is a very common issue for teachers across the United States: A newcomer with minimal or no English skills is parachuted into a mainstream class and the teacher is just told to integrate the student into his or her instruction—with little support.

Here are some suggestions for how you or your colleagues can help students in this situation.

Provide Emotional Support

Learn their story—why their family came here, what their interests are, goals they might have for their life. If you cannot speak their home language or can't find another staff person or student who can, using Google Translate is a very viable option. Using the audio translation mode will automatically provide verbal interpretation.

STRATEGY 32: DIFFERENTIATION FOR ELLs IN CONTENT CLASSES 359

Provide Academic Support

Provide access to a computer or tablet. If a student has zero or next-to-zero English, the best help any teacher—no matter what subject they are teaching—can provide is to support students in developing basic English communication skills. Duolingo, LingoHut, USA Learns, and many new artificial intelligence–powered sites are the best online tools for that kind of support (find links to those and other sites in the Technology Connections section). Doing this—for a short time at least—can help these students begin to develop self-confidence, get them familiar with online tools they can also use at home (if they have Internet access there), and give you some time to develop a longer-term plan on how you are going to teach them your content matter and pull together needed resources.

If the newcomer is literate in their home language, you can also provide access to online materials in that language that are comparable to what you are teaching in English. Links to many such resources can be found in the Technology Connections section. Providing a home language "preview" of a topic you will be teaching in class is an element of a preview, view, review strategy that is often used in a dual language classroom. In this strategy, the lesson is "previewed in the home language, "viewed" (or taught) in English, and then "reviewed" in the home language. Teachers may not be able to do that third part, but a "preview" can be better than nothing! Teachers can use an AI tool to generate resources on any topic in any language or access human-created multilingual materials online.

There are a number of online sites that provide grade-level materials for multiple subjects in English that an ELL can have automatically translated with a click of their mouse. Though, again, the translation quality will likely be uneven at best, using these resources can be an easy way for a content teacher juggling many responsibilities to make lessons more accessible to an ELL newcomer. See the Technology Connections section for a list of these kinds of sites.

There are many sites that provide high-quality materials on multiple subjects using different levels of English text (some also provide Spanish versions). For example, an article on the electoral college might be edited for three or four different reading levels. Using a high-English-level version of one for most of your students and a simplified version for your newcomer is a fairly easy way to make content accessible. In fact, there are tools that let you do the same for any text you copy and paste into them. You can find links to all these options in the Technology Connections section.

There are a number of content-specific books that are designed to be particularly accessible to ELLs. You can see a link to a few of them that we use in our classes in the Technology Connections section. Providing these textbook alternatives, which likely cover similar subjects to the ones you use with the majority of your students, could be a useful scaffold.

And there are several sites that provide videos on content topics in multiple languages, and links to them can be found in the Technology Connections section.

With recent advances in technology, it's not that difficult to automatically have what is said in English in the classroom by the teacher and students appear on a screen in English text or in the newcomer's home language. The translation, obviously, will be imperfect but, depending upon the language, can be passable. Google Translate and several other tools can read aloud text that is input. There are also rapid advancements in tech that are allowing simultaneous audio translation; however, at the time of this book's publication, they are not as far along. See the Technology Connections section for resources.

You can also "engineer" your English texts so that they are more accessible to all your students (Billings & Walqui, 2021). This could mean adding bold headings, images, more white space, and definitions of key vocabulary terms to your classroom materials. See the Technology Connections section for more resources, as well as visiting Strategy 2: Text Engineering.

At the very least, make sure you have a bilingual dictionary in your newcomer's home language or let them use one on their laptop or cell phone. Google Translate also lets users translate photos of textbook pages or text written on whiteboards.

At our school, seniors often get a class period when they are teaching assistants (TAs) or peer tutors. With support and minimal training from us, a student who doesn't even speak the newcomer's home language can provide invaluable support to them. In addition, having the title *peer tutor* can look better on a senior's transcript when applying to college. You can learn more in Strategy 39: Peer Teaching and Learning.

Even if your school doesn't have a peer tutor program, you can still have a "buddy" for your newcomer. This student (you could also have more than one to take turns) may, or may not, speak the home language of the newcomer. What they must have, though, is an openness and interest in helping them, and an understanding that this help does not mean just giving them the "answers." Links to resources to support peer tutors, "buddies," or volunteers can be found in the Technology Connections section. It's also critical that this "buddy" system not be unilaterally created by the teacher—genuine conversations need to be had with potential buddies and newcomers to ensure that everyone wants to do it. Research found in Strategy 39: Peer Teaching and Learning documents that these kinds of arrangements benefit both the tutor and the student being tutored.

Inductive teaching emphasizes pattern-seeking, which is a skill found to be particularly important to those learning a new language (and it's important for everybody else, too!). If you presently employ inductive methods in your instruction, creating simpler versions of data sets for your newcomer should be fairly easy (especially with AI tools). If you are not using inductive teaching now, we encourage you to consider experimenting with it. Also see Strategy 11: Inductive Learning.

If your newcomer does not have Internet access at home (or even if they do), providing them with accessible books that can be read at home can be a big help—plenty of research documents the importance of home libraries (Ferlazzo, 2010, May 17b). Our local friends of the library have provided thousands of free books for our newcomer students, and you can also print out many free books available online (see the Technology Connections section for useful sites).

STRATEGY 32: DIFFERENTIATION FOR ELLs IN CONTENT CLASSES

If your school has a specialized class where newcomers learn English, regularly talk with the teacher to learn more about the students and brainstorm how you can both support them in classes. If this teacher is available to co-teach with you, please see Strategy 40: Co-Teaching.

Also, don't forget to turn on the English subtitles feature when watching any videos in class.

Provide Social Support

Provide a peer mentor to your newcomer—ideally, someone who speaks his or her home language. At our school, peer mentors leave one of their classes for 15 minutes each week to chat with their mentee. You can read more about it in Strategy 39: Peer Teaching and Learning.

Ask individual students who have previously demonstrated empathy to reach out to your newcomer. Perhaps share stories with them of how other students have done the same (see the Technology Connections section for links).

Teaching Online

Teaching a primarily English-proficient class online that has a few intermediate ELLs is probably manageable if teachers follow the do's and don'ts listed earlier. If a teacher doesn't follow them, it likely won't lead to particularly successful outcomes.

Some tools are beginning to provide simultaneous audio translation in a student's home language so you can use it—if your video conferencing tool is compatible with them. See the Technology Connections for up-to-date developments.

It's challenging enough to support one or two newcomers in a predominantly English-proficient class that's meeting face-to-face. Candidly speaking, doing so in an online environment will require an exceptional amount of teacher time and energy. Having a peer tutor, "buddy," or student teacher to specifically support the newcomer is probably a requirement if you want to have any hope of providing the newcomer with adequate support.

What Could Go Wrong?

The main answers to this question can be found in the list of don'ts in the Application section. In addition, not everything do you try is going to be wildly effective. When that happens, don't get frustrated, and try to keep this story from Larry in mind: Many years ago, he met a man who worked with Mahatma Gandhi in the campaign for Indian independence. The key to Gandhi's success, the man told Larry, "was that he looked at every problem as an opportunity, not as a pain in the butt." We hope that you will look at the challenge of teaching ELLs in the same way—as an opportunity to become a better teacher for all your students.

Differentiation Recommendations

Newcomers (Preliterate or Low Literacy in Home Language): Provide home language support, both in translated text and video resources and with tools that provide simultaneous text and audio translation (if available). Make sure students know how to use Google Translate or several other tools to read aloud text that is inputted into it. Provide additional support from a peer tutor, a class "buddy," or an adult volunteer. Try to "engineer" English texts to make them more accessible. Learn and conscientiously apply the do's and don'ts listed in the chapter.	**Newcomers (Literate in Home Language):** Provide home language support, both in translated text and video resources and with tools that provide simultaneous text and audio translation, if available. Provide additional support from a peer tutor, a class "buddy," or adult volunteer. Try to "engineer" English texts to make them more accessible. Include inductive learning and collaborative learning in your toolbox of instructional strategies. Learn and conscientiously apply the do's and don'ts listed in the chapter.
Intermediate ELLs: Try to "engineer" English texts to make them more accessible. If there is more than one student, consider grouping for mutual support. If possible, provide additional support from a peer tutor, a class "buddy," or an adult volunteer. If there are newcomers in the same class, consider making an intermediate ELL student their "buddy." Include inductive learning and collaborative learning in your toolbox of instructional strategies. Learn and conscientiously apply the do's and don'ts listed in the chapter, and don't assume that because your students may appear to speak English easily that they have a full grasp of academic English.	**Advanced ELLs:** Remember that the do's and don'ts listed in the chapter can benefit both ELLs and English-proficient students, and apply them as much as possible. Try to integrate them into your instructional mind-set. Everyone will benefit!

Technology Connections

To see short videos of some of these differentiation strategies in action, go to The Best Videos for Content Teachers with ELLs in the Classroom (http://larryferlazzo.edublogs.org/2017/07/14/the-best-videos-for-content-teachers-with-ells-in-their-classes-please-suggest-more/).

Even more ideas on how to help content teachers support ELLs can be found at The Best Sites for Learning Strategies to Teach ELLs in Content Classes (http://larryferlazzo.edublogs.org/2011/09/07/the-best-sites-for-learning-strategies-to-teach-ells-in-content-classes/).

For specific math support, go to The Best Resources for Teaching Common Core Math to English Language Learners (http://larryferlazzo.edublogs.org/2014/11/22/the-best-resources-for-teaching-common-core-math-to-english-language-learners/), and for specific science support, go to The Best Resources for Teaching the Next Generation Science Standards to English Language Learners (http://larryferlazzo.edublogs.org/2014/11/22/the-best-resources-for-teaching-the-next-generation-science-standards-to-english-language-learners/) and to The Best Resources for Teaching Science to ELLs – Please Contribute

STRATEGY 32: DIFFERENTIATION FOR ELLs IN CONTENT CLASSES

More! (https://larryferlazzo.edublogs.org/2019/12/07/the-best-resources-for-teaching-science-to-ells-please-contribute-more/).

For history, go to The Best Places to Get Accessible History Texts for ELLs (https://larryferlazzo.edublogs.org/2021/04/24/the-best-places-to-get-accessible-history-texts-for-ells/).

Multilingual sites with materials for math, social studies, and science are at The Best Multilingual and Bilingual Sites for Math, Social Studies, and Science (http://larryferlazzo.edublogs.org/2008/10/03/the-best-multilingual-bilingual-sites-for-math-social-studies-science/).

Teachers can find sites that offer high-quality materials in English, along with the ability for students to translate them with a click of their mouse, at The Best Tools Where Content Teachers Can Have Materials Automatically Translated for ELLs – Help Me Find More! (https://larryferlazzo.edublogs.org/2023/09/05/the-best-tools-where-content-teachers-can-have-materials-automatically-translated-for-ells-help-me-find-more/).

The same text written at different Lexile levels is available at a number of sites. Those links can be accessed at The Best Places to Get the "Same" Text Written for Different Levels (http://larryferlazzo.edublogs.org/2014/11/16/the-best-places-to-get-the-same-text-written-for-different-levels/).

Free printable books can be found at The Best Sources for Free and Accessible Printable Books (http://larryferlazzo.edublogs.org/2009/07/31/the-best-sources-for-free-accessible-printable-books/). Multilingual books can be found at The Best Places Where You Can Order Bilingual Books (https://larryferlazzo.edublogs.org/2023/03/11/the-best-places-where-you-can-order-bilingual-books/).

Support for students to learn note-taking strategies is at The Best Resources on Effective Note-Taking Strategies (http://larryferlazzo.edublogs.org/2015/06/23/the-best-resources-on-effective-note-taking-strategies-help-me-find-more/).

If you're wondering why we're not big fans of lectures, check out The Best Research Demonstrating That Lectures Are Not the Best Instructional Strategy (http://larryferlazzo.edublogs.org/2014/06/14/the-best-research-demonstrating-that-lectures-are-not-the-best-instructional-strategy/).

For links to help students with little or no English skills that have been placed in a class with English-proficient students, please visit Ways a Content Teacher Can Support an ELL Newcomer in Class (http://larryferlazzo.edublogs.org/2016/11/24/ways-a-mainstream-teacher-can-support-an-ell-newcomer-in-class/).

Links to the sites we recommend for newcomer students can be found at Larry Ferlazzo – Online Tools (www.teachingenglish.org.uk/blogs/larry-ferlazzo/larry-ferlazzo-online-tools) and The Online Tools I Had Students Use Most This Year (https://larryferlazzo.edublogs.org/2023/06/16/the-online-tools-i-had-students-use-most-this-year/).

See The Best Resources to Help ELL Students with Simultaneous Translation in the Classroom (https://larryferlazzo.edublogs.org/2023/07/18/the-best-resources-to-help-ell-students-with-simultaneous-translation-in-the-classroom/) for automatic translation resources.

Find more ideas on "text engineering" to make your classroom materials more accessible to all students at The Best Strategies for "Engineering" Text So That It's More Accessible to ELLs (https://larryferlazzo.edublogs.org/2022/02/16/the-best-strategies-for-engineering-text-so-that-its-more-accessible-to-ells/).

Resources to support volunteers, "buddies," and peer tutors helping newcomer students can be found at The Best Resources to Help Prepare Tutors and Volunteers in ELL Classes – And, Boy, Do I Need Suggestions! (https://larryferlazzo.edublogs.org/2021/08/29/the-best-resources-to-help-prepare-tutors-volunteers-in-ell-classes-and-boy-do-i-need-suggestions/).

And, if you're still looking for more scaffolding suggestions, go to The Best Resources on Providing Scaffolds to Students (http://larryferlazzo.edublogs.org/2017/01/05/the-best-resources-on-providing-scaffolds-to-students/).

Attribution

Versions of some of these ideas appeared in our book, *The ESL/ELL Teacher's Survival Guide* (Ferlazzo & Sypnieski, 2022, p. 12).

STRATEGY 33

Supporting ELL Students with Interrupted Formal Education (SIFEs)

What Is It?

Students with interrupted formal education (SIFEs), also called *students with limited or interrupted formal education (SLIFEs),* are ELLs who may have very little formal schooling, may not be literate or only have very low literacy in their home language, or may come from a preliterate culture (one that does not have a written language or has only recently developed one). This term is also sometimes used to describe students who, though they may face challenges related to missing months or years of schooling, do not necessarily face the more severe issues of the first group.

This strategy will focus on that first group. We are not trying to minimize the challenges faced by this second group of students. Some ways to help them can be found in Strategy 32: Differentiation for ELLs in Content Classes with English-Proficient Students. Those activities, as well as ones discussed in Strategy 36: Culturally Responsive Teaching and Strategy 41: Working with Parents and Guardians, can also be particularly helpful to all SIFEs.

The number of SIFEs entering the United States can come in waves and may vary by location. For example, in 2004 many Hmong came to California and Minnesota when their main refugee camp in Thailand closed. However, the wave of unaccompanied minors who fled gangs in Central America in 2014–2015 went to more geographically dispersed areas. SIFEs, however, are not limited to these groups or time periods—they come from all over the world and continue to arrive here. Note that not all newcomers are SIFEs. Although all of the chapters in this book discuss strategies that can be used with newcomers and also include detailed differentiation recommendations, we have also included links in the Technology Connections section to even more specific resources.

Why We Like It

Even experienced ELL teachers can feel at a loss when working with SIFEs for the first (or second or third) time. We still remember years ago on the first day Larry taught his class of Hmong refugee students. He came to Katie's room after the first period in a panic telling her, "I don't know how to teach students to hold a pencil!" Larry and his students persevered that day and beyond using the strategies here and in other portions of this book. His time with them became the most memorable of his teaching career (his students might or might not characterize them the same way!).

The suggestions in the Application section of this strategy, and in Strategy 32: Differentiation for ELLs in Content Classes with English-Proficient Students, Strategy 36: Culturally Responsive Teaching, and Strategy 41: Working with Parents and Guardians, should provide a good start for teachers who are working with SIFEs for the first time (and may even have some good ideas for more experienced educators, too!).

Supporting Research

The activities listed here and in Strategies 34, 36, and 39 are consistent with the kind of support researchers have identified that best assist SIFEs in making a successful transition to U.S. schooling (Robertson & Lafond, n.d.) and "SLIFE: Students with Limited or Interrupted Formal Education" (WIDA Consortium, 2015).

Common Core Connections

We're talking here about assisting adolescents who have minimal or no experience with schooling and who often have had extensive periods filled with traumatic experiences. We think it's a little ridiculous to talk about meeting Common Core Standards in this situation—these activities are designed to assist our students to get to the point where they can begin to do some of the other activities in this book, which do address the Standards. It's less about building connections to Common Core Standards and more about building connections to basic literacy and an academic mind-set as well as basic human connections.

Application

Here are four important ways that we support SIFE students.

TECHNOLOGY SUPPORT

Many of the bilingual and multilingual sites accessible to most English language learners are not usable by many SIFEs because they show a word in a home language and then show it and say it in English (though it could be helpful to some students with low literacy). That's not very helpful if you can't read your home language. There are a few learning sites that provide audio and text in English and Spanish. Others show images of actions and objects along with short audio descriptions in English. In addition, there are some sites designed for young English speakers who are just beginning to read that provide limited support to nonliterate students. You can find links to these free sites in the Technology Connections section. In addition, there are helpful sites that can assist students as they begin to acquire handwriting skills, and you can find those links in the same place. Obviously, Google Translate and several other tools including AI chatbots can provide both audio and text support in many students' home languages, which can work well in individual conversations, as well as make text written in English accessible through audio and text translation. Presentation tools can translate audio in English and closed caption slides into student home languages. Other, newer tools are being developed that offer simultaneous audio translation, though those are not as far along at the time of this book's publication.

See the Technology Connections section for links to sites where you can access the most up-to-date information on these tools.

PHONICS INSTRUCTION

We shared in Strategy 11: Inductive Learning how we teach phonics inductively. We think this instructional strategy works for all ages but especially for adolescents because it requires higher-order thinking as they seek, find, and expand patterns. It minimizes the chances of secondary students feeling like they are being treated as young children.

In addition to doing those lessons with SIFEs and others, we also have students do follow-up phonemic awareness activities, particularly onset-rime (writing a word on the board such as *cat* and then changing the first letter so that it turns into different words that students can sound out—*fat, sat, bat,* etc.). Onset-rime is easy for teachers to do, easy for students to understand, and can easily be incorporated into all sorts of reading and writing activities. It can literally just take a few seconds.

We have links in the Technology Connections section to instructions for many phonemic awareness activities and to online exercises students can do to reinforce phonics knowledge.

HOME LANGUAGE INSTRUCTION

We've previously discussed in Strategy 1: Independent Reading how use of a home language can assist a student's acquisition of a new one. With Spanish-speaking students who are not literate in their home language, we've worked with our supportive Spanish teachers to provide peer tutors to help them gain reading and writing skills in their home language. There are also some, but not many, online sites that can support nonliterate Spanish speakers in learning basic Spanish literacy (see the Technology Connections section). In addition, we have recruited ELLs and English-proficient students who share the same home languages of SIFEs to act as peer tutors.

ENCOURAGEMENT, PATIENCE, AND SUPPORT

We want to make it very clear that our track record with SIFEs is decidedly mixed. Larry likes to illustrate his effectiveness with SIFEs by retelling a story about a heart-to-heart talk he had with Jose at the end of one school year. Jose, who was an unaccompanied minor refugee from Central America, had experienced many challenges in his first year of schooling. As Larry walked with him on his prep period, Jose shared his goals for the following year. "I want to show teachers more respect," he emphasized, "and I want to be more serious about learning." Larry was thrilled and supportive as they walked back to Jose's class. Jose entered and Larry began to walk away. Five seconds later, his teacher walked out with Jose in tow, "Mr. Ferlazzo," she said, "can you talk with Jose? He just walked in and yelled "Hello, b-t-hes, I'm back!"

Unfortunately, Jose dropped out of school shortly afterwards.

His decision is reflective of the high drop-out rate for SIFES in general (WIDA Consortium, 2015, p. 2). Support, including counseling and legal assistance to deal with immigration issues, is critical to helping SIFEs not feel overwhelmed by the many challenges they face.

Fortunately, the legislature in our state of California voted to provide Medi-Cal (the state's name for Medicaid) to all children under the age of 18—whether they are documented or not (Ferlazzo, 2016, April 30). These benefits include mental health services, which are important for many of our SIFEs who suffer from PTSD (post-traumatic stress disorder). So, assuming our school's support staff members can find counselors who speak the home language of our SIFEs, and assuming that they accept Medi-Cal reimbursement (two big assumptions), our students can receive some support through that avenue.

We're also lucky to have nearby law schools with immigration clinics that, depending on how overwhelmed they are at the time, can relieve some additional stress on our students by providing legal representation in immigration courts.

To maximize this kind of support and to increase the odds of SIFEs overcoming the challenges they face, being able to work as a team with their family or guardians can be very helpful. Oftentimes, that requires overcoming language challenges, connecting with foster parents, or working with older siblings or relatives who are not the student's parents. In our experience, they always want the student to succeed, but it may require a little extra time on our part to make those connections (see Strategy 41: Working with Parents and Guardians for ideas).

With all of these pressures and the resulting stress, our SIFEs need all the patience and compassion that we teachers have to give. And they often require a great deal of that patience and compassion—some may be unfamiliar with the "norms" of school life and need extra support in the area that many call "classroom management." The trauma that many SIFEs have experienced can be displayed in different ways, and becoming more familiar with trauma-informed instructional practices can benefit SIFE students, as well as others. See Strategy 37: Social Emotional Learning for suggestions, as well as the Technology Connections section.

One piece of advice we would offer related to trauma-informed instruction is to carefully consider how your lessons may affect your students' emotional health. For example, before Larry taught a lesson on gangs in Central America, he met with his SIFE students to see how they would feel about it. They were universally enthusiastic but also asked if there could be another place they could go if their feelings grew too strong during the class.

All students, including the SIFEs, were highly engaged in the lesson, but one was overcome by their emotions and knew that he could leave and go to another classroom (where Larry had made arrangements) to take a break.

Another example is the common ELL lesson where students are asked to talk, write, or draw about their migration journey to the United States. Teachers should consider offering alternative assignments to SIFEs and others whose journey may have been traumatic (Digby, 2019).

Admittedly, we sometimes fall short in assisting our students—the challenges facing some SIFEs may just be too much for them and for us. But the ideas we share here, and the strategies we offer in the rest of the book, increase the odds of success for all of us.

What Could Go Wrong?

Sometimes the challenges facing SIFEs can seem overwhelming to teachers and students alike. Certainly, our track record with SIFEs is nothing to brag about. However, the recommendations we make in this strategy, remembering the assets these students bring, *and* reminding them of these assets have all helped us and them.

Teaching Online

This is a difficult situation. Larry did have one SIFE student in his distance learning plan during the pandemic, and it was a struggle to engage the student and make the class content accessible (even though the student was Spanish-speaking and Larry speaks Spanish). Though his literacy was low, it was high enough for him to read at least some of the close captioned translations shown on the screen, and Larry was able to provide some quick supplemental instruction in Spanish. Luckily, they also had a Spanish-speaking peer tutor who was able to often work with him one-on-one in a breakout room. This support, along with online work he was able to do on his own, helped set him up for a successful high school career that led to his graduation.

If you don't have peer tutors, volunteers, or a student teacher available, though, our best advice would be to team your SIFE up with a "buddy" (see Strategy 32: Differentiation For ELLs in Content Classes with English-Proficient Students for details) who speaks the same home language and have them do a lot of partner work together.

Some tools can provide simultaneous audio translation in a student's home language; see the Technology Connections section for up-to date developments. Students with low literacy in their home language might benefit from the several online tools that provide simultaneous text or audio translation.

Technology Connections

For links to language-learning sites accessible to SIFEs (including sites to help nonliterate Spanish speakers learn Spanish vocabulary) and for more ways to support them (including through technology), visit The Best Online Resources for Teachers of SLIFEs (http://larryferlazzo.edublogs.org/2008/12/06/the-best-online-resources-for-teachers-of-pre-literate-ells/).

You can find links to step-by-step instructions for teaching phonemic-awareness activities and to online exercises for phonics reinforcement at The Best Articles and Sites for Teachers and Students to Learn About Phonics (http://larryferlazzo.edublogs.org/2011/03/01/the-best-articles-sites-for-teachers-students-to-learn-about-phonics/).

See The Best Ways for Responding to Student Trauma – Help Me Find More (https://larryferlazzo.edublogs.org/2016/11/11/the-best-ways-for-responding-to-student-trauma-help-me-find-more/) for advice on trauma-informed instruction.

See The Best Resources to Help ELL Students with Simultaneous Translation in the Classroom (https://larryferlazzo.edublogs.org/2023/07/18/the-best-resources-to-help-ell-students-with-simultaneous-translation-in-the-classroom/) for automatic translation resources.

Obviously, not every newcomer is a SIFE. Though all of our chapters contain strategies to use with all newcomers, additional support for non-SIFE newcomers can be found at The Best Resources to Help Educators Teach ELL Newcomers (https://larryferlazzo.edublogs.org/2019/12/30/the-best-resources-to-help-educators-teach-ell-newcomers/).

STRATEGY 34

Working with Long-Term ELLs

What Is It?

The title of this chapter, "Working with Long-Term ELLs," is less of a strategy and more a sharing of a few different strategies to support a large percentage of the U.S. ELL population. The State of California appears to be the only state that has determined an official definition of a long-term ELL (LTELLs): basically, a student who has been an ELL for six years or more (REL West, 2016a). Certain districts in other states and some researchers say more than five years is the duration required for that label (Cashiola et al., 2022). Regardless, there is no one reliable number identifying how many LTELLs are in U.S. schools, but the best estimate available suggests that it is between one-quarter and one-half of all ELLs.

LTELLs tend to have higher absenteeism, an increased likelihood of suspensions and other disciplinary actions, and lower graduation rates than either their English-proficient or their newer ELL counterparts (Cashiola et al., 2016; REL West, 2016b).

Researchers have found multiple factors that may have a role in students becoming LTELLs. These include (Buenrostro & Maxwell-Jolly, 2021):

- Elementary and middle schools and their teachers not having adequate knowledge on how to support ELLs so they can access grade-level content
- Increased absenteeism
- Changing schools
- Not receiving needed special education support
- May have minimal literacy in their home language
- Have more advanced speaking and listening skills but struggle to connect them to academic reading and writing tasks

Why We Like It

We educators, and state and district policies, cannot ignore the challenge LTELLs present to us and their needs that must be met. Putting our heads in the sand is not an effective, or ethical, strategy.

This chapter is a beginning attempt to provide educators with a few strategies to support the huge number of our students who have fallen into this category.

Supporting Research

Research about who LTELLs are, the factors that contribute to their becoming LTELLs, and the challenges they face was included in the "What Is It?" section. Here, we will share ways research suggests we can intervene and support LTELLs:

- Support students' home language development because improved home language literacy can have a positive impact on English language acquisition (Hanover Research, 2017).
- Intervene before student absenteeism and disciplinary issues increase.
- Pay particular attention to supporting ELLs in middle school to reduce the chances of their becoming LTELLs (Cashiola et al., 2016).
- Provide professional development to all teachers on how to support ELLs and also provide culturally relevant instruction.
- Enroll them in a support class that supplements, but does not replace, a core academic class such as English.
- Cohort LTELLs in academic classes, though not exclusively. In other words, they might stay together in the same classes, but there would also be non-LTELLs enrolled in the classes as well.
- Regularly monitor student progress and provide support and intervention when needed.
- Create an inclusive school climate (Olsen, 2014).

Common Core Connections

The focus of this chapter is to discuss ways LTELLs can successfully achieve *all* the Common Core standards.

Application

There are no easy answers for supporting LTELLs.

Providing regular professional development to ensure that all teachers are practicing ELL-appropriate instructional strategies to make content accessible to everyone may be one of the most important actions schools can make. We believe, and research tends to support our position (Ferlazzo, February 2024), that good ELL teaching means better teaching for everyone, including LTELLs and English-proficient students. Using many of the teaching strategies discussed in this book can make academic content more accessible to everyone. See the rest of this book and especially Strategy 32: Differentiation for ELLs in Content Classes with English-Proficient Students for ideas.

In schools that provide world language instruction in the home language of ELL students, ensuring that they are placed in those classes is another obvious way to support LTELLs.

One way Larry's school implemented several of the research-based recommendations for LTELL support was by creating a special support class for a group of LTELLs.

We have described it in great detail in our previous book, *The ESL/ELL Teacher's Survival Guide*, second edition, Jossey Bass, 2022 (page 329) and elsewhere (i.e., Ferlazzo, 2019).

Twenty students were enrolled in the support class, and they were also cohorted throughout the day in all their other academic classes (other English-proficient students were also in those other classes). Students in the support class regularly met with peer mentors—older students who met with them each week for 15 minutes to "check in" and provide additional support. Larry was in regular contact with student families and offered multiple social emotional learning lessons.

Students also created retrieval practice notebooks—see Strategy 12: Retrieval Practice for more information.

Most importantly, every week their content teachers would e-mail Larry a few sentences describing what they would be covering the next week and what prior knowledge would be helpful for students to have in order to access that material.

Larry used that information to teach simple lessons on those topics, including showing videos and having follow-up class discussions, so that students would enter those academic classes being as prepared and, in most classes, more prepared than their English-proficient counterparts.

By the end of the year, students in Larry's support class posted a higher increase in grades and English language assessments than those in the control group. Several entered the school's International Baccalaureate program the following year.

Teaching Online

Good online teaching for ELLs is better teaching for everyone else, too, so implementation of the many strategies discussed in this book can also benefit LTELLs.

What Could Go Wrong?

There are many other school challenges competing for attention with LTELL support. Because of this situation, the main thing that can go wrong is doing nothing at all.

In addition, there's nothing like theoretical, "preachy," or boring professional development that will discourage teachers from changing their practices to make instruction accessible to ELLs. See the Technology Connections section for resources on ways to increase the odds of offering effective professional development to your school's teachers.

If your school decides to create an LTELL support class, please don't put it on the least experienced educator or on one who doesn't want to teach it. Competency and desire will be critical to its success.

Technology Connections

Additional resources on LTELLs and how to support them can be found at "The Best Resources on Supporting Long-Term English Language Learners" (https://larryferlazzo.edublogs.org/2016/12/03/the-best-resources-on-supporting-long-term-english-language-learners/).

For suggestions on how to create useful and effective professional development opportunities for teachers, see The Best Resources on Professional Development for Teachers — Help Me Find More (https://larryferlazzo.edublogs.org/2014/03/27/the-best-resources-on-professional-development-for-teachers-help-me-find-more/).

STRATEGY 35

Multilevel Classes

What Is It?

Many schools might not have enough students for one newcomers class or one intermediate class. Instead, they may combine them into one (with, perhaps, some advanced ELLs also placed there).

If it's not an "official" multilevel class, most ELL classes are de facto ones. It's not unusual for an ELL class to receive new students each month (and, in some cases, every week!).

With so many different English language proficiency levels, what are strategies teachers can use to support, and challenge, all of them?

Why We Like It

Teaching a multilevel class well does not happen without careful planning. Every year we teach de facto ones with new students coming in regularly with little or no English skills. And, if we teach summer school (or, if we don't teach it because we're busy writing books, we help plan it), it's almost always a multilevel class. The ideas in this chapter, and in every chapter, come from our practical experience in trying our best to create optimal learning conditions for our students, as well as sane conditions for us.

Supporting Research

Though it's surprising to us that there seems to be little research on what tends to work and not work in multilevel ELL classes, the few studies there are support the use of small group instruction (including partner work), translanguaging, project-based learning, and self-access materials (Mathews-Aydinli & Van Horne, 2006; Shank & Terrill, 1995).

Common Core Connections

All the different instructional strategies described in this chapter actually have their *own* chapters elsewhere in this book. We didn't feel a need to repeat them all here again.

Application

We're dividing this section into two parts:

- First, a summary of the overall strategies we recommend for teaching a multi-level ELL class
- Second, our concrete and specific plans for teaching a multilevel class: what it looks like hour by hour

OVERALL STRATEGIES

As many teachers already know, the three key elements in any kind of differentiation strategy, which we first learned from educator Carol Ann Tomlinson (ASCD, 2020), are:

- Content
- Process
- Product

In other words, we differentiate by modifying the knowledge and skills students are learning, providing activities students can use to learn the knowledge and skills, and offering ways students can show that they have actually learned the information and developed the skills. Of course, there may very well be "fuzzy" lines between some of these categories, but it's far less important to be able to place a task in an exact differentiation category and far more important to appropriately differentiate the task itself!

What specific strategies can work for each element?

CONTENT

- Jigsaws (see Strategy 9: Jigsaw) can work well in all classrooms and are particularly suited for a multilevel one. More simple texts can be given to student groups with students less proficient in English and more complex ones to groups composed of more English-proficient students. Not only the text can be differentiated, but also the topic. For example, in a jigsaw on Abraham Lincoln's life, newcomers might be given text and need to prepare a class report on "Family Life," while intermediates or advanced ELLs might do one on "Challenges Lincoln Faced."

- Students can work on completely different "leveled" workbooks. For example, we use the Pearson "True Stories" series (https://www.pearson.com/languages/en-us/educators/connected-english-learning-program/adult/true-stories.html) as a warm-up. Students work in small groups with classmates at similar levels using the appropriate leveled "True Stories" books. See the Technology Connections section for a link to learn more about those particular workbooks and similar ones.

- Have one group of students receive an explicit lesson from the teacher for a period of time while other students are using self-access materials that they can use independently (on paper or online). See the Technology Connections section for suggestions of online sites.

PROCESS

- Provide a simple text accessible to everyone, but assign different tasks for students to do with it. For example, perhaps newcomers need to identify all the words in the text that are new to them and make a slideshow with a slide for each one showing the word, what it means in their own words, what the word is in their home language, the word in an original sentence, and an image. Intermediates and advanced ELLs might need to take the same text and write another paragraph mimicking its style of writing, or add several sentences that might naturally follow that paragraph.

- The previous activity is an example of a "flexible" task (Kiczkowiak, 2014). In other words, the initial lesson is the same for all students, but what they have to do with it depends on their language level. Some ways a flexible task can be differentiated include by quantity (newcomers do one task; intermediates do more); complexity (when using the picture word inductive model lesson from Strategy 11: Inductive Learning, newcomer students can complete clozes about the image while more advanced students can write their own sentence); or in roles (either a dialogue where a newcomer has lines with the fewest words or one in which the newcomer asks the questions and the intermediate/advanced student has to create original responses).

- Another lesson that "shouts" this kind of flexibility is the language experience approach (see Strategy 8: Language Experience Approach (LEA)). In LEA, the entire class does an activity (watches a video, plays a game, does an art project, etc.) and then comes together to write about it. In LEA, newcomers can write a sentence at a time, while more advanced students can write a mini-essay (perhaps with scaffolded graphic organizers).

- In project-based learning and problem-based learning (see Strategy 22: Project-Based Learning and Problem-Based Learning), similar ability groups can take on projects of differing levels of language complexity.

PRODUCT

- Students may need to take a test of vocabulary learned through the picture word inductive model (see Strategy 11), while intermediate and advanced ELLs might be challenged to actually create that test, or other activities that would demonstrate mastery of the vocabulary such as an online game, a crossword puzzle, or a series of cloze sentences (see Strategy 7: Clozes).

- A variation of the previous activity is having intermediate/advanced students prepare a lesson *and* a test on it. For example, during one of the times newcomers are working on self-access materials, the teacher can explain the parameters of a lesson (related to the theme the class is studying) they will be teaching the newcomers and how they will assess them. One strategy that we use is the picture word inductive model. See Figure 35.1: Student-Led Picture Word Inductive Model Lesson. This lesson is in three parts taught over a series of three days. We work with the more advanced students to prepare one part each day. See the lesson guide in the figure for more details.

WHAT OUR MULTILEVEL SUMMER SCHOOL CLASS LOOKS LIKE

The following sequence is a version of a four-hour multilevel summer school class (including breaks and lunch) we periodically have at our high school:

1. Conversation Practice (20 minutes)

    If peer tutors are available (see Strategy 39: Peer Teaching and Learning):

    Peer tutors work in small groups with newcomers in simple conversation practice (see Strategy 25: Conversation Practice), while more advanced students work in small groups with peer tutors in more advanced conversation practice. Newcomers might answer questions in a few words, while more advanced students can be expected to answer in multiple sentences and also ask questions in return.

    If peer tutors are not available:

    Newcomers work independently on artificial intelligence–powered sites to practice conversation and pronunciation. More advanced students would do the same with higher expectations. The teacher can work with students who have the lowest English proficiency during this time.

2. Grammar (30 minutes)

    The teacher gives a grammar lesson to the entire class. Our district uses the National Geographic Edge series. Though we have questions/concerns about its curriculum, its grammar books are ideal for multilevel classes. All their different leveled books cover the same grammar topics in the same order but provide more complex examples, along with questions and exercises for students to complete.

    If peer tutors are available, all students can return to their small groups and work with them to complete the exercises. In the absence of peer tutors, students can work in partners to complete the work.

3. Language Experience Approach (30 minutes)

    The entire class does a Language Experience Approach activity together—playing a game outside, going to the art room to do a project, watching a video, etc.—and then comes together to write sentences about what they just did. Newcomers can write simple sentences, while more advanced students can write longer and more complex ones.

4. Peer Teaching (30 minutes)

    This is the time for student-led lesson preparation and for actually teaching it (see Figure 35.1). The first time advanced students prepare the lesson, the teacher will need to assist them while newcomers are doing independent practice on one of the self-access sites. After the advanced students learn how to do it, the teacher can work with newcomers while advanced students prepare the lessons on their own. While the advanced students are doing that, the teacher can work with newcomers on various activities using sentences they wrote about the language experience approach (turning them into sentence scrambles or clozes, for example). Two or three days during the week the teacher can supervise the advanced students teaching the newcomers.

5. Reading (30 minutes)

    If peer tutors are available, newcomers can read books of their choice in small groups. They can take turns reading sentences/pages aloud, peer tutors can dictate some sentences to have students write them on mini-whiteboard, and tutors can ask comprehension questions. More advanced students can organize similar book clubs, and peer tutors can periodically offer comprehension questions or lead dictation and also help with questions.

    If peer tutors are not available, this could be a time for another "flexible task" that was mentioned earlier: dialogue, reading a text with differentiated follow-up tasks, a picture word inductive model activity where newcomers complete clozes about the image while more advanced students write multiple sentences, etc.

6. Jigsaw, PBL, and/or game (30 minutes)

    This could be the time for another flexible activity, perhaps a jigsaw (see Strategy 9), a project- or problem-based learning lesson (see Strategy 22), and/or a game. In the game, it's important to create the conditions where the advanced students don't always "win." We do this by using one of the many games discussed in this book that use whiteboards and unilaterally announce, depending on the game, something like, "These groups get one point for one answer, but these other groups have to produce three answers to get one point." We always get lots of boos, but students "get it."

Teaching Online

Theoretically, everything in this chapter can be done online. However, we've never tried teaching a multilevel class in an online environment, and we hope never to have that experience. It's a lot of balls to juggle in face-to-face instruction, and we are just not confident that we could pull it off successfully online. More power to you if you can do it!

What Could Go Wrong?

A multilevel class can be like managing a three-ring circus, even in the best of situations. We try to pre-empt the most egregious potential classroom management problems by explaining at the beginning it's a challenging environment for everyone and asking for students to help us out. Having peer tutors can make it much more manageable but, without them, things can get out of hand pretty quickly. There are many opportunities for off-task student behavior. Teachers need to plan well, be organized, develop solid student relationships, and plan for brisk transitions (which are easy times for things to begin to fall apart). Repeat the activities that seem to work well, and quickly condemn failures to oblivion.

Technology Connections

For even more ideas, visit The Best Resources on Teaching Multilevel ESL/EFL Classes (https://larryferlazzo.edublogs.org/2011/09/05/the-best-resources-on-teaching-multilevel-eslefl-classes).

Learn more about leveled "True Stories" books and other similar workbooks at "The 'True Stories' Book Series Is An Extraordinary Match for My ELL Newcomers Classroom – Do You Know of Other Similar Titles?" (https://larryferlazzo.edublogs.org/2023/01/13/the-true-stories-book-series-is-an-extraordinary-match-for-my-ell-newcomers-classroom-do-you-know-of-other-similar-titles/).

Find online sites that students can use independently at There Are Tons of Resources On This Blog to Help Educators Teach ELLs – This Post Is a Good Place to Start (https://larryferlazzo.edublogs.org/2023/12/29/there-are-tons-of-resources-on-this-blog-to-help-educators-teach-ells-this-post-is-a-good-place-to-start/).

All figures from this chapter, as well as 11 additional chapters, references, hyperlinked Technology Connections, and more online resources, can be found at www.wiley.com/go/ellteacherstoolbox2.

STRATEGY 35: MULTILEVEL CLASSES *381*

Names of Teachers:_____

Names of Your Students: _____

Lesson Topic: _____

What is the picture you are using to illustrate your topic (copy and paste it here):

At least eight words you will teach to your students using this picture:

1.
2.
3.
4.
5.
6.
7.
8.

At least eight cloze sentences using those words that your students will have to complete.

1.
2.
3.
4.
5.
6.
7.
8.

Figure 35.1 Student-Led Picture Word Inductive Model Lesson

LESSON GUIDE

FIRST DAY

1. Choose a topic.
2. Choose a picture.
3. Copy and paste the picture on the lesson plan and insert it in a Google Drawing that you will share with the teacher. Your teacher will share the Google Drawing with your students.
4. Decide who will teach each word to your students by saying the word, writing it on the Google Drawing, and making a line connecting the word to the object in the image.
5. Write your cloze sentences in the lesson plan. Make sure they are about the picture, and use each of the words you have taught.
6. Write your cloze sentences on a mini-whiteboard and number them. Make sure they are not in the same order you have taught the words! Decide who will read each one to your students.
7. Make sure each of your students has a mini-whiteboard they can write their answers to each of the cloze sentences.

SECOND DAY

8. The next day, review the words and the sentences with your students. Show the sentence, say it, and have each student repeat it. Then cover up the sentences, and dictate them to your students while they write them on their whiteboards. Plan which "teacher" is going to lead which activity.
9. Tell your students you will be testing them on the words the following day.

THIRD DAY

10. Prepare a test for your students. Say the words—not in the same order—and have students write them down on a sheet of paper. Then, prepare the same cloze sentences as "scrambled sentences" (the words and punctuation marks for each sentence are out of order). Write them on a mini-whiteboard and ask your students to put them in order on their test paper. Decide which teacher will lead which activity during the test.
11. Correct the tests and give students, and the teacher, the score.

Figure 35.1 (*Continued*)

STRATEGY 36
Culturally Responsive Teaching

What Is It?

Although the majority of students in U.S. schools are students of color from linguistically and culturally diverse backgrounds (NCES, 2024), the vast majority of educators who teach them are white (Spiegelman, 2020). Teaching practices that help teachers of all races be better teachers to students of diverse backgrounds—known as *asset-based pedagogies*—view students' cultural identities and experiences as strengths in the classroom (California Department of Education, 2024).

Two of the most well-known asset-based pedagogies are culturally responsive teaching and culturally sustaining pedagogy.

Culturally responsive teaching, a term introduced by Geneva Gay (2000), builds on the framework of *culturally relevant pedagogy* pioneered by Gloria Ladson-Billings (1995). Culturally responsive teaching isn't a strategy or even a set of strategies; rather, it is a mindset that underlies and guides everyday classroom practices. Its focus is on validating the cultural learning tools that diverse learners bring to the classroom and leveraging them to effect positive learning outcomes for all students.

Culturally sustaining pedagogy is an emerging perspective that builds on the tenets of culturally relevant and responsive teaching. This educational stance was first proposed by professor Django Paris (2012), who defines it as a pedagogy that "seeks to perpetuate and foster—to sustain—linguistic, literate, and cultural pluralism as part of the democratic project of schooling." In other words, this concept makes sure our educational practices not only *respond* to the diversity of languages and cultures in our classroom but also that they aim to *sustain* these elements at the center of teaching and learning.

These approaches may differ in their frameworks, but they share the goal of directly countering a "deficit" model of education and, instead, focusing on the strengths and assets of diverse students. We hope you agree that many of the practices included in this book embody these philosophies.

Why We Like It

As we've stated many times, looking at ELLs through the lens of assets and not deficits guides what we do in the classroom and the choices we make about how to do it. Instruction that is culturally responsive and sustaining explicitly challenges the deficit perspective. Rather, students are viewed as possessing valuable linguistic, cultural, and literacy tools. Recognizing, validating, and using these tools—in our experience—ultimately provides the best learning environment for our students and ourselves!

Supporting Research

Much research points to links between culturally responsive teaching and positive learning outcomes for all students (Gay, 2002; Krasnoff, 2016). Culturally responsive pedagogy has also been shown to have positive impacts on student motivation, student interest in content, and students' perceptions of themselves as capable learners, among other benefits (Aronson & Laughter, 2016). In addition, research has found culturally responsive teaching to be vitally important to educating ELLs with disabilities (University of Kansas, 2017).

Common Core Connections

Although the focus of culturally responsive teaching isn't on meeting certain Standards, it is on leveraging students' cultural and linguistic tools in order for them to learn at high levels. This learning can meet any number of Standards.

Application

So what does culturally responsive teaching look like in the ELL classroom? For us, it is an awareness that we try to bring to everything we do. It is a process we are constantly working on as we learn from our students and their experiences. Have we made mistakes along the way? Many. However, like we tell our students, mistakes are opportunities for learning, and we try our best to model this mind-set.

The following section contains several critical questions we ask ourselves when considering how our work with ELLs can be more culturally responsive and sustaining. Although these questions don't cover every aspect of culturally responsive teaching, they do represent foundational best practices we use in our classroom.

HOW WELL DO I KNOW MY STUDENTS?

In order to build on the rich linguistic and cultural experiences of our students, we must get to know them! This doesn't mean doing interrogations on the first day of school, however. It means building positive relationships with our students so they feel safe sharing their experiences with us. It involves daily interactions with students to learn about their struggles, their joys, and their goals.

It means taking the time to gather information that the school may possess about our students—their English proficiency levels, assessment results, home language surveys, health information, transcripts from previous schooling, and so on. It can also be making time to learn about students' home countries, the conflicts that may be going on there, the cities or towns they come from, and the languages they speak. See Strategy 43: Beginning the School Year for ideas on how we get to know our students.

Of course, a key factor in knowing our students is getting to know their families as well. See Strategy 41: Working with Parents and Guardians for resources on building connections between home and school.

DO MY WORDS REFLECT A CULTURALLY RESPONSIVE MIND-SET WHEN I AM TALKING TO STUDENTS AND ABOUT STUDENTS?

One of the simplest ways to honor students' cultural backgrounds and identities is to correctly pronounce their names. Mispronouncing a student's name and not making any attempt to get it right can cause them to feel embarrassed and can heighten their anxiety. Correctly pronouncing a student's name signals respect and a validation of who they are. It is a critical first step in building strong, trusting relationships with students. In addition, providing space for students to share their preferred pronouns with us is critical in creating a feeling of safety and inclusion. For more information and research on the value of correctly pronouncing students' names, see the Technology Connections section at the end of this chapter and the Student Names section in Strategy 43: Beginning the School Year.

As teachers, we also need to be mindful of the words we are using when discussing cultural experiences with students. Characterizing our students' beliefs as "right" or "wrong" through our words or our facial expressions may not only be inaccurate but also removes students from the center of the teaching and learning process. We want students to feel comfortable sharing with each other to build a community of learners in which all experiences are valued. As teachers, we can be far more effective in raising questions than in making judgments.

At the same time, it is also our job to teach U.S. cultural norms and/or laws (e.g., equal treatment of women and LGBTQ individuals) and create a classroom environment where everyone feels safe and respected. We can do this by teaching in a way that is cognizant of our students' home cultures, which may or may not promote different perspectives. These may require difficult conversations privately and publicly.

For those of us who work in schools located in high-poverty areas, we can often be asked questions by well-meaning people, such as, "How do you do it?" and "Aren't you afraid working in that neighborhood?" and "How can the students learn when their lives are so crazy?" In these situations, one can feel any number of emotions including anger, frustration, or hopelessness. It can be tempting to tell the stories of our students (the challenges or trauma they have faced) in an attempt to demonstrate their resilience.

Unfortunately, sharing these details can often do more to perpetuate stereotypes than to shatter them. Instead, we can promote culturally sustaining pedagogy by sharing with others the rich cultural and linguistic contributions our students make to our school and to the community.

We must be intentional with our words and in the actions that we discuss in other portions of this Application section. In addition, we must educate ourselves so we truly believe in what we are saying and doing. This involves becoming aware of any implicit biases we hold and working to address them. If we don't, students will see right through us, and we speak from direct experience.

HOW ARE MY INSTRUCTIONAL PRACTICES CULTURALLY RESPONSIVE?

Many of us have tried to engage our students by dropping a cultural reference into a lesson (mentioning an important person or event from our student's culture). Although it usually gets students' attention, it isn't an instructional practice that can maximize student learning, and it isn't a culturally responsive instructional practice.

Educators, however, *can* increase learning outcomes by teaching in ways that build on the cultural and linguistic experiences of their students. These methods, in turn, lead to increased engagement. Zaretta Hammond, educator and author of the book *Culturally Responsive Teaching and the Brain* (2015), explains this when she states:

> The most common cultural tools for processing information utilize the brain's memory systems—music, repetition, metaphor, recitation, physical manipulation of content, and ritual. The teacher is "responsive" when she is able to mirror these ways of learning in her instruction, using similar strategies to scaffold learning. (Aguilar, 2015)

We can illustrate this point with several simple examples from our classroom. We know that many of our ELL students come from cultural backgrounds that particularly value and practice working together to accomplish tasks (Krasnoff, 2016, p. 13). We mirror this in our instruction by providing daily opportunities for our students to work collaboratively in small groups.

A more-specific example comes from our experience working with Hmong refugees. While in refugee camps, many Hmong women created "story cloths" (embroidery that told stories about their lives). In a series of lessons, our Hmong students created their own hand-drawn versions of story cloths and helped the non-Hmong students to do the same. We then used their creations as springboards to learn the English words needed to talk and write about these stories. Students were more engaged in this language-learning activity because it mirrored, valued, and respected an important part of their home culture.

We have used the process of building on cultural experiences to create language-learning opportunities in many other lessons. These include ones in which students have made presentations about their home cultures (see Strategy 22: Project-Based Learning, Problem-Based Learning, and Bonus Strategy 7: Class Presentations available at www.wiley.com/go/ellteacherstoolbox2) and have done language-learning activities related to their favorite contemporary music (see Strategy 27: Music) and ancient cultural music. In addition, when learning about the elements of feudalism students questioned the textbook authors' claim that it ended hundreds of years ago when, in fact, their families recently experienced it in their own lives. This connection led to high-interest studying of the socio-economic conditions of various countries as well as direct student communication with textbook authors.

Here are a few more ideas of this kind of asset-based teaching:

- When studying weather and climate vocabulary, have students write and draw about how they experience it in their home countries, including how climate change has affected it.
- In an ELL world history class, ask Muslim students to contribute to teaching about Islam. One time, our students found an error in that section of our textbook, and their correction was confirmed by other sources.
- In an ELL U.S. history class, Afghan refugee students shared their experiences when learning about the Afghanistan War. Note that we had private conversations with students prior to that unit. See our later discussion about trauma-informed instruction.
- In another ELL U.S. history class, our Marshallese students contributed their families' experiences about nuclear bomb testing near their homes when studying the history of nuclear weapons.
- See Strategy 21: Problem Posing for ways we use Freirian instructional strategies to engage students in writing and discussions around problems facing their families and communities.
- In a math class, students can be asked to apply math skills while studying issues related to their lives, such as rising food and gas prices. Teachers can also incorporate cultural references into word problems to make them more relevant to students' experiences.
- In a science class, students can collect and analyze local data (e.g., health statistics) from their community.

Culturally responsive instruction is ultimately student-centered. It requires the teacher to help students build on their prior knowledge and cultural and linguistic experiences as they are challenged to read, write, speak, and think at high levels. For ELLs, in particular, it requires using best practices, such as modeling, instructional scaffolding, and collaborative learning, just to name a few, to build the language, academic, and critical thinking skills they need to be successful lifelong learners.

Instructional practices that are culturally responsive must also be trauma-informed. We want to learn about how our students have been impacted by trauma, what supports we can offer, but not cause further harm in the process. This starts with the critical strategy, described in many parts of this book, of building positive, trusting relationships with students. It does not mean teachers need to be what educator Alex Shevrin Venet (2019, p. 2) calls "trauma detectives." As teachers, most of us are not trained to offer students counseling or help them process traumatic experiences and could cause further trauma by trying to fill this role. We can be, however, what Venet (2019, p. 6) describes as "bridge builders" and work to connect our students with professionals who *can* help, including school counselors and social workers. Familiarizing ourselves with the resources available to students and families through the school and the surrounding community can help us offer specific interventions to students in need of support.

See the Technology Connections section for more resources on what culturally responsive instruction and trauma-informed practices look like in the classroom.

HOW IS THE CURRICULUM I AM USING CULTURALLY RESPONSIVE?

We, like most teachers, want to have an idea of what we will be teaching before we actually start teaching it! However, culturally responsive teachers must be flexible with their curriculum and allow for modifications based on student interests and experiences. Curriculum that is culturally responsive doesn't mean having to incorporate texts and information about every student's culture into every lesson. It also doesn't mean having a token "multicultural day" once a year to "celebrate" different cultures.

In our experience, culturally responsive curriculum involves the following:

- Trying our best to choose materials that represent diverse cultures and perspectives.
- Encouraging students to share their cultural and linguistic knowledge with each other.
- Allowing students to choose books they want to read from a diverse classroom library so they can see themselves and their experiences reflected in their reading (see Strategy 1: Independent Reading for our discussion on this idea of windows, mirrors, and sliding glass doors).
- When teaching about historical events or contemporary issues, incorporating role models representing diverse communities, including students' home cultures.
- Valuing literacy in the home language and English (see Strategy 1: Independent Reading, Strategy 32: Differentiation for ELLs in Content Classes with English-Proficient Students, and Strategy 42: Translanguaging for more on home language use).
- Inviting family and community members to the classroom to share cultural knowledge (see Strategy 41: Working with Parents and Guardians for ideas).
- Using digital content to instantly connect students to cultural and linguistic resources.
- Creating lessons on issues directly affecting students' lives, including ones related to current political dynamics that might affect their immigration status or the situation in their home countries (see the Technology Connections section for more information).
- Facilitating open classroom dialogue about the role of race, racism, and religious prejudice (e.g., Islamophobia) in our students' daily lives, including at school (see the Technology Connections section for resources on having these types of conversations with students).

Using assessments with asset-based language focusing on what students *are* doing instead of what is missing or incorrect. For an example, see Figure 19.1 in Strategy 19: Error Correction Strategies.

How Does My Physical Classroom Reflect Diversity?

When students enter our classrooms each day they receive critical messages about the learning environment and their place in it. Students feel more safe, supported, and valued when they see themselves reflected in the classroom: Do the posters on the walls reflect multiple cultures and languages? Is student work displayed? Are the books in the classroom library written by diverse authors? Do students have access to bilingual dictionaries and books in their home languages? How are the seats arranged? Can students easily move into groups? Considering these questions and others is an important step toward creating a learning environment that values student diversity.

Teaching Online

Culturally responsive instruction isn't something that can be "left out" in a distance learning situation. Teachers will need to put even more effort into building relationships with students and in maintaining a safe and welcoming "online" classroom. One way to do this is to regularly ask students for feedback (in the chat, Zoom poll, Google form, or other online survey) about which online activities and tools they are finding most helpful and engaging. Being flexible in responding to students' needs and interests helps to keep learners at the center of instruction. In addition, incorporating interactive activities where students can share their knowledge and experiences in a Zoom chat, an online collaborative application, or in breakout rooms helps to promote an assets-based learning environment.

What Could Go Wrong?

We are not martyrs, nor are we saviors. If you think you are, perhaps you should consider seeking a different profession. We still remember the time one of our former colleagues who lived in a predominantly white, middle-class suburb of Sacramento spoke to students at a school pep rally. He exhorted the students to work hard in class. He continued, "People ask me why I drive all the way down to this neighborhood to teach you. It's because I want to help you!" This is not a culturally responsive mind-set. However, it is a mind-set that we have probably had during different times of our career. The important thing is to be aware of our biases, work toward overcoming them, and be open to having them pointed out to us.

With that said, even teachers who spend time reflecting on their implicit biases may not be providing culturally responsive instruction. Ultimately, it comes down to student learning. Culturally responsive teaching is focused on leveraging the cultural knowledge and learning processes students bring to the classroom to boost their *cognitive abilities* and *academic success*.

As Zaretta Hammond wisely points out:

> The simplest way to judge whether your teaching is culturally responsive is whether your diverse students—students of color, English language learners, immigrant students—are learning. If they are not succeeding *academically* within your classroom norms, your approach might need to be more culturally responsive (Gonzalez, 2017).

Technology Connections

For links to many resources on culturally responsive and sustaining pedagogy, see The Best Resources About "Culturally Responsive Teaching" and "Culturally Sustaining Pedagogy" (http://larryferlazzo.edublogs.org/2016/06/10/the-best-resources-about-culturally-responsive-teaching-culturally-sustaining-pedagogy-please-share-more/).

More resources on the value of correctly pronouncing student names can be found at The Best Resources on the Importance of Correctly Pronouncing Student Names (http://larryferlazzo.edublogs.org/2016/06/11/the-best-resources-on-the-importance-of-correctly-pronouncing-student-names/).

For additional advice on talking with students about race, religious prejudice, and other challenges, see A Collection of Advice on Talking to Students About Race, Police and Racism (http://larryferlazzo.edublogs.org/2016/07/14/a-collection-of-advice-on-talking-to-students-about-race-police-racism/), A Beginning List of the Best Resources for Fighting Islamophobia in Schools (http://larryferlazzo.edublogs.org/2017/03/22/a-beginning-list-of-the-best-resources-for-fighting-islamophobia-in-schools/), and The Best Practical Resources for Helping Teachers, Students and Families Respond to Immigration Challenges (http://larryferlazzo.edublogs.org/2017/02/26/the-best-practical-resources-for-helping-teachers-students-families-respond-to-immigration-challenges/).

For resources related to trauma-informed instruction see the Best Lists on Responding to Student Trauma at https://larryferlazzo.edublogs.org/2020/10/29/here-are-my-best-lists-on-responding-to-student-trauma/.

Research and resources on assets-based pedagogy can be found at the Best Posts on Looking at Our Students Through the Lens of Assets and Not Deficits (https://larryferlazzo.edublogs.org/2016/09/14/the-best-posts-on-looking-at-our-students-through-the-lens-of-assets-not-deficits/).

STRATEGY 37
Social Emotional Learning

What Is It?

Social emotional learning (SEL) is often described as the "soft skills" we all need to be successful in multiple aspects of our lives, including building and maintaining positive relationships, managing emotions, showing empathy, and being able to make wise decisions (CASEL, n.d.). It's pretty difficult, if not impossible, to effectively learn professionally or academically without at the same time having at least a beginning grasp of some of these SEL skills. Though mini-lessons and modeling of SEL skills need to be integrated into all aspects of our teaching every day, this chapter will highlight a few key areas we believe may need to be explicitly taught to ELLs and to all students.

Why We Like It

English language learners face a number of pressures that highlight the need for teachers to include SEL in their "toolbox." These pressures include the stresses of immigrating to a new country, with a different culture and language; the challenge of being scapegoated by some public officials who threaten them and their families with imprisonment and deportation; and the reality that many may be living in poverty.

Research conclusively attributes the majority of factors that affect academic achievement to these kinds of issues outside of the schoolhouse doors (Ferlazzo, 2010, December 28). The consequences of these pressures on our students obviously can be found in our classes every day. Given these facts, and given most teachers' moral commitment to their students, how can we not help provide our students with SEL support to help them better navigate those challenges outside and inside the school environment?

Supporting Research

Many studies have found that assisting students to develop competences in social emotional learning skills results in both increased mental health and high academic engagement and achievement (Ferlazzo, 2015, June 18). Though there are far fewer studies focusing on ELLs, researchers have found that helping ELLs develop SEL competencies enhances the speed of language acquisition (Najarro, 2022; Lee & Soland, 2022), appears to enhance their mental health (Shi et al., 2023), improves their relationship skills (Olivo et al., 2020), and increases their sense of resiliency (Castro-Olivo, 2014).

Common Core Connections

There are many ways to align social emotional learning with the Common Core. In fact, there are so many that there is not enough space to list them here. Instead, we have created a resource list sharing more examples than you can shake a stick at. See the Technology Connections section for the link.

Application

There are many aspects of social emotional learning, and there is not enough space in this chapter to cover them all. In fact, Larry has written four specific books on student motivation and SEL!

We've decided to highlight in this chapter three key elements that we have found particularly helpful when working with ELLs: developing an asset-based mindset, building a sense of belonging, and teaching about a growth mindset.

ASSET-BASED MINDSET

Looking at our students through the lens of assets instead of deficits is a prerequisite to implementing effective social emotional learning (and, in our opinion, effective teaching) in the classroom.

Though there are specific actions we can take to implement this perspective (and we'll share them later in this chapter), it is much more of a mindset (see Figure 37.1: Changing Mindsets Infographic created by educator Valentina Gonazalez) and not a formula. We are not trying to sugarcoat the challenges our ELLs face. There are many of them, and it is not difficult for us to see them. But, putting just a little energy and intentionality into changing to an asset-based mindset can pay huge dividends. When teachers apply this perspective, students may be more likely to take the risks we are asking them to take in the classroom: to learn a new language, to move into a growth mindset perspective, to struggle through making mistakes and learning from them, and to develop greater perseverance in academic and other tasks.

Even more importantly, when students see us viewing them through an asset-based lens, they may be more likely to view *themselves* the same way. Self-efficacy—having confidence in one's self to accomplish goals—has been shown to enhance English language acquisition through learners stretching themselves toward higher expectations of themselves (Raoofi et al., 2012).

Here are some specific actions teachers can take to apply an asset-based mindset:

- Support and incorporate the use of students' home language as they acquire English (see Strategy 42: Translanguaging for specific ideas). As Professor Ryan Pontier points out, "It's the way people are" (Education Week, 2024)—our students *will* use their home language to communicate, so let's figure out ways to take pedagogical advantage of it!

> Though we share many ways to use translanguaging in our chapter on the topic, one of our favorites is the preview, view, review plan. In this strategy, the lesson is first previewed in the students' home language, then taught in English, and finally reviewed in the home language. Even if the teacher is not fluent in the students' home language, there are many online resources in different languages on just about every subject. See the Technology Connections section for resources.
>
> Of course, artificial intelligence is likely to make this process much easier for everyone, including having the teacher record the lesson in English, followed by AI translating it and using the teacher's voice!

- Look for opportunities to highlight and connect students' prior knowledge (also known as their funds of knowledge (OSPI, n.d.)) to what is being studied in class:
  - In an ELL newcomers class, students can make presentations about the climate and weather in their home countries and learn weather-related terms. Turn it into a Geography and Science lesson, too! Or when teaching about holidays celebrated in the United States, be sure to have students present about the holidays celebrated in their home countries and cultures, too.
  - When teaching about the American Revolution and U.S. Civil War, have students talk with their families and research revolutions and civil wars in their home countries. Presentations and Venn diagrams can follow, not to mention more in-depth knowledge about those events than may be present in classes only consisting of English-proficient students.
  - Look for opportunities to demonstrate their expertise on topics to the entire class. We've had Muslim students present on Islam when studying history and world religions. As we mentioned in the previous chapter, when studying the elements of feudalism in a textbook that said it had been fully eliminated hundreds of years ago, students talked with parents and wrote a letter to the textbook authors disputing their contention based on their families' experiences.

- Ask students to reflect on their life's experiences and identify strengths they have developed as a result of them. Research has shown that this kind of activity can result in students persisting more in the face of academic challenges (Hernandez et al., 2021). Some of the questions the authors of that study recommend we ask include:
  - "What about you has been overlooked or undervalued? What strengths have you gained from your unique life experiences? How can you use these abilities to help you achieve your goals—and help the world?" (Character Lab, 2021). In this

activity, and in others described in this chapter, it is important to provide sentence starters, sentence frames, and word banks to students with lower English proficiency so they can respond to questions.

- Build positive relationships with students while learning about their experiences, interests, and goals by . . . asking them and sharing your own. ELL newcomers can use images on a slideshow or develop a photo collage, while students with a higher English proficiency can respond in English to more specific questions ("What are three things you are most proud of doing in your life?"; "Tell me about a time when you showed kindness/courage/that you were a good friend/student/family member."). It's likely that artificial intelligence translation tools may provide the ability for teachers to also have strength-based conversations with parents/guardians, including questions like "What particular talents and skills would you like me to know about your child?" and "Is there particular expertise or skills that you would feel comfortable sharing in a presentation to our class?" (Alpert, 2020).

- Teach cognates! Cognates are words that have similar spellings, pronunciation, and meaning in more than one language, and 30% to 40% of English words are related to Spanish ones (Colorado, 2007). Obviously, these won't be helpful to speakers of other languages in our ELL classes, but helping our Spanish-speakers understand that they may already understand more than one-third of the English language could be a big confidence-booster!

- Incorporating additional aspects of culturally responsive instruction (see Strategy 36: Culturally Responsive Teaching for more details). Along with the ideas already mentioned in that chapter, and in this one so far, an obvious strategy could be including diverse texts. When teaching about folktales, for example, it could be relatively simple to incorporate ones from students' home cultures as mentor texts.

- Highlight the many economic and cognitive advantages of multilingualism (including the fact that many of our ELLs speak more than one language before they even begin to learn English!). See Strategy 38: Motivation for more ideas on this topic.

- While error correction is an important teacher responsibility (see Strategy 19: Error Correction Strategies), also look for opportunities to both privately and publicly affirm good specific student work and effort. There has been some attention to strength-based statements in math education (Kalinec-Craig, 2017; Jilk, 2016). We try ("try" because it's not always easy to remember or to fit them in) our own version of this idea by looking for opportunities to both praise students for doing specific good work, whether it's in language, in other academics, or in SEL, *and* stating why it's worthy of praise (they remembered a particular grammar rule, they made it a priority to do their homework, they recognized how important community is by helping a classmate, etc.). This idea also fits into developing growth mindsets, which is discussed later in this chapter.

STRATEGY 37: SOCIAL EMOTIONAL LEARNING

SENSE OF BELONGING

Creating the conditions for our students to feel like they "belong" in our classes and at our school is a critical element of social emotional learning. "Belonging" means they feel part of something bigger that supports them and that they can contribute to—a reciprocal arrangement (Fisher & Frey, 2024).

For obvious reasons, English language learners face potential obstacles to feeling a sense of belonging: they are not proficient in English, while most of the people around them are. Likewise, most come from a different country and culture, and many may have been out of school for an extended period of time (see Strategy 33: Supporting ELL Students with Interrupted Formal Education (SIFEs)).

Researchers have found that students who do feel a greater sense of belonging at school tend to have an increased sense of self-efficacy, reach higher levels of academic achievement, and have fewer negative behavioral experiences (Hennessey, 2018). Feeling a sense of belonging can be particularly helpful to students who are experiencing transitions (Walton, 2018), which is what is happening to many of our ELL students.

All of the ideas discussed in the asset-based mindset section can help contribute to ELL students developing a sense of belonging. Here are a few other research-based actions we can take:

- Hang posters on the classroom walls of figures representative of our students' cultures and ones with welcoming multilingual messages. Teachers (and students) can make their own, or many can be found online by searching for "Posters to Support Belonging in the Classroom" (Young, 2024).

- Demonstrate an "empathetic mindset" in classroom management (Young, 2024). This perspective doesn't mean to not enforce an ordered learning environment but to do so with flexibility and caring. "Hard" conversations always need to happen, but we try to do them often with the advice of educator and author Marvin Marshall in mind: "Will what I am about to do or say bring me closer or will it push me away farther from the person with whom I am communicating?" (Ferlazzo, 2009, November 20).

- Listen to students about how they are feeling about school and their personal lives, what ideas they have for improving the class, and if they have any particular concerns (Leonard, 2023). We use a simple weekly multilingual Google form where students can rate how they are feeling about a number of issues on a 1–5 scale, as well as providing questions requiring short written responses. It's critical, of course, to respond to what students write. If not, it can create a worse situation than if we had never asked to begin with!

- Provide mentors to support students. Peer mentoring has been used in many universities to support first-generation college students (Craig, 2016) develop a sense of belonging, and there is no reason to think it can't be equally effective with ELLs in the K-12 environment. We have older students, who are often more advanced

ELLs, meet with newcomer and intermediate ELL students once each week for 10 minutes. You can find additional resources about these efforts in the Technology Connections section.

- Make all school extracurricular activities accessible to ELLs, and explore creating others that speak specifically to ELL students' interests. Research supports the idea that these activities promote a sense of belonging (Mahoney & Cairns, 1997; Mahoney, 2000). Our school's athletic coaches make a point of recruiting from our ELL classes, and we have supported ELLs who wanted to begin clubs for Latinas and one for Afghans (both clubs were open to all, and we were pleasantly surprised that students from other cultures chose to join their friends in them).

- Create opportunities for well-structured small group learning in class. These learning groups can help students develop a sense of teamwork (Nifoussi, n.d.), and the Jigsaw method (see Strategy 9: Jigsaw) in particular has been found to contribute to a sense of student belonging (Leonard, 2023).

- Pronounce students' names correctly. Not doing this basic respectful gesture is linked to student alienation and disconnection (Thomas, n.d.). This holds true for student pronouns, too. If you have a problem with this, we suggest you get over yourself.

- Developing strong teacher/student relationships. Substantial research and common sense point to the role of positive teacher/student relationships contributing to all student's sense of belonging (Allen et al., 2021) and particularly to ELL students (Yough et al., 2023). Many of the recommendations already mentioned in this chapter can be implemented by teachers to develop these kinds of relationships, and there are additional ways, including:
  - Personally greeting students each day (and we don't believe it has to be at the front door as they come in)! We find it helpful just welcoming each student by name as they come in, even if we're at the front getting things set up for the class.
  - Getting to know students' interests and looking for commonalities (sports, music, movies, TV, etc.).
  - Learning about how a student's day and week has been going, and providing emotional support when needed (Allen et al., 2021).

GROWTH MINDSET

Having a growth mindset means you view problems and mistakes as opportunities to learn and obstacles to get through, not as "stop signs." It's a belief that through effort and practice, we can learn and improve. This means we aren't born with natural limitations on what we can learn.

This idea contrasts with a "fixed mindset," which basically indicates the opposite of most or all of these attributes. With such a "fixed mindset," we might not also want to take risks because of fear we could not look "smart."

It's a concept originally developed by researcher Carol Dweck, who also frames it as "The Power of Yet" (TED, 2015). In other words, "I just haven't learned _____ yet."

We might have different mindsets on different days or about different topics. It's not an all or nothing proposition but, rather, a question of which one do we tend to have more of the time.

We also need to be careful about not viewing everything as a mindset "problem." Our students can't "growth mindset" themselves out of societal or institutional challenges like racism or wealth inequity.

However, helping our students develop more of a growth mindset can be a useful skill to develop in their learning journey. Research indicates that having a growth mindset can lead to ELLs being more successful language learners (Hu et al., 2022; Sunman, 2023).

Here are some ways teachers can help their students develop a growth mindset:

- Teach them about a growth mindset. We do a simple lesson that begins with either explicitly defining the words "grow" and "mind" or asking students to define them (depending on their English language proficiency). We then explain that a growth mind-set means that we "grow our mind" by looking at problems as opportunities to learn.

    We then show some short accessible videos such as Yoda's "Do . . . or do not. There is no try" or a clip from the *Meet the Robinsons* cartoon with their signature line, "Keep moving forward!"

    Then, we share some simple mindset stories. You can see examples in Figure 37.2: Growth Mindset Stories. Next, we share a simple paragraph frame (see Figure 37.3: Growth Mindset Paragraph Fame) that students use to write their own, which they then share with each other in a "speed dating"–style process.

- Praise specifics and/or process instead of ability. For example, instead of saying "You're such a great student!" say, "I am so impressed that you studied so hard last night!" The latter comment can reinforce the idea that we improve through effort and not natural ability (Romero, 2015).

- Do not praise effort unconditionally! Dr. Dweck calls this mistake a "false growth mindset." Yes, praise effort, even if it is not successful. But then follow up by saying "Let's talk about what you've tried and what you can try next" (Dweck, 2015).

Teaching Online

Most, if not all, of the suggestions about asset-based learning and developing a growth mindset can be implemented in an online environment. Developing a sense of belonging in an online class, however, is an entirely different "kettle of fish." We can listen to students, use jigsaws in breakout rooms, greet students by name, and do our best to develop positive student/teacher relationships (during distance learning, we tried to schedule monthly short individual meetings with each student to build relationships). But, extracurricular activities, mentors, and posters supporting belonging, not so much.

What Could Go Wrong?

Incorporating students' background knowledge is, in most cases, going to result in a better learning experience for everybody. However, the beliefs that some might have in certain situations could be contrary to the values we have the responsibility to teach. There have been times when we have had to have more than one private conversation with students, and multiple classroom lessons, about the role of women, LGBTQ+ rights, and how to respect different religious beliefs. Keeping eyes open to watch for these issues and carefully planning to deal with them can be exceptional teaching and learning opportunities. Ignoring them can be a recipe for disaster.

We need to build relationships and provide emotional support to our students. But, as educator Alex Venet suggests (we quoted this in the previous chapter, but it's worth repeating), we should not be "trauma detectives" (Venet, 2023). When our students need assistance from professionals with expertise beyond our own, we should refer them to school counselors and to others (assuming, of course, our schools and communities have them available).

Technology Connections

Find many examples of how to connect SEL to academic standards, including the Common Core, at The Best Resources About Connecting SEL to Academic Standards (https://larryferlazzo.edublogs.org/2024/06/18/the-best-resources-about-connecting-sel-to-academic-standards/).

For more ideas on moving away from a "deficit mindset" and toward an "assets mindset," visit The Best Posts on Looking at Our Students Through the Lens of Assets and Not Deficits (https://larryferlazzo.edublogs.org/2016/09/14/the-best-posts-on-looking-at-our-students-through-the-lens-of-assets-not-deficits/).

For resources on incorporating students' home languages into classes, explore The Best Multilingual and Bilingual Sites for Math, Social Studies, and Science (https://larryferlazzo.edublogs.org/2008/10/03/the-best-multilingual-bilingual-sites-for-math-social-studies-science/).

For more ideas on how to promote a sense of belonging, visit The Best Resources for Learning How to Promote a Sense of "Belonging" at School (https://larryferlazzo.edublogs.org/2019/08/15/the-best-resources-for-learning-how-to-promote-a-sense-of-belonging-at-school/).

See The Best Resources on the Value and Practice of Having Older Students Mentoring Younger Ones (https://larryferlazzo.edublogs.org/2013/02/03/the-best-resources-on-the-value-practice-of-having-older-students-mentoring-younger-ones/) for additional resources on peer mentoring programs.

Learn more about developing a growth mindset in the classroom at The Best Resources On Helping Our Students Develop a Growth Mindset (https://larryferlazzo.edublogs.org/2012/10/13/the-best-resources-on-helping-our-students-develop-a-growth-mindset/).

STRATEGY 37: SOCIAL EMOTIONAL LEARNING 399

Attribution

Thanks to Valentina Gonzalez (www.valentinaesl.com) for permission to reprint her infographic.

All figures from this chapter, as well as 11 additional chapters, references, hyperlinked Technology Connections, and more online resources, can be found at www.wiley.com/go/ellteacherstoolbox2.

Changing Mindsets
@ValentinaESL

from:
- My ELLs can't speak English.
- My ELLs aren't able to read on grade level.
- I don't know how to help my ELLs.
- My ELLs seem off task, angry or unhappy.

to:
- What language can my ELLs speak?
- How can I accommodate this text? What resources are available?
- Who can I reach out to for support? Where can I learn more?
- How can I make the classroom environment inviting and safe?

Figure 37.1 Changing Mindsets Infographic   *Source:* Infographic created by Valentina Gonzalez, https://www.valentinaesl.com/, and published with permission

Growth Mindset Stories

From Mr. Ferlazzo:
I have shown a growth mindset here at school. Last year, I taught a very bad lesson on writing a story. Students didn't really know what I was talking about, and I didn't provide them enough support. I was very disappointed in myself. I could have just moved on to the next lesson and forgotten about my mistake. Instead, that night I spent time thinking about what I did wrong and what I could do better. I made a new lesson. The next day, I apologized to the class, and I taught students how to write a story in a much better way. Everybody learned how to write a story. I felt better because I learned from my mistake and did a better job.

From a Student:
I have been able to show a growth mindset. When I came to the United States, I didn't speak that much English. I was afraid to speak English. My friends didn't understand me. Then I started reading books in English and working harder in English class. I didn't give up. My friends began to understand what I was talking about, and that made me feel happy. That's how I learned English.

From a Student:
I showed a growth mindset at home. I was trying to learn how to change the transmission in a car. My dad was trying to teach me, but I was getting frustrated because I couldn't get it right. That night, I tried to remember everything my father had shown me and replayed it in my mind. The next day, I tried again. I remembered what I did wrong before. I learned how to do it. I didn't give up the first time. Now I can do it on my own. I feel successful.

Figure 37.2 Growth Mindset Stories *Source:* Reprinted with permission from *The Student Motivation Handbook,* Larry Ferlazzo, Routledge 2023

Name:	
	My Growth Mindset Story
Topic Sentence:	I have shown a growth mindset at (school, home, playing sports, etc.)
The Problem:	
How the problem affected me and made me feel:	
What action I took to show a growth mindset:	
How showing a growth mindset made me feel:	
Now, put it all together into one paragraph:	

Figure 37.3 Growth Mindset Paragraph Frame *Source:* Reprinted with permission *from The Student Motivation Handbook,* Larry Ferlazzo, Routledge 2023

STRATEGY 38

Motivation

What Is It?

All the many strategies discussed in this book are research-based and very practical. Though we're not big fans of the term "best practices" because we believe so much is dependent on one's local situation, we do think they've all been "best practices" for us!

At the same time, Larry has criticized some education researchers for how they identify ideas to attack and come up with all sorts of "best practice" recommendations, without recognizing that none of it matters if students won't do it! Many have tested these ideas with the most motivated students they can find and in ideal situations (Ferlazzo, 2024, May 29).

We have tried to avoid being guilty of the same mistake by only writing about strategies that we have regularly used successfully in our classrooms. One of the main reasons they've generally (though certainly not always) been successful is because we try to be intentional about creating the conditions where intrinsic motivation can flourish (though we are not averse to giving an occasional extrinsic boost).

This chapter will provide a short overview of what it takes to create those conditions to support student intrinsic motivation, where the desire to learn comes primarily from inside *them*, as opposed to a classroom culture of the extrinsic kind, where the incentive for them to learn comes primarily from *us*.

Why We Like It

Many of us are only with our students for less than 10 percent of their day—and that's just counting school days. It's possible that the allure of carrots we can offer and sticks we can wield during that tiny portion of the day can influence student conduct during the rest of the time, but we're doubtful that can work for most.

Instead, the best strategy for us and our students is to cultivate an environment where their intrinsic motivation can grow. This way, we hope that their desire to learn and practice English will continue far past when the bell rings bringing our class to a close.

Supporting Research

Much research has documented the importance of motivation in language learning (Alizadeh, 2016) and specifically intrinsic motivation (Zhuang, 2023 & Ardasheva et al., 2012).

In addition, there are a massive number of studies identifying the importance of intrinsic motivation in learning *anything*. Larry has written four books on the topic where much of the research is discussed. In summary, intrinsic motivation has been found to lead to higher academic achievement, provides a greater sense of well-being, is long-lasting, and promotes critical and higher-order thinking. Extrinsic motivation, on the other hand, tends to reduce long-term interest, effort, and creativity (Ferlazzo, 2023).

Researchers have identified four major elements of what is needed to support the development of intrinsic motivation (Ryan & Deci, 2000):

1. Autonomy: Does the learner have some degree of control over what they are being asked to do and how it can be done?
2. Competence: Does the learner feel like they have good odds of being successful in doing the task or project?
3. Relatedness: Does the learner feel that the activity helps them feel more connected to others whom they like and/or respect?
4. Relevance: Does the learner feel that the work is interesting, valuable, and/or fun to them, and useful to their present lives and/or hopes and dreams for the future?

Zoltán Dörnyei and Kata Csizér (1998), researchers of motivation among language learners, have identified many similar elements in their conclusions about what is required to support student motivation.

Common Core Connections

Depending on how you use the two read alouds in this chapter and how you ask students to respond to them, they can easily be connected to multiple reading and writing standards. However, as in Strategy 39: Social Emotional Learning, the main purpose behind the activities in this chapter is to help create the conditions where students *want to do* the many other strategies in this book that directly connect to the standards. The standards won't matter if students won't do the work corresponding to them!

Application

Many things in our world are not an either/or proposition, and that includes motivation. We can be motivated by both intrinsic and extrinsic rewards—just as we are motivated to write this book by both the excitement of learning from the process *and* the additional income that it can produce for us.

In addition, there are certainly times we use extrinsic rewards and negative consequences in our classroom, and we don't beat ourselves up over it!

It's a question of which side do we tend to fall on, and we like to believe it tends to be on the intrinsic side of things.

Here are a few ways we've tried to create the conditions where intrinsic motivation can thrive.

ACTIONS TO SUPPORT AUTONOMY

Providing opportunities for student choice supports autonomy. We discuss some ways to do this in Strategy 16: Choice Boards/Learning Menus, in Strategy 22: Project-Based Learning/Project-Based Learning, and in Strategy 11: Inductive Learning.

Other ways to provide choice include giving students the option to decide who they want to work with in small groups, where they want to sit, and what ways they want to make presentations (with digital tools or with a paper poster).

If you are going to offer time in class for independent language learning practice, there are many excellent online tools. See the Technology Connections section for suggestions.

GOAL-SETTING

Setting goals and, specifically, students setting their own goals, has been found to be an effective way to support student autonomy and can lead to increased motivation (Orzechowska & Polok, 2019) and increased language learning (Ferlazzo, 2023, February 18).

We've tried *many* different types of goal-setting strategies and forms. You can see two of the forms we've used with our students in Figure 38.1: Goal-Setting Form One and Figure 38.2: Goal-Setting Form Two (we generally make both multilingual depending on the home languages of our students that year).

Based on our experience, we're not really sure any actual goal-setting form is more effective than any other.

Rather, the key factor in determining the goal-setting strategy's success is if time can be made for a regular system of students reviewing the progress they are making—or not making—in achieving their goals and creating opportunities to adjust them.

We have used Figure 38.2: Goal-Setting Form One as more of a "reset" activity midway through the school year, but it can be used at any time. We initially complete a section a day on the first page (numbers 1 to 11), and they share their answers with classmates. It could be called a "visioning exercise" to get students seriously thinking about their future—perhaps for the first time in their lives. Of course, we also complete our own as a model.

Then, they complete the second page, consisting of more immediate actions they can take to help realize those longer-term goals, what challenges they might experience in taking those actions, and how we as teachers can best support them.

Students turn in both sheets to us. We make copies for us (and in case students lose theirs), return the originals, and have students tape or glue them into their class notebooks. Then, perhaps once each week, we'll include these questions in our Warm-Up or

STRATEGY 38: MOTIVATION

Do-Now: "Please review both of your goal sheets. Which, if any of the actions you said you wanted to take, have you done this week? Were there any times you didn't feel like doing them but you did anyway? If so, what helped? Are there any changes you want to make to your long-term goals or on any other part of the sheets?"

Connecting very long-term goals with very short-term ones, and regularly revisiting them, has sometimes had some success.

Figure 38.2: Goal-Setting Form Two is another sheet we've used with some success, though it tends to take more time.

Once each month, we meet individually with each student (usually while the whole class is working more independently on a project), and have them complete the form.

Each Friday after they complete their weekly formative assessment (see Strategy 49: Assessment), they generally do independent work of their choice on laptops. During that time, peer tutors or a student teacher or a bilingual aide have quickly scored their assessments and returned them. While they're working on their laptops, they complete Figure 38.3: Goal Review Form, and, importantly, we walk around and check in with them about how they did in relation to their goals and if they want to make any changes.

We should point out that we don't view these goal-setting forms and the ongoing review processes themselves as primarily a language acquisition activity. That's why we use Google Translate to make sure that all the forms are very accessible to all students. It's a form of translanguaging (see Strategy 42: Translanguaging) that helps students maximize their "appetite" for learning English. Having students clear on their English learning goals and their strategies to accomplish is are more important than their potential learning (or not) a few more words in English and having less clarity on their goals.

A final note on goal-setting. We typically preface any goal-setting conversation with students with a simple one-on-one conversation starter. We begin by drawing a line across a sheet of paper, with a "0" on one end and a "100" on the other. We explain that the "0" would signify they were putting no effort into learning English and the "100" would indicate they were doing everything possible to learn it. We then gave them the paper and asked them to make a mark where they think they fall on the line.

During our career, practically *every* student marked where we would have said they were based on our observations.

We then ask them about their future hopes and dreams, and we discuss how learning English is going to be critical for them achieving those goals. Next, we put a mark on the line that is perhaps 20 or 30 points higher than they had said they were presently at and ask, "What would it take for you to get here?" (Chance, 2022).

That conversation then leads into whatever goal-setting form we may be using at that time.

ACTIONS TO SUPPORT COMPETENCE

Several strategies discussed elsewhere in this book can contribute toward students' feelings of competence. These include teaching classmates through jigsaws (see Strategy 9: Jigsaw), helping students develop a growth mind-set (see Strategy 37: Social Emotional Learning), and the many scaffolds we discuss throughout the book, like sentence starters and writing frames (Strategy 14: Writing Frames and Writing Structures), along with others discussed in the differentiation infographics located in many chapters.

Here are a few strategies we like to use that can promote students competence.

VISUALIZATION

Professor Zoltán Dörnyei did extensive research on motivation and language learning. One area he found particularly effective was visualization, also known as mental imagery (Powels, 2019; Dörnyei, 2008; Cambridge University Press ELT, 2016). We have applied this kind of guided visualization in many of our classes to great positive effect (you can see a link in the Technology Connections section to many posts on the topic, including the results of "teacher action research" in Larry's classes).

When we do guided visualizations, we first begin with a lesson on its value, including showing videos of athletes practicing it. We also review extensive research showing its effectiveness (see Figure 38.4: Visualization Read Aloud). The next day, students enter a darkened classroom with low-meditative music playing in the background. We explain that our research shows that students will improve their English if they participate, but if they don't want to, they can put their heads down and rest.

We then lead the class through a guided visualization where they are being successful in some kind of language acquisition or practice, including the following:

- We lead them through a specific activity where they have to use English (writing an essay, making a presentation, going on a date), perhaps face a challenge, and then overcome it and succeed.

- We ask students to think of several activities they would like to do well when speaking English (order a meal in a restaurant, go on a date, make a presentation, write an essay, etc.). We then ask students to imagine themselves doing those activities smoothly and easily. They silently visualize themselves doing it.

- We ask students to quickly review their goal sheet and choose to silently visualize themselves accomplishing one of their goals. Researchers suggest visualization can be particularly effective when people see themselves accomplishing the tasks needed to achieve their goals (Dean, 2023), so we try to encourage that kind of imagery. For example, in addition to having students see themselves speaking English fluently on a date, we also suggest they visualize seeing themselves studying English successfully for a test or practicing speaking English with friends.

- We might explain to students what we will be doing in class that day and do a guided visualization of them doing it well.

We've even had students who asked if they could try leading the class in a visualization, and those have usually turned out well. Now, *that's* an opportunity to develop a sense of competence!

The added benefit of doing this kind of visualization activity at the beginning of a class is that student calmness and focus tend to carry over to the remaining class time.

You can find more resources about visualization, including the results of Larry's Teacher Action Research on it, in the Technology Connections section. An easy way he evaluates how students feel about it is by having them answer two questions anonymously: Are you actively participating in the visualizations? Do you think it's helping you learn English?

TEMPORAL COMPARISONS

"Temporal comparisons" is a fancy term for comparing how you're doing with your own past results, instead of comparing yourself to how others are doing (known as "social comparisons"). Temporal comparisons have been found to help students develop insight and pride (Gürel et al., 2020) instead of feelings of dissatisfaction that can result from social comparisons (Tyler, 2001).

Here are some ways we promote temporal comparisons with our ELLs so that students can see their own progress (some of these also come from Larry's book, *The Student Motivation Handbook*):

- Students record themselves reading the same text for a minute or two at various times during the year and can listen to their improved fluency.
- Give students a list of vocabulary words they will be using at the beginning of a unit. Have them check off the ones they know, and then collect the sheets. After the unit is completed, return the same papers and ask them again to check words they know.
- Ask students to keep the essays or stories they write at the beginning of the year (or we keep them). Then, at the end of the year, return them and have students rewrite them using the skills they've developed since that time.
- Have students complete a set of clozes near the beginning of the year. Then, have them complete the same ones midyear and at the end of the year so they can compare their scores and see their progress.
- In Strategy 49: Assessment, we share how we have students periodically view their weekly formative assessment scores, and they are displayed visually as a bar graph. When appropriate, students can take photos of their progress to show their families.

SHOUT-OUT WHITEBOARD

We borrowed the idea of a shout-out whiteboard from our colleague Nicole Scrivner. We have a medium-sized portable whiteboard where, at the end of each class, we write the names of a few students highlighting their success ("Most Cooperative Classmates"; "Best Players in Today's Game"; "Today's Best Sentence Writer"). We, of course, make sure that everyone's name appears on it for some reason at least once every two or three weeks.

Students tend to love it and generally take photos when their name is on it so they can show their families.

ACTIONS TO SUPPORT RELATEDNESS

Some studies suggest that schools taking steps to promote a sense of student belonging could be the most effective way that they can enhance student motivation (Xie, 2022), and "belonging" is just another word for "relatedness."

So many of the strategies discussed in this book can promote relatedness, including the teacher/student and student/student kind. Specifically, Strategy 37: Social Emotional Learning has a list of activities under belonging, and there's no need to repeat them all again here.

We would just like to highlight three of the most important and easiest relatedness strategies to implement:

1. Correctly pronounce students' names! As one of Larry's students once told him: "I remember when several teachers mispronounced my name and it made me feel different. When a teacher tried making an effort in trying to pronounce my name, it made me feel like they actually care."
2. Use the weekly online Google form for students to rate how they are feeling, discussed in more detail in Strategy 37: Social Emotional Learning.
3. Implement introductory activities described in Strategy 43: Beginning the School Year, particularly the "Partner Introductions" section and "I Am" project.

ACTIONS TO SUPPORT RELEVANCE

Of course, most of the strategies discussed in this book hit the mark on student "relevance," since most of our students want to stay in the United States and need to learn English to be successful. We do, however, try to make it even more concrete whenever possible. For example, when we study jobs vocabulary, we'll incorporate an accessible lesson where students can research careers. The methods we use to connect to student background knowledge (discussed in Strategy 5: Activating Prior Knowledge and in Strategy 37: Social Emotional Learning) can enhance students' feelings that classroom lessons are relevant.

Remember, the word "relevance" can also be used to describe something that we enjoy doing. Larry found a lengthy article on door-to-door salespeople fascinating, but it isn't relevant to what he is doing in his life. This perspective can be applied to playing games in the classroom (see Strategy 23: Learning Games for Reading and Writing and Strategy 31: Learning Games for Speaking and Listening). The "relevance" can be the fun of playing the games with friends, whether or not the content in the game is interesting to them.

An activity that we find useful in helping students feel like our class is especially relevant to their hopes and dreams is a series we do throughout the year on the advantages of being bilingual.

We have a lengthy lesson plan on the topic in our book, *The ESL/ELL Teacher's Survival Guide*, but it's pretty easy to construct your own with the resources that are in the Technology Connections section.

We have also included a simple Read Aloud on the topic that could be a good introduction to the idea in any ELL class. See Figure 38.5: Bilingual or Multilingual Advantages Read-Aloud.

Teaching Online

Nothing about teaching online is easy, but most of the activities listed in this chapter can be done online without too much trouble. Visualization, however, is probably the exception. Especially with cameras off, we would not bet on many students actually participating in the activity when they could be looking at their phone or surfing the Web instead.

What Could Go Wrong?

As with all the strategies in this book, some of the ideas in this chapter may very well not work the first (or even the second) time you try them, and they may never work with the particular class you have that year. As education researcher Dylan Wiliam has said, "Everything works somewhere; nothing works everywhere" (Smith, 2016). For example, sometimes one kind of goal sheet works well with one class, but not with another. If something doesn't work, don't worry about it and move on.

We've always found that the vast majority of our students actively participate in the visualization activities. However, even though they can easily opt out of it by just sleeping, now and then a student will feel like they want to disrupt it by talking or making noise. We try to pre-empt this potential problem by asking students to respect the "rules" when we introduce the idea. But sometimes a serious conversation is required after a violation takes place.

Keep track of the names you're putting on the shout-out whiteboard! If not, you might miss putting someone's name up there every two or three weeks. If you do, they may or may not say something to you about it, but they will remember!

Technology Connections

More information on student motivation can be found at The Best Posts and Articles On "Motivating" Students (https://larryferlazzo.edublogs.org/2010/05/17/my-best-posts-on-motivating-students/).

The Best Sites Students Can Use for Independent Practice (https://larryferlazzo.edublogs.org/2022/07/19/the-best-sites-students-can-use-for-independent-practice/) provides links to many online language learning tools we use in our classroom.

Learn more about visualization activities at Best Posts on Helping Students "Visualize Success" (https://larryferlazzo.edublogs.org/2010/12/23/my-best-posts-on-helping-students-visualize-success/).

For more information on the advantages of speaking more than one language, including many videos that could be shown in class, visit "The Best Resources for Learning the Advantages to Being Bilingual or Multilingual" (https://larryferlazzo.edublogs.org/2011/02/16/the-best-resources-for-learning-the-advantages-to-being-bilingual/).

Attribution

Our asking students what they wanted others to say about them far in the future was inspired by Dan Pink's "One Sentence Project" (https://www.danpink.com/2011/01/whats-your-sentence-the-video/).

Thanks to Luther Burbank High School teacher Nicole Scrivner for inspiring us with her shout-out whiteboard idea!

All figures from this chapter, as well as 11 additional chapters, references, hyperlinked Technology Connections, and more online resources, can be found at www.wiley.com/go/ellteacherstoolbox2.

Name _____

NEXT YEAR

1. My school goal for next year is _____.
2. My outside-of-school goal for next year is _____.
3. Next year, I want my friends to describe me by saying I am _____.
4. Next year, I want my teachers to describe me by saying I am _____.
5. Next year, I want my parents/family to describe me by saying I am _____.

10 YEARS FROM NOW

6. In 10 years, I want to _____.
7. In 10 years, I want my friends to describe me by saying I am _____.
8. In 10 years, I want my parents/family members to describe me by saying I am _____.

20 YEARS FROM NOW

9. In 20 years, I want to _____.
10. In 20 years, I want my partner/wife/husband/friends to describe me by saying I am _____.
11. In 20 years, I want my children (if I have them) to describe me by saying I am _____.

Figure 38.1 Goal-Setting Form One

Things I can do NOW to help achieve these goals:

1.
2.
3.

When I don't feel like doing these things, actions I can take to help me get back on track:

1.
2.
3.

When I don't feel like doing these things, actions my teachers can take to help me get back on track:

1.
2.
3.

Figure 38.1 (*Continued*)

Name _____ Date _____

1. **These are things I've done well to learn English during the past month (circle all that apply):**

   Worked hard and was not distracted

   Helped my classmates

   Attended Zero Period English class before school

   Practiced English at home (did computer work, watched English language movies/videos/tv shows, spoke English with family and friends, read a book in English)

   Studied and did well on tests

2. **These have been the scores on my last four Friday tests:**

   _____ _____ _____ _____

3. **I want the scores on my next four Friday tests to be:**

   _____ _____ _____ _____

4. **These are actions I'm going to take to learn English better (circle all that apply):**

   Work on the computer 15 minutes at home each school day on Quill, Raz Kids, ESL Video, Brainpop, Adobe Express, Blooket, Quizizz, Wordwall, other (write here) _____

   Attend Zero Period English class before school

   Work harder in class and not be distracted

   Be an assistant peer tutor (help classmates focus more, help classmates understand things)

   Study on my own before the Friday test

   Read a book and complete the "Reading a Book" form

   Speak English with my family and friends

   Watch English language movies/videos/television shows

Figure 38.2 Goal-Setting Form Two

Name: _____

1. What did you do to learn English in the past week? Check all that apply:
   ☐ Worked hard and was not distracted.
   ☐ Helped my classmates.
   ☐ Went to the 7:45 a.m. class.
   ☐ Practiced English at home (did work on the computer, watched English language videos, spoke English with friends/family, read a book in English).
   ☐ Studied a lot for the test.

2. What was your goal for today's test?

3. What was your actual score in today's test?

4. Did you meet your goal?

5. Look at your goal for next week's score. You can keep it the same, or change it. If you want to change it, cross out the old goal and write the new one. Write your goal for next week here, too.

6. What can you do to learn English in the next week? Check all that apply.
   ☐ Work harder and not be distracted.
   ☐ Help my classmates.
   ☐ Go to the 7:45 a.m. class.
   ☐ Practice English at home (do work on the computer, watch English language videos, speak English with friends/family, read a book in English).
   ☐ Study a lot for the test.

7. Do you have other ideas of actions *you* can take to learn English, or ideas on how Mr. Ferlazzo can help you learn English?

Figure 38.3 Goal Review Form

Visualization means seeing yourself in your mind doing things very well before you have to do them. Many athletes use visualization to improve their skills—like soccer players Pele[1] and Lionel Messi. Messi said, "Visualization is a key part of my training. I imagine myself scoring goals and making a difference in every game."[2] Basketball and baseball players say the same thing.[3] Members of the U.S. Special Forces use visualization, too.[4] Scientists have found that people who visualize doing well in job interviews are more likely to get a job.[5] Scientists say visualization works best where you have to do the most thinking to be successful. A lot of thinking is involved in learning a new language![6] Some scientists think that people who visualize themselves speaking English may be able to learn the language faster.[7]

Sources:

1. SportsShrinkTV (2013). *Mental Rehearsal for Sport - the Pele Way.* www.youtube.com/watch?v=Vw5C7AelwZ8
2. MindTraining.net (n.d.). *Lionel Messi - Motivational Soccer / Football Quotes, Mental Profile & Biography.* https://mindtraining.net/motivational-quotes/sports-champions/lionel-messi.php#
3. James, C. (2018, December 26). In baseball, mental coaches were once seen as for the "weak-minded." Now they're essential. *The Washington Post.* https://www.washingtonpost.com/sports/2018/12/26/baseball-mental-coaches-were-once-seen-weak-minded-now-theyre-essential/
4. Akil, B. (2009, November 9). How the Navy Seals increased passing rates. *Psychology Today.* https://www.psychologytoday.com/intl/blog/communication-central/200911/how-the-navy-seals-increased-passing-rates
5. Barker, E. (n.d.). Can your imagination improve your next job interview? *Barking Up the Wrong Tree.* https://bakadesuyo.com/2012/01/can-your-imagination-improve-your-next-job-in/
6. Ferlazzo, L. (2010, April 1). Mental imagery success. *Larry Ferlazzo's Websites of the Day.* larryferlazzo.edublogs.org/2010/04/01/mental-imagery-success/
7. Thornbury, S. (2011, December 26). V is for visualization. *An A-Z of ELT.* https://scottthornbury.wordpress.com/2011/12/26/v-is-for-visualization/

Figure 38.4 Visualization Read Aloud

We are going to try this in our classroom.

When you come into the classroom tomorrow and each day for the next two weeks, the room will be dark and the lights will be out. Please come silently and close your eyes. I will talk and ask you to imagine yourselves using English in some way. If you want to do it, please just sit up with your eyes closed. It's okay if you don't want to do it. If you don't, you can sit up with your eyes closed or put your head down. But please don't speak during the visualization. It may last five minutes.

At the end of two weeks we'll decide together if we want to continue it or stop.

Figure 38.4 (Continued)

Scientists and others have recently found that people get many benefits from learning English (and other languages):

Learning English can increase your income by 20 percent to 25 percent. It's a skill that employers want.

Learning another language "exercises" the brain as if it were a muscle. Because of that increased flexibility, bilingual people are better learners, have a better memory, and can do more things at once and better than people who speak only one language. They are also better at solving problems.

People who are bilingual can delay the beginning of Alzheimer's disease by an average of four years over people who speak only one language. Being bilingual strengthens the part of the brain that gets attacked first by the disease.

Sources: M. de Lotbiniere, "Research Backs English as Key to Development," *The Guardian,* July 5, 2011; "Why It Pays to Be Bilingual," Voxy, Feb. 15, 2011, retrieved from http://voxy.com/blog; D. Marsh, "Languages Smarten Up Your Brain," *The Guardian,* Jan. 25, 2010; C. Dreifus, "The Bilingual Advantage," *New York Times,* May 30, 2011; S. S. Wang, "Building a More Resilient Brain," *Wall Street Journal,* Oct. 12, 2010.

Figure 38.5 Bilingual or Multilingual Advantages Read Aloud *Source:* Republished from *The ESL/ELL Teacher's Survival Guide,* second edition, Jossey-Bass, 2022. Used with permission

STRATEGY 39
Peer Teaching and Learning

What Is It?

Our students have many abilities, and those can include assisting their classmates to acquire language, academic, and life-skills knowledge. In several previous strategies, we've included activities in which students have prepared materials and lessons to teach their classmates. This strategy highlights five additional ways we've encouraged our ELL students to act as teachers.

Why We Like It

We like this strategy for so many reasons! It puts into action the value of looking at our students through the lens of assets instead of deficits; it heightens levels of student engagement; and, as we discuss in the next section, it is exceptionally effective in facilitating learning for the teacher and the student.

Supporting Research

Researchers have found that knowing you will be teaching others enhances your own learning ability (Washington University, St. Louis, 2014). The results of other studies reinforce this conclusion and suggest that peer tutoring helps the academics of the tutor and the student receiving the assistance (McIntyre, 2022). In addition, researchers found that the tutor didn't have to be an academic star in order to be effective (Sparks, 2015).

Common Core Connections

The Standards being met in this strategy depend on which activity students are doing at the time. All five of the exercises described here meet multiple Standards in all four domains.

Application

Here are five ways we have facilitated peer teaching and learning with English language learners.

EMPATHY PROJECT

Luther Burbank High School, where Larry teaches and where Katie formerly taught (she now works at another high school), has a heavy emphasis on restorative practices and social emotional learning. School administrators made *empathy* a focus of one month and asked Pam Buric, a talented colleague, if she would have her intermediate ELLs write short vignettes about their immigrant experiences (see the Technology Connections section for links to access them). Though they didn't use a graphic organizer to plan their writing, they later used Figure 39.1: Personal Story Outline to teach ELL beginners. This figure represents the same outline used in the intermediate students' stories. After the intermediates completed writing their stories, Pam reserved the library for several periods each day over the course of a week and invited other teachers to sign up for a one-period visit to listen and learn from some of our school's ELLs. The response was overwhelming, and there wasn't enough space or time to accommodate all the interested classes.

Prior to coming to the library, teachers from the visiting classes used the lesson plan in Figure 39.2: Story Sharing and had their students complete the prompt in Figure 39.3: Writing Prompt: Building Empathy. They arrived at the library to find the ELL students seated on one side of various tables. Each student from the listening class arrived with copies of Figure 39.4: Story-Sharing Listening Chart and took a seat across from the ELL students. The students began to tell their stories as the listeners took notes. Every several minutes, the teachers would announce it was time to move, and the listening students moved down a seat in a sort of speed-dating progression. This process took the entire class period. The following day, the ELL class debriefed about the previous day's experience while waiting for a new class to arrive at the library. The listening students also reflected in their own classroom at the same time.

It was universally hailed as a powerful experience by students and faculty members alike and will become a regular occurrence at the school. However, it didn't stop there.

The week after the ELL intermediates completed this exercise at the library, they went into Larry's beginners class. There, using the graphic organizer in Figure 39.1, the intermediates worked one-on-one with the beginner students to help *them* write their own stories (you can find those at a link in the Technology Connections section). Then, while spread between two different classrooms, the beginners did a speed-dating process with the intermediates and told them their stories.

As mentioned previously, the school has made a decision to do this activity annually. However, we are making one change—in the future, the non-ELL students will also be writing their own personal stories (about a challenge that they have faced that may or may not be a story of immigration), which they will share with the ELL students. We feel that making it a reciprocal process will further strengthen our school's sense of community.

STRATEGY 39: PEER TEACHING AND LEARNING

PEER TUTORING

Luther Burbank High School supports juniors and seniors who might ordinarily have a period as a teacher's assistant to consider, instead, becoming a peer tutor (it's an official class on their transcript). Some of these peer tutors are advanced ELLs, others are proficient bilinguals, and others are English-only students. Peer tutors don't necessarily have to speak the home language of our ELL beginning and intermediate students. One thing they all share, however, is a desire to help ELLs.

Sometimes this help means circulating around the class as we are teaching and stepping in to assist students who are experiencing challenges with the lesson. Other times it's working intensively one-on-one with a new arrival to the school. More recently, the school has made an effort to increase the number of peer tutors so that there is a ratio of one peer tutor for every three ELLs and sometimes it's even one-to-one. With these numbers, each peer tutor can be "assigned" to regularly work with the same small group of ELL students.

All these situations begin with the peer tutors watching a brief video created by English teacher Carol Salva sharing suggestions on how volunteers can assist ELLs (a link to it can be found in the Technology Connections section). Peer tutors also receive an advice sheet (see Figure 39.5: Peer Tutor Advice/Guidelines). We also take a few seconds at the beginning of each class to brief them on the upcoming lesson. Oftentimes, this means that we have a slide open at the teacher's computer, and a "lead" peer tutor takes a photo of the slide which shares what they will be doing that day; then they share the image in a group text. Peer tutors provide us weekly feedback on their experiences through a weekly Google form.

Peer tutors work with ELL students doing a variety of tasks, including:

- Following up with projects being done in the class that they have not completed
- Practicing English conversations (see Strategy 25: Conversation Practice)
- Playing games (see Strategy 23: Learning Games for Reading and Writing and Strategy 33: Learning Games for Speaking and Listening)
- Having students complete worksheets reinforcing what we are doing in class (see the Technology Connections section for sources of free—and high-quality—ELL worksheets)

In addition, during time when we are giving whole-class instruction that peer tutors don't need to pay attention to in order to subsequently work with students, they can do other work, including:

- Preparing personalized online games for the class, reinforcing concepts we have been learning
- Writing "text walk-throughs" for online video games (see Strategy 33: Learning Games for Speaking and Listening)
- Creating Sentence Navigators (see Bonus Strategy 3: Sentence Navigators and Sentence Builders) that reflect the thematic units we are studying

But the peer tutors are not working all the time. They are students, after all, and not paid staff. Our expectation is that they are fully present to the ELL students or the work of the class at least 60 percent of the time (though they are welcome to work more!). The rest of the time, they can use our class as a study hall to complete work from other classes, enjoy a snack (twice a year they can choose one that we'll order for them and keep in a cabinet), or step outside and look at their phone for a few minutes.

Here's what a typical day in Larry's class looks like with peer tutors:

- **Beginning of class:** Lead peer tutor takes a photo of the plan for the day and shares it on a group text with the other peer tutors. Other peer tutors distribute folders and materials to students (this maximizes learning time because students don't have to pick them up on their own). Students go directly into their small learning groups led by peer tutors.

- **First 10 minutes of class:** Students work in small groups—leveled by English proficiency—led by peer tutors. They might use the class grammar book, a "True Stories" book (Ferlazzo, 2023), or another workbook. Midway through the time, peer tutors lead an activity where they dictate some of the sentences they have just read and students write them down on mini-whiteboards.

- **Next 10 minutes:** All students return to learn about the next activity. Two or three times a week, it's oral practice. Students have glued hundreds of conversational starters and "fill-in-the-blank" frames for responses in their notebooks. On those days, students work in peer tutor groups practicing ones of their choice for 8 to 10 minutes. See Strategy 8: Vocabulary and Strategy 25: Conversation Practice for copies of those prompts. On days they don't do oral practice, the class moves directly into the next activity and spends that extra time on it.

- **Next 20 minutes:** Larry briefly introduces an activity that the peer tutors will lead in small groups for about 15 or 20 minutes focused on the theme the class is studying during that week (school, food, health, home, community, etc.). It might be the picture word inductive model (see Strategy 17: Using Photos or Other Images in Reading and Writing), a sequencing activity (see Strategy 6: Sequencing), an activity from a textbook, or a frame for writing (see Strategy 14: Writing Frames and Writing Structures). About once a week students spend a longer time period practicing with peer tutors and performing short humorous dialogues (related to the theme) that they will perform to another small group and then in front of the entire class with a mic.

- **Next 10 minutes:** Next, the class comes back together and Larry will give a brief grammar lesson. Students then go back into their peer tutor-led groups for 10 minutes or so to complete the exercises related to the lesson.

- **Final five minutes:** Larry finishes up the class with some games from Quizizz, Kahoot, or Blooket that are related to either the theme or the grammar topic they are studying.

There are often exceptions to this schedule, including a formative assessment every Friday and weekly time for a dialogue journal (see later in this chapter). But this routine is more typical than atypical for Larry's class in recent years, and the accelerated learning that has resulted from making peer tutors integral to his instructional practice has paid off with more rapid student acquisition of English.

PEER MENTORING

Having peer mentors, especially for ELL newcomers, enhances student-to-student relationships and provides needed support. Peer *mentors* are distinguished from peer *tutors* by the fact that their job is not to assist with daily academic tasks. Instead, mentors are there to provide overall school and life counsel. Older (though that is not always the case) trained student mentors who are ELL intermediates or English-proficient students meet weekly with their mentees to build relationships, discover problems (at school and at home), offer advice, and regularly strategize with teachers on how they can best be helpful.

Oftentimes, these peer mentors are students in Larry's other classes, and he makes arrangements with the teachers of ELL students (students from his class and from other ELL classes) during that period to have them briefly pulled out of class.

See Figure 39.6: Peer Mentor Guidelines for an example of the kind of training these mentors receive from us. The mentor and mentee are excused from one of their classes for at least 15 minutes each week to take a walk around the school campus and chat about their experiences. Mentors then complete Figure 39.7: Peer Mentor Form, which is returned to Larry for his use or for the use of other ELL teachers.

In addition, peer mentors are often given a "focus question" each week to ask their mentees. Figure 39.8 Peer Mentor Focus Questions shares a few examples.

SISTER CLASSES

Dialogue journals are a well-known practice in ELL classrooms (VanderMolen, 2011) in which students typically write letters to their teachers in notebooks, and teachers then respond back, often by including some recast sentences (ones that were originally written by their students with mistakes and are now rewritten correctly by the teacher in their response). They can be a very effective learning tool. However, we can't imagine how any secondary teacher can find the time to do them.

But that doesn't mean we can't modify the idea and use it in our classrooms. We periodically use dialogue journals with the difference being that we arrange with the teacher of a mainstream class to have their students agree to be journal partners with our ELLs. In these cases, the mainstream teacher recognizes the benefits that his or her students gain from being teachers and recasting sentences as well as the opportunity to learn about the lives of ELL students.

We've found that this kind of activity works best when all students write using pseudonyms for the first few weeks, each writing in the dialogue journal once each week. This anonymity creates an air of suspense and mystery that culminates in a joint social gathering with food that occurs either during class time or during a special lunch when identities are unveiled. Dialogue journals continue for a few more weeks afterwards, but we end it while enthusiasm is still high—we would recommend a two-month period of time at most. However, the relationships that students gain during the process often continue through the rest of the school year and beyond. See Figure 39.9 Dialogue Journal Prompts for a sample of the weekly prompts we use in our dialogue journals.

These kinds of sister classes don't have to be restricted to the physical location of your school. Larry's ELL geography classes often connect with English classes in the regions of the world they are studying. Typically, after learning about a country, Larry's students will record themselves asking questions about the country they are studying and post them on their class blog. Then, an English class in that country will record themselves responding to those questions and posing their own questions about life in the United States. Larry's students respond, and then this short and sweet project is done. You can find links in the Technology Connections section for ways to find classes around the world who might be interested in doing this kind of activity with your school.

EVERYONE IS A TEACHER

We regularly emphasize that our class is a learning community and that we all need to help each other learn. One day, however, we made this idea more of a central focus to our lesson. We explained to our students that English is hard to learn (no surprise to them!), they only had a few years of high school left, and that it was going to take more than one or two teachers to help everybody learn. So, we all had to be teachers. We shared some ideas to illustrate the concept ("I'm a teacher when I speak English because I'm an example"; "I'm a teacher when I come to school because I'm a model for others") and then invited students to contribute other ideas. They came fast and furious, and students made posters such as the one in Figure 39.10: Everyone Is a Teacher Poster.

Students took it seriously on different levels, but there was clearly one huge benefit—it was far more energizing to students and to us if we said to an off-task student "Everyone is a teacher!" instead of saying "Angela, please get back to work."

We also created a simple form listing the actions the class had determined they could do as teachers and had them glue it in their writer's notebook (see Figure 39.11: Everyone Is a Teacher Goal-Setting Chart). Each Friday, students graded themselves on how they had done in that area during the previous week, but we didn't look at it. We had students share their grades with a partner of their choice and also identify one—just one—area they wanted to improve on in the coming week. They then shared that goal with the entire class.

Though we made it clear that the grades were for their own personal assessments, we found that many students made a point of showing it to us—they were proud of their honesty in the self-assessment. See Figure 39.12: Student Example of Goal-Setting Chart for an example.

We've tried lots of goal-setting strategies over the years, but this appears to be among the most effective, if not *the* most effective.

Teaching Online

Though it's more challenging to do so online, we have had peer tutors work with small groups or one-on-one with ELL students in breakout rooms. We have also found that working with Sister Classes from other countries and sharing Dialogue Journals is also doable in an online environment.

Realistically, though, The Empathy Project and Everyone Is a Teacher is a "bridge too far" to do online.

What Could Go Wrong?

Peer tutors are not teachers, no matter how competent they may appear to be at times. Don't dump too much responsibility on them. And keep them happy—encouraging words and special treats now and then can't hurt (we also always pay their way when we go on field trips)! Remember, they are not getting paid to be tutors.

Differentiation Recommendations

Newcomers (Preliterate or Low Literacy in Home Language): Ideally, there are enough peer tutors so that the ratio can often be one-to-one for students in this category. However, you probably want to ensure that this is "fluid," so that, if there is only one student in this category, they also have a chance to work with other students. Students can also be encouraged to draw in their dialogue journals.	**Newcomers (Literate in Home Language):** Work in small groups with peer tutors and write with dialogue journal prompts.
Intermediate ELLs: Can fully participate in empathy project activities. Can be a student to whom newcomers are writing to in dialogue journals. Can be a peer mentor to newcomer students.	**Advanced ELLs:** Fully participate in Empathy Project activities. Can be a student to whom newcomers are writing to in dialogue journals. Can be a peer mentor to newcomer and intermediate students.

Technology Connections

To learn more about the empathy project and to read our students' stories—which you can feel free to use as models with your students—visit What ELLs Taught Our School in a Week-Long Empathy Project (http://larryferlazzo.edublogs.org/2017/04/21/guest-post-what-ells-taught-our-school-in-a-week-long-empathy-project/).

For additional ideas on how we use peer tutors to support ELLs, visit The Best Resources on Peer Tutors (https://larryferlazzo.edublogs.org/2023/02/04/the-best-resources-on-peer-tutors/).

See the video created by Carol Salva that we show our peer tutors, as well as other resources we use to help them learn to support ELL students, at The Best Resources to Help Prepare Tutors and Volunteers in ELL Classes – And, Boy, Do I Need Suggestions! (https://larryferlazzo.edublogs.org/2021/08/29/the-best-resources-to-help-prepare-tutors-volunteers-in-ell-classes-and-boy-do-i-need-suggestions/).

To find free—and good—worksheets peer tutors can use with ELLs, go to The Best Sites for Free ESL/EFL Hand-Outs and Worksheets (http://larryferlazzo.edublogs.org/2009/02/18/the-best-sites-for-free-eslefl-hand-outs-worksheets/).

For additional ideas on how mentors can support ELLs, visit The Best Resources On the Value and Practice of Having Older Students Mentoring Younger Ones (https://larryferlazzo.edublogs.org/2013/02/03/the-best-resources-on-the-value-practice-of-having-older-students-mentoring-younger-ones/).

Learn about other ways to use Dialogue Journals at The Best Resources for Learning How to Use Dialogue Journals (https://larryferlazzo.edublogs.org/2022/09/02/the-best-resources-for-learning-how-to-use-dialogue-journals/).

See how Larry's ELL geography classes have worked with sister classes around the world at Links to the Joint Projects My ELL Geography Class Did with Classes Around the World—Want to Join Us This Year? (http://larryferlazzo.edublogs.org/2015/08/01/links-to-the-joint-projects-my-ell-geography-class-did-with-classes-around-the-world-want-to-join-us-this-year/).

If you'd like to connect with classes in different countries and do similar projects, check out The Best Ways to Find Other Classes for Joint Online Projects (http://larryferlazzo.edublogs.org/2009/05/30/the-best-ways-to-find-other-classes-for-joint-online-projects/).

There are many other ways students can help their classmates learn, and you can find them at The Best Posts on Helping Students Teach Their Classmates (http://larryferlazzo.edublogs.org/2012/04/22/the-best-posts-on-helping-students-teach-their-classmates-help-me-find-more/).

Attribution

Thanks to our colleague Nichole Scrivner for letting us reprint her materials and to Pam Buric for letting us tell her story.

Thanks to Carol Salva for creating the video we show our peer tutors about how they can assist ELLs to best learn English.

All figures from this chapter, as well as 11 additional chapters, references, hyperlinked Technology Connections, and more online resources, can be found at www.wiley.com/go/ellteacherstoolbox2.

Name: _____

Summary of Event:

Emotions Involved:

When:

Who Else Was Involved:

Where:

What Happened:

First:

Second:

Third:

Fourth:

Conclusion (Includes What I Learned):

Figure 39.1 Personal Story Outline

> ### Message to the Visiting Teacher
>
> Thank you for bringing your classes to visit our students. Please prepare your student listeners on the following *before* their visit:
>
> - Instruct them to use active listening—being a respectful and engaged audience; using eye contact, leaning in, nodding and responding, and so on.
> - For each student they visit, they will take notes in one of the boxes on their graphic organizer (please remind them to bring a pen or pencil).
> - After the student is done telling their story, the visiting listener should ask one or two questions. A list of possible conversation starters is provided on the graphic organizer. The idea is to engage in conversation and build relationships. Please review the graphic organizer's layout and preread the possible prompts with your students so that they are prepared for these interactions.
> - **Discussion About Empathy.** The students sharing their stories are taking a huge risk. Discuss being empathetic about language and speech issues, as well as about the content of the shared story. (Prewriting activity for building empathy follows in Figure 33.3.)

Figure 39.2 Story Sharing   *Source:* Reproduced with permission of Nichole Scrivner.

> (To be done *pre*-visit. Have students journal write and then discuss as a class.)
>
> Imagine yourself suddenly and unexpectedly in a new country. You've left your home, friends, and some members of your family behind. Everyone around you speaks a brand-new language, celebrates different cultural holidays, and practices different customs.
>
> Now imagine being in that situation and then being asked to share a sensitive story about your past to a total stranger in your new school.
>
> - How might you feel in this situation?
> - How would your ideal listener behave while listening to your story? What might they do or say? How might they respond?
> - What would help you feel comfortable and safe?

Figure 39.3 Writing Prompt: Building Empathy   *Source:* Reproduced with permission of Nichole Scrivner.

STRATEGY 39: PEER TEACHING AND LEARNING

Listener's Name: _____

Conversation Starters:

- How do you feel about . . . (ask something related to the story you heard or anything else that comes to mind)?
- What are your favorite . . . (hobbies, interests, musical tastes, sports, classes, books, etc.)?
- Can you share something about your home country (culture, music, food, sports, customs, etc.)?
- How does the current political climate make you feel? What about your family?
- Do you feel safe and comfortable at [name of school]? If so, why? If not, what could be done to make you feel more comfortable?

Name of storyteller:
One thing I found interesting . . .
Notes on our conversation:

Name of storyteller:
One thing I found interesting . . .
Notes on our conversation:

Figure 39.4 Story-Sharing Listening Chart *Source:* Reproduced with permission of Nichole Scrivner.

You will be a peer tutor working with students who are learning English, most of whom have recently arrived in this country.

You, in effect, will be working with the teacher as a "co-teacher." You can have a huge impact on helping students in class improve their lives, and you can develop important teaching skills that can benefit you personally and professionally in the future. Being able to list "peer tutor" on a job or college application can also benefit you.

You will NOT be a typical teaching assistant (TA). You will not be filing papers or running errands.

You will TEACH.

It's not an exaggeration to say that most—though not all—students over the years have loved doing this work. If you decide, however, that peer tutoring is not for you, just let the teacher know and you can be moved to a different class.

Here are some things to keep in mind as you work as a peer tutor:

1. Relationships are everything! Get to know students you will be working with. Take time periodically to learn about their lives, interests, goals, and concerns. Ask them to show images on their phone to you of their families, their friends, and their home country. If you feel comfortable doing so, share your images, too. If you speak their home language, it will be easy to have these types of conversations. If you don't, using Google Translate, a bilingual dictionary, or pantomiming works, too.

2. You'll be working with some students individually and some students in small groups. We'll have to see how it goes, but you will likely be working regularly with the same students. Here are some activities you'll be doing with them:

   - Having them read a paper or online book to you, where you can be encouraging and help them with pronunciation and comprehension.
   - Practice conversations. We have a conversation "cheat sheet" with many typical questions and answers that you can role-play.
   - Teach and practice academic vocabulary. We'll be learning higher-level words used in school work and putting them into sentences.

Figure 39.5 Peer Tutor Advice/Guidelines

- Helping students complete work in the textbook. Remember, you are *teaching*, not just giving answers. When students write down answers, ask them to explain why they think that's the answer.
- Helping students write sentences—either about pictures or about text. If they write something that might not be correct, try first pointing to the error with your finger and asking them to think about why that's wrong. This way, they have an opportunity to fix it without your giving them the answer.
- Using flashcards with students. We have lots of boxes filled with images on one side and the word describing it on the other.
- Playing games, including the many English-learning board games we have in the cabinets.
- Leading total physical response (TPR) groups. You'll be teaching words verbally and modeling the word physically (stand up, sit down, etc.).

3. Try to keep track of your students' strengths and challenges, and look for opportunities to build on their strengths and help them with their weaknesses—where do they need more practice, for example. There will be plenty of times when you can decide what you and your student(s) want to work on.

4. Help your teacher be better by offering them feedback on what seems to be working and not working in class and sharing ideas you have for activities. You'll also be creating some materials to use with students. You will never have any homework for this class! But I may ask you to be creative when students don't need your help.

Figure 39.5 (*Continued*)

1. Meet with your mentee at least one time each week for at least 15 minutes. Talk with Mr. Ferlazzo about the best time for you two to meet, and Mr. Ferlazzo will make arrangements with teachers.

2. First, get to know your mentee—ask about their life, family, interests, goals. Share your own stories with them, too. It's especially important for them to hear from you about your challenges (especially if you have moved to a new school or country) and what has helped you overcome them.

3. Some questions to regularly ask your mentee could include these:
   - What have been the best things that have happened to you this week—in and out of school?
   - What have been the biggest challenges or problems you've faced this week—in and out of school?
   - What classes are you doing well in, and what classes are you having problems in? What are some things you can do to help deal with those problems?
   - Do you feel like anyone is bullying you or making fun of you?
   - Are there any questions you have about the school or life in the United States?

4. If your mentee shares something that makes you feel worried or uncomfortable (e.g., if you feel like your mentee might be in danger), please notify Mr. Ferlazzo or another teacher immediately.

Figure 39.6 Peer Mentor Guidelines

STRATEGY 39: PEER TEACHING AND LEARNING 431

Date: _____

Name of Mentor _____ Period _____

Name of Mentee (first name is fine) _____

Teacher of Mentee _____

How did it go? What did you learn that might be helpful for the mentee's teacher to know so that the teacher could make the class a better experience for your mentee (two or three sentences are sufficient):

_____

_____

_____

_____

_____

Figure 39.7 Peer Mentor Form

These are questions you should ask your mentee:

What do you like to do for fun? How are you feeling about your classes? What challenges are you facing in your classes and your life right now? What is going well for you right now?

The holidays can be stressful for many people. How are you feeling about the holiday season? Are you looking forward to it or do you feel stressed? Or both? If it might be stressful, what can you do to make it less stressful?

How would your teachers describe you? Are you pleased by your answer? Would you like them to say something different about you? What would you have to do to make that happen?

How would your different family members describe you? Are you pleased by your answer? Would you like them to say something different about you? What would you have to do to make that happen?

Can you tell me about the best three moments in your life, and why they were so great? Then, mentors share about your three best moments.

When you're feeling stressed, what do you do to feel better? When you don't feel like doing something—school or something else—but you know it's important, how do you motivate yourself to do it?

What is one thing you think one of your teachers should do (or stop doing) to make the class a better environment for everyone? How do you think you could approach that teacher to talk with him/her about it?

How do you feel about your first semester grades? What, if anything, would you like to do differently during the second semester?

If you could have dinner with three other people—living or dead, fictional or real—who would they be and why? What qualities do those three people have that you would like to develop in yourself?

What is one thing—related to school or your personal life—that you want to improve about yourself? Why? What is your plan to make that improvement happen?

If you could change three things about this school, what would they be and why?

What new after-school club, activity, or sport would you like to see the school offer?

Figure 39.8 Peer Mentor Focus Questions

I want to tell you about my family. I live with _____. What can you tell me about your family?

I would like to tell you about what job I would like to do. I want to be a _____ because _____. If I was a _____ I would be able to _____. What kind of job would you like to have?

I do lots of things for fun. I like to _____, _____ and _____. What do you do for fun?

These are the three best things that have happened in my life. One, _____. Two, _____. Three, _____. What are the best things that have happened to you?

These are some of my favorite holidays that we celebrate in my home country:

What are your favorite holidays?

These are my favorite movies and television shows: _____
What are your favorite movies and television shows?

My favorite musical groups or singers are: _____

What are your favorite musical groups or singers?

These are my favorite classes, and the classes I don't like:

I like _____ because _____.

I like _____ because _____.

I don't like _____ because _____.

I don't like _____ because _____.

What are your favorite classes and the ones you don't like?

These are my goals for the second semester:

What are your goals for the second semester?

Figure 39.9 Dialogue Journal Prompts

Figure 39.10 Everyone Is a Teacher Poster

STRATEGY 39: PEER TEACHING AND LEARNING   435

	Date:	**Date:**	**Date:**	**Date:**
I will speak English.				
I will be serious.				
I will be a model.				
I will come to school.				
I will practice in class.				
I will help students.				
I will listen.				
I will only use my phone to translate.				
I will sing.				
I will repeat words.				
I will practice Raz-Kids.				

Figure 39.11   Everyone Is a Teacher Goal-Setting Chart

March 24

I will speak English.	B	
I will be serious.	D	
I will be a model.	F	
I will come to school.	D	
I will practice in class.	A	
I will help students.	B	
I will listen.	C	
I will only use my phone to translate.	A	
I will sing.	B	
I will repeat words.	A	
I will practice Raz-Kids.	C	

Figure 39.12 Student Example of Goal-Setting Chart

STRATEGY 40

Co-Teaching

What Is It?

Many ELL teachers are in situations in which they either go into a class to support students when a content teacher is teaching or pull ELLs out to support content instruction. This practice is often done when a school doesn't have enough beginning and intermediate ELLs to financially justify having courses exclusively for them or when schools believe that this form of instruction is best for their students.

While every teacher's situation is unique, co-teaching experts Andrea Honigsfeld and Maria Dove have named several common co-teaching models, which vary according to how students are grouped and the role of each co-teacher during instruction (Honigsfeld & Dove, 2017):

One Group: One Leads, One "Teaches on Purpose" (Whole class instruction with one teacher "leading" the instruction and the other teacher circulating, checking for comprehension, providing feedback, scaffolding, etc.).

One Group: Two Teach Same Content (Whole class instruction with both teachers leading the lesson together).

One Group: One Teach, One Assess (Whole class instruction with one teacher leading instruction and the other observing for the purpose of assessing students).

Two Groups: Two Teach Same Content (Class is divided into two groups with each teacher providing instruction on the same content to one group. Teachers can exchange groups part way through the lesson so that all students experience being taught by both teachers).

Two Groups: One Preteaches, One Teaches Alternative Information (Class is divided into two groups. Students who may need more background knowledge and vocabulary frontloading work with one teacher, while the rest of the students do alternative activities to promote interest in the topic with the other teacher. The two groups can then come back together to learn about the topic).

Two Groups: One Reteaches, One Teaches Alternative Information (This arrangement is similar to the previous one and students who need extra support or more instruction are grouped with one teacher who focuses on reviewing or reteaching content, while the other engages the rest of the students in an alternative activity).

Multiple Groups: Two Monitor and Teach (Students are divided into multiple groups while both teachers circulate to provide support. Teachers can also remain stationary and meet with small groups to provide mini-lessons as students rotate through learning stations).

Honigsfeld and Dove also make the important point that for any of these models to work, teachers must engage in "collaborative planning, instruction, assessment, and reflection" (Ferlazzo, 2019). And, we know this means school administration must be committed to providing teachers the time and resources to make this happen.

Why We Like It

We have actually applied every other strategy in this book multiple times in our own classrooms. The only times, however, when we have co-taught classes were when we did it with each other. Having two veteran ELL educators co-teach exclusively ELL classes is rare, and our experience is unlikely to be similar to what most ELL teachers face.

Unlike some who write on education issues, we do not feel comfortable writing about situations we know little about. So we have invited veteran ELL co-teacher Carlota Holder to share some of her experiences. You can also find links to additional co-teaching resources in the Technology Connections section.

Supporting Research

Substantial research supports the recommendations included in this strategy. There are many different kinds of co-teaching models, and all have their own advantages and disadvantages (Burgess, 2011; Hendrickson, 2011; Honigsfeld & Dove, 2008).

Common Core Connections

When an ELL educator is co-teaching in content classes, the ELL educator is responsible for working with their colleague in supporting ELL students to access the Standards in that content area.

Application

This section was written by Carlota Holder. Carlota is the Director of Academic Language for Enlace Academy on the west side of Indianapolis. Her grade-level experience ranges from kindergarten to eighth grade with English language and Spanish instruction. Her roles have ranged from ELL assistant, ELL teacher, sheltered instruction observation protocol (SIOP) co-teacher, ELL coach, and Spanish teacher.

CO-TEACHING DON'TS AND DOS

Having finally graduated from my ELL courses in grad school, I never knew that I'd be going into a field in which most of my instruction would be taking place with a co-teacher. Who would have thought? I began working with ELL students as an instructional assistant pushing into classrooms, and I was lucky enough to have mentors let me assist and observe their ELL classes. Then I became a teacher who was responsible for ELL students in a completely different environment—a co-teaching one. No one taught me how to co-teach. Here's what I have learned:

- Don't assume that the teachers with whom you're co-teaching have background knowledge on second language acquisition.
- Do help them learn through trial and error. This will help them build their background knowledge and shows that you trust them and their content.

    I have wanted to tell teachers how to teach their materials to *our* students many times, but I learned the hard way that this was not the most-effective communication strategy. Instead, let teachers achieve successes and make mistakes. Jump in and say, "I like how you did . . ., maybe next time we could do . . ." Then, add second-language acquisition data to support your suggestion. I would often take what they had developed back to my classroom and play with it. I would remake it with the suggestions I gave them and attach it in a follow-up e-mail. This practice also showed my co-teacher that I was willing to put in hard work to improve instruction for everyone.

- Don't refer to students as *my* students when talking with your co-teachers.
- Do refer to students as *our* students when talking with your co-teachers.

    How many times do we refer to our students as *my* students? However, it is important that you refer to students as *our* students when you're in a co-teaching situation. In a co-teaching situation you are working toward the same goal: to improve the language and content knowledge of *all* students. You are both responsible for their education. This action acknowledges that you're working as a team.

- Don't avoid planning and collaboration.
- Do take time to plan and collaborate.

    Complaints I sometimes hear from co-teachers include "My school doesn't give me time to plan and collaborate with my co-teachers" or "I don't have time to plan and collaborate with my co-teachers." A supportive school would give you time, but we live in the real world. Try to eat lunch with your co-teacher and collaborate. Stay an extra half-hour after school to make plans together or offer to visit them on their prep. You could even collaborate off campus with some margaritas. (You'll be surprised how much you can get done!) Planning and collaboration can begin to happen digitally after you have broken the ice in person. You can then start sharing your plans and assignments electronically. Google Drive is the best collaborative resource to ever exist! If planning and collaboration can't happen physically, be sure to use whatever you can digitally and continue to be persistent and patient.

- Don't allow one teacher to take all the responsibilities for instruction.
- Do share responsibilities for instruction.

    Your co-teacher is an expert in his or her content area and you are an expert in language acquisition. Together, you can make a phenomenal team. Share responsibilities with each other. Offer to do some grading. Offer to make assignments for certain groups of students. My favorite is offering to make visual supports for my teachers. I tell them my ideas and then ask for their advice on the content portion, because I am not the content expert. I want my supports to be valuable, not only to our students but also to my co-teacher. This way we can build our resources and continue to use them year after year.

- Don't undermine the other teacher's authority or question the teacher in front of students.
- Do treat each other as equals in the classroom.

    We want to model respectful relationships in front of our students. I had a co-teacher once who was very set in her ways. We had 100-minute English language arts blocks and she refused to let any student go to the bathroom for any reason. I did not agree with that policy—if a student needs to go, then a student needs to go. One day I decided to let one of our students use the bathroom. On her return I was reprimanded in front of the *entire class,* as if I were a student. Thankfully, this co-teaching "relationship" only lasted a year.

- Don't force it.
- Do keep trying!

    If you have the power to choose your co-teacher, find someone who is willing to *learn* and keep trying. Not everything you do will work. It's a fail-and-learn process.

Thankfully, there's a book with seven different co-teaching styles that you can try and has a plethora of resources: *Collaboration and Co-Teaching* by Andrea Honigsfeld and Maria G. Dove (2010). There are also many ELL teachers to connect with on Twitter on other social media platforms. *Together* we can meet and exceed the high expectations we set for our English language learners.

Teaching Online and Technology Connections

You can find lots of additional information on co-teaching, including co-teaching in an online environment, at The Best Resources on Co-Teaching with ELLs (http://larryferlazzo.edublogs.org/2017/07/07/the-best-resources-on-co-teaching-with-ells-please-suggest-more/).

Attribution

Thanks to Carlota Holder for contributing her recommendations! A version of her dos and don'ts originally appeared at Co-Teaching Dos and Don'ts (2017, August 1b, http://larryferlazzo.edublogs.org/2017/08/01/guest-post-co-teaching-dos-and-donts/).

STRATEGY 41

Working with Parents and Guardians

What Is It?

Parents or guardians can be critical partners in supporting ELLs. Unfortunately, it's not unusual for ELL family members to be working multiple jobs. This kind of schedule and economic pressure can be a barrier to traditional family involvement in a school's physical location, but it does not diminish a family's commitment to supporting their children in academic success. In addition, the prior school experience of the parents or guardians, including how schools and teachers were viewed in their home countries, can provide further obstacles to effective engagement. As a result of this experience, some parents of ELLs might feel reluctant to ask questions or make suggestions about their child's academic work (Smith, 2005).

Another potential issue is that sometimes our students are not living with their parents. Instead, they may be living with an older sibling or an aunt or uncle or a foster parent who does not necessarily have the same kind of parental relationship with them. When we use the word *parent* in this strategy, we are including this broader definition.

The recommendations we share in the Application section take all of these challenges into account.

Why We Like It

In our work with families, we always try to keep in mind the difference between *parent involvement* and *parent engagement*.

Simply put, parent involvement is often more of a *doing to* and engagement is a *doing with*. When emphasizing involvement, schools tend to lead with their *mouths*—generally telling parents what they should be doing. Engagement, however, has schools leading with their *ears*. By listening to parents' ideas, and by eliciting from them what they have found works best with their children, school staff members can develop more genuine partnerships that are helpful to young people. We have gained great insight over the years by asking parents a simple question: "Can you please tell me about the times when your child has seemed to be learning the most and working hard in school, and what you think teachers were doing at that time to encourage it?"

Another example of parent involvement is a school's focus on *communication,* which is often one-way. Schools across the country emphasize sending sheets of information home (which often do not arrive or, if they do, can be in a language that parents don't understand) and using automated phone calls. Engagement tries to use two-way *conversation,* through efforts such as making home visits and phone calls that don't necessarily happen only when there's a problem with a child.

During Larry's 19-year community-organizing career, he often talked about the difference between irritation and agitation—we irritate people when we challenge them to do something about what *we* are interested in, and we agitate people when we challenge them to act on *their* interests. Involvement often leans toward irritation—schools might have a predetermined and limited list of ways they want parents to help, such as making copies, organizing bake sales, and so on. Engagement, instead, looks through the lens of agitation and emphasizes discovering the parents' interests and goals. See the story of Burbank High School's home computer project in the Application section to get an idea of results that can come from agitation.

Another important difference is that there is a tendency with involvement to focus solely on improving what goes on within the four walls of the school, whereas in engagement there is recognition that the school must be participating as an institution in neighborhood-wide improvement efforts. This kind of engagement acknowledges the fact that many of the elements affecting student academic achievement have their roots outside of the classroom.

All the suggestions in the Application section fall under the engagement category.

Supporting Research

Years of research have demonstrated the importance of family engagement to student academic achievement (Ferlazzo, 2011, October 30). This kind of engagement can mean parents participating in activities on the school site and supporting their children's school work at home. This same research highlights the benefits of *engagement* over *involvement*.

Common Core Connections

Looked at in one way, parent engagement has no specific connection to any Common Core Standards. Looked at in a different way, it can be critical to every one of them. We'll leave it up to you and your administrator to look at the research, reflect on your experience, and decide which of those perspectives you should take.

Application

Our parent engagement efforts have fallen into three primary categories over the years: communicating with parents, supporting them in the challenges they face, and inviting them to participate in our classroom learning.

COMMUNICATING WITH PARENTS

Communicating with parents of our students is a key element of family engagement. This can be a particular challenge for teachers of ELLs who do not speak the home language of their students.

Schools are required by federal law (Mathewson, 2016; US Department of Justice and US Department of Education, 2015) to communicate "essential information" effectively with immigrant parents, so schools must bring in bilingual staff members or contracted interpreters for critical meetings such as ones related to a child's future (discipline issues, evaluation for special needs, etc.), as well as having important documents professionally translated into the parents' home language. Depending on your school district's policies, "essential information" may or may not include the kind of regular communication many teachers want to have with the parents of their students.

There are several ways we try to address this challenge. One way is to use Google Translate or one of the many other tools that are available to assist schools in communicating with parents who speak languages other than English. See the Technology Connections section for links to those resources.

Even if we do not fluently speak the home language of our students' parents, we can certainly learn a few words. Being able to say "hello," "We love having your child in our class," and "good-bye" in what is likely to be a poorly accented and garbled version of their language can go a long way toward beginning to build a trusting relationship.

Home visits to the parents of ELL students (with an interpreter if the teacher doesn't speak their home language) are another excellent way to build communication and relationships. Our local teachers union helped begin the national Parent-Teacher Home Visit Project, which you can learn more about through links in the Technology Connections section.

During one home visit Larry made to an immigrant family, the father spoke at length about how thrilled he was at our use of the Internet at school to help his daughter learn English. He explained how he wished he could afford a computer and web connection at his house so the entire family could learn, too. Instead of just listening politely and leaving (and forgetting), or going back to see if our school could organize such a program for parents, Larry asked him if he knew other parents who felt the same and if he would be willing to organize a meeting of them to see if there might be something we could do together. He agreed, and then parents worked with our school to develop a project that provided free home computers and Internet service to immigrant families. It was later named one of the most effective uses of technology to teach reading in the world by the International Literacy Association. See the Technology Connections section for more information on this project.

STRATEGY 41: WORKING WITH PARENTS AND GUARDIANS

Even if your district does not have a large number of materials available for parents in their home languages, there are many other sources of these kinds of important resources. See the Technology Connections section for links to multilingual explanations of the Common Core Standards, requirements that districts have to meet to provide resources to English language learners (including those with special needs), and videos and written materials about how their children can further pursue their academic career beyond high school. More and more artificial intelligence-powered tools are also becoming available that will automatically dub videos that you create into different languages of your choice.

Another simple way to communicate with parents is through their children themselves. Larry has his students write a simple weekly letter to their parents/guardians explaining the most important things they learned in each of their classes that week. Students write them in their home languages and use the template found in Figure 41.1: Template for Student Family Letter (Larry uses Google Translate to provide the template to students in different languages). The homework is to give the letter to their parents/guardians; the guardians are to ask them at least one question about it; the student answers it and writes the question they were asked at the bottom of the letter, and then the parent/guardian signs the letter.

Students write the letter every Thursday; it works better than doing it on Friday because they are more likely to remember to bring it back. Larry gives them extra credit for returning it and has an approximately 70 percent turn-in rate.

Writing the letter is obviously not an English language acquisition exercise. Rather, it's an opportunity for students to reflect on their learning and to solidify the connection between the classroom and the student's family. If students are not literate in their home language, they can "write" their letter by using Google Docs Voice Typing. If parents or guardians are not literate in their home language, students can read it to them.

Finally, parents who do not speak English may have questions about how they can best support their children's academic work. A message we consistently give to parents is that asking their children questions about what they are doing in school, making sure they have time and a place to study at home, regularly encouraging them to have big dreams for their future, and discussing the issues going on in the world around them are all extraordinarily effective actions that parents can take—whether they speak English or not.

SUPPORTING PARENTS

Many parents of ELLs are experiencing challenges in their lives. Here are a few ways we try to support them.

Parent academies are increasing in popularity across the country. This is when schools organize classes for parents where they are taught about how schools work. At schools where involvement takes the lead (remember our discussion of *involvement* versus *engagement*), the curriculum for these classes is often predetermined by the school, and classes are led and taught by school staff members.

At schools where engagement is the priority, families work with the parent coordinator to identify topics that should be covered—which might or might not be focused on the school (e.g., the citizenship process was one recent topic)—run the meetings, and own the entire project. You can learn more through the Technology Connections section.

Of course, it's not that uncommon for schools to sponsor adult English classes for parents of their students. Because schools are often in the neighborhoods where their ELL students live, having an accessible location for these educational opportunities can be very convenient for their parents.

Last, the changing political climate can create pressures and stresses for ELL families. Schools and districts can help in different ways. For example, our Sacramento City Unified School District launched a Safe Haven program to support undocumented students and their families. This effort includes informing them of their rights and publicizing the contributions they have made and are making to our community (Ferlazzo, 2017, March 8).

INVITING FAMILIES TO PARTICIPATE IN CLASSROOM LEARNING

We always seek ways to involve families in our classroom learning. One year, we invited a father who created Hmong flutes to show our class how he made them. When we are studying the U.S. Civil War, we often have students interview family members about civil wars in their home countries. In addition, we ask students to interview their family as part of participating in the StoryCorps program that stores the recordings in the Library of Congress.

The Technology Connections section contains links to scores of other ideas on how teachers can encourage students to leverage the funds of knowledge held by their families for learning in the classroom.

What Could Go Wrong?

It's not easy for overworked teachers to find time to communicate with families. We've got our hands full with everything we have to do in the classroom! We will be the first to admit that family engagement sometimes falls off the radar for us, too. All we can do is fit it in when we can, and we always find the benefits outweigh the time costs.

It can be easy for teachers to rely on students to carry the burden of translation for their parents. Do everything within your power to resist that choice and, instead, push your school to provide professional assistance. On occasion, however, absent that professional support, we *might* ask a student to help interpret informal *positive* feedback from us about their work to the parent (e.g., "Xeng worked very hard on his presentation and it showed. It was excellent!"). We would *never* use a student to communicate behavior or academic concerns or official school information or policy.

Technology Connections

For many related resources, including suggested apps teachers can use to communicate with immigrant parents, visit The Best Parent Engagement Resources for Immigrant Families (http://larryferlazzo.edublogs.org/2017/08/06/the-best-parent-engagement-resources-for-immigrant-families/).

STRATEGY 41: WORKING WITH PARENTS AND GUARDIANS

For tools to communicate with families, even if you are fluent in their home language, visit The Best Resources to Help ELL Students with Simultaneous Translation in the Classroom (https://larryferlazzo.edublogs.org/2023/07/18/the-best-resources-to-help-ell-students-with-simultaneous-translation-in-the-classroom/). There is a section on that blog post focusing on multilingual parent communication tools.

To learn more about teachers making home visits, and to learn about the home computer project that came out of our visits, check out The Best Resources for Learning About Teacher Home Visits (http://engagingparentsinschool.edublogs.org/2011/10/10/the-best-resources-for-learning-about-teacher-home-visits/) and The Best Resources for Learning About Schools Providing Home Computers and Internet Access to Students (http://larryferlazzo.edublogs.org/2011/03/19/the-best-resources-for-learning-about-schools-providing-home-computers-internet-access-to-students/).

Multilingual resources accessible to immigrant parents can be found at The Best Multilingual Resources for Parents (http://engagingparentsinschool.edublogs.org/2013/05/16/the-best-multilingual-resources-for-parents/).

Information on effective parent academies is at My Best Posts on Parent "Academies" and "Universities" (http://engagingparentsinschool.edublogs.org/2013/02/23/my-best-posts-on-parent-academies-universities/).

For additional resources on ways schools can support immigrant families, visit The Best Practical Resources for Helping Teachers, Students and Families Respond to Immigration Challenges (http://larryferlazzo.edublogs.org/2017/02/26/the-best-practical-resources-for-helping-teachers-students-families-respond-to-immigration-challenges/).

You can find lots of suggestions on how to involve families in student homework at The Best Places Where Students—and/or Their Families—Can Tell Their Immigration Story (http://larryferlazzo.edublogs.org/2016/10/12/the-best-places-where-students-can-tell-their-andor-their-families-immigration-story/) and at The Best Student Projects That Need Family Engagement (http://engagingparentsinschool.edublogs.org/2014/02/09/the-best-student-projects-that-need-family-engagement-contribute-your-lessons/).

For even more parent engagement resources and ideas, you can visit Larry's blog, "Engaging Parents in School" (https://engagingparentsinschool.edublogs.org/).

Attribution

Portions of this section originally appeared in "The Difference Between Parent 'Involvement' & Parent 'Engagement,'" *Education Week* (http://blogs.edweek.org/teachers/classroom_qa_with_larry_ferlazzo/2012/03/response_the_difference_between_parent_involvement_parent_engagement.html).

All figures from this chapter, as well as 11 additional chapters, references, hyperlinked Technology Connections, and more online resources, can be found at www.wiley.com/go/ellteacherstoolbox2.

Dear Mom and Dad (or Uncle/Aunt or Guardian),

I finished another week of school!

Here are the things I liked about it:

Here are the most interesting or important things I learned in each class:

In English, I learned _____.

In Math, I learned _____.

In Biology, I learned _____.

In PE, I learned _____.

In Geography, I learned _____.

In Theater, I learned _____.

Here are the things I didn't like about my school week, and hope they will get better:

Please ask me at least one question about what I have written in this letter and I will tell you my answer (you can ask me more than one question!).

I need to write down one of the questions you ask me, and then have you sign at the bottom of this letter.

Figure 41.1 Template for Student Family Letter

STRATEGY 42
Translanguaging

What Is It?

Translanguaging[1] can have different meanings. In the classroom, it basically means honoring students' use of their home languages to help learn English and understand the academic content that is being taught. It doesn't really mean "translating," though translating some words could be a part of it. It's a pedagogical strategy to view students' home languages as an asset they can use to more actively engage with the lesson that is being taught. It's about strategically using a student's home language as a scaffold to help them achieve English language acquisition success, in addition to being a scaffold for an English language learner to learn higher-level academic content that they might not be able to access yet in English.

Why We Like It

We discuss the importance of teachers having an "asset-based mind-set" in Strategy 37: Social Emotional Learning. Why wouldn't we want to leverage one of our students' biggest assets—their home language—to help them learn what we are teaching?

Supporting Research

Extensive research finds that translanguaging results in increased English language acquisition (Najarro, 2023; Champlin, 2016; McLaughlin, 2022). At the same time, however, researchers have found that teachers can be unsure of its meaning and how it can benefit their students (Champlin, 2016). We hope this chapter can be helpful in dealing with these concerns.

[1] We've been experimenting with how ChatGPT and Google's Gemini chatbots can assist in the classroom. This is the only chapter in the book where AI assistance was provided in writing the narrative and AI provided approximately 5% of the content. It was interesting to see how useless it was as a resource.

Common Core Connections

Translanguaging can be used to help ELLs achieve any and all of the Common Core Standards, depending on how it's being used and in what class or lesson. It increases the odds of ELLs being able to meet those standards prior to gaining academic fluency in English, which can take many years (Hesson et al., 2014).

Application

We think that the best way to describe how translanguaging can work in the ELL classroom is by writing this section in a different way from any of the other chapters, and sharing a chart of "What It Is and What It Looks Like" and "What It Is Not and What That Looks Like."

Each italicized point is followed by a practical classroom example.

What Translanguaging Is	What Translanguaging Is Not
Flexibility in Language Use.	*A strict "English-only" classroom policy.*
Students can use Google Translate, a bilingual dictionary, or ask a classmate using their home language the meaning of a word.	A student is penalized or admonished by the teacher for speaking their home language or using a tool to learn a word's meaning.
Culturally responsive instruction that builds on students' cultural knowledge and includes having bilingual and other books that allow students to see themselves and their culture in lessons and texts.	*Just uses U.S.-centric cultural examples and texts that don't represent students in the class.*
Students use English and their home language to make presentations about holidays important to their culture.	Uses a text data set (see Chapter 11: Inductive Teaching and Learning) on holidays that only includes popular ones celebrated in the United States.
Uses a student's home language as a scaffold to acquire language and academic content.	*Ignores the potential benefit of leveraging students' home languages.*
Teacher uses the preview, view, review method—previews the lesson in the student's home language, teaches the lesson in English, reviews it in the home language. If the teacher doesn't speak the home language, online materials on the topic can be used. Other strategies could be to have a bilingual interactive word wall (see Chapter 48) or to encourage students to research information in their home language to prepare a class report in English on that topic.	Does not provide multilingual resources and links in students' home languages that support the academic content being taught in the classroom.
Creates a bridge between languages.	*Nothing or everything is translated.*

What Translanguaging Is	What Translanguaging Is Not
Cognates (words in more than one language that come from the same root) and false cognates (words that sound like they come from the same root, but don't) are explicitly taught.	Cognates and student home language grammar similarities or similarities are not discussed *or* students are just told to use Google Translate all the time if they don't understand something.
Creates opportunities for monolingual parents/guardians to support their children academically.	Feels that there really isn't any way for monolingual parents to support their children in English language acquisition.
Includes a weekly assignment where students write a letter to their parents/guardians in their home language explaining what they learned in class that week and encourages family members to ask their children questions about it.	The only contact made with family members or guardians about the class is when there is misbehavior by the child.
Opportunities for linguistic diversity are sought out.	Obvious opportunities for students to share their home language aren't even on the teacher's "radar."
Students are invited to share home language words, terms or sayings that might be relevant to the lesson topic to help create a more inclusive environment.	When teaching a lesson on folktales or fables, students are never asked to share knowledge from their home cultures.
Recognizes that a student's home language is a valuable asset and gift.	Views a student's home language as an "inconvenience," "hindrance," or "unimportant."
The teacher periodically asks students to teach them (and perhaps other students) keywords in their home languages.	The teacher communicates no curiosity about students' home languages or their cultures.
Collaborative work is encouraged so that students can provide each other mutual support, including assistance conveyed through shared home languages.	Students do most classwork entirely on their own.
Students who share a home language work as partners on a grammar workbook, checking their answers with each other and discussing questions—in English and in their home language.	Silently, students work (or try to work) on grammar practice with the teacher being the only acceptable person to provide assistance.

It's important to note that, though we framed this section as an either/or proposition, there are many gray areas in translanguaging.

Supporting a student's home language does not mean you can't have rules about use of Google Translate when students are writing (ours is "Use it for words and not sentences") or even have a five-minute "English-only" time for an activity.

Teaching Online

All of these translanguaging strategies can be used in an online environment. However, it's critical for the teacher to initiate clear discussion about what translanguaging is and when it's appropriate to use. If not, some students might decide, instead, to go "all in" on translating everything.

What Could Go Wrong?

The key to translanguaging success is to use it strategically. The teacher needs to proactively plan for it and discuss reasons and times for its use with students. If not, learning English is hard, and a not insignificant number of students may very well choose to use their home language to avoid some of the challenging, yet necessary, tasks involved in learning a language.

We also suggest that teachers try to become familiar with common classroom inappropriate words (i.e., curse words) in your students' home languages. Trust us, those will be among the first words some students will want to learn and others will want to teach them!

Technology Connections

Additional resources to support translanguaging can be found at:

The Best Resources for Learning About Translanguaging (https://larryferlazzo.edublogs.org/2022/07/17/the-best-resources-for-learning-about-translanguaging/).

The Best Resources Explaining Why We Need to Support the Home Language of ELLs (https://larryferlazzo.edublogs.org/2017/04/10/the-best-resources-explaining-why-we-need-to-support-the-home-language-of-ells/).

The Best Places Where You Can Order Bilingual Books (https://larryferlazzo.edublogs.org/2023/03/11/the-best-places-where-you-can-order-bilingual-books/).

STRATEGY 43

Beginning the School Year

What Is It?

Teachers must consider many factors at the beginning of the school year. These include how to build relationships with students, what content they will be teaching, the instructional strategies they will use, how they will manage behavior, what resources they will need, how their classroom will be physically organized, and many others.

Teachers of ELLs must also consider these questions in relation to their students' cultural, linguistic, and academic experiences.

Why We Like It

We know that the choices and causes we make at the beginning of the school year can have many effects as we progress through the rest of the year—and we want these effects to be positive! In our experience, focusing on two elements at the beginning of the year—building positive relationships with students and their families and creating a safe, effective learning environment—lay a strong foundation on which to build throughout the school year. We will share ideas for cultivating these elements in the Application section.

Supporting Research

Extensive research shows that students who have positive, supportive relationships with teachers tend to be more engaged in learning, have fewer behavior issues, and experience higher levels of social and academic development (Rimm-Kaufman & Sandilos, n.d.). Supportive school-based relationships have been found to play an especially important role in engagement and academic performance for immigrant students (Suarez-Orozco et al., 2009).

Common Core Connections

The relationship and community building activities in this section can support some of the Standards in each domain. Although they may not hit every Standard, these activities are absolutely necessary to create the conditions in which students feel safe and supported as they work toward meeting them.

Application

Building strong relationships and creating a positive, safe learning environment can't be accomplished the first day or week of school. It also doesn't involve checking off certain activities on a to-do list. It is a dynamic process that starts on the first day of school (or even before) and needs to be continually nurtured and modified *every day* as the school year progresses. Some of the activities we share in this section can be used for introductory lessons and ones throughout the year to maintain positive relationships and foster an effective learning environment. This is by no means an exhaustive list. It does contain new activities not discussed in our first two books, along with a few that we have improved since then. All of the activities can be easily adapted to meet the needs of students at various English proficiency levels. In addition, building relationships with parents is also an important piece of community building at the start of the year. See Strategy 41: Working with Parents and Guardians for resources on building connections between home and school.

GREETING STUDENTS

Greeting students on the first day of school is an easy way to make them feel welcome and to assure them that they are in the right class. Establishing this practice as part of a teacher's *daily* routine can be more challenging but, in our experience, well worth the effort.

Though we applaud those teachers who choose to offer this kind of greeting at the door, we personally prefer to be in front of the classroom and encouraging/supervising students to begin their warm-up activities and making sure peer tutors are getting organized.

We find that greeting each student *by name* with a smile is much more important than where we do it. Unfortunately, it's probably not uncommon that some students can go an entire school day without an adult saying their name in a friendly manner. We try to make sure that none of our students finds themselves in that category.

Once this practice is established, students are quick to remind us when we forget!

STUDENT NAMES

Making it a priority to learn students' names and how to correctly pronounce them by the end of the first week is another way to develop positive relationships in the classroom. As we discuss in Strategy 36: Culturally Responsive Teaching, making sure we are correctly pronouncing students' names signals respect and a validation of who they are. This respect also includes asking students if they want to be called a name other than the one printed on the roster.

We find that writing down the phonetic spellings of students' names on our seating chart is a good way to learn them. We also have students make quick name plates by folding a piece of paper into a triangle and writing their name on it using a colored marker. They then place it on top of their desk during the first week of school and can fold it up each day and keep it in their folder. This helps students to learn each other's names as well.

Teachers can also have students create short introductory videos where they themselves pronounce their names for everyone's benefit.

Though we don't want to put students "on the spot" by publicly asking every student about the pronoun they want us to use, we do announce that we will use whatever pronoun they prefer and that they can let us know that choice publicly or privately.

COURSE EXPECTATIONS ACTIVITY

During the first week of school (usually the second day), we give students Figure 43.1: Course Expectations, which contains general information about the class in simple language. We quickly go over each section and have beginning students translate the headings (materials, grading, class rules, etc.) into their home language. Then, we make it an interactive lesson by allowing students to work in partners or small groups to complete Figure 43.2: Course Expectations Questions. We may first demonstrate how to do Question 5 by writing the first rule "Be on time" and drawing a clock with the starting time for the class. We also might model how to quickly sketch the classroom for Question 6. Students then work together to reread Figure 43.1 in order to answer all of the questions in Figure 43.2. They get to walk around and tour the classroom so they can draw a map for Question 6. We circulate during the process to check for comprehension and to offer assistance.

As an extension, the class can be divided into groups and given a poster paper. Each group can create a poster for one of the class rules containing the rule in English, the translation in any home languages, and a picture showing what the rule means. These can then be hung on the wall for daily reference.

LETTER EXCHANGE

This activity comes from our first book, *The ESL/ELL Teacher's Survival Guide* (Ferlazzo & Sypnieski, 2022, p. 28) that shares basic information about us—our teaching experience, family, interests outside of school, and so on. We read the letter to students and then ask students to write a letter back. Depending on the level of the class, our letter can be simplified and we may provide sentence frames for students to use (e.g., "My name is. I am _____ years old. I was born in _____. My favorite thing about school is _____.") This activity is a great way for us to learn about students and to get a quick sample of student's writing. Students and teachers can also exchange letters at different points during the year. We've found it particularly helpful to do at the end of a quarter to reflect on growth and highs and lows of those months.

PARTNER INTRODUCTIONS

ELLs may feel anxious being asked to introduce themselves on the first day. It can be much more comfortable for them to talk about someone else. One way to do this is by dividing students into pairs and providing them with a short list of simple questions to use to interview each other. The teacher can provide a sheet with the questions and space for students to write the answers or they can fill in the answers if using sentence frames. See Figure 43.3: Partner Introductions for a sheet we use with beginners. Students can practice the questions first by listening to the teacher say the question and then repeating it. Then, after students ask each other the questions and write down the answers, they can practice introducing each other using the answers or sentence frames as a guide. This rehearsal can be followed by asking students to introduce their partners to the whole class or in small groups.

"I Learn Best When . . ." Cards

This activity was introduced to us by educator and author Rick Wormeli (2016). It involves giving students an index card and asking them to list all the things that help them learn best. We structure this activity for intermediate ELLs at the beginning of the year (our newcomers find it a bit too challenging initially, so we do this activity with them several months after the start of school) by using the sentence stem "I learn best when . . ." and providing students with a few models (e.g., "I learn best when the teacher shows pictures"; "I learn best when I work with other students"; "I learn best when I can see an example first"). After students have had a few minutes to write, we ask them to share their ideas in small groups in order to see if any of the ideas that help their classmates learn best could also apply to themselves. We then create a class list of "I learn best when . . ." ideas that can be posted on the wall and added to throughout the year. We collect the students' index cards and periodically hand them back out to students (usually at the beginning of a new quarter) so students can reflect on how they learn best and make any modifications or additions to their list.

"I Am" Project

There are many variations of *I am* activities—students can create a poem, a poster, a slideshow, a brief oral presentation, a collage, and so on (you can find many examples by searching *"Who am I?" activities* online). This activity encourages students to describe themselves in a creative format. At the beginning of the year, it serves as a way for teachers and students to learn about each other's experiences and interests. We change the format up from year to year, but we always provide sentence frames along with a model about ourselves. We also give the option for students to add illustrations. The sentence frames we shared in *The ESL/ELL Teacher's Survival Guide:*

I love because _____.
I wonder _____.
I am happy when _____.
I am scared when _____.
I worry about because _____.
I hope to _____.
I am sad when _____.
In the future, I will _____.

We modify the activity for newcomers by encouraging them to complete it in their native language. Students can also add drawings or pictures cut from magazines to visually

STRATEGY 43: BEGINNING THE SCHOOL YEAR

represent their feelings, interests, and goals. We then have students share their projects in small groups of three to four and ask them to look for two similarities and two differences. Each group then shares their observations with the whole class.

SELF-PORTRAITS

There are many different variations of self-identity portrait activities, and you can find a link to many of them in the Technology Connections section. These "portraits" can lead to more student self-awareness, emphasize student assets, and create opportunities for students to make connections and become aware of commonalities with classmates (many of the activities in this chapter serve similar purposes).

We do a fairly simple version with our students—one that we adapted from the variety of similar activities that can be found online, but probably borrowed the most from the English Teaching 101 blog (https://englishteaching101.com/self-portrait-ideas-esl/). First, we model a graphic organizer with one of our names in the middle and then have circles or boxes surrounding our name labeled:

Interests

Languages

Family

Culture/Home Country/Religion/Race

Hopes for the Future

Important Possessions

We then list the items, beliefs, etc., that are appropriate for us in the boxes or circles, generally up to three in each. We list them using English words.

Next, we ask students to create their own graphic organizer reflecting their identities.

Then, we share poorly drawn (since we're terrible artists) images of ourselves, with images representing the items and beliefs that we wrote down on the graphic organizer. Students do the same and create their own pictures (we print out blank images for students who are artistically challenged like ourselves; just search "blank images of people" online) with smaller images representing their graphic organizer items.

Students then share and explain their images in a "speed-dating" style.

LANGUAGE MAPS

Language Portraits have been a tool of linguistics researchers to help them learn how children and adults connect to language (Notre Dame Center for Literacy Education, 2021). You can see many by searching online, but we prefer a very modified version of what English teacher Alycia Owen uses with her students, which she calls a "Language Map."

In our version, we show a paper on a document camera titled "English" and divided into fourths—Speaking, Listening, Reading, Writing. Under each of those language domains, we write examples of when we use English. For example, under "Speaking," we'll write "teaching, talking with family, in the store." Then, we'll do the same under each of the other domains. We may draw small images, as well.

Next, we'll show another paper that looks similar, but is labeled "Spanish." Then, we'll write under each domain when we use that language. Under speaking, we might write, "teaching, speaking with students, talking with their parents."

We'll then ask students to do their own sheets for English and for any other language that they speak.

Students then share their "Language Maps" through a speed-dating system.

Searching online for "Language Portraits" will lead you to images similar to the "Self-Portraits" that we described earlier. You might want to try having students make those kinds of illustrations. We've just found these kinds of "Language Maps" seem to be easier for our students.

MY SUMMER CLOZE ACTIVITY

When returning to school in the fall, many students get asked to write or talk about what they did over the summer. Although we may want to know what students did while they weren't in school, we also want to be sensitive to the fact that not all our students have positive summer vacation experiences, especially if they were moving. We can give them the opportunity to express their feelings, positive and negative, by writing about the summer in an honest way. We model this by writing a couple of quick sentences about our own summer, sharing something positive that happened and something challenging.

Figure 43.4: My Summer is a cloze activity we used with our returning high-beginner and low-intermediate students during the first week of school to scaffold the process of writing and talking about their summer experiences. We first read it aloud to students and clarify any new vocabulary. Then students work independently to fill in the blanks. When finished, students can work in pairs or small groups and take turns reading parts or all of their completed *my summer* activity.

Teaching Online

Even though students might keep their cameras "off," teachers can still cheerfully greet each student as they enter the video conference. Most student activities can be done through online documents and screen sharing, including drawing images with on-line drawing boards (see Technology Connections for replace options for Google Jamboard). It will be important to emphasize that students should only use Google Translate for "words" and not "sentences" because teacher monitoring of translation tools will be impossible to do in an online environment. We can only hope that students understand the importance of trying to write in English on their own, at least, at first.

What Could Go Wrong?

As Rick Wormeli (2016) wisely states, "The most urgent questions students ask as they begin a new school year are, 'Am I safe?' and 'Do I belong?'" We want our words and actions to represent a *yes* answer to these critical questions. Teachers who spend a large amount of time going over the rules and projecting a "this is how *I* do things" attitude may have the intention of creating a safe environment for students, but these actions don't cultivate a sense of belonging, where student input is sought and valued. Similarly, the classroom can feel like it belongs to the teacher when educators overshare and talk all about their interests or what they did over the summer. Instead, we want our students to feel safe, supported, and that they are the stars of the show. Once they feel this, real learning can happen!

Differentiation Recommendations

Newcomers (Preliterate or Low Literacy in Home Language): The "I Am" project and "Self-Portraits" can be done fairly easily because of the drawing involved, and students can use Google Translate or other similar tools to write the appropriate words in English. They will need a peer tutor or a classmate's help to access other activities.	**Newcomers (Literate in Home Language):** Students should be able to access all chapter activities (albeit some with translation help with technology or a peer tutor) in the chapter at the beginning of the year except for the "I Learn Best" cards.
Intermediate ELLs: Students should be able to access all chapter activities. They could be challenged to write more extensively and use more complex language in the Self-Portrait and Letter Exchange lessons.	**Advanced ELLs:** Students should be challenged to write even more extensively and use more academic vocabulary and writing structures in writing activities. They can be encouraged to act as peer tutors with less English-proficient students.

Technology Connections

For additional ideas and resources on building community in the classroom, see The Best Resources on Developing a Sense of Community in the Classroom (http://larryferlazzo.edublogs.org/2017/07/18/the-best-resources-on-developing-a-sense-of-community-in-the-classroom/).

Further resources for the beginning of the school year can be found at The Best Resources for Planning the First Days of School (http://larryferlazzo.edublogs.org/2011/08/08/the-best-resources-for-planning-the-first-day-of-school/).

For more ideas on student "self-identity" projects, visit Three Excellent Student Identity "Self-Portrait" Activities (https://larryferlazzo.edublogs.org/2022/07/30/three-excellent-student-identity-self-portrait-activities/).

More ideas for student "getting to know you" activities can be found at The Best Lists of "Icebreaker" Prompts – Please Share Your Own (https://larryferlazzo.edublogs.org/2022/07/31/the-best-lists-of-icebreaker-prompts-please-share-your-own/).

For different options of free virtual whiteboards, see "The Best Alternatives to the Soon-to-Be-Deceased Google Jamboard" (https://larryferlazzo.edublogs.org/2023/10/03/the-best-alternatives-to-the-soon-to-be-deceased-google-jamboard/) and/or "The Best Online Virtual 'Corkboards'" (https://larryferlazzo.edublogs.org/2011/03/30/the-best-online-virtual-corkboards-or-bulletin-boards/).

Attribution

Versions of some of these ideas appeared in our book, *The ESL/ELL Teacher's Survival Guide* (Ferlazzo & Sypnieski, 2012, p. 21–23).

Thank you to Rick Wormeli (2016) for the great ideas contained in his article, "What to Do in Week One?" (www.ascd.org/publications/educational-leadership/sept16/vol74/num01/What-to-Do-in-Week-One%C2%A2.aspx).

All figures from this chapter, as well as 11 additional chapters, references, hyperlinked Technology Connections, and more online resources, can be found at www.wiley.com/go/ellteacherstoolbox2.

Welcome to English Language Development!

In this class, we will be working on our English listening, speaking, reading, and writing skills.

Listening and speaking: You will practice saying English words and sounds every day.

Reading: You will read English books together as a class and by yourself every day. You will learn new words through your reading. You will learn reading strategies that will help you in your other classes.

Writing: You will do a lot of writing in English every day. You will practice using new words in your writing. You will learn writing strategies that will help you in your other classes.

Thinking: You will be thinking a lot! You will practice thinking skills every day.

Figure 43.1 Course Expectations

Materials

Students need to have the following every day:

- A school-issued laptop
- #2 pencil
- Blue or black pen
- A book for independent reading (students may check out books from the classroom, school library, or public library)

Grading

Student grades will be based on three areas:

- Product (quality of student work)
- Process (how students do their work)
- Progress (evidence that students are progressing)

Students will earn points for class assignments and homework. Students are expected to come to class every day; participate in class activities; and demonstrate their growth as readers, writers, and speakers of English.

Class Rules

Along with the expectations listed in the student handbook, here are five class rules that students are expected to follow:

1. Be on time (in your seat when the bell rings).
2. Be prepared. Bring a pen or pencil, paper, and your book every day.
3. *Show respect* for yourself, your classmates, the class materials, and the teacher.
4. Follow classroom procedures and stay on task.
5. Work hard and make mistakes (that's how you learn!).

I am happy you are here! Let's have fun and learn a lot!

Figure 43.1 (*Continued*)

1. My teacher for this class is _____.
2. Which English skills will we be practicing in this class?
   _____
   _____

3. What materials do you need to bring to class with you every day?
   _____
   _____

4. What do you need to do to be successful in this class?
   _____
   _____

5. Write down the five class rules. Then draw a picture next to each one to show that you understand what it means.
   - _____
   - _____
   - _____
   - _____
   - _____

6. Take a minute to look or walk around the classroom. Draw a map of our classroom below. Label the following things: bookshelves, dictionaries, classroom supplies (pencils, class folders, paper, notebooks), garbage cans, pencil sharpener, TV, computers, and anything else you think is important.

7. Please write down two questions you have about this class, this classroom, this school, or your teacher.
   _____
   _____

Figure 43.2 Course Expectations Questions

Ask your partner the following questions and write down his or her answers.

Question: What is your name?
Answer: His or her name is _____.

Question: How old are you?
Answer: He or she is _____ years old.

Question: Where are you from?
Answer: He or she is from _____.

Question: What languages do you speak?
Answer: He or she speaks _____.

Question: What is your favorite food?
Answer: His or her favorite food is _____.

Now, write your partner's answers in this paragraph and practice introducing him or her to the class.

This is _____. He or she is _____ years old. He or she is from _____. He or she speaks _____. His or her favorite food is _____.

Figure 43.3 Partner Introductions

My summer was _____ (great, good, okay, bad). I did _____ (many, a few) things.

One thing I did was _____. Another thing I did was _____.

My favorite part of the summer was _____ _____. The worst part of my summer was _____ _____.

I practiced my English _____ (a lot, some, a little) over the summer. I practiced it by _____ (reading books, using Duolingo, watching TV, going to summer school). I think my English is _____ (better, worse, the same) as it was when school ended in June.

I feel _____ (happy, feeling okay, sad) about being back in school. The best part about school is _____ (seeing friends, learning new things, seeing my teachers).

My big goal for this year is to _____ (work hard, work harder than I did last year, practice speaking English more, behave better in class, do my best).

I think it's going to be a _____ (great, good, okay, bad) year.

Figure 43.4 My Summer

STRATEGY 44
Ending the School Year

What Is It?

The end of the school year can be a challenging time for students to stay engaged in learning and for teachers to maintain their energy. Incorporating end-of-year activities that encourage ELLs to celebrate their growth can be energizing and can keep students learning up until the last bell rings.

Why We Like It

Teachers and students may feel like they are limping across the finish line at the end of the school year. During the last quarter, when testing is finished and spring is in the air, teachers and students can be tempted to go on cruise control. However, this attitude can result in a loss of valuable learning and practice time, especially for ELLs who benefit from as many language-learning opportunities as possible. Although these last several weeks definitely present challenges, they also provide opportunities for students to consider what it means to finish strong, set goals and plan to make it happen, and experience success.

Supporting Research

As we mentioned earlier in Strategy 17: Using Photos or Other Images in Reading and Writing, research by Daniel Kahneman, a Nobel Prize winner, has found that we tend to make future decisions based on the peak-end rule (Holt, 2011)—that we primarily remember how particular events and time periods *ended* along with the best moments that we experienced during those times (Ferlazzo, 2010, March 8). Those memories then influence our future decision making. From this perspective, asking students at the end of the year to reflect on the positive learning experiences they've had (the peaks) and the progress they've made can influence their feelings about—and future decisions related to—school and learning.

Common Core Connections

Depending on how the activities described in this strategy are structured, they can support multiple Standards in all four domains.

Application

This section will share ideas for encouraging ELLs to finish strong during the *last few months* of school and to boost learning in the *last few days* of school. We don't necessarily do all of them every year, but this list provided a menu for you, and us, to choose from depending on our unique classes and personal and professional circumstances.

ACTIVITIES FOR THE LAST FEW MONTHS OF SCHOOL
Finishing Strong Goal-Setting Activity

ELLs can be taught the concept of a strong finish by using simple sports metaphors to illustrate the idea of pushing through fatigue and other difficulties in order to play our best until the end of the school year (e.g., runners don't slow down at the end of a race, basketball teams don't stop playing defense or shooting the ball in the last quarter, etc.). Understanding this concept is easier than actually applying it, however! One of the ways we help students do this is through a goal-setting activity.

After students understand the concept of finishing strong, we ask them to think about what they would like to accomplish in order to finish the school year strong (ideas may be related to learning English, academic skills, behavior, etc.). We pass out Figure 44.1: Finishing Strong Goal Sheet, put a copy under the document camera, and model writing down three goals for ourselves using the sentence frame "I want to _____" (e.g., "I want to finish two books by the end of the school year" or "I want to call three parents a week for positive reasons").

We then model writing down the actions we will need to take in order to accomplish these goals using the sentence frame "To do this, I will" (e.g., "To do this, I will ask my friends to recommend a book that will keep me interested and I will read 20 minutes each night before bed" or "I will make a note when a student does something positive that I want to share with their family").

Students are given time to write down their goals and what actions they can take to accomplish them. We circulate and help students who may need ideas for action steps. We also allow students to work together and to share their goals with each other in order to generate more ideas. For beginners, their goals and action steps might be "I want to learn to talk to my counselor about college. To do this, I will make a list of questions and translate them into English" or "I want to get better at writing sentences in English. To do this, I will write about my book every day and ask my teacher to check it."

We have students glue or staple this sheet in their writer's notebooks. Then, every Friday for the last several weeks of school, students are given time to reflect on their progress and fill out one row of the weekly goal check-in chart on the bottom half of Figure 44.1. They use the chart to reflect on how they did in terms of each goal during that week, what changes they will make the next week if needed, and what help they may need to do this. We complete our weekly check-in on our copy of Figure 44.1 on the document camera. Students love holding us accountable for our goals! See the Technology Connections section for links to multiple other examples of student goal-setting sheets.

Free-Choice Unit

A great way to keep engagement high and to promote language learning is to have students work in pairs or small groups to create a unit on a topic of their choice and teach it to their classmates. Students can select any topic that they want to learn more about or the class could vote on a category to choose from (e.g., famous people, cities, cultures, etc.). The teacher can ask students to generate a list of questions they have about the topic and incorporate time for Internet research. Students can use a graphic organizer (such as a KWL chart) to capture new learnings.

Students can teach their classmates about their topic in a number of ways, depending on how extensive the teacher wants the project to be. For example, students could use higher-order teaching strategies described in this book—inductive data sets, clozes, and sequencing activities—to teach their peers about their topic. Student instructions for creating these activities can be found in Figure 6.5: Strip Story Instructions in Strategy 6: Sequencing, Figure 7.15: Instructions for Making a Cloze in Strategy 7: Clozes, and Figure 11.6: Data Set Instructions in Strategy 11: Inductive Learning. Of course, students should be asked to use these instructional strategies only if they have applied them on multiple occasions throughout the year. Students can also be asked to create a visual aid or to use technology (a slideshow, video, infographic) to teach their topic. The teacher can provide students with a lesson plan format (see Figure 44.2: Lesson Plan) so students can think through how they will teach their classmates about their topic. These lessons can be taught in small groups with groups taking turns to teach each other, or small groups can teach the whole class over a several-day period.

A modified version of this activity could be done with a beginning class. Students could work in groups to identify a topic and five questions they want to research. Then they could be given time to look online for the answers and write them down in English (with teacher or peer tutor assistance if needed). Each group could then create a poster or slideshow containing the information they learned about the topic with images or drawings.

Students could teach their classmates about their topic using the poster and teacher-provided sentence frames (e.g., "We learned that _____" or "One interesting fact about is _____"). Another option is to use the student-led lesson plan described in Strategy 47: Using Technology.

Visual Displays of Learning

The final quarter is a great time to ask ELLs to reflect on the progress they've made throughout the year. In our experience, asking them to create visual displays of their learning makes this process even more creative and engaging.

In Strategy 1: Independent Reading, we describe an activity we do with students to celebrate the reading they've done during the year. Students design a visual representation of their reading journey (a chart, a time line, a map, a bookshelf, etc.) that contains the titles of the books they've read. See Figure 1.2: My Year of Reading Visual Project for the directions and Figure 1.3: My Year of Reading Student Example.

There are many other ways for students to visually represent what they've learned (here are just a few):

- Students can make a top-ten list (most important skills or content learned).
- Students can be divided into groups with each one being assigned a topic the class has studied. Students then work as a group to create a poster containing the five most important things they learned about this topic, along with an image to represent each one.
- Each student can draw a picture or create a storyboard of their best moment in class during the year. This could then be used as a springboard for writing about the experience.
- Students could create a map or time line of the school year on a large sheet of paper. It could include important learning topics, memorable activities, school events, field trips, when new students entered the class, holidays, and so on.
- See the year-in-review activity in the upcoming Reflecting on Growth section for another visual project.

Visiting Other Classes

Making arrangements to visit an elective teacher's classroom at the end of the year can be another way to increase engagement and to encourage ELL and English-proficient students to learn from each other. In the past we have taken our beginning and intermediate classes to participate in art, ceramics, and music classes. We make plans with the elective teacher for their students to teach a simple lesson to our ELLs (e.g., how to play an instrument, how to make an origami bird, how to make a simple ceramic pot, etc.). Many times, these activities turn into natural language lessons for all students involved—ELLs are learning new words in English and the non-ELLs often learn a few new words in their partner's home language. Other times, we pre-teach a set of vocabulary particular to the class we will be visiting. We have received positive feedback from our students and the student teachers in the elective classes about these activities.

STRATEGY 44: ENDING THE SCHOOL YEAR

Using Technology

The last several weeks of the school year is a good time to take advantage of the instant engagement and authentic audiences that technology provides. Students can make digital book trailers (see Bonus Strategy 1: Literary Conversations, available at www.wiley.com/go/ellteacherstoolbox2) on a favorite book that can be shared with next year's students. They could play any of the online learning games listed in Strategy 23: Learning Games for Reading and Writing. Ending the year with an oral presentation that incorporates technology can also be motivating for students. See Bonus Strategy 7: Oral Presentations, available at www.wiley.com/go/ellteacherstoolbox2, for ideas on short and long student presentations.

Field Trips

The end of the year can be a great time to get outside and take field trips. This could be an out-of-town trip or a simple one to a neighborhood store where students have to complete a scavenger hunt. See the Technology Connections section for lots of other field trip ideas.

ACTIVITIES FOR THE LAST FEW DAYS OF SCHOOL

Advice for Future Students

During the last week of school, we often ask students to reflect on the class (the routines, topics of study, learning strategies, projects, etc.) and think about what would be helpful information to share with new students the following year. Students can work in small groups to brainstorm ideas and can then choose from a menu of options—writing a letter to new students, making a list of tips and advice for how to be successful, creating a handbook for the class, and so on. These projects can be shared with incoming students during the first week of the new school year—and we've found that students really pay attention to what their peers have to say!

The Year in Review

It's easy for students, and all of us, to forget what we've done and learned over the past 12 months. Creating opportunities to revisit them can help pull them into our long-term memory (see Chapter 12: Retrieval Practice).

We have our intermediate ELL students use Figure 44.6: Year-in Review Instructions and Planning Sheet to prepare a slideshow that they either present speed-dating style or in front of the class.

You can see a link in the Technology Connections sections to access slideshow examples of student presentations.

Personal Reflections

Borrowing from a *New York Times* Learning Network post (Schulten, 2023), we share the following questions with students (with newcomers, we also provide sentence starters to help them with responses) and ask them to create a slideshow. They can choose any five of them to answer, which they share speed-dating style:

> What do you want to remember about this school year? Why?
> What surprised you?
> What challenged you?
> What successes are you most proud of?
> What did you learn, whether in or out of school?
> How have you grown?
> How could you build on that growth next year?

Expressing Gratitude

Research has found that people gain many benefits from expressing gratitude, and we try to create opportunities for our students to do it various times during the year (with the added benefit from the English required to express it in class!).

This kind of activity is an especially nice one to do to finish up the year. We ask that each student complete this writing frame for three separate students in class:

> *I want to thank* _____ *because he/she/they* _____.
> *When they do that, it makes me feel* _____.
> *OR*
> *When they did that, it made me feel* _____.
> *I am glad I got to know them, and am happy they are in our class!*

Reflecting on Growth

Asking ELLs to reflect on their personal and academic growth can be a powerful culminating activity. One way we do this is by having students create a year-in-review poster. We give students Figure 44.3: My Year Directions and explain that they will draw a chart like the one in the figure on a large sheet of paper (with the months of the school year on the x-axis and positive numbers 1 to 5 on the top of the y-axis and negative 1 to 5 on the bottom of the y-axis). We create an example based on our experiences during the year that serves as a model for students to reference.

We have students start by reflecting on their year and choosing seven important things that happened (meeting a new friend, changing into a new class, doing a project). They then plot these events on their chart. They need to think about where to place them—which month it happened and where it would go on the positive or negative y-axis. Once they plot the event, students need to write a short description of what happened and draw a picture to represent it. If they label an event as negative, they must describe what happened along with what they learned from this event. They could even draw a line connecting the negative event and what they learned from it up to the positive section—after all, learning from mistakes and challenges is always a good thing!

Another way we encourage ELLs to reflect on their progress is by using an improvement rubric for students to evaluate their work. This kind of rubric, unlike many others, does not contain deficit language. Instead, it emphasizes what students *have done* instead of what they *have not done*. Although this process could be used to compare any two similar pieces of work done over the course of a semester or school year, we typically use it with ELLs to analyze their growth in writing.

First, we give students time to review all the essays they've written during the year and to choose two of them—one, preferably from earlier in the year and the other a later one. Students then analyze each essay using an improvement rubric. Figure 44.4: Writing Improvement Rubric is an example of one we used with our high-beginning and low-intermediate class. This rubric can also be found in Strategy 19. We are reprinting here for the reader's convenience. Once students complete this scoring process, we give them a few reflection questions to answer (see Figure 44.5: Improvement Rubric Reflection Questions). Students can then pick one of the two essays to revise and rewrite with their reflections in mind.

Class and Teacher Evaluations

Asking ELLs to evaluate the class and our teaching can offer valuable feedback for us while prompting students to consider their own learning strengths and challenges. Over the years we have given students surveys about our class and our teaching in different formats (multiple-choice, question-answer, fill-in-the-blank, number rankings, etc.).

However, what they all have in common, and what makes them effective, is that they are anonymous and give students a chance to offer honest feedback. The teacher can consider in which areas to receive feedback and then work backward to design the questions. For example, if we want feedback on our relationship-building efforts, we might include the following fill-in-the-blank question on a survey: "My teacher cares about what is happening in my life _____ (a lot, some, a little, not at all)." If we are interested in how students felt about the level of challenge in our class we might ask, "The work in this class was _____ (too hard, just right, too easy)." Some of the questions can also be designed to prompt student reflection on their learning processes, such as "Which activities helped you learn English the most this year and why?" or "What could you do differently or better to help yourself in this class?" See the Technology Connections section for different versions of teacher and class evaluations.

Also, see Figure 44.7: Sample Anonymous ELL Class Evaluation Sheet for an example of questions Larry includes in a Google Form that is set not to record student e-mail addresses.

We also try to have students complete versions of these evaluations at different points during the year so we have time to make any changes during the school year.

ENCOURAGING SUMMER PRACTICE

As students are taking time to reflect on and celebrate their progress at the end of the year, they can also be prompted to think about how to capitalize on these gains over the summer and not experience a summer slide. Many of us are familiar with the research on the summer slide, which shows that many young people, especially in low-income communities, experience academic losses during the time they're out of school (Ferlazzo, 2011, June 26).

We familiarize our ELLs with this research and brainstorm as a class ways to continue to build their skills over the summer. Ideas usually include reading books in English, watching movies with English subtitles, practicing their English-speaking skills out in the community, and doing online practice (see the Technology Connections section for the resources we recommend for online summer learning). We make arrangements with the teachers our students will have in the fall to give them extra credit for any work done over the summer, including online activities and reading books. We allow students to check out books from our classroom library. We also invite a librarian to come and issue library cards to our students so they can use the public library during the summer and the rest of the year. The library is a great summer resource for students who don't have easy access to computers at home. We also have students practice on their laptops before they leave for the summer so they can familiarize themselves with the sites and register for them if needed.

What Could Go Wrong?

It's difficult for students to finish strong when their learning environment doesn't reflect this spirit. Don't take work off the walls and pack all your books away when you are expecting students to be engaged and learning during the final week of school. Nothing says "School's out!" like bare walls and bookshelves. Don't do a countdown of the number of days left in the school year on your board.

For some of our students, the summer doesn't represent a carefree time of rest and rejuvenation. They may already be experiencing feelings of anxiety that can be heightened by the constant reminder of how the school year is quickly coming to an end. It is not helpful when teachers talk about how much they are looking forward to their summer plans. It is important for our students to know that we *want* to be there with them (even if we have momentary dreams of vacation that we keep to ourselves).

Differentiation Recommendations

Newcomers (Preliterate or Low Literacy in Home Language): Assuming these students have been in class for the bulk of the year, they should be able to access most of the end-of-year activities described in this chapter.	**Newcomers (Literate in Home Language):** Students should be able to access all of the activities in this chapter.
Intermediate ELLs: Students should be able to access all of the activities in this chapter. The teacher might want to consider not providing sentence starters for all of them.	**Advanced ELLs:** Students should be able to do all activities while writing longer and more complex sentences and paragraphs.

Technology Connections

For additional resources on ending the school year, see The Best Ways to Finish the School Year Strong (http://larryferlazzo.edublogs.org/2015/04/17/the-best-ways-to-finish-the-school-year-strong/).

Many examples of student goal sheets can be found at The Best Posts on Students Setting Goals (http://larryferlazzo.edublogs.org/2010/05/18/my-best-posts-on-students-setting-goals/).

Explore ideas for virtual and real-life field trips at The Best Resources for Organizing and Maximizing Field Trips—Both "Real" and "Virtual" (http://larryferlazzo.edublogs.org/2016/06/24/the-best-resources-for-organizing-maximizing-field-trips-both-real-virtual/).

To see many examples of teacher evaluations, along with results, visit The Best Posts on Students Evaluating Classes (and Teachers) (http://larryferlazzo.edublogs.org/2010/05/08/my-best-posts-on-students-evaluating-classes-and-teachers/).

More resources and research on the summer slide are available at The Best Resources on the "Summer Slide" (http://larryferlazzo.edublogs.org/2011/06/26/the-best-resources-on-the-summer-slide/).

For a list of updated, free online sites where teachers can easily create virtual classrooms and track student progress, see Larry's post "Updated: Here Are the Sites I'm Using for My Summer School 'Virtual Classroom'" (http://larryferlazzo.edublogs.org/2016/05/23/updated-here-are-the-sites-im-using-for-my-summer-school-virtual-classroom/).

To see student examples of "Year-in-Review" presentations, visit Here's the Year-in-Review Presentation Plan My Students Used This Week – Handouts and Slideshow Examples Included! (https://larryferlazzo.edublogs.org/2019/05/30/heres-the-year-in-review-presentation-plan-my-students-used-this-week-handouts-slideshow-examples-included/).

Attribution

Figures 42.2, 42.4, and 42.5 were modified from Larry's book *Helping Students Motivate Themselves* (2011).

All figures from this chapter, as well as 11 additional chapters, references, hyperlinked Technology Connections, and more online resources, can be found at www.wiley.com/go/ellteacherstoolbox2.

Name_____

What I Want to Do and How I Will Do It

1. I want to _____.
   To do this, I will _____.
2. I want to _____.
   To do this, I will _____.
3. I want to _____.
   To do this, I will _____.

Weekly Goal Check-In

Date	My Goal—(1, 2, or 3)	How did I do? Did I make progress?	What will I do differently next week?	What help do I need to do this?

Figure 44.1 Finishing Strong Goal Sheet

STRATEGY 44: ENDING THE SCHOOL YEAR

Group Members: _____

Our Topic: _____

Make a list of the strategies you will use to teach your classmates about the topic (e.g., cloze, sequencing, data set):

We will be using _____ *to teach about* _____.

How will you introduce your lesson and get students' attention (show a video clip, ask a question for students to discuss in pairs or to answer on a sticky note, etc.)?

We will start our lesson by _____.

What do you want students to do during your lesson (complete a cloze, read and categorize a data set, answer a question, etc.)? How much time will students need to do each part?

Students will _____.

They will need _____ *minutes.*

How will you give directions to students (write them on the board, say them, give them a copy of the steps, etc.)? Can students work together? Alone? With a partner?

We will give directions by _____.

Students will work _____.

What tools will you need to teach your lesson (document camera, computer, whiteboard markers, copies of activities, etc.)?

To teach our lesson we will need _____
_____.

Figure 44.2 Lesson Plan *Source:* Modified from *Helping Students Motivate Themselves* (www.routledge.com/Helping-Students-Motivate-Themselves-Practical-Answers-to-Classroom-Challenges/Ferlazzo/p/book/9781596671812) by Larry Ferlazzo (2011, p. 111).

What tools will students need during your lesson (pencil, paper, colored markers, etc.)?
During our lesson, students will need _____
_____.

How will you help students learn during your lesson (without giving them the answers)?
We will help students learn by _____
_____.

How will you end your lesson? Will students need to turn in any work to you?
We will end our lesson by _____
_____.

Figure 44.2 (Continued)

1. Make a chart like this on a poster:

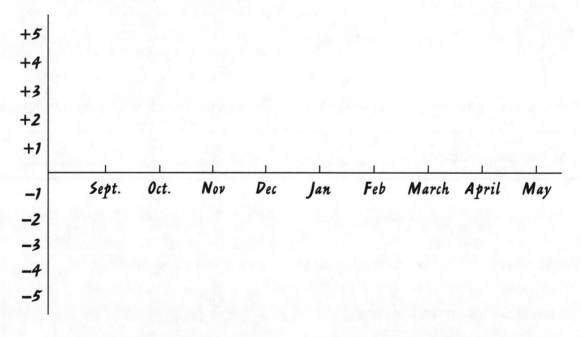

2. Think of seven important things that happened during this school year in any of your classes — a lesson, learning something new, meeting a new friend, doing a project. You can include things that were not too good, too. Plot them on your chart — describe it in words and then draw it.

Figure 44.3 My Year Directions *Source:* Modified from Helping Students Motivate Themselves (https://www.routledge.com/Helping-Students-Motivate-Themselves-Practical-Answers-to-Classroom-Challenges/Ferlazzo/p/book/9781596671812) by Larry Ferlazzo (2011, p. 79).

ESSAY 1:	ESSAY 2:
I opened my essay with an attention grabber (a hook). 1 2 3 4	I opened my essay with an attention grabber (a hook). 1 2 3 4
I used a thesis statement saying the main idea of the essay. 1 2 3 4	I used a thesis statement saying the main idea of the essay. 1 2 3 4
I wrote a list in the introduction paragraph saying what topics I would cover in the essay. 1 2 3 4	I wrote a list in the introduction paragraph saying what topics I would cover in the essay. 1 2 3 4
I organized my essay into paragraphs. 1 2 3 4	I organized my essay into paragraphs. 1 2 3 4
I used topic sentences in all my paragraphs. 1 2 3 4	I used topic sentences in all my paragraphs. 1 2 3 4
I used the correct verb tenses (past or present). 1 2 3 4	I used the correct verb tenses (past or present). 1 2 3 4
Punctuation was correct throughout the essay, including in dialogues. 1 2 3 4	Punctuation was correct throughout the essay, including in dialogues. 1 2 3 4
I wrote a conclusion in which I summarized my main points and left the reader with something to think about. 1 2 3 4	I wrote a conclusion in which I summarized my main points and left the reader with something to think about. 1 2 3 4

Figure 44.4 Writing Improvement Rubric *Source: Modified from Helping Students Motivate Themselves* (https://www.routledge.com/Helping-Students-Motivate-Themselves-Practical-Answers-to-Classroom-Challenges/Ferlazzo/p/book/9781596671812) *by Larry Ferlazzo (2011, p. 79).*

1. Look at the scores you gave yourself on both essays. Overall, which essay was your strongest? Why?

2. Look at the scores on your strongest essay. What did you do well?

3. Look at the scores on your strongest essay. What are three things you need to get better at next year?

4. In what areas of your writing would you like your teacher to help you with next year?

Figure 44.5 Improvement Rubric Reflection Questions *Source:* Reproduced with permission of Routledge Company.

Year-in-Review Instructions

You will be making a three- to five-minute presentation, using Google Slides and index cards, on what you think are the most important things you learned this year in school and why you think they are important. You can use your daily notebooks and any other materials to help you reflect back on the year.

Identify **two things you learned in each of your academic classes** (*English, geography/ethnic studies, math, biology*).

You will explain **why each thing is important and how it can be applied in another area**.

For example: One important thing I learned in biology *was about fat. I can apply it when thinking about the food I am going to eat. I will look for foods that have less fat in them.*

In addition, your presentation must also include **two things you did in school that you liked and explain why you liked them**.

Finally, you must also talk about **two things you want to improve in your school work for next year and why you want to improve them**.

Figure 44.6 Year-in-Review Instructions and Planning Sheet

Only put two to five key words on each slide, and use appropriate images that emphasize your points.

Year-in-Review Planning Sheet

ENGLISH:
One important thing I learned in English was _____.
I can apply it when _____.
Another important thing I learned in English was _____.
I can apply it when _____.

GEOGRAPHY/ETHNIC STUDIES:
One important thing I learned in geography/ethnic studies was _____.
I can apply it when_____.
Another important thing I learned in geography/ethnic studies was _____.
I can apply it _____.

MATH:
One important thing I learned in math was _____.
I can apply it when _____.
Another important thing I learned in math was _____.
I can apply it _____.

BIOLOGY:
One important thing I learned in biology was _____.
I can apply it when _____.
Another important thing I learned in biology was _____.
I can apply it when _____.
WHAT I LIKED:
One thing we did _____ class was _____. I liked it because _____.
Another thing I liked happened in _____class. We _____.
I liked it because _____.
WHAT I WANT TO IMPROVE:
I want to improve _____
because _____.
I also want to improve _____
because _____.

Figure 44.6 (Continued)

1. How did you generally feel about this class?

   1   2   3   4   5

   It was terrible!   It was great!

2. How much English did you learn in this class?

   1   2   3   4   5

   I didn't learn any English!   I learned a lot of English!

3. How hard did you work in this class?

   1   2   3   4   5

   I was very lazy!   I worked hard all the time!

4. How interesting was the content of this class?

   1   2   3   4   5

   Boring!   Really Interesting!

5. How organized was the Google Classroom for this class

   1   2   3   4   5

   Really Confusing!   Excellent!

6. How fair was grading for this class?

   1   2   3   4   5

   Really Unfair!   Very Fair!

7. How did you feel about the quantity of work that was required for this class?

   1   2   3   4   5

   Way too much!   Just the right amount!

8. How did you feel about Mr. Ferlazzo's teaching ability?

   1   2   3   4   5

   He's a really bad teacher!   He's great!

Figure 44.7 Sample Anonymous ELL Class Evaluation Sheet

9. How did you feel that Mr. Ferlazzo related to you?

   1   2   3   4   5

   He didn't seem to care much about me.   He was very concerned about me.

10. Which helps you learn the most? (choose three)
    - Book groups that begin each class
    - Picture words and other activities with peer tutors
    - Quizizz and other Games
    - Practicing in the grammar book
    - Writing paragraphs and essays
    - Practicing conversations and dialogues
    - Studying for, and taking, the Friday tests
    - Other _____

11. Which helps you learn the least? In other words, which DO NOT help you learn? (choose three)
    - Book groups that begin each class
    - Picture words and other activities with peer tutors
    - Quizizz and other Games
    - Practicing in the grammar book
    - Writing paragraphs and essays
    - Practicing conversations and dialogues
    - Studying for, and taking, the Friday tests
    - Other _____

12. What was the most interesting thing you learned in this class?

13. What was the best thing about this class?

14. What was the worst thing about this class and how do you think it could be improved?

Figure 44.7 (Continued)

STRATEGY 45
Beginning and Ending of Class

What Is It?

As educators know, what happens during the first and the last few minutes of class can have a big impact on student learning. *Do nows, walk-in procedures, bell ringers,* or *warm-ups* are all names for activities that students do right at the beginning of class or, as we try to do in our schools, a minute or two prior to the bell ringing. For our purposes, we will refer to these types of openers as "do nows."

Closure activities are designed to wrap up the lesson in the last few minutes of class and provide students the opportunity to respond to their learning in some way.

Why We Like It

"Do nows" can take many forms (which we will discuss in the Application section). In our experience, the most-effective "do nows" for ELLs share two features—they are meaningful activities connected to student learning *and* students can do them independently as part of a routine. Establishing a daily routine—one in which students come into class and immediately know what to do—sets the tone for learning and is a great management tool. Having all students engaged in a learning activity gives us the opportunity to check in with individuals who may need extra support or direction. We also make a point to periodically share with students how the do-now activity can benefit them (e.g., how improving their reading skills in English and in their home language can directly help them in school and in life). Ultimately, we like this practice because it sets a focused and supportive tone in the classroom where students know what they are expected to do, when to do it, and why they are doing it.

Closure activities, which can also include a variety of options, give students a chance to process, summarize, and reflect on their learning. As teachers, we can use them for formative assessment and to gather valuable student feedback. We like closure activities because we can get a lot of bang for our buck. Taking just a few minutes to do one of these activities can yield a wealth of information about our students, our teaching, our curriculum, and ourselves!

Supporting Research

Research shows that "do nows" can be used to create a sense of purpose. Sharing with students not only what they will be learning about that day but also *how it can benefit them* has been found to increase student learning, motivation, and engagement (Busch, 2017). Beginning class with a "do now" further serves as an excellent classroom management technique when incorporated as part of a daily routine. Students can immediately be engaged and on task from the moment they enter class. This effectively sets the tone for the rest of the lesson (Shen & Frances, n.d.).

In Strategy 17: Using Photos or Other Images in Reading and Writing and in Strategy 44: Ending the School Year, we shared research on Daniel Kahneman's peak-end rule, which can also be applied to closure activities. This research stresses the importance of good endings, because we tend to primarily remember the *endings* of events and time periods, and these memories can shape our feelings and decisions in the future (Ferlazzo, 2010, March 8).

Common Core Connections

Depending on which "do nows" and closure activities are included in a lesson, they can support multiple Standards in all four domains.

Application

This section is divided into two parts—ideas for how to *start* and how to *end* class.

DO-NOW ACTIVITIES

As we stated previously, effective "do nows" in our experience share two key qualities—they are meaningful activities connected to student learning *and* students can do them independently as part of a routine. The "do nows" included here best meet these criteria. They can also be modified for use with all proficiency levels and, even though they are part of our classroom routine, they don't feel routine. They allow for student choice and take students' diverse interests into account. This list is not long, but the three main activities described here encompass all of these qualities and have worked best for our students.

Independent Reading

Strategy 1: Independent Reading describes how we support our ELLs in reading books of their choice in class on a daily basis. This practice becomes an established routine in the first few weeks of school as we help students select books, familiarize them with the classroom and school library, and begin to share with them the research on the positive impacts of reading on the brain and on learning (see Strategy 1: Independent Reading for this research).

Once independent reading is an established routine, it serves as an excellent do-now activity. When students enter the room, they can immediately get their book and begin reading. Some students keep their books in their backpacks, and others leave them in plastic crates that we have labeled for each class and are placed near the door for easy access. Most students are engaged in their reading because we encourage them to read books that interest them. For the few students who are struggling to stay engaged, we can use this independent reading time to help them find a new book or to read one-on-one with them. If we are fortunate enough to have a peer tutor or two in the class, we'll have each of them take a student to a quiet corner or outside. The ELL student can then read their book to the peer tutor.

This "do now" works for students at all English proficiency levels because they can read a book at their level or even in their home language. Our classroom library is leveled and contains a section of books in other languages (but we never restrict which levels students can choose from). This type of organization does, however, make it easier for students to quickly find books on their own.

We find that most of our students prefer reading a hard-copy book, as long as the topics are high-interest and accessible (books written for young children are not appropriate for older ELLs). However, there are many options for online reading, as well, including sites that provide audio and visual support for the text. A possible negative to online reading can be the temptation to go to other sites.

When we have peer tutors (see Strategy 39: Peer Teaching and Learning), we often ask them to take turns taking students outside and having them read their books aloud to them. Peer tutors can then provide comprehension and pronunciation support.

Partner Reading

As we described in Strategy 2: Literary Conversations, we do a partner reading activity as a "do now" in our beginner-intermediate class once a week. Students enter to see the directions posted on the document camera (Figure 2.3: Partner-Reading Instructions). They form partners (or we have the names of pairs listed on the front board), choose a book, and start reading. They then complete the rest of the steps listed on Figure 2.3. Of course, the first few times we do this activity, it requires teacher modeling and support. Once students are familiar with the process, it becomes another do-now routine that actively engages students in learning within a few minutes of entering class. Students enjoy it because they are working together and are free to choose any book they like.

Peer Tutor–Led Small Groups

If we have enough peer tutors, one of our favorite "do now" activities is having leveled (by English-proficiency level) small groups led by them. In these groups, students work on either a workbook, a book in the *True Stories* series (Ferlazzo, 2023), or some other activity. Peer tutors are briefed the previous day or are familiar enough with the activity so that all they have to do is be informed at the beginning of class.

STRATEGY 45: BEGINNING AND ENDING OF CLASS

Online Skills Practice

There are many online sites available for practicing various English skills (see the Technology Connections section for links to them). If your students have laptops or other devices, as most do, it can simply be a matter of having a note on the board directing them to what site to do that day or providing them with a variety of choices. If you have peer tutors, they can distribute headphones, or they can be available in a location for students to easily access them (preferably in multiple containers organized alphabetically so they don't have to spend excess time looking to find their own; we keep them in plastic bags marked with each student's name).

Oral Practice

Having students enter and see a question and sentence-starter response that they need to complete and write down in a notebook is another "do now" we often use. We use the prompts found in either Strategy 4: Vocabulary or Strategy 25: Conversation Practice. Then, students break into pre-assigned small groups (led by peer tutors if we have them, led by student leaders if we do not) and practice asking and answering the "question-of-the-day" and previous ones if there is extra time. Then, depending on the size of the class, one group goes to another and practices it again, or each group chooses a pair to "perform" in front of the entire class.

Visualization

Research has shown that visualization techniques have helped enhance performance in many areas, including in second language acquisition (Vlaeva & Dörnyei, 2021). We have applied this technique at various times as a "do now" activity to both enhance language learning and to help students get into a "learning frame of mind," especially for classes who might be starting right after lunchtime, when they might be distracted.

On the day we introduce this activity, we show videos illustrating well-known athletes applying visualization techniques (see the Technology Connections section for links to them, as well as to additional information on how we use this strategy), explain the research behind it, and explain that we will begin each class with a few minutes of visualizing activities. We tell students that they do not have to actually participate in the activity, but they will be required to at least close their eyes and be silent.

Then, in subsequent days, students enter a darkened room with meditative music playing. We greet them at the door to remind them to enter silently and close their eyes. Then, we lead them through a short visualization exercise where they are imagining themselves in a situation where they are successfully communicating in English (at a store, restaurant, in another class, etc.).

As mentioned earlier, other research has found this kind of exercise to be effective in language acquisition. We don't have any concrete data on its English-learning impact for our students, but we do give them anonymous surveys where we ask, one, if they actually participated in the visualization exercise and, two, if they liked it and thought it helped them feel more motivated and confident in learning English. The vast majority of students always respond positively to both questions.

We have generally used this activity with classes that tend to be less focused and we have *always* found that it has had a dramatic impact on students being more serious about their work. See Strategy 38: Motivation for more ideas on using visualization.

Writer's Notebook Prompts

We have also used writer's notebook prompts to engage students at the start of a lesson. We usually teach our ELLs in two-hour block classes. Oftentimes we will have students read at the start of the first hour and then respond to a prompt in their writer's notebook at the beginning of the second hour. The prompts can vary with students responding to their reading, answering questions related to the upcoming lesson, or choosing a topic from their heart map or writing territories to write about (all of these ideas are described in Bonus Strategy 5: Writer's Notebook).

We post the prompt on the document camera during the break between classes and students get their notebooks as they enter the room. Then when they go to their seat, they can immediately begin thinking and responding to the prompt. Because we want them to be able to work independently, we are careful to write the prompt in simple language and provide any synonyms for challenging words. Beginners can translate the question with the help of a more English-proficient classmate or Google Translate and can respond in their home language if needed.

An Additional Note on "Do Nows"

Some educators suggest that "do nows" should directly connect to the lesson being taught that day or review concepts from the previous lesson. We agree with them but may have a broader definition of *connect* than they have in mind. Literacy skills relate to everything that students are doing. And, we know these reading and writing "do nows" are engaging our students because many times they don't want to stop doing them!

Some also suggest that "do nows" must be assessed and feedback must be provided to students in order for them to be effective so they don't become, as educator David Ginsburg (2011) says, "do laters" or "do nevers." We agree that assessment and feedback are important to inform our practice and enhance students' learning.

However, we've also found that attaching points to enjoyable literacy practices (such as free reading and journaling) can make them less enjoyable for students, thus decreasing motivation and engagement. We seek to find a balance by periodically collecting students' notebooks to check their progress and to offer brief written feedback.

CLOSURE ACTIVITIES

Meaningful closure activities only need to take a few minutes, yet they are so hard to do! Before we know it, the class period has whizzed by and our closure consists of calling out "Have a good day everybody!" The most effective closure activities, in our experience, share the following characteristics—they are short, they involve student reflection, and they require active processing from all students. The activities described here contain these elements.

Shining Moments

This activity was introduced to us by secondary teacher Paige Price (Your Shining Moment, n.d.) and involves asking students to think about what they did best on an assignment, an essay, or in class that day. They then write down this shining moment on a notecard or at the bottom of the assignment and turn it in before they leave. We like to use this as a closing activity with ELLs because it encourages them to reflect on their progress and to leave the classroom on a positive note (remember the research about good endings!). It also gives us valuable information about our students and their confidence levels. We usually have students write on notecards and may provide sentence frames such as "My shining moment today was _____" or "Today, what I did best was _____." Sometimes, we leave a few extra minutes so students can share their shining moments with a partner or in a small group.

A variation on this activity that we use when students are doing a longer piece of writing is to stop a few minutes before the end of class and ask students to read over what they've written. We then ask them to highlight or underline what they believe is their best sentence—a shining sentence. They also have to think about *why* it is the best and be prepared to share their sentence and reasoning with a partner. We provide the sentence frames: "My best sentence is _____." "I think it is the best because _____."

Question Menu

One way to ensure that you always have a closing activity on hand is to create a menu of reflection questions and tasks that students can choose from. This question menu can be stapled into their notebooks for easy reference. There are numerous options to include on the menu—students can be asked to summarize their learning, make connections, reflect on their learning processes, list something they did well and something that was a challenge, draw a quick sketch to represent their learning, write a new word they learned, and many others. The Technology Connections section contains resources for many more closure questions.

Everybody Think...

This quick closure activity is short and can be done on the fly, but it is highly effective. At the end of the class, the teacher simply asks a closing question (about content, the learning process, etc.) and says, "I will give you all 45 seconds to think of your answers and then will call on three students to share."

Self-Assessment Exit Tickets

Exit tickets, or exit slips, are typically responses that students write on a card, slip of paper, or sticky note and hand in as they exit the classroom. We frequently use this type of closing activity as a quick and easy way for students to assess their comprehension. At the end of class, we ask students to reflect on their understanding of the lesson and to choose from a list of responses on the board. Examples could include "I've got it!"; "I need more practice"; "I don't get _____"; or "I still need help with _____." Students can quickly write down the response that is closest to how they're feeling. The teacher can review these responses and address any needs the following day.

We generally have students put their names on exit tickets, but sometimes we make them anonymous. This works when we want to confirm or not confirm our gut feelings about how the class is doing on a specific project or comprehending a specific concept. Even though we often emphasize that mistakes are opportunities for learning, some students might still be hesitant to disclose their lack of understanding. For example, if we're in the middle of a project and feel that students are not being entirely candid with us about how they're doing ("I got it! I got it!"), we will have them complete an anonymous exit ticket rating their feelings about the project (1 = excellent, 2 = okay, 3 = lost). We can then plan next steps based on the results. For example, maybe we need to give students additional time to complete it or provide further scaffolding.

Sticky Note Compliments

This activity encourages student reflection while cultivating positive student–student relationships. At the end of the lesson, the teacher quickly passes out sticky notes to each student and displays the following prompt on the document camera:

> On your sticky note, write something you learned from a classmate today or write a positive comment about one of your classmates.

The teacher then collects student responses as they leave. The next day, the teacher can share the positive comments that students have written about each other with the whole class.

3–2–1

The 3-2-1 activity described in Strategy 9: Jigsaw can be varied in multiple ways. One way to use it as a closing activity is to have students write down on a notecard three things they learned from the day's lesson, two questions they still have about the topic, and one thing they did well during the lesson.

One-Minute Reports

Another activity we've previously described that could work for closure is the one-minute report in Strategy 30: Listening. In this activity, students work together to develop a short oral report (no more than one minute long) summarizing what they learned from the day's lesson. The teacher then calls on five or six (could be more or less depending on time) students from various groups to share their one-minute report with the class or in small groups. Everyone must participate and have his or her report ready to go because students will be chosen at random by the teacher.

Teaching Online

All these activities can be conducted online through online documents, slideshows and virtual white boards (see Technology Connections for different options), shared screens, and breakout rooms. However, regular reinforcement will be needed so students remember to use Google Translate and Artificial Intelligence tools appropriately. Again, as we've previously mentioned, without the ability to accurately monitor student actions, use of those tools in an online environment is based on an "honor" system.

"Do nows" are important. However, as we've mentioned in earlier chapters, we also think one of the most important ways to begin classes is by welcoming and acknowledging each student individually by name. We feel that saying, "Hi, (student's first name)" is even more important in an online environment where making a personal connection is so much more difficult. And it's easy to offer that welcome as you let people into the video conference.

What Could Go Wrong?

"Do nows" are meant to engage students as they walk in the door for a short period of time (usually 5 to 10 minutes, a bit longer with independent reading). Stick to the time limit and move on while students are still engaged. Don't sabotage this time by telling students all about your weekend or asking them to run errands for you. Do circulate to offer support and encourage students who seem less engaged. It is tempting to use this time (and we sometimes succumb to this temptation) to attend to our own business (checking e-mail, stapling copies, etc.), but we will see better results when we stay tuned in.

As we said, we are sometimes guilty of closing our lesson as the bell is ringing and we are shouting our good-byes or clean-up instructions. Try to avoid this by devoting some thought to each lesson's closing activity. Using a question menu (such as the one previously described in the Application section) for students to reference in their folders on any day can help address this challenge. Asking students to be in charge of reminding you when it is time to close the lesson or of developing and implementing their own closure ideas can also work well.

Differentiation Recommendations

Newcomers (Preliterate or Low Literacy in Home Language): Students can use many of the online tools listed in Strategy 33: Supporting ELL Students with Interrupted Formal Education (SIFEs) and/or work with a peer tutor or with another ELL student who speaks the same home language for "do now" activities. Many of the closure activities can be completed with drawings, or they can use Google Translate or other previously described supportive online tools to participate, as well as working with a peer tutor or another student.	**Newcomers (Literate in Home Language):** Students should be able to participate in all of the "do now" and closure activities described in the chapter.
Intermediate ELLs: Students can do all the activities described in the chapter and should read more complex texts and provide longer written responses using more complex language.	**Advanced ELLs:** Students can do all the activities described in the chapter and should read even more complex texts and provide even longer written responses using even more complex language. Some could function as peer tutors to students with lower English proficiency.

Technology Connections

For accessible online sites for reading resources, go to The Best Websites to Help Beginning Readers (https://larryferlazzo.edublogs.org/2008/01/22/the-best-websites-to-help-beginning-readers/), The Best Websites for Beginning Older Readers (https://larryferlazzo.edublogs.org/2008/01/23/the-best-websites-for-beginning-older-readers/), or The Best Websites for Intermediate Readers (https://larryferlazzo.edublogs.org/2008/01/26/the-best-websites-for-intermediate-readers/).

For sites where students can practice various skills, go to The Best Sites Students Can Use for Independent Practice (https://larryferlazzo.edublogs.org/2022/07/19/the-best-sites-students-can-use-for-independent-practice/).

Learn more about visualization techniques at Best Posts on Helping Students "Visualize Success" (https://larryferlazzo.edublogs.org/2010/12/23/my-best-posts-on-helping-students-visualize-success/).

For different options of free virtual whiteboards, see The Best Alternatives to the Soon-to-Be-Deceased Google Jamboard (https://larryferlazzo.edublogs.org/2023/10/03/the-best-alternatives-to-the-soon-to-be-deceased-google-jamboard/) and/or The Best Online Virtual "Corkboards" (https://larryferlazzo.edublogs.org/2011/03/30/the-best-online-virtual-corkboards-or-bulletin-boards/).

For more on "do nows," see The Best Resources for "Do Now" Activities to Begin a Class (http://larryferlazzo.edublogs.org/2016/09/10/the-best-resources-for-do-now-activities-to-begin-a-class/).

For further information on closure activities, including a long list of sample questions, see The Best Questions to Use for Class Closing Activities—What Are Yours? (http://larryferlazzo.edublogs.org/2013/09/19/here-are-some-questions-i-use-for-class-closing-activities-what-are-yours/).

Attribution

Thank you to Paige Price for her helpful ideas in the Teaching Channel video "Your Shining Moment" (www.teachingchannel.org/videos/celebrating-student-achievement).

STRATEGY 46
Zero-Prep Activities

What Is It?

"Zero prep" means exactly what it says—a high-value English acquisition activity (not "busywork") that requires no preparation time by the teacher. In our definition, when we say "zero prep," we mean "zero prep." This means no copying, no distributing books, nada. It also means a minute or less of teacher thinking is required before launching the activity.

The only physical preparation that may be required in some of these activities is distribution of mini-whiteboards, markers, erasers (in some cases, to each student; in other situations, to small groups), and/or sheets of paper.

Perhaps you have to cover an ELL class during your planning period because of an absence or emergency and the teacher hasn't left a sub plan. Or, perhaps a family situation or your own illness has put you in a bind and you haven't had time to plan a lesson for that day. Or, maybe, despite your years of experience, you've badly miscalculated how much time your lesson will take and you've ended up with 20 minutes before the bell rings (it happens!). Or, finally, if you are called away from your class at the last minute and you need to explain to the sub and your students a simple activity for them to do.

When those situations arise, the activities described in this chapter can be a huge help!

Why We Like It

Things happen, and when they do, it's not fair to our students if we waste their time. The activities listed in the chapter all offer excellent language learning opportunities—no "busywork" options here. Our students can't afford to waste their time, and we are morally and professionally obligated not to create situations where their time is wasted.

Supporting Research

We share several games in this chapter, and Strategies 23 and 32 detail extensive research on their effectiveness in language teaching. This chapter also includes zero-prep activities involving images, and you can find the research connections for them in Strategy 17: Using Photos or Other Images in Reading and Writing. We share a cooperative writing activity, and research for that one can be found in Strategy 16: Choice Boards/Learning Menus. Finally, research supporting the dictation activities here can be found in Strategy 24: Dictation.

Common Core Connections

Most of these zero-prep activities can be connected to one or more of the Reading and Writing Standards. As we explained in Strategy 24: Dictation, the dictation activities inexplicably don't fall under Speaking and Listening Standards but do fall under the Language Standard of "comprehend more fully when . . . listening."

Application

A few of these activities are discussed in more detail elsewhere in the book. In that case, we provide brief descriptions and basic instructions about how to do it, along with a reference to which chapter has more information. That majority of games in Strategy 23: Learning Games for Reading and Writing and in Strategy 31: Learning Games for Speaking and Listening fit into the "zero-prep" category, and we didn't just want to repeat listing them all here. Other activities are new to the book, including some very simple games that are not listed in those games chapters.

We've grouped these activities into five categories: Games, Using Images, Reading and Writing, and Dictation.

GAMES

Word Searches with Clozes

We're not big fans of the typical word search and feel that those generally fall into the "busywork" category. However, if you have graph paper available to distribute, having students create cloze (gap-fill) sentences on one sheet of regular paper and then having students create the word search including the answers to the clozes—now that's a different story! Students can then exchange their creations and complete them.

Countdown

Write nine letters on the front whiteboard—a mixture of vowels and consonants. Divide students into small groups with one mini-whiteboard each. Depending on the English-proficiency level of the class, give them a minute or two to write as many words as they can using letters from the board—the longer the word, the more points they receive (one point for each letter). Then, put up another group of nine letters to continue the game.

Word Chain

Again, get students in small groups with one whiteboard for each group. Give students a word, and tell them they have 30 seconds to write as many words as they can that begin with the last letter of the word you gave them. Groups receive a point for each correct word.

Then, choose the last letter from the first word on the whiteboard belonging to the group that gained the most number of points in that round, and that's the letter students have to use to create the next group of words.

Word Association

Give students a word, let's say "dog." Students, again in small groups with whiteboards, have to come up with as many words as they can that are connected to that word in some way (bone, bite, fur, toy, ball, collar, etc.) and receive a point for each one. If they put a questionable word on their board, any group or the teacher can challenge it. If they can't give a good explanation, they lose three points. The game continues to another word, chosen by the teacher or by a student.

USING IMAGES

"What Are These Animals Saying?"

We collect photos and videos, and they're also easy to find, of animals that look like they're talking to one another. You can see the Technology Connections section for a link to them. Showing them to students (perhaps in small groups) and challenging them to write a dialogue for the picture/video is often a fun assignment—which they also have to act out!

"Spot the Difference" Pictures

If you have access to a computer, the Internet, and a projector, search the Internet for "Spot the Difference" pictures. You'll find many examples. Project them on the screen, and have students work in groups to write about the differences they see. If you want to personalize it more to what the class is studying at the time, many artificial intelligence–powered text-to-image tools will create these Spot the Difference images on demand.

We modified the next two ideas from ELL teacher Brent Warner (2022).

Share an Image

The teacher begins by modeling, showing an image from their phone, and telling the story behind it. Then, students begin "speed-dating" (every other row moving clockwise so every few minutes they have different partners) by showing a picture from their phone and telling its story. They can show the same picture to everyone, or change it.

Scavenger Hunt

Students get in partners or in small groups with their phones out. The teacher tells the class what they have to find in one of their photos (something green, a baby, a rollercoaster), and they are given one minute to find it, write it on a whiteboard in a sentence ("The woman is wearing a green shirt") and show it. This could be played as a game with points for the groups who are successful, or just as a fun learning activity.

READING AND WRITING

Scrambled Sentences

Student groups are given paper clips, paper (or index cards), scissors, and their textbook or another book. They are asked to identify 10 sentences from the book and write them so each word is on a small piece of paper or index card (including punctuation marks). Then, they take the papers or cards from each sentence and mix them up and then paper clip them together. It's important to point out that they shouldn't mix up all 10 sentences together—they should just mix up and clip together the words from the same sentence. Each group passes on their 10 sentences to the next one, who have to unscramble the sentences correctly. After five or seven minutes, the sentences are switched again.

Partner Reading

Students are asked to choose a partner with whom they want to read a book together and then are given a minute or two to choose a book. They are told they will take turns reading aloud to each other for 10 minutes. At the end of that time, they have to answer these questions on a sheet of paper—the questions will be on the board:

1. What are your names?
2. What is the title of the book?
3. What are three words in the book that are new to you, and what do they mean?
4. Can you please draw two pictures that represent some things that happened in the book and write a sentence about what each drawing is?
5. Did you like the books? Why or why not? ("We liked this book because....." or "We didn't like this book because....")

Cooperative Storytelling

We describe this activity in Bonus Strategy 4: Cooperative Writing. Students are given a regular sheet of paper or, ideally, an easel sheet. In small groups, they have to answer the questions we ask to help them create their own story (What is the setting? Who is the protagonist, etc.). See Strategy 16 for more details.

DICTATION

We describe these next activities more fully in Strategy 24: Dictation.

Picture Dictation

The teacher quickly draws a picture and hides it from students. They describe it, and students have to replicate it on their sheets based on the description. Hilarity often ensues when students share their versions with the entire class. Next, students put folders upright on their desks so that others can't see what they are drawing, and they are given 5 or 10 minutes to create their own "masterpiece." In partners, they then take turns dictating descriptions of their image so that their partner can try to replicate it.

Dictogloss and Variations

We describe multiple variations of this activity in Strategy 24. Basically, it's a matter of taking a simple text and first having students only listen to it as the teacher reads it slowly. Next, the teacher reads it at a typical pace, and students can write notes about it. Then, the teacher reads it again with students only listening. Afterward, students can work in partners to try and recreate the original text. After a while, the teacher shows the text on the smartboard or document camera for students to compare it to their versions.

Teaching Online

The games in this chapter just won't work in an online environment, since it would be very easy for students to use their phone, laptop, and/or artificial intelligence to get the answers. However, all the other activities may be "AI proof"—or relatively so.

What Could Go Wrong?

Students "cheating" at the games by using their phone will certainly happen, and the only ways to minimize that are by talking to them beforehand about how that won't help their language acquisition (which probably won't help much when their competitive juices get going) and by watching them like hawks while they're playing (which tends to be more effective).

Differentiation Recommendations

Newcomers (Preliterate or Low Literacy in Home Language): When playing the zero-prep games, an easy modification is to ask them to try to participate without use of the translation devices on their phones but if they're "stuck," they can use them. Generally, we find that students appreciate the support, and respect our request that they don't use it as too much of an "unfair" advantage over the rest of the students, who don't get to use their phones. Depending on their numbers in our classes, they are either grouped all together or mixed with others in the game groups.	**Newcomers (Literate in Home Language):** These students should be able to access all or most of the zero-prep activities. Teachers, though, need to ensure that the game questions and dictation texts are accessible.
Intermediate ELLs: Students should be able to develop some of the game questions. Text levels, and teacher expectations, should be higher in all activities.	**Advanced ELLs:** Students should be able to develop some of the game questions. Text levels, and teacher expectations, should be even higher in all activities.

Technology Connections

Get even more ideas at The Best Resources for Zero-Prep ELL Lessons (https://larryferlazzo.edublogs.org/2022/11/26/the-best-resources-for-zero-prep-ell-lessons/). If you want to expand the definition of "zero prep" a bit further, you can find links to many free worksheets that can be easily downloaded and printed for students to use.

Of course, if you want to expand the zero-prep definition, any artificial intelligence–powered chatbot can also help with creating a worksheet on just about any topic imaginable and at any student language level.

For images to use for the "animal talking" lesson, check out The Best Resources for Using "If This Animal or Image Could Talk" Lesson Idea in Class" (https://larryferlazzo.edublogs.org/2015/08/01/the-best-resources-on-using-if-this-animal-or-image-could-talk-lesson-idea-in-class/).

There are many online sites that ELL students can access for language practice, and having them work on them during class time is always another zero-prep activity that can work. You can see our recommended ones at "There Are Tons of Resources on This Blog to Help Educators Teach ELLs – This Post Is a Good Place to Start (https://larryferlazzo.edublogs.org/2023/12/29/there-are-tons-of-resources-on-this-blog-to-help-educators-teach-ells-this-post-is-a-good-place-to-start/).

STRATEGY 47
Using Technology

What Is It?

When we say *technology* in this strategy, we are specifically talking about smartphones, desktops, laptops, and tablets. Most strategies in this book have featured Technology Connections. The point of this particular strategy is to discuss broader issues about tech use and share some specific tech projects we've done with ELLs.

Why We Like It

In Strategy 38: Motivation, we briefly discussed the four pillars that promote intrinsic motivation:

1. **Autonomy:** having a degree of control over what needs to happen and how it can be done
2. **Competence:** feeling that one has the ability to be successful in doing it
3. **Relatedness:** doing the activity helps students feel more connected to others and feel cared about by people whom they respect
4. **Relevance:** work must be seen by students as interesting and useful to their present lives and hopes and dreams for the future (Ryan & Deci, 2000)

Not every lesson must have the maximum level of all four of these elements, but we don't think it's too difficult, or too much to ask, to suggest that most lessons have some degree of all of these qualities. When they are combined, these qualities promote a sense of *student agency,* when students feel that they have and, in fact, do have a greater ability to proactively determine their life's path. Student agency, in turn, also encourages a higher likelihood of being able to transfer what they learn to other contexts (Lindgren & McDaniel, 2012).

Technology—used well—can provide superior opportunities to integrate these four qualities with language instruction and particularly create possibilities to personalize learning. In other words, it can assist students to pursue highly relevant topics to their lives while connecting them to strong academic challenges.

Most of the student activities we highlight in this strategy clearly make those connections. We also feel it is important to include the fourth one—learning to type or keyboard—because it is often overlooked in secondary classrooms (the assumption is students have developed that ability in earlier grades). This is an important skill our ELL students need to develop if they haven't already done so in their countries of origin.

In addition to discussing how artificial intelligence can support our students' English acquisition, we also discuss here, and in other chapters, how it can help us be better teachers to them.

The ability to comfortably use technology has become essential in our social, academic, and professional worlds. Our ELLs (and us educators) can benefit by using it in ways we suggest in this chapter and in previous Technology Connections sections.

Supporting Research

Extensive research has documented the positive impact the use of technology can have on ELLs' reading abilities (Sullivan, 2007); motivation and engagement (Baker et al., 2015; Diallo, 2014, p. 6; Lee, 2012); and writing, speaking, and listening skills (Kasapoğlu-Akyol, 2010, p. 237).

Common Core Connections

The first three activities listed in the Application section support many different Standards. They involve reading, writing, speaking and listening, and teachers need to be mindful that students are regularly increasing the complexity of the work being done. Autonomy can be a two-edged sword, and though most of our students are eager to challenge themselves, left to their own devices they may not know *how* to go about doing so.

Student skill in typing and keyboarding is important so they can meet the Standard of using "technology, including the Internet, to produce and publish writing and to interact and collaborate with others."

Application

We will discuss specific recommendations on how students can use technology to teach their classmates, how tech can be used to promote independent learning, and how online resources can provide opportunities for meaningful homework. In addition, we'll be discussing ways to effectively teach typing and keyboarding and how artificial intelligence can specifically help English Language Learners.

TEACHING OTHERS

In a multilevel English language learner class (and what ELL class *isn't multilevel?*), it's not always easy to keep all students engaged all the time. Periodically, we have a group (usually two or three) of more advanced ELLs choose a topic and, using laptops or cell phones, work together to prepare a lesson they then teach to another small group (see Figure 47.1: Student-Led Lesson Plan). Using Figure 47.2: Lesson Guide and teacher guidance, students identify a short and simple read aloud of four to seven sentences from an online text about a topic of interest, identify several new vocabulary words from it that they will need to preteach, and find a related image they can use for a picture word inductive model (see Strategy 11: Inductive Learning) mini-lesson. We give them time to practice teaching their lesson, and then they give it a try with another small group using laptops, mini-whiteboards, and often plain paper. Though the quality tends to be mixed, the teachers and the students seem to benefit from this change-of-pace activity. We shared research about the value of peer-led instruction in Strategy 39: Peer Teaching and Learning.

These lessons usually take 20 minutes or so. If you want to use less time, have students do only one or two of the steps.

INDEPENDENT STUDY

As you might note from all of our previous sections on Technology Connections, we are often very specific in the technology-related assignments we give to our students. However, we also provide them time to pursue their own choices to study. This freedom, though, comes with some guidance from us.

Researchers have found that providing different kinds of choice in learning encourages autonomy. Teachers are familiar with organizational choice (in this case, for example, it might be letting students choose who they want to work with and where they would like to sit) and procedural choice (e.g., providing a list of final presentation options). However, a third kind—*cognitive choice*—is thought by some researchers to stimulate even more self-motivation (Stefanou et al., 2010). Both of these independent projects try to promote cognitive choice so students are given a wide latitude in determining what they learn and how they are assessed.

We use these next two activities to promote disciplined independent study—one on a weekly basis, the other for individual days. Of course, this schedule assumes that teachers and students have regular access to technology.

Weekly Independent Project

Every other Monday, ELL students in our class complete a form (Figure 47.3: Weekly Computer Independent Study Plan) on which they can identify anything they want to learn so long as it promotes their language development: verbs, the history of Mexico, vocabulary about food, and so on. They also choose how their learning will be assessed on that

Friday—through a test (see Figure 47.4: Personalized Learning Weekly Test), a class presentation, or a student-generated assessment idea. For the most part, students research their topics using the wide variety of resources that we make available on Google Classroom (see the Technology Connections section), including ChatGPT or other artificial intelligence-powered sites (see the Artificial Intelligence section later in this chapter), or any paper-based resource (such as a workbook) we have available in the classroom.

Daily Independent Work

We sometimes give students a portion of a class period to use their choice of several activities we make available on Google Classroom (see the Technology Connections section). As we've discussed, online tools can help students reinforce their sense of competence by promoting risk-taking. Making mistakes in grammar, articulating new knowledge, or experimenting with pronunciation feels less scary when we know that our missteps will remain a secret between us and our computer. If students have demonstrated that they can work with a partner and still stay focused on the task, they can work in pairs.

In fact, immediate feedback from a computer program can serve as a limited form of coaching—a crucial component of deliberate practice that supports mastery. Deliberate practice is intentional goal-oriented repetition with regular reflection and subsequent readjustment of one's study (Ferlazzo, 2012, July 21). Effective practice also requires feedback and coaching. Such support might be adequately provided by a combination of feedback from the computer program and regular conversations between a student and teacher. But it also requires constant reflection by the learner on what they're doing right, could be doing better, and must do in order to reach the next level.

Online tools seldom provide this reflective space, so we need to consider how we can make students' work on the computer more comparable to deliberate practice. With ELL students, we provide a simple form (Figure 47.5: Daily Computer Plan and Reflection) they can use, in combination with our one-on-one conversations, for goal setting and reflection on their work online. It contains three sentence starters or guidelines (the figure also includes multiple examples and models):

- [Before you log in] Today, I want to . . .
- [At the end of class] Did I achieve my goal? (yes or no)
- [At the end of class] What things helped me learn today or didn't help me learn today?

For example, after using the reflection form and thinking about additional questions we had discussed in class, Rodrigo realized that although he had enjoyed using a site filled with English language–learning games the most, he had learned more when he used an independent reading tool that provided audio and visual support. His realization didn't mean that he never played the language games again, but he began spending more time—at home and at school—on the reading site to reach his goal of being able to read more-challenging text in English.

HOMEWORK

In our classes, students probably have a little non-online homework once or twice a week if they don't complete some of the writing tasks we do in class. But that's pretty minimal. Online homework is a different kettle of fish and first requires some prep work with our students.

As part of more than one personal conversation we have with each student, we learn their goals, their personal situations (including age, work schedules, family and living situations, and access to the Internet). We discuss the difficulties of learning a new language, what the research says about the length of time it takes, and how much time they have left in high school. We explain that we make individual contracts with students about online homework based on their goals, age, and access to the Internet.

At the end of our conversation(s), we ask each student how much time they think they can spend on one of the sites we use (we have this conversation after students have become familiar with using them during class time). Sixty percent of the time, students say an unreasonably high amount, and we say, "That's great, but why don't we start at a lower amount and then build up to that time?" We're happy with 15 minutes a day, five days a week. However, that amount can be challenging for students who are working full-time or who have had minimal prior school experience or who have weak or no Internet connections at home. In those situations, we make different agreements.

In each case, we try to make the time to call home to talk with a family member and explain the agreement. We do this to support the student and to help ensure there's a little more accountability support at home.

All the sites students can use—and choice is important—provide teachers with reports on student progress (in the case of ChatGPT or other chatbots, we just ask students to copy and paste or share screenshots of what they did). Students know this, and we show the reports to them. The atmosphere, however, that we work hard at creating in our classroom is not one of "If you don't do it, then your grade will go down." Instead, it's more of "What's going on? Has something changed? Do we need to readjust the time expectation?" We use a system in which students have a major influence in grading themselves and grades don't function as a big motivator in our classrooms. But it's clear that most students want us to believe that they do follow through on what they say they are going to do.

Links to the homework sites our students use can be found in the Technology Connections section. In addition, we've included a link there to more details about our thoughts and practices on grading. Learn more about our assessment strategies at Strategy 49: Assessment.

ARTIFICIAL INTELLIGENCE

Though we are not subscribers to the belief that artificial intelligence will "revolutionize" education (no matter what Bill Gates and Sal Khan say), we do believe that it can provide substantial benefits to those who are learning a new language and also to their teachers.

We have shared in many chapters the different ways AI can be incorporated into English language instruction. Many of the sites we recommend to our students for language learning use AI to provide feedback on pronunciation, to teach grammar through adaptive learning, and to help teach vocabulary.

Also, ChatGPT and similar chatbots can supply countless opportunities for motivated students to use for language acquisition. We don't feel a need to use up space listing its responses, but you can help students develop prompts like these that they can write in English or in their home languages:

What are ways you can help a Beginning English language learner like me learn English on my own?

What are games I can play with you to help learn English?

As we mentioned earlier, there are many examples in different chapters of how AI can assist teachers. If you want to learn about additional ones, ask ChatGPT or another chatbot this question:

What are the best ways a teacher of English language learners can use you?

See the Technology Connections section for links to additional AI resources.

LEARNING TO TYPE AND USE THE KEYBOARD

Many of our students come to us with limited typing or keyboarding skills. This can be yet another challenge to writing and test-taking success in school, so we believe it's important to help them develop this ability.

We have a link in the Technology Connections sections to free online typing and keyboarding sites. All of them are good, though Dance Mat typing from the BBC is far and above the best for ELLs because of the audio and visual support it provides to users. The link to the list that includes all of the typing sites is in the Technology Connections section.

OTHER TECH EQUIPMENT

Though we don't go in for lots of bells and whistles with the technology we use in the classroom, there are two pieces of equipment—apart from laptops—that we feel are essential.

One is having enough headphones with microphones for each student. We put one in a plastic bag labeled with the student's name, and peer tutors pass them out and pick them up each day we will be using them.

The other is some sort of microphone to amplify student speech when they are in front of the class for when groups are performing dialogues or making presentations. Though students may be self-conscious about using the mic at first, they get used to it quickly and ensures that everyone can hear what is said and frees us from having to regularly say, "Please speak louder." See a link in the Technology Connections section for teacher-recommended microphones.

We describe equipment that can be used for simultaneous translation in both Strategy 33: Supporting ELL Students with Interrupted Formal Education (SIFEs) and in Strategy 41: Working with Parents and Guardians.

Teaching Online

All these activities can be done during distance learning, and we have, in fact, done just that (except for extensive use of artificial intelligence sites, which did not exist during that time).

Again, though, it is critical to have early, and regular, conversations about the ethical use of AI, since it would be easy for students to misuse it in an all online environment.

What Could Go Wrong?

Students, like all of us, can find it hard to resist the siren call of Internet distractions (social media, YouTube music and sports videos, games, etc.) when they are supposed to be working on other more academic or professional projects online. One way we try to preempt these challenges is by teaching a lesson on the famous "marshmallow test" so students can see the long-term value of self-control. A link in the Technology Connections section will lead you to that lesson. Then, prior to each time we use technology, we are able to remind students to not "eat the marshmallow."

Sometimes, prior to working on a tech task, we will also just ask students to raise their hands if they agree to not use other sites while working on their devices. Does this mean that all our students will show self-control? No, of course not. But usually a gentle reminder (or two or three) will take care of the problem. As always, teachers should not be sitting behind their desks catching up on other tasks while students are working. We need to be constantly circulating, checking in with students, offering encouragement, asking and answering questions, and, yes, checking computer screens.

In Strategy 14: Writing Frames and Writing Structures, we discussed the benefits and challenges Google Translate offers to our students. Please see that strategy if you'd like to review the suggestions we offered there.

A final point we'd like to make in this section is recognizing that not all teachers and students have adequate access to school technology. If that is the case for you, and your school or district is strapped for cash, you might want to consider grant sources, including Donors Choose. We have included links to resources and advice in the Technology Connections section on seeking those kinds of funds.

Differentiation Recommendations

Newcomers (Preliterate or Low Literacy in Home Language): Online sites that provide audio and image support for text can be a huge help for students in this category. See Strategy 33: Supporting ELL Students with Interrupted Formal Education (SIFEs) and the Technology Connections section in this chapter for recommendation. ChatGPT and other AI-powered chatbots can be used for language practice while providing audio support in the student's home language.	**Newcomers (Literate in Home Language):** Students should be able to do all the activities listed in the chapter. Can be encouraged to become proficient in keyboarding.
Intermediate ELLs: Students should be able to do all the activities listed in the chapter. They should be encouraged to do higher English-level tasks, however. Can be encouraged to become proficient in keyboarding.	**Advanced ELLs:** Should be encouraged to do all the listed tasks at a higher English level.

Technology Connections

For even more research on technology and language learning, you can explore The Best Places to Find Research on Technology and Language Teaching/Learning (http://larryferlazzo.edublogs.org/2011/02/23/the-best-places-to-find-research-on-technology-language-teachinglearning/).

To find sites that students can use for independent practice, visit The Best Sites Students Can Use for Independent Practice (https://larryferlazzo.edublogs.org/2022/07/19/the-best-sites-students-can-use-for-independent-practice/).

You can find links to the online sites our students use for homework at The Best Online Homework Sites for English Language Learners (http://larryferlazzo.edublogs.org/2017/07/30/the-best-online-homework-sites-for-english-language-learners-please-offer-your-own-suggestions/).

If you'd like more information on how we handle grading, check out The Best Resources on Grading Practices (http://larryferlazzo.edublogs.org/2013/01/09/the-best-resources-on-grading-practices/).

For additional resources on using artificial intelligence in the classroom, see The Best Posts About Using Artificial Intelligence with ELLs (https://larryferlazzo.edublogs.org/2023/06/04/the-best-posts-about-using-artificial-intelligence-with-ells/) and A Collection of "Best" Lists About Using Artificial Intelligence in Education (https://larryferlazzo.edublogs.org/2023/01/01/a-collection-of-best-lists-about-using-artificial-intelligence-in-education/).

One way artificial intelligence can save teachers time is by automatically creating quizzes and other exercises from videos and texts. Though they definitely have to be reviewed and edited prior to being given to students, they can provide a good starting point for teachers to create custom materials. See The "Best" Tools for Automatically Turning Texts and Videos into Interactive Language Learning Tools (https://larryferlazzo.edublogs.org/2022/08/03/the-best-tools-for-automatically-turning-texts-videos-into-interactive-language-learning-tools/).

We've listed links to typing and keyboarding sites at The Best Sites Where Students Can Learn Typing/Keyboarding (http://larryferlazzo.edublogs.org/2017/07/30/the-best-sites-where-students-can-learning-typingkeyboarding/).

Find a list of teacher-recommended microphones at Around the Web in ESL/EFL/ELL (https://larryferlazzo.edublogs.org/2021/10/24/around-the-web-in-esl-efl-ell-128/).

For lesson plans on the marshmallow test and other ideas on how to encourage our students to develop more self-control, go to The Best Posts About Helping Students Develop Their Capacity for Self-Control (http://larryferlazzo.edublogs.org/2010/06/03/my-best-posts-about-helping-students-develop-their-capacity-for-self-control/).

If you need to raise your own funds for classroom technology (or for anything else), visit The Best Advice for Using Donors Choose (http://larryferlazzo.edublogs.org/2015/04/05/the-best-resources-on-advice-for-using-donors-choose-please-share-your-experiences/).

Attribution

Portions of the text in this strategy originally appeared in Larry's article in ASCD *Educational Leadership*, "Student Engagement: Key to Personalized Learning" (Ferlazzo, 2017, www.ascd.org/publications/educational-leadership/mar17/vol74/num06/Student-Engagement%40-Key-to-Personalized-Learning.aspx) and is used with permission.

All figures from this chapter, as well as 11 additional chapters, references, hyperlinked Technology Connections, and more online resources, can be found at www.wiley.com/go/ellteacherstoolbox2.

STRATEGY 47: USING TECHNOLOGY *507*

Names of Teachers: _____

Lesson Topic: _____

Six words your students need to know: Write the word, definition, and how you will teach it (gesture, picture, acting, etc.). Remember, the words need to come from the read aloud:

1.

2.

3.

4.

5.

6.

Copy your read aloud here:

Show a picture on the whiteboard about your topic. Ask students to tell you words about the picture. Add at least four new words to the picture. Write one sentence on the board about the picture. Then, ask students to write one or more sentences about the picture and share with the class.

Figure 47.1 Student-Led Lesson Plan

1. Choose a topic.

2. Ask the teacher for advice on what to read or watch online to learn about the topic.

3. Find a written passage of four to seven sentences about the topic. Copy and paste it on a document to print out and write at the bottom the URL address of where you found it.

4. Choose six words that students need to know so they can understand the read aloud.

5. Decide who will be teaching the six words and how they will teach them.

6. Decide who is going to read the read aloud.

7. Choose a picture online that relates to the topic and print it out.

8. Decide who is going to teach about the picture and what words you are going to use to label the picture.

9. Find a picture about your topic and copy-and-paste it to show it on your screen using an online whiteboard. Ask students to tell you words about the picture. Add at least four new words to the picture. Write one sentence on the board about the picture. Then, ask students to write one or more sentences about the picture and share with the group.

Figure 47.2 Lesson Guide

STRATEGY 47: USING TECHNOLOGY *509*

Name _____

This week, when you are working on the computer, think about what you would like to learn about or do. Examples could be "learn 20 words used in construction and how to use them"; "learn eight irregular verbs and how to use them"; "learn more about the history of Mexico—in English"; "read enough books in Raz-Kids to increase two levels"; "earn 600 points in Duolingo"; and so on. List them here:

1.

2.

3.

4.

How do you want to show what you have learned at the end of the week (check one; if you check more than one, you will get extra credit):

____ Taking a test
____ Making a presentation to the class with a slideshow or poster
____ Creating a poster
____ Writing a song and performing it
____ Creating and performing a short play
____ Other (write your idea here _____)

Figure 47.3 Weekly Computer Independent Study Plan

Name _____

Vocabulary

Write six new words in the area you studied and use them in sentences.

The area I studied was _____.

1. Word _____
   Sentence_____

2. Word _____
   Sentence_____

3. Word _____
   Sentence_____

4. Word _____
   Sentence_____

5. Word _____
   Sentence_____

6. Word _____
   Sentence_____

Figure 47.4 Personalized Learning Weekly Test

Conversation

If you practiced conversations on the computer or with someone else, write them here:

First Conversation:

You: "_____"

Someone else: "_____"

You: "_____"

Someone else: "_____"

Second Conversation:

You: "_____"

Someone else: "_____"

You: "_____"

Someone else: "_____"

Figure 47.4 (*Continued*)

Name _____
Date _____

Examples

[Before you log-in] Today, I want to:

- ☐ Learn about clothes words
- ☐ Read a new level of books on Raz-Kids
- ☐ Try a new site on the class blog

[At the end of class] Did I achieve my goal? yes or no_____
[At the end of class] What things helped me learn today or didn't help me learn today:

- ☐ Working with someone else helped me learn better.
- ☐ Working with someone else did not help me learn better.
- ☐ I liked a new site called _____ because _____ _____.
- ☐ I played some games, but they didn't really help because they were too easy. I should have gone to the site called _____.

Today's Plan and Reflection

[Before you log-in] Today, I want to:

[At the end of class] Did I achieve my goal? _____
[At the end of class] These things helped me learn today or didn't help me learn today:

Figure 47.5 Daily Computer Plan and Reflection

STRATEGY 48

Interactive Word Walls

This chapter is written by our good friend and talented educator Valentina Gonzalez. She is a former classroom teacher with more than 20 years in education serving also as a district facilitator for English learners, as a professional development specialist for ELs, and as an educational consultant. She is the co-author of *Reading and Writing with English Learners: A Framework for K-5* and the author of the children's book *Krofne with Baba*.

What Is It?

An interactive word wall is a thematically and graphically organized wall of words with related visuals. While traditional word walls are teacher created, alphabetic, and rarely include visuals, interactive word walls are co-created with students, making them more student-centered. They are deliberately tied to the unit of study and intentionally planned to maximize thinking, participation, engagement, and overall learning.

Imagine a large graphic organizer (that might otherwise be on a single sheet of paper) on the classroom wall with labeled visuals, words, anchor charts, and real objects that the teacher and students co-create. Interactive word walls include organizers such as Venn diagrams, treemaps, cycles, etc. The word wall becomes interactive when students add to it and engage with it. Students are contributors to the learning.

Why We Like It

Interactive word walls make grade-level content understandable to students and help develop their language. Students speak and listen to grade-level peers using academic vocabulary and language from the interactive word wall. The interactive word wall is a scaffold many students use when they are paired or grouped for peer discussion. This social aspect supports English learners through practice with English as well as by working with peers at various levels of English proficiency. Listening and verbalizing are both important parts of acquiring language. A convenient by-product of the interactive word wall may also be that it builds community by asking learners to interact with one another and as a class.

Labeled visuals and real objects on the interactive word wall position learners from their assets, providing entry points for grasping new vocabulary. This is especially important for students who are learning English and new content. New vocabulary can be made understandable quite easily through the use of visuals and then aided with words and labels. Vocabulary can be described as the currency of the classroom. The more you know, understand, and can use, the richer you are as a reader, writer, and thinker.

Graphic organizers displayed on an interactive word wall assist students to connect ideas. Some examples of commonly used organizers are concept maps, circle maps, T-charts, sequence charts, and Venn diagrams. When used effectively by students, these organizers provide learners with a tool to take ownership of their thinking.

Interactive word walls come alive through student interaction rather than being stagnant features on the wall. Students can be asked to find and bring pictures representing words listed on the wall and tape them there.

English learners' language development and instruction are further supported and scaffolded by the contextual richness of the visuals, objects, labels, experiences, and organization. As words and visuals are added and explained, ELLs are able to make connections with the new vocabulary. Learners can also make cross-linguistic connections by adding words in the languages they speak to the words in English.

Supporting Research

Studies have found that students benefit from interactive word walls and use them as resources and reference points when participating in classroom instruction (Jackson, 2013). Words taught in context and used repetitively are more likely to be understood and retained as information than words merely memorized.

A key component of interactive word walls is visuals, photographs, and/or real objects. Studies provide evidence that using media like visuals does increase students' vocabulary achievement (Khafidhoh & Carolina, 2019). When pictures are added to words during the instructional process, students were found to also engage and participate more readily. In studies, it has been found that "the more visual the input becomes, the more likely it is to be recognized—and recalled" (Medina, 2014). Researchers named this the picture superiority effect.

Learning is strengthened by collaboration and active participation (Vygotsky, 1978). Active learning and engagement are facets of the interactive word wall. Students act as co-creators of it and participate in discussing the contents of it.

Graphic organizers have been found to help students with retention and comprehension (Wang, Mayer, Zhou, & Lin, 2021). Studies have also found that interactive graphic organizers such as ones used with interactive word walls can produce higher performance in students. Deeper knowledge is reported when students interact with graphic organizers (Fisher, Frey, & Hattie, 2017).

Common Core Connections

Interactive word walls can be used to support nearly every Standard depending on the topic of the IWW. Beyond supporting vocabulary, the IWW can be used as leverage to support the development of speaking and listening, reading, and writing.

Application

Planning ahead for interactive word walls pays off in the long run. Begin by examining an upcoming unit of study and determine the learning goals. This will uncover the topic for the interactive word wall and the type of graphic organizer that fits the learning. The Learning Goals Organizer can help you think through options.

Learning Goals Organizer

Students will . . .	Possible Type of Graphic Organizer
Learn about different literary genres.	Tree map (see Figure 48.1)
Explore the hierarchy or natural order of organisms or elements.	Pyramid/triangle chart (see Figure 48.2)
Analyze types of energy, volcanoes, books, or governments.	Content frame (see Figure 48.3 and Figure 48.4)
Compare two/three countries, leaders, environments, books, or characters.	Venn diagram (see Figure 48.5)
Describe people, places, or things or explore the connection between things, such as food webs.	Bubble map/web diagram (see Figure 48.6)
Analyze the parts of a story.	Story map (see Figure 48.7)
Learn about the life of a historical figure or explore a timespan of events.	Time line chart or a BME sequence chart (see Figure 48.8)
Analyze the order and relationship between elements of a system.	Onion diagram (see Figure 48.9)
Learn new vocabulary and their relationships among each other.	Scene or backdrop (see Figure 48.10)

Then plan out the organizer on a small scale to identify desired specific academic vocabulary and language. Produce a large-scale blank blackline graphic organizer that only includes the title and place it prominently in the classroom for students. This will be their canvas for interaction and learning throughout the unit of study. It is helpful to share the expectations with students explicitly since some may not know or be comfortable with co-creating word walls. This type of participation may be new and the invitation and encouragement to add to the wall might be necessary daily.

It may sound something like this:

Teacher: Class, we are going to be learning about the types of energy. Read this with me. (*The teacher points to the title of the IWW.*)

Class: (*The class chorally reads the title.*) Types of energy.

Teacher: As we learn each type of energy, we are going to add words, pictures, and objects to this graphic organizer on the wall. Today we will explore heat energy. (*The teacher writes "**heat**" in the first column.*) Read this with me (*the teacher points to a sentence stem at the bottom of the IWW and the class reads together*). One type of energy is . . . (*the teacher points to the word **heat**).

Class: (*They chorally read as the teacher points to the sentence stem and the word heat in the graphic organizer.*) One type of energy is heat.

(*The lesson continues with instruction that includes looking at different heat sources, watching videos, reading about heat energy, and discussing heat energy. The teacher provides students with time to add images, visuals, and real objects to the IWW. Finally, the teacher will model a sentence for students and ask them to try one with their group or a partner.*)

Teacher: Listen and watch as I make a sentence using the information we have learned today and added to the wall. (*The teacher points to the words and visuals on the IWW wall while saying the following sentence.*) "<u>Fire</u> is an example of <u>heat</u> energy." Now you pick a word and make a sentence using the sentence stem ___ is an example of ___ energy.

Class: (*Students turn to their groups or partners and practice using the IWW and sentence stem.*)

Students will be directed to the IWW each day in similar and different ways in the following days. As the unit and days go on, reminders may be needed for students to continue to add visuals and labels. The teacher will frequently stop to provide time for students to discuss what has been added and create opportunities for students to elaborate by adding words such as "because" or "however" to their responses. The teacher will also deliberately make connections with students' home languages when appropriate. For instance, if the interactive word wall is titled "Types of Energy" and the student says that in their home language energy is "energije," they will take time to discuss this cognate and invite the student to add the word to the word wall.

The addition of sentence stems that fit the content and context of the learning provides students with English language structures to produce academic language using academic vocabulary. In the example of Types of Energy, one might be, "A __ is a type of ___ energy because . . ." Model the use of the sentence stem verbally while pointing to the respective areas of the interactive word wall and provide students with opportunities to practice sharing with peers.

See Figure 48.11 for two classroom examples of IWWs.

Teaching Online

The initial planning ahead remains the same as in online teaching and learning circumstances. Once the topic and type of graphic organizer have been identified, a platform for the online IWW will need to be selected. This can be as easy as creating a shared slide with the blackline master of the graphic organizer or using one of the many available online whiteboards (see Technology Connections). Then as the unit progresses, students are invited to add to the shared document.

Having students practice speaking and listening using the domain-specific vocabulary in complete sentences online with peers is possible with the use of breakout rooms and video recordings (such as through Padlet).

What Could Go Wrong?

Including young minds in classroom creation is messy. When we envision what the interactive word wall will look like, it seldom turns out exactly that way with students because they bring their own set of background experiences and knowledge to the wall. Sometimes it is difficult to let go of the idea of a picture-perfect classroom wall and let students grapple with ideas and get messy.

Teachers with many classes in one day face a logistics problem around how to have two, three, or even six interactive word walls. There just isn't enough wall space in a classroom to have that many IWW, and it's not feasible to take each IWW down after the class period is over. Teachers who have multiple classes daily may want each class to have their own interactive word wall yet physically the space is unavailable to display, and if the first-period class is already added to the word wall, then the subsequent classes will see what has been shared. Do they hide the interactive word walls from previous classes? And if so, where? How do you manage all the interactive word walls? Teachers with multiple classes daily have been creative with interactive word walls. Some have one shared interactive word wall. Others layer the interactive word walls on top of one another hiding them from previous classes.

While a traditional word wall stays up all year, the interactive word wall only stays up during a unit of study. This poses a storage and retrieval problem for teachers and students. Where can teachers store all of these useful interactive word walls yet also make them available for students to easily access throughout the school year? Again, some teachers have been resourceful by using clothing hangers and hanging the interactive word walls on racks. Other teachers take pictures of the interactive word walls and create albums with them.

Technology Connections

Environmental print provides easy access to students and is preferred over online versions. However, it is possible to create alternative versions of interactive word walls using technology, primarily for online teaching situations. You can find various online tools to do that

518 THE ELL TEACHER'S TOOLBOX 2.0

at The Best Alternatives to the Soon-to-Be-Deceased Google Jamboard (https://larryferlazzo.edublogs.org/2023/10/03/the-best-alternatives-to-the-soon-to-be-deceased-google-jamboard/).

For additional ideas on how to use classroom walls, visit The Best Ideas About How to Use Classroom Walls – Please Recommend More Resources (https://larryferlazzo.edublogs.org/2018/01/18/the-best-ideas-about-how-to-use-classroom-walls-please-recommend-more-resources/).

All figures from this chapter, as well as 11 additional chapters, references, hyperlinked Technology Connections, and more online resources, can be found at www.wiley.com/go/ellteacherstoolbox2.

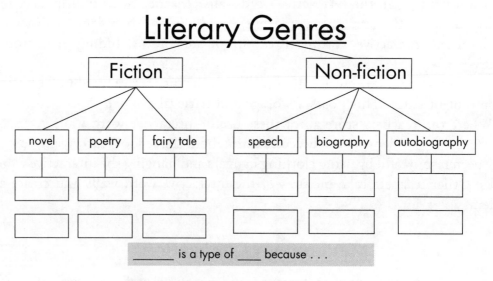

Figure 48.1 Literary Genres Tree Map

STRATEGY 48: INTERACTIVE WORD WALLS 519

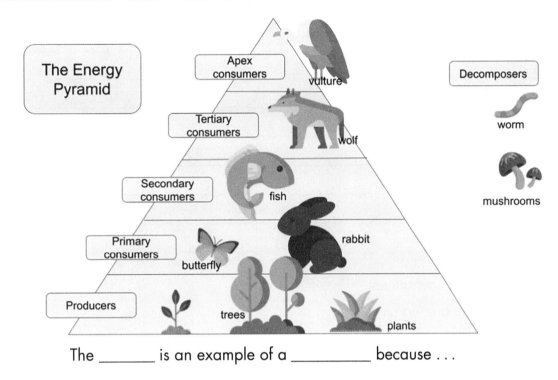

The _____ is an example of a _____ because . . .

Figure 48.2 Pyramid/Triangle Chart

Word (English)	Word (Other Languages)	Picture	Meaning (English)	Meaning (Other Languages)
Characters				
Protagonist				
Antagonist				
Setting				
Conflict				
Events				
Dialogue				
Resolution				
Theme				

In the story, _____, the main characters are . . .

_____ is a protagonist/antagonist because . . .

The conflict in this story arises when . . .

Figure 48.3 Narrative Words Content Frame

Government	Definition	Characteristics	Examples
Direct democracy			
Representative democracy			
socialism			
communism			
monarchy			
oligarchy			
autocracy			

_____ is a type of government.

In _____ people are led by . . .

_____ has an example of _____ government because . . .

In my opinion, _____ is the best type of government because . . .

Figure 48.4 Forms of Government Content Frame

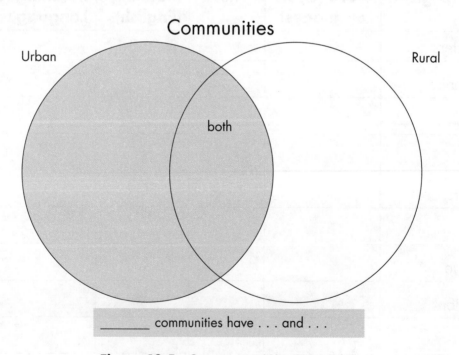

_____ communities have . . . and . . .

Figure 48.5 Communities Venn Diagram

STRATEGY 48: INTERACTIVE WORD WALLS

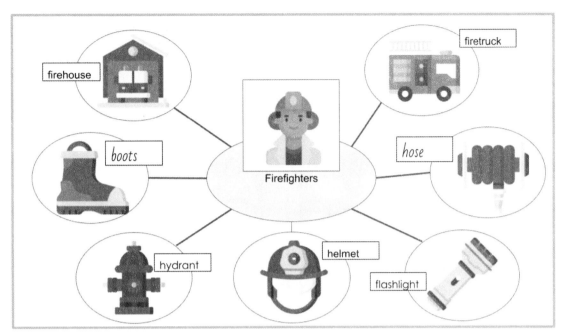

A firefighter has . . .

Firefighters use . . .

Figure 48.6 Bubble Map/Web Diagram Example

The main characters in the story _____ are . . .

The setting takes place in . . .

The problem was that . . .

The problem was solved when . . .

Figure 48.7 Story Map Example

STRATEGY 48: INTERACTIVE WORD WALLS

| Beginning | Middle | End |

In the beginning of the story . . .
In the middle, . . .
At the end . . .

Figure 48.8 BME Sequence Chart

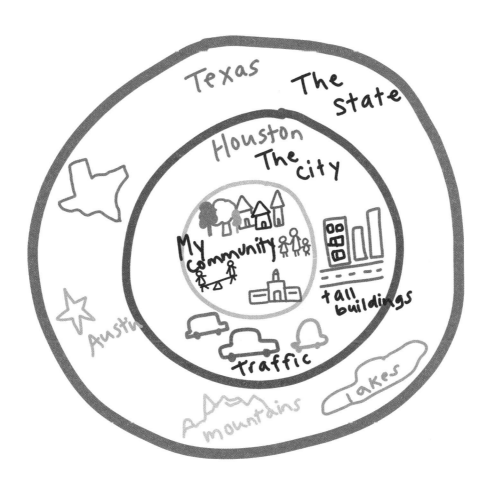

Figure 48.9 Communities Example of an Onion Diagram

Figure 48.10 Elementary Prepositions Interactive Word Wall Example

Figure 48.11 Photographs of Classroom Examples   *Source:* (A) Photo: Suzy Matias-Fitzgerald, (B) Photo: Pamela Guajardo

STRATEGY 49

Assessment

What Is It?

All teachers understand the importance of assessment. Though there are various types of assessment, for all practical purposes, we consider three types—diagnostic, formative, and summative—to be the most important. From our perspective, formative assessments are the most critical for our day-to-day teaching.

Diagnostic assessments indicate the current state of a student's language proficiency. If being done in a class other than English, it could also assess content knowledge.

Formative assessments are an ongoing process for teachers (and students) to gather and evaluate evidence so that teachers can make adjustments to their teaching and students can make adjustments to their learning.

Summative assessments are given at the end of an instructional sequence or grading period to measure student learning.

Why We Like It

Diagnostic assessments can quickly give us a somewhat accurate picture of a student's current language level. "Quickly" is the operative word here since many ELLs come to classes after the school year has begun and we typically have to do a diagnostic assessment at the same time that we're teaching a class. As most teachers know, many ELLs arrive with little or no paperwork or assessment data from previous schools, and those who do may have data that is far out-of-date with their current knowledge.

Formative assessments can literally inform our teaching minute to minute, and if we want to support student self-efficacy and want them to be co-creators of their learning (and we, at least, do), we need to put a significant amount of energy into planning, implementing, recording, and sharing their results.

Summative assessments, including standardized tests, have a place in our schools. However, we tend to feel the pressure they place on students does not help create the best conditions for our students to learn, and often, practically speaking, we learn the results too late to take action on them.

We have a chapter on assessment in the second edition of *The ESL/ELL Teacher's Survival Guide*. We feel it's exceptionally thorough. In this chapter, however, we plan to focus on a few of the ways assessments help our students and us the most.

Therefore, we'll use some space on diagnostic and more on formative (though some might call one or two of our formative assessments summative). For a more thorough examination of these issues, please check out our other book.

Supporting Research

Researchers are almost universal in their support of formative assessments as a key and valuable way to inform instruction (REL Northwest, 2020). Fewer studies, but valid ones, support our perspective on the value of formative *over* summative assessments for teaching and learning. Specifically for ELLs, researchers have found that formative assessments do a better job of enhancing academic motivation and self-regulation skills, as well as reducing test anxiety (Ismail et al., 2022).

Common Core Connections

There's only one way to determine if students have successfully mastered *any* standard, and that is to conduct a valid assessment!

Application

We will be focusing this section on diagnostic and formative assessments. As we mentioned earlier, to learn even more about them and other forms of assessments, including summative, grading in "mainstream" content classes, and standardized tests, we recommend you visit the chapter on assessment in our previous book, the second edition of *The ESL/ELL Teacher's Survival Guide*. In fact, this section on diagnostic assessments is largely taken from that chapter, and portions of the section on formative assessment are, too (*ESL/ELL Teacher's Survival Guide*, 2022, Jossey Bass). There just isn't room in this chapter for us to cover all those topics—we already couldn't fit in 11 chapters that are online!

INITIAL OR DIAGNOSTIC ASSESSMENTS

When students enter a class, it can be helpful to assess their reading, writing, and speaking skills to get an idea of their current proficiency level. The purpose of these initial assessments is to gain information about students' levels of English in order to tailor future instruction to meet students' specific language needs. These types of assessments can also indicate whether a student has been placed in the appropriate class for their level of proficiency. Most schools and/or districts have protocols for assessing ELLs as they enter school. However, ELL teachers are the ones who interact with these students on a daily basis in a comfortable and safe environment and therefore may be more capable of making accurate judgments about students' language abilities. Teachers can initially assess students' English abilities in a variety of ways, but here are a few we have found effective.

Reading and Writing

Having students read a short piece of text and then write to a prompt can offer the teacher valuable information about students' reading comprehension skills and writing skills. Figure 49.1 is an example of an initial assessment we have used with our intermediate ELLs to gather information on students' reading, writing, and thinking skills. The teacher can select a piece of text that they believe may fit the level of the students and adjust the language of the prompt as needed.

For beginners, we sometimes use Figure 49.2. If they have next-to-zero English proficiency, we tell them they can write a response in their home language (we use Google Translate for the instructions and to understand their response). Their ability (or inability) to write in their home language is important information for us to also know. If they have some English language ability, we still ask them to write in their home language, too.

In both cases, we assure students that they will not be graded on what they write—its purpose is just to give us a better idea of their English-language proficiency so that we can be better teachers for them. We ask them to please not use Google Translate for assistance. We assure them that they will be able to use it during class, but this time we'd like them to just keep their phone in a backpack.

A major advantage to this kind of assessment is that students can work on it independently while we're teaching our class.

Of course, one piece of writing is not going to fully illustrate a student's English abilities, but it can be a quick snapshot that the teacher can use to plan further assessments and conversations with students to get to know them at the beginning of the year.

Speaking and Listening

Given the fact that we are generally teaching while doing an initial "intake," our conversation with students about the writing assessment also functions as a quick speaking and listening assessment.

We have found that this process generally provides us with an accurate assessment of the new student's English proficiency and their academic background. But it's not a high-stakes assessment with permanent consequences—in the unlikely event that we discover after the first day, two days, or even three days that we made the wrong call and the student should be placed in a different class, we explain that situation to the student and our administrators, and just make the switch.

FORMATIVE ASSESSMENTS

Formative assessment is not a type of test or assessment but is a *process* that combines teaching, learning, and assessment. It is an ongoing process where teachers and students evaluate assessment evidence to make adjustments to their teaching and learning. Gathering this assessment evidence can be done in multiple ways—including more formal measures, such as written tests, and informal practices, such as student self-evaluation or observation.

The formative assessment process is an effective way for teachers to check students' understanding throughout the learning process and then use this information to guide instruction.

This type of ongoing assessment process is critically important when teaching ELL students in order to identify when and how students need extra support. As WestEd researcher Robert Linquanti points out, "Formative assessment practices have enormous potential to strengthen teachers' capacities to developmentally stage or 'scaffold' ELLs' language and content learning" (Working Group on ELL Policy, 2010).

The formative assessment process serves to strengthen students' abilities to assess their own progress, to set and evaluate their own learning goals, and to make adjustments accordingly. Formative assessment also elicits valuable feedback from students about what teachers are doing effectively and what they could do better.

The following activities can be used by teachers and students to collect evidence of student learning and progress. It is important to remember that *how* the teacher chooses to use this information ultimately determines whether it is "formative" in nature. Effective teaching and assessment involve using this evidence to make decisions about what students need and how best to meet those needs and encourage students to use this information in the same way.

Weekly "quizzes." Assessing students on a weekly basis on what has been taught over the week can help the teacher check for student understanding. This information can help the teacher identify which students need more help and which concepts need to be further practiced. Both the teacher and the students can gain valuable information from these tests about what they need to do differently. For these "tests" to be helpful to students and the teacher, they need to be short and low stakes (not used as a "gotcha" or in a punitive way). It is also important that these assessments reflect what has already been taught and not be new concepts. When administered in a positive learning environment, these types of weekly tests can build students' confidence as they are able to demonstrate what they have learned. They can also be used as a teaching opportunity, as the teacher identifies questions or parts of the test that students struggled with and reteaches those concepts. Weekly tests can take various forms—labeling pictures, multiple choice, writing to a prompt, performing a role-play—depending on the level of the class and the concepts being assessed. For an example of a weekly assessment used with beginners, see the Sample Friday Quiz in Figure 49.3.

Note that this sample quiz was about our Story Writing Unit, which typically comes near the end of the school year. This very low-stakes quiz, however, is representative of the kind we give during the entire year. We pass out the first part of the figure, which is generally 25 questions. You'll note in the answer sheet that most of the first part of the test consists of vocabulary words. In some cases, the teacher just says the word (followed by using it in a sentence) and students write the word. For example, "Author. Munro Leaf is the author of *The Story of Ferdinand*." In other cases, the teacher gives the word's definition, and students have to recall and write down the word the teacher is referring to. For example, ""What is the word for the hero in a story?"

That's followed by a related sentence that is written with no spaces between words—students have to rewrite it correctly. Then, some grammar questions, followed by a question requiring a short written response. It ends with five "scrambled sentences" connected to that week's topic.

Writing prompts. Teachers can assess student learning by having students write to a prompt. These prompts can take many forms, such as a question to answer, a statement with which to agree or disagree, a picture to describe, or a response to a text or video clip. It is important that writing prompts for ELLs contain clear directions and take into account the cultural and linguistic knowledge that students currently possess. Asking students to write about content they have not yet learned or about cultural situations they are not familiar with will not yield valuable information about students' true abilities. For example, giving students a prompt asking them to describe their favorite carnival or fair ride might be confusing for students who haven't attended this type of event or aren't familiar with the term *carnival*.

When all our students have laptops (which is most of the time since the pandemic), we will often (sometimes once each week) create a shared Google Slides presentation with a simple "personal" prompt and additional scaffolded instructions. Students write their responses on the slide that has their name on it. That night, we'll change the text color when appropriate to indicate important errors (not all of them!), give students time the next day to fix them, and then students will share their slide and present it to the entire class or in small groups. Not only do these responses function as important formative assessments to teacher and student alike, but they also provide grammatical teaching opportunities, and the information shared can help build classroom community. Of course, students can also write out their responses on paper, too.

Figure 49.4 shows some of the main prompts that we have used.

After students begin to develop a degree of English proficiency, we ask that they only use Google Translate for *words* and not for *constructing sentences* when writing their responses. We repeatedly explain that they will not be graded on the accuracy of their spelling or grammar, only on their effort. We emphasize that what they are writing is just a "draft." We tell students that by showing us what they actually know without Google Translate's assistance, we can be better teachers for them. We also say that after we have looked at what they wrote, we'll give them some individual feedback and then they can use our feedback and Google Translate to develop a final version.

Student self-assessment and reflection. Activities that promote metacognitive thinking and ask students to reflect on their learning processes are key to the formative assessment process. When students are asked to think about *what* they have learned and *how* they have learned it (the learning strategies they've used), they are better able to understand their own learning processes and can set new goals for themselves. Students can reflect on their learning in many ways: answering a set of questions, drawing a picture or set of pictures to represent their learning process, talking with a partner, or keeping a learning log or journal, for example. Students can be prompted to reflect on their learnings of academic concepts as well as life lessons and personal growth. Teachers can pause in the middle of a lesson—or at its end—and ask students to share the part of the lesson that was least clear to them. The teacher can use these responses to check for student understanding, but also to check the pulse of the class in terms of student motivation, confidence levels, and levels of metacognition.

To assist students in both their self-reflection and in determining their future goals (see the next section), we find it helpful to periodically meet with students and show them a visual representation of their past quiz results. See Figure 49.4: Visual Representation of Student Quiz Scores.

Goal sheets. As we explained in Strategy 38: Motivation, having students set their own goals and evaluate progress toward achieving them is an effective part of the formative assessment process. It is important to help students distinguish between learning goals and performance goals. Research has shown the advantages of emphasizing learning goals ("I want to take more leadership in small groups") over performance goals ("I want to get an A in this class"). Both are important, but the issue is which one is given greater weight. Goal sheets are an effective way to help students set goals and track their progress. It can be helpful to identify specific goals. For example, "I will read in English for 20 minutes each night" is more specific than "I will read more." Also, goals need to be achievable in a short period of time and not impossibly difficult. The teacher can model how to set effective goals and also how to evaluate one's progress toward achieving them by asking students to periodically write or talk about what they have achieved, what they still would like to achieve, and *how* they will do it.

Examples of goal-setting exercises and sheets can be found in Strategy 38.

Use of mini-whiteboards. If you don't have a class set of inexpensive mini-whiteboards, we strongly recommend you get one as soon as possible. Not only are they invaluable tools for use in the many games we've discussed in various chapters in this book (which are also formative assessment activities), they can be used in countless other activities, as well. We use them in grammar lessons ("What verb goes in the blank, 'Javier and Ruben _____ to the game yesterday'—write what you think is the correct verb, but don't raise your board until I say to"), vocabulary review, to test listening comprehension—you name the lesson, we've used mini-whiteboards in it. See the Technology Connections section for more ideas.

Choice Board assessments. You can see how we've used choice boards for assessment in Strategy 16: Choice Boards/Learning Menus.

Games. All the games we've discussed elsewhere in this book are excellent formative assessment activities. We're also big fans of online games like Quizziz, Kahoot, Blooket, and whichever new sites will be online by the time you read this book. Not only do students love playing them, and they serve as excellent tools to review concepts already taught, but you gain immediate access to detailed data about every student and their game performance on each question—at a glance.

There are obviously many other strategies teachers can use for formative assessment. The real key, of course, is not which strategy you use, but what you do with the knowledge you gain from it. All the data in the world is useless if it's not put to use.

Teaching Online

All these examples of assessment in the classroom can also be used online. The key challenge here, as we've discussed in other chapters, is how to ensure that students are not using tech tools to "fake" their mastery of certain academic skills and content. It's a lot easier in the physical classroom to apply the old saying, "Trust, but verify" than it is to do so in an online environment. Candid conversations are always helpful in the classroom, but they are absolutely critical when teaching online.

What Could Go Wrong?

Good teachers collect tons of formative assessment data. Very good and great teachers put it to good use. If students are showing that they are having problems with putting the Friday quiz sentence scrambles in the correct order, and that's happening week-after-week, then it's time to re-evaluate how you are teaching sentence structure—students are not going to improve unless you make teaching it a priority. And if what you have been doing hasn't been successful, then it's time to switch things up. Don't take it personally! Doing more of the same stuff that didn't work before means it probably is unlikely to work in the future with the same students.

Technology Connections

Find more formative assessment ideas at The Best Resources for Learning About Formative Assessment (https://larryferlazzo.edublogs.org/2010/08/22/the-best-resources-for-learning-about-formative-assessment/).

Explore Some "Best" Ideas for Using Mini-Whiteboards in the Classroom (https://larryferlazzo.edublogs.org/2023/05/07/some-best-ideas-for-using-mini-whiteboards-in-the-classroom/ for more ideas on how to use them in class).

Attribution

As we noted, two of the figures and a portion of the narrative for this chapter originally appeared in our book, *The ESL/ELL Teacher's Toolbox*.

All figures from this chapter, as well as 11 additional chapters, references, hyperlinked Technology Connections, and more online resources, can be found at www.wiley.com/go/ellteacherstoolbox2.

My Day:

Main prompt: Please go to the slide with your name and write as much as you can about your day.

What time do you get up?

What do you do first?

What happens during the day?

Who do you see?

What do you eat?

What do you do at night?

What time do you go to sleep?

Your Favorite Place:

Main prompt: Please go to the slide with your name and write as much as you can about your favorite place in the whole world.

What is it?

Where is it?

Why is it your favorite place?

What do you do there?

What else is there?

Who else is there?

Summer Plans:

Main Prompt: Please go to the slide with your name and write as much as you can about what you want your summer to look like.

What are the top three things you want to do this summer?

What will people around you be doing this summer?

Where do you want go?

Do you want to go to summer school? Why or why not? If you do, what do you want to learn?

Write about some of the favorite things you've done in past summers.

Figure 49.1 Intermediate-Level Initial Assessment

> Please write as much as you can about a close friend. Tell about how and where you met them, why they are your friend, what you do together, what their family is like, etc.
>
> Please try to write in English, without using Google Translate. This is not a test.

Figure 49.2 Beginner-Level Initial Assessment *Source: Originally published in* The ESL/ELL Teacher's Survival Guide, *Jossey Bass, 2022. Reprinted with permission.*

> Name _____
>
> Date _____
>
> **Excerpt**
>
> The older you are, the younger you get when you move to the United States. Two years after my father and I moved here from Guatemala I could speak English. I learned it on the playground and by watching lots of TV. Don't believe what people say—cartoons make you smart. But my father, he worked all day in a kitchen with Mexicans and Salvadorans. His English was worse than a kindergartener's. He would only buy food at the bodega down the block. Outside of there he lowered his eyes and tried to get by on mumbles and smiles. He didn't want strangers to hear his mistakes. So he used me to make phone calls and to talk to the landlady and to buy things in stores where you had to use English. He got younger. I got older.
>
> **Writing Prompt**
>
> Read the paragraph above and write more than one paragraph responding to the following questions. Describe Gonzalo's experience of moving to the United States. Write your opinion about Gonzalo's experience: What do you think about his experience? How is his experience similar to or different from your own? Be sure to use specific examples from the paragraph above, anything else you've read, and/or your own life.

Figure 49.3 Sample Friday Quiz *Source: P. Fleishman, "Gonzalo," in* Seedfolks *(New York: Harper Trophy, 1997), 17–18; Originally published in* The ESL/ELL Teacher's Survival Guide, *Jossey Bass, 2022. Reprinted with permission.*

STRATEGY 49: ASSESSMENT 535

Name _____ Date _____

1.
2.
3.
4.
5.
6.
7.
8.
9.
10.
11.
12.
13.
14.
15.
16.
17. Ferdinand likes to smell the flowers.
18. Ferdinand _____ a bull.
19. The title of the book _____ *The Story of Ferdinand*.
20. Did you like *The Story of Ferdinand*? Why or why not?

_____
_____
_____
_____

21. characters story . are people in the the and animals

_____

22. the the author wrote story .

_____

23. story . of the the is the title name

_____

Figure 49.4 Example Prompts with Scaffolding

24. talk each to when . dialogue is characters a other

_____

25. story . for illustrator pictures the draws the

_____

(answer sheet)

Name _____ Date _____

1. **plot**
2. Teacher asks, "What are the five senses?" **touch, smell, taste, see (exact words may vary)**
3. **beginning**
4. **senses**
5. Teacher asks, "What is the word for the hero in a story?" **protagonist**
6. Teacher asks, "What is the word of the hero's enemy in the story?" **antagonist**
7. Teacher asks, "What is the word for when and where the story takes place?" **setting**
8. **author**
9. **title**
10. Teacher asks, "What is the word for the fight in the story?" **conflict**
11. Teacher asks, "What is the word for the main message of the story?" **theme**
12. **illustrator**
13. **characters**
14. **dialogue**
15. **middle**
16. **end**
17. **Ferdinand liked to smell the flowers.**
18. Ferdinand **is** a bull.
19. The title of the book **is** *The Story of Ferdinand*.

Figure 49.4 *(Continued)*

20. Did you like *The Story of Ferdinand*? Why or why not?

_____
_____
_____
_____

21. Characters are the people and animals in the story.
22. The author wrote the story.
23. The title is the name of the story.
24. A dialogue is when characters talk to each other.
25. The illustrator draws pictures for the story.

Figure 49.4 (*Continued*)

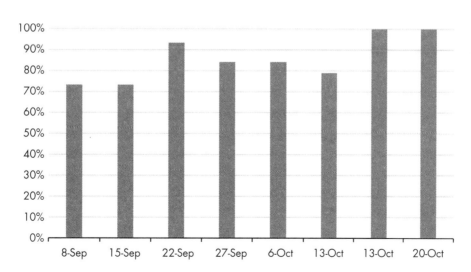

Figure 49.5 Visual Representation of Student Quiz Scores

STRATEGY 50
Accelerated Learning

What Is It?

The term "accelerated learning" became popular as educators began to explore strategies to help students compensate for their so-called "learning loss" due to the pandemic. (We have BIG issues with the term "learning loss," and many ideas connected to it, but we don't think it's necessary to go into that here.)

"Accelerated learning" is often contrasted with "remediation." In acceleration, educators are supposed to teach only the concepts and information that might have been missed that are absolutely essential for students to access grade-level content. It has been described as moving from "just in case learning," which requires an extensive review of all information that may be needed to access grade level work, to "just in time learning," which focuses just on the prior knowledge needed to access the content being taught next (Morton & Hashim, 2023).

Hmm, we wonder why this might sound familiar to teachers of English language learners? It's because that's what we've done all the time for years!

Especially for those of us teaching in secondary classrooms, we need to help our students learn a new language and culture, while they are learning new content at the same time, while they have missed out on much of the content that their peers have been exposed to for years.

Even though most ELL teachers have been doing this for years, and many are experts at accelerated learning, and even though we have issues with the term "learning loss," we have still recognized that many of our students have been harmed by the pandemic. So, we have stepped up our game over the past few years, as have others. This chapter will highlight some of the ways researchers, other teachers, and us have accelerated learning recently, and how we plan to continue it into the future.

STRATEGY 50: ACCELERATED LEARNING

Why We Like It

Though ELL teachers have been doing "accelerated learning" forever, the pandemic and the increased interest in the term and the concept pushed us to think more strategically about what was "accelerated" about what we had been doing and what more we could do.

Because of ELL teachers' experience with this idea, all of us are uniquely positioned to reflect and deepen our work. We don't need to buy high-cost "off-the-shelf" programs that are unlikely to work anyway—as one vendor said, "We're huge in learning loss!" (MacGillis, 2023).

As we describe in the "Supporting Research" section, the key elements required in accelerated learning are the existing elements of our, and most ELL teachers', instructional practice. Refining them further to maximize benefits to our students is a no-brainer.

Supporting Research

Research finds that small-group tutoring, adding instructional time, utilizing advantages of educational technology, providing scaffolds to support learning new content, prioritizing social emotional learning skills, and ensuring positive and regular parent communication are some of the key elements of successful accelerated learning (Morton & Hashim, 2023). One of the results of enhanced parent engagement can be increased student attendance, which is also a critical element of accelerated learning (Wolforth & Newman, 2024).

In addition, acceleration requires a high degree of student engagement and lessons that students feel are clearly relevant to their lives. Regular formative assessments, and analyses of them, are required to best inform instruction (New Jersey Department of Education, 2021).

Ensuring that lessons promote "active learning" and that are relevant to students' lives has also been found to be important in acceleration (Sarr et al., 2020).

Specifically for ELLs, researchers recommend teachers connect instruction to students' prior knowledge, including home languages and cultural resources (Thomas B. Fordham Institute, 2021).

Common Core Connections

All the instructional strategies discussed in this chapter are designed to make even more grade-level content accessible to English language learners sooner than they would otherwise learn it. A number of the strategies listed here are discussed in more detail in chapters specifically devoted to them, and you can find their direct Common Core connections in those chapters.

Application

"Accelerated learning" sounds good on paper and in talks, but it's a very different animal in real life. Here are some of the ways we have implemented the different elements identified as key to acceleration.

TUTORING

In an ideal world, schools would have the money to pay experienced adult tutors well, they would be able to find lots of qualified candidates to hire, and they would be able to fit in tutor sessions during the school day.

In our real world, there are not many districts and schools who can make all three of those things happen. In fact, there are not many who can even do one of those things!

Since the strategies in this book reflect "the world as it is" and not "the world as we would like it to be," we are advocates for using peer tutors to work with ELLs, which Strategy 39: Peer Teaching and Learning discusses in depth. We talk about another way to use peer tutors in the next section.

ADDING INSTRUCTIONAL TIME

Summer school is often offered as an answer to this issue. However, it's important to note that summer time learning taught in the same way as the rest of the year has often been found to be ineffective (Ferlazzo, 2023, August 10). Summer school programs focused more on social emotional learning and heavily on student high-interest topics tend to be more successful (Sparks, 2024; Barshay, 2021). Of course, if teachers follow the recommendations we're making in this book, their classes during the year would use those latter strategies, too!

During the school year itself some years we've been able to add "instructional time" with peer tutors through two ways—one, before the school day officially begins and, two, after the school day officially ends.

During both cases, peer tutors work with our ELL students. At Larry's school, students in the International Baccalaureate program must spend a substantial amount of time performing volunteer work (known as CAS). Some do it by tutoring ELL students in the morning in Larry's room (he always arrives early, anyway) and/or after school, under the supervision of staff running the regular after school program.

See Figure 50.1: Instruction for After-School Tutors to see how this effort operates. Though it's focused on tutoring after school, with just a few exceptions it works as well for before-school tutors, also.

USING EDUCATIONAL TECHNOLOGY

We discuss many ways to use educational technology in Strategy 47: Using Technology. There are multiple online tools that students can use independently to reinforce their language acquisition. In the Technology Connections section, you will find links to the sites we have students use, and that list is always evolving.

SCAFFOLDS

Graphic organizers, writing frames, sentence starters—you name a scaffold, we have it covered in this book!

STRATEGY 50: ACCELERATED LEARNING

SOCIAL EMOTIONAL LEARNING

Strategy 37: Social Emotional Learning and Strategy 38: Motivation share many "tips" on how to incorporate SEL skills into class.

Goal-setting is discussed at length in Strategy 38. The related idea of Individual Student Learning Plans has recently been tried as part of accelerated learning efforts in some districts (McFarlane, 2023; Blume, 2023). These plans, developed by districts, are supposed to communicate to students and their parents where they are academically in relationship to grade levels and, it seems to us, tend to focus more on student deficits. We like the idea of an individual plan for each student and sometimes have used an asset-based version we create *with* students that are also shared with their parents/guardians. See what we have used in Figure 50.2: Student Personal Report Form.

PARENT/GUARDIAN COMMUNICATION

As we discussed in Strategy 41: Working with Parents and Guardians, we place a high priority on maintaining positive relationships with the families of our students. Creating time to make calls home when we have positive news about their children is just as important, if not more important, than calling when there are challenges to discuss with them.

FORMATIVE ASSESSMENTS AND BEING DATA-INFORMED

To accelerate learning, it's critical that the teacher be data-informed about their students. Formative assessments are key to this; they inform both the teacher and the student about what they know and what they don't know.

We generally do many formative assessments each week and often two or more each day. Having each student use mini-whiteboards to answer questions and using online quiz sites like Quizizz or Kahoot are low-stakes strategies to determine prior knowledge before lessons begin and how successful our lessons have been and with whom.

When we're teaching an ELL newcomers class, we don't really find it necessary to do any assessment of student knowledge of the English topic prior to a lesson—the vast majority of time, students have had no prior study. It's a different story when teaching an intermediate, advanced, or multilevel class. In those situations, we'll often do quick prior assessments and find a diversity of knowledge. As Douglas Fisher and Nancy Frey have pointed out, even though some researchers suggest that 40 percent of class time may be spent on topics students have already mastered, it might be a different 40 percent for each student in class (Fisher & Frey, 2022).

If we're teaching in those situations, we generally have two plans: one, a lesson to quickly provide some needed priority knowledge, along with the new content and follow-up practice; and two, the same lesson, include the essential prior knowledge, along with some additional practice on the essential prior knowledge and follow-up practice on the new content. Then, based on the formative assessment results, we'll divide students into different peer tutor groups based on skills.

If we have a student teacher, sometimes we'll have them take the more proficient (or less proficient) group outside or in another room (Larry has two adjoining classrooms) to work with them after a lesson.

We're generally not big fans of tracking with "ability" groups in schools. However, in ELL classes, especially since the groups are very fluid, neither we nor the students are generally bothered by it. It's clear that the grouping is not based on ability or intelligence; it's just based on how long students have been in the United States.

STUDENT ENGAGEMENT, RELEVANCE, AND CONNECTION TO PRIOR KNOWLEDGE

Researchers suggest that active learning, not lecture, and asset-based lessons (see Strategy 37: Social Emotional Learning) make a difference in acceleration. They caution that it's not a matter of slowing down—that's what happens in remediation. Acceleration doesn't mean speeding through lessons, but it does mean we should be energetic and fast-paced (Fisher & Frey, 2022).

SIMULATIONS

Some say there is a difference between "simulations" and "role-plays," but we think it's more like "you say tomato, I say tomato." Dialogues, like the ones found in Strategy 25: Conversation Practice, can be used for students to practice for situations they'll find themselves in outside of school. Students with a higher English language proficiency can be told a situation ("You're bringing your car into a mechanic") and asked to create their own dialogues. Searching "role plays simulations ESL" online will find many ideas. Artificial intelligence tools can create role-plays, too. See the Technology Connections section for more information.

Online simulations have been found to assist ELLs with language acquisition. See the Technology Connections section for more resources on simulations.

It's very important to keep these simulations closely connected to situations our students might find themselves in. Historical simulations and simulations of current world events, though they can be useful if crafted well, can also often be ethically questionable and potentially traumatic for students involved (Onion, 2019).

Teaching Online

In theory, all of these instructional strategies can be applied online. In practice, however, we think it will be a big challenge to actually "accelerate learning" online for the majority of students, except for the most highly motivated ones. As we teachers discovered during the pandemic era distance learning, face-to-face instruction is the gold standard of instruction that's needed to maximize student learning.

What Could Go Wrong?

Plenty can be wrong with the activities in this chapter. Peer tutors need to be trained well, or researchers (and our own experiences) suggest they'll just give students the answers

STRATEGY 50: ACCELERATED LEARNING 543

(Ferlazzo, 2024, April 27). You might get students as peer tutors who don't really want to do it (in that case, we move them out quickly). Teachers can feel a bit overwhelmed at first by having to plan two follow-up practice activities for each lesson—one for students who had prior knowledge and one for those who didn't—but don't hesitate to use artificial intelligence or resources off the Web to help make it easier.

It's possible that even with all of our efforts at accelerated learning, our students may not make the progress we hoped they would make. Teachers need to remember that the majority of factors influencing student academic achievement lay outside the schoolhouse doors (Ferlazzo, December 18). The bottom line is that all we can do is be research-informed, be informed by our past experience and present judgment, and do our best (2017, July 16).

Technology Connections

For more information on Accelerated Learning, visit The Best Resources About Accelerated Learning (https://larryferlazzo.edublogs.org/2021/09/06/the-best-resources-about-accelerated-learning/).

Find recommendations of websites students can use to enhance their English language acquisition at There Are Tons of Resources on This Blog to Help Educators Teach ELLs – This Post Is a Good Place to Start (https://larryferlazzo.edublogs.org/2023/12/29/there-are-tons-of-resources-on-this-blog-to-help-educators-teach-ells-this-post-is-a-good-place-to-start/).

For more information on simulations, check out The Best Online Learning Simulation Games and Interactives – Help Me Find More (https://larryferlazzo.edublogs.org/2014/07/23/the-best-online-learning-simulation-games-interactives-help-me-find-more/). This site also includes AI tools specifically designed to create role plays.

All figures from this chapter, as well as 11 additional chapters, references, hyperlinked Technology Connections, and more online resources, can be found at www.wiley.com/go/ellteacherstoolbox2.

Thank you for being willing to be after-school tutors! Not only will you be earning CAS hours and adding an impressive activity to future job applications and resumes, but you will also be providing a great deal of help to a student who is new to this country dealing with a new culture and a new language!

You will be paired to tutor a student one-on-one. However, if you want, you can decide with other tutors to form small groups of two to three tutors and two to three students. Then, you just have to decide to do the same activities and still provide one-on-one support to your student. If you do not speak Spanish and need occasional help to communicate with your student, you can ask a tutor who is bilingual or ask the after-school staff person.

Your goal is to help your students learn English and, at the same time, try to have some fun doing it.

Mr. Ferlazzo will help get things started each day but then will have to leave for meetings. The after-school staff will be your "supervisor" and helper if you have any problems or questions.

You and your student are expected to work for one hour. You are expected to complete the "Tutor Reflection Form" after each tutoring session and give it to Mr. Ferlazzo the next day. The form will be signed and returned after he reviews it, and you can use it for your CAS materials.

See the next page for ideas for activities to do with your students.

Figure 50.1 Instruction for After-School Tutors

STRATEGY 50: ACCELERATED LEARNING

ACTIVITIES TO DO DURING TUTORING SESSION:

Mr. Ferlazzo will bring a milk crate or two filled with materials you can use with your student. YOU – and your student – have the freedom to decide which you want to use for how much of the time. Return all materials to the crates, and Mr. Ferlazzo will pick them up the next morning. These activities could include:

1. Using the *English in Action* book. Students should write their name in one of the books, and they can write in it, too. You should start at the beginning for most students, but some might be more advanced. In those cases, it's fine to begin where they want.

2. Using the bilingual dictionaries. You can teach students some of the words and phrases in the dictionaries by modeling them and asking them to repeat them. Then, "test" them by covering up the words and asking what the items are.

3. Using the mini-whiteboards and markers. After students have learned and practiced words and sentences, you can dictate them to the students and they can try writing them down on the whiteboards, which you can then check.

4. Practice conversations. There are copies of short conversation sheets in the box that you can practice with students – and you can modify them. Again, follow up with having them write them on the whiteboards.

5. Reading. There are simple books in the crate. You and your student can look at them, you read a sentence pointing to the words, and then they repeat them. Again, you can use the whiteboards to follow up.

6. Use what is called the Language Experience Approach. This means you do an activity with your student that takes 10 to 15 minutes. Then you ask them to write sentences about what you both did – you can help them write those sentences and you can write simple ones, too, to help them out. For example, you can take a frisbee from the box and play a game of catch outside of the library and come back and write about what you did first, second, third, etc. Play a board game. There will be some board games in the box you can play to help your students learn English.

7. Any other classwork. For example, your students may want help in math.

Figure 50.1 (*Continued*)

TUTOR FORM TO COMPLETE AFTER YOUR SESSION

NAME _____

DATE OF TUTORING _____

NAME OF YOUR STUDENT _____

WHAT ACTIVITIES DID YOU DO WITH YOUR STUDENT?

1. _____
2. _____
3. _____

WHAT DO YOU THINK WENT WELL AND WHY?
_____
_____
_____

WHAT WOULD YOU DO DIFFERENTLY?
_____
_____
_____

WHAT HELP DO YOU NEED FROM MR. FERLAZZO?
_____
_____

Figure 50.1 (*Continued*)

STRATEGY 50: ACCELERATED LEARNING 547

Student Name _____ Date _____

Current Class Grade _____

On a scale from 0 to 100, with 0 being the student is not trying to learn English at all and 100 being they are doing everything possible to learn English, where is this student right now? Red mark is where student thinks they are; Green mark is where teacher thinks they are:

0_____100

Student Strengths Circle any: **Where Student Could Improve:**

Student Strengths	Where Student Could Improve
Works hard in class	Could work harder in class
Respectful to teacher and peers	Could be more respectful to teacher and peers
Does extra work to learn more English	Needs to do more extra work to learn English
Reading and writing in English	Reading and writing in English
Listening and speaking in English	Listening and speaking in English
School attendance	School attendance
Weekly test scores	Weekly test scores

Actions students can take to continue strengths and make improvement:

1. Work for 20 minutes each day at home on online sites like _____ _____.

2. Write in English about a picture for homework three nights a week.

3. Record themselves describing a picture three nights a week.

4. Attend 7:45 a.m. class with Mr. Ferlazzo four times a week.

5. Study in Mr. Ferlazzo's room during lunch for 15 minutes each day.

6. Read a simple English book each week at home and write about it in English.

7. Other _____

Student Signature _____ Parent Signature _____

Figure 50.2 Student Personal Report Form

Appendix: English Language Arts Standards—Anchor Standards

Reprinted from https://www.thecorestandards.org/ELA-Literacy/. Copyright 2010, National Governors Association Center for Best Practices and Council of Chief State School Officers. All rights reserved.

College and Career Readiness Anchor Standards for Reading

Key Ideas and Details

CCSS.ELA-LITERACY.CCRA.R.1

    Read closely to determine what the text says explicitly and to make logical inferences from it; cite specific textual evidence when writing or speaking to support conclusions drawn from the text.

CCSS.ELA-LITERACY.CCRA.R.2

    Determine central ideas or themes of a text and analyze their development; summarize the key supporting details and ideas.

CCSS.ELA-LITERACY.CCRA.R.3

    Analyze how and why individuals, events, or ideas develop and interact over the course of a text.

APPENDIX: ENGLISH LANGUAGE ARTS STANDARDS—ANCHOR STANDARDS

Craft and Structure

CCSS.ELA-LITERACY.CCRA.R.4

Interpret words and phrases as they are used in a text, including determining technical, connotative, and figurative meanings, and analyze how specific word choices shape meaning or tone.

CCSS.ELA-LITERACY.CCRA.R.5

Analyze the structure of texts, including how specific sentences, paragraphs, and larger portions of the text (e.g., a section, chapter, scene, or stanza) relate to each other and the whole.

CCSS.ELA-LITERACY.CCRA.R.6

Assess how point of view or purpose shapes the content and style of a text.

Integration of Knowledge and Ideas

CCSS.ELA-LITERACY.CCRA.R.7

Integrate and evaluate content presented in diverse media and formats, including visually and quantitatively, as well as in words.[1]

CCSS.ELA-LITERACY.CCRA.R.8

Delineate and evaluate the argument and specific claims in a text, including the validity of the reasoning as well as the relevance and sufficiency of the evidence.

CCSS.ELA-LITERACY.CCRA.R.9

Analyze how two or more texts address similar themes or topics in order to build knowledge or to compare the approaches the authors take.

Range of Reading and Level of Text Complexity

CCSS.ELA-LITERACY.CCRA.R.10

Read and comprehend complex literary and informational texts independently and proficiently.

---

[1] Please see "Research to Build and Present Knowledge" in **Writing** and "Comprehension and Collaboration" in **Speaking and Listening** for additional standards relevant to gathering, assessing, and applying information for print and digital resources.

College and Career Readiness Anchor Standards for Writing

Text Types and Purposes

CCSS.ELA-LITERACY.CCRA.W.1

Write arguments to support claims in an analysis of substantive topics or texts using valid reasoning and relevant and sufficient evidence.

CCSS.ELA-LITERACY.CCRA.W.2

Write informative/explanatory texts to examine and convey complex ideas and information clearly and accurately through the effective selection, organization, and analysis of content.

CCSS.ELA-LITERACY.CCRA.W.3

Write narratives to develop real or imagined experiences or events using effective technique, well-chosen details, and well-structured event sequences.

Production and Distribution of Writing

CCSS.ELA-LITERACY.CCRA.W.4

Produce clear and coherent writing in which the development, organization, and style are appropriate to task, purpose, and audience.

CCSS.ELA-LITERACY.CCRA.W.5

Develop and strengthen writing as needed by planning, revising, editing, rewriting, or trying a new approach.

CCSS.ELA-LITERACY.CCRA.W.6

Use technology, including the Internet, to produce and publish writing and to interact and collaborate with others.

Research to Build and Present Knowledge

CCSS.ELA-LITERACY.CCRA.W.7

Conduct short as well as more sustained research projects based on focused questions, demonstrating understanding of the subject under investigation.

CCSS.ELA-LITERACY.CCRA.W.8

Gather relevant information from multiple print and digital sources, assess the credibility and accuracy of each source, and integrate the information while avoiding plagiarism.

CCSS.ELA-LITERACY.CCRA.W.9

Draw evidence from literary or informational texts to support analysis, reflection, and research.

Range of Writing

CCSS.ELA-LITERACY.CCRA.W.10

Write routinely over extended time frames (time for research, reflection, and revision) and shorter time frames (a single sitting or a day or two) for a range of tasks, purposes, and audiences.

College and Career Readiness Anchor Standards for Speaking and Listening

Comprehension and Collaboration

CCSS.ELA-LITERACY.CCRA.SL.1

Prepare for and participate effectively in a range of conversations and collaborations with diverse partners, building on others' ideas and expressing their own clearly and persuasively.

CCSS.ELA-LITERACY.CCRA.SL.2

Integrate and evaluate information presented in diverse media and formats, including visually, quantitatively, and orally.

CCSS.ELA-LITERACY.CCRA.SL.3

Evaluate a speaker's point of view, reasoning, and use of evidence and rhetoric.

Presentation of Knowledge and Ideas

CCSS.ELA-LITERACY.CCRA.SL.4

Present information, findings, and supporting evidence such that listeners can follow the line of reasoning and the organization, development, and style are appropriate to task, purpose, and audience.

CCSS.ELA-LITERACY.CCRA.SL.5

Make strategic use of digital media and visual displays of data to express information and enhance understanding of presentations.

CCSS.ELA-LITERACY.CCRA.SL.6

Adapt speech to a variety of contexts and communicative tasks, demonstrating command of formal English when indicated or appropriate.

College and Career Readiness Anchor Standards for Language

Conventions of Standard English

CCSS.ELA-LITERACY.CCRA.L.1

Demonstrate command of the conventions of standard English grammar and usage when writing or speaking.

CCSS.ELA-LITERACY.CCRA.L.2

Demonstrate command of the conventions of standard English capitalization, punctuation, and spelling when writing.

Knowledge of Language

CCSS.ELA-LITERACY.CCRA.L.3

Apply knowledge of language to understand how language functions in different contexts, to make effective choices for meaning or style, and to comprehend more fully when reading or listening.

Vocabulary Acquisition and Use

CCSS.ELA-LITERACY.CCRA.L.4

Determine or clarify the meaning of unknown and multiple-meaning words and phrases by using context clues, analyzing meaningful word parts, and consulting general and specialized reference materials, as appropriate.

CCSS.ELA-LITERACY.CCRA.L.5

Demonstrate understanding of figurative language, word relationships, and nuances in word meanings.

CCSS.ELA-LITERACY.CCRA.L.6

Acquire and use accurately a range of general academic and domain-specific words and phrases sufficient for reading, writing, speaking, and listening at the college and career readiness level; demonstrate independence in gathering vocabulary knowledge when encountering an unknown term important to comprehension or expression.

Index

1-2-3 activity, 288
3-2-1 activity, 488
3-2-1 graphic organizer, 103
3-2-1 ideas, 103
3-2-1 poster, instructions, 102–103
3-2-1 structure, variation, 102
"3 Strategies for Deep Virtual Learning" (Perini/McTighe/Silver), 142
4-3-2 fluency activity, 288
5, Warm-ups, 482
7 Steps to a Language-Rich, Interactive Classroom (Seidlitz/Perryman), 218

A

ABC. *See* Answer, Back it up, Comment
Ability groups, 542
Academic language development, QSSSA tool (usage), 217
Academic Language Oral Practice, 44; prompts, 57f
Academic Language Sentences (game), 268–269
Academic vocabulary, 43–44; teaching, word lists (usage), 51
Accelerated learning: after-school tutors, instruction, 540, 544f–546f; application, 539–542; Common Core connections, 539; data awareness, 541–542; defining, 538; educational technology, usage, 540; formative assessments, 541–5421; instructional time, addition, 540; online teaching, 542; parent/guardian communication, 541; preference, reason, 539; prior knowledge, connection, 542; problems, 542–543; relevance, 542; remediation, contrast, 538; scaffolds, usage, 540; simulations, 542; social emotional learning, 541; student engagement, 542; Student Personal Report form, 547f; supported research, 539; technology connections, 543; tutoring, 540
Action mazes, 337
Activating prior knowledge: anticipation guides, 61; application, 60–63; assessment, 41; Common Core connections, 60; defining, 59; differentiation recommendations, 64; field trips, 63; home language materials, usage, 63; KWL charts, 60–61; multimedia, usage, 61; online teaching, 63; preference, reason, 59; preparatory texts, 62–63; problems, 64; quickwrites, usage, 62; supporting research, 60; technology connections, 64–65; vocabulary, usage, 62
Activating schema, 59
Active learning, promotion, 539
Active listening, 333, 334, 337
Active viewing, 322
Adjectives, Concept Attainment Example, 148f
Adkins, Jen, 173
Adobe Express, 327
Adobe Flash, 347
Advanced students, Jigsaw materials, 102–104
After-school tutors, instruction, 540, 544f–546f
Agentic feedback, 229
Albano, Larissa, 348
Alinsky, Saul, 49
Amazon Alexa, usage, 337
Amazon Echo, 337
Animals, images (usage), 316
Anonymous ELL Class Evaluation Sheet, sample, 471, 480f–481f
Answer, Back it up, Comment (ABC): format, 169; model, 168; paragraphs, usage, 184; Writing Structure, 169, 178f
Answer-Question (game), 343–344
Anticipation guides, 61, 66f–67f
AREE. *See* Assertion, Reason, Evidence, Explanation
Argument (higher-order thinking skill), 153
Aronson, Elliot, 105

553

INDEX

Artificial intelligence (AI): chatbots, usage, 48, 189, 234, 240, 271; dialogues, 287–288; ethical use, 188, 241; quality, 166; revolution, 7; technology, usage, 502–503; text-to-image tools, usage, 204–205; tools, language skills limitations, 8, 167; videos, 327
Asher, James J., 296
Ask-answer-add, 289–290
Assertion, Reason, Evidence, Explanation (AREE) Writing Structure, 160, 181f; Teaching Grid, 182f
Assess. *See* Question, Signal, Stem, Share, Assess
Assessment: application, 527–531; beginner-level initial assessment, 534f; Choice Board assessments, 531; Common Core connections, 527; defining, 526; formative assessments, 528–531, 541–542; Friday quiz, sample, 529, 534f; games, usage, 531; goal sheets, 537; initial/diagnostic assessments, 527–528; intermediate-level initial assessment, 533f; mini-whiteboards, usage, 531; online teaching, 531–532; preference, reason, 526–527; problems, 532; prompts, scaffolding (inclusion), 530, 535f–537f; reading/writing, 528; speaking/listening, 528; strategy, 151; student quiz scores, visual representation, 537f; student self-assessment/reflection, 530; supporting research, 527; technology connections, 532; weekly "quizzes," 529; writing prompts, 530
Asset-based mindset, 392–395, 449
Asset-based pedagogies, 383
Asset-based teaching, ideas, 387
Asynchronous conversations, structuring, 221
Audio, quality, 322
Autonomy: actions, support, 404; intrinsic motivation development element, 403
Avalos, Alma, 306

B

Back and forth activity, 316; page, 319f
Back and Forth: Photocopiable Cooperative Pair Activities for Language Development (Rodgers, et al.), 316, 318
Back-to-back (listening activity), 336
Banville, Sean, 128
Bassano, Sharron, 137
Beene, Tina, 214
Beginner students, Jigsaw application, 100–101
Bell ringers, 482
Belonging, sense, 395–396
Benefits of Reading Unit, writing prompt, 122
Bennett, Colette M., 207
Bernabei, Gretchen, 170, 173
Beuckens, Todd, 289, 292
Bilingual/Multilingual advantages read aloud, 409, 416f
Bishop, Rudine Sims, 7
Blooket, usage, 420, 531
Bloom's Questions for Images, 201, 210f–211f
BME Sequence Chart, 523f
Boggle (game), 273
Books: interview, conducting, 8; selection, 7–8; trailer, creation, 8; writing/talking about, 8
Boosting Achievement: Reaching Students with Interrupted Our Minimal Education (Salva), 214
Brain dumps, 151
Brainpop, Jr., usage, 286
Brandi, Nati Gonzalez, 305, 309
Bridge builders, 388
Bubble Map/Web Diagram example, 521f
Buric, Pam, 418
Busywork, 492, 493
Buy a Mistake (game), 230

C

Cabal, Cristina, 274
Calhoun, Emily F., 142
Callan, Nancy, 101, 105
Categories (game), 269–270
Categorizing (higher-order thinking skill), 153
Change-of-pace activity, 500
Changing Mindsets Infographic, 392, 399f
Chants, 307; Information Chants, 307, 313f–314f; jazz chants, 302, 307
Chatbots, 287; ethical use, 241
ChatGPT, 63, 287, 501; prompt, 141; question, 272; student usage, 290; usage, 231, 234, 239, 243, 271, 503; encouragement, 167
ChatGPT-Created Text Data Set, 141, 149f
Chavez, Cesar (cloze passage), 82
Choice boards (learning menus), 404, 493; application, 194; assessments, 531; Choice Board Makeover, 198f; Common Core connections, 193; defining, 193; differentiation recommendations, 194; Homework Choice Board, 194, 197f; Newcomers Quarterly Assessment, 196f–197f; Online Choice Board, 194; online teaching, 194; preference, reason, 193; problems, 194; supporting research, 193; technology connection, 194
Choose Your Own Adventure (listening activity), 337
Claim (teaching), images (usage), 201
Class, beginning/ending, 5; 3-2-1 activity, 488; application, 483–489; closure activities, 486–489; Common Core connections, 483; defining, 482; differentiation recommendations, 490; Do Nows, 483–486; Everybody Think… activity, 487; independent reading, 483–484; One-Minute Reports activity, 489; online skills, practice, 485; online teaching, 489; oral practice, 485; partner reading, 484; peer tutor-led small groups, 484; preference, reason, 482; problems, 489; Question Menu, 487; self-assessment exit tickets, 488; Shining Moments activity, 487; Sticky Note compliments, 488; supporting research, 483; technology connections, 490–491; visualization, 485–486; writers, notebook prompts, 486
Class Dojo, usage, 216, 222
"Classical" LEA version, 94–95

Classroom: learning, family participation, 446; risk-taking culture, 233; small group learning, opportunities (creation), 396; walls, posters (usage), 395

Classroom-appropriate reading material, student selection, 6

ClassTools, 266–267

Clines, 44–45, 58f, 61

Closed-ended questions, usage, 219

Close reading, 114–115, 122–126

Close-read photos/images, discussion, 200–201

Closure activities, 486–489

Clozes, 135; application, 81–82; captions, writing, 202; Common Core connections, 81; defining, 80; differentiation recommendations, 83; exercise, follow-up exercise, 305; Letter Blanks—Juan and Maria (Student Handout), 89f; Letter Blanks—Juan and Maria (Teacher Answer Key), 90f; making, instructions, 92f, 467; No Answers Show—Art and Music (Student Handout), 81, 85f; No Answers Show—Art and Music (Teacher Answer Key), 86f; No Answers Show—Jobs (Student Handout), 85f; No Answers Show—Jobs (Teacher Answer Key), 85f; No Blanks—US History (Student Handout), 90f; No Blanks—US History (Teacher Answer Key), 91f; online teaching, 82–83; Persuading My Parents (Student Sample), 92f; Persuading My Parents Cloze and Mimic Write, 82, 91f; Phrase Blanks—Kamala Harris (Student Handout), 88f–89f; Phrase Blanks—Kamala Harris (Teacher Answer Key), 89f; preference, reason, 80; problems, 83; supporting research, 80; technology connections, 84; usage, 493; Word Bank at End of Sentences—Cesar Chavez (Student Handout), 87f; Word Bank at End of Sentences—Cesar Chavez (Teacher Answer Key), 88f; Word Bank—Helen Keller (Student Handout), 86f; Word Bank—Helen Keller (Teacher Answer Key), 87f

Cognates, 47

Cognitive choice, 500

Collaboration and Co-Teaching (Honigsfeld/Dove), 440

Collaborative learning, 103; opportunities, 358

College and Career Readiness Anchor Standards for Language, 552

College and Career Readiness Anchor Standards for Listening, 551

College and Career Readiness Anchor Standards for Reading, 548–549

College and Career Readiness Anchor Standards for Speaking, 551

College and Career Readiness Anchor Standards for Writing, 550–551

Comic strips, 71

Common Core Anchor Standards, 23

Common Core connections: accelerated learning, 539; assessment, 527; choice boards (learning menus), 193; class, beginning/ending, 483; clozes, 81; conversation practice, 286; co-teaching, 438; culturally responsive teaching, 384; dictation, 279; ELLs, differentiation, 354; error correction strategies, 229; grammar, teaching, 158; graphic organizers, 23; independent reading, 6; inductive learning, 134; Interactive Word Walls (IWWs), 515; jigsaw, 100; Language Experience Approach (LEA), 93; Long-Term ELLS (LTELLs), interaction, 372; motivation, 403; multilevel classes, 375; music, 303; parents/guardians, interaction, 443; peer teaching/learning, 417; photos/images, usage, 200, 315; prior knowledge, activation, 60; problem posing, 245; project-based learning/problem-based learning, 252; QSSSA, 218; quoting/summarizing/paraphrasing, 184; reading/writing, learning games, 264; retrieval practice, 151; revision, 238; school year, beginning, 453; school year, ending, 466; sequencing, 69; social emotional learning, 392; speaking/listening, learning games, 343; strategy, 334; Students with Interrupted Formal Education (SIFEs), 366; technology, usage, 499; text engineering, 16; total physical response, 296; translanguaging, 450; video, 321; vocabulary, 40; writing frames/writing structures, 166; zero-prep activities, 493

Common Core ELA Standards, student reading rule, 6

Common Core Standards, 43, 103, 187

Communities Venn Diagram, 520f

Community Problem Research Form, 254, 261f

Compare and contrast methods, 202–203

Competence: intrinsic motivation development element, 403; support, actions, 405–406

Comprehensible input, 321

Concept attainment, 138–139

Concept Attainment Paraphrasing 1, 186, 191f

Concept Attainment Paraphrasing 2, 187, 191f–192f

Conflict map, 35f

Connecting Four (game), 270–271

Consonant-consonant pattern, 137–138

Content classes, ELL differentiation, 353

Context clues, 43; teaching, steps, 56f

Conti, Gianfranco, 159, 161

Conversation cheat sheets, 290

Conversation practice, 116, 167, 378; 1-2-3 activity, 288; application, 286–291; ask-answer-add, 289–290; Common Core connections, 286; critical thinking dialogues, 287; defining, 285; Dialogue Scramble, 293f; Teacher Answer Key, 294f; dialogues, usage, 286–288; differentiation recommendations, 291; Holiday Dialogue, 286, 293f; Mexican American War Critical Thinking dialogue, 287, 294f; online teaching, 291; preference, reason, 285;

problems, 291; pronunciation feedback, 290; self-assessment, 291; supporting research, 285–286; technology connections, 292
Conversation Starters, example, 295f
Cooperative learning opportunities, 358
Cooperative Storytelling, 495
Cooperative writing, 103, 104, 199, 200, 495; activity, 492–493
Correct a Sentence (game), 230
Co-teaching: advice, 439–440; application, 438–440; Common Core connections, 438; defining, 437–438; models, 437–438; online teaching, 441; preference, reason, 438; supporting research, 438; technology connections, 441
Course expectations. *See* School year
Creativity in the English Language Classroom (Fehér), 51
Critical thinking dialogues, 287
Csikszentmihalyi, Mihaly, 69
Csizér, Kata, 403
Culturally relevant pedagogy, 383
Culturally responsive curriculum, factors, 388
Culturally responsive mind-set, words (usage), 385–386
Culturally responsive teaching, 244, 394, 454; application, 384–389; Common Core connections, 384; defining, 383; online teaching, 389; preference, reason, 384; problems, 389–390; supporting research, 384; technology connections, 390
Culturally Responsive Teaching and the Brain (Hammond), 386
Culturally sustaining pedagogy, 383
Curiosity gap, 100

D

Davies, Genesis, 348
Delayed dictation, 281
Details, listening, 338
Dialogue: artificial intelligence dialogues, 287–288; critical thinking dialogues, 287; example, 37f; Holiday Dialogue, 286, 293f; Journal prompts, 422, 433f; puppet dialogue, 288; usage, 286–288

Dialogue Scramble, 293f; Teacher Answer Key, 294f
Dictation, 334, 493, 495; application, 280–283; Common Core connections, 279; defining, 279; delayed dictation, 281; Dictogloss (word usage), 280–281; differentiation recommendations, 284; information gap activities, 282–283; online teaching, 283; paired dictation, 280; picture dictation lesson, 282; preference, reason, 279; problems, 283; running dictation (messenger-and-scribe), usage, 231, 282–283; supporting research, 279; technology connections, 284
Dictogloss (word usage), 280–281, 946
Difference picture, spotting/finding, 202–203
Different or Same? (listening activity), 337
DIY PD: A Guide to Self-Directed Learning for Educators of Multilingual Learners (Salva), 214
Donors Choose (grant source), 504
Do-Now (do now), 5, 482; activities, 483–486; questions, inclusion, 404–405; text inspiration, 125–126
Dörnyei, Zoltán, 403, 406
Dove, Maria G., 437–438, 440
Drill-and-kill, 158
Driving question, 254
Duolingo, usage, 359
Dusbiber, Dana, 118, 121
Dweck, Carol, 396–397

E

Ebbinghaus, Hermann, 150
Educational technology, usage, 540
Edutopia (blog), 125
Elementary QSSA examples, 221, 225f
Elish-Piper, Laurie, 126
Ello (listening activities), 289
ELL Teacher's Toolbox, The, update, 1
Emergent bilinguals, term (replacement), 2
Emotional learning, 405
Empathetic mindset, demonstration, 395
Empathy, building (writing prompt), 418, 426f
Empathy Project, 418

End-of-Quarter Reading Reflection, 9, 13f
Engagement, benefits, 443
Engineered text, example, 18f–21f
English language acquisition, writing importance (learning), 167–168
English Language Arts Standards—Anchor Standards, 548–552
English Language Development (ELD), 214
English language learner (ELL): Anonymous ELL Class Evaluation Sheet, sample, 471, 480f–481f; Dictogloss, usage, 281; extracurricular activity access, 396; newcomers, handling, 358–361; problem-based learning, examples, 253; problems, 10; project-based learning, examples, 252–253; school support, 6; sentence: development, 49; frames, usage, 7; students: home visit, 444; support, 365; visual processing opportunities, 22; term, usage, 2; writing lesson, 167–168
English language learner (ELL), differentiation: academic support, providing, 359–361; advice, 355–358; application, 354–361; Common Core connections, 354; cooperative/collaborative learning opportunities, 358; defining, 353–354; emotional support, providing, 358; graphic organizers, providing, 357; home language, development (encouragement), 357; modeling, usage, 355; nonlinguistic cues, usage, 356; note-taking strategies, 357–358; preference, reason, 354; sentence-starters, providing, 357; social support, providing, 361; speech, rate (control), 356; student assets, recognition, 355; supporting research, 354; understanding, checking, 356–357; verbal/written instructions, giving, 356; wait time, control, 356
English-proficient students, content classes (ELL differentiation), 353

Equity, QSSSA tool (usage), 217–218
Error correction strategies: application, 229–233; Common Core connections, 229; concept attainment (attainment plus), 229; defining, 228; differentiation recommendations, 233; games, 230; growth mind-sets, encouragement, 230; Improvement Rubric, 231, 232, 236f; individual feedback, giving, 230–231; online teaching, 233; preference, reason, 228; problems, 233; recasts, usage, 232–233; self-correction, 231–232; support research, 228–229; technology connections, 234–235
ESL/ELL Wordle (game), 272–273
ESL Jigsaws, 101
Essay: ChatGPT, usage, 239; electronic version, 240; hard copy, review, 239; pre-planning, graphic organizer (usage), 238–239
Essential question, 254
Everette, Meghan, 173
Everybody Think… activity, 487
Everyone Is a Teacher. *See* Peer teaching/learning
Evidence (teaching), images (usage), 201
Example of a Structured Visual, 219, 224f
Example Signals, 220, 224f
Example "Who First" Indicators, 220, 224f
Expanded Sentence Scramble & Answer Sheet, 160, 162f–164f
Experiencing self, 205–206
Extensive reading, 5
Extrinsic motivation, 403

F

Face-to-face teaching, 26
Feedback, 234, 264, 501; agentic feedback, 229; incorporation, 239; individual feedback, giving, 230–231; opportunity, 238; pronunciation feedback, 290; student feedback, 482
Fehér, Judit, 51
Field trips, 63
Figlewicz, Agnieszka, 235, 240
Fill-in-the-blank, 189, 265; frames, 420; outlines, extensions, 168–169; sentences, 166; sheets, 80

Finished books wall, online version (creation), 9–10
First language (L1) (home language): abilities, 6; diglot story, writing, 48; skills, transfer (research), 357; usage, 357
Fisher, Douglas, 125, 128, 541
Fishtank Learning, 17
Five senses chart, 24, 29f; student example, 30f
Flashcards, retrieval practice example, 150–151
Fleenor, Stephen, 214, 223
Flipgrid, usage, 221
Flow, development (promotion), 69
Flyswatter (game), 265–266
Formative assessments, 528–531, 541–542
Four Truths and a Lie (game), 345–346
Four Words sheet, 40–41, 46, 52f
Frames. *See* Writing frames: photos/images. *See* Photos/images.; prompt, usage, 122
Frayer, Dorothy (Frayer Model), 41–42
Free-choice unit, 467
Free recall, 152
Free voluntary reading, 5
Frey, Nancy, 115, 125, 128, 541
"Fun" stories, 298–299

G

Games, usage, 139, 342
"Gamified" LEA version, 95–96
Gandhi, Mahatma, 361
Gap-fills, 80, 135
Gates, Bill, 502
Gay, Geneva, 383
Gemini (Google), usage, 63, 234
George Washington Writing Frame, 168, 173f
Germany, Antoine, 173
"Get Up, Stand Up" (Marley), 303
Gill, Michelle, 223
Ginsburg, David, 486
Goals: review form, 414f; setting, forms, 404, 411f–413f; sheets, 531
Goal-setting activity, completion, 466–467
Goal-Setting chart, student example. *See* Peer teaching/learning
Goldenberg, Claude, 114
Golden line, identification/writing, 8
Gonzalez, Valentina, 392, 399, 513
Google Assistant, 337
Google Bard, 189
Google Classroom, 140, 205, 291, 501

Google Docs: add-ons, usage, 84; drag-and-drop activities, 71; usage, 139, 140, 239; Voice Typing, 445
Google Drawings, 205
Google Drive (collaborative resource), 440
Google Form, 471
Google Home, 337
Google Jamboard, 141, 458
Google Slides, 71, 205, 327
Google Translate, 445, 452, 458, 486, 504, 530; audio/text support, 367; avoidance, 528; benefits/pitfalls, 167, 171–172; ethical use, 241; pictures, usage, 357; student usage, 238–239; usage, 358
Graham, Carolyn, 302
Grammar concepts: discussion, 281; teaching, 159
Grammar, teaching: application, 159–160; Common Core connections, 158; defining, 158; differentiation recommendations, 160; Expanded Sentence Scramble & Answer Sheet, 160, 162f–164f; online teaching, 160; preference, reason, 158; problems, 160; scrambled sentences, expansion, 160; sentence navigators, completion, 159; Sentence Puzzle, 159, 162; supporting research, 158; technology connections, 161
Graphic organizers, 45, 119, 184, 291, 514; application, 23–25; Common Core connections, 23; defining, 22; differentiation recommendations, 26; online teaching, 25; preference, reasons, 22; Problem-Posing Graphic Organizer, 246, 250f; problems, identification, 26; supporting research, 22–23; technology connections, 26–27; usage, 120–121, 357, 514
Gratitude, expression, 470
Growth Mindset: Paragraph Frame, 401f; Stories, 400f
Growth Mindset (growth mindset), 397
Growth mind-set, encouragement, 230
Guardians. *See* Parents/guardians
Guess the Word (game), 345
Guess Who (game), 273

H

Hamilton: An American Musical (music), appreciation, 303, 306
Hammond, Zaretta, 386, 390
Hangman (game), 269
Harris, Kamala (cloze passage), 82
Has/Have, Concept Attainment Example, 148f
Headbands (game), 273
"Heads, Shoulders, Knees, and Toes" (song), 303
Hearing, listening (contrast), 333
"Hello, Goodbye" (song), 303
Helping Students Motivate Themselves (Ferlazzo), 73, 205, 473
Herron, Jan, 329
Hess, Natalie, 324, 329
Higher-order thinking skills, incorporation, 153
High-interest books, ELL student access, 10
High-interest reading materials, online sites, 11
High-intermediate students, Jigsaw materials, 102–104
Holder, Carlota, 438, 441
Holiday Dialogue, 286, 293f
Home Culture Project, 253, 257f–260f
Home language: development, encouragement, 357; instruction, 367; materials, usage, 63; reading, encouragement, 6; student illiteracy, interaction, 90
Homework: revision, 240; technology, usage, 502
Homework Choice Board, 194, 197f
Honigsfled, Andrea, 437–438, 440

I

"I Am" Project, 456–457
"I Just Called To Say I Love You" (song), 304
"I Learn Best When. . ." cards, 456
Images. *See* Photos/images
Improvement Rubric, 231, 232, 236f, 471; Reflection Questions, 471, 478f; Writing Improvement Rubric, 477f
Independent reading, 5, 167, 468; application, 6–9; Common Core connections, 6; defining, 5; differentiation recommendations, 10; online teaching, 9–10; problems, identification, 10; technology connections, 11–12; term, enjoyment, 5; usage, 483–484
Independent study, technology (usage), 500–501
Individual feedback, giving, 230–231
Individual Student Learning Plans, 541
Inductive learning, 169, 199, 228, 367, 404, 467; adjectives/periods, Concept Attainment Example, 148f; application, 134–139; ChatGPT-Created Text Data Set, 141, 149f; Common Core connections, 134; Concept Attainment Example, 138–139; data set instructions, 146, 467; defining, 133; differentiation recommendations, 140; Has/Have, Concept Attainment Example, 148f; International New Year's Traditions Data Set, 136, 144f; John F. Kennedy Data Set, 136, 145f; Kitchen Picture Cloze Sentences, 135, 143f–144f; Man in the Kitchen, 143f; online teaching, 139–140; phonics data set, 136, 137–138; picture data sets, 136, 138; Picture Word Inductive Model (PWIM), 134–136; preference, reason, 133; problems, 140; Seasons of the Year Data Set, 136, 145f; *Sounds Easy!* example page, 147f; supporting research, 133–134; technology connections, 141–142; text data sets, 136–137; teaching, sequence (example), 137; Writing an Essay Flow Chart, 139, 149f
Inductive strategies, 139; games, usage, 139; pre-reading, 139; scaffolding writing, 139
Information Chants, 307, 313f–314f
Information gap activities, 99, 282–283
Ingham, Jonny, 51
Instructional practices, cultural responsiveness, 386–388
Instructional time, addition, 540
Interactive picture dictionaries, online availability, 51
Interactive read alouds, 117–118
Interactive Word Walls (IWWs), 41, 45–47; application, 515–516; BME Sequence Chart, 523f; Bubble Map/Web Diagram example, 521f; classroom examples, 516, 525f; Common Core connections, 515; Communities Venn Diagram, 520f; defining, 513; Elementary Prepositions Interactive Word Wall example, 524f; elements, 46; Forms of Government Content Frame, 520f; Literary Genres Tree Map, 518f; Narrative Words Content Frame, 519f; Onion Diagram, communities example, 523f; online teaching, 517; preference, reason, 513–514; problems, 517; Pyramid/Triangle Chart, 519f; Story Map example, 522f; supporting research, 514; technology connections, 517–518
International New Year's Traditions Data Set, 136, 144f
Intrinsic motivation, development (elements), 403

J

Jazz chants, 302, 307
Jigsaw, 376; application, 100–104; beginners/low-intermediates, materials, 100–101; Common Core connections, 100; defining, 99; differentiation recommendations, 104–105; Driver's License Activity, 101, 106f; Driver's License Jigsaw, 100, 106f; high-intermediates/advanced, materials, 102–104; Nina's Break-In: How to Use This Jigsaw, 101, 109f; Nina's Break-In Part 1, 101, 107f; Nina's Break-In Part 2, 101, 108f; online teaching, 104; preference, reason, 99; problems, 104; process, steps, 101; Student Jigsaw Instructions, 103, 110f; Student Sentence Starters, 112f; Student Textbook Jigsaw Instructions, 103, 111f; supporting research, 99–100; technology connections, 105; topics/categories, usage, 102
John F. Kennedy Data Set, 136, 145f
Johnson, Elisabeth, 136, 142
Just in time learning, 538

K

Kahneman, Daniel, 465, 483
Kahoot!, usage, 160, 189, 420, 531, 541

Keller, Helen (cloze passage), 82
Kernel essays, 170, 173
Keyboard, usage/learning, 503
Khan, Sal, 502
Kitchen Picture Cloze Sentences, 135, 143f–144f
Knowledge Read Aloud, 155f
Knowledge transfer (higher-order thinking skill), 153
Know, Want, Learn (KWL) charts, 22, 60–61, 119, 467; digital copies, student completion, 63; information, addition, 81
Krashen, Stephen, 321, 342
Krofne with Baba (Gonzalez), 513

L

Ladson-Billings, Gloria, 383
Language: College and Career Readiness Anchor Standards, 552; techniques, student knowledge, 25
Language Experience Approach (LEA), 71, 232, 377; application, 94–96; "classical" version, 94–95; Common Core connections, 93; defining, 93; differentiation recommendations, 97; "gamified" version, 95–96; Model, 94, 98f; online teaching, 96; preference, reason, 93; problems, 96; supporting research, 93; technology connections, 97
Language-learning classrooms, information gap activities (usage), 282
Language Maps, 457–458
Language Portraits, usage, 457–458
Learning. *See* Problem-based learning; Project-based learning: acceleration, 286; active learning, promotion, 539; cooperative/collaborative learning opportunities, 358; games. *See* Reading; Writing. ; goals, organizer, 515; just in time learning, 538; loss, 538; menus. *See* Choice boards. ; object-based learning, 255; plan, development, 254; self-regulated learning, practice, 152; small group learning, opportunities (creation), 396; strategy, 151; visual displays, 468

Learning and Remembering Read Aloud, 152, 157f
Learning Games for Reading and Writing, 228
Learning Management System, 291
Learning Network (NYT), 201, 469
Leisure reading, 5
Leon, Claudia, 201
Letter exchange. *See* School year
Letter Scavenger Hunt, 344
Letter sounds scavenger hunt, 344
LingoHut, usage, 359
Linquanti, Robert, 529
"Lion Sleeps Tonight, The" (song), 303
Lip-syncing, 304
Listening: active listening, 333, 334, 337; assessment, 528; benefits, 334–336; College and Career Readiness Anchor Standards, 551; dialogue, sample, 336, 341f; frames, 340f; free listening, 304; hearing, contrast, 333; ideas, 336–337; language frames, 335–336; lip-syncing, 304; metacognitive listening, 334–335; practice sheet, 340f; pre-listening, 304–306; reading, relationship, 304; saying/singing, 304–305; video usage, guidelines, 321–322
Listening, learning games, 151; Answer-Question, 343–344; application, 343–347; Common Core connections, 343; defining, 342; differentiation recommendations, 347; Four Truths and a Lie, 345–346; Guess the Word, 345; Letter Scavenger Hunt, 344; Nine Box Grid, 343, 349f; online teaching, 347; preference, reason, 342; problems, 347; Running Dictation, 345; sound effects, 344; supporting research, 342; technology connections, 348; Telephone, 345; Video Game Walk-Throughs, 347
Listening, photos/images: application, 316; Common Core connections, 315; defining, 315; differentiation recommendations, 317; online teaching, 317; preference, reason, 315; problems, 317;

supporting research, 315; technology connections, 317
listening/reading, 304
Listening strategy: adventure, selection, 337; applications, 334–338; Common Core connections, 334; defining, 333; differentiation recommendations, 338; online teaching, 338; preference, reason, 333; problems, 338–339; supporting research, 333; technology connections, 339
Literacy development, support, 10
Literary Genres Tree Map, 518f
Long-Term ELLs (LTELLs): application, 372; Common Core connections, 372; defining, 371; factors, 371; online teaching, 373; preference, reason, 372; problems, 373–374; supporting research, 372; technology connections, 374
Lorenzutti, Nico, 309
Low-intermediate students, Jigsaw application, 100–101
Lyneis, Anne, 16, 17

M

Main characters, delineation, 32f
Markman, Betsy, 201
Marley, Bob, 303
Marshmallow test, 504
Marzano, Robert, 39, 264
Masterpiece, creation, 496
McGrath, Irina, 194, 195
McTighe, Jay, 139, 142
Memory Read Aloud, 156f
Mental imagery, 406
Mentimeter (web app), 222
Messenger-and-scribe, 282
Metacognitive listening, 334–336
Metacognitive processes, modeling, 118
Mexican American War Critical Thinking dialogue, 287, 294f
Mexico Writing Frame, 168, 174f
Mexico Writing Structure, 169, 177
Microsoft 365 Online, 139
Microsoft Flip, 327
Microsoft Word, usage, 239
Miguez, Miguel, 194, 195, 203, 207
Millington, Neil T., 289, 292
Millin, Sandy, 275
Mini-posters, creation, 24

Mini-whiteboards, usage, 117, 152, 264–268, 297, 531
Mistakes, correction, 338
Modeling, usage, 355
Montemagno, Margaret, 201
Motivation strategies: application, 403–409; autonomy, support (actions), 404; Bilingual/Multilingual advantages read aloud, 409, 416f; Common Core connections, 403; competence, actions (support), 405–406; defining, 402; extrinsic motivation, 403; goal review form, 414f; goal-setting, 404–405; forms, 404, 411f–413f; intrinsic motivation, development (elements), 403; online teaching, 409; preference, reason, 402; problems, 409; relatedness, support (actions), 408; relevance, support (actions), 408–409; shout-out whiteboard, 407–408; supporting research, 403; technology connections, 409–410; temporal comparisons, 407; visualization, 406–407; Read Aloud, 406, 415f–416f
Multilevel classes: application, 376–379; Common Core connections, 375; defining, 375; online teaching, 379; preference, reason, 375; problems, 379–380; Student-led Picture Word Inductive Model lesson, 381f–382f; supporting research, 375; technology connections, 380
Multilingual learners, term (replacement), 2
Multimedia, usage, 61
Music, 322; application, 303–307; chants, 307; cloze exercise, follow-up exercise, 305; Common Core connections, 303; comprehension activities, 305; defining, 302; differentiation recommendations, 308; extension activities, 305; free listening, 304; *Hamilton* (music), appreciation, 303, 306; Information Chants, 307, 313f–314f; lyrics, visual representation (creation), 306; My Favorite Song activity, 306–307, 309, 311f–312f; online teaching, 307; personalized song lessons, 306–307; personal theme song, activity, 307; preference, reason, 302; pre-listening, 304–306; problems, 308; sequence, 303–305; Song Lyric Analysis sheet, 306, 310f–311f; supporting research, 302; technology connections, 308–309; topical projects, 305–306
My Favorite Song activity, 306–307, 309, 311f–312f
My Summer Cloze activity, 458
My Year of Reading (visual project), 9, 13f; student example, 14f, 468

N

Name It (game), 266
Narrative Word Chart, 23, 24, 28f, 41, 54f
Narrative Words Content Frame, 518f
Nation, Paul, 288
Nearpod (app), 222
Newcomer ELL, support, 9
Newcomers Quarterly Assessment, 196f–197f
Nine Box Grid, 264–265, 343, 349f; Health Care Words example, 264, 276f; template, 264, 276f
Nonlinguistic cues, usage, 356
Notebooks (retrieval practice), 152–153
Note-taking: process, 281; scaffold, 357; strategies, 357–358

O

Object-based learning, 255
Object Writing Frame, 255, 262f
One-Minute Reports activity, 489
One-on-one conversation starter, 405
Ones-and-dones, 232
"One Sentence Project" (Pink), 410
Onion Diagram, communities example, 523f
Online skills, practice, 485
Online teaching, 9–10
Online whiteboards, usage, 140
Only Connect (game show), 139, 270
Open-ended questions, usage, 2190
Oral language development (facilitation), practices (usage), 115–116
Oral practice, 485
Oral presentations, 122, 469, 489
Organizational structure, student knowledge, 25
Osteen, Mary, 173

P

Padlet, usage, 221, 517
Paired dictation, 280
Parallel texts (digital sites usage), 10
Paraphrasing, 103, 167, 271; application, 186–187; Common Core connections, 184; Concept Attainment Paraphrasing 1, 186, 191f; Concept Attainment Paraphrasing 2, 187, 191f–192f; defining, 183; differentiation recommendations, 188; online teaching, 188; Paraphrase Sheet, 187, 192f; preference, reason, 183; problems, 188; supporting research, 184; technology connection, 189
Parent involvement/engagement, difference, 442, 445
Parents/guardians, communication, 541
Parents/guardians, interaction, 384, 504; application, 444–446; classroom learning, family participation, 446; Common Core connections, 443; defining, 442; parental support, 445–446; preference, reason, 442–443; problems, 446; Student Family Letter, template, 445, 448f; supporting research, 443; technology connections, 446–447
Paris, Django, 383
Partner reading, 484, 495
Pause and Predict sheet, 326, 331
Peak-End Rule (peak-end rule), 205, 465, 483
Peck, Carissa, 275
PEE. *See* Point, Evidence, Explain
Peer Mentor (peer mentor), 421; Focus Questions, 421, 432f; form, 421, 431f; guidelines, 421, 430f; providing, 361; Writing Prompt: Building Empathy, 418
Peer reviewing process, usage, 239–240
Peer review, opportunity, 238

Peer Review Sheet, 239–240, 243f
Peer teaching/learning, 500;
    application, 418–422;
    Common core connections,
    418; defining, 417; Dialogue
    Journal prompts, 422, 433f;
    differentiation
    recommendations, 423;
    Empathy Project, 418;
    Everyone Is a Teacher: activity,
    422; goal-setting chart, 422,
    435f; Poster, 422, 434f;
    goal-setting chart, student
    example, 422, 436f; online
    teaching, 423; Personal Story
    outline, 418, 425f; preference,
    reason, 417; problems, 423;
    sister classes, 421–422; Story
    Sharing, 418, 426f; listening
    chart, 418, 427f; supporting
    research, 417; technology
    connections, 423–424; Writing
    Prompt: Building
    Empathy, 418, 426f
Peer-to-peer conversation, 220
Peer tutors: advice/guidelines, 419,
    428f–429f; classroom,
    description, 420; impact,
    48–49; tutor-led small
    groups, 484
Pen-pal activity, 232
Perini, Matthew J., 139, 142
Periods, Concept Attainment
    Example, 148f
Personalized Learning Weekly Test,
    501, 510f–511f
Personalized online games,
    preparation, 419
Personalized songs: elevation, 309;
    lessons, 306–307
Personal Story outline, 418, 425f
Personal theme song, activity, 307
Peterson, Jim, 245
Phonicball (game), 265
Phonic darts, 265
Phonics: data set, 136, 137–138;
    debate, 115; instruction, 367
Photo collages, usage, 316
Photos/images, usage, 245, 465, 483,
    494. *See also* Listening;
    Speaking; AI text-to-image
    tools, usage, 204–205;
    application, 200–205; Bloom's
    Questions for Images, 201,
    210f–211f; captions, writing,
    202; close-read photos/images,
    discussion, 200–201; Cloze

captions, writing, 202;
    Common Core Connections,
    200; compare-and-contrast
    methods/activities, 202–203;
    defining, 199; difference
    picture, spotting/finding,
    202–203; differentiation
    recommendations, 206;
    display, online tools (usage),
    203; Examining an Image, 200,
    209f, 210f; online teaching,
    205; parts, unveiling, 202;
    picture story, 203–204;
    preference, reason, 199;
    problems, 205; questions, 201;
    sensory details, 204; slideshow
    annotation, 200; Slideshow
    Notes, 200, 208f; supporting
    research, 199; teaching
    purpose, 201; technology
    connections, 205; Window
    Swap Assignments, 203, 212f;
    Wonders Of Street
    View, 203, 213f
Pictionary (game), 269
Picture: data sets, 136, 138;
    dictionaries, usage, 48–49;
    selection, 245; song pictures,
    304; story (stories),
    71, 203–204
Picture Dictation, 495; lesson, 282
Picture Word Inductive Model (PWIM),
    45, 134–136, 199
Pink, Dan, 410
Pleasure reading, 5
Poe, usage, 234
Point, Evidence, Explain (PEE) Writing
    Structure, 169, 179f
Pollard, Laurel, 324, 329
Poster creation, sentence starters
    (usage), 168
Pre-listening, 304–306
Preparatory texts, 62–63
Price, Paige, 491
Prior knowledge, activating/building,
    118–119, 408; proactive
    strategies, usage, 355
Prior knowledge, connection, 542
Problem-based learning, 377;
    application, 252–255;
    Common Core connections,
    252; Community Problem
    Research Form, 254, 261f;
    conclusions, deriving/
    acting, 255; defining,
    251; differentiation
    recommendations, 256;

examples, 253; Home Culture
    Project, 253, 257f–260f; Object
    Writing Frame, 255, 262f;
    online teaching, 256; plan,
    implementation, 255;
    preference, reason, 251;
    problems, 256; supporting
    research, 251–252; technology
    connections, 257
Problem-based project
    process, 253–255
Problem-posing: application, 245–247;
    Common Core connections,
    245; defining, 244;
    differentiation
    recommendations, 248;
    Graphic Organizer, 246, 250f;
    online teaching, 248;
    preference, reason, 244;
    problems, 248; students,
    questions, 246–247;
    supporting research, 244;
    technology connections, 249
Project-based learning, 377, 386, 404;
    activities, 255; application,
    252–255; Common Core
    connections, 252; Community
    Problem Research Form,
    254, 261f; conclusions,
    deriving/acting, 255;
    defining, 251; differentiation
    recommendations, 256;
    examples, 252–253; Home
    Culture Project, 253,
    257f–260f; Object Writing
    Frame, 255, 262f; online
    teaching, 256; plan,
    implementation, 255;
    preference, reason, 251;
    problems, 256; supporting
    research, 251–252; technology
    connections, 257
Project-based project process, 253–255
Project, focus (identification), 254
Pronunciation feedback, 290
Protagonist-antagonist,
    understanding, 24
Protagonist, term (teaching), 42
Puppet dialogue, 288
Pyramid/Triangle Chart, 519f

Q

Question and Sentence
    Starters list, 53f
Question Menu, 487
Question, Signal, Stem, Share, Assess
    (QSSSA): application, 218–221;

Common Core connections, 218; defining, 214–216; differentiation recommendations, 222; Elementary QSSA examples, 221, 225f; Example of a Structured Visual, 219, 224f; Example Signals, 220, 224f; Example "Who First" Indicators, 220, 224f; online teaching, 221; preference, reason, 216–218; problems, 221; routine, 215–216; Script, 117, 221; Secondary QSSA examples, 221, 226f; supporting research, 218; technology connections, 222–223; tool, usage, 217

Quickwrites, usage, 62

Quill (grammar tool), 160

Quizizz, usage, 160, 189, 274, 420, 531, 541

Quizzes: retrieval practice example, 150–151; sample, 529, 534f; usage, 151–152

Quoting, 103, 169, 271; application, 184; Common Core connections, 184; defining, 183; differentiation recommendations, 188; online teaching, 188; preference, reason, 183; problems, 188; supporting research, 184; technology connection, 189

R

RACE. *See* Restate, Answer, Cite, Explain/examples

Random Name Picker, feature (usage), 267

Read alouds: Bilingual/Multilingual advantages read aloud, 409, 416f; interactive read alouds, 117–118; Knowledge Read Aloud, 155f; Learning and Remember Read Aloud, 157f; Memory Read Aloud, 156f; usage, 114, 117–118; visualization read aloud, 415f–416f

Reading, 23–24; assessment, 528; College and Career Readiness Anchor Standards, 548–549; listening, relationship, 304; partner reading, 484; photos/images. *See* Photos/images. ; strategies, 114, 116–117; videos, showing, 324

Reading Aloud (Heads Up) (Thornbury), 117

Reading Anchor Standards, 200

Reading and Writing with English Learners: A Framework for K-5 (Gonzalez), 513

Reading comprehension, 62; application, 115–126; close reading, 114–115, 122–126; comprehension/decoding, 124; in-depth meaning, 124; options, 125; text, analysis/comparison, 125; text, function (determination), 124; text, inspiration, 125–126; text, previewing, 123; Common Core connections, 115; defining, 113; differentiation recommendations, 127; online teaching, 126; preference, reason, 113–114; prior knowledge, activation/building, 118–119; problems, 126; read alouds, usage, 114, 117–118; Reading Data Set, benefits, 120, 131f–132f; Reading Strategies Word Chart, 116, 129f; supporting research, 114–115; technology connections, 127–128; text structure, previewing, 119; Think Aloud Example, 130f; think alouds, usage, 114, 117–118; vocabulary, usage, 118; "What People Say About. . .," 132f; whole-class readings, 118–122; graphic organizers, usage, 120–121; post-reading, 121–122; pre-reading, 118–119; purpose, setting, 119; during reading, 119–121; text, annotation, 120; text, reading, 119–120; text, response, 122; text, summarization, 121–122

Reading, learning games, 71, 151, 228, 408, 419; Academic Language Sentences (game), 268–269; application, 264–273; board game adaptations, 273; Categories (game), 269–270; Common Core connections, 264; Connecting Four (game), 270–271; defining, 263; differentiation recommendations, 274; ESL/ELL Wordle (game), 272–273; fill-in-the-blanks, 265; Flyswatter (game), 265–266; Hangman, 269; Name It (game), 266; Health Care Words, example, 276f; template, 276f; Nine Box Grid, 264–265; online teaching, 273; phonic darts, 265; Pictionary (game), 269; preference, reason, 263; problems, 273; Round-and-Round She Goes (game), 266–267; sentence scrambles, usage, 267–268; Summarize This! (game), 271–272; supporting research, 264; team-writing sentences, 269; technology connections, 274–275; What Doesn't Belong? (game), 270; Writing Bingo (game), 267; Writing More (game), 271

Reading Wars, 115

Reading words: identification, 29f, 55f; teaching, 42

Recasts, usage, 232–233

Reinforcing exercises, 40

Relatedness: intrinsic motivation development element, 403; support, actions, 408

Relevance: acceleration, relationship, 542; intrinsic motivation development element, 403; support, actions, 408–409

Relevance + Accessible Chorus + Movement equation, 306

Remediation, accelerated learning (contrast), 538

Remembering self, 205–206

Research-based actions, 395–396

Restate, Answer, Cite, Explain/examples (RACE) Writing Structure, 169

Retrieval practice, 469; application, 151–153; Common Core connections, 151; defining, 150; differentiation recommendations, 154; higher-order thinking skills, incorporation, 153; Knowledge Read Aloud, 151, 155f; Learning and Remember Read Aloud, 157f; Memory Read Aloud, 151, 156f; notebooks, 151–153; online teaching, 153; preference, reason, 150; problems, 153; quizzes/tests, usage, 151–152; supporting

research, 150–151; technology connections, 154; usage, 152
Revised Bloom's Taxonomy, 201
Revision, 167; application, 238–240; Common Core connections, 238; defining, 237; differentiation recommendations, 241; homework revision, 240; online teaching, 241; Peer Review Sheet, 239–240, 243f; preference, reason, 237–238; problems, 241; supporting research, 238; technology connections, 242
Role-plays, simulations (contrast), 542
Roth, Maggie, 16, 17
Round-and-Round She Goes (game), 266–267
Running dictation (messenger-and-scribe), usage, 231, 282–283, 345

S

Safe Haven program, 446
Salva, Carol, 214, 424
Scaffolding writing, 139
Scaffolds, usage, 540
Scavenger Hunt (image usage), 494
School: communication focus, 443; extracurricular activities, ELL accessibility, 396
School Strip School, first day: Student Handout, 74f; teacher answer key, 75f
School year, beginning, 385; application, 454–458; Common Core connections, 453; Course Expectations, 460f–461f; activity, 455; questions, 455, 462f; differentiation recommendations, 459; "I Am" Project, 456–457; "I Learn Best When..." cards, 456; initiation, 453; Language Maps, usage, 457–458; Language Portraits, usage, 457–458; Letter Exchange, 455; My Summer, 464f; Cloze activity, 458; online teaching, 458; partner introductions, 455–456, 463f; preference, reason, 453; problems, 458–459; Self-Portraits, activities, 457; students: greeting, 454; names, learning, 454–455; supporting research, 453; technology connections, 459
School year, ending: Anonymous ELL Class Evaluation Sheet, sample, 471, 480f–481f; application, 466–472; classes: evaluations, 471; visiting, 468; Common Core connections, 466; defining, 465; differentiation recommendations, 472; field trips, 469; final days, activities, 469–472; final months, activities, 466–469; free-choice unit, 467; goal-setting activity, completion, 466–467; goal sheet, finishing, 474f; gratitude, expression, 470; growth, reflection, 470–471; learning, visual displays, 468; lesson plan, 475f–476f; My Year Directions, 470, 476f; personal reflections, 469–470; preference, reason, 465; problems, 472; students, advice, 469; summer practice, encouragement, 472; supporting research, 465; teacher evaluations, 471; technology: connections, 473; usage, 469; Writing Improvement Rubric, 471, 477f; reflection questions, 478f; year in review, 469; Year-in-Review instructions/planning sheet, 478f–479f
Scrambled sentences, 495; expansion, 160
Scrivner, Nicole, 410, 424
Seasons of the Year Data Set, 136, 145f
Secondary QSSA examples, 221, 226f
Second language (L2): acquisition, 6; skills, transfer, 357; vocabulary, 48
Self-assessment, 291; capacity, 232; exit tickets, 488
Self-correction, 231–232
Self-explanation, 134
Self-Portraits, activities. See School year
Self-regulated learning, practice, 152
Self-selected books, reading (benefits), 6
Sentence: builders, 419; construction, 530; fill-in-the-blank sentences, 166; frames, usage, 7; navigators, 95; completion, 159; creation, 419; scrambles, 70–71, 267–268; starters, usage, 168, 357; strips, 325
Sentence Puzzle, 159, 162f
Sequencing, 80, 286; activities, differentiating recommendations, 72; application, 69–71; comic strips, 71; Common Core connections, 69; defining, 68; online teaching, 71–72; preference, reason, 68; problems, 72; sentence scrambles, 70–71; strip stories, 69–70; Day of the Dead Strip Story (Student Handout), 70, 78f; Day of the Dead Strip Story (Teacher Answer Key), 79f; First Day of School Strip Story (Student Handout), 70, 74f; First Day of School Strip Story (Teacher Answer Key), 75f; instructions, 78f; Mexico Strip Story (student handbook), 70, 76f; Mexico Strip Story (Teacher Answer Key), 77f; supporting research, 69; technology connections, 73
Serravallo, Jennifer, 116
Shackelford, Molly Lange, 223
Shanahan, Timothy, 43
Share. See Question, Signal, Stem, Share, Assess
Share an Image (image usage), 494
Sheltered instruction observation protocol (SIOP), 439
Shining Moments activity, 487
Shory, Michelle Makus, 194, 195
Shout-out whiteboard, 408
Signal. See Question, Signal, Stem, Share, Assess: example, 220, 224f
Silent sustained reading, 5
Silver, Harvey F., 139, 142
Simulations, role-plays (contrast), 542
Singing, 304; activities, 305
Sister class, 421–422; response, 232
Slideshow annotation, 200
Slideshow Notes, 200, 208f
Small group learning, opportunities (creation), 396
Small-group tutoring, 439
Social comparisons, 407
Social emotional learning, 252, 408; application, 392–397; asset-based mindset, usage, 392–394; belonging, sense, 395–396; Changing Mindset

Infographic, 399f; Common Core connections, 392; defining, 391; growth mindset, 396–397; Growth Mindset: Paragraph Frame, 401f; stories, 400f; online teaching, 397; preference, reason, 391; problems, 398; supporting research, 391–392; technology connections, 398

Song: drawing, idea, 305; pictures, 304

Song Lyric Analysis sheet, 306, 310f–311f

Sorting Tool (Smithsonian Learning Lab), usage, 142

Sound Effects (game), 344

Sounds Easy! (Bassano), 137–138; example page, 147f

Spanish-speaking English language learners, diglot story (sentence examination), 48

Speaking: assessment, 528; College and Career Readiness Anchor Standards, 551; video, usage (guidelines), 321–322

Speaking, learning games, 151; Answer-Question, 343–344; applications, 343–347; Common Core connections, 343; defining, 342; differentiation recommendations, 347; Four Truths and a Lie, 345–346; Guess the Word, 345; Letter Scavenger Hunt, 344; Nine Box Grid, 349f; online teaching, 347; preference, reason, 342; problems, 347; running dictation, 345; Sound Effects, 344; supporting research, 342; technology connections, 348; Telephone (game), 345; video game walk-throughs, 346

Speaking, photos/images (usage): application, 316; Common Core connections, 315; defining, 315; differentiation recommendations, 317; online teaching, 317; preference, reason, 315; problems, 317; supporting research, 315; technology connections, 317

Speed-dating procedure/style, 25, 204, 327, 457, 494

"Spot the Differences" pictures (image usage), 203, 494

Stems, 166. *See also* Question, Signal, Stem, Share, Assess

Sticky Note compliments, 488

Story (stories): action mazes, 337; Cooperative Storytelling, 495; events, 36f; "fun" stories, 298–299; Map, example, 522f; Personal Story outline, 418, 425f; practical stories, 298; setting, 31f; writing, 38f

Story of Ferdinand, The (Leaf), 23, 25, 27, 185, 423, 529

Story Planning Sheet, 298, 301f

Story Sharing, 418, 426f; listening chart, 418, 427f

Strip stories, 69–70; Day of the Dead Strip Story: Student Handout, 78f; Teacher Answer Key, 79f; instructions, 78f, 467; Mexico Strip Story: Student Handout, 76f; Teacher Answer Key, 77f; School Strip School, first day: Student Handout, 74

Structured Visual, example, 219, 224f

Structures. *See* Writing structures

Student-Led Lesson Plan, 500, 507f

Student-led Picture Word Inductive Model lesson, 378, 381f–382f

Student Motivation Handbook (Ferlazzo), 407

Students: advice, 469; agency, sense, 498; assets, recognition, 355; autonomy, support, 6; communication ability, 285; culturally responsive mind-set, words (usage), 385–386; dialogue journal, sister class response, 232; downtime, 159; element knowledge, 24–25; engagement, acceleration (relationship), 542; English proficiency, 240; feedback, 482; feelings, listening, 395–396; goal sheet, review, 406; greeting, 454; guided visualization, 406; home language illiteracy, interaction, 9; learning, visual representation, 468; mini-whiteboards, usage, 264; names, learning, 454–455; Personal Report form, 547f; prior knowledge possession, 24; questions, 246–247; quiz scores, visual representation, 537f; reviewing, exercise, 186–187; self-assessment/reflection, 530; self-efficacy, support, 526; stress levels, reduction, 166; successes, publishing, 8; understanding, level, 384–385; vocabulary level, defining, 25

Students with Interrupted Formal Education (SIFEs), 9, 138, 214, 395, 504; application, 366–367; Common Core connections, 366; defining, 365; encouragement/patience/support, 367–369; home language instruction, 367; online teaching, 369; phonics instruction, 367; preference, reason, 366; problems, 369; supporting research, 366; technology: connections, 369–370; support, 366–367

Students with Limited or Interrupted Formal Education (SLIFEs), 365

Student-teacher check-ins, 8

Summarize This! (game), 271–272

Summarizing, 103, 169, 271; application, 185–186; Common Core connections, 184; defining, 183; differentiation recommendations, 188; examples, 185, 190f; higher-order thinking skill, 153; online teaching, 188; preference, reason, 183; problems, 188; supporting research, 184; technology connection, 189

Summer practice, encouragement, 472

Supporting characters, example, 33f

Synchronous conversations, structuring, 221

Synonyms/antonyms, visual display, 50

T

Teacher Clarity, impact, 215

"Teacher Clarity," impact, 215

Teacher from the Black Lagoon, The (Thaler), 24, 25, 42

Teacher-generated scaffolds, nonusage, 166

Teacher-planned activity, 94

Teachers, end of year evaluations, 471

Teaching Beginning Reading and Writing with the Picture Word Inductive Model (Calhoun), 142
Team-writing sentences, 269
Technology connections: accelerated learning, 543; assessment, 532; choice boards (learning menus), 194; class, beginning/ending, 490; clozes, 84; conversation practice, 292; co-teaching, 441; culturally responsive teaching, 390; dictation, 284; ELL differentiation, 362; error correction strategies, 234; grammar, teaching, 161; graphic organizers, 26; independent reading, 11; inductive learning, 141; Interactive Word Walls (IWWs), 517; jigsaw, 105; Language Experience Approach (LEA), 97; long-term ELLs, interaction, 374; motivation, 409; multilevel classes, 380; music, 308; parents/guardians, interaction, 446; peer teaching/learning, 423; photos/images, usage, 206, 317; prior knowledge, activation, 64; problem-posing, 249; project-based learning/problem-based learning, 257; QSSSA, 222–223; quoting/summarizing/paraphrasing, 189; reading comprehension, 127; reading/writing, learning games, 274, 348; retrieval practice, 154; revision, 242; school year, beginning, 459; school year, ending, 473; sequencing, 73; SIFEs, 369; social emotional learning, 398; speaking/listening, learning games, 348; strategy, 339; technology, usage, 505; text engineering, 17; total physical response (TPR), 299; translanguaging, 452; video, 328; vocabulary, 50; writing frames/writing structures, 172; zero-prep activities, 497
Technology, usage, 540; application, 499–504; artificial intelligence, 502–503; cognitive choice, 500; Common Core connections, 499; connections, 505–506; Daily Computer Plan and Reflection, 501, 512f; daily independent work, 501; defining, 498; differentiation recommendations, 505; educational technology, usage, 540; homework, 502; independent study, 500–501; Lesson Guide, 500, 508f; online teaching, 504; Personalized Learning Weekly Test, 501, 510f–511f; preference, reason, 498; problems, 504; Student-Led Lesson Plan, 500, 507f; supporting research, 499; typing/keyboard, learning, 503; Weekly Computer Independent Study Plan, 500–501, 509f; weekly independent project, 500–501
Tekhnologic blog, 71
Telephone (game), 345
Temporal comparisons, 407
Tennant, Adrian, 337, 339
Terrell, Shelly, 309
Tests, usage, 151–152
Text: annotation, 120; data sets, 136–137; creation, ChatGPT prompt, 141; teaching, sequence (example), 137; previewing, 123; reading, 119–120; response, 122; structure, previewing, 119; summarization, 121–122; walk-throughs, 419
Text-dependent questions, asking (Common Core-supported strategy), 123
Text engineering, 15; application, 16–17; Common Core connections, 15; defining, 15; methods, 16; online teaching, 17; preference, reasons, 15; problems, identification, 17; supporting research, 15–16; technology connections, 17
Thematic Report: My Favorite Story, 332f
Theme: example, 34f; understanding, 24
They Say, I Say: The Moves that Matter in Academic Writing (Graff/Birkenstein), 169
Think alouds: example, 130f; usage, 114, 117–118
Thinking skills, usage, 307
Thornbury, Scott, 117
"Three Little Birds" (song), 303
Tier Three words, 43
Tomlinson, Carol Ann, 376
Toppel, Katie, 264–265, 275, 343, 348
Total physical response (TPR), 46; application, 296–299; commands, 298; Common Core connections, 296; defining, 296; differentiation recommendations, 299; extension activities, 297–299; "fun" stories, 298–299; mini-whiteboards, usage, 297; online teaching, 299; practical stories, 298; preference, reason, 296; problems, 299; Story Planning Sheet, 298, 301f; supporting research, 296; technology connections, 299
Translanguaging, 166; application, 450–451; Common Core connections, 450; defining, 449, 450–451; language use flexibility, 450–451; online teaching, 451–452; preference, reason, 449; problems, 452; supporting research, 449; technology connections, 452
Trauma detectives, 387–388
"True Stories": book, usage, 420; series, usage, 376
Two Truths and a Lie (game), 345–346
Typing, learning, 503

U

Upstander word chart, 62, 67f
USA Learns, usage, 359

V

Velcro boards, 265
Venet, Alex Shevrin, 387
Venn diagram, creation, 203
Verbal instructions, giving, 356
Videos: access, 322; accessible vocabulary, 321; active viewing, 322; AI videos, 327; application, 321–327; clips, selection, 245; Common

Core connections, 320; defining, 320; differentiation recommendations, 328; Game Walk-Throughs, 347; length, control, 321; online teaching, 327–328; Pause and Predict sheet, 326, 331f; preference, reason, 320; problems, 328; quality, 322; selection, 323; sequence, 322–323; showing, 324; student creation, 50; subtitles, usage, 322; supporting research, 320; technology connections, 328–329; Thematic Report: My Favorite Story, 332f; thinking sheet, 330f; usage: guidelines, 321–322; purpose, 321; vocabulary videos, 327; watching, 323

Virtual field trips, 63

Visualization (mental imagery), 406–407, 485–486; guided visualization, 406; Read Aloud, 406, 415f–416f

Visual summary activity, execution, 121

Vocabulary: academic vocabulary, 43–44; teaching, word lists (usage), 51; application, 40–48; clines, 44–45, 58f; cognates, 47; Common Core connections, 40; context clues, 43; defining, 39–40; differentiation recommendations, 50; instruction: online tools, usage, 50; support, technology (usage), 50–51; Interactive Word Walls, 41, 45–47; knowledge, increase (student monitoring), 50; Narrative Word Chart, 54f; online teaching, 49; picture dictionaries, usage, 48–49; preference, reasons, 40; problems, identification, 49; supporting research, 40; technology connections, 50–51; usage, 62, 118; videos, 327; word webs, usage, 45

W

Walk-and-talk, 245
Walk-in procedures, 482
Walqui, Aída, 15

Warm-Ups, 482; questions, inclusion, 404–405

Weekly Computer Independent Study Plan, 500–501, 509f

"What Are These Animals Saying" (image usage), 494

What Doesn't Belong? (game), 270

Wheel of Names, usage, 216, 222

Whole-class instruction, 419

Whole-class readings, 117–122

Wiliam, Dylan, 229, 233

Willingham, Daniel, 120

Window Swap Assignments, 203, 212f

Wonders Of Street View, 203, 213f

Word Association, 494

Word Chain, 493–494

Word-lay activity, usage, 286

Words: active processing, student needs, 39; chart, usage, 41–42; clues, 47–48; identification, 29f, 55f; pronunciation, 39; teaching, 42; webs, usage, 45

Word Searches, Clozes (usage), 493

Wormeli, Rick, 456, 458, 460

WRITE Institute, 27, 51

Writers, notebook, 297, 486; prompts, 486

Writing, 24–25; assessment, 528; College and Career Readiness Anchor Standards, 550–551

Writing About a Book, 169, 176f

Writing About a Movie, 169, 175f

Writing an Essay Flow Chart, 149f

Writing Bingo (game), 267

Writing frames, 188, 203, 241, 406, 504; application, 166–170; Common Core connections, 166; defining, 165; differentiation recommendations, 172; English language acquisition, writing importance (learning), 167–168; fill-in-the-blank outlines, extensions, 168–169; George Washington Writing Frame, 168, 173f; Mexico Writing Frame, 168, 174f; online teaching, 170; preference, reason, 165–166; problems, 170–171; Restate, Answer, Cite, Explain/examples (RACE) Writing Structure, 169, 180f–181f; structures, 169–170; supporting research, 166; Table A Memory, 170; technology connections, 12; Writing About a Book, 169, 176f; Writing About a Movie, 169, 175f

Writing Improvement Rubric, 471, 477f

Writing, learning games, 71, 151, 228, 408, 419; Academic Language Sentences (game), 268–269; application, 264–273; board game adaptations, 273; Categories (game), 269–270; Common Core connections, 264; Connecting Four (game), 270–271; defining, 263; differentiation recommendations, 274; ESL/ELL Wordle (game), 272–273; fill-in-the-blank, 265; Flyswatter (game), 265–266; Hangman, 269; Name It (game), 266; Nine Box Grid, 264–265; Health Care Words example, 276; template, 276f; online teaching, 273; Pictionary (game), 269; preference, reason, 263; problems, 273; Round-and-Round She Goes (game), 266–267; sentence scrambles, 267–268; Summarize This! (game), 271–272; supporting research, 264; team-writing sentences, 269; technology connections, 274–275; What Doesn't Belong? (game), 270; Writing Bingo (game), 267; Writing More (game), 271

Writing More (game), 271

Writing structures, 188, 203, 241, 406, 504; Answer, Back it up, Comment (ABC) Writing Structure, 169, 178f; application, 166–170; Assertion, Reason, Evidence, Explanation (AREE) Writing Structure, 169, 181f; Teaching Grid, 182f; Common Core connections, 166; defining, 165; differentiation recommendations, 172; English language acquisition, writing importance (learning), 167–168; example, 169–170; Mexico Writing Structure, 169, 177f; online teaching, 170; Point, Evidence, Explain (PEE) Writing Structure, 169, 179; preference, reason, 165; problems, 171; Restate, Answer, Cit, Explain/examples (RACE) Writing Structure, 169, 180f–181f; supporting research, 166; Table A Memory, 170; technology connections, 172

Written instructions, giving, 356

Y

Year-in-Review instructions/planning sheet, 478f–479f

"You Are So Beautiful" (song), 303

Z

Zeigarnik effect, 166

Zero-prep activities: application, 493–496; Common Core connections, 493; Cooperative Storytelling, 495; Countdown, 493; defining, 492; Dictation, 495; Dictogloss, 496; differentiation recommendations, 496; games, 493–494; images, usage, 494; online teaching, 496; Partner Reading, 495; Picture Dictation, 495–496; preference, reason, 492; problems, 496; reading/writing, 495–496; Scavenger Hunt, 494; Scrambled Sentences, 495; Share an Image, 494; "Spot the Difference" pictures, 494; supporting research, 492–493; technology connections, 497; "What Are These Animals Saying?," 494; Word Chain, 493–494; Word Searches, Clozes (usage), 493

Zero Prep: Ready-to-Go Activities for the Language Classroom (Pollard/Hess/Herron), 324, 329